Reflections in a Glass Darkly

HIPPOCAMPUS PRESS LIBRARY OF CRITICISM

S. T. Joshi, *Primal Sources: Essays on H. P. Lovecraft* (2003)
S. T. Joshi, *The Evolution of the Weird Tale* (2004)
Robert W. Waugh, *The Monster in the Mirror: Looking for H. P. Lovecraft* (2006)
Scott Connors, ed., *The Freedom of Fantastic Things: Selected Criticism on Clark Ashton Smith* (2006)
Ben Szumskyj, ed., *Two-Gun Bob: A Centennial Study of Robert E. Howard* (2006)
S. T. Joshi and Rosemary Pardoe, ed. *Warnings to the Curious: A Sheaf of Criticism on M. R. James* (2007)
Lovecraft Annual
Dead Reckonings

Reflections in a Glass Darkly

Essays on J. Sheridan Le Fanu

Edited by
Gary William Crawford, Jim Rockhill, and Brian J. Showers

Hippocampus Press

New York

Published by Hippocampus Press
P.O. Box 641, New York, NY 10156.
http://www.hippocampuspress.com

Cover illustration Jason Van Hollander from a photograph by Laura
Anzuoni.
Cover design by Barbara Briggs Silbert.
Hippocampus Press logo designed by Anastasia Damianakos.

First Edition
1 3 5 7 9 8 6 4 2

ISBN13: 978-1-61498-005-6

For the Le Fanu Family,
Past and Present

Contents

Foreword

W. J. Mc Cormack

*S*heridan Le Fanu and Victorian Ireland was published on Saint Patrick's Day 1980, with a reception in the Brotherton Library, University of Leeds.

The event was further distinguished by the display of selected papers from a Bennett Family collection in the process of being acquired by the library from (the late) Mrs. Susan Digby-Firth. Oxford University Press was represented by Jon Bell, my editor. I think the original proposal was vetted by Jon Stallworthy, who later wrote the biography of Louis MacNeice, but Jon Bell was the most able intermediary. Since 1980, two paperback editions from other publishers have appeared. Le Fanu, reasonably documented, has been with us for over thirty years.

What has changed since then in the milieu which produces and consumes scholarly books? Or, to be more modest, what has changed with reference to Le Fanu and his milieu? First, the Web and the Internet have made possible the rapid searching of such basic sources as newspapers; in this case, the *Irish Times*, which was established in 1859, just in time for the second productive period of Le Fanu's career as novelist. A few "search-and-find" experiments would suggest that the results will not add much to our knowledge of him, though his younger brother emerges more fully documented in his social and philanthropic activities.

When I was writing the biography, William Le Fanu's diaries were in the possession of his namesake and descendent, a distinguished librarian and bibliographer, who gave me access to them in his home. They passed shortly afterwards into the manuscripts department of the library at Trinity College Dublin and, somewhat later, were catalogued. These offer an astonishing view of the hard-working mid-Victorian Irish (Protestant) professional man, over a very long period, with yearly tallies of fish caught which now beggar belief.

In 1980, the Blackwood Papers (at the Public Record Office of Northern Ireland) were in the process of being catalogued, and I was given privileged access to portions of the collection relating to Le Fanu and his Sheridan/Blackwood relatives. One would expect this collection to reveal more of such material today. Only very recently did I discover that Nelson Browne, author of a pioneering brief study of the novelist, was a Belfast-based teacher and art collector, who (with the poet John Hewitt) represented the Belfast centre of P.E.N. at the 1948 re-interment of W. B. Yeats.

The great northern influence of Le Fanu's period in Irish history was [Sir] Samuel Ferguson (1810–1886), archeologist, poet, public administrator, translator, and more. Though Eve Patten has given us a very useful introduction to Ferguson's career and significance, we await a full biography. The same need attaches itself to the names of Charles Lever (1806–1872) and William Carleton (1794–1869), both novelists competing for the Irish reader's attention as Le Fanu's contemporaries. Biography has gone out of fashion, partly because the shrinking of a standard Ph.D. to "whatever can be said on the topic within three years" frightens off researchers, and partly because ideological shifts render the "bourgeois individual subject" unattractive because "incorrect."

These same ideological shifts have in some regards served Le Fanu well. Analyses drawing on feminism have been rewarding, and items in the bibliography that I had been inclined to discount as the product of an exhausted imagination (e.g., *Willing to Die*, 1873) now respond to new lines of enquiry. Post-colonialism has also taken up Le Fanu (see the work of Nicholas Allen). It is disappointing that no hitherto unrecognized texts have been identified as Le Fanu's; my suggestion of 1980, that [*My Own Story; or*] *Loved and Lost* (in the *Dublin University Magazine*, 1868–1869) might be sympathetically considered, has won some endorsements but thereafter the trail of clues runs cold.

Le Fanu's re-emergence in the last years of the nineteenth century deserves close examination, especially by tracing the movement of individuals in the publishing business. In his early days, Edmund Downey worked for William Tinsley who issued *The House by the Church-yard* in London under the Tinsley Brothers imprint. Downey, Waterford-born, also employed George Brinsley Le Fanu to illustrate some of the novels in the 1890s. What else did the novelist's son illustrate, and why?

Paperback editions have made far more of the material available, but the parlous condition of the British publishing trade discourages the reissuing of anything that will not feature on undergraduate reading-lists. By far the most urgently needed text is a thoroughly annotated *House by the Church-yard*, the apparatus to which ideal edition would illuminate the relations between mid-Victorian Ireland and its Elizabethan-Jacobean-Georgian roots, or the tending of what are taken as roots.

Is this possible for the 2014 bicentenary of the novelist's birth?

Claraghy, Rockcor
County Monaghan
Republic of Ireland
June 2011

Introduction

Gary William Crawford, Jim Rockhill, and Brian J. Showers

In recent years Joseph Sheridan Le Fanu (1814–1873) has attained only a measure of the fame he so rightfully deserves. While not a household name like Edgar Allan Poe (with whom he is often compared), Le Fanu is earning an increasingly venerable place as "the father of the English ghost story." This book is a tribute to him, in which we offer scholars, students, and readers of Le Fanu a sourcebook into the works of Dublin's—and Gothic literature's—"Invisible Prince."

Starting with a selection of classic commentaries on the author, and enriched by new essays written especially for this book, we have grouped the contents into several subject areas and provided an index in order to make the information in this volume accessible for readers new to Le Fanu and seasoned scholars alike.

Our book comes on the heels of several academic and Internet studies, journals, and databases made available in recent years. Victor Sage's *Le Fanu's Gothic: The Rhetoric of Darkness* (Basingstoke, UK: Palgrave Macmillan, 2003) and James Walton's *Vision and Vacancy: The Fictions of J. S. Le Fanu* (Dublin: University College Dublin Press, 2007) offer impressive revisionist analyses of Le Fanu's body of work. Similarly, Gavin Selerie's metafictional *Le Fanu's Ghost* (Hereford, UK: Five Seasons Press, 2006) displays not only an imaginative series of interrelated prose and verse fantasias on Le Fanu's family, life, work, and legacy, but an extensive nonfictional apparatus, much of it based on new research—it is as if a splinter from one of the oblique references to Le Fanu's *The House by the Church-yard* in James Joyce's *Finnegans Wake* (1923–1939) had grown into an independent work and provided its own glosses. Consolidation of current research is being done by Gary William Crawford, who published *J. Sheridan Le Fanu: A Bio-Bibliography* (Westport, CT: Greenwood Press, 1995). Crawford maintains the Internet continuation of its secondary bibliography, and edits the online journal *Le Fanu Studies*.[1] Our hope in this book is to crystallize past scholarship, while bringing fresh perspectives to both familiar works and works that are either undeservedly neglected or maligned.

The book opens with biographical pieces, including excerpts of longer works by Le Fanu's friend Alfred Perceval Graves and his brother William Richard Le Fanu, and a selection of obituaries compiled and introduced by Brian J. Showers. With these we hope to present a portrait of the author that strips away the near century and a half of Gothic caricature that is sometimes attached to his life. Also included are extracts from *Wilkie Collins, Le Fanu and Others* (1931) by S. M. Ellis, whose 1916 essay, from which the present essay was expanded, originated the most familiar and sensational account of the author's death. These have been supplemented by reproductions of all known portraits of Le Fanu, some printed here for the first time, with commentary.

The section devoted to general studies includes a number of notable pieces by M. R. James, E. F. Benson, and V. S. Pritchett, with a valuable early essay by Edna Kenton on Le Fanu's possible influence on the Brontës, which also offers a glimpse of how far Le Fanu had fallen into obscurity by the early decades of the twentieth century. There follow several essays on special topics, such as Wayne Hall's essay concerning how Le Fanu marketed his fiction to gain recognition in the fiercely competitive world of London publishing. Simon Cooke provides an essay detailing Le Fanu's relationship with his editor Charles Dickens and the impact this had on his own fiction. Also included are two essays discussing Carl Theodor Dreyer's *Vampyr* (1932), one of the earliest adaptations of Le Fanu in film, loosely based on *In a Glass Darkly* (1872).

The last and largest section of the book contains essays that explore individual works by Le Fanu. Here you will find Elizabeth Bowen's influential introduction to *Uncle Silas* characterizing it as an Irish novel transposed to an English setting and its heroine to the bride of Death, as well as Bowen's less frequently encountered introduction to *The House by the Church-yard*. Jack Sullivan's classic analysis of "Green Tea" as an archetypal ghost story, from *Elegant Nightmares: The English Ghost Story from Le Fanu to Blackwood* (1978), leads a series of essays on Le Fanu's supernatural and mystery fiction.

Since the early decades of the twentieth century, writers have adopted varying modes and tools to discuss Le Fanu, focusing upon perceived Freudian,[2] Swedenborgian,[3] colonialist,[4] sociocultural,[5] gender,[6] and other themes

---

1. www.lefanustudies.com

2. E.g., Peter Penzoldt's and V. S. Pritchett's essays included in this book. Ivan Melada's 1985 study for Twayne tends to pigeonhole Le Fanu's fiction into either psychological studies or allegories, omitting consideration of stories and novels that fit

noted within his work. Recent criticism of Le Fanu has tended to move away from psychological readings or from Le Fanu's position in the Anglo-Irish Ascendancy class to newer, more original vantage points. Thus, this book premieres several essays by Carol A. Senf, John Langan, Stephen Carver, Jarlath Killeen, Sally C. Harris, William Hughes, Peter Bell, and Victor Sage, which discuss Le Fanu's works from new perspectives and present for consideration some of Le Fanu's less commonly considered works, generally regarded as inferior, such as *All in the Dark, The Wyvern Mystery,* and *Willing to Die.*

The wisest course the editors can take at this point is to step out of the way, lest any shadows we cast distract the reader from these reflections in a glass darkly.

May 2011

---

neither category. It is further compromised by a sprinkling of factual errors, as basic as the incorrect date of death provided in the chronology.

3. E.g., "*Uncle Silas:* A Habitation of Symbols," Chapter 5 in W. J. Mc Cormack's *Sheridan Le Fanu and Victorian Ireland* (Oxford: Clarendon Press, 1980), Robert Tracy's editorial material for *In a Glass Darkly* (Oxford: Oxford University Press/World's Classics, 1993), Jim Rockhill's introductions and afterwords for the three-volume collected supernatural fiction of Le Fanu (Ashcroft, BC: Ash-Tree Press, 2002, 2003, 2005), and Anne Ashman's dissertation "A Psychobiographical Study of Death, Mourning, and the Swedenborgian After-Life in the Later Works of Joseph Sheridan Le Fanu" (University of Aberdeen, 2005).

4. E.g., Jamieson Ridenhour's editorial material for *Carmilla* (Kansas City, MO: Valancourt, 2009); Andrew Smith's "Colonial Ghosts: Mimicry, History, and Laughter" in *The Ghost Story 1840–1920: A Cultural History* (Manchester: Manchester University Press, 2010); Nicholas Allen's "Sheridan Le Fanu and the Spectral Empire," in Helen Conrad O'Briain and Julie Anne Stevens, ed., *The Ghost Story from the Middle Ages to the Twentieth Century* (Dublin: Four Courts Press, 2010).

5. E.g., Michael Begnal's *Joseph Sheridan Le Fanu* (Lewisburg, PA: Bucknell University Press, 1971) and W. J. Mc Cormack's *Sheridan Le Fanu and Victorian Ireland.*

6. E.g., Jarlath Killeen's essay in this volume.

Acknowledgments

The editors wish to thank Laura Anzuoni, Anna and Francis Dunlop, Nicola LeFanu, David Lumsdaine, Sarah LeFanu, Mark Le Fanu, Catherine Porteous; Christian Digby-Firth, Derrick Hussey, N. J. R. James, S. T. Joshi, Elizabeth McCarthy, Bernice W. Murphy, Sorcha Ní Fhlainn, Rosemary Pardoe, Robert Lloyd Parry, Barbara and Christopher Roden, David E. Schultz, Jason Van Hollander; Glen Graham, Robyn A. Williams, and Dorothy Jean Williams of the Detroit Public Library, the Public Records Office of Northern Ireland, and each of the contributors for their assistance in the preparation of this volume.

I. Some Notes on Biography

A Memoir of Joseph Sheridan Le Fanu

Alfred Perceval Graves

A noble Huguenot family, owning considerable property in Normandy, the Le Fanus of Caen were, upon the revocation of the Edict of Nantes, deprived of their ancestral estates of Mandeville, Sequeville, and Cresseron; but, owing to their possessing influential relatives at the court of Louis the Fourteenth, were allowed to quit their country for England, unmolested, with their personal property. We meet with John Le Fanu de Sequeville and Charles Le Fanu de Cresseron, as cavalry officers in William the Third's army; Charles being so distinguished a member of the King's staff that he was presented with William's portrait from his master's own hand. He afterwards served as a major of dragoons under Marlborough.

At the beginning of the eighteenth century, William Le Fanu was the sole survivor of his family. He married Henrietta Raboteau de Puggibaut, the last of another great and noble Huguenot family, whose escape from France, as a child, by the aid of a Roman Catholic uncle in high position at the French court, was effected after adventures of the most romantic danger.

Joseph Le Fanu, the eldest of the sons of this marriage who left issue, held the office of Clerk of the Coast in Ireland. He married for the second time, Alicia, daughter of Thomas Sheridan and sister of Richard Brinsley Sheridan; his brother, Captain Henry Le Fanu, of Leamington, being united to the only other sister of the great wit and orator.

Dean Thomas Philip Le Fanu, the eldest son of Joseph Le Fanu, became by his wife Emma, daughter of Dr. Dobbin, F. T. C. D., the father of Joseph Sheridan Le Fanu, the subject of this memoir, whose name is so familiar to English and American readers as one of the greatest masters of the weird and the terrible amongst our modern novelists.

Born in Dublin on the 28th of August, 1814, he did not begin to speak until he was more than two years of age; but when he had once started, the boy showed an unusual aptitude in acquiring fresh words, and using them correctly.

The first evidence of literary taste which he gave was in his sixth year,

17

when he made several little sketches with explanatory remarks written beneath them, after the manner of Du Maurier's, or Charles Keene's humorous illustrations in *Punch*.

One of these, preserved long afterwards by his mother, represented a balloon in mid-air, and two aeronauts, who had occupied it, falling headlong to earth, the disaster being explained by these words: "See the effects of trying to go to Heaven."

As a mere child, he was a remarkably good actor, both in tragic and comic pieces, and was hardly twelve years old when he began to write verses of singular spirit for one so young. At fourteen, he produced a long Irish poem, which he never permitted anyone but his mother and brother to read. To that brother, Mr. William Le Fanu, Commissioner of Public Works, Ireland, to whom, as the suggester of Sheridan Le Fanu's "Phaudrig Crohoore" and "Shamus O'Brien," Irish ballad literature owes a delightful debt, and whose richly humorous and passionately pathetic powers as a raconteur of these poems have only doubled that obligation in the hearts of those who have been happy enough to be his hearers. [. . .]

But besides the poetical powers with which he was endowed, in common with the great Brinsley, Lady Dufferin, and the Hon. Mrs. Norton, young Sheridan Le Fanu also possessed an irresistible humor and oratorical gift that, as a student of Old Trinity, made him a formidable rival of the best of the young debaters of his time at the "College Historical," not a few of whom have since reached the highest eminence at the Irish Bar, after having long enlivened and charmed St. Stephen's by their wit and oratory.

Amongst his compeers he was remarkable for his sudden fiery eloquence of attack, and ready and rapid powers of repartee when on his defense. But Le Fanu, whose understanding was elevated by a deep love of the classics, in which he took university honors, and further heightened by an admirable knowledge of our own great authors, was not to be tempted away by oratory from literature, his first and, as it proved, his last love.

Very soon after leaving college, and just when he was called to the Bar, about the year 1838, he bought *The Warder*, a Dublin newspaper, of which he was editor, and took what many of his best friends and admirers, looking to his high prospects as a barrister, regarded at the time as a fatal step in his career to fame.

Just before this period, Le Fanu had taken to writing humorous Irish stories, afterwards published in the *Dublin University Magazine*, such as the "The Quare Gander," "Jim Sulivan's Adventure," "The Ghost and the Bone-Setter," etc.

These stories his brother William Le Fanu was in the habit of repeating for his friends' amusement, and about the year 1837, when he was about twenty-three years of age, Joseph Le Fanu said to him that he thought an Irish story in verse would tell well, and that if he would choose him a subject suitable for recitation, he would write him one. "Write me an Irish 'Young Lochinvar'," said his brother; and in a few days he handed him "Phaudrig Crohoore"—*Anglice,* "Patrick Crohoore [Connor]."

Of course this poem has the disadvantage not only of being written after "Young Lochinvar," but also that of having been directly inspired by it; and yet, although wanting in the rare and graceful finish of the original, the Irish copy has, we feel, so much fire and feeling that it at least tempts us to regret that Scott's poem was not written in that heart-stirring Northern dialect without which the noblest of our British ballads would lose half their spirit. Indeed, we may safely say that some of Le Fanu's lines are finer than any in "Young Lochinvar," simply because they seem to speak straight from a people's heart, not to be the mere echoes of medieval romance.

"Phaudrig Crohoore" did not appear in print in the *Dublin University Magazine* till 1844, twelve years after its composition, when it was included amongst *The Purcell Papers.*[1]

[. . .] Mr. William Le Fanu, the suggester of this ballad, who was from home at the time, now received daily instalments of the second and more remarkable of his brother's Irish poems—"Shamus O'Brien" (James O'Brien)—learning them by heart as they reached him, and, fortunately, never forgetting them, for his brother Joseph kept no copy of the ballad, and he had himself to write it out from memory ten years after, when the poem appeared in the *Dublin University Magazine* [July 1850].

Few will deny that this poem contains passages most faithfully, if fearfully, picturesque, and that it is characterised throughout by a profound pathos, and an abundant though at times a too grotesquely incongruous humor. Can we wonder, then, at the immense popularity with which Samuel Lover recited it in the United States? For to Lover's admiration of the poem, and his addition of it to his entertainment, "Shamus O'Brien" owes its introduction into America, where it is now so popular. Lover added some lines of his own to the poem, made Shamus emigrate to the States, and set up a public-house. These added lines appeared in most of the published versions of the poem. But they are indifferent as verse, and certainly injure the dramatic effect of the poem.

"Shamus O'Brien" is so generally attributed to Lover (indeed we re-

---

1. ["Phaudrig Crohoore" first appeared in "Scraps of Hibernian Ballads" (*DUM,* June 1839).—Ed.]

member seeing it advertised for recitation on the occasion of a benefit at a leading London theatre as "by Samuel Lover") that it is a satisfaction to be able to reproduce the following letter upon the subject from Lover to William le Fanu.

Astor House,
New York, U.S. America.
Sept. 30, 1846.

My dear Le Fanu,

    In reading over your brother's poem while I crossed the Atlantic, I became more and more impressed with its great beauty and dramatic effect—so much so that I determined to test its effect in public, and have done so here, on my first appearance, with the greatest success. Now I have no doubt there will be great praises of the poem, and people will suppose, most likely, that the composition is mine, and as you know (I take for granted) that I would not wish to wear a borrowed feather, I should be glad to give your brother's name as the author, should he not object to have it known; but as his writings are often of so different a tone, I would not speak without permission to do so. It is true that in my programme my name is attached to other pieces, and no name appended to the recitation; so far, you will see, I have done all I could to avoid "appropriating," the spirit of which I might have caught here, with Irish aptitude; but I would like to have the means of telling all whom it may concern the name of the author, to whose head and heart it does so much honour. Pray, my dear Le Fanu, inquire, and answer me here by next packet, or as soon as convenient. My success here has been quite triumphant.

Yours very truly,
Samuel Lover.

We have heard it said (though without having inquired into the truth of the tradition) that "Shamus O'Brien" was the result of a match at pseudo-national ballad writing made between Le Fanu and several of the most brilliant of his young literary *confrères* at Trinity College, Dublin. But however this may be, Le Fanu undoubtedly was no Young Irelander; indeed he did the stoutest service as a press writer in the Conservative interest, and was no doubt provoked as well as amused at the unexpected popularity to which his poem attained amongst the Irish Nationalists. And here it should be remembered that the ballad was written some eleven years before the outbreak of '48, and at a time when a '98 subject might fairly have been regarded as legitimate literary property amongst the most loyal.[2]

---

2. [Graves is referring to two unsuccessful uprisings in Ireland, the Insurrection of 1798 and the Rebellion of 1848. Cf. Albert Power's "Sheridan Le Fanu and the Spirit of 1798" included in this volume.—Ed.]

We left Le Fanu as editor of *The Warder*. He afterwards purchased the *Dublin Evening Packet,* and much later the half-proprietorship of the *Dublin Evening Mail*. Eleven or twelve years ago he also became the owner and editor of the *Dublin University Magazine*, in which his later as well as earlier Irish stories appeared. He sold it about a year before his death in 1873, having previously parted with *The Warder* and his share in the *Evening Mail*.[3]

He had previously published in the *Dublin University Magazine* a number of charming lyrics, generally anonymously, and it is to be feared that all clue to the identification of most of these is lost, except that of internal evidence.

The following poem, undoubtedly his, should make general our regret at being unable to fix with certainty upon its fellows:

> One wild and distant bugle sound
> Breathed o'er Killarney's magic shore
> Will shed sweet floating echoes round
> When that which made them is no more.
>
> So slumber in the human heart
> Wild echoes, that will sweetly thrill
> The words of kindness when the voice
> That uttered them for aye is still.
>
> Oh! memory, though thy records tell
> Full many a tale of grief and sorrow,
> Of mad excess, of hope decayed,
> Of dark and cheerless melancholy.
>
> Still, memory, to me thou art
> The dearest of the gifts of mind,
> For all the joys that touch my heart
> Are joys that I have left behind.

Le Fanu's literary life may be divided into three distinct periods. During the first of these, and till his thirtieth year, he was an Irish ballad, song, and story writer, his first published story being the "The Fortunes of Sir Robert

---

3. [Le Fanu's term as editor and proprietor of the *DUM* has been given various dates beginning as early as 1860 and ending as late as 1871. According to *The Wellesley Index of Victorian Periodicals, 1824–1900*, Le Fanu was editor from July 1861 to June 1869 and proprietor from 27 July 1861 to March 1870. William Mc Cormack's *Sheridan Le Fanu and Victorian Ireland* (Oxford: Clarendon Press, 1980) accords with this date of purchase and states that Le Fanu sold the magazine to the London printer Charles F. Adams in 1869 (pp. 198, 203).—Ed.]

Ardagh," which appeared in the *Dublin University Magazine* of 1838.[4]

In 1844 he was united to Miss Susan Bennett, the beautiful daughter of the late George Bennett, Q. C. From this time until her decease, in 1858, he devoted his energies almost entirely to press work, making, however, his first essays in novel writing during that period. *The Cock and Anchor, a chronicle of old Dublin City*, his first and, in the opinion of competent critics, one of the best of his novels, seeing the light about the year [1845]. This work, it is to be feared, is out of print, though there is now a cheap edition of *The Fortunes of Colonel Torlogh O'Brien*, its immediate successor. The comparative want of success of these novels seems to have deterred Le Fanu from using his pen, except as a press writer, until 1863, when *The House by the Churchyard* [first serialized in the *Dublin University Magazine* from October 1861 to February 1863] was published, and was soon followed by *Uncle Silas* and his five other well-known novels.

We have considered Le Fanu as a ballad writer and poet. As a press writer he is still most honorably remembered for his learning and brilliancy, and the power and point of his sarcasm, which long made the *Dublin Evening Mail* one of the most formidable of Irish press critics; but let us now pass to the consideration of him in the capacity of a novelist, and in particular as the author of *Uncle Silas*.

There are evidences in "Shamus O'Brien," and even in "Phaudrig Crohoore," of a power over the mysterious, the grotesque, and the horrible, which so singularly distinguish him as a writer of prose fiction.

Uncle Silas, the fairest as well as most familiar instance of this enthralling spell over his readers, is too well known a story to tell in detail. But how intensely and painfully distinct is the opening description of the silent, inflexible Austin Ruthyn of Knowl, and his shy, sweet daughter Maude, the one so resolutely confident in his brother's honour, the other so romantically and yet anxiously interested in her uncle—the sudden arrival of Dr. Bryerly, the strange Swedenborgian, followed by the equally unexpected apparition of Madame de la Rougierre, Austin Ruthyn's painful death, and the reading of his strange will consigning poor Maude to the protection of her unknown Uncle Silas—her cousin, good, bright devoted Monica Knollys, and her dreadful distrust of Silas—Bartram-Haugh and its uncanny occupants, and foremost amongst them Uncle Silas.

---

4. [Graves, whose memoir accompanied the posthumous collection of Le Fanu's *The Purcell Papers* somehow overlooks this story's predecessor, "The Ghost and the Bone-Setter," also included in that volume, which first appeared in the January 1838 issue of the *DUM*.—Ed.]

This is his portrait:

A face like marble, with a fearful monumental look, and for an old man, singularly vivid, strange eyes, the singularity of which rather grew upon me as I
looked; for his eyebrows were still black, though his hair descended from his
temples in long locks of the purest silver and fine as silk, nearly to his shoulders.

He rose, tall and slight, a little stooped, all in black, with an ample black
velvet tunic, which was rather a gown than a coat. . . .

I know I can't convey in words an idea of this apparition, drawn, as it
seemed, in black and white, venerable, bloodless, fiery-eyed, with its singular
look of power, and an expression so bewildering—was it derision, or anguish,
or cruelty, or patience?

The wild eyes of this strange old man were fixed on me as he rose; an habitual contraction, which in certain lights took the character of a scowl, did
not relax as he advanced towards me with a thin-lipped smile.

Old Dicken and his daughter Beauty, old L'Amour and Dudley Ruthyn, now
enter upon the scene, each a fresh shadow to deepen its already somber hue;
while the gloom gathers in spite of the glimpse of sunshine shot through it by
the visit to Elverston. Dudley's brutal encounter with Captain Oakley, and
vile persecution of poor Maude till his love marriage comes to light, lead us
on to the ghastly catastrophe, the hideous conspiracy of Silas and his son
against the life of the innocent girl.

It is interesting to know that the germ of *Uncle Silas* first appeared in the
Dublin University Magazine of 1838, as the short tale, entitled, "Passage in
the Secret History of an Irish Countess." It next was published as "The Murdered Cousin" in a collection of Christmas stories,[5] and finally developed
into the three-volume novel we have just noticed.

There are about Le Fanu's narratives touches of nature which reconcile
us to their always remarkable and often supernatural incidents. His characters are well conceived and distinctly drawn, and strong soliloquy and easy
dialogue spring unaffectedly from their lips. He is a close observer of Nature,
and reproduces her wilder effects of storm and gloom with singular vividness;
while he is equally at home in his descriptions of still life, some of which remind us of the faithfully minute detail of old Dutch pictures.

Mr. Wilkie Collins, amongst our living novelists, best compares with Le
Fanu. Both of these writers are remarkable for the ingenious mystery with
which they develop their plots, and for the absorbing, if often over-

---

5. [Le Fanu's first, anonymous, collection of tales, *Ghost Stories and Tales of Mystery*
(Dublin: James McGlashan, 1851).—Ed.]

sensational, nature of their incidents; but whilst Mr. Collins excites and fas-
cinates our attention by an intense power of realism which carries us with
unreasoning haste from cover to cover of his works, Le Fanu is an idealist,
full of high imagination, and an artist who devotes deep attention to the
most delicate detail in his portraiture of men and women, and his descriptions of the outdoor and indoor worlds—a writer, therefore, through whose
pages it would be often an indignity to hasten. And this more leisurely, and
certainly more classical, conduct of his stories makes us remember them
more fully and faithfully than those of the author of *The Woman in White*.
Mr. Collins is generally dramatic, and sometimes stagy, in his effects. Le
Fanu, while less careful to arrange his plots, so as to admit of their being
readily adapted for the stage, often surprises us by scenes of so much greater
tragic intensity that we cannot but lament that he did not, as Mr. Collins has
done, attempt the drama, and so furnish another ground of comparison with
his fellow-countryman, Charles Maturin (also, if we mistake not, of French
origin), whom, in his writings, Le Fanu far more closely resembles than Mr.
Collins, as a master of the darker and stronger emotions of human character.
But, to institute a broader ground of comparison between Le Fanu and Mr.
Collins, whilst the idiosyncrasies of the former's characters, however immaterial those characters may be, seem always to suggest the minutest detail of
his story, the latter would appear to consider plot as the prime, character as a
subsidiary element in the art of novel writing.

From this society he vanished so entirely that Dublin, always ready with
they, can form any idea of the true character of the man; for after the death
of his wife, to whom he was most deeply devoted, he quite forsook general
society, in which his fine features, distinguished bearing, and charm of conversation marked him out as the beau-ideal of an Irish wit and scholar of the
old school.

From this society he vanished so entirely that Dublin, always ready with
a nickname, dubbed him "The Invisible Prince;" and indeed he was for long
almost invisible, except to his family and most familiar friends, unless at odd
hours of the evening, when he might occasionally be seen stealing, like the
ghost of his former self, between his newspaper office and his home in Merrion Square; sometimes, too, he was to be encountered in an old out-of-the-
way bookshop poring over some rare black letter Astrology or Demonology.

To one of these old bookshops he was at one time a pretty frequent visitor, and the bookseller relates how he used to come in and ask with his peculiarly pleasant voice and smile, "Any more ghost stories for me, Mr. ——?"
and how, on a fresh one being handed to him, he would seldom leave the
shop until he had looked it through. This taste for the supernatural seems to

have grown upon him after his wife's death, and influenced him so deeply that, had he not been possessed of a deal of shrewd common sense, there might have been danger of his embracing some of the visionary doctrines in which he was so learned. But no! even spiritualism, to which not a few of his brother novelists succumbed, whilst affording congenial material for our artist of the superhuman to work upon, did not escape his severest satire.

Shortly after completing his last novel, strange to say, bearing the title *Willing to Die,* Le Fanu breathed his last at his home No. 18, Merrion Square South, at the age of fifty-[eight].

"He was a man," writes the author of a brief memoir of him in the *Dublin University Magazine,* "who thought deeply, especially on religious subjects. To those who knew him he was very dear; they admired him for his learning, his sparkling wit, and pleasant conversation, and loved him for his manly virtues, for his noble and generous qualities, his gentleness, and his loving, affectionate nature." And all who knew the man must feel how deeply deserved are these simple words of sincere regard for Joseph Sheridan Le Fanu.

Le Fanu's novels are accessible to all; but his "Purcell Papers" are now for the first time collected and published, by the permission of his eldest son (the late Mr. Philip Le Fanu), and very much owing to the friendly and active assistance of his brother, Mr. William Le Fanu.

Anecdotes from Seventy Years of Irish Life

W. R. Le Fanu

I was born on the 24th of February, 1816, at the Royal Hibernian Military School in the Phoenix Park, Dublin; my father being then chaplain to that institution. I was the youngest of three children—the eldest was Catherine Frances; the second, Joseph Sheridan, author of *Uncle Silas* and other novels, and of "Shamus O'Brien" and other Irish ballads. [p. 1]

In the year 1826, my father having been appointed Dean of Emly and Rector of Abington, we left Dublin to live at Abington, in the county of Limerick. Here our education, except in French and English, which our father taught us, was entrusted to a private tutor, an elderly clergyman, Stinson by name, who let us learn just as much, or rather as little, as we pleased. For several hours every day this old gentleman sat with us in the schoolroom, when he was supposed to be engaged in teaching us classic lore, and invigorating our young minds by science; but being an enthusiastic disciple of old Isaak,[1] he in reality spent the whole, or nearly the whole, time in tying flies for trout or salmon and in arranging his fishing gear, which he kept in a drawer behind him. Soon after he had come to us, he had wisely taken the precaution of making us learn by heart several passages from Greek and Latin authors; and whenever our father's foot step was heard to approach the school room, the flies were nimbly thrown into the drawer, and the old gentleman, in his tremulous and nasal voice, would say, "Now, Joseph, repeat that ode of Horace" . . . As soon as our father's step was heard to recede, "That will do," said our preceptor; the drawer was reopened, and he at once returned, with renewed vigor, to his piscatory preparations, and we to our games. Fortunately my father's library was a large and good one; there my brother spent much of his time in poring over many a quaint and curious volume.[2] [pp. 7–8]

---

1. [William refers to the British writer Isaak Walton (1593–1683), whose most popular work was *The Compleat Angler*, first published in 1653 and reprinted frequently thereafter.—Ed.]

2. [William paraphrases Poe's "The Raven" (1845): "Once upon a midnight dreary,

26

When scarcely fifteen years of age my brother Joseph had written many pieces of poetry, which showed a depth of imagination and feeling unusual in a boy that age . . . He let no one see these poems but his mother, his sister, and myself. Whether he feared his father's criticism I cannot tell, but he never let him see them; still, he certainly had no great dread of my father, for whenever he had incurred his displeasure he would at once disarm him by some witty saying. One thing that much distressed the Dean was his being habitually late for prayers. One morning breakfast was nearly over and he had not appeared; and when he at last came in it was near ten o'clock. My father, holding his watch in his hand, said in his severest voice, "I ask you, Joseph, I ask you seriously, is this right?" "No, sir," said Joe, glancing at the watch; "I'm sure it must be fast." [pp. 9, 11]

Practical jokes, I am glad to say, are seldom practiced now, but in my early days they were much in vogue. Here is one my brother played on me:—I was in Dublin, and had a long letter from my father, who was at home at Abington, giving me several commissions. In a postscript, he said, "Send me immediately *Dodd's Holy Curate*. If Curry has not got it you will be sure to get it at some other booksellers'; but be sure to send it, if possible, by return of post." Curry had it not; in vain I sought it at other booksellers, so I wrote to my father to say that it was not to be had in Dublin, and that Curry did not know the book, but had written to his publishers in London to send it direct to Abington. By return of post I had a letter from my father saying he was utterly at a loss to know what I meant, that he had never asked me to get him *Dodd's Holy Curate*, and had never known of the existence of such a book. There is, in fact, no such book. What had happened was this: my father had gone out of the library for a few minutes, and had left his letter to me, which he had just finished, open on his writing-table; Joseph had gone into the library and took the opportunity of my father's absence to add the postscript, exactly imitating his writing, and on his return my father duly folded the letter and sent it to the post without having perceived my brother's addition to it.

Another, not so harmless—but boys are mischievous—he played on an elder woman, whom he met near Dublin when he was staying on a visit with some friends. He had never seen the woman before, and never saw her after;

---

while I pondered, weak and weary, / Over many a quaint and curious volume of forgotten lore." This is likely an attempt to root his brother's interest in the Gothic and macabre to his youth, even though Joseph would have been in his thirties when the "The Raven" was first published.—Ed.]

but she looked at him as if she recognized him, stopped and stood before him looking earnestly at his face, when the following dialogue ensued:—

Woman. "Oh, then Masther Richard, is that yourself?"

Joseph. "Of course it is myself. Who else should I be?"

Woman. "Ah, then, Masther Richard, it's proud I am to see you. I hardly knew you at first, you're grown so much. Ah, but it's long since I seen any of the family. And how is the mistress and all the family?"

Joseph. "All quite well, thank you. But why don't you ever come to see us?"

Woman. "Ah, Masther Richard, don't you know I daren't face the house since that affair?"

Joseph. "Don't you know that is all forgotten and forgiven long ago? My mother and all would be delighted to see you."

Woman. "If I knew that, I'd have been up to the house long ago."

Joseph. "I'll tell you what to do—come up on Sunday to dinner with the servants. You know the hour; and you will be surprised at the welcome you will get."

Woman. "Well, please God, I will, Masther Richard. Good-bye, Masther Richard, and God bless you."

What sort of welcome the old lady (she had very probably been dismissed for stealing silver spoons) received on her arrival on the following Sunday has not transpired; but I dare say she was "surprised" at it. [pp. 11–13]

To return to my brother:—the tone of those early verses . . . as well as that of some of his later ballads, was due to his mother, who, as a girl, had been in her heart more or less a rebel. She told him of the hard fate which, in '98,[3] befell many of those whom she knew and admired. She told him much of Lord Edward Fitzgerald and the fight he made for his life, and showed him the dagger with which he fought for it. It is many years now since she gave me that dagger, and with it the account of how it came into her possession. [p. 16]

Amongst our neighbors was a Mr. K——, who lived about five miles from us, and had a very pretty daughter, with whose beauty and brightness my brother, when about nineteen, was much taken. In those days it was a custom on St. Valentine's Day for every lover to send a "valentine" to the lady of his heart, so to Miss K——he sent the following:—

---

3. [A reference to the failed though much romanticized 1798 Irish Rebellion in which semi-disparate factions of the United Irishmen rose against the British establishment, first in the counties nearest Dublin, then spreading to other parts of Ireland. The uprising was excessively bloody and led to the Act of Union in 1800.—Ed.]

Life were too long for me to bear
　　If banished from thy view;
Life were too short a thousand year,
　　If life were passed with you.

Wise men have said, "Man's lot on earth
　　Is grief and melancholy,"
But where thou art there joyous mirth
　　Proves all their wisdom folly.

If fate withhold thy love from me,
　　All else in vain were given;
Heaven were imperfect wanting thee,
　　And with thee earth were heaven. [p. 43]

After our return to Abington we occasionally spent a few weeks in summer at Kilkee, in the county of Clare, now a much-frequented watering place, then a wild village on the wildest coast of Ireland. A new steamboat, the *Garry Owen,* had then begun to ply between Limerick and Kilrush, a considerable town, about eight miles from Kilkee. On the voyage, which generally took about four hours sometimes five or more if the weather was bad the passengers were cheered by the music and songs of a famous character, one Paddy O'Neill, whose playing on the fiddle was only surpassed by his performances on the bagpipes. He was, moreover, a poet, and sang his own songs with vigor and expression to his own accompaniment.

One summer evening my brother, who was a prime favorite of his, persuaded Paddy to drive across with him from Kilrush to Kilkee, and there they got up a dance in Mrs. Reade's lodge, where some of our family were sojourning at the time. I am sorry to say I was away somewhere and missed the fun. The dance music was supplied by Paddy's pipes and fiddle, and between the dances he sang some of his favorite songs. Next day my brother wrote some doggerel verses celebrating the dance and in imitation of the "Wedding of Ballyporean," a song then very popular in the south of Ireland. One verse ran:—

But Paddy no longer his fiddle could twig,
And the heat was so great that he pulled off his wig;
But Mary McCarthy being still for a jig,
He screwed his old pipes till they roared like a pig.
　　Oh! they fell to their dancing once more, sir,
　　Till their marrow bones all grew quite sore, sir,
　　And they were obliged to give o'er, sir,
　　　　At the dance in the lodge at Kilkee.

A copy of the verses was presented to Paddy, who was highly delighted with them, and for years after sang them with much applause to the passengers on the *Garry Owen*. A few days after the dance he came to see my brother, and said he would be for ever obliged to him if he would alter one little word in the song.

"Of course I shall, with pleasure," said my brother. "What is the word?"

"Pig, your honor," said Paddy. "I'm sure your honor doesn't think my beautiful pipes sounded like a pig."

"Oh," he answered, "you don't think I meant that they sounded like the grunt or squeak of a pig? I only meant that they were as loud as a pig."

"As loud as a pig!" said Paddy, rather indignantly; "as loud as a pig! They wor a great deal louder; but if your honor wouldn't mind changing that one word, I think it would be a great improvement, and would sound more natural like. This is the way I'd like it to go:—

> But Mary McCarthy being still for a jig,
> He screwed his old pipes till they roar'd like a nymph.

You see, your honor, the rhyme would be just as good, and I think it would be more like the rale tune of it."

The suggested improvement was at once made, to Paddy's great satisfaction.

My brother told me that it was a favorite song of Paddy's that suggested to him the plot of "Shamus O'Brien." [pp. 84–87]

In 1839 my brother became connected with the *Dublin University Magazine*, of which he was subsequently the proprietor; to it he contributed the many interesting and amusing Irish stories, afterwards collected in *The Purcell Papers*. Some of them I used occasionally to recite, and wishing to have one in verse, I asked him to write one for me. He said he did not know what subject I would like. I said, "Give me an Irish 'Young Lochinvar'," and in a few days he sent me "Phaudrig Crohoore" ("Patrick Connor"; or, more correctly, "Patrick the Son of Connor").

When "Phaudrig Crohoore" appeared in the *Dublin University Magazine*, my brother, under his *nom de plume*, wrote a preface to it, in which he said that it had been composed by a poor Irish minstrel, Michael Finley, who could neither read nor write, but used to recite it, with others of his songs and ballads, at fairs and markets.

Many years afterwards, one evening, after I had recited it at Lord Spencer's, who was then Lord Lieutenant of Ireland, the late primate, Beresford, said to Lady Spencer, who was sitting near me, "I can tell you a curious fact, Lady Spencer; that poem was composed by a poor Irish peasant, one

Michael Finley, who could neither read nor write." Then turning to me, "Were you aware of that, Mr. Le Fanu?" I was, your Grace," said I; "and you may be surprised to hear that I knew the Michael Finley who wrote the ballad intimately—he was, in fact, my brother. But in one particular your Grace is mistaken; he could read and write a little." The primate took it very well, and was much amused. [pp. 93, 96–97]

In a very hot July five and fifty years ago, a walking party left my father's house to visit some places of note in the counties of Limerick, Cork, and Tipperary. Our party consisted of John Walsh, afterwards Master of the Rolls in Ireland; John Jellett, the late Provost of Trinity College, Dublin; Gaetano Egedi, an Italian friend of ours; my brother, and myself. The weather being unusually warm, our plan was to start each day late in the afternoon, arriving at our destination about midnight, and visiting next day whatever was of interest in the neighborhood. Towards the end of our tour we arrived late one night at Mitchelstown, famous for its caves, and now also of sacred political memory.[4] Next morning we set off, immediately after breakfast, for the caves, which are about six miles from the town, near the village of Ballyporeen, celebrated in the old Irish song, "The Wedding of Ballyporeen," in which the wedding feast is thus described:—

> There was bacon and greens, but the turkey was spoiled;
> Potatoes dressed every way, roasted and boiled;
> Red herrings, plum-pudding the priest got a snipe;
> Cobladdy, stiff dumpling, and cow-heel and tripe.
> Oh! they ate till they could ate no more, sir;
> Then the whisky came pouring galore, sir.
> How Terence McManus did roar, sir,
> At the wedding of Ballyporeen!

The caves are in the cavernous limestone formation, and not unlike those of Derbyshire. We entered by a sort of ladder, which, after a descent of about thirty feet, leads to a long and narrow sloping passage, ending in a chamber about eighty feet in diameter, and thirty feet high. From this lofty hall a series of passages lead to other chambers of various sizes and heights; in many of them the stalactites from the roof uniting with the stalagmites from

---

4. [The Mitchelstown Caves are today, as they were in Le Fanu's time, a tourist attraction located near Burncourt, County Tipperary. The impressive limestone cave system (with passages totaling three kilometers) was discovered in 1833. The "Mitchelstown Massacre" occurred in 1887 when three campaigners for the Irish Land League were shot dead by police officers for inciting the non-payment of unfair rent.–Ed.]

the floor form white pillars of glistening brightness; the whole effect of these halls when lighted up is very beautiful.

Having spent most of the day in the caves, we started about seven in the afternoon for Tipperary, which we hoped to reach by midnight. To go there by road would have been a walk of some five and twenty or thirty miles, while straight across the Galtee mountains[5] was little more than half the distance; we therefore adopted the latter route. Lest we should lose our way, we secured the services of a guide, a fine young peasant, who said he knew the way across the mountains well. He could speak but little English; this however did not matter much, as we only wanted him to lead us. Off we set on this splendid summer evening, bright and calm. After a while we sat down for a little rest among the heather, high up on Galtee More. It was a glorious sight as we looked back on the great plain below us, with its green pastures and waving cornfields bathed in the light of the setting sun. We could not rest long, and were soon on foot again, and had nearly reached the crest of the range, when suddenly a fog rolled down upon us, so thick that we could not see more than thirty or forty yards. On we trudged, vainly hoping that the fog would lift; but, far from doing so, it grew darker every hour. We wandered on till we had crossed the summit; but soon after we and our guide had completely lost our way. On reaching the edge of a lake we asked the guide in which direction we should go round it, and found, as we had suspected, that he was as hopelessly lost as we were, and saw plainly that he had never known that there was a lake there. We went round by its margin till we came to a small stream flowing from it; we followed its course, knowing that it must lead us to the lower lands.

It was night now, and though the fog was as thick as ever, it was not altogether dark, as some little moonlight shone through it. The guide tried to cheer us up by constantly saying, "Na-bochlish"[6] (never mind), "the houses is near, the houses is near." Once, some fifteen or twenty yards from us, a horse galloped past; as well as we could see he was of a chestnut color. We were too anxious to find our way to think much of this; but our guide brightened up immensely. "See the *coppel*"[7] (the horse), "gentlemen," he said; "I tell'd ye the houses is near." But, alas! near the houses were not, and we had yet before us many a scramble through brakes of gorse, and many a tumble

5. [The Galtee Mountains, sometimes "Galty," in County Tipperary, are Ireland's highest inland mountain range.–Ed.]

6. ["Na-bochlish" is William Le Fanu's phonetic spelling of *ná bac leis*, Irish for "never mind."–Ed.]

7. ["*Coppel*" is the phonetic spelling of *capall*, Irish for "horse."–Ed.]

over rocks and tussocks. By this time the moon had gone down, and we were in complete darkness. The fog lifted as suddenly as it had come upon us. I forget which of us suggested that we should all shout together as loudly as we could, and thus, perhaps, attract the notice of some dweller on the slope of the mountain. After several shouts, to our joy, we heard in the distance an answering shout, and soon saw a bright light in the direction from which the welcome sounds had come. Shout answered shout as we hurried down; at times the light went out, but soon blazed up again.

At last, on the opposite side of a narrow glen full of rocks and brush-wood, we saw the figures of men and women lighted up by a flaming sheaf of straw, which one of the men held up high in his hands. We quickly crossed the glen, and were at once surrounded. "Who are ye?" "What do ye want?" "Are ye peelers?"[8] "What sort of gentlemen are ye at all to be on the mountains this time of night?" To these and many such-like questions we gave the best answers we could.

After a brief conversation, in Irish, with our guide, they led us to a large thatched farm-house; the habitation highest on the hills. They explained to us that they and some of their neighbors had been at the fair at Bansha and stayed out late, and just as they got home had heard our shouts. A huge turf fire was blazing on the hearth, at which we sat drying our nether garments, which were thoroughly drenched; great mugs of hot goat's milk were supplied to warm our insides, our host informing us that he had upwards of eighty goats on the mountain. He and the boys (all unmarried men are boys in the south) and girls sat up with us by the cheery fire, talking, joking, and telling stories. After some time my brother happened to say to the man of the house, "I suppose that was your horse that passed us on the mountain?"

All were silent, and looked one at another half incredulous, half frightened. One of them, after a pause, said, "There is no horse on the mountain. What sort of a horse was it that ye thought ye seen?"

"A chestnut horse," said we.

"Oh, begorra!" said our friend; "they seen the yalla horse!" Then turning to us, "It's a wonder ye all cum down alive and safe; it is few that sees the yalla horse that has luck after."

This was one of the superstitions of the dwellers on the Galtees. We afterwards thought that it might have been a red deer that passed us, as at that time it was supposed that there were a few of them, wild ones, still on the mountain. From what our entertainers told us it appears that had not the night been so calm, we should have been in considerable danger of an attack

---

8. ["Peeler" is slang for police officer.–Ed.]

by the enchanted "wurrum," who had his abode in the dark lake we had passed; but fortunately for us it is only on wild and stormy nights that, with fearful roars, he emerges from the lake to waylay benighted wanderers.

One of the boys now asked us whether we had heard what had happened that day. As we had not, he told us that "a very responsible man," as he called him, had been shot dead that morning hard by towards Bansha. (He was, I think, Mr. Massey Dawson's steward or forester.) He did not exactly know, he said, why the man had been shot, but thought he was hard on the people about the price of timber, and had also dismissed some laborers.

Another of the boys said, "Now, why didn't they give him a good batin', and not to go kill him entirely?"

"Ah, then, I suppose," said the other, "they kem from a distance and didn't like to go home without finishing the job."

"But," said the other very seriously, "what will them chaps do on the day of judgment?"

"Oich," said his friend, "what does that signify? Sure many a boy done a foolish turn."

It is not improbable that our friends knew perfectly well who had been engaged in the murder. However that may be, early next morning we bid our entertainers a hearty farewell, and, again refreshed with hot goat's milk, started for the town of Tipperary, passing through the glen of Aherlow, then one of the most disturbed places in Ireland, about which the saying amongst the people was, "Wherever the devil is by day he is sure to be in the glen of Aherlow by night." It was the only time my brother saw that lovely valley, which he made the home of Shamus O'Brien in the popular ballad. [pp. 116–22]

The ballad [Shamus O'Brien] was written in a very few days, in the year 1840, and sent to me day by day by my brother as he wrote it to Dundalk, where I was then staying. I quickly learned it by heart, and now and then recited it. The scraps of paper on which it was written were lost, and years after, when my brother wished for a copy, I had to write it out from memory for him. One other copy I wrote out in the same way and gave to Samuel Lover when he was starting on his tour through the United States . . .

Notwithstanding his disclaimer of authorship, I afterwards, more than once, heard the poem attributed to Lover. He did, indeed, add a few lines, by no means an improvement to it, in which he makes Shamus emigrate to America, where he sets up a public-house, and writes home to his mother to invite her to come out and live with him in his happy home. I suppose he thought that this would suit the taste of the Irish-Americans.

Many years after this, when I had recited the poem at the house of my friend, Sir William Stirling Maxwell, he said, "I was afraid poor Shamus would be hanged." "I didn't think so for a moment," said Lord Dufferin. "Why?" said Sir William. "Possibly," said Lord Dufferin, "it may have been because I have heard William Le Fanu recite it once or twice before." [pp. 127–29]

In the spring of 1841 a great grief befell us in the death of our only sister, the constant and loved companion of our young days. Her cleverness, her sweet temper, and, above all, her wondrous goodness, had endeared her, not to us alone, but to all who knew her. Without a particle of that cant or one of those shibboleths which spoil the conversation and mar the usefulness of so many, she influenced for good all who came in contact with her. She was the idol of the poor in our neighborhood. There are still old people at Abington who speak of her as "the good Miss Catherine," and tell of all the good she did.

She had been early a contributor to the *Dublin University Magazine*, in which she wrote most pleasantly,[9] but fell into ill-health and died when she was twenty-seven. She was her father's darling. After her death he never was the same, and did not very long survive her. We were summoned from Dublin to her death-bed. Great was her joy at seeing us and having us with her. She had feared that we would not arrive in time to see her.

It was in this same year, 1841, that my brother took his B. A. degree in the University,[10] and soon afterwards was called to the Irish Bar.[11] But he almost immediately became connected with the Press, and proprietor and editor of *The Warder*, a paper of note in Ireland; and shortly afterwards he purchased another paper, which he also edited. This was injurious to his future prospects, as it prevented his applying himself to a profession, for which his eloquence and ready wit fitted him, and of which his contemporaries had hoped to see him a distinguished member. Later on he purchased, and for some time edited, the *Dublin University Magazine*. It was in that periodical he published the first of Rhoda Broughton's novels. She was first cousin to my brother's wife, Susan Bennett, the charming daughter of the late George Bennett, Q. C., whom he married in the year 1844.

In 1845 the first and one of his best novels, *The Cock and Anchor, a*

9. [Catherine Frances Le Fanu (1813–1841): "The Botheration of Billy McCormack—Showing that Innocence Leads to Ruination" (*DUM* 16 [November 1840]: 539–44) appears to be her only contribution to the *Dublin University Magazine.*—Ed.]

10. [Trinity College, Dublin; founded in 1592. In Joseph Sheridan Le Fanu's lifetime it was Ireland's most prestigious Protestant university.—Ed.]

11. [Le Fanu was called to the Bar in 1839.—Ed.]

Chronicle of old Dublin City, appeared; and very soon his second, *The Fortunes of Torlogh O'Brien.* They were published in Dublin, and were unsuccessful. I know not why, for they were quite equal to some of his most
successful novels.

Owing to their want of success, and to the amount of time he was
obliged to devote to the Press, he did not for eighteen years again take up his
pen as a novelist. It was not until 1863 that his next [novel], *The House by
the Church-yard,* appeared. It was soon followed by *Uncle Silas,* the best
known of his novels, and afterwards by [several] others.

His wife, to whom he was devotedly attached, died in 1858, and from
this time he entirely forsook general society, and was seldom seen except by
his near relations and a few familiar friends. In the year 1871, almost immediately after the publication of his last novel, *Willing to Die,* he breathed his
last in his house in Merrion Square.[12] One who knew him long and well thus
speaks of him in a short memoir which appeared, in the *Dublin University
Magazine,*[13] soon after his death: "He was a man who thought deeply, especially on religious subjects. To those who knew him he was very dear. They
admired him for his learning, his sparkling wit, and pleasant conversation,
and loved him for his manly virtues, for his noble and generous qualities, his
gentleness, and his loving, affectionate nature."

All who knew my brother will feel the truth of these few simple words.
[pp. 138–40]

---

12. [*Willing to Die* was completed shortly before Sheridan Le Fanu's death in 1873,
and serialized posthumously. Curious that William, who visited his brother on his
death-bed and was in the house to help the family with funeral arrangements and
other business affairs following his brother's death, should have supplied the wrong
date in this instance.—Ed.]

13. [An anonymous obituary; *Dublin University Magazine* (March 1873): 319–20. See "A
Void Which Cannot Be Filled Up" by Brian J. Showers included in this volume.—Ed.]

Extracts from
Wilkie Collins, Le Fanu and Others

S. M. Ellis

The outstanding characteristic of Le Fanu is his amazing literary versatility. As Mr. Edmund Downey has well put it, "Sober, orderly historical romance; stories charged with boisterous fun and frolic; stories of the supernatural, which of their kind have no equal; stirring ballads; lyrics full of sweetness and sympathy; tender love stories; novels with plot and purpose and passion, alive with creatures of flesh and blood—all were creations of the same brain." In England Le Fanu's fame rests upon his

---

[S. M. Ellis's famous biographical essay on Le Fanu, expanded from a piece first published in the *Bookman* (London) 51 (October 1916), remains as vivid, entertaining, and gracefully written now as it was when it first appeared in print nearly a century ago. This essay was among the main sources of information for scholars of Le Fanu and the weird tale between the time of its revised publication in 1931 and the appearance of the first full-length biography, W. J. Mc Cormack's *Sheridan Le Fanu and Victorian Ireland*, in 1980. Unfortunately, Ellis, in accordance with the standards of his time, does not always cite his sources, which makes the most dramatic event described in both essays (see the final extract included here) rather puzzling. There is no reason to believe, given Ellis's diligence in this and other works, that he had not received this information from a source he considered reliable; but the absence of citation for that particular source proved critical once Mc Cormack published correspondence written by the Le Fanu family written within two days of the same tragic event, which directly contradicts key details in Ellis's account. Thus, we are left with a charming but not altogether verifiable portrait of Le Fanu, informed by previous accounts, and deepened further by Ellis's own research and his friendship with the author's youngest son, the illustrator George Brinsley Le Fanu (1854–1929), which is consistent with the habits and character described by the author's family and close associates. Ellis makes it so easy for the reader to summon up a "willing suspension of disbelief" that even those anecdotes since cast into doubt have taken on a death-in-life of their own.—Ed.]

stories of the supernatural and of murder, but other aspects of his work are almost unknown. In Ireland he is remembered for his ballads of national aspirations and studies of native character and types. To understand these latter phases of his literary expression it is necessary to look back to the author's origin and boyhood. [p. 140]

Joseph was ever a lover of practical jokes, and one of the earliest perpetrated by himself and his brother, William, occurred at Abington Rectory. There was a huge watch-dog there of uncertain temper; one time he would be playful as a kitten, and another as ferocious as a lion. One day when the dog's mood was mild, the boys decided to dress him up in some ancient garments they had discovered in a cupboard. Accordingly Carlo was attired in an old blue cloth tail-coat, ornamented with brass buttons, while a green cocked-hat was placed on his head. Enjoying the joke, the dog pranced up and down in his finery, but when the boys tried to divest him of his clothes he showed fight and turned on his savage mood, he set himself down by the front steps, snarling, and there the boys had to leave him. Some time later, the Dean, chancing to look out of one of the front windows, noticed that a large number of people were assembled outside the gate, all gazing in the direction of the hall-door, and laughing heartily. He went out, and found the masquerading dog to be the cause of the excitement, but all his efforts to remove the animal were in vain. Both lost their tempers, and the Dean's annoyance was increased by the fact that every idler of the neighborhood was assembled to witness the contest. The dog won, and remained on the steps in his fancy dress for days, having much the appearance of a disheveled reveler from a ball shut out from his own door. As Le Fanu used to say, when telling this story, the vain hound of Abington set the fashion for a philosophy of clothes long before Carlyle's Teufelsdröckh[1] evolved his system. [pp. 141–42]

At Abington, where, as I have said, Joseph Le Fanu spent most of his boyhood, there was constant excitement, and often danger, when, in 1831, came the Tithe troubles.[2] Both Le Fanu's sister and brother were stoned, and the Rectory people were well armed. One day William Le Fanu and a cousin, Robert Flemyng, when out riding were saluted by a considerable crowd with

---

1. [A reference to the Philosopher of Clothes in Thomas Carlyle's (1795–1881) satirical *Sartor Resartus* (1833–34).—Ed.]

2. [The Tithe War (1830–33) was a widespread campaign by the Catholic majority against paying tithes assessed on property and chattels to support the "official" church attended by the ruling Protestant minority.—Ed.]

cries of "Down with the Orangemen! Down with the Tithes!" A cart was pushed across the road, but the boys drew their pistols and got away under a shower of stones. A quarter of a mile further on they came upon another band of disaffected who flung volley after volley of stones. The boys were covered with blood, but fortunately were not stunned. [pp. 144–45]

Such were the quaint and plaintive people, passionate, often treacherous and murderous, yet often lovable and faithful, among whom Le Fanu spent some of his most impressionable years, whose qualities of mind and character he grew to understand more truly perhaps than any other author who has sought to present his humble fellow-countrymen in poetry and prose. Thus it came about that in the first phase of his literary career Le Fanu interpreted the lives and aspirations of the Irish peasantry, particularly those of Limerick and the neighboring counties; and no better vantage ground for his observation could have been found than his home at Abington in the seething Thirties. Here the faction fights and the superstitions of the peasantry were of immense interest to the Le Fanu boys. . . . Concurrently with his interest in the peasantry of Ireland, Le Fanu had naturally, being an imaginative boy, from his earliest youth found an equal pleasure in the wild legends, the superstitions, and ghost stories of his native land. As he said, "In my youth I heard a great many Irish traditions, more or less of a supernatural character, some of them very peculiar, and all, to a child, at least, highly interesting"; and he goes on to picture the appropriate setting in which he heard these mysterious tales—"the old-fashioned parlor fire-side and its listening circle of excited faces, and, outside, the wintry blast and the moan of leafless boughs, with an occasional rattle of the clumsy old window-frame behind shutter and curtain, as the blast swept by. . . . " [pp. 146, 149]

Even as a boy, Le Fanu became an authority on the superstitions and archeology of Ireland, as is vouched for by Samuel Carter Hall, who has related:

> I knew the brothers Joseph and William Le Fanu when they were youths at Castle Connell, on the Shannon; both became famous—one as an author, the other as a civil engineer. . . . They were my guides throughout the beautiful district around Castle Connell, and I found them full of anecdote and rich in antiquarian lore, with thorough knowledge of Irish peculiarities. They aided us largely in the preparation of our book, *Ireland: its Scenery and Character.* [p. 154]

Wylder's Hand was highly praised by the author's friend, Charles Lever, who wrote to Le Fanu in 1864:

I cannot wait for the end of the month, and the end of your story, to tell you of a very serious blunder you have made in it—a mistake perhaps more palpable to myself than to many of your readers; but which, recognised or not, is still grave. Your blunder was in not holding back your novel some twelve or fifteen years, for you will never beat it—equal it you may, but not pass it. It is first rate, and I feel assured it will have a high success. The two women are beautifully drawn, and the touches of nature in your blackest characters attract the sympathy of the reader to individuals who, if handled by an inferior artist, would have repelled by their cold rascality. In this day of serial deluge, one is driven to hourly comparison; and I tell you frankly, that at my fire-side you carry off the palm from all competitors . . . . Though I said it will be hard for you to beat *Wylder's Hand*, by all means try, at all events. Write on and write fast. I am sure that the imaginative faculty is never the better for lying fallow, and if you be able to falsify my prediction and do greater work, none of your friends will be more rejoiced than myself. [pp. 160–61]

It is curious that Le Fanu was never attracted by the dramatic possibilities of *Uncle Silas* and others of his stories on the stage. He was fond of the theatre and often attended the performances of the old Theatre Royal in Dublin, where on one occasion he found himself seated behind an immensely tall man, wearing an immensely tall top-hat, who completely blocked his view of the stage. On request, the man removed his hat, but the view of the play was not much improved thereby. "I wish," said Le Fanu to his young son Brinsley, who was with him, "that I could muster up courage to ask him to remove his head also." Concerning this point of Le Fanu's neglect of his stage possibilities, Brinsley related:

I never heard my father say that he thought any of his novels would dramatise well, and I fancy had he been constructing a plot for a play he would have worked on very different lines from those he adopted in constructing a plot for a novel. He had considerable knowledge of the conditions with which dramatic literature is bounded, as well as a very keen love of drama itself. Remember, too, that dramatic authors in his day had no opportunity of reaping the golden harvest of a *Charley's Aunt* or *Private Secretary*. This may have had something to do with my father's indifference to this form of authorship. I feel sure that had he turned his attention to it he could have constructed a play fit to rank with the best of his novels.

There has been a dramatic version of *Uncle Silas* adapted by other hands—Laurence Irving and Seymour Hicks—which was produced for a matinée performance at the Shaftsbury Theatre on February 13th, 1892, and afterwards on a provincial tour. William Haviland played the part of Uncle Silas; Holman Clark that of Charke; Violet Vanbrugh played Maud, and

Irene Vanbrugh her cousin Milly; Laurence Irving and Gordon Craig were in small parts, and Dudley Ruthyn, a dialect part, was taken by Mr. Seymour Hicks, who informs me that one of the critics said he "spoke one of the seven unknown languages of the stage." Henry Irving was present at the rehearsal, and perhaps it was the hope of the producers that he would be tempted to assume the role of Silas, which, however, in the provincial run was taken over by his son Laurence. Certainly Henry Irving would have made a fine thing of the macabre Silas and his physical characteristics would have been wonderfully adapted to the description in the book . . . . [pp.163–64]

Mr. T. P. Le Fanu, in his *Memoir of the Le Fanu Family* [1924], has made the interesting suggestion that in the character of Austin Ruthyn, the brother of Silas, the author drew a sketch of himself, which Mr. T. P. Le Fanu says coincides with his own recollections of his uncle:

> It was peculiar figure, strongly made, thick-set, with a face large, and very stern; he wore a loose, black velvet coat and waistcoat . . . he married, and his beautiful young wife died . . . he had left the Church of England for some odd sect . . . and ultimately became a Swedenborgian.

Mr. T. P. Le Fanu records another personal touch in the book. At Knowl there was a portrait of Uncle Silas in youth which represented "a singularly handsome young man, slender, elegant, in a costume then quite obsolete, through I believe it was seen at the beginning of this century—white leather pantaloons and top-boots, a buff waistcoat, and a chocolate-colored coat, and the hair long and brushed back." There was an actual picture with these details hanging in Joseph Le Fanu's dining-room in Merrion Square supposed to be a portrait of George Colman the Younger. [pp. 164–65]

In the Sixties other guests at Le Fanu's house were his gifted cousins on the Sheridan side, Mrs. Norton and Lady Gifford. Percy FitzGerald was also welcome, though Le Fanu did not care by now to see many people for he was rapidly becoming a recluse. FitzGerald has left a pleasant picture of the nights in Merrion Square, the warm, fire-lit dining-room, on the walls of which hung Sheridan family portraits to the number of a dozen and a pastel portrait of Swift given by the author to a Sheridan. Sometimes the niece of Le Fanu's wife, Rhoda Broughton, would be there, and she would read aloud her early literary efforts—tales of fragile heroines and rugged heroes of the school of *Guy Livingstone*. Le Fanu perceived her promise and printed *Not Wisely but Too Well* and *Cometh Up as a Flower* in 1867 in the *Dublin University Magazine*, which he owned. He said to Miss Broughton: "You will succeed, and when you do, remember that I prophesied it." He introduced her to his own publisher in London, Bentley, and by the time *Red as a Rose is She* appeared, in 1872, Rhoda Broughton was famous. Percy FitzGerald says Le Fanu was a very sensitive man and compact of moods, passing from grave to gay, with ever a desire to tell or hear a ghost story. He still, at this time, preserved his predilection for a practical joke, and played quite an elaborate one on Percy FitzGerald. They were discussing the effects of reviews and criticisms, and FitzGerald, who had lately been enjoying some good notices of his books, was discanting on the utter unimportance of such things—the philosopher would be unmoved by them, smile tranquilly if the review was good and contemptuously if it proved to be bad. Le Fanu said nothing, but a few days later FitzGerald received from him a local newspaper which quoted from a London weekly a very stinging notice of FitzGerald's last book which was, indeed, a most bitter attack. FitzGerald rushed round for sympathy to Le Fanu, who condoled and observed: "Well, the only thing is to summon up your philosophy—and smile when a review is bad: but you are *not* smiling?" He smiled himself, however, and owned up to his joke. As the owner of the newspaper, he had been able to have a portion of the type lifted out and inserted in its place this imaginary review of FitzGerald's book which he had composed himself. Only one copy was printed off the introduced type and the other "make-up" was then put back.

Another trick Le Fanu played was on one of his contributors to the *Dublin University Magazine*, the antiquarian writer Patrick Kennedy, who was so ardent an Irish patriot that he frequently claimed famous men of other nationalities as his fellow-countrymen. This amused Le Fanu, who, one evening when he and his friend were discussing race superiority, said, "I suppose you know that Shakespeare was of Irish extraction?" "Was he?" exclaimed Kennedy, very excited. "Yes, there is hardly a doubt of the fact," replied Le Fanu; "he was descended from a branch of the famous O'Shaughnessys— The O'Shaughnessy-Spears; but realizing in England the awkwardness of the name, the family shortened it to Shaugspeare or Shakespere." Mr. Kennedy, much impressed, spent several weeks of research in endeavoring to find the records of The O'Shaughnessy-Spears, but in vain, and he was ashamed to admit that he could not trace Shakespeare to his Celtic source.

More reprehensible was the earlier jest he had practised on William Keogh, later the judge to whom he dedicated *The Wyvern Mystery*. The two were having supper at an old-fashioned tavern in Dublin. Keogh was a nervous, irascible man who eventually committed suicide. He was suspicious of all political opponents, and on this night sat with oysters before him inveighing against some person or movement, when, to continue the story in the words of Brinsley Le Fanu (who related this anecdote to Edmund Downey):

In the course of his philippic he frequently raised his eyes to the ceiling. My father (for some reason which he could not account for except it was the spirit of mischief had suddenly taken possession of him) put a shake of cayenne pepper on Keogh's oysters every time the future judge raised his eyes. "These oysters are rather hot, Le Fanu," he said after the first mouthful. "I don't find them so," replied his friend. "Oh, they're fearfully hot," persisted Keogh. "Nonsense, man!" cried the mischief-maker; "there's nothing the matter with them. It's some trick of your imagination. They are exactly the same oysters I am eating,"—giving them another surreptitious dose of cayenne while Keogh was shooting another glance at the ceiling. Again did Keogh attack the oysters, determined this time not to be daunted by his imagination, though his mouth was like a furnace and his eyes running water. But the ordeal was too much for him, and starting to his feet, his face aflame, he cried: "I know what's the matter. It's that villain Foley" (the proprietor of the tavern). "He has poisoned my oysters!" Le Fanu succeeded in pacifying Keogh; but to the end of his life the judge was ignorant of the cause of the trouble, and he often spoke of the mysterious fiery bivalves which had turned to live coals in his mouth. [pp. 167–69]

His son, Brinsley Le Fanu, gave me a remarkable account of his father's methods of work. He wrote mostly in bed at night, using copy-books for his manuscript. He always had two candles by his side on a small table; one of these dimly glimmering tapers would be left burning while he took a brief sleep. Then, when he awoke about 2 a.m. amid the darkling shadows of the heavy furnishings and hangings of his old-fashioned room, he would brew himself some strong tea—which he drank copiously and frequently throughout the day—and write for a couple of hours in that eerie period of the night when human vitality is at its lowest ebb and the Powers of Darkness rampant and terrifying. What wonder then, that with his brain ever peopled by day and by night with mysterious and terrible beings, he became afflicted by horrible dreams, which, as I have suggested, were the bases of his last stories of the supernatural. Apart from imbibing much strong tea—which apparently was not of the Green variety!—he was a most abstemious man, and a non-smoker. Le Fanu always breakfasted in bed, and at mid-day went down to the dining-room at the back of the house, where he would resume work, writing at a little table which had been a favorite possession of his grand-uncle, Richard Brinsley Sheridan. This room opened out to a small garden, pleasant in spring with lilac and flowering shrubs and fruit blossoms, and in this small monastic-like close he took the little exercise book in hand, his mind still and ever with

> The dark folk who live in souls
> Of passionate men, like bats in the dead trees;
> And with the wayward twilight companies.[3]

During these last years he rarely went out into the city. Only under cover of the darkness of night would be venture out, and then generally to the old book-shops in search of works dealing with demonology and ghost lore . . . . He became altogether a recluse, and would now see no one except his family, and even his old and congenial friend, Charles Lever, was refused admittance on the last occasion, as it proved to be, when he visited Dublin. Le Fanu soon had cause to regret the lost opportunity, for Lever died soon after, in 1872. [pp. 175, 176]

Horrible dreams troubled him to the last, one of the most recurrent and persistent being a vision of a vast and direly foreboding old mansion (such as he had so often depicted in his romances), in a state of ruin and threatening imminently to fall upon and crush the dreamer rooted to the spot. So painful was this repeated horror that he would struggle and cry out in his sleep. He mentioned the trouble to his doctor. When the end came, and the doctor stood by the bedside of Le Fanu and looked in the terror-stricken eyes of the dead man, he said: "I feared this—that house fell at last."[4]

Joseph Sheridan Le Fanu died at 18 Merrion Square, Dublin, on February 7th, 1873, at the age of fifty-eight. He was buried in Mount Jerome Cemetery. [p. 177]

The books of Le Fanu have a remarkably wide appeal and apparently are read with pleasure by the most differential types of mind. He has been, thus, praised by Swinburne, James Payn,[5] Seymour Lucas (the historical painter), and even by the fastidious Henry James, who in one of his short stories, "The

---

3. [From "To Some I Have Talked with by the Fire" by William Butler Yeats.—Ed.]

4. [It has not proven possible to determine who gave Ellis this version of Le Fanu's final hours, but there could be no greater contrast than between this famous account published nearly fifty years after the author's death and the one written within two days of the event by Emma Lucretia Le Fanu, who had been at her father's bedside throughout his final illness. See Brian J. Showers' "A Void Which Cannot Be Filled Up: The Obituaries of J. S. Le Fanu" included in this volume.—Ed.]

5. [James Payn, in *Some Literary Recollections*, writing of the late Prince Leopold, Duke of Albany, says: "I had the satisfaction of introducing him to the works of Le Fanu, and his admiration of that author (so strangely neglected by the general public, notwithstanding the popularity of some of his imitators) vied with my own."—Ed.]

Liar," is describing the arrival of a guest in an English country house, where, in his bedroom, "There was the customary novel of Mr. Le Fanu for the bedside; the ideal reading in a country house for the hours after midnight"; and so anxious was Oliver to commence the enthralling tale that he could not forbear to turn the pages, with the result that his dressing was delayed and he was late for dinner—a truly Jamesian situation for analysis. One must predicate that Le Fanu's reader possess some measure of culture, for he writes with the outlook of a gentleman; his books attest literary allusion and classical knowledge. He is indeed an archaeologist, and I think it is his blend of learning with mystery and crime which created romances that hold the attention of readers who would have no liking for the ordinary sensational novel. For in Le Fanu's work there is something akin to the panoramic pilgrimage of human life, the sunshine and the shadows, the joy and the tragedy, the happy song and the dirge of sorrow, the high lights of the hills of romance and the dark valley through which all must shudderingly pass ere they reach the oblivion of the tomb. [pp. 178–79]

Portraits of Joseph Sheridan Le Fanu

Jim Rockhill, Brian J. Showers, and Douglas A. Anderson

Considering that printed portraits of Le Fanu (28 August 1814–7 February 1873) are few, and fewer still are currently available, we were pleasantly surprised to discover a dozen portraits surviving in a variety of media, from pen and ink to oils to photographs to a plaster mask of the author's face. Many of the portraits included here, reproduced from museums and private collections, have never before appeared in print. Others had been reproduced incomplete, while a few additional images had been printed in only one previous source, where they languished for decades. Although though some of the images reproduced here were originally in color, we regret that we have only been able to reproduce them here in black and white.

This gathering of all known portraits of the author would not have been possible without the kind and greatly appreciated assistance of Anna and Francis Dunlop, David Lumsdaine, Nicola LeFanu, and Sarah LeFanu; W. J. Mc Cormack, Christian Digby-Firth, Robert and Sarah Lloyd Parry; Glen Graham, Dorothy Williams, and Robyn A. Williams of the Detroit Public Library; and Erika Ingham of the National Portrait Gallery, London.

Every effort has been made to locate the original of each portrait as well as provide full details about its creation, current owner, and location.

Dates and inscriptions for these portraits have survived only in part, and are occasionally contradictory; therefore the chronological arrangement in the following gallery is conjectural, though reasonably accurate.

I.   Miniature in Decorative Wooden Frame

Date: c. early 1830s

Artist: Unknown

Medium: Possibly oil on card, with a decorative wooden frame

Dimensions: 8.5 cm × 10 cm (with frame: 16 cm × 22 cm)© Courtesy of Anna and Francis Dunlop. Mrs. Anna Dunlop is the great granddaughter of William Richard Le Fanu.

This miniature painting is one of the earliest known portraits of Le Fanu. The youthful features suggest a date earlier than the National Portrait Gallery of London's watercolor (II) dated December 1842, or the "wedding portrait" (III) from c. 1843. Le Fanu's youthful countenance along with the book in his hand may very well imply that he was a schoolboy when he sat for this portrait, suggesting the early 1830s. It appears in print here for the first time.

The inscription on the back of the portrait, written in William Richard Le Fanu's hand, reads, "My brother / Joseph Sheridan leFanu / Author of Uncle Silas etc etc / W R LeFanu 31 [Ma?]y 1893." Some of the inscription is no longer legible, thus the shape of the first letter and terminal "y" suggests May, but is not definite.

A card affixed to the back by the framer reads "Daniel Egan, / Carver, Gilder, and Printseller, / 26, Lower Ormond Quay, / Dublin." A second card states that the portrait was once the property of William R. Le Fanu.

II. Watercolor in the National Portrait Gallery, London

Title: *Joseph Thomas Sheridan Le Fanu* (NPG 4864)

Date: c. 1842

Artist: Unknown

Medium: Watercolor

Dimensions: 14.6 cm × 19.4 cm

© Courtesy of the National Portrait Gallery, London.

Although the National Portrait Gallery's records state "c. 1842," inscribed on the portrait's reverse is "Joseph Thomas Sheridan Le Fanu / December 1842 aged 27." The portrait was a gift to the National Portrait Gallery in 1972 by the gallery's Chairman of Trustees, Lloyd Tyrell-Kenyon, 5th Baron Kenyon (1917–1993). The portrait's provenance prior to Lord Kenyon's ownership is unknown. The portrait is not generally on display at the gallery.

III. Wedding Portrait

Date: c. 1843

Medium: Watercolor

Dimensions: 24 cm × 30 cm

© Courtesy of Christian Digby-Firth.

This painting, and its companion piece depicting Susanna Bennett, was probably commissioned on the occasion of Le Fanu's marriage to Miss Bennett in December 1843. Although originally in color, the painting is reproduced in black in white on the cover of W. J. Mc Cormack's *Sheridan Le Fanu and Victorian Ireland* (Oxford: Clarendon Press, 1980) and within *The Illustrated J. S. Le Fanu*, selected and edited by Michael Cox (Wellingborough: Equation, 1988). The colors on the cover of the second enlarged edition of *Sheridan Le Fanu and Victorian Ireland* (Dublin: Lilliput Press, 1991) are tinting added to the previous black and white image.

Emery Walker ph. sc.

Joseph Sheridan Le Fanu

IV. Photogravure Plate by Emery Walker

Title: *Joseph Sheridan Le Fanu*
Medium: Photogravure
Photogravure: Sir Emery Walker (1851–1933)

This photograph was first published in T[homas] P[hilip] Le Fanu's *Memoir of the Le Fanu Family* (privately printed, 1924). It is signed "Emery Walker ph. sc."

Emery Walker was a noted photographer and engraver who lived and worked most of his life in London. Walker's home at 7 Hammersmith Terrace in London is preserved and open to the public.

Since the part in the subject's hair is opposite to that in all other known portraits, it is reasonable to assume that this image was reproduced in reverse, possibly during the process of reproducing it in photogravure. Cf. the photograph printed by Werner & Son (V). The whereabouts of the original and its photographic source is unknown.

Werner & Son

39 GRAFTON ST
DUBLIN.

V. Photograph Printed by Werner & Son

Medium:　　　Photograph
© Courtesy of Anna and Francis Dunlop.

This photograph is apparently a copy of an original whose whereabouts is currently unknown. The reverse of the card onto which this photograph is affixed bears the Werner & Son logo and the date "1888," clearly indicating that this print was made a decade and a half after the author's death. According to the National Portrait Gallery, London, Alfred Werner & Son (of 39, Grafton Street, Dublin) were active between the 1880s and the first decade of the twentieth century; therefore it is probable that Werner & Son were responsible only for this copy, and not the original photograph.

This photograph would appear to have been taken near the same time as the source for Emery Walker's photogravure (IV), if not at the same sitting.

JOSEPH SHERIDAN LE FANU.

VI. Plate from *Seventy Years of Irish Life*

Artist: H. Fitzner Davey (c. 1861–1935)
Medium: Engraving

This rarely reproduced image first appeared in *Seventy Years of Irish Life: Being Anecdotes and Reminiscences* by William Richard Le Fanu (London: Edward Arnold, 1893). The work is signed "H. Fitzner Davey."

Henry "Harry" Fitzner Davey was a British wood engraver, active between 1883 and 1900. He was best known for his work in portraiture and magazine illustration, having contributed to both the *English Illustrated Magazine* and the *Illustrated London News*.

The whereabouts of this engraving and its probable photographic source are unknown.

VII. Photograph of Le Fanu with a Cane

Date: Possibly c. 1860s

Medium: Photograph

© Courtesy of Anna and Francis Dunlop

This photograph was first printed as a frontispiece in *The Poems of Joseph Sheridan Le Fanu* (London: Downey, 1896). That version, cropped into an oval focusing exclusively on the author and extending no further than the hands, has been reprinted many times, including in *The Illustrated J. S. Le Fanu*, selected and edited by Michael Cox (Wellingborough, UK: Equation, 1988). A less severely cropped version of the photo, depicting the author from head to knees, appeared twenty years later in S. M. Ellis's "Joseph Sheridan Le Fanu," *Bookman* (London) 51 (October 1916): 15. Despite the quality of the illustrations throughout the *Bookman*, and presumably working from a secondary source rather than the original, reproduction there is less satisfactory than its predecessor, the dark and amorphous shapes in its foreground conspiring with the blotches in the background to lend it an air akin to Dorian Gray.

Fortunately, although we feared that the original was already sufficiently damaged by the time Graves reproduced it in 1896 to necessitate cropping, and possibly no longer directly available by 1916, the original has indeed survived and appears in print here, uncropped, for the first time.

This photograph would appear to capture Le Fanu near the same time in life as the posthumous portraits (VIII, IX, X, XI) created by his son, George Brinsley Le Fanu, and the similarity in dress and pose suggest it may have served as at least one of the references for those portraits.

To S.M. Ellis Esqr
    From Brinsley Le Fanu.
            Oct. 1916.

VIII. Pen and Ink Drawing by Brinsley Le Fanu

Date: October 1916

Artist: George Brinsley Le Fanu (1854–1929)

Medium: Pen and ink

This is one of the most reproduced images of Le Fanu. It was first printed in S. M. Ellis's *Wilkie Collins, Le Fanu and Others* (London: Constable, 1931). The inscription reads: "To S. M. Ellis Esq. / From Brinsley Le Fanu. / Oct. 1916." Given the sketch's similarity to the artist's other known portraits of his father (IX, X, XI), this drawing may have served as a study for those works. The sketch is reproduced in *Best Ghost Stories of J. S. Le Fanu*, edited by E. F. Bleiler (New York: Dover, 1964) and in *The Illustrated J. S. Le Fanu*, selected and edited by Michael Cox (Wellingborough, UK: Equation, 1988). The whereabouts of the original are unknown.

IX. Oil Painting in the National Gallery of Ireland

Title: Joseph Sheridan Le Fanu (NGI 919)

Date: 1916

Artist: George Brinsley Le Fanu (1854–1929)

Medium: Oil on canvas

Dimensions: 26 cm × 36 cm

Reproduced courtesy of the National Gallery of Ireland Collection; Photo © National Gallery of Ireland.

Painted in 1916 by the author's son, the artist and illustrator Brinsley Le Fanu. It was presented to the National Gallery of Ireland by Mr. T[homas] P[hilip] Le Fanu in 1929. The pose and dress are similar to the three other portraits Brinsley made of his father (VIII, X, XI), suggesting he could have used one or more images for reference, including the photograph with a cane (VII). Rarely reproduced, this painting appeared in Ann M. Stewart's *National Gallery of Ireland: Fifty Irish Portraits* (Dublin: National Gallery of Ireland, 1984).

Brinsley also illustrated some posthumous editions of his father's works including *The Wyvern Mystery* (1889), *The Watcher and Other Weird Stories* (1894), and *The Evil Guest* (1895).

X. Portrait in the Bookman by Brinsley Le Fanu

Date: Unknown

Artist: George Brinsley Le Fanu (1854–1929)

Medium: Likely oil on canvas

This portrait appeared in S. M. Ellis's article "Joseph Sheridan Le Fanu" for the *Bookman* (London) 51 (October 1916): 21, where it is described, "From a painting by his son, Brinsley Le Fanu." It was very likely cropped for its inclusion in the *Bookman*. The whereabouts of the original are unknown. This portrait is similar in pose to Brinsley's other portraits of his father (VIII, IX, XI).

XI. Oil Painting by Brinsley Le Fanu

Date: Possibly c. 1916

Artist: George Brinsley Le Fanu (1854–1929)

Medium: Oil on canvas

Dimensions: 30 cm × 40 cm (with frame: 34 cm × 45 cm)

© Courtesy of Nicola LeFanu and David Lumsdaine. Professor LeFanu is the great granddaughter of William Richard Le Fanu and the granddaughter of T. P. Le Fanu.

The pose and dress in this portrait are identical to those in the painting in the National Gallery of Ireland (IX), the pen and ink drawing reproduced by S. M. Ellis (VIII), and the portrait in the *Bookman* (X). Whether one oil painting is a preliminary study for the others is debatable, as both the expression and background are considerably brighter in the NGI portrait than they are in this dark and strikingly dour portrait, which seems to depict a much older, more troubled man.

XII. Plaster Mask

Date: Possibly early February 1873

Artist: Unknown

Medium: Photographs of a plaster mask

© Courtesy of Anna and Francis Dunlop.

These three photographs of a plaster mask—said to be the author's death mask—depict a peaceful countenance that is decidedly at odds with the sensational account of Le Fanu's death given in S. M. Ellis's *Wilkie Collins, Le Fanu and Others* (1931). Le Fanu's serene expression here is more in keeping with the letter from Emmie Le Fanu, Joseph's daughter, to Lord Dufferin on 9 February 1873 (Cf. "A Void Which Cannot Be Filled Up" by Brian J. Showers included in this volume).

Nonetheless, although it is possible that family tradition is correct in assigning the creation of this mask to the week of 7 February 1873; the absence of any reference or other documentation contemporary to this artefact, coupled with the disappearance of the artefact itself, makes it difficult to determine that fact definitively. Since life masks were also fashionable during Le Fanu's lifetime—among the more famous examples from this era are life masks of Ludwig van Beethoven from 1812 and two made of Abraham Lincoln in 1860 and 1865—the possibility that this may have been produced late in the author's life, rather than at its end, cannot be ruled out.

As with the photograph of Le Fanu with a cane (VII), the plaster mask may have served as reference for Brinsley Le Fanu's four posthumous portraits (VIII, IX, X, XI). The plaster mask of Le Fanu has never been seen in print before. Although the photographs and negatives are in the possession of Anna and Francis Dunlop, the whereabouts of the actual mask is unknown.

A Void Which Cannot Be Filled Up: Obituaries of J. S. Le Fanu

Brian J. Showers

On a dull, overcast February afternoon in 1873, Irish author Joseph Sheridan Le Fanu was laid to rest in Mount Jerome Cemetery in south Dublin. A light pall of snow descended from the solemn, gray sky onto a field of equally solemn and gray monuments. It is not now known exactly who or how many people attended the semi-reclusive author's funeral, though we definitely know that Joseph's younger brother William Richard Le Fanu, who diligently recorded the day's weather in his diary, was present.[1] Thomas "Philip" Le Fanu, Joseph's errant son who signed the *Register of Burials*, also likely attended the interment. Philip, or "Philly" as he was affectionately known, would join his father in the very same vault less than seven years later.

Erected on the gravesite beside which the funeral party had assembled was a large granite vault measuring eight feet by six. The capstone of Keane limestone, which today lies atop the two-tiered granite base, was on that day shifted to one side so that the mortal remains of the distinguished author could be lowered into the subterranean vault below. This vault, along with "Perpetual Right of Burial," was purchased in 1841 by Le Fanu's father-in-law George Bennett. Joseph's coffin was placed in the vault beside his wife Susanna, the latter of whom preceded him in death by some fifteen years.[2]

Today the nondescript vault of the Bennett/Le Fanu family can be found on the interior apex of the Nun's Walk, adjacent the cemetery wall.[3] The

---

1. "N. [i.e. wind out of the north] cloudy very cold—a few small flakes of snow in morning. At Dear Joe's funeral, Tommy F[__?] + William C[arwood?], + poor Emmy [JSLF's daughter]—at office till [4?], then to see Emmy, [P__?] took walk with B[ailey?, Brinsley?], Philip + B[ennett?] [discussed? dined?] with us." From William Le Fanu's diary, 11 February 1873. Supplied by Jim Rockhill.

2. *Mount Jerome Cemetery Register of Burial 1871–1876*, Reel #910606, Dublin City Library and Archive.

3. The description of the vault as recorded in the *Mount Jerome Cemetery Register of Per-*

vault is subtly anachronistic as it sits among other markers and memorials that were erected in more recent times. The capstone and its inscription are perfectly horizontal, like a tabletop, facing the open sky. As such, the cap-stone is particularly susceptible to the elements, hence the severe erosion during the 150-odd years since the first stonecutter's marks. At a casual glance the surface of the stone appears smooth and blank, but upon closer inspection one can see faint indentations. On a bright day, one can with relative ease make out the faded name in block capitals:

JOSEPH SHERIDAN LE FANU

There seems to be a trend to portray the author as one who was doggedly haunted—perhaps a character from one of his own stories: a man whose torments were larger than life. These embellishments are traceable to the publication of S. M. Ellis's 1931 book, *Wilkie Collins, Le Fanu and Others*, in which are contained a number of anecdotes based on the recollections of the author's son, George Brinsley Le Fanu (1854–1929). The veracity of some of these anecdotes is unsubstantiated (though they seem to contain elements of truth); but one in particular, which is often repeated, seems overly lurid and sensational:

> Horrible dreams troubled him to the last, one of the most recurrent and persistent being a vision of a vast and direly foreboding old mansion . . . in a state of ruin and threatening imminently to fall upon and crush the dreamer rooted to the spot. . . . When the end came, and the doctor stood by the bedside of Le Fanu and looked in the terror-stricken eyes of the dead man, he said: "I feared this—that house fell at last."[4]

The "terror-stricken eyes of the dead man" are doubtful given his daughter Emma Lucretia's contradictory observations in a letter to Lord Dufferin dated 9 February 1873: "His face looks so happy with a beautiful smile on it." Her use of the present tense, and the date of the letter being between Le Fanu's death and his burial, gives one the impression that she wrote these words in the presence of her father's corpse.[5] Likewise, a plaster mask of Le Fanu, very

---

petuities is inaccurate. An amendment clarifying the vault's description was added in 2003. For full details of this inaccuracy and the subsequent confusion it caused, see "Mix-Up at the Boneyard," *Le Fanu Studies*, Volume 1, Issue 2.

4. For the full passage, see "Extracts from *Wilkie Collins, Le Fanu and Others*" by S. M. Ellis reproduced in this volume.

5. The sentences both before and after are in the past tense. It is almost as if Emmie paused in between these two sentences to look upon her dead father's face. There are

possibly his death mask, is devoid of a tormented *rictus;* instead we see a face that would seem to be at peace.[6]

No doubt Le Fanu endured many hardships in the latter half of his life: the premature losses of both his sister and his wife, a questioning of faith, and increasing financial difficulty—but this does not seem to warrant such a haunted caricature. We should not forget that Le Fanu also wrote several humorous tales and, according to his brother's reminiscences in *Seventy Years of Irish Life,*[7] was a lifelong devotee of the practical joke. Clearly there was more to Le Fanu than the gloom that is generally portrayed. One might rightfully wonder, should Joseph Sheridan Le Fanu walk into the room this very moment, what would he be like?

In the days following Le Fanu's passing a number of obituaries appeared in newspapers and journals throughout Ireland and England. Over fifty years after Le Fanu's death, another writer of ghostly tales, M. R. James, stated, "I do not . . . claim for this author any very exalted place."[8] Although James continued his summation with unreserved praise, the former sentiment is the general tone of the obituaries published in the wake of the Irish author's death. And even though words like "genius" and "uncommon merit" are used, they are often tempered with qualifying phrases like "[journalism] prevented him applying himself to his profession" and "he ran too swiftly, and he frustrated his own dearest ambition." Most of his obituarists seem to agree that Le Fanu was by no means a *great* writer, but was indeed a very good one; one who lamentably might have been better, or one still yet to reach his zenith. Reprinted here is a selection of obituaries, which constitute a snapshot of how the general public might have viewed Le Fanu at the time of his death.

There seems to be a distance between the obituarists and their subject, and given Le Fanu's gradual withdrawal from society this is not surprising. Even in life, "his handsome . . . face was wholly missed from society; and he

---

no other verb tense inconsistencies in the letter.

6. Photographs of Le Fanu's plaster mask are printed for the first time in "The Portraits of Le Fanu" in this volume.

7. See "Anecdotes from *Seventy Years of Irish Life*" by William Richard Le Fanu; S. M. Ellis also relates some of Le Fanu's practical jokes, which can be found in "Extracts from *Wilkie Collins, Le Fanu and Others.*" Both pieces are included in this volume.

8. "I do not then claim for this author any very exalted place, but I desire to advance the claim that he has attained supremacy in one particular line: he succeeds in inspiring a mysterious terror better than any other writer." From notes for a speech entitled "The Novels and Stories of J. Sheridan Le Fanu," given to the Royal Institution of Great Britain on 16 March 1923. Reprinted in *Ghosts & Scholars* 7.

was only known on the title page of his books," observes one obituarist. "To the public he was scarcely known apart from his books," echoes another. The rather charming nickname "Invisible Prince" is well-known Le Fanu lore, but the appellation becomes downright grim if one considers his financial hardships and likely emotional decline. One gets the impression that Le Fanu was at the time of his death not personally known by many outside of his close circle. To the people of Dublin he was a prominent stranger, an apparition whose presence was keenly felt, but rarely seen. Fortunately through these obituaries we are also offered clues as to the author's character and personality in happier times.

The *Freeman's Journal* notes Le Fanu's "vigour and pungent sarcasm which he possessed in an uncommon degree," a characteristic also mentioned by family friend Alfred Perceval Graves (1846–1931) in a "Memoir" he wrote as an introduction to *The Purcell Papers* (1880).[9] The *Freeman's Journal* obit also recalls Le Fanu's "handsome, even distinguished face"[10] and goes on to state that "his manners were so impressive that you thought of him long after you have seen him. He was in every sense a gentleman. He bore himself with dignity and self-reliance." The *Dublin University Magazine* obituary, possibly written by one close to Le Fanu, more elaborately lists the congenial qualities the author possessed. He was admired for his "learning, his sparkling wit and pleasant conversation, and loved . . . for his manly virtues, his noble and generous qualities, his gentleness, and his loving, affectionate nature." M. R. James, who never knew Le Fanu, wrote, "I believe that he was a singularly striking personality both in looks and in conversation."[11] Clearly the aforementioned nickname "Invisible Prince," regardless of its disheartening nuances, is one of respect and possibly sympathy for a man whose "life was a most troubled one."[12]

---

9. "As a press writer he is still most honourably remembered for his learning and brilliancy, and the power and point of his sarcasm, which long made the *Dublin Evening Mail* one of the most formidable of Irish press critics." (*The Purcell Papers*, pp. xxii–xxiii)

10. This sentence in *The Freeman's Journal* obituary is paraphrased nearly verbatim by the *Dublin University Magazine*. Compare the *Journal's*: "His handsome, even distinguished face was wholly missed from society; and he was only known on the title page of his books," with the *DUM*'s: " . . . he led a secluded life, mixing little in society, from which his handsome, distinguished face was missed. To the public he was scarcely known apart from his books."

11. M. R. James, "The Novels and Stories of J. Sheridan Le Fanu." *Ghosts & Scholars* 7.

12. Emma L. Le Fanu. 9 February 1873. "He lived only for us, and his life was a most troubled one."

All the obituaries that speak of Le Fanu's novels are unanimous in identifying *Uncle Silas* and *The House by the Church-yard* as his most accomplished and commercially successful novels; the latter of which M. R. James
famously wrote was "a book to which I find myself returning over and over
again and with no sense of disappointment."[13] But it is *Uncle Silas* that is
shown the slight edge of favoritism in these eulogies. Without even mentioning *The House by the Church-yard*, the *Irish Times* regards *Uncle Silas* in particular as "marked with great richness of invention, and force in the
conception and delineation of character." The *Freeman's Journal* lauds *The
House by the Church-yard* for its good style, cheerful tone, and clever construction, but pulls out all stops in its subsequent praise for *Uncle Silas*,
which it begins by calling, "a marvel of mystery and a prodigy of power" and
goes on from there. The *Dublin University Magazine*, after mentioning *The
House by the Church-yard* and *Uncle Silas* ("perhaps the best of all his
works"), goes so far as to state that of Le Fanu's other novels, "it is unnecessary to speak." Indeed, apart from his ghost stories, *The House by the Church-
yard* and *Uncle Silas* still today seem to be the most popular and readily
available of his novels. Interestingly enough, in the years since Le Fanu's
death *Wylder's Hand*, written between the two aforementioned books, has
steadily become at least as popular as *The House by the Church-yard*. Both
past and modern critics seem to agree that Le Fanu was at his creative peak
near the beginning of his career as a novelist.

An interesting observation regarding the *Dublin University Magazine*
obituary comes from Jim Rockhill: "The *DUM* obit was obviously written by a
family member or close associate—perhaps Alfred Perceval Graves or William
Le Fanu?—who knew Le Fanu well enough to express how he would have
liked to be remembered. I sometimes get the sense while reading this that Le
Fanu himself is speaking. There is too much detailed family information for
this to have come from anyone outside the man's immediate circle. Note also
the attention paid to the family's nobility since the late 16th century."[14]

Le Fanu owned the *DUM* from 1861 until he "gave up control" in 1869.[15]
Le Fanu's successor was a poet by the name of James F. Waller (1810–1894)
who resumed editorship of the magazine in 1870 until 1873. Waller had ini-

---

13. From M. R. James's prologue to *Madam Crowl's Ghost and Other Tales of Mystery*
(London: G. Bell and Sons, Ltd., 1923). James goes on to declare that, "I think [*Uncle
Silas*] is his best novel."

14. Private correspondence.

15. See Jim Rockhill's introduction to *The Haunted Baronet and Others* (Ashcroft, BC:
Ash-Tree Press, 2003).

tially served as editor of the *DUM* from 1846 to 1854 and was responsible for publishing a number of Le Fanu's early tales including "The Watcher" (1846), "The Mysterious Lodger" (1850), "Ghost Stories of Chapelizod" (1851), and "An Account of Some Strange Disturbances in an Old House in Aungier Street" (1853). Given their history, Waller and Le Fanu most likely had an affinity for one another. It is entirely possible that Waller was in contact with and commissioned the obituary either directly from the family or from one of Le Fanu's close friends. The *DUM* obituary is one of the lengthiest and most detailed published. Regarding the possibility of Alfred Perceval Graves as its author, it should be noted that much of the same intricate ancestral details are reproduced in his own "Memoir" published seven years later.

Finally, from these obituaries we see that Le Fanu was remembered primarily as a novelist, a journalist and even a balladeer. What he is mainly known for today, rightly or wrongly, are his innovative tales of the supernatural. Yet these are not once mentioned among his many accomplishments, and indeed constitute a comparatively small portion of his body of work. I am not sure whether the man himself would have placed his ghost stories highly on his list of achievements, although I am sure that M. R. James's sentiments, applied equally to both short stories and novels, would have brought a smile to the author's lips: "Nobody sets the scene better than he, nobody touches in the effective detail more deftly. . . . [Le Fanu] succeeds in inspiring a mysterious terror better than any other writer."[16]

Letter from Emmie Le Fanu to Lord Dufferin, 9 February 1873.[17]

18 Merrion Square
Dublin
Feb. 9th /73.

Dear Lord Dufferin

I write a line to tell you of our terrible loss. My darling father died on Friday morning [7 Feb.] at 6 o'Clock. He had almost got over a bad attack of Bronchitis but his strength gave way & he sank very quickly & died in his sleep. His face looks so happy with a beautiful smile on it. We were quite unprepared for the end. My brother Philip & I never left him during his

---

16. The first line is from M. R. James's "The Novels and Stories of J. Sheridan Le Fanu," the second line is from the prologue to *Madam Crowl's Ghost* (1923).

17. Public Records Office of Northern Ireland, Dufferin and Ava Papers, D/1071/H/B/305/11.

illness & we were hopeful and happy about him even the day before he seemed to be much better. But it comforts me to think he is in Heaven, for no one could have been better than he was. He lived only for us, and his life was a most troubled one. I know you will feel this Dear Lord Dufferin. He loved you very much and very often spoke of you.

Ever your affectionate Emmie L. Le Fanu

Irish Times (8 February 1873): 2.

DEATH OF J. S. LE FANU, ESQ.

The Irish public will learn with much regret that Mr. Joseph Sheridan Le Fanu, one of the ablest of Irish writers, is no more. His death took place yesterday at his residence, Merrion square. Mr. Le Fanu was for many years connected with the Dublin press, and was, until a very few years ago, part proprietor of the *Evening Mail*. For several years past he directed his energies to the composition of works of fiction, and many of these—*Uncle Silas* in particular were marked with great richness of invention, and force in the conception and delineation of character. The *Dublin University Magazine* owed to him much of its reputation at the time that it was really an Irish periodical. Mr. Le Fanu's powers allowed no symptoms of decline to the last. His readers, and those who knew him in private life; fully expected that his pen would yet give to the world productions equal, or superior, to the best of those he had already written. Had Mr. Le Fanu begun his career as a novelist at an earlier period of life, he might have approached the fame of a Lever or Carleton. As it is, he leaves a blank which will be sensibly felt. It is somewhat remarkable that the best known, or the most promising Irish novelists now remaining are all of the female sex—Miss Broughton, Lady Wilde, Miss Godkins, Miss Maunsell, and Miss Mulholland.

Freeman's Journal (10 February 1873): 6.

DEATH OF MR. LE FANU.

The death of Mr. Le Fanu, the novelist, will be learned with regret by all who are interested in the maintenance of our national repute for literary effort. He died on Friday at his residence Merrion-square, in the 58th year of his age. Mr. Le Fanu was called to the Bar in 1839, but found the pursuit of that profession averse from his disposition. He entered the ranks of the press, and became editor and joint proprietor of *The Warder* newspaper, with no

less a colleague than Mr. Isaac Butt. At that time, when Protestant
Ascendancy was at its zenith, *The Warder* was a splendid property, and Mr.
Le Fanu became a successful journalist in every sense of the word. The
brilliant services of Terry Driscoll added greatly to the popularity of the
paper. Gradually the times changed, and *The Warder* ceased to be splendid.
Mr. Le Fanu then purchased the *Evening Packet,* which a few years since was
amalgamated with our able contemporary, the *Evening Mail.* In the columns
of the *Mail* Mr. Le Fanu found free scope for that vigor and pungent sarcasm
which he possessed in an uncommon degree. His first novel (of the later
series) *The House by the Church-yard—a Souvenir of Chapelizod,* was, it may
be fairly said, the book of the season. For good style, a cheerful tone, clever
construction, and maintained power it must take rank with the better order
of novels. He soon after published *Uncle Silas;* and in this he placed himself
in the foremost ranks of popular-novelists. All the critical journals, all the
daily newspapers were loud in eulogy, and Mr. Le Fanu took then a place
which he never lost with library readers. *Uncle Silas* is certainly a marvel of
mystery and a prodigy of power. The reader is rapt in painful attention from
first to last. There is a nerve, a fierce intensity in the book which keeps the
reader spell-bound; and it has this uncommon merit—you can read it a
second time with vivid delight. Mr. Le Fanu then, at the height of his
success, resolved on a course which eventually injured his fame. He wrote at
least a couple of novels every year. They poured from his pen with
Braddonian rapidity. Hardly a magazine exists to which he has not
contributed the leading serial, sometimes with success, often with
satisfaction, always with punctuality—for he was now a devotee. But he ran
too swiftly, and he frustrated his own dearest ambition. His labor for the last
seven years must have been immense, for he did not write with ease; his
manuscript was very irregular, for he never lost his careful disposition. His
handsome, even distinguished face was wholly missed from society; and he
was only known on the title page of his books. This was the more to be
lamented, inasmuch as Mr. Le Fanu, though by no means an enthusiast, was
always attractive. He had that quickness which mayhap his French blood
gave him; and his manners were so impressive that you thought of him long
after you have seen him. To those who knew him no phenomena could be
more striking than that he, of all men, should have written "Shamus
O'Brien"—the '98 ballad—and "Phaudrig Crohoore"—two really splendid
specimens of Irish ballad poetry. They are full to excess of rollicking Irish
humor, fine quaint wit, homely phrase, and bold description. Conscientiously
he could write them easily—for politics were not a law unto him; but
naturally they must have been a great effort, or he a many-sided man. In this

rapid sketch of Mr. Le Fanu's work, we hope we have not erred in coldness from a desire to keep the reputation of a really brilliant man free from the extravagant nonsense with which it is the habit to follow the little lives of local literati. We desire to say in real earnestness the plain truth; for Mr. Le Fanu's fame has no need of that villainous puffery which bedaubs indiscriminately the "mechanical mediocrity" which torments us every day. In one respect he was entitled to the praise of every man connected with the guild of letters, whether he be bond or free. Too often, clever Irishmen lack that self-respect and self-control which bring dignity and honor and the praise of good men. We need not pause to name the men of genius who have lived miserably and died meanly, to become immortal as master minds, and be remembered as self-hostile dupes. In our own generation we have had many; memories vivid with shame and pain, burning, albeit, in intellectual glory. In this matter Mr. Le Fanu was above reproach. He was in every sense a gentleman. He bore himself with dignity and self-reliance. In his death we lose a man whom Ireland and literature will not lightly forget, and to whom generations to come will be indebted for days and nights of keenest pleasure.

[This article was also reprinted in the *Irishman* (15 February 1873).]

Times (London) (10 February 1873): 7.

IRELAND.

[. . .] A blank is left in literary circles by the death of Mr. J. S. Le Fanu, the Irish novelist, which occurred yesterday at his residence in Merrion-square. In early life Mr. Le Fanu devoted his talents to the press, to which he was for many years an able contributor. He was the author of many successful and popular novels, and two or three years ago withdrew from journalism in order that he might concentrate his attention on more permanent literature and increase his reputation as an author. In private life he was highly esteemed. [. . .]

Irish Builder (15 February 1873): 50.

OBITUARY.
THE LATE J. SHERIDAN LEFANU.

Since our last issue Ireland has lost another racy novelist, for many years well known in English as well as Irish literary circles. He was a member of the Irish Bar, and contributed to the *Dublin University Magazine* and other Irish and English publications. He was also for some time proprietor of the above magazine, and chief editor and proprietor of the *Warder* newspaper. Of late years he relinquished all active connection with the newspaper press, and devoted his time to the production of some very successful novels. Mr. Le Fanu was the son of the Dean of Emly, a dignitary of the Irish Church, and brother to William Le Fanu, Commissioner of Public Works. At his death the late novelist was in his fifty-eighth year.[18]

All the old compeers and colleagues who worked together on magazines and newspapers during the past thirty years in this city are disappearing, and soon we will have scarcely one left. The *Dublin University Magazine* possesses memories that are bright, though the fate of the magazine itself is a wayward one of late years. It still lives; but men who, like Le Fanu and Lever, helped to preserve its fame as well as its name, are gone from us.

J. Sheridan Le Fanu deserves a fitting memoir and tribute to his memory, and we hope that some of his old companions of the pen will supply it on an early occasion.

Illustrated London News (15 February 1873).

OBITUARY OF EMINENT PERSONS.
MR. LE FANU.

Joseph Sheridan Le Fanu, Esq., died, on the 7th inst., at 18, Merrion-square South, Dublin, in his fifty-eighth year. Descended from the sisters of the Right Hon. Richard Brinsley Sheridan, Mr. Le Fanu inherited no small share of the genius of the Sheridan family. He was called to the Irish Bar in 1839, but soon deserted law for literature. His first contributions appeared in the *Dublin University Magazine*, which, at a later period, he edited. He was also for several years proprietor and editor of *The Warder*, and also part proprietor of the *Dublin Evening Mail*. As a novelist he gained considerable distinction, his most popular works being *The House by the Church-yard* and *Uncle Silas*.

Dublin University Magazine (March 1873): 319–20.

JOSEPH SHERIDAN LE FANU.

Since the last issue of this Magazine, there has passed away one who for several years controlled its destinies as Editor and Proprietor,—one who was

---

18. [Although Le Fanu was indeed fifty-eight when he died, he was technically in his fifty-ninth year.—Ed.]

well known in the best Dublin society—and one who inherited a large share of the genius that came to him on his mother's side, relinquishing the bright prospects which the influence of his family would have enabled [him] to wield for the arduous and uncertain paths of literature.

Joseph Sheridan Le Fanu, author of *Uncle Silas* and many other well-known novels, died at his house, Merrion Square, Dublin, in the fifty-ninth year of his age, on the 7th of February. He was the representative of a noble Huguenot family of Normandy, who possessed in that province in the *generalité* of Caen, many estates, among which were Mondeville, Sequeville, Cresseron, &c.; the certificate of noblesse, officially signed by Guy Chamillart, bearing date 1671, and now in the possession of his son, Philip S. Le Fanu, Esq., of Merrion Square, proves their nobility by charter to the year 1595.

On the revocation of the Edict of Nantes, they were deprived of their estates; but having influential relatives at the Court of Louis XIV, they were permitted to leave France with their personal property without molestation, two members of the family, John Le Fanu de Sequeville and Charles Le Fanu de Cresseron, held cavalry commissions in the army of William III. Charles was on the King's staff, and afterwards served as Major of Dragoons, under Marlborough.

Joseph Sheridan was son of Thomas Philip Le Fanu, Dean of Emly, whose father, Joseph Le Fanu, formerly Clerk of the Coast in Ireland, married Alicia, sister of the Right Honorable Richard Brinsley Sheridan; his brother, Captain Henry Le Fanu, having married Sheridan's only other sister. The Subject of this notice was born in August 1814, and at an early age, gave promise of the powers which he afterwards attained. His wonderful acting in private theatricals, as a mere boy, is still fresh in the recollection of many, and when scarcely fifteen years of age he wrote many pieces of poetry, which show an unusual depth of imagination and feeling. He entered Trinity College, Dublin, in 1833, and was there distinguished by classical knowledge, but still more by his power in debate in the College Historical Society; many of his contemporaries there now occupying distinguished positions in life, remember him as one of its most eloquent members. He was called to the Bar in 1839, but almost immediately afterwards became connected with the press, having purchased *The Warder* newspaper, then a paper of note in Ireland, which he edited. This was injurious to his future prospects, as it prevented him applying himself to his profession, for which he was admirably suited, and of which, there can be little doubt, he would have become a distinguished member.

His earliest contributions to literature appeared in this Magazine, of which, years afterwards, as we have said, he became proprietor and editor. Among his earliest articles were several stories, some serious, others replete with wit and humor, and highly illustrative of the habits and feelings of the Irish peasantry. Amongst his contributions to the Magazine were also many short poems, some full of tenderness and feeling, others of powerful dramatic effect. Foremost amongst the latter were "Shamus O'Brien", a ballad of '98, and "Phaudhrig Crohoore", two of the best specimens of Irish ballad poetry, abounding in rollicking humor and vivid description, combined with touches of the deepest pathos. He married, in 1844, Susan, daughter of the late George Bennett, Q. C.; from that time until her death, which occurred in 1858, he wrote little, except for the press. The death of his much-loved wife was an overwhelming blow to him, from which he never recovered. From that time till his death he led a secluded life, mixing little in society, from which his handsome, distinguished face was missed. To the public he was scarcely known apart from his books. In 1863 he published *The House by the Church-yard*, which was soon followed by *Uncle Silas*, and other novels of which it is unnecessary to speak. *Uncle Silas* was, perhaps, the best of his works, the plot the most skillfully contrived, the interest the most absorbing. Of his latest work, *Willing to Die*, the last pages were written a few days before his death. He was a man who thought deeply, especially on religious subjects. To those who knew him he was very dear. They admired him for his learning, his sparkling wit and pleasant conversation, and loved him for his manly virtues, his noble and generous qualities, his gentleness, and his loving, affectionate nature. His death has left in many hearts a void which cannot be filled up.

II. General Studies

M. R. James on J. S. Le Fanu

M. R. James

Only one novelist known to me ever refers to Sheridan Le Fanu as an acknowledged authority or master in the particular line to which he devoted himself: the name of this writer is respectable but not more. It is James Payn.[1] Probably if the works of Andrew Lang ever have a concordance made to them, the name of Le Fanu will be found to occur in it. But the fact remains that Le Fanu is not at the moment the occupier of any particular pedestal. There has never been a boom in his writings. I am not anxious for one, though if it comes I shall be prepared to concede the great author of booms, Poet Gosse,[2] several points or bisques.

I do not then claim for this author any very exalted place, but I desire to advance the claim that he has attained supremacy in one particular line: he succeeds in inspiring a mysterious terror better than any other writer. I have heard the proposition advanced that Edgar Allan Poe stands at the head of those who have written *terrible* stories in English, but I can in no sort of way agree with those who think so. For one thing, the effect of this kind of literature depends largely, I fancy, upon its modernity: in style, at any rate, it must not be antiquated, however remote the scene or date of the events described. To be really *frightful,* the story must seem possible and near for the moment. But Poe's tales have to my mind such an essential flavor of 1830–1840 as takes the whole edge off them, and suggests the costume, furniture and art of the time when they were written. Moreover, there is usually a sug-

---

1. [James Payn (1830-1898) was a prolific novelist, poet and essayist who, like Le Fanu, was a contributor to one of Dickens's journals and was educated at Trinity College. Unlike Le Fanu, the journal was *Household Words* instead of *All the Year Round,* and his alma mater was located in Cambridge, not Dublin.–Ed.]

2. [Sir Edmund William Gosse (1849-1928) was an influential poet, lecturer, and biographer, who became official librarian to the House of Lords. His circle of friends included many of the most prominent writers in England and the Continent. H. G. Wells referred to him as the "official man of letters."–Ed.]

gestion or introduction of the mad element, which accounts for anything supernatural, and brings everything horrible into the range of everyday life; for, though the things that madness do may be horrible and no doubt would be if one was to experience them, yet they are so constantly being done that they fail to stimulate the imagination.

So when I read "The Fall of the House of Usher" which by some is thought the most horrific of all stories, I merely feel that it is like a bad dream. Reality is there none. This low estimate may perhaps be influenced by my abhorrence of his verses.

However, it is time to say something about Le Fanu—and what he wrote. His life is easily dismissed: he came of an old Huguenot stock, lived all his days in Dublin, and died in 1873—a widower. For many years he edited the *Dublin University Magazine* and another Dublin organ, a newspaper whose name I don't remember.

I believe that he was a singularly striking personality both in looks and in conversation. During the last years of his life—and after and in consequence of his wife's death—he became almost entirely a recluse, having been before that a very prominent figure in Dublin society.

The novels and collections of stories which have been published with his name attached to them (I will explain this qualification in a moment) are: *The Cock and Anchor, Torlogh O'Brien, Uncle Silas, The House by the Church-yard, Checkmate, Guy Deverell, The Tenants of Malory, Haunted Lives, A Lost Name, The Wyvern Mystery, Wylder's Hand, All in the Dark, The Rose and the Key*, and *Willing to Die*—these are his novels. The collections of stories are *Chronicles of Golden Friars, In a Glass Darkly* and *The Purcell Papers*—this last is a posthumous publication, with a memoir by Mr. Graves prefixed to it. But besides these, there are a number of anonymous stories in magazines which are identifiable with moral certainty as productions of Le Fanu. For example: "Squire Toby's Will" in volume 22 of *Temple Bar*, one of the best of his ghost stories; "Dickon the Devil," a ghost story which appeared in a Christmas number of *London Society* or *Belgravia* in or before 1871;[3] and a fair number of similar stories in the early volumes of the new series of *All the Year Round* (e.g. "Sir Dominick's Bargain," "The White Cat of Drumgunniol," "Tom Chuff's Vision," "The Child that went with the Fairies," "Stories of Lough Guir").

I will say something about such of the novels as I know or remember. *The Cock and Anchor* was probably never republished after its appearance in a Dublin journal. I have never seen it, but it would seem to be a story of Old Dublin. *Torlogh O'Brien* is a romance of the Battle of the Boyne period; it

---

3. ["Dickon the Devil" first appeared in *London Society* (Christmas Number, 1872).—Ed.]

was illustrated by Phiz[4] and I know at least three editions. It shows strongly the influence of Harrison Ainsworth,[5] but is a far better constructed book than any that Ainsworth ever wrote. In one chapter, where the villain of the book falls into the hands of rebels and is tortured with the strappado, an absolute mastery of the horrible is shown—and yet there is nothing disgusting.

Uncle Silas may perhaps be spoken of in the next place. The leading episode appeared twice in stories of much less compass before the novel took its present shape and name. It is probably the best known of Le Fanu's books—and I think it is his best novel. The framework of the story is easily sketched. A girl is left by her father's death heiress to an immense property. There is an uncle who, years before, had been suspected of murdering a man—a disreputable gambling acquaintance—who was found dead, and might have committed suicide, in his house. This uncle had lived a reclusive life ever since, and the father of the heiress—in order to demonstrate his confidence in the baselessness of the accusation—leaves his daughter in the sole guardianship of her uncle. The masterly way in which the coils are gradually drawn close round the girl by her uncle, and the final terrific murder-scene and escape can hardly be forgotten by those who have read the book. Extraordinarily powerful, too, is the drawing of the spectral uncle ("venerable, bloodless, fiery-eyed"), of the dreadful Madame de la Rougierre, and in a less degree, of Dudley Ruthyn and Dr. Bryerly.

In *Checkmate* and *The House by the Church-yard* we have a situation of which Le Fanu is plainly very fond: the idea of a formidable and almost supernaturally wicked man returning after years of absence and living quite unsuspected, in one case on the very scene of an early crime, and in the other among men who had known him in early years. Dangerfield and Longcluse are such men—and they strangely resemble one another.

I think it is in *Tenants of Malory* that the same idea crops up again. *Checkmate* has moreover some tremendous episodes: not least, that of the

---

4. [Hablot Knight Browne (1815–1882) was a popular illustrator who published under the names of N. E. M. O. and Phiz. His most famous work accompanies ten novels by Charles Dickens, including *The Pickwick Papers*, *Nicholas Nickleby*, *Martin Chuzzlewit*, and *David Copperfield.*—Ed.]

5. [William Harrison Ainsworth (1805–1882) was a successful writer of picaresque and historical novels bristling with swordplay, desperate escapes, glamorized rogues, dramatized folklore, and supernatural elements of varying degrees of development. *The Lancashire Witches* (1849) has received praise from such respected genre scholars as Montague Summers and E. F. Bleiler as "one of the major English novels about witchcraft."—Ed.]

German Baron whose trade it is to change the faces of people who are "wanted." *The House by the Church-yard* seems to be a typical book of the author's. The construction is by no means faultless and, indeed, I can but agree that any one not in sympathy with the author might be frightened off by reading the first third of the book. But with all this there is the most curiously successful atmosphere of horror and mystery; and the background—a suburb of Dublin in the last century—is far more vivid and real, in spite of an absence of word painting, than anything in the vast majority of recent novels. There is but one chapter in the book which introduces the supernatural, but that whets the appetite for more. It is the description of appearances at a haunted house: foremost among them the hand of an old man, which is seen resting toadlike on the pillow of some sleeping member of the family, and once the mark of it is found on a dusty table in the parlor.

Wylder's Hand and *A Lost Name* are probably the best of the remaining novels; in both of them we find the same power of infusing into every moment of the story a coloring, sometimes only melancholy, more often somber and mysterious. In nearly all his books this quality is present in varying degrees. I shall return to it again.

The Wyvern Mystery introduces a character not unlike Madame de la Rougierre; a blind Dutch woman, almost insane, and in this author's hands a terrific apparition who almost succeeds in murdering the heroine. *Guy Deverell* I have totally forgotten. Weakest of all the novels is *All in the Dark*—a domestic story with a sham ghost: an offence hard to forgive in any writer but much harder in Le Fanu's case, seeing that he could deal so magnificently with realness without incurring any more expense.

When we turn to the three collections of stories, and to the short anonymous tales in the magazines, we come upon some of Le Fanu's best work. There are one or two humorous quick stories in dialect in *The Purcell Papers*, which seem to me admirable. In the same collection is the truly horrifying "Episode in the Life of Schalken the Painter." A motif not unlike that of Bürger's ballad "Lenore" is employed here: a living corpse marries a girl, and when she has escaped from the vault, comes to reclaim her—with success only too marked.

"The Drunkard's Vision" again has considerable power—and so certainly have one or two of the non-supernatural stories in the collection. The *Chronicles of Golden Friars* contains two good stories and one less good: so far as I remember one only introduces anything like a ghost and I shall have a little more to say about it.

The volume called *In a Glass Darkly* is probably the best known, next to *Uncle Silas*, of all the author's works, and to those who have read it, the titles

"The Familiar," "Mr. Justice Harbottle," "Carmilla" and "Green Tea" will suggest the remembrance of an agreeable thrill. The two first, and "Squire Toby's Will," I should assert to be the best ghost stories in the English language.

This is more than enough of a catalogue: my business is now to notice some favorite ideas and devices of Le Fanu, and to try and arrive at some analysis of his peculiar powers.

But perhaps his weaknesses may be mentioned first. Among these I should rank the tendency to use over and over again certain devices in themselves striking. I have spoken of one of these—the motif of the banished villain returning to the society of men in a new shape. This thought is closely connected in my mind with another which dominates several of the ghost stories. I may call it the Vampire-idea. Of course, one story, "Carmilla," is a real Styrian Vampire story, but the idea I speak of is rather a wider one. It takes two forms: in one the dead returns to earth in a form sometimes human sometimes animal—thus the owl in "The Familiar" and the bull-dog in "Squire Toby's Will" are embodiments of the "Watcher" and of Squire Toby. In the other form, a human soul or else an evil spirit takes possession of a body and uses it. Minheer Vanderhausen, in the Schalken story, is a case in point, and so is the young man in "The Haunted Baronet." He has been drowned and after every effort to recover him has failed, and he has lain for the greater part of the night a corpse, he suddenly revives; and there can be no doubt from what follows that the reader is meant to understand that the evil genius of the Mardyke family has taken up its abode in his body. There is a hint of the same in Miss Agnes Marbyn (in *A Lost Name*). Even in *Uncle Silas*, Lady Knollys says of that worthy: "Silas Ruthyn is himself alone, and I can't define him, because I don't understand him. Perhaps other souls than human are sometimes born into the world and clothed in flesh."

The conception is one which Le Fanu has certainly used with tremendous effect and the recurrence of it would be probably not obvious until one had read nearly all his work with attention. And further it must be remembered that a good many of the stories in which it occurs are incomplete or fugitive sketches which ought not perhaps to be strictly reckoned with.

A similar weakness is the recurrence of types of character. The old servant (both malignant and kindly), lunatic or visionary, whose rhapsodies are written it seems to me with great skill, the hard-drinking squire, the broken man of pleasure—these may all be found in several of his books. But they are always used with effect.

There is really only one element which I would wish away, and that is a certain vein of almost maudlin writing into which he falls—though rarely—and which induces him to give hopeless pet names to some of his characters, and otherwise makes his reader blush for him. Three books err in this way: in *Wylder's Hand* I find a number of scenes connected with a little boy; in *A Lost Name* there are a brother and sister whose names I really cannot bring myself to repeat; and *All in the Dark* contains more than a fair proportion of such matter. However, the whole amount of it is small.

As to his peculiar power: I think the origin of it is not far to seek. Le Fanu had both French and Irish blood in his veins, and in his works I seem to see both strains coming out, though the Irish predominates. The indefinable melancholy which the air of Ireland and its coloring inspire—a melancholy which inspires many Irish writers—is caught by Le Fanu and fixed in words with an almost complete success. He dwells very fondly and very frequently on sunset scenes over a horizon of dark hanging woods, on moonlight shining on a winding river with wooded banks, on a heavily-timbered park, a black tarn in a lonely glen, an old air heard in the distance at night, a ruined chapel or manor-house, a torchlight funeral in a gloomy church. Pictures like these strike his fancy and he makes them stand out for his readers. They have been made commonplace enough by worse writers; but we indeed have [bad] pictures of ruined castles on the Rhine or Melrose Abbey by moonlight, yet it is possible to have good pictures of these subjects, and most likely had there been no good pictures of them there would have been no bad ones. I think Le Fanu's are good pictures, and I am certain they have inspired a great many that are not good.

But how does he contrive to inspire horror? It is partly, I think, owing to the very skilful use of a crescendo, so to speak. The gradual removal of one safeguard after another, the victim's dim forebodings of what is to happen gradually growing clearer; these are the processes which generally increase the strain of excitement. "The Familiar" and the concluding chapters of *Uncle Silas* are the best specimens of this. And again the unexplained hints which are dropped are of the most telling kind. The reader is never allowed to know the full theory which underlies any of his ghost stories, but this Le Fanu has in common with many inferior artists. Only you feel that he has a complete explanation to give if he would only vouchsafe it.

Who was the person who, in *Uncle Silas*, was heard to say "Fly the Fangs of Belisarius"? Where did Minheer Vanderhausen take his wife to? What was the rationale of the mysterious coach and the lady and her servants who brought Carmilla the Vampire to the house where she was to find a new victim? And what exactly was it that passed when Lewis Pyneweck and the hangman came to see Mr. Justice Harbottle? We are never told. The trick of omission or suppression may be used in a very banal fashion, but Le Fanu uses it well.

As to his real beliefs and theories, we can gather something: to spirit rapping he was, I am glad to think, a decided foe—*All in the Dark* is partly a hit at the system. Was he a Swedenborgian? I think not, but he was greatly attracted by Swedenborg's speculations. They are quoted in "Green Tea" and *Uncle Silas:* in the latter book a speech of Dr. Bryerly gives us a clue to the sort of view Le Fanu half-entertained.

It would be a plausible thing to compare the place of Le Fanu in fiction with that of Doré[6] in art. In so far as they possess a style easily distinguishable from others, and like rather cognate subjects, they have something in common; but there the plausibility of the comparison ceases, to my mind, for apart from the general fallaciousness of these comparisons I cannot see that Doré's merits are nearly equal to Le Fanu's, when both men are taken at their best. The name of Wiertz,[7] again, might occur to some as supplying a fit analogy in painting to Le Fanu's written works. After my first visit to the Wiertz Gallery at Brussels I might have said so too. After my second, nothing could seem unfairer to Le Fanu. Almost all that had before seemed strong appeared merely *outré,* and what I had thought really tragic and terrible was either disgusting or mad.

No: if an analogy to Le Fanu in pictorial form be desired, I would suggest that Bewick,[8] where he treats a supernatural subject, is not unsuitable to

---

6. [Louis Auguste Gustave Doré (1832-1883) was a prolific and popular French painter, sculptor, and illustrator whose engravings ranged from the contemporary splendors and squalors of Blanchard Jerrold's *London: A Pilgrimage* to the grotesquery of Rabelais's *Gargantua and Pantagruel,* the high fantasy of Ariosto's *Orlando Furioso.* His most famous work—for the Bible, Dante's *The Divine Comedy,* Milton's *Paradise Lost,* and Coleridge's *The Rime of the Ancient Mariner*—achieved a rare melding of the horrible and the sublime.—Ed.]

7. [Antoine Wiertz (1806-1865) was a Belgian painter and sculptor whose work prefigures the Symbolists in its use of a highly detailed, classical technique to depict scenes with implicitly or overtly grotesque, sensual, or delirious content. James would undoubtedly have been familiar with "The Premature Burial" (1847), depicting a cholera victim breaking out of his coffin, and "La Belle Rosina" (1847), in which a nearly naked young woman stares up at the fleshless face of a skeleton.—Ed.]

8. [Thomas Bewick (1753-?) was an English engraver, ornithologist, musicologist, and memoirist best known for his illustrations to various books of fables, poetry, and natural history. His work received praise from writers as diverse as William Wordsworth, Thomas Carlyle, John Ruskin, and John James Audubon. M. R. James was not the only writer impressed by Bewick's penchant for placing horrors nearly out of sight in the corners of otherwise mundane illustrations. In the opening chapter of *Jane Eyre,* Charlotte Brontë refers thus to one of the illustrations in *A History of British*

cite. There is, for instance, an excellent vignette which shows us a tired ped-lar with a pack on his back approaching a cave surrounded by lichen, and evidently intending to spend the night there. Look twice at the picture and you will see that the cave mouth and the trees around it are crowded with bird hobgoblins. They will only wait till the poor man is asleep, then they will come out, and if anyone leaves the place at all it will be a raving maniac. But more probably no-one will leave it alive.

In this sketch, I have left a great many points untouched: Le Fanu on death; Le Fanu as a master of felicitous quotation; Le Fanu as a writer of bal-lads. These and other aspects of my author must remain for you to discover if, as I hope, you peruse his works well enough to be able to do so. Were I asked to give in a few words and in literary slang an estimate of his position, I should be inclined to say that he occupies a very important place as an ex-ponent of the Celtic imagination, and with this I must leave you.

Birds (1797): "The fiend pinning down the thief's pack behind him, I passed over quickly: it was an object of terror." The woodcut to which James refers appeared in the same volume at the end of the chapter entitled "Of the Shrike."–Ed.]

A Forgotten Creator of Ghosts— Joseph Sheridan Le Fanu, Possible Inspirer of the Brontës

Edna Kenton

He foresaw that the proprietors of Stayes would do him very well. In his bed-room at a country house he always looked first at the books on the shelf and the prints on the walls; he considered that these things gave a sort of meas-ure of the culture and even of the character of his hosts. Though he had but little time to devote to them on this occasion a cursory inspection assured him that if the literature, as usual, was mainly American and humorous, the art consisted neither of the water-colour studies of the children nor of "goody" engravings . . . . There was the customary novel of Mr. Le Fanu for the bedside; the ideal reading in a country house for the hours after mid-night. Oliver Lyon could scarcely forebear it while he buttoned his shirt.

Henry James, "The Liar"

I.

To a searcher in the barren field of Le Fanuana, who had run through innumerable indexes of literary "Histories" and "Studies" on the steadily diminishing chance of finding anywhere even bare mention of Joseph Sheridan Le Fanu, it was almost a shock to come upon a sturdy little row of figures following his name in one of the volumes of *The Cambridge History of*

[Kenton's essay is a curious case of insight compromised by the obscurity into which Le Fanu had fallen by the early decades of the twentieth century. Until the efforts of S. M. Ellis, M. R. James, and others finally bore fruit, only a small portion of Le Fanu's work was known to even the most diligent twentieth-century reader, as witness the efforts of Lovecraft and his associates to locate truly representative samples of that author's work. Thus, the reader will note a smattering of errors due not only to the paucity of reliable secondary literature on the author, but the scarcity of even primary texts.—Ed.]

English Literature.[1] Was it that in this dignified compendium of criticism he was at last recognized, "revived"? But no! Only in light of the ever-projected Brontës did he shine on a few of their particular pages.

Straight into Charlotte Brontë's centenary year—1916, when this thirteenth volume of *The Cambridge History* was issued—Professor A. A. Jack, of the University of Aberdeen, who wrote the Brontë chapter, shot a little shell which somehow failed to explode. With a theory of his own regarding the "sources" of *Jane Eyre*, he suggested that "the tale of actual and intended bigamy which Sheridan Le Fanu contributed to the *Dublin University Magazine*[2] in 1839" might have been at once the source of the famous "plot" and the source of Thackeray's vague disturbance over *Jane Eyre's* reminiscent quality.

It is Le Fanu's odd fate that his name should pass. Suggestions wilder than this have sufficed to rally the Brontëans for annihilation of the unfortunate suggestor; witness that naïve victim of Irish amiability, The Rev. William Wright, who looked up *The Brontës in Ireland*, or that unlucky prey of the deadly parallel who "proved" that Branwell Brontë wrote *Wuthering Heights* is more sacrosanct than *Jane Eyre*. Yet, if he had gone further, as he might have, and had suggested probable? origins in *The Purcell Papers* for Emily Brontë's "greatest villain in fiction," Le Fanu's predestined obscurity would doubtless have worked to hush even that profane pronouncement into silence. However, a book might be written (let us hope it will not be) on the correspondences between *The Purcell Papers* of Le Fanu and the Brontë novels.

Surely the unmitigated famelessness of Sheridan Le Fanu can be ranked among the outstanding curiosities of literature. One of the literal "best sellers" of the 1860–1880s, he has disappeared even from cursory addenda to Victorian literary history. Author of some of the really remarkable ghost stories of our literature, he is remembered today only by "occultists"—the people, by the way, who really recognize a really ghostly tale. You will find his "Green Tea," his "Carmilla" and his "The Room in the Dragon Volant" referred to still in occult literature. But if you should glance through Miss Dorothy Scarborough's exhaustive work, *The Supernatural in [Modern English] Fiction* [New York: G. P. Putnam's Sons, 1917], you will search in vain for even passing mention of Sheridan Le Fanu as a craftsman of parts in the delicate art of

---

1. [Kenton is referring to A. A. Jack's "The Brontës" in Sir Adolphus William Ward and Alfred Rayney Waller, ed., The Cambridge History of English and American Literature. Vol. XIII. English—The Victorian Age. Part One. The Nineteenth Century, II (Cambridge: Cambridge University Press, 1917).

2. "A Chapter [in the History of a Tyrone Family]: Being the Tenth Extract from the Legends of the Late Francis Purcell, P. P., of Drumcoolagh" [*DUM*, October 1939].

transferring shadows to the printed page; and this omission from her extensive survey is high evidence of how completely he has passed away from the literary earth. Curious are the fates of little books and little writers—most curious of all sometimes when they are called great. Le Fanu was not a great writer, but he wrote a few great ghost stories. And even as the "sensation" author of *Uncle Silas, The House by the Church-yard, Checkmate* and *Wylder's Hand,* to mention no others of a list so famous fifty years ago, his unqualified passing within a half-century's short span is hardly comprehensible.

Only one biographer—and he a personal friend—has tried to keep his name alive. Alfred Perceval Graves wrote Le Fanu's obituary in 1873 for the *Dublin University Magazine* which Le Fanu had owned.[3] He wrote the preface for *The Purcell Papers,* the legends of the "wonderful priest of Drumcoolagh," collected from the old *Dublin University Magazine* files of 1838–1839[4] and published in 1880. In 1886 he prefaced the posthumous *Poems,* and in the 'nineties assisted Le Fanu's son, Richard Brinsley Sheridan Le Fanu, in editing a short-lived series of reprints of his father's work with illustrations by his son. In 1904 Mr. Graves published another edition of the *Poems* with another preface and, as recently as 1913, in his *Irish Literary and Musical Studies,* he gave many pages to what is probably his final tribute to his friend—a study pathetically reminiscent of all his others. He had so early said it all. Only a brother, William Le Fanu, in his autobiography, has contributed further to the picture of this charming Irish gentleman, littérateur, raconteur and occultist of old Dublin.

In the *Lives* of the multitudinous Sheridans we find him now and then. Contemporary of all the great Victorians (he lived from 1814 to 1873) his blood was that of some of the greatest English lights, social and otherwise, of his age. Through his grandmother, Alicia, daughter of "Tom" and Frances Sheridan and sister of Richard Brinsley and Elizabeth, he was direct descendant of a family whose members have kept unbroken claim to fame for two hundred years. The Sheridan connection was double, for the two Sheridan sisters married two Le Fanu brothers. In Le Fanu's Merrion Square home in

---

3. [Although there are definite similarities between this obituary and some passages in the "Memoir of Joseph Sheridan Le Fanu," which Graves used to introduce *The Purcell Papers,* his composition of the unsigned obituary has not been confirmed.—Ed.]

4. [The full series of Purcell Papers collected by Graves was published between January 1838 ("The Ghost and the Bone-Setter") and June 1850 ("Billy Malowney's Taste of Love and Glory"). Kenton alternates between referring to the entire collected series and those stories in which she sees the greatest similarities to the work of the Brontës, published during 1838 and 1839.—Ed.]

Dublin hung a dozen Sheridan portraits, all his by inheritance; "Tom" Sheridan, actor, father of the brood; Frances Sheridan, author of the eighteenth century *Memoirs of Miss Sidney Biddulph*, with their children and their children's children. Richard Brinsley Sheridan's granddaughters, the famous "Sheridan Sisters" of London when Victoria was its girl-queen, were cousins of the Dublin Sheridan-Le Fanus—Caroline, the Hon. Mrs. Norton, Georgina, loveliest of all the Duchesses of Somerset, and Helen, Lady Dufferin. The family ramifications stretched back and forth across the Irish Sea, and the whole family, all sides of it, wrote, from the old mother lioness down.

No wonder, then, that Sheridan Le Fanu scribbled from his earliest years. His *métier* was the mysterious, when it was not the ghostly and the lurid, and for a score of years, from the 1860s on, he was read enormously on both sides of the Atlantic, for he was issued in America as fast as he was published in England. But, famous contemporary of another famous "mystery" writers—Collins, Braddon *et al.*—their names remain on any roll call of the Victorians while his is literally obliterated. His one-time vogue is noted by a no less meticulous recorder of his times than Henry James. In "The Liar," one of three tales published in 1889 under the title of *A London Life*, Mr. James remarks that, upon his hero's arrival at Stayes to paint Sir David's portrait, he looked, for omens and signs, at the pictures and the books, and they promised well: "There was the customary novel of Mr. Le Fanu for the bedside; the ideal reading in a country house for the hours after midnight."

For Le Fanu, better than most of his lurid school, could "write;" more than others of his school, with the exception of Bulwer-Lytton, he was "occult;" his backgrounds were distinguished, they were thick with medieval lore and his pages were whimsical as well as lurid.

He had, however, a special gift for dealing with luridities. He was a real forerunner of the "psychic horror school" which Arthur Machen later on was to proceed to make his own and, after Machen, Blackwood. Why Le Fanu's "Dr. Hesselius," whose "case histories" furnish the material for the ghostly tales of *In a Glass Darkly*, does not lead the long modern list of "psychic doctors" in fiction is another mysterious mischance. His "Notes" on maladies of the mind were pioneer excursions into a field much over-cultivated today; he is the true father of Machen's Dr. Raymond, of Blackwood's Dr. Silence, even of that great degreeless, lay scientist, Mr. Sherlock Holmes himself.

In his *Victorian Novelists* (1906), Louis Benjamin includes Sheridan Le Fanu, but all mistakenly devotes his rather shallow, critical attention to the "sensation" novels. This irritating study, the later Graves essays and the disregarded niche Professor Jack hollowed for him beside the Brontë sisters in *The Cambridge History of English Literature* are the only twentieth century recognitions of Le Fanu's life and works that a tolerably comprehensive search has salvaged from the modern flood of printed matter. Others may have been missed, but his exclusion from Miss Scarborough's exhaustive research into supernatural fiction, Le Fanu's veritable field, is fair evidence that Sheridan Le Fanu, for all modern cognizance, might never have lived at all.

II.

If, in that pathetic list of Charlotte Brontë's reading sources for 1829, set down in Mrs. Gaskell's extraordinary *Life*, the old *Dublin University Magazine* had been listed with *Blackwood's*, or if it had figured in the later catalogue of the Haworth parsonage library, this at least can be asserted fairly—Professor Jack would not have been the first to suggest, in 1916, *The Purcell Papers* as a plot source for *Jane Eyre*. Long before her centenary year the extent of Charlotte Brontë's indebtedness to Sheridan Le Fanu would have been the subject of more than one profound *opus*.[5] It is inexplicable, however, that Professor Jack's theory of sources stops short with one of the Purcell Papers and one of the Brontë novels; for, the further the comparison is carried, the stronger the case becomes. But, midway in his chapter on the Brontës, he springs, with disconcerting suddenness, a merely partial "case." He quotes a letter of Charlotte's to Mr. Williams in the autumn of 1847, that one which refers to Thackeray's well-known remark on the "reminiscent quality" of the *Jane Eyre* plot and carries her own asseveration of her belief that it was original. Then he comments as follows:

> Charlotte Brontë's possible forgetfulness, if she had seen the story, and Thackeray's dim recollection are equally explicable. The tale of the actual and intended bigamy which Sheridan Le Fanu contributed to the *Dublin University Magazine* in 1839 was just one of those stories eminently adapted to floating in the back of the mind. In the strange fictions of Le Fanu the reader's feelings are deeply moved without his either seeing the actual occurrences face to face or believing them to be real . . . . While nothing could be more probably than that the author of *The Irish Sketch Book* and *Barry Lyndon* had read this story, it is clear that Charlotte could have had access to it . . . . Charlotte Brontë herself, in requesting Messrs. Aylett & Jones to send out review copies of the *Poems*, mentions alone among Irish papers the *Dublin University Magazine*. A favourable notice appeared in writing the editor to thank him for it, 6th October, 1846, she signs herself, "Your grateful and constant

---

5. [There is a brief mention of similarities between "A Chapter in the History of a Tyrone Family" and *Jane Eyre* in an anonymous review of *The Purcell Papers* printed in the *Saturday Review* (19 June 1880): 802–3.—Ed.]

reader." Later, 9th October, 1847, she makes a special request that Messrs. Elder & Smith should send *Jane Eyre* to the same review. It is not improbable that a forgotten remembrance of Le Fanu's story, read years before, supplied what was never a fertile inventiveness with the machinery it wanted.

Le Fanu's story of "actual and intended bigamy," "A Chapter in the History of a Tyrone Family," the tenth of the Purcell Papers, is the story of Fanny Richardson, told by herself and set down by Father Purcell. Lord Glenfallen pretends to marry her and takes her to Cahergillagh Court which boasted legends in plenty, with an old housekeeper, Martha, for teller of tales. Martha's first recital concerned the ominous fate of Lady Jane. There is a mysterious part of the castle which Fanny is forbidden to visit, but its mysterious dweller visits her, announcing herself as the true Lady Glenfallen and demanding that Fanny depart. This and succeeding visits Lord Glenfallen explains by saying that the lady is mad. She is blind, not mad; but at the end there is a murderous attack upon Fanny in her bedroom which is more than a little reminiscent of many things. The blind woman is hanged; Lord Glenfallen cuts his throat in mania and Fanny retreats to a convent. So much—and so very little—for one of the Purcell Papers in a Brontëan light. Professor Jack does much more with it; but nothing, of course, can convey the same delightfully piquant analogy as the Le Fanu story itself, to which, if he can obtain it today, the reader is cheerfully referred.

III.

Now there are many reasons why the anonymous Purcell Papers, all of them, should have keenly interested the Brontë sisters in their fanciful girlhood. The tales were "Irish," they were "ghostly," above all, they were filled to running over with "coincidences," "correspondences," "identifications." Brontë family names abounded—Patricks and Emilys and Janes and Marys and Hughs. If Lady Glenfallen had for servant an "old Martha," so had the Haworth parsonage. If Father Purcell, "the wonderful priest of Drumcoolagh," lived in a mythical parish, Patrick Brontë, priest of Haworth, had served his tutor apprenticeship in the literal Irish Parish of Drumgooland.

Professor Jack's suggested sources for plots end with "A Chapter in the History of a Tyrone Family" and *Jane Eyre*. But speculation can go further and fare more abundantly with others of *The Purcell Papers* and their correspondences with Emily Brontë's *Wuthering Heights*. For the Second, Fifth and Sixth of the Papers bear the oddest resemblances to that novel with its "greatest villain," and they too are tales "eminently adapted to floating in the back of the mind." In each of them there is a Lady Emily, and in each of them there is an arch villain. In each of them there is a superlatively lonely house, and in two of them the revengeful inferior becomes the brutal master. In the first, "The Fortunes of Sir Robert Ardagh," there are three sisters, the second of whom, Lady Emily, lives with her husband in Castle Ardagh. Sir Robert has a mysterious valet, whose malignant will dominates his master's fortunes and who at last destroys him. "A Passage in the Secret History of an Irish Countess," has the forced-marriage plot, wickedly maneuvered by Sir Arthur T—n, father of an Emily and an Edward, and uncle of a Margaret, sincerely intent upon acquiring his niece's fortune either through her marriage with his son or by her murder. Murder it is, but all mistakenly not of the heroine—Emily is slain, and Margaret ends her story in the very mood of the end of *Wuthering Heights,* the wish that Emily "had been spared and that in her stead *I* was mouldering in the grave, forgotten and at rest."

But "The Bridal of Carrigvarah" yields the most of reminiscent likenesses, of suggestions of Heathcliff's villainy, revenge and love, of "correspondences" and "identifications." Here also is a Lady Emily, sadly figuring as a minor deserted character.

It will be recalled that the old servant, Ellen Dean, tells the tangled tale of *Wuthering Heights,* most of it, of Healthcliff's servitude and later mastership. In "The Bridal of Carrigvarah," Ellen Heathcote, daughter of a stern father, has at the outset two loves, Richard O'Mara and Edward Dwyer, the latter a servant of the O'Maras, malignant, revengeful, plotting their downfall. Having forced his young master into insincere assertion of his indifference to Ellen, Dwyer dickers for Heathcote's farm lease and his daughter. Refused both, he muses thus:

> Insolent young spawn of ingratitude and guilt, how long must I submit to be trod upon thus; and yet why should I murmur—his day is even now declining . . . . But I must wait—I am but a pauper now . . . . Were I independent once, I'd make them feel my power, and feel it *so,* that I should die the richest or the best avenged servant of a great man that has ever been heard of.

Through Dwyer's devices, O'Mara, though betrothed to Lady Emily, marries Ellen Heathcote secretly, "madly, fervently, irrevocably in love," and hides her in the lonely Lodge, set in black and heathy hills. Again, through Dwyer's villainy, O'Mara is challenged by Lady Emily's brother and slain. While believing herself deserted, Ellen gives birth to a child and at its death sends for "the wonderful priest of Drumcoolagh," who finds the Lodge as dreary as ever Ellen Dean found Heathcliff's Wuthering Heights. Ellen Heathcote dies, glad to know she was widowed, not deserted, and Dwyer completes the overthrow of the hated O'Maras.

"Correspondences" are, of course, a most delicate matter of shades, even shares of shades; things to be felt, not seen. Professor Jack's launching of his little boat of surmise, on so cool an ocean of documents as make up *The Cambridge History of English Literature,* argues strongly for the strength of his feeling. Taking his tip and playing it farther, his "measure of correspondence," as he calls it, between the Purcell Papers and the Brontë novels is largely increased. There is also, for the added amusement of "connections," Le Fanu's *Uncle Silas,* published nine years after Charlotte Brontë's death, but of interest notwithstanding. This is no more than a three-volume extension of "The Secret History of an Irish Countess," with many names changed and with a governess, Madame de la Rougierre, added to brim the cup of villainy. On *Uncle Silas* Sheridan Le Fanu won his first wide fame. It is a queer old book, yet queerer books have survived, by their titles at least, to keep the memories of their authors green. But *Uncle Silas* too has passed—until the other day when it was included in an "old novels" series. And, once again, Le Fanu's fate of frustration has been operative. Since he was to be reprinted, why *Uncle Silas,* instead of those "occult" old tales by which alone, and by the smallest of small groups, the author has been remembered!

IV.

It was some years ago, during an evening of talk on "horror" tales (the cataleptic, the vampiric, the "buried alive," the tangible ghostly and the intangible obsessionistic) that a title, "Green Tea," floated suddenly to the surface. Just the title, nothing more. I recalled it (no one else had ever heard of it) as a tale, vaguely, of a physician, a clergyman and an obsession—a little black monkey visible always by a halo of reddish light. Nothing of the story remained—only the impression of its effect, which is indeed all any old forgotten tale can ask. Most of us who like to read can recall "the look of the page," but this too had vanished.

A few days later the arm of coincidence reached across an old bookstall and laid a finger on *Ignorant Essays,* by Richard Dowling (1888). Both book and author were unknown, but a note of authority rang out on the contents page: "The Only Real Ghost in Fiction," and the book fell open at the fifteenth page and at this paragraph:

> I am very bad at dates, but I think Le Fanu wrote "Green Tea" before a whole community of Canadian nuns were thrown into the most horrible state of nervous misery by excessive indulgence in that drug. Of all the horrible tales that are revolting, "Green Tea" is I think, the most horrible. The bare statement that an estimable and pious man is haunted by the ghost of a monkey is at first blush funny. But if you have not read this story read it and

see how little of fun there is in it. The horror of the tale lies in the fact that this apparition of a monkey is the only *probable* ghost in fiction . . . .

Sheridan Le Fanu, of course, and *In a Glass Darkly!* I saw again the little volume of ghostly tales of which "Green Tea" was one. I read on, and, in face of Mr. Richard Dowling's naïve summary of it, interest lapsed. It seemed too sufficiently obvious; I explained its enduring impression by the surmise that a youthful faith in the goodness of all clergymen must have been extreme; better never go back to the story itself.

But later I was to go back to its author for other reasons, and I reread "Green Tea" and the other case histories of Dr. Hesselius. Le Fanu's Father Purcell of Drumcoolagh may or may not lie back of *Jane Eyre* and *Wuthering Heights,* but his Dr. Hesselius was John the Baptist for the gods of later fiction— the psychic doctors. (Balzac's Dr. Desplein is the great father of them all!)

> "In Dr. Martin Hesselius," writes his "Watson," a young surgeon frustrated of a great career by the loss of two fingers, "I found my master . . . . his knowledge was immense, his grasp of a case was an intuition . . . . For nearly 20 years I acted as his medical secretary. His immense collection of papers he has left in my care to be arranged, indexed, and bound. His treatment of some of these cases is curious. He writes in two distinct characters. He describes what he saw and heard, as an intelligent layman might, and when in this style of narrative he has seen the patient either through his own hall door to the light of day or through the gates of darkness to the caverns of the dead, he returns upon the narrative, and in the terms of his art and with all the force and originality of genius proceeds to the work of analysis, diagnosis, and illustration."

On these lines precisely "Green Tea" is done, in letters to a friend, Professor Van Loo of Leyden. These letters trace the strange case of the Rev. Mr. Jennings, a wealthy bachelor clergyman, beginning with Dr. Hesselius's first observations of him at an evening party.

> "Mr. Jennings," writes the good doctor, "has a way of looking sidelong upon the carpet as if his eye followed the movements of something there. This, of course, is not always. It occurs now and then. But often enough to give a certain oddity to his manner, and in this glance travelling along the floor there is something both shy and anxious."

Mr. Jennings drinks too much green tea, but his troubles are not born of that. Later he brings his hallucination to the doctor, who traces its developments, observing, after some time, "He has not yet given me his full and unreserved confidence." He never does, and goes down to a bitter death. And, after Dr. Hesselius has seen him "through the gates of darkness to the caverns of the dead," he "returns upon the narrative" and sums up.

No bad pattern, this, by which to cut one's dark psychologic cloth, in 1872.[6] Dr. Hesselius was a gold mine for any novelist interested in the psychologic and the occult. In this German physician and metaphysician of the mind and soul, Le Fanu had hit upon more than a cunning device in the way of a reservoir for learning, intuition, magic or psychology to be tapped at will; he had hit upon a character as well, one that, had he lived to work with it, might have towered high in the heavens of ghostly fiction. But he had come upon it too late; he died the following year. The rest is silence, complete mysterious silence. He was famous; he was read; he "sold;" he was of the Sheridan blood; he was filially reprinted no more than a quarter century after his death, and that death is only half a century back. But his very name is lost to present-day historians of his age. His novels, so multitudinously printed and reprinted, have simply disappeared. They are as rare on old bookstalls as black swans on old lakes.

Sheridan Le Fanu himself was "rare," after his wife's death, which occurred in 1858. He had been wit and scholar of old Dublin society; but, says Graves:

> From this society he vanished so entirely, that Dublin, always ready with a nickname, dubbed him "The Invisible Prince," and, indeed, he was for a long time almost invisible, except to his family and most familiar friends, unless at odd hours of the evening, when he might occasionally be seen stealing, like the ghost of his former self, between his newspaper office and his home in Merrion Square. Sometimes, too, he was to be encountered in an old, out-of-the-way book shop, pouring over some rare Astrology or Demonology. . . .

If it is ever discovered that the *Dublin University Magazine* of 1838 and 1839 was in the parsonage at Haworth—was even in the little circulating library at Keighley where the Brontë sisters walked for books to read—was even in the libraries of those purgatorial homes where the sisters were sad governesses, Sheridan Le Fanu's *The Purcell Papers* may easily become the generating cause of a little literary thunderclap.

Meantime, Dr. Hesselius of "Green Tea" of *In a Glass Darkly* stands as the forerunner of the "soul doctors" so liberally employed by later writers in the supernatural field. On "Green Tea" alone (let pass the rest of his occult tales) Le Fanu, particularly charming descendant of the famous Sheridans, earned his right of way into any studies of the supernatural in fiction. That he had disappeared so completely from lists and records, even from the footnotes, of the Victorians, is so inexplicable as to be of itself almost "supernatural."

---

6. ["Green Tea" was first serialized in *All the Round*, New Series (23 October–13 November 1869) before appearing in *In a Glass Darkly*.—Ed.]

Sheridan Le Fanu

E. F. Benson

The writer of ghost stories and of tales which are designed to make the flesh creep embarks on hazardous voyages. If he does not scare his readers or inspire in them those precious uncomfortable impulses that cause them to glance hastily round in order to make sure that the creaking board or the wail of the wind did not betoken some dreadful presence even now making itself manifest to their horrified eyes, he has failed more ruinously than can any other class of narrator. The writer of humorous stories, though he may not amuse, may still interest his readers, the writer of serious psychological stuff may, though unwittingly, amuse; but no such adventitious good fortune can befall the author whose sole aim is to terrify. If he does not do that, he is naught, he falls completely flat, and no interest in side issues, whether intentional or not, will put him on his feet again. He must be an artist of no common sort, for the fearful lies but a hairbreadth away from the grotesque and the ludicrous, and his phantoms will terrify none unless they are surrounded by the phantasmal atmosphere in which alone they can live and breathe. Of all atmospheres, that is the most difficult to produce: it is easier to amuse, it is even easier to edify than, by suggestion, to alarm.

Sometimes a novelist whose *métier* and methods are purely psychological brings off a tremendous hit in the creepy line. The classical instance of such a happening was when Henry James wrote The Turn of the Screw. Not one of his most fervent admirers ever imagined that he could frighten them, but that appalling tale has probably alarmed more readers than the collected ghost stories of most other authors who make a speciality of creepiness. He tried it again, but with less success, in The Sense of the Past. Perhaps he would have been wiser to rest on one unfading laurel.

But there is one author, far too little known by those in search of creepy lore, who seldom fails in his high mission: his name is Sheridan Le Fanu. He produces, page for page, a far higher percentage of terror than the more widely read Edgar Allan Poe, and whether he deals in ghosts direct or in more material horrors, his success in making his readers very uneasy is amaz-

105

ing. Though we may already know the story we select to give us some insupportable moments on a lonely evening, there is a quality about most of his tales which seldom fails to alarm: familiarity with them does not breed comfort. Many ghost stories are efficacious for a first reading, but few, when we already know the worst that the author has to tell us, preserve untainted the atmosphere of horror as do the tales in In a Glass Darkly. The best of these, "Green Tea," "The Familiar," and "Mr. Justice Hartbottle," are instinct with an awfulness which custom cannot stale, and this quality is due, as in The Turn of the Screw, to Le Fanu's admirably artistic methods in setting and narration. They begin quietly enough, the tentacles of terror are applied so softly that the reader hardly notices them till they are sucking the courage from his blood. A darkness gathers, like dusk gently falling, and then something obscurely stirs in it. . . . Dickens, in his Christmas Carol, which is one of the most famous ghost stories in literature, goes the other way about it, and the wrong way. He leads off with the appearance of Marley's ghost, and then he has done his worst. The darkness brightens and we end on a grievous anti-climax of roast goose, Tiny Tim and a regenerated Scrooge. The moral is excellent, but who wants a moral in a ghost story? We can unbend our minds over morals afterwards.

This quiet, cumulative method leading up to intolerable terror is characteristic of all Le Fanu's best work, and it is that which makes him so wholesale a fear-monger. He employs this technique not only in his short stories, but when he is engaged on a full-length, novel. Far the best of these, to my mind, is Uncle Silas, which in skill of narration, of gradual crescendo towards that most hideous chapter called "The Hour of Death," is a sheer masterpiece in alarm. The book is a long one: it is not till we come to the four hundred and fiftieth page or thereabouts that the climax arrives, but from the first page onwards there is no pause in the relentless drip, drip, drip of ominous and menacing incident. Without the aid of the supernatural (though we are once or twice, rather unfairly, threatened with a ghost that does not mature), Le Fanu piles up, in the growing dusk, chapter by chapter, the horror of great darkness. Out of this dusk, intermittently at first, peer the grim faces of the French governess, of Dudley Ruthyn, of Uncle Silas, creatures of flesh and blood, but more ghastly than any ghost. Occasionally, as when Madame de la Rougierre is sent about her business, or when Dudley has apparently sailed for Australia, or when Uncle Silas seems like to die, we try to persuade ourselves that the darkness is lifting, but we are aware in our quaking consciousness that we are but buoying ourselves up with idle hopes. We do not see them for the moment because night is gathering, but we are sure that they are awfully whispering together in that shroud of blackness from which they will presently emerge for some murderous business. We cannot close the book, we cannot skip a word, we are altogether in the author's grip, and these compulsions are due to the consummate art with which he handles and develops his hideous theme. . . . Already, after a dreary period of fiction in which so many of our eminent writers have seemed to aim at producing flat and interminable chronicles, there are signs that the public craves for stories again, and, if such signs portend a change, we may be sure that among the authors of the mid-nineteenth century Le Fanu will come into his own, for technically, as a story-teller, his best work is of the first rank, while as a flesh-creeper he is unrivalled. No one else has so sure a touch in mixing the mysterious atmosphere in which horror darkly breeds.

From *The Supernatural in Fiction*

Peter Penzoldt

Joseph Sheridan Le Fanu (1814–1873) was a novelist above all, but for certain reasons which I shall try to analyze later he is nowadays remembered only for his short tales, while, except for *Uncle Silas*, all his novels have been forgotten.

During his lifetime Le Fanu's thrillers were best-sellers, and so great was his fame that Henry James paid him a lasting tribute in "The Liar," where we read:

> There was the customary novel of Mr. Le Fanu for the bedside: the ideal reading in a country house for the hours after midnight.

and learn that the hero was so fascinated by the book that he was late for dinner.

After his death, however, Le Fanu soon disappeared from the publisher's records, and so completely was he forgotten, that in 1917 Dorothy Scarborough did not even mention him in her standard work on the supernatural in modern English fiction. Then, after half a century of unmerited neglect, came the Le Fanu revival started by Dr. M. R. James's prologue and epilogue to *Madame Crowl's Ghost and Other Tales of Mystery* (London: G. Bell & Sons Ltd., 1923),[1] by Joseph Sheridan Le Fanu. This was followed by Professor Jack's article on the Brontës,[2] in which Le Fanu's *Purcell Papers* are sug-

---

1. [As in his analyses of M. R. James and H. P. Lovecraft, Penzoldt is most perceptive in his analysis of the author's aesthetic and the manner in which an author's work employs structure and language to create immediate effects and imply more than is on the written page. Unfortunately, his uncritical acceptance of Freud's theories also leads to occasional biographical extrapolations like that based on the mistaken initial publication date of "Green Tea" noted below. Details related to publication in Penzoldt's footnotes have been standardized and, when possible, incorporated into the text.—Ed.]

2. [Penzoldt is referring to A. A. Jack's "The Brontës" in Sir Adolphus William Ward and Alfred Rayney Waller, ed., The Cambridge History of English and American Literature. Vol. XIII. English—The Victorian Age. Part One. The Nineteenth Century, II (Cambridge: Cambridge University Press, 1917).

gested as the source of inspiration of *Jane Eyre,* Edna Kenton's article on the same subject, published in 1929,[3] and E. F. Benson's remarks in *The Spectator* of February 1931. In the same year S. M. Ellis published his *Wilkie Collins, Le Fanu and Others* (London: Constable and Co., 1931), which contains the first, and only, complete Le Fanu bibliography. Finally, sixteen years later, in 1947, Elizabeth Bowen wrote an introduction to *Uncle Silas*[4] which is proba-bly the best study ever written on this particular novel. But, as far as I know, Miss Bowen's introduction is the only evidence of recent interest in the works of Le Fanu, whose writings can now be found only in the better an-thologies of ghostly tales. These, however, are never complete without one or other of his stories. Unfortunately, the critics to-day are again inclined to neglect him. H. P. Lovecraft in his *Supernatural Horror in Literature*[5] barely mentions him, while Edward Wagenknecht, a great specialist in the field of the ghost story, hardly touches the subject in his *Cavalcade of the English Novel* [New York: Henry Holt and Company, 1943].

With the Le Fanu revival of about 1930 came the general over estima-tion of his work that was to be expected. Edna Kenton thought that the ap-parition in "Green Tea" was "the only probable ghost in fiction." To S. M. Ellis (p. 157) "The Haunting of the Tiled House" was "the most terrifying ghost story in the language," while E. F. Benson (p. 263) went so far as to say that "Le Fanu produces, page for page, a far higher percentage of terror than the more widely read Edgar Allan Poe."

But there is no need to resort to such exaggerations to demonstrate the importance of Le Fanu's ghost fiction. His influence alone on contemporary and later authors entitles him to a better place in the history of English lit-erature than he is generally given. This influence is a threefold one. Firstly, Le Fanu undoubtedly influenced the Brontës. Secondly, he created Dr. Hes-selius, the spiritual father of Machen's Dr. Reymond and Dr. Black, and of Blackwood's John Silence. Thirdly, Dr. M. R. James acknowledged him as his master and chief inspiration.

Le Fanu's influence on the Brontës was first discovered by Professor

---

3. [Edna Kenton, "A Forgotten Creator of Ghosts—Joseph Sheridan Le Fanu, Possible Inspirer of the Brontës," *Bookman* (New York) (July 1929): 528–35. Included in this volume.—Ed.]

4. *Uncle Silas,* by Joseph Sheridan Le Fanu, with an introduction by Elizabeth Bowen. The Cresset Press, London 1947.

5. *Supernatural Horror in Literature,* by Howard Philips Lovecraft. Ben Abramson, New York 1945. [First appeared in W. Paul Cook, ed., *The Recluse* (1927). Revised 1933–35.—Ed.]

Jack.[6] There is, indeed, a marked resemblance between the tenth narrative of the *Purcell Papers*, "A Chapter in the History of a Tyrone Family," a tale of "actual and intended bigamy,"[7] and *Jane Eyre* (1847). Le Fanu's story is about a certain Lord Glenfallen, who keeps his blind wife in a secret part of his castle. He subsequently marries the girl Fanny Richardson. But the wife nightly escapes from her apartments, and informs the unfortunate girl that she is the real Lady Glenfallen. Finally there is a murderous attack on Fanny in her bedroom, which Edna Kenton rightly calls "more than a little reminiscent of many things." The end of the story is, however, more tragic than that of *Jane Eyre*. Lord Glenfallen cuts his throat, his wife is hanged, and Fanny retreats to a convent.[8]

Edna Kenton, in her article in *The Bookman* of 1929, goes even further than Professor Jack, and points out the correspondence between *Wuthering Heights* and the second, fifth and sixth narratives of the *Purcell Papers*.[9] Miss Kenton bases her study on numerous details, such as the frequent use of Brontëan family names, and the recurrent theme of the revengeful inferior who later becomes the brutal master. (Second and sixth of the *Purcell Papers*.) In view of the many resemblances she discovers, I find Miss Kenton's theory rather convincing. But to-day one has to be a Brontë specialist to say anything definite on the subject, which has been so studied and over-studied.

The figure of Dr. Hesselius had an influence on later writers no less important than that of the *Purcell Papers*. Even if Balzac's Dr. Desplein was the ancestor of the long line of "psychic doctors," which include Dr. Reymond, John Silence, and perhaps even that great lay scientist, Sherlock Holmes, it was certainly Le Fanu who introduced the prototype into English fiction.[10]

---

6. Cf. *Cambridge History of English Literature*. Chapter XII. *The Brontës*, by A. A. Jack, M. A., Peterhouse, Chalmers Professor of English Literature in the University of Aberdeen.

7. First printed in the *Dublin University Magazine* in [October]1839 and reprinted in *The Purcell Papers* (1880).

8. Edward Wagenknecht in his *Cavalcade of the English Novel* finds the first outlines of *Jane Eyre* in the Brontëan "Saga of Angria." But this was composed between 1829 and 1845, so that there is still a good chance that Le Fanu's influence showed even in this earlier work.

9. Second narrative. "The Fortunes of Sir Robert Ardagh," March 1838; fifth, "Passage in the Secret History of an Irish Countess," November 1838; sixth, "The Bridal of Carrigvarah," April 1839. All were first published in the *Dublin University Magazine*, and later reprinted as *The Purcell Papers* (1880).

10. It is Edna Kenton in her article on Le Fanu who mentions Sherlock Holmes in this connection, and she is not completely wrong. But it must be remembered that

Had not Le Fanu died the year after he created Dr. Hesselius,[11] the German doctor might well have become as much a little demigod of fiction as any of those later characters who are spiritually descended from him. As it is, he lacks many of the qualities of his successors. To begin with, he theorizes too much. Algernon Blackwood's Dr. Silence does so too, but Blackwood knew how to avoid Le Fanu's greatest mistakes. Though John Silence develops long theories, they are at least on subjects with which human science does not pretend to deal. His theories do not, therefore, provoke the reader to a fierce denial, as do those of Dr. Hesselius in "Green Tea." Everybody knows that green tea contains a stimulant which may produce nervous depression and even hallucinations, but it does not open an "interior sense" or lead the reveler towards a direct contact with the other world.

We shall see in the next two chapters that the drug theme is hardly ever convincing. Neither Stevenson nor Machen used it with much success. Algernon Blackwood's "A Psychical Invasion" (from *John Silence*), though it has some excellent features, is one of his weakest tales. Only De Quincey in his *Confessions of an English Opium Eater* is really convincing. But for him the drug motif was not merely a means of introducing the supernatural, it was also the main theme of the book. He was clever enough to present the visions of the opium eater as what they were: namely, as hallucinations, and did not suggest that they were supernatural. This strict adherence to reality, which leaves no loophole whereby the visions could be dismissed as supernatural and scientifically impossible, increases their horror a hundred-fold.

Another rather annoying feature of Dr. Hesselius is his infallibility. He is constantly astonishing the reader with his perspicacity. In "Green Tea," for instance, he immediately knows that the father of a gentleman whom he had barely met has seen a ghost, that this gentleman is writing a book, and that he is unmarried. When asked how he has learned these details, he answers with silence and a superior smile. It is all rather childish; but is not this improbable power of detection precisely the same as that which made Sherlock Holmes one of the most popular figures in literature? We have no right to blame Le

---

above all Holmes belongs to a tradition which began with Poe's Dupin, and is to-day carried on by the host of infallible private detectives such as Agatha Christie's The Saint, Maurice Leblanc's Arsène Lupin, Mr. Moto, Charlie Chan, and so on, and is at least closely related to a class of literature inferior to that which produced John Silence and Dr. Reymond.

11. Dr. Hesselius appears for the first time in the collection *In a Glass Darkly*, 1872. ["Green Tea" first appeared as a serial in *All the Year Round* (New Series) between 23 October and 13 November 1869.–Ed.]

Fanu for a *naïveté* which delights us in the writings of his successors.

Le Fanu, like Bulwer-Lytton, was a very learned man, and like Bulwer-Lytton he had an unfortunate tendency to display his knowledge in his tales. Dr. Hesselius was an excellent vehicle for this purpose. But despite this character's tedious digressions, and the narrow scientific basis on which they balance, ever less securely, the creation of Dr. Hesselius still has its importance even beyond the fact that a new figure was thus introduced into English fiction. To a certain extent, his advent marks the beginning of the psychological ghost story.

Towards the end of his life, Le Fanu, who had always been extremely sensitive, and was probably a neurotic, became definitely abnormal. He was troubled by horrible nightmares, which S. M. Ellis suggests were perhaps the origin of some of his stories. One dream of a terrible, forbidding old mansion, which threatened to crush the paralyzed dreamer, was particularly painful and persistent. S. M. Ellis relates how, when the end came, and the doctor, standing by his bedside, looked into the terror-stricken eyes of what had been Le Fanu, he said "I feared this, that house fell at last."[12] Evidently Le Fanu had consulted a doctor about his ghostly visions, and probably knew that they were, at least partly, pathological. But it is also probable that his doctor disappointed him as much as the "materialistic doctors" had disappointed Dr. Hesselius's patient in "Green Tea." Le Fanu invented Dr. Hesselius one year before he died. Was not the creation of this "ideal doctor" a pathetic attempt at a self-cure? In any case the tales of *In a Glass Darkly* show a curious mixture of deep psychological insight and quaint esoteric beliefs. As "Green Tea" shows, Le Fanu never ceased to believe that the ultimate cause of such sufferings as his own lay in another world, yet at the same time he seemed to think, in some curious way, that the evil could be cured in the body. In this respect, all authors before the Freudian era were more materialistic than the later champions of the psychological ghost story. Like Kipling and many others Le Fanu wrote fictional psychiatry rather than true psychological ghost stories as we know them to-day.

Le Fanu describes the symptoms of mental and nervous disease with almost uncanny accuracy, though the causes he suggests for the maladies are woefully inadequate. As is often the case with neurotics, the constant preoccupation with his own problems must have developed his natural gift of intuition, and given him an empirical, but uncommonly penetrating,

---

12. S. M. Ellis, *Wilkie Collins, Le Fanu and Others*. [Cf. discussion of Ellis's version of Le Fanu's death in the notes to Ellis's article and Brian J. Showers's "A Void Which Cannot Be Filled Up" elsewhere in this volume.—Ed.]

knowledge of psychology. Again, like many neurotics, he became interested in problems which were not his own. Like Baudelaire, he was fascinated by lesbianism. "Carmilla" from *In a Glass Darkly* contains a description of a real "love scene" between two girls, one of whom is the vampire. The description of the mental attitudes of the seducer and the seduced in the following example is psychologically almost perfect. Of course the technical term "lesbianism" is never used, and it is doubtful whether Le Fanu ever knew it, or was aware of the true nature of what he was describing. But even if this is so, we must admit that his intuition did not fail him in the following paragraph:

> She used to place her pretty arms about my neck, draw me to her, and laying her cheek to mine, murmur with her lips close to my ears, "Dearest, your little heart is wounded; think me not cruel because I obey the irresistible law of my strength and weakness; if your heart is wounded, my wild heart bleeds with yours. In the rapture of my enormous humiliation I live in your warm life, and you shall die—die, sweetly die, into mine. I cannot help it; as I draw near to you, you in your turn will draw near to others, and learn the rapture of that cruelty, which yet is love: so, for a while, seek to know no more of me and mine, but trust me with all your loving spirit."
>
> And when she had spoken such a rhapsody, she would press me more closely in her trembling embrace, and her lips in soft kisses gently glowed upon my cheek.
>
> Her agitations and her language were unintelligible to me.
>
> From these foolish embraces, which were not of very frequent occurrence. I must allow, I used to wish to extricate myself; but my energies seemed to fail me. Her murmured words sounded like a lullaby in my ear, and soothed my resistance into a trance, from which I only seemed to recover myself when she withdrew her arms.
>
> In these mysterious moods I did not like her. I experienced a strange tumultuous excitement that was pleasurable, ever and anon mingled with a vague sense of fear and disgust. I had no distinct thought about her while such scenes lasted, but I was conscious of a love growing into adoration, and also of abhorrence. This I know is paradox, but I can make no other attempt to explain the feeling.[13]

The reader will admit that hardly anything else like this was written in the Victorian era.

Le Fanu shows a marked interest in all aspects of feminine psychology. He portrays in his work nearly all the emotions and peculiarities of women,

13. Joseph Sheridan Le Fanu, *In a Glass Darkly*, with numerous illustrations by Edward Ardizzone, (London: Peter Davies, 1929): 317. First published 1872.

except normal love between man and woman. Bigamy held great fascination for him, as we have seen, but he wrote no straightforward love stories. When normal love appears in one of his stories it is usually merely mentioned and quickly passed by. Elizabeth Bowen called *Uncle Silas* an entirely "sexless" novel, and the term might rightly be applied to all Le Fanu's work, if one can call perverse or illegal love relations "sexless." Another striking feature is that many of his short stories and novels are written in the first person, and told by a feminine character. It is particularly remarkable that all his heroines are either children, very young girls, or at least somewhat infantile in their behavior. In this respect there is a strong analogy between Le Fanu and our contemporary Franco-American author Julien Green.

These features of Le Fanu's tales, the childish heroines, the identification with feminine characters, and the "sexlessness" of the stories, indicate, when taken together, that he suffered from a severe neurosis, and that many of the terrors he invented arose from this pathological state. The kind of neurosis from which he suffered is of no importance, and in any case can hardly be decided post-mortem. One of the first rules of psychoanalysis is never to advance a theory without a knowledge as complete as possible of the patient's subconscious and personal history. Thus throughout this book I shall limit my psychological investigations to the analysis of independent stories, and shall only occasionally draw some very general conclusions about the author's personality. In Le Fanu's case, psychoanalysis is of use only because it helps us to ascertain four very important facts.

The first of these is that, being a neurotic, he was prone to neurotic fears which are reflected in his work. The symbolism of his tales has, therefore, a genuine basis in experience, and is always effective and never artificial.

Secondly, his self-identification with weak, feminine, child-heroines shows that in the face of neurotic terrors he reacted as a helpless child. No fear is so great as that of the utterly helpless. If the reader sympathises with the heroine, he too is likely to experience some of this terror. Thus Le Fanu's neurosis helped him to write tales of terror more affecting than those of most of his less neurotic rivals.

Thirdly, as we have already mentioned, Le Fanu's neurosis kindled his interest in psychological problems which were not, or at least not directly, his own. It helped to develop his natural intuition.

Fourthly, the creation of Dr. Hesselius was an attempt to fight his own problems.

In "Green Tea," Le Fanu's psychological insight is probably at its most evident, and his symbolism at its most striking. Disregarding Dr. Hesselius's fantastic theories, the story is the case history of a schizophrenic, or rather

an account of the neurotic symptoms which are often observed in connection with this mental disease. The Reverend Dr. Jennings is haunted by an
ape-like demon which at first watches him, annoying him merely by its presence, but later he begins to speak, uttering terrible blasphemies. Finally it
drives the unfortunate clergyman to suicide. The omniscient Dr. Hesselius
explains this affair as the result of hereditary suicidal mania, and the opening
of an "interior sense" can be created as easily as a "cold in the head or a trifling dyspepsia." One of his remedies is "iced eau-de-Cologne." But for all
this nonsense, which must have sounded a little naïve even when the story
was first published, "Green Tea" contains a strikingly accurate description of
the gradual decline of a man suffering from split personality. Le Fanu went so
far as to divide it into stages, one, two and three. The ghost monkey, if one
may be allowed to regard it as a product of a schizoid neurosis rather than of
green tea, is the symbol of suppressed sex desire. Dr. Hesselius is for once
really perspicacious, when he immediately observes that Jennings must be
unmarried. Unfortunately he draws the wrong conclusions from this statement, and perhaps Le Fanu simply wished to suggest that a solitary man is
more easily given to nervous brooding. He must have known this better than
anyone. But the fact remains that animal ghosts are often the symbols of
suppressed sex desire. It is significant that the monkey frequently disturbs its
victim when he is praying. If sex is consciously or unconsciously considered
as sinful, this fact would be one more point in favour of the theory.[14]

Le Fanu's great gift for psychology is also evident in his stories of guilty
conscience. Conscience in fact was one of his favourite themes, and dominates such little masterpieces as "Madam Crowl's Ghost," "Squire Toby's
Will," "The Familiar" and "Mr. Justice Harbottle." No previous author of
ghost stories, and perhaps not even Shakespeare himself, has handled the
theme with such deep comprehension of human nature. Though Le Fanu's
characters are not always lifelike, their obsession is nevertheless real, and
makes the stories convincing. He knew that a guilty conscience manifests itself by degrees, and this gradation gives his tales an additional firmness of
structure and helps to build up the suspense. He knew, moreover, that any
event, even if it had no outward connection with a deeply-rooted guilt, could,
by its symbolical connection with the crime, suddenly awaken the feeling of

---

14. It must never be forgotten that all the tales studied in this book are fiction. No
author exactly observed the dividing line between mental and neurotic disease, and
Le Fanu certainly did not even know of this distinction. It is, therefore, not surprising
that we find what are really neurotic symptoms described in connection with mental
disease. Besides, modern psychiatry knows that they often appear together.

guilt. This knowledge allowed him to make the transition from the natural to the supernatural in his tales with uncommon ease, and so to overcome the greatest difficulty of all ghost-story writers. But this brings us to the question of structure in Le Fanu's tales, and to his influence on Dr. M. R. James.

Dr. Montague Rhodes James is generally considered to be Le Fanu's disciple. Personally, I believe that Le Fanu's influence on the English scholar hardly went beyond the fact that both were interested in a good ghost story, and Dr. James's sincere admiration for his forerunner.[15] Indeed one can hardly imagine two more dissimilar characters than Le Fanu and James. A common taste for ghost fiction is the only link between the visionary Anglo-Irish Swedenborgian, a queer mixture of the *grand seigneur* and the haunted recluse, and the matter-of-fact English doctor, who has as little doubt about God and the Church as about the scientific integrity of his countless bibliographical works.[16] Le Fanu was a poet, James a scholar. The first would spend his nights writing tales of the supernatural, trembling before the creations of his own morbid imagination. The second divided his spare time between bicycling and composing ghost stories, which he intended as Christmas stories for his pupils.

This difference in character is, of course, visible in their respective writings. Le Fanu's stories impress by their terrible air of authenticity, their visionary quality. James holds us by his brilliant structure, in which no ghost-story writer has ever equaled him. But he gives us intellectual rather than emotional pleasure. One is never rid of the feeling that he is somewhat artificial. Nevertheless, he is indebted to Le Fanu for his particular structural technique. In his introduction to *Ghosts and Marvels*, he envisages the perfect ghost story in terms that might be a description of his own art and, to a certain extent, of Le Fanu's:

> Let us, then, be introduced to the actors in a placid way; let us see them going about their ordinary business, undisturbed by forebodings, pleased with their surroundings; and into this calm environment let the ominous thing put out its head, unobtrusively at first, and then more insistently, until it holds the stage. It is not amiss sometimes to leave a loophole for a natural explanation, but, I would say, let the loophole be so narrow as not to be quite practicable.[17]

---

15. Cf. James's introduction to *Ghosts and Marvels*. (The World's Classics, Oxford University Press, 1927.) "But 'Schalken' conforms more strictly to my own ideals. It is indeed one of the best of Le Fanu's good things."

16. Cf. Stephen Casely, "Montague Rhodes James, O. M., 1862–1936," from *The Proceedings of the British Academy*, Vol. XXII. London, Humphrey Milford.

17. M. R. James, Introduction to *Ghosts and Marvels*, p. vi.

A little earlier in the same paragraph James speaks of this process as a "nicely managed crescendo." Now with the one exception of his contemporary, Wilkie Collins, Le Fanu was the first author to use this "nicely managed crescendo," thus creating the prototype of the modern ghost story, with the climax placed at the end. Poe, for example, used quite another technique, introducing most of his tales with dreary, half-philosophical reflections on occult subjects, thus preparing the reader emotionally for the climax, which usually followed after a rather short dramatic action. Le Fanu, on the other hand, succeeded where most of his forerunners failed, in starting the action at the beginning of the story, and in developing it through pages of steadily increasing suspense to a final grisly climax. He invented a most telling device to heighten the effect of this technique. Having introduced us to the actors, according to James's formula, "in a placid way," letting us "see them going about their ordinary business, undisturbed by foreboding, pleased with their surroundings," he breaks the calm, not with the first appearance of the "thing" as M. R. James would have done, but with an unusual, yet in no way supernatural, event. Thus in "Mr. Justice Harbottle" a stranger disguised as an old man comes to warn the hanging judge of a "supreme court of judges" that will sentence him for the legal murders he has committed. Harbottle makes his footman follow the man, but the stranger knocks him down and escapes. Everything points to the fact that the stranger's masquerade is merely an attempt to intimidate the judge, who hardly seems to give the incident a second thought. Yet later the "supreme court of judges" becomes a terrible supernatural reality. Harbottle is finally sentenced to death, and either is hanged or hangs himself in his own house (the reader is left to decide which). The following extract is taken from the trial scene, in which the hanging judge is sentenced by the image of his own impure soul. At this stage the atmosphere is already ghostly, and manifestly belongs to the domain of the supernatural.

> The chief-justice seemed to feel his power over the jury, and to exult and riot in the display of it. He glared at them, he nodded to them; he seemed to have established an understanding with them. The lights were faint in that part of the court. The jurors were mere shadows, sitting in rows; the prisoner could see a dozen pair of white eyes shining, coldly, out of the darkness; and whenever the judge in his charge, which was contemptuously brief, nodded and grinned and gibed, the prisoner could see, in the obscurity, by the dip of all these rows of eyes together, that the jury nodded in acquiescence.[18]

---

18. "Mr. Justice Harbottle" from *In a Glass Darkly*. Compare this scene with the trial scene in Stephen Vincent Benét's "The Devil and Daniel Webster." Even if neither of them has influenced the other, there is still a great resemblance between the two scenes.

Another example of this technique is found in "The Familiar" (*In a Glass Darkly*). A shot is fired at the chief character, before he is haunted to death by the man he once killed. This shot is as little explained as is the intervention of the stranger in "Mr. Justice Harbottle," but there is good reason to believe that this, like the other, is not a supernatural event. In any case, these incidents aid the transition from the natural to the supernatural, both from the psychological and from the structural point of view. Considered from the structural point of view, it is clear that Le Fanu's device of beginning a story with a strange but natural event spares him the long troublesome preparation for the appearance of the ghost, which always presents the greatest difficulty. In Le Fanu's tales the reader is already in the midst of the action, and has suffered several surprises before the "thing" finally appears. His "willing suspension of disbelief" is thus more easily secured.

But this sequence of events is also what one would expect in a mental case-history. This astonishingly accurate psychiatry marks Le Fanu as one of the earliest masters of the psychological ghost story. Though he always insists strongly on the supernatural explanation he leaves the "loophole" which James suggests for a natural explanation. He asks the question "insanity or ghostly vision?" which is peculiar to the true psychological ghost story. In "Mr. Justice Harbottle" this problem is put quite explicitly. The following paragraph refers to the warrant the hanging judge receives from the supreme court of judges:

> What of the paper I have cited? No one saw it during his life; no one after his death. He spoke of it to Dr. Hedstone; and what purported to be "a copy," in the old Judge's handwriting, was found. The original was nowhere. Was it a copy of an illusion, incident to brain disease? Such is my belief.

Le Fanu's technique, as described above, places the incidents of the story in the exact order in which one would expect them to occur, if one was regarding them as symptoms of persecution mania arising from a guilty conscience. When it is latent, mental or neurotic disease of this kind still needs some outward inducement, such as a shock, or physical threat, to bring it to the surface. Thus Le Fanu comes very near to the psychological truth when he exposes his characters to some natural danger before they become the victims of ghostly visions.

Another reason for the structural perfection of Le Fanu's work was probably his curious predilection for presenting the same tale in the form of stories of varying lengths. As S. M. Ellis points out,[19] the theme of "The Fortunes of Sir Robert Ardagh" (*Dublin University Magazine*, March 1838) was

---

19. *Wilkie Collins, Le Fanu and Others.*

used again in "Sir Dominick's Bargain," [*All the Year Round* (New Series), 6 July 1872] and in "The Haunted Baronet" [*Belgravia*, July–October 1870]. "Passage in the Secret History of an Irish Countess" (*Dublin University Magazine*, November 1838) was the original short form of a story which was later enlarged into "The Murdered Cousin" (*Ghost Stories and Tales of Mystery*, Dublin: James MacGlashan, 1851), and finally made a full-length appearance in the famous *Uncle Silas* (London: Richard Bentley, 1864). In the same way, "A Chapter in the History of a Tyrone Family" (*Dublin University Magazine*, October 1839) was, years later, extended into the novel entitled *The Wyvern Mystery* (London: Tinsley Brothers, 1869), while "Some Account of the Latter Days of the Hon. Richard Marston, of Dunoran" (*Dublin University Magazine*, April 1848) became somewhat longer as "The Evil Guest" (*Ghost Stories and Tales of Mystery*, Dublin: James MacGlashan, 1851), and reached three-volume form as *A Lost Name* in 1868.

There is good reason to believe that Le Fanu considered his earlier short stories, at least, as detailed plans for novels. They represent his first attempts to master some of the themes that haunted him. Many of them already show a sub-division into separate chapters. Now it is undoubtedly more difficult to retain the interest of the reader throughout the four hundred pages of a novel like *Uncle Silas*, than to maintain suspense for the forty or fifty pages of a longish ghost story. Critics unanimously agree that Le Fanu was capable of both. But there is no doubt that his mastery of both genres is partly due to his habit of presenting his themes first in the form of a short tale, then as a novel. His short stories were more rigorously constructed than those of his contemporaries because they were the plans for the more exacting achievement of a novel, while his novels retained some of the structural simplicity of the short tale, and avoided the tedious digressions and sub-plots of the Gothic writers.

As many of Le Fanu's short tales were originally written as sketches or detailed schemes for novels, it may be supposed that he was more of a novelist than a short-story writer.[20] This was indubitably the case. One might well ask why, in that case, he still lives on in his short stories, while all his novels except *Uncle Silas* have been forgotten.

Le Fanu has often been called the "Irish Wilkie Collins," and a comparison between Collins and Le Fanu may yield the answer to my question. Both were writers of sensational novels, and both were famous in their day. Both wrote short stories of the supernatural, which they thought relatively unim-

---

20. In his day, Le Fanu was also a well-known poet. He wrote lyrics and ballads, amongst which "Shamus O'Brien" ([*Dublin University Magazine*] July 1850) was the most famous.

portant compared with their novels. Both were aware of the fact that in general the supernatural is better fitted to the short story than to the novel: that the reader's "willing suspension of disbelief," though it may last for thirty or fifty pages, is liable to disappear before the end of a long novel. Thus Collins's and Le Fanu's most famous novels are not typical stories of the supernatural, like, for example, Bram Stoker's *Dracula*. In their longer narratives the supernatural does not so much appear in the plot as pervade the atmosphere. Their books are, above all, mystery stories and thrillers. Now the true mystery story demands accuracy in detail, and a certain realism. In fact, the closer we come to modern times, the more the public demand precision from this particular genre. To-day, the mystery and detective novel is almost a mathematical problem, of which the reader can find the solution if he is careful enough not to miss a clue. Woe to the author who forgets to furnish these clues in the right place! No true devotee will read him again. Moreover, the merit of the modern mystery story depends upon the degree of probability it possesses. It has thus developed considerably since the time of the Gothic novel, when supernatural fiction and the mystery story were hardly even distinct genres.

Wilkie Collins's novels have all the qualities of the most modern detective story. They are accurate in detail, time is usually well accounted for, they rarely lack probability, and Collins wrote with more realism than most of his contemporaries. It is no wonder that his novels are still in favor with the public. Le Fanu's novels on the contrary lack all these qualities. He is superb at creating suspense, so long as the reader is willing to overlook the fact that his heroines invariably do everything they can to get themselves into trouble, and would rather walk into a death trap than out of an open door; that months seem to pass without being accounted for, and that important elements of the plot are simply forgotten *en route*, or finish in a dead end. On the other hand, Le Fanu was skilled in drawing characters who, although they are anything but lifelike, are yet drawn with an imagination equaled only by that of E. T. A. Hoffmann. Indeed, the following paragraph could be from Hoffmann's pen:

> As he spoke one of the strangest-looking men I ever beheld entered the chapel at the door through which Carmilla had made her entrance and her exit. He was tall, narrow-chested, stooping, with high shoulders, and dressed in black. His face was brown and dried with deep furrows; he wore an oddly-shaped hat with a broad leaf. His hair, long and grizzled, hung on his shoulders. He wore a pair of gold spectacles, and walked slowly, with an odd shambling gait, while his face, sometimes turned up to the sky and sometimes bowed down towards the ground, seemed to wear a perpetual smile; his long thin arms were swing-

ing, and his lank hands, in old black gloves, were ever so much too wide for them, waving and gesticulating in utter abstraction. ("Carmilla")

The most famous of Le Fanu's characters, Uncle Silas and Madame de la Rougierre, are completely divorced from those "puppet characters" with which the modern detective novel revived the Gothic tradition. They are also far more colorful, even if less real, than Wilkie Collins's characters.

The fact is that Le Fanu had more imagination than Collins, and this is probably why the Irish master outpaced his English rival whenever they chose to make use of the supernatural, even though his fanciful, but highly improbable, novels are no longer read by the public. Indeed, Collins was not much of a ghost-story writer, and his "A Terribly Strange Bed," a half-breed between a modern detective story and a Gothic tale, is still a more exciting thriller than his "Dream Woman," or the other ghostly tales in *The Queen of Hearts.*

I have given Le Fanu the place of honour amongst those authors whose tales form the transition from the Gothic tale to the true short story of the supernatural.[21] Having discussed his important influence on later authors, and the innovations he made, it is now time to study the Gothic features of his work, which place him in this period of transition.

The Gothic influence was undoubtedly more important in his novels than in his short stories. *Uncle Silas* abounds in gloomy descriptions of cemeteries and old mansions; and the scene in which Maude Ruthyn searches the attics of Bartram-Haugh for the skeleton of Mr. Clark, and discovers instead the horrible presence of Madame de la Rougierre, is pure Gothic. During her search, the heroine herself has the novels of Mrs. Radcliffe in mind. The trick-window, by which Uncle Silas gains access to the supposedly sealed room, is nothing but a development of the Gothic trapdoor and secret passages. *The House by the Church-yard* and *Wylder's Hand* are full of gothic descriptions of gloomy mansions and landscapes. Typically Gothic gloom pervades the opening pages of *Uncle Silas,* and many, if not most, of the later scenes. Even the characters show this influence to a certain extent. Uncle Silas, though far more colorful, is descended from the prototype of the Gothic villain.

There is one further point to be noticed, which definitely places Le Fanu in the Gothic tradition. Like Scott and Marryat, he includes one of his best ghost stories in a novel: "The Haunting of the Tiled House" [sic] appears in *The House by the Church-yard.* Thus at least one of his ghost stories originated in very much the same manner as Marryat's "Werewolf" and Scott's "Wandering Willie's Tale," namely, as a Gothic sub-plot.

As far as the short stories are concerned, the Gothic element is less ob-

---

21. With one exception, the peerless Edgar Allan Poe.

vious, but there are sufficient traces of it to indicate a direct influence. In "The Room in the Dragon Volant" there are subterranean passages, and in "Madam Crowl's Ghost" a secret chamber. The Gothic setting is always present. The word "Gothic" itself is introduced in the two following examples:

> The little I saw bore the character of Gothic gloom, and helped my fancy to shape and furnish the black void that yawned all round me. I heard a sound like the slow tread of two persons walking up the flagged aisle. A faint echo told of the vastness of the place. An awful sense of expectation was upon me, and I was horribly frightened when the body that lay on the catafalque said (without stirring), in a whisper that froze me, "They come to place me in the grave alive; save me." ("The Room in the Dragon Volant")

> Under a narrow arched doorway, surmounted by one of those demoniacal grotesques in which the cynical and ghastly fancy of old Gothic carving delights, I saw very gladly the beautiful face and figure of Carmilla enter the shadowy chapel. ("Carmilla")

Bloody horror scenes, of the type beloved by the Gothic masters, abound in the short tales, as well as in the novels. The example quoted below is only one of dozens. The torture scenes in "Mr. Justice Harbottle" are quite as horrible as this, the conclusion of "Carmilla":

> The two medical men, one officially present, the other on the part of the promoter of the inquiry, attested the marvellous fact that there was a faint but appreciable respiration and a corresponding action of the heart. The limbs were perfectly flexible, the flesh elastic; and the leaden coffin floated with blood, in which to a depth of seven inches the body lay immersed. Here, then, were all the admitted signs of vampirism. The body, therefore, in accordance with ancient practice, was raised, and a sharp stake driven through the heart of the vampire, who uttered a piercing shriek at the moment, in all respects such as might escape from a living person in the agony. Then the head was struck off, and a torrent of blood flowed from the severed neck. The body and head were next placed on a pile of wood and reduced to ashes, which were thrown upon the river and borne away; and that territory has never since been plagued by the visits of a vampire.[22]

22. "Carmilla" probably inspired Bram Stoker's *Dracula*, and this result of Le Fanu's work can be added to the other more important ones already mentioned. In any case the various attributes of the vampire as they are described in the above paragraph are the same as in *Dracula*; but it is difficult to determine whether this is due to direct influence or coincidence, for the vampire theme is nearly always treated in this manner. Still, it is more than probable that Bram Stoker had read Le Fanu.

The characters in Le Fanu's short stories are less convincing, and thus closer to the Gothic "puppet characters" than those of the novels. This may be due to the brevity of the tales which makes it more difficult to produce convincing personalities. Generally speaking, Victorian authors were not masters of the modern art of sketching a character, they needed space in which to create something really lifelike.[23]

Yet there are numerous features in Le Fanu's work that show his superiority over the Gothic masters. I have tried to analyze his use of structure, and his psychological accuracy in the description of neurotic disease, both of which were definitely new. I shall now turn to consider the type of ghost he created.

Compared with the Gothic spook, Le Fanu's apparitions are what Dorothy Scarborough called "the modern ghost." They are no longer pallid shades, but alarming and pugnacious specters. In "A Strange Event in the Life of Schalken the Painter" the dead fiend actually kidnaps his "bride" and the joint efforts of several strong men avail of nothing against him. The demon in "Green Tea" is particularly fascinating. The idea of presenting him as a small and seemingly innocent monkey makes him all the more horrible.

> The interior of the omnibus was nearly dark. I observed the corner opposite to me at the other side, and at the end next the horses, two small circular reflections, as it seemed to me, of a reddish light. They were about two inches apart, and about the size of those small brass buttons that yachting men used to put upon their jackets. I began to speculate, as listless men will, upon this trifle, as it seemed. From what centre did that faint but deep red light come, and from what—glass beads, buttons, toy decorations—was it reflected? We were lumbering along gently, having nearly a mile still to go. I had not solved the puzzle, and it became in another minute more off, for these two luminous points, with a sudden jerk, descended nearer the floor, keeping still their relative distance and horizontal position, and then, as suddenly, they rose to the level of the seat on which I was sitting and I saw them no more.
>
> My curiosity was now really excited, and, before I had time to think, I saw again these two dull lamps, again together near the floor; again they disappeared, and again in their old corner I saw them.
>
> So keeping my eyes upon them, I edged quietly up my own side, towards the end at which I still saw these tiny discs of red.
>
> There was very little light in the bus. It was nearly dark. I leaned forward to aid my endeavour to discover what these little circles really were. They shifted their positions a little as I did so. I began now to perceive an outline of something black, and I soon saw, with tolerable distinctness, the outline of a small black monkey, pushing its face forward in mimicry to meet mine;

---

23. Cf. Bates, *The Modern Short Story*, Ch. I. "Retrospect."

those were its eyes, and I now dimly saw its teeth grinning at me.

I drew back, not knowing whether it might not meditate a spring. I fancied that one of the passengers had forgot his ugly pet, and wishing to ascertain something of its temper, though not caring to trust my fingers to it, I poked my umbrella softly towards it. It remained immovable—up to it—*through* it. For through it, and back and forward it passed, without the slightest resistance.

I can't, in the least, convey to you the kind of horror that I felt. When I had ascertained that the thing was an illusion, as I then supposed, there came a misgiving about myself and a terror that fascinated me in impotence to remove my gaze from the eyes of the brute for some moments. As I looked, it made a little skip back, quite into the corner, and I, in a panic, found myself at the door, having put my head out, drawing deep breaths of the outer air, and staring at the lights and trees we were passing, too glad to reassure myself of reality.

I stopped the bus and got out. I perceived the man looked oddly at me as I paid him. I dare say there was something unusual in my looks and manner, for I had never felt so strangely before.

Few authors have succeeded so well in the presentation of a garrulous and ubiquitous ghost. Kipling's Mrs. Keith Wessington ("The Phantom Rickshaw") becomes the less convincing the more she talks and the more frequently she appears; but Le Fanu's monkey demon becomes all the more terrible by his continuous presence. Le Fanu's superiority probably lies in greater psychological insight. Moreover, he knew how to maintain an even tone throughout a ghost story and avoids Kipling's occasional insipid jokes. His tales are written in a style that fits the tragic subject perfectly. Another important point is that the demon's speech is never directly reproduced, but is simply described by the victim. Le Fanu knew that too much precision is dangerous in the direct presentation of the supernatural. Again, he was far before his time. One need only compare him with Dickens, Stevenson, and even Kipling, to measure the extent of his advance.

Finally Le Fanu was the inventor of the extremely effective main motif, the disembodied hand. Why his "The Haunting of the Tiled House" should never have met with the tremendous success of W. F. Harvey's "The Beast with Five Fingers"[24] is as incomprehensible as the failure of Dr. Hesselius.

His general attitude to the supernatural was also new in his day, and

---

24. Harvey's story has recently been turned into a film with Peter Lorre in the lead. It even appeared in translation in *Samedi Soir,* which is good proof of its enormous popularity, when one considers the lack of interest which the French public normally display in ghost stories.

shows traces of some of Blackwood's principal ideas. He believed that men were constantly surrounded by preternatural powers, and that in certain abnormal physical and psychical conditions they could establish direct contact with the other world. This idea is, of course, Swedenborgian, and Le Fanu, who was an ardent student of the great Nordic mystic, quotes some relevant passages in "Green Tea" (Chapter III). But, so far as I know, he was the first to introduce these ideas successfully into the English ghost story.

In conclusion, a few words should be said about Le Fanu himself, for he was certainly as extraordinary as a personality as he was great as an innovator.

Except for Edgar Allan Poe and H. P. Lovecraft, he is the only author of ghost fiction whose personal habits aided him in his writing. In short, Le Fanu was what the public generally expect a ghost story writer to be. S. M. Ellis, in his *Wilkie Collins, Le Fanu and Others*, gives a startling account of the author's last years. After the death of his wife he retired from the world, living as a recluse and finally closing the door even to his most intimate friends. He rarely went out, and then only at night, when he went to visit the old bookshops in quest of the volumes of ghostly lore and demonology which, towards the end, were his only reading. His methods of work, too, were in accordance with his other eccentricities. If one is to believe S. M. Ellis, he was not averse to creating the right atmosphere for composition artificially if necessary:

> He wrote mostly in bed at night, using copybooks for his manuscript. He always had two candles by his side on a small table; one of these dimly glimmering tapers would be left burning while he took a brief sleep. Then, when he awoke, about 2 a.m., amid the darkling shadows of the heavy furnishings and hangings of his old-fashioned room, he would brew himself some strong tea, which he drank copiously and frequently throughout the night when human vitality is at its lowest ebb, and the Powers of Darkness rampant and terrifying. What wonder, then, that, with his brain ever peopled by day and night with mysterious and terrible beings, he became afflicted by horrible dreams, which, as I have suggested, were the basis of his stories of the supernatural. (p. 175)

Le Fanu was an ardent Swedenborgian, but he always remained hostile to spiritualism, which he despised for its ineffectual messages and mild manifestations. "His mind," says Ellis, "savoured stronger and more frightful meat."

Mr. Ellis could have mentioned that Le Fanu drew his own portrait in *Uncle Silas*. Maud Ruthyn's father, the Swedenborgian Count, certainly has many of the qualities of his creator, and it is strange to see how in this character Le Fanu portrays himself with a queer mixture of vanity and clairvoyance. Count Ruthyn is feared and admired for his knowledge of spiritual things: Le Fanu describes him almost as a saint. But his complete innocence of the ways of the world nearly causes the death of his only daughter, whom he leaves as ward with his wicked and criminal brother.

Even from his childhood Le Fanu showed a strong tendency to escape from reality. Fortunately his escapism took other forms beside a morbid taste for supernatural horror. Although he was known, even as a boy, for his wide knowledge of Irish ghostlore, he was also renowned as a practical joker. According to Mr. Ellis, his taste for this particular form of amusement never left him, and there was no end to the delightful tricks he played. Once, he informed a scholarly friend and ardent Irish patriot that Shakespeare was descended from the Irish O'Shaughnessy-Spears and changed his name on coming to England. It seems that the poor man spent months trying to prove the theory. Le Fanu was fond of all kinds of jokes, even the crudest ones. One of his favorite stories was about the family friend, Anthony Trollope, who arrived late one evening at an Irish country inn, and not knowing that he was to share the room with another guest, nearly beat a poor parish priest to death when the latter considerately tried to climb into bed as noiselessly as possible. Perhaps this anecdote inspired Dr. M. R. James with the idea for his famous "Oh, Whistle, and I'll Come to You, My Lad."

But Le Fanu was not all queerness and eccentricities. Besides being an author, he was also a successful journalist. Having studied Law at Trinity College, Dublin, he was called to the Irish Bar in 1839. In 1841 he left this uncongenial profession, and became the proprietor and editor of *The Warder*. In the following year he bought *The Protestant Guardian* and later owned a third share in *The Statesman*, *The Dublin Evening Packet* and *Evening Mail*. It was only in the later years of his life that he became the recluse to whose pen we owe some of the finest ghost stories in English literature.

Le Fanu's importance in the history of the development of the ghost story is largely due to the fact that so many of his ideas were later taken up by other writers. His accurate description of mental disease foreshadowed the modern psychological ghost story. His Dr. Hesselius was the forerunner of numerous infallible scientists and detectives. He was the first to make a ghost form a disembodied hand. He was a pioneer, too, in the structure of his stories, and was one of the first writers to use the gradual building-up of suspense to a final climax that was perfected by James. Even his attitude to the supernatural was new, and at times seems akin to that adopted far later by Blackwood. Yet these innovations are so mingled in his tales with relics of the Gothic tradition, that he has fallen out of favor with the modern world, and his very real contribution to the development of the ghost story has often been overlooked.

An Irish Ghost

V. S. Pritchett

The leaves fly down, the rain spits and the clouds flow like a dirty thaw before the wind, which whines and mews in the window cracks and swings the wireless aerial with a dull tap against the sill; the House of Usher is falling, and between now and Hogmanay, as the drafts lift the carpets, as slates shift on the roof and mice patter behind the wainscot, the ghosts, the wronged suitors of our lives, gather in anterooms of the mind. It is their moment. It is also the moment to read those ghosts of all ghosts, the minor novelists who write about the supernatural. Pushed into limbo by the great novelists with their grandiose and blatant passion for normality, these minor talents flicker about plaintively on the edges of fame, often excelling the masters in a phrase or a character, but never large enough to take the center of the stage. Such a writer is J. Sheridan Le Fanu. In mid-Victorian literature, Le Fanu is crowded out by Dickens and Thackeray, talked off the floor by Lever, that supreme raconteur, surpassed or (should one say?) by-passed on his own ground by Wilkie Collins: yet he has, within his limits, an individual accent and a flawless virtuosity. At least one of his books, a collection of tales republished sixteen years ago with Ardizzone's illustrations and entitled *In a Glass Darkly* is worth reading; it contains the well-known "Green Tea." His other books show that, like so many talented Irishmen, he had gifts, but too many voices that raise too many echoes.

Le Fanu brought a limpid tributary to the Teutonic stream which had fed mysterious literature for so long. I do not mean that he married the Celtic banshee to the Teutonic poltergeist or the monster, in some Irish graveyard; what he did was to bring an Irish lucidity and imagination to the turgid German flow. Le Fanu's ghosts are the most disquieting of all: the ghosts that can be justified, blobs of the unconscious that have floated up to the surface of the mind, and which are not irresponsible and perambulatory figments of family history, mooning and clanking about in fancy dress. The evil of the justified ghosts is not sportive, willful, involuntary or extravagant. In Le Fanu the fright is that effect follows cause. Guilt patters two-legged behind its victims in the street, retribution sits adding up its account night after night, the secret doubt scratches away with malignant patience in the guarded mind. We laugh at the headless coachman or the legendary heiress grizzling her way through the centuries in her nightgown; but we pause when we recognize that those other hands on the wardrobe, those other eyes at the window, those other steps on the landing and those small shadows that slip into the room as we open the door, are our own. It is we who are the ghosts. Those are *our* own steps which follow us, it is *our* "heavy body" which we hear falling in the attic above. We haunt ourselves. Let illness or strain weaken the catch which we keep fixed so tightly upon the unconscious, and out spring all the hags and animals of moral or Freudian symbolism, just as the "Elemental" burns sharp as a diamond before our eyes when we lie relaxed and on the point of sleep.

Some such idea is behind most of Le Fanu's tales. They are presented as the cases of a psychiatrist called Dr. Hesselius, whose precise theory appears to be that these fatal visitations come when the psyche is worn to rags and the interior spirit world can then make contact with the external through the holes. A touch of science, even bogus science, gives an edge to the superstitious tale. The coarse hanging judge is tracked down by the man whom he has unjustly hanged and is hanged in turn. The eupeptic sea captain on the point of marrying an Irish fortune is quietly terrorized into the grave by the sailor whom, years before, he had flogged to death in Malta. The fashionable and handsome clergyman is driven to suicide by the persecutions of a phantom monkey who jumps into his Bible as he preaches, and waits for him at street corners, in carriages, in his very room. A very Freudian animal this. Dark and hairy with original sin and symbolism, he skips straight out of the unchaste jungle of a pious bachelor's unconscious. The vampire girl who preys on the daughter of an Austrian count appears to be displaying the now languid, now insatiate, sterility of Lesbos. I am not, however, advancing Le Fanu as an instance of the lucky moralist who finds a sermon in every spook, but as an artist in the dramatic use of the evil, the secret, and the fatal, an artist, indeed, in the domestic insinuation of the supernatural. With him it does not break the law, but extends the mysterious jurisdiction of nature.

Le Fanu might be described as the Simenon of the peculiar. There is the same limpid narrative. He is expert in screwing up tension little by little without strain, and an artist in surprise. The literature of the uncanny scores crudely by outraging our senses and our experience; but the masters stick to the simple, the *almost* natural, and let fall their more unnerving revelations as if they were all in the day's work. And they are. The clergyman in "Green Tea" is describing the course of his persecution, how it abates only to be renewed with a closer menace.

"I traveled in a chaise. I was in good spirits. I was more—I was happy and grateful. I was returning, as I thought, delivered from a dreadful hallucination, to the scene of duties which I longed to enter upon. It was a beautiful sunny evening, everything looked serene and cheerful and I was delighted. I remember looking out of the window to see the spire of my Church at Kenlis among the trees, at the point where one has the earliest view of it. It is exactly where the little stream that bounds the parish passes under the road by a culvert; and where it emerges at the roadside a stone with an old inscription is placed. As we passed this point I drew my head in and sat down, and in the corner of the chaise was the monkey."

Again:

"It used to spring on a table, on the back of a chair, on the chimney piece, and slowly to swing itself from side to side, looking at me all the time. There is in its motion an indefinable power to dissipate thought, and to contract one's attention to that monotony till the ideas shrink, as it were, to a point, and at last to nothing—and unless I had started up, and shook off the catalepsy, I have felt as if my mind were on the point of losing itself. There are other ways," he sighed heavily, "thus, for instance, while I pray with my eyes closed, it comes closer and closer, and I see it. I know it is not to be accounted for physically but I do actually see it, though my lids are closed, and so it rocks my mind, as it were, and overpowers me, and I am obliged to rise from my knees. If you had ever yourself known this, you would be acquainted with desperation."

And then, after this crisis, the tortured clergyman confides once more to his doctor and makes his most startling revelation in the mere course of conversation. The doctor has suggested that candles shall be brought. The clergyman wearily replies:

"All lights are the same to me. Except when I read or write, I care not if night were perpetual. I am going to tell you what happened about a year ago. The thing began to speak to me."

There is Henry James's *second* turn of the screw.

We progress indeed not into vagueness and atmosphere, but into greater and greater particularity; with every line the net grows tighter. Another sign of the master is Le Fanu's equable eye for the normal. There is a sociability about his stories, a love of pleasure, a delight in human happiness, a tolerance of folly and a neat psychological perception. Only in terms of the vampire legend would the Victorians have permitted a portrayal of Lesbian love, but how lightly, skillfully and justly it is told. Vigilance is a word Le Fanu often uses. We feel a vigilance of observation in all his character drawing, we are aware of a fluid and quick sensibility which responds only to the essential things in people and in the story. He is as detached as a *dompteur;* he caresses, he bribes, he laughs, he cracks the whip. It is a sinister but gracious performance.

One doesn't want to claim too much for Le Fanu. For most of his life he was a Dublin journalist and versatility got the better of him. He is known for two of his many novels: *Uncle Silas* and *The House by the Church-yard. Uncle Silas* has ingenious elements. Le Fanu saw the possibility of the mysterious in the beliefs and practices of the Swedenborgians, but the book goes downhill halfway through and becomes a crime puzzle. A good man dies and puts his daughter in his brother's care, knowing his brother is reputed to be a murderer. By this reckless act the good man hopes to clear his brother's name. On the contrary, it puts an idea into his head. This brother, Uncle Silas, had married beneath him, and the picture of his illiterate family has a painful rawness which is real enough; but such a sinister theme requires quiet treatment, and Le Fanu is too obviously sweating along in the footsteps of Dickens or Wilkie Collins. Lever is another echo. It is his voice, the voice of the stage Irishman which romps rather too nattily about *The House by the Church-yard*, into which Le Fanu seems to have thrown every possible side of his talent without discrimination. There are ghosts you shrink from, ghosts you laugh at, cold murder is set beside comic duels, wicked characters become ridiculous, ridiculous ones become solemn and we are supposed to respect them. It is all a very strange mixture, and Sterne and Thackeray, as well as Lever, seem to be adding their hand. A good deal is farcical satire of the military society in eighteenth-century Dublin, and Le Fanu is dashing and gaudy with a broad brush:

> "Of late Mrs. Macnamara had lost all her pluck and half her colour, and some even of her fat. She was like one of those portly dowagers in Nubernip's select society of metamorphosed turnips, who suddenly exhibited sympathetic symptoms of failure, grew yellow, flabby and wrinkled, as the parent bulb withered and went out of season."

His comic subalterns, scheming land agents and quarreling doctors, his snoring generals and shrill army wives, are drawn close up, so close up that it is rather bewildering until you are used to the jumpy and awkward angles of his camera. One gets a confused, life-size impression, something like the impression made by a crowded picture of Rowlandson's, where so much is obviously happening that one can't be sure exactly what it is and where to begin. Le Fanu was spreading himself as Lever had done, but was too soaked in the journalist's restless habits to know how to define his narrative. He became garrulous where Lever was the raconteur. He rambles on like some rumbustious reporter who will drop into a graceful sketch of trout fishing on the Liffey or into fragments of rustic idyll and legend, and then return to his duels, his hell-fire oaths and his claret. I can see that this book has a flavor, but I could never get through it. The truth is that Le Fanu, the journalist, could not be trusted to *accumulate* a novel. You can see in *Uncle Silas* how the process bored him, and how that book is really a good short story that has unhappily started breeding. His was a talent for brevity, the poetic sharpness and discipline of the short tale, for the subtleties and symbolism of the uncanny. In this form Le Fanu is a good deal more than a ghost among the ghosts.

Excerpts from the "Prologue" and "Epilogue" to *Madam Crowl's Ghost*

M. R. James

Joseph Sheridan Le Fanu, who died just fifty years ago, was in his own particular vein one of the best story-tellers of the nineteenth century; and the present volume contains a collection of forgotten tales by him, and of tales not previously known to be his. [. . .]

He stands in the absolutely first rank as a writer of ghost stories. That is my deliberate verdict, after reading all the supernatural tales I have been able to get hold of. Nobody sets the scene better than he, nobody touches in the effective detail more deftly. I do not think it is merely the fact of my being past middle age that leads me to regard the leisureliness of his style as a merit; for I am by no means inappreciative of the more modern efforts in this branch of fiction. No, it has to be recognized, I am sure, that the ghost-story is in itself a slightly old-fashioned form; it needs some deliberateness in the telling: we listen to it the more readily if the narrator poses as elderly, or throws back his experience to "some thirty years ago."

I digress. Ghost stories and tales of mystery are what this volume contains, and, in order to lure the reader on, I have placed the most striking and sensational of them at the beginning of it. These are also the most recent in date; for, as was natural, Le Fanu made improvements in the proportions and in the conception of his short stories as time went on. If the reader likes "Squire Toby's Will" and "Madam Crowl's Ghost," as I think he must, he will go on to the earlier stories and find in them the same excellent qualities, only slightly overlaid by the mannerisms of the forties and fifties. [. . .]

I need only add that the stories in this volume have been gleaned from extinct periodicals. They are the result of a fairly long investigation, but I am sure that some anonymous tales by my author must have eluded me, and I shall be very grateful to any one who will notify me of any that he is fortunate enough to find.

M. R. James
Provost's Lodge,
Eton, July, 1923

Note:—I have omitted three other stories of a similar nature, *viz:* "The Mysterious Lodger" (*Dublin University Magazine*, Vol. 50) which, though it contains some excellent detail, is more in the nature of a religious allegory than a ghost story proper; "My Aunt Margaret's Adventure" (*ibid.* 1864) which belongs to a class of which I disapprove—the ghost-story which peters out into a natural explanation; and also a fragment called "Hyacinth O'Toole" which appeared posthumously in *Temple Bar* (1884).

[. . .]

Anyone who reads through the whole range of volumes that I have enumerated will be struck by certain habits of the writer, quite apart from any question of style or quality. I shall enlarge upon two of these. One very marked one is his *penchant* for rewriting a story in a different setting, and for developing a long story out of a short one.

Take examples of this. *The Cock and Anchor,* his first novel, was, as I have said, reissued with some changes as *Morley Court.* But there—it is a story of the eighteenth century. In 1870 the plot and many of the incidents reappear in *Checkmate* in a nineteenth century setting. True, another, and a very striking thread is now interwoven with them: the coarse villain of *The Cock and Anchor* is replaced by the refined, but far more formidable figure of Walter Longcluse; and the atmosphere is of Le Fanu's most impressive. But the earlier story has been incorporated into the later. In *Torlogh O'Brien* (1847) a story of 1840 ("[An Adventure of] Hardress Fitzgerald, [a Royalist Captain]") is used: it will be found in *The Purcell Papers.*

Again, the main incidents of the story of Uncle Silas appeared first in the *Dublin University Magazine* in 1839 as "Passage in the Secret History of an Irish Countess," one of *The Purcell Papers,* and again in 1851 in the anonymous book [*Ghost Stories and Tales of Mystery*], under the title of "The Murdered Cousin." In this case too the setting was shifted, in the novel, from the eighteenth to the nineteenth century.

A Lost Name is a three-volume novel developed out of a longish story called "The Evil Guest" (one of the 1851 collection). "The Evil Guest" is practically identical with "Richard Marston, of Dunoran" (1848). For the third time the nineteenth century replaces the eighteenth. But if I am not mistaken, the central incident in the three stories—the murder—is derived from a tale once widely current. Dickens in the *Holly Tree Inn* tells of a chapbook he used to read, of Jonathan Bradford; and, says he, "Then I remembered how the landlord was found at the murdered traveler's bedside with his own knife at his feet and blood upon his hand: how he was hanged for the murder, notwithstanding his protestations that he had indeed gone there to kill the traveler for his saddle-bags, but had been stricken motionless on finding him already slain; and how the ostler, years afterwards, owned the deed." Now the plight of the landlord is exactly that of Carmel Sherlock in *A Lost Name*, who goes to kill Sir Roke Wycherley, and finds his throat already cut. The master of the house is the real culprit.

I have not been able to search out the story of John Bradford, but I think my identification of it with Le Fanu's source must stand.

The fourth example of this odd habit is in *The Wyvern Mystery*. The episode which describes the blind cast-off mistress of the hero making her way into the bedroom of his young wife and trying to cut her throat was first embodied in a short story ("An Episode in the History of a Tyrone Family") which will be found in *The Purcell Papers*.

Lastly, in *Chronicles of Golden Friars*, two stories out of the three of which the book consists show the same, or a like trait. In "Laura Mildmay" is the fine ghost story of Dame Crowl of Applewale which will be found, anonymous, in *All the Year Round* [New Series]; and in "The Haunted Baronet" another older story, "The Fortunes of Sir Robert Ardagh," is worked up and expanded.

I do not know whether many parallels to this procedure can be cited. I do not defend or repudiate it; I merely record it as a marked feature in Le Fanu's work and pass on to call attention to another equally curious. That is, my author's fondness for repeating a certain *motif*—again in varied contexts—so varied that I think the reader need not resent it. The theme is this: the villain of the piece returns after the lapse of many years to surroundings where some who knew him of old still live, and, until the catastrophe, passes unrecognized. In most cases his old crime has been committed before the book begins—we are only told of it as a past event and we only see the criminal in his new avatar. The examples of this are: first, in *The House by the Church-yard*, Dangerfield (whom Le Fanu, with odd carelessness, calls sometimes Giles and sometimes Paul) is really the murderer and consummate villain Charles Archer. He comes as an elderly man to a place where there are but two people living who might know him; one does know him at once and keeps silence; the other is long puzzled and suddenly enlightened, and does not keep silence and suffers for it.

In *Checkmate* the murderer—Yelland Mace—reappears as the elegant but mysterious Walter Longcluse. But this time he has had his face entirely changed by an elaborate operation.

In *The Tenants of Mallory*, the outlawed Arthur Verney (of right Viscount Verney), for years an outcast in Constantinople, returns to England at the peril of his life as "Mr. Dingwell, the great Greek Merchant."

In all of these cases the suspicion and the steps that lead to the ultimate detection are a great element of interest in the story. But these are not all the examples.

In "Laura Mildmay" (*Chronicles of Golden Friars*) the wicked Captain Torquil figures at the beginning of the story as trying to kidnap the baby heroine, and then, after years have passed and he has long been reputed dead, turns up again as the excellent and pious Mr. Burton, and is only prevented, at the last moment, from making the said heroine fall over a precipice.

In *Guy Deverell* Herbert Strangways, injured long years before by Sir Jekyl Marlowe, takes up his abode as a visitor, supposed to be a Frenchman, at Marlowe Hall, and by his machinations Sir Jekyl's thread is cut short.

And the strange book *Haunted Lives* has a very similar strain of an unsuspected identity of the villain (so to call him) and the hero running throughout it.

Le Fanu himself, who lets a year or two lapse after using this favorite theme before he touches it again, may well have applauded himself for his moderation. To the critic who reads the whole series of his works from start to finish, he may well seem to have indulged his predilection for it (predilection I am sure it is, and not poverty of invention) too much. Personally I find the settings of the theme so satisfactorily varied that I do not resent its recurrence. But if any one is inclined to cavil, I cannot put up a very strong defense. Only, I would represent that Le Fanu is pretty obviously one who writes stories for his own (and his readers') pleasure; he has no axe to grind; no cause to champion; no crusade to preach; in none of his books do I find any *tendency*—unless it be in the one in which he makes fun of spiritualism. His object is to tell a story, usually one that will mystify and alarm his reader, and in his favorite theme he sees the possibility of many effective variations. I do not blame him for making trial of them.

There are, to be sure, really weak places in his armor. For one thing he is certainly a hasty and rather careless writer. His text admits of many small emendations, which shows him to have been a bad proof reader; there are a certain number of definite mistakes and inconsistencies in the stories, and you may often find sentences which are not only too long, but do not construe. That is one blemish, due, I cannot doubt, in part to the conditions under which he wrote—I mean the serial form which he employed for twelve out of his fourteen novels.

A more serious fault affects the texture of the work: it is what I will call his mawkishness. He can write of sad things with true and moving pathos; he can write love-scenes that appeal as genuine; but he does, not and again, also indulge in a sentimentality which calls the blush to the cheek: it is at the worst perhaps in *A Lost Name*.

Perhaps, by way of conclusion, I may be allowed to offer a brief characterization of the novels.

Of the two early ones, *The Cock and Anchor* and *Torlogh O'Brien*, the former has been sufficiently described. The other is not very readable now; but in one or two places the author has been quite relentless in his description of horrors, and is ably backed up by the terrible illustrations of Phiz.

Of the later and larger group, six are markedly superior to the rest. These are *The House by the Church-yard, Wylder's Hand, Uncle Silas, Guy Deverell, The Tenants of Malory, Checkmate*.

Uncle Silas and *The House by the Church-yard* divide the honors of the first place. Probably the first-named is too well known to require description; but the second, I think, is not, and it is a book which seems to me to bring together in a concentrated form all Le Fanu's best qualities as a story-teller. It is a costume-novel, the scene is Chapelizod, near Dublin, and the date the year 1767.

From the prologue, in which the scene is set and the tale started by the digging-up of a strangely battered skull in the churchyard, you pass to an amazingly fine description of a dark night of storm and a funeral, and these strike the note of ominous mystery which runs through all the book. Not that the book is a gloomy one: it is full of live, gay people, and there is rollicking farce of excellent quality, side by side with ghosts and murders, and a somber ballad (unsurpassed in its way) which has a decisive bearing on the catastrophe. In short, this is a book to which I find myself returning to over and over again and with no sense of disappointment.

The other four novels all have strong points. The intrigue of *Wylder's Hand* defies detection; *Guy Deverell* is full of good small character sketches; *Checkmate* has moments of breathless interest; *The Tenants of Malory* is marked out by the glorious talk of Mr. Dingwell; frequenters of Beaumaris, by the way, will soon recognize that there and at Penmon Priory the scene of the story is laid.

Personally I find the remaining six worth reading, but I do not wish persons unacquainted with Le Fanu to approach him by way of *A Lost Name* or *All in the Dark*. Let them begin with *In a Glass Darkly*, where they will find the very best of his shorter stories, and go on to *Uncle Silas* and *The House by the Church-yard*. It is on these three volumes that I principally base the claim I make for Le Fanu, that he is one of the best story-tellers of the last age.

Doubles, Shadows, Sedan-Chairs, and the Past: The "Ghost Stories" of J. S. Le Fanu

Patricia Coughlan

Man has not been able to describe himself as a configuration in the *episteme* without thought at the same time discovering, both in itself and outside itself, at its borders yet also in its very warp and woof, an element of darkness, an apparently inert density in which it is embedded, an unthought which it contains entirely, yet in which it is also caught. The unthought (whatever name we give it) is not lodged in man like a shriveled-up nature or a stratified history; it is, in relation to man, the Other: the Other that is not only a brother but a twin, born not of man, nor in man, but beside him and at the same time, in an identical newness, in an unavoidable duality. This obscure space so readily interpreted as an abyssal region in man's nature, or as a uniquely impregnable fortress in his history, is indispensable to him: in one sense, the shadow cast by man as he emerged in the field of knowledge; in another, the blind stain by which it is possible to know him. In any case, the unthought has accompanied man, mutely and uninterruptedly, since the nineteenth century. Since it was really never more than an insistent double, it has never been the object of reflection in an autonomous way. . . . For though this double may be close, it is alien, and the role, the true undertaking, of thought will be to bring it as close to itself as possible; the whole of modern thought is imbued with the necessity of thinking the unthought . . . of ending man's alienation by reconciling him with his own essence, of making explicit the horizon that provides experience with its background of immediate and disarmed proof, of lifting the veil of the Unconscious, of becoming absorbed in its silence, or of straining to catch its endless.

Michel Foucault, *The Order of Things*

Le Fanu's supernatural stories number about thirty and are dated between 1838 and 1872. This essay starts from the premise that these haunting-tales form a coherent *oeuvre* and deserve to be discussed as one. I shall not engage in a lengthy commentary on individual stories, but shall proceed by identifying and interpreting some of the stories' most striking and frequently recurrent narrative motifs. These are: the domestic interior and its furniture; the *doppelgänger* and shadow; and landscape as the locus of an otherness which is frequently apprehended as a buried layer of the past. Within the body of Le Fanu's haunting-tales these motifs form a constellation of significance; I shall try to suggest where it lies by discussing a few representative instances in each case, and generalizing from those. My purpose is to suggest that this body of work is not adequately described as a scattered series of slight, whimsical contributions to the genre of the Victorian ghost-story, but rather that it has a unity of purpose and meaning and that it may represent Le Fanu's most significant achievement. I propose that it would be more appropriately interpreted as being in the European genre of the metaphysical and psychological *nouvelle*, a genre whose characteristic strategy is to frame—within supernatural plots of various kinds—important questions about the concept of the self and the constitution of what is called reality.

Le Fanu began writing in a literary climate which was extremely receptive to the influences of German Romanticism. Recent German literature was enthusiastically and copiously translated and discussed in Irish periodicals in the 1830s.[1] It is likely that its peculiar combination of the perspectives of science and occultism had a strong, though equivocal, influence on Le Fanu. The boundaries between the two were then far less clearly drawn than in later periods. Subjects in the trance cast by hypnotists using the newly discovered "animal magnetism" seemed to reveal the possible existence of other personalities within the self, and in fact the development of psychology toward the discoveries of the psychoanalysts did happen as a curious combination of rational and avowedly surrational inquiry. The status of dual or multiple personality and of apparent haunting and visionary experiences of all kinds remained uneasily undefined throughout Le Fanu's period: such experiences might be attributed to electrical or magnetic activity in the body, or to otherworldly intervention in the traditional way. These issues were discussed by James Clarence Mangan and by Henry Ferris in the *Dublin University Magazine* in 1841, 1842, and 1846.[2] The *DUM* articles arose chiefly from the work

---

1. See Patrick O'Neill, "The Reception of German Literature in Ireland: 1750–1850, Pt. 2," *Studia Hibernica* 17–18 (1978): 91–106; and "German Literature and the *Dublin University Magazine*, 1833–50," *Long Room* 14–15 (Autumn 1976–Spring 1977): 20–31.

2. See J. C. Mangan's "Chapters on Ghostcraft," *DUM* 19 (January 1842): 1–17; Ferris's "German Ghosts and Ghost-Seers," *DUM* 17 (January 1841): 33–50 and *DUM* 18 (February 1841): 217–32; and "Miscellanea Mystica No. II," *DUM* 27 (February 1846): 155–70. See O'Neill, loc. cit., note 1 above.

of Justinus Kerner, author of *Die Seherin von Prevorst* (1829), an investigation of a "ghost-seeress," a case of alleged psychic experiences in a German town. Le Fanu indeed invents a scientist, the pompous Dr. Hesselius, somewhat along the lines of Justinus Kerner the "ghost-craftsman," to introduce a batch of his later haunting-stories in the guise of case-histories: the superb "Carmilla," as well as "Green Tea" and "The Familiar," is framed in this way. Hesselius's limitations are clear to the reader, and though he is himself quite confident of the validity of his point of view, he is fairly savagely undermined by irony. Seen against the psychological experiences they claim but fail to account for, Hesselius's positivist explanations compound the problematic nature of the mind and thus represent a formal analogue to the smooth surfaces in the troubling of which I discern the chief project of these stories. The most important feature of Le Fanu's work in this genre is his insistence on keeping open the question of the origins or causes of psychological malaise, and not letting it collapse into glib explanations, whether moral or medical. In this indeterminacy lies one of the greater strengths of Le Fanu's haunting-stories; he knew that "to explain was to explain away," as Beckett puts it, and therefore frequently gives a plurality of explanations that cancel one another out. It seems clear that this indeterminacy represented his own real state of mind before the phenomena of apparent hauntings; this is evident in the questionable status enjoyed in his novel *Uncle Silas* by Swedenborgianism, another tradition combining the occult and the scientific.[3]

Like the German tale-writers, Le Fanu uses legend and folktale motifs quasi-allegorically to go behind the apparently calm face of contemporary assumptions about the psyche and explore states of discontinuity, intolerable psychological strangeness (such as is captured by the notion of ghosts), and especially the fragmentation of the self. Le Fanu repeatedly and very effectively uses the motif of the double or shadow, a motif which was brought to prominence in Jean Paul Richter's *Siebenkäs* (1796) and Adalbert Chamisso's *Peter Schlemihl* (1814), as well as in a large number of Hoffmann's stories. This motif is particularly expressive of some of the psychological concerns of the first and second generations of Romantics. Le Fanu's repeated use of it reveals his capacity to introduce highly individual variations on those themes.

The German Romantic tale not only used contemporary psychological experiment and study but also had, particularly in its form, another source of inspiration, from outside official literary tradition: the folk or fairy tale. In Chamisso's highly influential *Peter Schlemihl* (1814), for instance, the story of

---

3. See for example the vision ascribed to Maud by the Swedenborgian sage, Dr. Bryerly, near the beginning; it is never clear whether she sees it, or takes it on faith.

the man who barters away his shadow to a devil-figure then lives to regret it, is narrated in a naïve and whimsical style that handles marvels of all kinds in a deadpan manner. Yet the effect of the story is very remote from that of genuine folktale: it is evident to the reader that allegory is intended, and that one is called upon to consider whether it is political, moral, or epistemological, or a combination of these. The clarity and apparent simplicity of the folktale provided these writers with a narrative means of breaking the molds of existing literary forms, and therefore of implicitly challenging the prevailing psychological assumptions embedded in those forms.[4] Further, in folklore, marvels, and metaphysics—magic journeys and feats, demonic lovers and bargains, haunting-plots of all kinds—was found a rich source of images of disturbance and strangeness, which could be used metaphorically to explore the concept of the individual self, newly problematic in the post-Enlightenment period.

Le Fanu had the stimulus not only of foreign literary appropriations of folk and fairy tales but, in common with his Irish contemporaries of various ethnic backgrounds, he had the opportunity of direct contact with folk material. He put that opportunity to very good use, most obviously in the trio of folktale retellings he published in 1870—"Stories of Lough Guir," "The Child That Went with the Fairies," and "The White Cat of Drumgunniol." But the whole body of his ghost stories shows deeply the impress of the folk material he assimilated, partly in his childhood and youth in County Limerick, and partly through his friendship with the Dublin folklorist Patrick Kennedy in the 1870s. Of his remaining haunting-stories, at least five contain a demonic bargain of some kind, four a demon-lover who tries whether successfully or not to carry off a young girl, and six an otherworldly double or shadow, generally malevolent. Many stories combine several of these with one another and with other recurring story motifs.

That material underwent certain transformations in its assimilation into his fiction, as folklore necessarily must in being drawn into literature. The analysis of those transformations may be made to lead toward the formulation of pertinent questions about Le Fanu. The primary way in which the transformation of folk story material can be seen in Le Fanu is in the relations between the level of *discourse* in his work, and the level of story, or between *sjuzhet* and *fabula*, as it has been formulated by modern narrative

---

4. Ralph Tymms, in his study *Doubles in Literary Psychology* (Cambridge: Bowes & Bowes, 1949), 37–38, describes the German Romantics' "penchant for merging fantasy with an awareness of the existence of problems in abnormal psychology," and remarks that "with Hoffmann the identification of the fairy-tale with the psychological case-book was to be deliberate, so as to invest the *Märchen* with a specifically symbolic meaning."

theory.[5] On the one hand we have the narrator communicating with the reader, both rational and modern people, sophisticates, probably city-dwellers, certainly middle-class. On the other, there is the world of the stories: removed in place and generally also in time from that implied reader. Far from attempting to conceal this gap, Le Fanu frequently thematizes it in his stories. Here is an example from the opening of "Ultor de Lacy" (1861):

> In my youth I heard a great many Irish family traditions, more or less of a supernatural character, one of them very peculiar, and all, to a child at least, highly interesting. One of these I will now relate, though the translation to cold type from oral narrative, with all the aids of animated human voice and countenance, and the appropriate *mise-en-scène* of the old-fashioned parlour fireside and its listening circle of excited faces, and, outside, the wintry blast and the moan of leafless boughs, with the occasional rattle of the clumsy old window-frame behind shutter and curtain, as the blast swept by, is at best a trying one. (BGS 444)[6]

This passage contains a constellation of features important in Le Fanu's work. It proposes two sets of contrasts which are of the greatest importance for any interpretation of the story which it introduces. First, there is the opposition between the present occasion of narration and reception, and those of a posited original occasion: for the reader, from animated and excited faces to cold type and solitary passivity; for the writer, from past to present, youth to maturity, listener to narrator. The circumstances of oral narration are presented as an idyll of participatory communality, and the impossibility of recreating them as a sad loss. But within this passage there is also another opposition: between the warm company within and the winter wind outside. This is the tension characteristic of Romance and Gothic fictions of various kinds. As David Punter says in *The Literature of Terror* (1980):

> Most ghost stories implicitly propose two alternate members of the audience, the second being by definition someone who is more credulous and thus more scared than oneself. This shadowy double is the residual form of Gothic's hypothetical previous audience, those people, conveniently located

---

5. See V. Erlich, *Russian Formalism* (2nd ed., The Hague, 1965), 240–41.

6. The most accessible collections of the stories are E. F. Bleiler (ed.), *Best Ghost Stories of J. S. Le Fanu* (New York: Dover, 1964) and *J. S. Le Fanu: Ghost Stories and Mysteries* (New York: Dover, 1975). All subsequent page-references are to these editions, which I abbreviate as BGS and GSM respectively.

in the past but more probably in the lower depths of society, from whose fears Gothic is supposed to have arisen.[7]

This amalgam of safety and fear is, however, imputed by Le Fanu to both the kinds of audience he describes. It is true that the appropriation of Irish folklore by the institution of literature raises ideological problems; but Le Fanu's use of Irish folklore characteristically avoids the condescension sometimes shown to it by his contemporaries. He is aware of its difference from literature and its otherness from him and his class, but clearly he finds in it a mode of vision alternative and analogous to his own, which enables him to frame problems pressing to him too. It is evident not only from his use of so many folktale types and motifs but also from his reworking of the Earl of Desmond legends in "Stories of Lough Guir" (1870) that he understood this material as a *langue* which carried an understanding of the world, and not as a quaint collection of outlandish or nugatory superstitions.

But in the passage quoted, though there is a doubleness, a dialectic of threat and safety in both kinds of social framework described, there is a difference in the apparatus of reassuring comfort. The fireside community of peasant oral narration is replaced by the more abstract and mediated order and sophistication of the bourgeois reader who feels safe enough to seek the sensation of fear in literature, and remains confident of his or her capacity to keep it within the proper bounds. The reader of Gothic and ghost stories is impelled by a half-shameful wish to transgress, to plunge virtually, but not actually, into strangeness. Hence the moralizing framework of most such stories, which is, however, no more than perfunctory and merely represents the putting away at the back of the mind of the temporarily prominent Other, rather as a very fancy party dress would be replaced in its drawer after a carnival occasion. Is Le Fanu's work any more than the pleasant diversion implied by this metaphor? Does he in fact preserve the security of the reader, by keeping his ghosts firmly in the realm of unreality? Or does he reveal that security as only a cover-up (in the sense of a corrupt deception)?

Schelling defined the uncanny as "anything which ought to remain in secrecy and has become manifest."[8] That "ought" sounds like a moral imperative, but in the discourse of psychoanalysis it is revealed rather as the conscious mind's suppression of anxiety, which it may choose to call moral. Ludwig Binswanger describes the uncanny as:

---

7. Punter, *The Literature of Terror: A History of Gothic Fictions* (London: Longmans, 1980), 422.

8. Quoted in Ludwig Binswanger, "The Case of Lola Voss," tr. E. Angel, in *Being-in-the-World* (New York, 1963), 306.

. . . the original existential anxiety, which now "has emerged." The feeling of uncanniness is aroused by anything that causes that anxiety to emerge, anything that is apt to shock us out of our familiarity with "world and life," as the (unwonted) recurrence of the similar, the *Doppelgänger*. . . . Through defensive measures, the existence tries to protect itself against the Emergence of the Uncanny. Through them, it still finds some foothold in "care," worrying, bargaining, being cautious, even though this caution serves exclusively to ward off the Uncanny, and completely spends itself in the service of the Uncanny.[9]

In the fiction of Le Fanu's period what we might call the order of the conscious mind is represented, in literary terms, by formally realistic works. Such narratives normally address themselves to the present, in time, and the proximate, in space. They make a claim to rationality in plotting and characterization and proclaim their distance from the enchantments of Gothic, folk and fairy tale, which they tend to represent as belonging to outgrown phases of mental development. As the name implies, realism sees itself exclusively as the form which confronts and holds the mirror up to actual social conditions, and aims to marginalize all other kinds of narrative and treat them as fantasy and decoration: the folktale as a toy for children, the ghost or horror story as mere entertainment. This is not the place for an extended justification of the seriousness of Gothic and romance narrative, a matter which has in any case been well explored in many recent discussions (for instance David Punter's *The Literature of Terror*, already mentioned). The old dismissal of it as a flight from social obligation has been replaced by a more mediated view that acknowledges the role of non-realist narrative forms in interrogating the status quo by tacitly rejecting its claims to full rationality. It is now possible to discern, as it was not in the period of realist dominance, in the practice and forms of other kinds of fiction, a challenging representation precisely of that which is excluded by realism, namely what Freud calls "the dark, inaccessible part of our personality."[10] He adds that it can mostly be known negatively, as a kind of shadow to the conscious part: a notion which is a challenge to the concept of the unitary and consciously structured personality on which realist narrative depends.

To use a metaphor: let us say realism is a house, in good order, with secure doors and windows, and fully furnished with wardrobes, cupboards, curtains, pictures and hangings. In this well-regulated house is, however, a poltergeist, who (which?) bangs thing around while no-one is in the room;

9. Op. cit., 306–7.

10. *New Introductory Lectures on Psychoanalysis*, tr. J. Strachey (Harmondsworth: Penguin, 1973), 105.

on its walls are shadows or stains, suggestive of blood, which do not disappear in better lighting or when painted over. Strangers whom no-one remembers admitting wander about familiarly in the passageways, entering bedrooms and rummaging in drawers. The inhabitants are alternately scornful and terrified; they end by moving house. This is inconsequential (it is incidentally a plot-summary of Le Fanu's "Authentic Narrative of a Haunted House" [1862]), and if one likes logic, and good sense, and finality, it is also somewhat irritating. In this metaphor the shadows, stains, traces, and inexplicable noise, and puzzling visitors stand for horror and supernatural fiction, which do not so much set themselves up as alternatives to realism, as loiter darkly in its interstices, as if waiting to pounce. One might add (at the risk of making this building dangerous) that the idea of the fully conscious and rational personality in the house, and the stains and shadows represent its neuroses and dreams. In the "Authentic Narrative" the head of the family takes all rational steps to try to solve the mystery:

> I had . . . a most careful examination made to discover any traces of an entrance having been made by any window into the house. The doors had been found barred and locked as usual; but no sign of any thing of the sort was discernable. I then had the various articles—place, wearing apparel, books, &c., counted; and after having conned up and reckoned up every thing, it became quite clear that nothing whatever had been removed from the house . . . (BGS 427)

But counting the spoons (a good example of Binswanger's *sorge*, care, fuss, worry) is quite comically the reverse of appropriate; something has been *added* to the house not taken away from it. The other world of the unconscious is always already within (on the level of *fabula*, of course, the crime has already been committed in the house before they arrived).

It will be noticed that his idea of shutting in and shutting out is also present in the "Ultor de Lacy" passage. The "shutter and curtain" and the "clumsy old window-frame" are set up as barriers between within and without, between the controlled environment and the Other, the uncanny, for which the sound of the wind is a metonymy. What Binswanger calls "the self-protection of the existence" is represented in Le Fanu by the domestic interior. Le Fanu is very interested in furniture. Most of it is a good deal more substantial and elaborate than this, but its function in the stories in general does not differ from that of this "shutter and curtain": to shut fear out, or sometimes in. Its solidity and weight stands for that of the protagonists, for their status in the world and their confidence of its continuance; for their initial or outward certainties, and against the past, retribution, moral debt. Furniture: great curtained beds, deep winged chairs, wainscot

and wooden paneling, ponderous oak or mahogany dressing-chests, and old
family portraits. All are at once possessions and signs of their owners' claim
to permanence and control, and all become the ground of the undoing of
control and the mocking of permanence.

Nearly all Le Fanu's protagonists are inhabitants of a time which the
reader can call the past—typically the eighteenth, but sometimes the seventeenth century—and they are also almost invariably members of the landed
gentry. But in their emphasis on domestic interiors the stories carry very
definitely the impression of their contemporary readers', rather than their
characters', social context. The original possessors of those great beds and
chests and ancestors' portraits did not need to have them so obsessively noticed and described; they are there for the Victorian middle-class reader, for
whom the domestic interior had a particular importance, as noted by Walter
Benjamin in his essay "Louis Philippe or the Interior." Discussing the period
beginning with 1830, he says:

> For the private citizen, for the first time the living-space became distin-
> guished from the place of work. The former constituted itself as the interior.
> The office was its complement. The private citizen who in the office took re-
> ality into account, required of the interior that it should support him in his
> illusions. . . . From this sprang the phantasmagorias of the interior. This rep-
> resented the universe for the private citizen. In it he assembled the distant in
> space and in time. . . . The interior was not only the private citizen's uni-
> verse, it was also his casing. Living means leaving traces. In the interior,
> these were stressed. Coverings and antimacassars, boxes and casings, were
> devised in abundance, in which the traces of everyday objects were moulded.
> The resident's own traces were also moulded in the interior. The detective
> story appeared, which investigated these traces . . .[11]

At first glance the interiors in Le Fanu seem no more than a canny move to
satisfy this bourgeois taste for grand antiques and "pieces." This is a
deceptive impression. It can be shown that Le Fanu's interiors are as far as
possible from mere decor. They have been fabricated for subversive purposes.
(Max Ernst's delightful "novel in collage," *Une Semaine de Bonté* (1934), with
its grand rooms in which skeletons and monsters of equivocal gender and
species ooze and peer out of heavy plush sofas and from behind brocade
hangings, provides an analogy to this subversion.)

---

11. "Paris—the Capital of the Nineteenth Century," tr. Q. Hoare, in Harry Zohn, ed.
Charles Baudelaire: A Lyric Poet in the Era of High Capitalism (London: NLB, 1976),
766–67.

> In the hall was placed, as was customary in those times, the sedan-chair
> which the master of the house occasionally used, covered with stamped
> leather, and studded with gilt nails, and with its red silk blinds down. In this
> case, the doors of this old-fashioned conveyance were locked, the windows
> up, and . . . the blinds down, but not so closely that the curious child could
> not peep underneath one of them, and see into the interior. ("Mr. Justice
> Harbottle," BGS 270)

What the child sees in the "interior" of the chair is the story's retributive
ghost, waiting for the appointed hour of the judge's death, presumably in
order—fittingly enough—to carry him off in his own sumptuous vehicle.
Earlier in the story old Harbottle has had a grisly dream-trial while he waits,
dozing in his carriage, for his drinking-companions. In both cases the terror
intrudes upon him even though he has shut himself up in the security of his
private domain. Neither his house nor his carriage turns out to be proof
against the invasion, which lies in wait *within* the very conveyance which is
the sign of his exalted status. Such heavy wooden pieces as these are rather
like the symbolizing of law and conformity in another contemporary non-
realistic fiction, Hawthorne's *The Scarlet Letter* (1850), by objects such as the
iron-bound and studded prison-door, the brazen-clasped bible lying on its
oak table and the great suit of armor in the Governor's hall which distorts in
its depths and hugely magnifies the scarlet "A" worn by Hester Prynne.

In both cases the signs of apparent order and authority are revealed as a
sham. Le Fanu's Judge Harbottle is cruel, arbitrary and corrupt, and clearly deserves his fate. The real interest of the story, however, does not lie in the moral
comeuppance he gets, but rather in the projected sense of the infestation of a
series of apparently secure interiors by alien energies, variously manifested.

These interiors are ostensibly domestic and material. On the level of the
story, they are settings and possessions; but on the level of discourse the
reader is impelled by the persistent foregrounding of what seem like mere details of décor, in tale after tale, to discover in them the trace of a theme. The
concept of the interior has a domestic, but also a psychic, referent. Within is
within the conscience, the mind, the consciousness, as well as within the
cupboard, the chest, the bed.

The beds in Le Fanu are nearly always great curtained ones, like the one
in "Carmilla," down the length of which eerily slithers the heroine's vampire
sweetheart; or the high majestic one in "Madam Crowl's Ghost" on which
the doll-like wicked old lady reclines, all dressed up to die; or the enormous
one in "Strange Events in the Life of Schalken the Painter" (1839) in the
gloom of which the predatory figure of the plutocrat Death awaits the lovely
Rose Velderkaust:

Abundance of costly furniture was disposed about the room and in one corner stood a four-post bed, with heavy black cloth curtains around it; the figure frequently turned towards him with the same arch smile; and when she
came to the side of the bed, she drew the curtains, and, by the light of the
lamp, which she held towards its contents, she disclosed to the horror-
stricken painter, sitting bolt upright in the bed, the livid and demoniac form
of Vanderhausen. (BGS 46)

This early story brilliantly frames the problem in relations between surface
and depths or appearance and reality. It is set in the studio of the
seventeenth century Dutch realist painter Gerard Douw, a highly successful
painter of still-lifes, interiors and commissioned portraits.12 The historical
Douw's pictures were famous for having a highly polished finish, a quality for
which they continued to be prized until the Impressionists began to stress
the uses of indeterminacy.[13] Le Fanu makes him smug about his profession
and firm in his dealings with his niece: she may not marry his indigent pupil,
Schalken, but must be preserved for a better match. The suitor Douw favors
turns out to be Death, clinking with gold but bluish-white about the face,
presumably with putrefaction. The story shows the bourgeois solidity of
Douw's paintings as the true expressive form of his acquisitiveness: and sure
enough, in Schalken's horrific vision of the doomed girl in Death's chamber
at the end, he finds she has led him: ". . . to his infinite surprise, into what
appeared to be an old-fashioned Dutch apartment, such as what the pictures
of Gerard Douw have served to immortalize" (BGS 46). Earlier on, Douw
has pooh-poohed Rose's objections to the ugliness of Vanderhausen-Death
by reading her a moral lesson about not being taken in by mere appearances:
"A man may be as ugly as the devil, and yet, if his heart and his actions are
good, he is worth all the pretty-faced perfumed puppies that walk the Mall"
(BGS 39). For the reader this is full of ironies, verbal and other ("as ugly as
the devil"): Douw proves himself to be taken in—and in part willfully—by
the most pleasant and substantial apparent good of the suitor's gold and fine

12. [The name of the Dutch painter Gerrit Dou is commonly Anglicized as "Gerard
Douw" (sometimes "Dow"). For a comparison between the painting techniques of
Douw and Schalken with the prose techniques of Le Fanu, see Kel Roop's "Making
Light in the Shadow Box: The Artistry of Le Fanu" included in this volume.–Ed.]

13. See J. Rosenberg, ed. *Pelican History of Art: Dutch Art and Architecture* (Harmondsworth: Penguin, 1972), 145–47; and Agnes Czober, *Rembrandt and His Circle* (New
York: Taplinger, 1970), commentary on Pl. 18–a Douw portrait that, however, treats
the person as merely decorative and stresses a collection of gleaming objects in the
foreground.

clothing (a high surface polish, one might say). In the darker depths of the
story, Rose is the victim of Douw's own hopeless sensual infatuation with
material wealth. She is the price paid by Douw for his financial security. Her
horrified lover, Schalken, is the author's stalking-horse, innocent and
powerless witness of the business.

Le Fanu opens the story with the description of a painting, which the
narrator says is the record of Schalken's haunted vision. This picture is double, like all pictures: a representation *of* something, but also an object, part of
the furnishings, a family heirloom of the narrator's. The events of the *fabula*
(story) are framed within this painting, unfolding from it and leading back to
it at the end. Thus there are two descriptions of Rose, smiling and silent.
Veiled and carrying a lamp, like a Truth-figure in traditional iconography,
she leads Schalken toward the dreadful vision in the church crypt, which is
itself done up like a Douw painting. But by the end the image of Rose,
Schalken and the bridegroom Death has ceased to be a flat, possessable
thing: the initial tableau with figures, complete with coyly mysterious gesture, has been invested with an intense and terrifying alien energy: "By the
light of the lamp . . . she disclosed . . . the livid and demoniac form of Vanderhausen" (BGS 46). Just as death waits inside the curtained bed, so, as often in these tales, the images apparently safely fixed on canvas can take on a
power related in some obscure way to the past, either of the individual or of
history, and return upon the protagonist.[14] At the very beginning of "Schalken" the narrator talks urbanely about the curious management of lights as
"the chief apparent merit" of the painting, but adds: "I say *apparent*, for in its
subject, not in its handling, however exquisite, consists its real value" (BGS
29). And from then on the tone alters from suavity to intense horror, as the
detached "pleasure in lights," or in fine surface gloss, is peeled away.

In Le Fanu the large-scale horrors of Gothic, the Gothic of Maturin,
Lewis, or Radcliffe, are absent. Terror in his work is a domestic matter, usually set back, to be sure, by a couple of generations, and mostly located in the
countryside, whether of Ireland or Cumberland, but without the cosmic
sweep of *Melmoth the Wanderer,* and eschewing exoticism of setting. The
strangeness in his work is achieved by other means, and has largely different
effects or purposes: it is to be met, as we have seen, inside the house, beneath the apparently straightforward surface and within the self.

This invasion may come from within, like the ghost sitting in the sedan-
chair, or it may break or creep in from without by rationally inexplicable

---

14. The cleaning of the portrait typically releases these catastrophic energies, as in
"Carmilla" and "The Haunted Baronet."

means. Another of the forms it takes is what Binswanger calls "the un-wonted recurrence of the similar." As in the motif of the double, this has a long history in the tale-telling of many periods, but in its modern forms the tradition was instituted in German literature at the end of the eighteenth century; the word *doppelgänger* was coined to name it by Jean Paul Richter. The double motif can take various forms.[15] The best known is that in which the character encounters a person exactly resembling him, but apparently with another quite independent existence. If one can isolate the main idea underlying the motif in its nineteenth-century versions, it is perhaps that the self is non-unitary and does not therefore present a single smooth surface to experience. The basic and highly subversive notion is usually masked or framed by an ethical motivation of the double's appearances and influence—as for instance in the case of the conscience-double, which accuses and re-tributively hands about the protagonist—but it remains deeply disturbing to realist characterization, which depends on the notions of coherent and pro-gressive personality development and full moral consciousness. The concept of the double has been suggestively compared to the hypothesis of the "sleeping-soul," considered by Locke: that a man's complete unconscious-ness of his thought while asleep may make him in effect into two separate entities.[16] Locke decisively rejects the idea of such a profound difference ex-isting within the personality, but its close relationship to the fundamental hypotheses of psychoanalysis is obvious. The conscience-double, the grue-some phantom-double, and the Mephistophelean sidekick-double all em-body the unsettling notion that whether by wickedness, or suffering, or as a result of a moment of inattention to some social or moral taboo, the self may undergo a process of fragmentation, and be ever after impossible to reunify. There is a brilliant social variant of this essentially psychological motif in Dostoevsky's early novel *The Double* (1846), which anatomizes the condition of rationalized bureaucratic man in the city. Wilde combined the legend of eternal youth with a double motif in *The Picture of Dorian Gray* (1897). Le Fanu shows interest in several varieties of doubling, with a particular empha-sis on sibling- or cousin-doubling, on the Faust-Mephistopheles type, and on phantom doubles. His doubles are peculiar within the tradition of the motif in being often complementary halves of a notional pair rather than the more usual mirror-images; but they are perhaps all the more eerie for that. (He does have one highly effective use of the similar and supplanting double: in

15. See Otto Rank, *The Double: A Psychoanalytic Study*, tr. and ed. H. Tucker, Jr. (Chapel Hill: Univ. of North Carolina Press, 1971).

16. *An Essay concerning Human Understanding* (1690) II 1, 10–11 (quoted in Tymms 214).

"Mr. Justice Harbottle," when the wicked judge is given a dream-trial and condemned by a dream-judge called Chief Justice Twofold.) Le Fanu's repeated use of doubles within the family—whether contemporary, or extended by the deployment of revivified ancestors, such as Carmilla—again reveals his stress on domesticity, and may even recall the Freudian emphasis on the family as ground for legendary reenactments. The first modern masters of the motif, Hoffmann and Chamisso, were fond of using the shadow—also a folktale motif—or the reflection in a mirror as doubles. Le Fanu shows some suggestive traces of this, too; there is a very eerie one at the end of "The Drunkard's Dream." The drunkard's wife sees, on the night of her husband's death, "two persons, one of whom she recognized as her husband, noiselessly gliding out of the room" (GSM 173). The narrator suggests it may have been his shadow, "but she told me that the unknown person had been considerably in advance of the other, and on reaching the door, had turned back to reveal something to his companion" (GSM 173). What he reveals is presumably the way to the other world. This seems to draw on the primitive idea of the soul-double, as the "wraith or visible counterpart of the person, seen just before or just after, or at the moment of, his death."[17] The double as used in nineteenth-century literature might be called, then, a submerged unconscious part of the personality; or sometimes "the insubstantial shadow of the truth, which a man prefers to reality."[18] In Justinus Kerner (the "ghost-craftsman" paraphrased extensively by Mangan in the *Dublin University Magazine*) it is used to embody "the essential truth of affinity, of the predestined marriage of like souls."[19] But what in Kerner is positive and uplifting, suggesting a cosmic harmony, in Le Fanu can combine desire and destruction. In "Carmilla" (1872), which we shall consider at more length, the fair-haired Laura is wooed and preyed upon by the dark-haired vampire Carmilla. But though Carmilla is seen at story level to arrive from somewhere else—ostensibly—to the reader the elsewhere she represents is a hidden Other within the heroine and her father's house. She turns out to be the original of an old family portrait (a favorite motif of Le Fanu's) and she woos the innocent and bemused Laura with the promise of a common and mutual transformation in being:

> "You are afraid to die?"
> "Yes, everyone is."

---

17. A. E. Crawley. "Doubles," in J. Hastings, ed., *Encyclopaedia of Religion and Ethics* (New York: Scribner's, 1925-35).

18. Tymms.38.

19. Loc. cit., 39 (the work referred to is *Reiseschatten*, 1811).

"But to die as lovers may—to die together, so that they may live together. Girls are caterpillars while they live in the world, to be finally butterflies when the summer comes; but in the meantime there are grubs and larvae, don't you see—each with their peculiar propensities, necessities and structure. So says Monsieur Buffon, in his big book, in the next room." (*BGS* 297)

Carmilla is the Other of desire. This is rare in Le Fanu; his other treatments of demonic-lover plots—such as "Laura Silver Bell" or "Ultor de Lacy"—do not attempt to show the lover to the *reader* as tempting, only to the object of seduction; in fact he goes out of his way to make those devil-figures clearly repulsive, and to show the victims as bewitched. The explanation for the extraordinary vividness and power of the character of Carmilla— unsatisfactory as her motivation would be if this were formal realism—may lie in Le Fanu's adaptation here of the *doppelgänger* motif.

Carmilla is of an age with the heroine. They share, and have shared before Carmilla arrived, the same dreams. They do not resemble each other physically, but are presented as like two halves of a pair: Carmilla's dark coloring is the pendent to Laura's fairness, her vivacity to Laura's meekness: and her predatory nature to Laura's submissive one. It is never made clear in the story whether Carmilla is conscious of her vampire being; there are hints that she well understands it and is deceitful and cunning, and also indications that she is quite unaware of it, and is its prisoner. This uncertainty is one of the finest effects in the tale, and raises it well above the normal crude simplicity of vampire plots. It would seem that what Le Fanu is investigating is the recesses of consciousness, Carmilla and Laura are twin fragments of a complete personality, which it is somehow difficult to join or keep together. This effect recalls the lost shadows and reflections of the German Romantic. writers: the reflection, for instance, which, in Hoffmann's story "The Lost Reflection," the hero Erasmus Spikker leaves behind in sunny sensuous Italy with the demonic lover Giulietta while he goes back to his wife and baby in Germany. The point is that Carmilla stands for the suppressed, or perhaps unrealized, half of Laura. The story frames reality within unreality: because of the apparent remoteness from everyday social life of the supernatural and particularly of the vampire tale, Le Fanu could give Carmilla, seduction speeches and extraordinary directness. The sexual pleasure she promises to Laura involves an exquisite mutual yielding up of consciousness. This is to enable the metamorphosis from grub to butterfly: a clear metaphor for the attainment of adulthood, the state Laura, motherless and childishly dependent on her father, fights shy of. Pursuing this strand of interpretation, one might find that to give herself over to Carmilla's desires and learn to share them is Laura's best bet. One might, that is, but for the cross-strand which links Carmilla on the other hand to death, and makes when the summer comes a moment in the other world. It is revealed at the *dénouement* that such moments are chimerical, and that the reality of Carmilla in her tomb is as follows: "The limbs were perfectly flexible, the flesh elastic; and the leaden coffin floated with blood, in which to a depth of seven inches, the body lay immersed" (BGS 336). The peculiar version of the double motif which Le Fanu sets up in "Carmilla" can be paralleled elsewhere among the stories. In "Ultor de Lacy" there are two sisters: one fair, one dark; one saved, the other doomed to a demon lover (this time male, but also, like Carmilla, of the race of historical ghosts). The saved one, Alice, has nocturnal visions of the seduction of the doomed one, Una. When she confesses her fears, Una replies dismissively: "'Dreams, Alice. My dreams crossing your brain; only dreams, dreams. Get you to bed, and sleep'" (BGS 464). In "The Haunted Baronet," the protagonist, Sir Bale Mardyke, has a kind of double in his kinsman Phillip Feltram, illegitimate descendant of a woman wronged by an earlier Mardyke. In the course of the story the weakling Philip finds the strength, by means of an uncanny communicating with the past, to reverse Sir Bale's initial domination of him. Bale and Philip, like Laura and Carmilla, appear to the reader as two halves of a self which have somehow come adrift from each other: feeling and yielding in Philip, harshness and moral stupidity in Bale.

There is also another kind of unfixing of the bounds of the self in "The Haunted Baronet." At the beginning of the story there is a frame-passage set in the local village inn, all good English cheer and honest country folk. The wronged and drowned woman of a past generation is alluded to, but it is never made quite clear that the wrong really does belong to the past: the present Sir Bale seems to carry in the people's mind the guilt associated with his ancestor's evil deed. It seems that he is not quite fully an individual, but as well as being himself, in some sense *is* also his ancestor.

The two cousins in "The Murdered Cousin" (1838)[20] represent a variation on the double-motif: one girl is murdered by the villains in mistake for the other. This sinister and intriguing device was, significantly, dropped by Le Fanu in the later, more famous and more sentimental version, *Uncle Silas*. It is suggestively similar to the *dénouement* of "Carmilla," in which also one half of a notional composite self must be sacrificed for the life of the other.

---

20. ["The Murdered Cousin" was originally published under the title "Passage in the Secret History of an Irish Countess" when it first appeared in the *Dublin University Magazine* in November 1838. It was re-titled "The Murdered Cousin" for its inclusion in *Ghost Stories and Tales of Mystery* (Dublin: McGlashan, 1851).–Ed.]

There are other Le Fanu stories which adapt rather differently the *doppelgänger* motif, notably "The Familiar" and "Green Tea" (1869). Both are among Le Fanu's most skilled and brilliant work, both set in cities and in or near the present of narrator and original readers. This, especially "Green Tea" (which uses Swedenborgian material) is as near as Le Fanu comes to a version of the motif which would explore the psychology of doubling at an individual level, in the characterization, in the realist manner.

Normally in his haunting-tales there is a large gap between the understanding of the characters, at story level, and that of the reader-narrator couple: if we take "Carmilla" as an example, we can say that Laura and her father can only interpret the events of the story as a demonstration of the existence of vampires, whereas it is open to the reader to construe the material more metaphorically and find other, quite different meanings in it: that the Carmilla figure embodies Laura's fear of maturity, for instance, and that though Laura (the narrator) is quite unconscious of the fact, Carmilla represents a part of her, Laura's, self. In these stories it is as if the psychology of the protagonist is objectified, whether in a double-motif of some kind, or in the domestic interior, or, as we shall see, in the landscape. Le Fanu shows little interest in producing the effect of depth, or interiority, in characterization; his haunted characters do not reflect on their condition, or if they do we are not told about it. Instead their whole houses, or demesnes, become the ground of their inner conflicts, the stages of which are represented by haunting-episodes of growing intensity. A classic example of this is "Squire Toby's Will," in which the protagonist has cut his elder brother off from his inheritance and is haunted by a type of conscience-double, in the shape of a dog, which attaches itself to him and follows him everywhere. Finally he has it shot by his gamekeeper. On story level, to him and his servants, the dog resembles his dead father, who thus seems to be accusing him; but to the reader, it seems the embodiment of the guilt he feels but will not acknowledge.

In Le Fanu the past, both personal and historical, leaves stains or traces in the world, or in our consciousness of the world (two things not easy to separate). Such traces are initially encountered as a residue, but actively lead back into that past. This is the case in "Sir Dominick's Bargain" (1872), in which the "rusty stain in the plaster of the wall" is made the starting-point of the story, which thus reverses the normal chronology and gives the ending first.

> "Do you mind that mark, sir?" he asked.
> "That's about seven or eight feet from the ground, sir, and you'll not guess what it is."
> "I dare say not," said I, "unless it is a stain from the weather."
> "'Tis nothing so lucky, sir," he answered . . . (BGS 33)

And so the story is unfolded by the "sharp-featured man" first encountered "in the dark recess, deep in the shadow of the castle window, as flashback from the present time of the detached frame-narrator who is an English visitor on business in rural Ireland. "The Haunted Baronet" provides another more striking version of this stain-motif. The unwilling but desperate Sir Bale crosses the lake to seek the man he thinks is a gipsy fortune-teller. He is told he will find his way through the woods by scrutinizing the surface of a "broad druidic stone, that stood like a cyclopean table on its sunken stone props before the snakelike roots of the oak" (BGS 133). When he carries out the instructions and stares at the stone

> it seemed not as if a shadow fell upon the stone, but rather as if the stone be-
> came semi-transparent, and just under its surface was something dark—a
> hand, he thought it—and darker and darker it grew, as if coming up towards
> the surface, and after some little wavering, it fixed itself movelessly, pointing,
> as he thought, towards the forest. (BGS 135)

Perception has the task of interpreting such scars and traces. In "Ultor de Lacy" (1861) the sardonic demon wooer can dematerialize before one's glance, passing back into the ancient building he inhabits: figure becoming one with ground, which means that ground must hold figure always eerily *in potentia*:

> As Larry gazed, the figure somehow dissolved and broke up without receding.
> A hanging tuft of yellow and red ivy nodded queerly in place of the face,
> some broken and discoloured masonry in perspective took up the outline and
> colouring of the arms and figure, and two imperfect red and yellow lichen
> streaks carried out the curved tracing of the long spindle shanks. Larry
> blessed himself, and drew his hand across his damp forehead, over his bewil-
> dered eyes, and could not speak for a minute. It was all some devilish trick;
> he could take his oath he saw every feature in the fellow's face, the lace and
> buttons of his cloak and doublet, and even his long finger nails and thin yel-
> low fingers that overhung the cross-shaft of the window, where there was
> nothing but a rusty stain left. (BGS 455–56)

Earlier in the story, the reverse happens: the apparently quite real castle fades away in the moonlight when the bewildered priest tries to visit it.

> At last, sure enough, he saw the castle plain as plain could be . . . but when
> he emerged at the top, there was nothing but the bare heath. . . . In a few
> minutes more he was quite close, all of a sudden, to the great front, rising
> gray and dim in the feeble light, and not till he could have struck it with his
> good oak "wattle" did he discover it to be only one of those wild, gray front-

ages of living rock that rise here and there in picturesque tiers along the slopes of these solitary mountains. (BGS 452)

But for the tone, this would resemble nothing so much as Lewis Carroll's "Mad Gardener's Songs" ("he looked again, and found it was a hippopotamus"), another apparently naïve Victorian "alternative" text.

But though the disappearing castle and the appearing ghost are motivated (sketchily, as usual, at the end) as historical retribution, the interest of such spellbinding moments in these stories surely does not lie in such motivation. When their editor, E. F. Bleiler (everywhere else a sensitive commentator) says they contain "a hidden, often diabolic morality, that will suffer evil to go unavenged or unbetrayed" (BGS, "Introduction" viii), he reverses the real interest of the matter. The numinous Other in nature and the past—the final motif we shall identify—usually functions retributively, it is true, at the level of *fabula* (story material). The haunted protagonists *are* evil, in the majority of cases. But the reader of more than one or two stories quickly sees that the working out of each individual damnation is hardly the point. Le Fanu's many repetitions of the same story-material confirm this perception; M. R. James was quite right to say that whatever the cause of such repetition, it was not poverty of invention.[21] The pleasure in the reading comes rather from the perception of larger patterns of psychic investigation than from the moralization of phantoms.

Le Fanu's construction of the Other in landscape and history owes a good deal to the influence of folklore, and is best examined by starting from the 1870 "Stories of Lough Guir." This piece opens with a prefatory reminiscence by the narrator, in which he recounts his first hearing of the tales. The structure of this reminiscence is important: it presents the past as three successive levels, in a pattern strikingly replicated at least twice more in these stories. The most recent stratum is that of the writer's boyhood, when he says he first heard the stories, from a named source, Miss Anne Baily. The second is that of the Whig and convivial past of the Baily family, as implied by the great drinking-cup, engraved "the glorious, pious, and immortal memory." The third stratum is that of the Earl of Desmond, paradigm of the old ruined Norman-Irish aristocracy whose rule was supplanted by the English claim to sovereignty.

In his folklore existence this Earl subsumes at least two, and probably more, figures from actual history (the chief two are Gearoid Iarla, the fourteenth-century Desmond who is also an important Irish poet, and the last Earl, around whom gathered the resistance in Munster to the Elizabethan

---

21. "Epilogue" of Madam Crowl's *Ghost and Others Tales* (London: Bell, 1923), 274.

conquest of Ireland).[22] It appears at first that Le Fanu was evidently thinking of this last Earl, because he describes the castle beside the lake as "a stronghold of the last rebellious Earl of Desmond, which defied the army of the lord deputy" (GSM 145). Yet the stories he then retells concern the Earl as a magical and otherworldly figure; the recession through the three stages of the past leads not just from his own childhood in this countryside to the 1688 Revolution, and thence to the Tudor conquest, but farther back, to a landscape from which the action of history has been elided.

The lake is the central symbol of this group of stories: "And beneath its waters lie enchanted, the grand old castle of the Desmonds, the great earl himself, his beautiful young countess, and all the retinue that surrounded him in the years of his splendour, and at the moment of his catastrophe" (GSM 145). Out of those waters, it is said, he can emerge every seven years and attempt converse with the human world. The "catastrophe" here mentioned is identified in this frame-narration as that of Desmond's political and military defeat; but within the first of the tales themselves, "The Magician Earl," a quite different version is given, in which his imprisonment within the lake waters has been caused by his necromancy. Thus the reader is left with two incompatible versions of events, one history, one romance. Irish history being the echo-chamber it is, all this must, of course, have implications for Le Fanu's own political position, since, as Disraeli puts it in Sybil, ruins are "the children of violence, not of time" and the picturesque is the Siamese twin of politics; but it is not as easy as it might initially seem to work out these implications.[23] It is not my intention here to try, but I shall point out that the "Stories of Lough Guir" taken in its totality, frame-passages and all, does preserve both versions without deciding between them: in Le Fanu, hauntings take place apparently for preference in the best-furnished houses, and the past is always returning, usually retributively, on the present.

The threefold layering of the past which opens "Lough Guir" strongly suggests a homologous layering of the self and of the landscape. We find it again in "The White Cat of Drumgunniol" (1870), where, once again at the threshold of the *fabula* (which concerns the retributive haunting of a family by the ghost of a wronged woman), the reader's eye is led along the scenery, through personal childhood memory ("I have myself seen") and historical reference (the rapparees), to an otherworld entrance (the liss):

---

22. See the discussion in D. Ó hÓgain, "An É an t-Am Fós É?" Bealoideas 42–44 (1974–76): 213–309; and "Gearoid Iarla agus an Draíocht," Scriobh 4 (1979): 234–9. I am grateful for these references to Diarmuid O Giolláin.

23. *Sybil*, in *The Works of Benjamin Disreali* (London: Dunne, 1904), 54.

I have myself seen the old farm-house, with its orchard of huge mossgrown apple trees. I have looked round on the peculiar landscape; the roofless, ivied tower, that two hundred years before had afforded a refuge from raid and rapparee, and which still occupies its old place in the angle of the haggard; the bush-grown "liss," that scarcely a hundred and fifty steps away records the labours of a bygone race. (BGS 409)

In this dream-vivid landscape (which is always the same one, lovingly reconstructed over and over again in Le Fanu's stories) everything is encrusted, the trees "mossy," the tower "ivied," the liss "bush-grown." But these sedimentary layers, too, can be penetrated, as can those of the personal and historical forgetfulness whose action they mime, and as can the thick coverings and concealments of plush and tapestry and oak chests. The feline ghost (perhaps an albino double of Poe's contemporary black cat, who also likes to sit on dead men's faces) recurs through the generations and it seems cannot be eluded, even by the innocent.

The other place where this recession into time and space is rehearsed is in "The Haunted Baronet," a story I have already mentioned in connection with the double motif. Several of Le Fanu's most important motifs are so skillfully interwoven in this story that it is difficult to unpick its fabric sufficiently to trace any one; so the discussion of landscape and memory will involve us again in traces, doubles and shadows.

When Sir Bale needs reliable racing tips, and ready cash with which to bet in order to save his estates, his half-double, half-sibling Philip Feltram leads him, as we have seen, to a source of both. To get there Bale must cross the lake and enter the forest. This forest, which is usually of aboriginal oak, makes repeated appearances in Le Fanu.[24] Sometimes it has suffered or is suffering denudation, which is the result and sign of evil-doing of some kind.[25] Many of these forests contain—are—the forest of the past. Sir Bale's version is the abode allegedly of the gipsy,[26] but in fact of the malevolent ancestor

---

24. Here in "The Haunted Baronet," in "The Last Heir of Castle Connor," and in "A Chapter in the History of a Tyrone Family."

25. As in "The Murdered Cousin" (1838), its later version *Uncle Silas* (1863), and "The Fortunes of Sir Robert Ardagh" (1838). The only crime which can be pinned on Silas during most of that novel is that of "waste," cutting down and selling timber from Maud's land.

26. Le Fanu often uses gipsies as figures standing at the threshold of the Other and possessing a knowledge denied ordinary characters: in *Uncle Silas* Maud encounters the gipsy camp on the journey from her father's house—secure and familiar—to Bartram-Haugh where they will plan to murder her; and in "Carmilla" only the gipsy

who thereafter haunts him and is (once again, to *the reader*) a version of himself. Even before Bale's wife polishes up the old portraits near the end of the story and reveals this ancestor, he is throughout described as if he partook of an existence in some other dimension: part-human, part-avian predator.

To reach the forest Sir Bale must cross the lake. This he is extremely reluctant to do, for reasons he does not state in so many words, but which to the reader are both clear and full of metaphorical implication. The village people believed the lake is haunted by the drowned woman; but to Bale it represents another kind of barrier: he has not visited the woods on the far side since childhood, when they were his playground. His adult life has (outside the bounds of the story, as always in Le Fanu) been one of profligacy, dissipation and brutality; the crossing of the lake constitutes a confrontation with that earlier, innocent self, and hence within the landscape of Sir Bale's psyche it is truly a haunted and fearful place. Here again the personal and the ancestral past are made to coincide, as are the outer and inner scenery. When eventually he is forced by his pressing debts to make the journey, the landscape prompts in him an outpouring of reminiscence:

> He looked round him as if in a dream. He had not been there since his childhood. There were no regrets, no sentiment, no remorse; only an odd return of the associations and fresh feelings of boyhood, and a long reach of time suddenly annihilated.
>
> The little hollow in which he stood; the three hawthorn trees at his right; every crease and undulation of the sward, every angle and crack in the lichen-covered rock at his feet, recurred with a sharp and instantaneous recognition to his memory.
>
> "Many a time your brother and I fished for hours together from that back there, just where the bramble grows. That bramble has not grown an inch since, not a leaf altered . . ." (BGS 131)

This hints that crossing the lake has led Bale into another dimension: a place which is changeless. In Irish folklore, lakes, like caves in hills, are frequently seen as otherworld entrances. Throughout "The Haunted Baronet," the lake seems to Bale to menace him: he feels imprisoned in this ancestral landscape:

> "There's nothing so gloomy as a lake pent up among barren mountains . . .
> We fancy the shore must look very pretty from a boat; and when we try it, we find we have only got down into a pit and can see nothing rightly. For my part, I hate boating, and I hate the water; and I'd rather have my house . . . at the edge of a moss . . . and an open horizon . . . then be suffocated among

pedlar notices Carmilla's long pointed vampire teeth (BGS 296).

impassable mountains, or upset in a black lake and drowned like a kitten . . .
" (BGS 74)

For Philip, by contrast, the lake becomes a source of energy: he returns from
his near-drowning in it as a changed man, who seems to have been invested
with uncanny powers. After this event, when Bale sees him one evening
standing on the steps of the house, in the evening sun, he is "throwing a long
shadow that was lost in the lake" (BGS 129)—a shadow that connects him
with the other world of whose existence he now partakes, and to which he
eventually brings Bale, through the agency of their common ancestor. When
Bale asks him who is the source of the money he suddenly has to lend, he
replies:

> "A friend, who is—*myself*."
> "Yourself! Then it is yours—*you* lend it?" . . .
> "Myself, and not myself," said Feltram oracularly; "as like as voice and
> echo, man and shadow." (BGS 118)

The lake in this story is a repository of the past and of guilt, inherited
ancestrally and also perhaps incurred individually, though this is not clear.
Together with the ancient house beside it, the fells surrounding it and the
forest at the other, magical side of it, the lake forms the focus of the reader's
and the narrator's attention. This landscape symbolically objectifies human
consciousness; in it all the fragments of the Mardyke family are unified: Sir
Bale, thinking himself safe behind the wainscot and stone of the great house;
his malevolent ancestor, waiting within the forest and on the old canvas to
be released into power; and Philip, who goes to encounter, within the lake
waters, the slighted woman from whom he is descended. He undergoes there
a transformation, fulfilling the prediction that he will "but go in weakness to
return in power" (BGS 94). This is evidently an inspired metamorphosis in
Le Fanu's imagination of the Earl of Desmond's folklore life in the
otherworld beneath Lough Guir. He, too, has undergone a transformation,
and his life beneath the lake is structurally analogous to all those states of
strangeness within the everyday which one encounters in various guises
everywhere in Le Fanu: the Swedenborgian realm of the newly dead in *Uncle
Silas*; the "summer" of "Carmilla" in which girls shall be butterflies; the aural
wraith-life of Una de Lacy after her departure with her demon-lover (when
she has dwindled to a voice singing in the glen). Those depths of the past
and the Other are so profound, but also so completely subject to the laws of
human history, that even the sound-stain of this ghost-voice will eventually
wear away:

The apparition has long ceased. But it is said that now and again, perhaps once in two or three years, late on a summer night, you may hear—but faint and far away in the recesses of the glen—the sweet, sad notes of Una's voice, singing those plaintive melodies. This, too, of course, in time will cease, and all be forgotten. (BGS 465)

Le Fanu's stories are haunted, then, not by phantoms from the realm of metaphysics, but by the various projections of otherness within the complexity of personality. Far from being amused essays in a trivial genre, they are forerunners of the revolutionary hypotheses of twentieth-century thought about human identity; forceful intimations of "the element of darkness" described by Foucault as "the unthought," revelations of the "obscure space" in man, a tracing of "the blind stain by which it is possible to know him."

III. Some Special Topics

Making Light in the Shadow Box:
The Artistry of Le Fanu

Kel Roop

Illuminated by infrequent scholarship, the stories of gothic writer Joseph Sheridan Le Fanu have remained hidden in the recesses of literary appreciation.[1] His admirers may, in fact, regard such obscurity as most appropriate for this author of the macabre tale who so effectively casts his characters in darkness. Horror seems masterly woven in the black textures of his stories; however, it most thoroughly infects the Le Fanu world through the eerie play of candle flames and moonbeams.[2] Indeed, in their depiction of an unholy cosmos, Le Fanu's stories suggest an intricate structuring of light patterned after the technique of the minor Dutch painter Godfrey Schalken. Although the influence of Schalken has essentially escaped critical attention, this lesser painter figures as subject and title of an early Le Fanu story and, perhaps even more significantly, as originator of the writer's luminous paradigm of evil.

As a student of Gerard Dou,[3] a master of *Helldunkelstudien*, Godfrey Schalken received a thorough introduction to the chiaroscuro popular with Dutch painters of the seventeenth century and appears to have adopted many of his mentor's candlelit subjects as his own.[4] But in his combination of

---

1. For the most recent and exhaustive of Le Fanu studies, see W. J. Mc Cormack, *Sheridan Le Fanu and Victorian Ireland* (Oxford, 1980); and Jack Sullivan, *Elegant Nightmares: The English [Ghost] Story from Le Fanu to Blackwood* (Athens, Ohio, 1978).

2. I challenge the critical emphasis on darkness in Le Fanu's stories. See, for instance, E. F. Benson who writes that "a darkness gathers, like dusk gently falling, and then something obscurely stirs in it." "Sheridan Le Fanu," *The Spectator* (21 February 1931): 263-64.

3. [The name of the Dutch painter Gerrit Dou is commonly Anglicized as "Gerard Douw" (sometimes "Dow").–Ed.]

4. For discussions of Dou's influence on Schalken, see Jacob Rosenberg, Seymour Slive, and E. G. tee Kuile, *Dutch Art and Architecture: 1600-1800*, ed. Nikolaus Pevs-

light sources (such as the blending of candle, pipe, and ember light in "A Comely Woman at an Arched Window"), Schalken exceeded Dou's instruction. In order to capture the hybrid gleam most effectively, he often arranged his subjects within a series of frames formed by windows and curtains for which his spots of light provided the focus.[5] Even more important is the larger frame Schalken apparently employed in the production of his paintings. Like his contemporaries, Schalken may have experimented with optics in order to achieve the most natural representation.[6] Although the details of his technique remain undisclosed, he is said to have painted his scenes by the means of an optical device: "he placed the object he intended to paint in a dark room, with a candle, and looking through a small hole, painted by day what he saw by candle-light."[7]

Le Fanu seems to have written "[Strange Even in the Life of] Schalken the Painter" and the four supernatural stories of In a Glass Darkly ("Green Tea," "The Familiar," "Mr. Justice Harbottle," "Carmilla") in a similar fashion. He leaves only the smallest opening of perception in his layered narrations, yet through his aperture he, the reader, and the characters see and plummet into scenes molded by flickering candlelight. Le Fanu's careful ordering finally betrays a universe permeated by a malignant glow which usurps human power.

Of the stories addressed in this essay, all but "The Familiar" make specific reference to art. "Schalken the Painter" (1839), an earlier story than those contained in In a Glass Darkly (1872), seems a dominant example of Le

---

ner (Harmondsworth, Eng., 1972): 358; and Hofstede de Groot, A Catalogue Raisonné of the Works of the Most Eminent Dutch Painters of the 17th (Seventeenth) Century, vol. 5, trans. Edward G. Hawke (Cambridge, 1976), 309.

5. De Groot, A Catalogue Raisonné, 5.310.

6. Although he recognizes that "little is . . . known about the importance of perspective treatise to Dutch artists," Arthur K. Wheelock, Jr. nonetheless offers several provocative speculations concerning their experimentation with optics. No mention is made of Schalken, but Wheelock notes one theory regarding Dou's technique: "Dou set up a screen between himself and the object to be painted and inserted a concave mirror into it. He squared his canvas and then stretched threads over the surface of the 'verre' in a similar fashion. He was then able to imitate both the composition and the colour in his painting." Dou's interest in perspective may have subsequently spurred Schalken on to create his own optical device. See Perspective, Optics, and Delft Artists Around 1650 (New York, 1977), 2–3, 158–63, 166.

7. Bryan's Dictionary of Painters and Engravers in Five Volumes, vol. 5, ed. George C. Williamson (New York, 1905), 32.

Fanu's later technique. The story opens with a description of a painting typical of Schalken's style: against an antique religious backdrop, a woman with an "arch smile" holds a lamp while a male figure gropes for his sword in alarm.[8] However, the reader slowly sees the painting through Le Fanu's viewfinder until the writer's own candlelight transforms the original "representation of reality"; by the end of the story, the enigmatic composition has unfolded into a complete vision of terror dominated by the ghastly addition of the demon Vanderhausen.[9] Contained within the frame formed by the two images, Le Fanu's story has become a study of preternatural evil. In its aptly titled chapter "A Wonderful Likeness," the story "Carmilla" also incorporates paintings as integral elements to be reformed by Le Fanu's spectroscope. Portraits of Laura's family, refinished by "something of an artist," appear to reveal the true identity of the vampire, for in the painting of Mircalla Karnstein "was the effigy of Carmilla" (299). The narrative, however, ultimately challenges a simplistic one-to-one correspondence between painting and subject. In similar fashion does the writer verbally extend and "refinish" the visual art in "Mr. Justice Harbottle" and "Green Tea"; the spectral hangman Harbottle sees resembles that in "the famous print of the 'Idle Apprentice'" (263), while the countenance of Jennings in "Green Tea" is "fleshed out, like a portrait of Schalken's, before its background of darkness" (192).

At first these portraits may simply enforce a recognition of a demonic hinterland: through these images of the vampiric Carmilla, the ghoulish hangman, the spectral Rose, and even the living yet possessed Jennings, Le Fanu delineates the supernatural world before the reader. Although the painting by Schalken contains the figure of the artist, the narrator informs the reader that it is "valuable for . . . presenting a portrait of his early [yet deceased] love, Rose Velderkraust" (46). For the narrator, Schalken is simply an inconsequential human embellishment. Likewise, the Le Fanu narrative may seem significant only for its sensational rendering of the macabre. Within his understated prose, the writer jars the reader out of earthly secu-

---

8. Although no specific model has been found for the painting described by Le Fanu, it seems a composite of Schalken elements. See, for example, "A Young Lady Drawing Aside a Curtain," "A Comely Woman at an Arched Window," and "Light and Fire." De Groot, 5.32.

9. Joseph Sheridan Le Fanu, *Best Short Stories of Joseph Sheridan Le Fanu*, ed. E. F. Bleiler (New York, 1964), 29. All further references to Le Fanu's works are from this edition and cited parenthetically in the text.

rity with rare yet striking depiction of unearthly beings. No corners or blankets can conceal the vision.[10]

The specter, however, seems arrested within the boundaries of the canvas. Despite the initial shock of seeing the other world, the reader may enjoy safety in the knowledge that the demon is caged by the paintings' or stories' edges. Especially in Schalken's painting does art clearly appear an attempt at objectification. In a "dream," the inspiration for the painting, the ghost of Rose leads the artist through a labyrinth to an old Dutch room where she draws back the curtains of a heavy bed to unveil her demon spouse Vanderhausen. Schalken's painting shields the viewer from this malignant vision unacceptable to the rational mind and offers the more benign image of Rose. In "Carmilla" and "Green Tea," such artistic containment appears a means of scientific discovery. Laura examines the painting with experimental precision: "Here you Carmilla are, living smiling, ready to speak, in this picture. Isn't it beautiful, papa? And see, even the mole on her throat" (299). A perfect reflection of the succubus, the painting has captured every feature. And Carmilla reacts to the threat of the painting as does the traditional vampire to the mirror: with avoidance. To Laura's exclamations she says nothing and at last diverts attention from herself to the moonlight. In "Green Tea," Jennings' resemblance to a Schalken painting becomes part of the whole scientific method of Dr. Hesselius, who "guessed well the nature, though not even vaguely the particulars of the revelations he was about to receive, from that fixed face" (192).

Through his narrative ordering of the supernatural, Le Fanu might thus resemble the "picture-cleaner" in "Carmilla," who arrives "armed with hammer, ripping chisel, and turnscrew" (298) for the unpacking, equipped to conquer the evil within the boxes. His mastery seems complete as the paintings are methodically checked off according to "corresponding numbers" and "restored to their places" (299). The paintings appear to capture, isolate, and control within their gallery the supernatural traces filtered into the temporal world. So too do Le Fanu's intersecting stories foster the illusion that evil may not transgress the frame's edge.

Yet neither painting nor printed word can, in fact, shield man from the fiend. The portraits actually efface the boundaries between earthly and unearthly forces, for their canvases often combine human with spectral forms. Although the narrator of "Schalken the Painter" ignores this human ele-

---

10. In his analysis of Le Fanu's novel *Uncle Silas*, W. J. Mc Cormack similarly describes a "duality of portrait/subject," suggesting that "a portrait represents a rigid projection of idealized personality, formal and remote" (166).

ment, the more perceptive viewer would not. Indeed, included within the "portrait of [Schalken's] early love" is the figure of the painter aggressively posed: "in an attitude of alarm, his hand is placed upon the hilt of his sword, which he appears to be in the act of drawing" (29). An emblem of the combat between the natural and supernatural, the painting belies the epigraphical edict: "Let him, therefore, take his rod away from me, and let not his fear terrify me" (29).

Recent scholarship explains this juxtaposition of worlds as representative of the psychological state of the human viewer or participant. The portraits merely symbolize the war between the unconscious and conscious, the heart and the mind.[11] But such attempts to fix the portraits in a post-Freudian interpretation may reveal more about contemporary interests than about the Victorian Le Fanu's artistic concerns. Admittedly, Le Fanu brings psychological nuances to the ghost story, but he ultimately subordinates them to tightly structured representations of supernatural evil.[12]

By reducing characters to emblems, Le Fanu forces the reader's attention to a powerful structure that does not contain but creates the evil into which it draws its victims. Actual and figurative galleries only offer the façade of restraint. In reality, Le Fanu's portraits undermine safety, for they supply no final limits, no enclosures; Carmilla's and Schalken's paintings noticeably lack frames.[13] Although painted as the culmination of ghostly events, Schalken's portrait provides the introduction to Le Fanu's story, the portal into the macabre. Even more explicitly does Schalken's drawing of Saint Anthony in the same story allow the entrance of the fiend. As Schalken curses the imperfections of the painting, the demon Vanderhausen simultaneously appears. Finally, in his writing of "Schalken the Painter," Le

---

11. See, for instance, Mc Cormack, *Sheridan Le Fanu*, 166, who distinguishes between a human being and the main character Maud's emotional response to him. William Veeder similarly interprets the portrait of Carmilla as "symptomatic of Laura's attempt to control passion by objectifying it" in "'Carmilla': The Arts of Repression," *Texas Studies in Language and Literature* 22 (1980): 208.

12. See Mc Cormack, *Sheridan Le Fanu*, 151. Within his psychological studies of character in *Uncle Silas*, he has paradoxically, yet quite accurately, identified Le Fanu's emphasis on form at the expense of characterization. He writes that characters lose "spontaneity" through Le Fanu's formalization of them.

13. See Veeder, "'Carmilla,'" 208, who interprets the frameless painting as an indication of Laura's uncertainty about her relationship. He notes that Laura is not attacked by Carmilla until she takes the painting to her room. But his analysis again seems too quickly to reduce the symbol to a representation of psychological duality.

Fanu distends the unbounded threshold of the artist's portrait of Rose into a sinister foyer. His story deepens the painting's original "interior of what might be a chamber in some antique religious building" with a corridor comprised of a narrow hallway, a Dutch compartment, a curtained bed, and even the "arch smile" of Rose (29, 46). Through a compounding of internal frames, the painting becomes a three-dimensional shadow box which draws the reader into terror.

As the title suggests, In a Glass Darkly narrows the portrait aperture to that of the window, a symbol of vision appearing repeatedly in "Carmilla," "Green Tea," "The Familiar," and "Mr. Justice Harbottle." But like the portrait, the window only creates a semblance of secure insight by uniquely blending barrier with peephole. The observer thinks that the plate of glass affords him an opportunity of seeing without interacting. In reality, the transparent window acts more as the slit of a Schalken viewfinder that at once arrests and creates, often forging the characters and even the readers into its creations.

Throughout the stories, Le Fanu's windows consistently resemble optic lenses. No expansive panes dominate the characters' cheerless façades; rather the houses, rooms, and even doors are equipped merely with elongated slivers of glass. "Tall" and "slender" windows open into the houses of both "Green Tea" and "Mr. Justice Harbottle" (185, 248); in "Carmilla," Laura confers with her priest in a room lit by a "small lattice" (278); and perhaps most ominous of all is the narrow transom in "The Familiar," a "*kind* of window" (emphasis added, 240). Like the paintings, windows also achieve a three-dimensional depth. Rarely flush with the wall, they are more often, as in "Green Tea," part of a deep "recess" formed by bookcases or other projections, frequently located in rooms suggestive of art. In "Schalken the Painter," the artist first strains to see Vanderhausen from the window of his studio. Such studio-window association becomes a source for repetitive punning in the stories of In a Glass Darkly, in which windows often appear in the "drawing room."

Although windows proliferate in the Le Fanu canon, they allow only the most imperfect vision. Those of Justice Harbottle's house are especially inefficient; in the course of the story, they are obstructed by "bills" (of sale), "turned . . . yellow by time," and even "stained with dust and rain of fifty years" (246, 247, 248). Attempts to view the temporal world through such openings can result only in frustration. Even those less encumbered panes of the other stories hinder willed sight. No matter how determined Schalken might be, the window will not yield the physical form of Vanderhausen. Yet at times the glass does provide capricious glimpses of the intangible. In "The

Familiar," the General sees from a window the darting figure of Barton's specter. Justice Harbottle is also permitted several views of his ghoulish prosecutors through the window of his carriage. But these images appear unsolicited and suggest containment by rather than of the supernatural.

Nonetheless, like the stories' portraits, windows seem to check the evil. Those lining Harbottle's house and the chateau in "Carmilla" are separated like paintings in a gallery, each sheet of glass rendering a distinct static image. As Harbottle's carriage winds its way past his spectral prosecutors, each scene framed by the window resembles a tableau in a Renaissance pageant of the seven deadly sins. But unlike Spenser's Red Cross Knight, Harbottle does not gain saving insight from the parade of evil. The window's edges provide a momentary false comfort; Harbottle awakens in the carriage mistakenly convinced that the ghouls were only actors in a nightmare. They soon slip beyond the windowsill, infiltrate Harbottle's house, and hang the corrupt judge. Le Fanu's compounding of window imagery throughout *In a Glass Darkly* only makes multifaceted prisms out of isolated windows, the houses, and even the volume; and these prisms release rather than control evil.

The window of the shadow box is thus an active medium, creating as well as framing supernatural forms. It does not reflect but "throws a rosy light" (319); it does not reveal but "commands a view" (233). And as the window acquires greater power, man steadily loses his. In "The Familiar," Barton sees the demon through the window and "staggers slowly back, like one who had received a stunning blow"; when Montague also sees the figure, he mindlessly and "mechanically" chases it (230), succumbing to the ultimate power of the window to suck the natural character into preternatural depths. Montague's plunge—unlike that of Rose Velderkaust, Captain Barton, Rev. Jennings, or Justice Harbottle—does not lead to the ends of the abyss. Yet for these less fortunate characters, the window is the impetus to a permanent fall into death. Rose disappears from her room, leaving behind her only an open window looking down on a quietly rippling canal.

The windows of *In a Glass Darkly* as well as "Schalken the Painter" do not reveal interiors dominated by the unexpected gloom but rather by light, especially Schalken candlelight. In "Schalken the Painter," the narrator "positions" the characters so that the reader might better understand events and uses candles as the focus for this "composition." Yet this same narrator attempts to undermine the importance of lighting in the Schalken painting, arguing that "the curious management of its lights constitutes, as usual in his pieces, the chief apparent merit of his pictures. I say *apparent*, for in its subject, and not in its handling, however exquisite, consists its real value" (29). Juxtaposed to the narrator's own artistic design, this statement loses credibility and through its adamant denial actually directs the reader's attention to the light. In a Schalken painting or a Le Fanu tale, the artist consistently subordinates subjects or forms—mere victims of preternatural illumination—to the "management of light."

Although myriad lights merge to cast a pernicious glow in Le Fanu's stories, the characters presume to forge a dichotomy distinguishing benign from malevolent light sources. Dr. Hesselius in "Green Tea" calls the twilight "odd" (191); for Captain Barton in "The Familiar" moonlight is "imperfect" (212); and the narrator of "The Familiar" identifies a division of light yielded by the transom, a window "intended in the day to aid in the lighting of the passage, and through which at present the rays of the candle were issuing" (240). But in the Le Fanu tale, such duality deceives. The writer does not offer a Platonic world in which the observer need only leave the shadowy cave to find perfect goodness. Rather, Le Fanu's light emanates from and remains within the shadow box, generating the essence of evil.

Most deceptive of all is daylight, in which the characters invest a naïve faith. Like a child clutching the blanket over his eyes, Captain Barton waits for the sun to dispel the boogieman; but still he hears the demon muttering in the "daytime as well as after nightfall" (216). Barton's minister is also surprised by the sensation of evil, "though it was broad daylight" (216). Only the six-year-old Laura in "Carmilla" does not hold a child's trust in the sun's glare, which cannot quell her fears from the nightmare of the night before. Like those best acquainted with the supernatural, she knows that daylight has no power over evil. If anything, it is a source of malevolent energy which imbues Carmilla with her beauty, evokes Jennings' demonic monkey, and animates Captain Barton's "familiar." The fiend jostles the arm of General Montague on a crowded, sunny street of Paris and becomes only more ominous in "familiar" daylight.

Le Fanu's window-prisms gradually divide the brilliance of daylight into its more elusive counterparts of moonlight and twilight. Although in the stories moonlight often accompanies the first appearance of demonic forms, its radiance beguiles the character caught within the shadow box. Barton wonders at the formless footsteps he hears, for "there was sufficient moonlight to disclose any object" (212). Rather than a means of vision, the moon is a mood shaper, whose mysterious properties are detailed at length by Laura's governess in "Carmilla." In the story, the seemingly objective rays of the sun surrender to the less transparent but more provocative "rosy" moonbeams at play in the windows of the chateaus. In "Green Tea," twilight supplies an even more expansive red-stained palette. As though the sun were actually setting in the midst of Jennings' room, "the red reflected light of the western sky" settled on Jennings and his figure is "faintly seen in the ruddy twilight" (191).

Although both moonlight and twilight appear "dusky" and "filmy," their foggy luminosity is more important for its effect on the forms beneath it than for its distortion of light.[14] In one sense, light does not become blurred at twilight but more distinct. With its ruddy color and "filmy" texture, it resembles a tangible being like the fog of Eliot's "Prufrock." But to gain life, it saps that of physical forms just as the vampire Carmilla drains the force from her victims. Edges dissolve under the hazy twilight. The daughter of Justice Harbottle's housekeeper plays in the house until "she can no longer discern the colors of the china figures on the chimneypiece or in the cabinets" (269). As the forms fade to nothing, twilight "deepens," allowing the entrance of Harbottle's hellish executioners.

Through the imagery of lamps and fire, light becomes more obviously animated, although it assumes a semblance of contained activity. The flame flickering within the glass enclosure seems as confined as a scene caught within the frame of a window or painting. Also, carried and positioned, lamps appear controlled by the stories' characters. In "Carmilla," they are at first frivolous and insignificant decorations: the general attends a ball at a chateau where the "trees were hung with colored lamps" (319). For both Justice Harbottle and Captain Barton they seem obedient instruments aligned in orderly rows. The "long lines of . . . oil lamps" encourages Captain Barton in his flight from the demon by appearing to be a refuge. But the warm glow of the lamps does not protect; Captain Barton hears the bullet's "whistle" as the lights "twinkle" before him (222).

Uncontained fire realizes the potential dynamism of the lamps. As evil pervades Justice Harbottle's house—as it has nearly enacted its execution of him—the maid imagines an infernal backdrop for his death: "the lamps seemed all to have gone out, and there were stoves and charcoal fires here and there" (266). Still the naïve initiate of the shadow box attempts to ignore the flame's tyranny. According to the narrator of both "Schalken the Painter" and "Mr. Justice Harbottle," the fires "blaze cheerily" as though they were part of a Dickens' Christmas (245, 269). Despite the narrator's optimism, the flames of both stories only usher in demonic servants. Within the maid's vision are hellish stokers feeding the evil blaze.

---

14. I here differ with Jack Sullivan, *Elegant Nightmares*, 24, who suggests that twilight is significant because "lights and shadows become so blurred and undefined as to become almost interchangeable."

At the core of the shadow box burns the candle. All the light that has been steadily diffused by the window-prism converges at moments of climax in the candle's flame. With its power to cast shadows that contrast with its distinct glow, the candle exposes and creates those forms usually kept in the crevices of man's mind. Entering her room during a brief escape from Vanderhausen, Rose thinks she sees the demon. By the candle's flame, Schalken too discerns a "shadow" dart around the corner. In "Carmilla" candlelight also casts an eerie backdrop from which evolve Laura's nightmares. As a black cat and female figure coagulate from the thick shadows of her room, a "candle burns all through the night" (304).

The demons that inhabit Le Fanu's stories seem in fact pasteboard figures which materialize at the candle's bidding. Despite their torment of the characters, they easily disappear into the darkness. Only the candle remains a constant malignant presence. By the end of "The Familiar," supernatural evil has abandoned its frenzied form; the force that ultimately damns Captain Barton to eternal terror is not that of the fiend. Rather, the candle's flame which the valet observes "slowly shifting" by the transom (240) signifies and abets Captain Barton's collapse. Rose too disappears as a result of candle management. Although she explains as the candle's light goes out, "the darkness is unsafe" (44), the gloom is only effected by the flickering flame. Shadows created by the candles so precisely arranged in the story gather around Rose until she succumbs to the final shadow of death. In fact, "by the bedsides" of all the unfortunate victims of evil, candles burn, ironic harbingers of the shadowy cavern into which man must fall.

Still, the victim's greatest shadow in the Le Fanu tale is not that of death but of depersonalization. The candle's flame not only creates supernatural forms, but makes mere shells of men as well. As the force of evil permeates the shadow box, it becomes concentrated in the features of its victims and demons alike. Le Fanu stories become true Schalken paintings in which parts of the form blaze against a backdrop of darkness. Those physical receptacles of personality and spirit—the eyes, the smile—no longer comfort with their mortal mutability, but terrify with their essential and eternal glow of horror. Rose's dress and "arch smile" reflect the light of her lamp; Jennings discovers the monkey demon through the increasingly specific focuses of "two luminous points," "two dull lamps," "tiny discs of red," "little circles," and finally "its eyes" (193); and Jennings himself is emptied of personality as evil luminosity gains power: "on the stony face of the sufferer—for the character of his face, though still gentle and sweet, was changed—rested that dim, odd glow which seems to descend and produce, where it touches lights, sudden through faint, which are lost, almost without gradation, in darkness" (191). Perhaps most dehumanizing of all is the light's power to make man its servant. Like the ghoul specifically called "lamplighter" (230, 253), man brings the light that dooms others. Rose's uncle, lover, and minister bear the candles that define the scene of her disappearance; the door slams shut and locks Rose away from her uncle as he goes to the anteroom to get yet another candle. Likewise, Jennings' devoted servant errs when he discovers Jennings sitting alone in the dark (for all lights were the same to him) by insisting on lighting the candles. Earlier, Hesselius also "made him have candles lighted" (201). Although Le Fanu's light-bearers may resemble the participants in certain death rites, such as the old Catholic sacrament of Extreme Unction, their light does not usher in the grace of God but fiends of unearthly horror. Indeed, through their ignorance they ignite the candle's wick.

The characters who fall victim to supernatural terror live in a society that often "makes light of" life. A false "gaiety" pervades the world of Captain Barton, whose fiancée, Miss Montague, especially exists in "gay society" (210). In "Carmilla," Laura's father repeatedly reacts to supernatural suggestions with laughter. Laura's governess is even said to have "made light of" the child's nightmare (277). Of all the characters in "Carmilla," only the vampire herself is overtly identified as not a lightbearer, for she "refused [Laura] . . . the least ray of light" (291). But those beings in whom man places his greatest trust and from whom he seeks the most security ultimately spread the light in the shadow box.

Although "through" in the biblical "through a glass darkly" (1 Cor. 13:12) suggests that one day man will pass beyond the shadows of the temporal world and into Christian light, Le Fanu offers his reader and characters no such encouragement. For Le Fanu, man is permanently caught *in* a Schalken shadow box sustained by continually flickering candlelight. Only with death can man escape light and dark, can the shadow box collapse, can the "house fall."[15]

---

15. According to Nelson Browne, Le Fanu often experienced a nightmare in which a structure like the house of Roderick Usher threatens to collapse: "In this vision he beheld one of those ill-omened houses he had often described in his romances—a mansion so ruinous and tottering that it looked as if it might at any moment fall upon and bury the dreamer, helpless with terror." See *Sheridan Le Fanu* (London, 1951), 30–31. [S. M. Ellis was the originator of this anecdote in print, cf. his entry in this volume.—Ed.]

Le Fanu's House by the Marketplace

Wayne Hall

Isaac Butt, one of the original founders of the *Dublin University Magazine* (DUM) and its editor from 1834 to 1838, took note during his term of the wide range of favorable reviews lavished on the DUM not only from the "leading Protestant journals of Ireland," such as the *Evening Mail,* but even from the "radical" and politically hostile *Freeman's Journal.* Such praise, Butt remarked, "could almost revive the dream that once filled our minds in our younger and more enthusiastic days—a dream that all party distinctions might one day be obliterated, and all Irishmen unite together in the bonds of fraternity and peace."[1] The dream was never realized, not even within the limited range of the DUM's own stable. By 1842 William Carleton, one of the earliest and perhaps the best of all the DUM's contributors, had defected to a new and vehemently nationalist paper, the *Nation,* from whose pages he issued a lengthy and stinging attack on the DUM's current editor, Charles Lever. Lever's work, Carleton charged, "offers disgusting and debasing caricatures of Irish life and feeling," all because this "buffoon" wishes so slavishly to impress his British readership.[2] The next month, Carleton expanded his attack to include Lever's magazine: since the DUM "came, unluckily, into his hands, it has, month after month, degenerated into such indescribable dullness, that it is, even with the best intentions, impossible to read it."[3] Following Lever's departure as editor, Carleton rejoined the DUM in 1846 with his serialized novel *The Black Prophet: A Tale of the Famine,* which drew its subtitle from nineteenth century Ireland's most shattering experience. Butt's dream of Irishmen united in fraternity and peace belonged, indeed, only to the past.

Carleton's attack on Lever provides only the most dramatic example of a

---

1. *Dublin University Magazine* 6 (December 1835): 711. All further citations are given parenthetically in the text by volume, date, and page number.

2. *Nation* (23 September 1843), cited in David O'Donoghue, *The Life of William Carleton: Being His Autobiography and Letters: and an Account of His Life and Writings, from the Point at Which the Autobiography Breaks Off,* 2 vols. (London: Downey, 1896), 2.60.

3. *Nation* (7 October 1843), cited in O'Donoghue, 2.61.

fundamental problem facing the *DUM* through the whole of its 45-year career: without some degree of cohesiveness and unity among the Irish writers, what chance did they have of realizing one of the *DUM*'s central aims from the start, the creation of a truly national Irish literature? When Joseph Sheridan Le Fanu purchased the magazine in 1861, the goal seemed as elusive as ever. During his tenure as editor from 1861 to 1869, Le Fanu serialized his own novels in the journal at the rate of one per year. Meanwhile, *Laurence Bloomfield in Ireland*, a long poem by William Allingham, was appearing in *Fraser's*, and several novels by Lever ran in *Blackwood's* and the *Cornhill Magazine*. Samuel Ferguson first published a poetic work, *Lays of the Western Gael*, with a London press. And Carleton, while he did issue his novel *Redmond Count O'Hanlon* with an Irish publisher, once again felt alienated from the *DUM* and, like the others mentioned here, had nothing to contribute to Le Fanu's magazine. The effect is one of bright, scattered fragments, many of them drawn to the same London market that Lever had courted. Limited publishing opportunities and a small reading public in Ireland left few Anglo-Irish writers immune from the lure of British commercial success in the nineteenth century. The literary conflicts over readership and culture that undercut the *DUM*'s hopes for unity continue to stand out sharply during that time when Le Fanu served as its last significant editor. His two best novels, *The House by the Church-yard* and *Uncle Silas*, exemplify the central dilemma that Le Fanu shared with his fellow writers: how to create a literature that was uniquely Irish while remaining attractive and marketable to its most likely audience, the English reader.

The House by the Church-yard: A Souvenir of Chapelizod was Le Fanu's first work as the new owner and editor of the *DUM*. The opening installment, in October, 1861, sets the scene of the novel, Chapelizod in 1767, at that time "about the gayest and prettiest of the outpost villages in which old Dublin took a complacent pride" (58, Oct. 1861: 387). The broad sweep of characters includes military and professional men, their wives, daughters, and lady friends, servants, minor blackguards, a Roman Catholic priest and a Protestant rector, and the new and mysterious young gentleman Mr. Mervyn—all of them quickly entwined in a plot that seems thoroughly shapeless when measured by the narrative conventions of the usual nineteenth century novel. The features of Le Fanu's tale, all of which lay claim to his interests, resist any hierarchical ordering and, thus, create a fictional technique that later drew Joyce's attention to this work. *Ulysses*, too, regards all details as worthy of attention and significance, and *Finnegans Wake* specifically acknowledges *The House by the Church-yard*, the most congenially Irish Le Fanu novel to appear in the *DUM*.

Within the intricacies of the novel's plot, the chatty gaiety and light-hearted courtships conceal several darker currents, the main one carrying us ever closer to the true identity of Charles Archer, the suave and polished land agent who lives under the name of Paul Dangerfield. To such neighbors as General Chattesworth, Dangerfield seems "the most principled man I think I ever met" (59, Feb. 1862: 137). To himself, Dangerfield can never escape his earlier identity as the murderer Charles Archer, and at times he even doubts the very nature of that identity: "Charles Archer living—Charles Archer dead—or, as I sometimes think, neither one nor t'other quite—half man, half corpse—a vampire—there is no rest for thee: no Sabbath in the days of thy work. Blood—blood—blood—'tis tiresome. Why should I be a slave to these d——d secrets" (60, Sept. 1862: 293). Dangerfield's villainy finally comes to light when his latest victim, Dr. Sturk, regains consciousness after a macabre trepanning. Yet, the framework of the novel suggests that nothing, after all, has been gained within a society that continues on its path to the grave whether evil is exposed or not. The narrator, Charles de Cresseron, is inspired to tell his story by the discovery of Sturk's battered skull after it has moldered in the coffin for half a century. Over and over, de Cresseron steps aside from his tale to remind us of the mortality of his characters: "Poor Nan! with thy fun and thy rascalities, thy strong affections and thy fatal gift of beauty, where does thy head rest now?" (58, Oct. 1861: 402).

The setting of the novel arises out of Le Fanu's nostalgia for the first dozen years of his own life, when his father served as Anglican chaplain for the Royal Hibernian Military School in Dublin. For Le Fanu's family, however, the security of this time, centering around the quaintness of Chapelizod and the bright pageantry of viceregal affairs, gave way in 1826 to a new parish assignment in Abington, on the borders of Limerick and Tipperary. In this remote rural village, faced with the relative apathy of the few Church of Ireland parishioners and the inexorable movement towards Catholic emancipation, the Le Fanus found life physically isolated and uncertain at best, violent and potentially apocalyptic at worst times. In *The House by the Church-yard*, the splendid details of an old time and place have suffered a similar transformation " . . . the earth, or rather that grim giant factory, which is now the grand feature and centre of Chapelizod, throbbing all over with steam, and whizzing with wheels, and vomiting pitchy smoke, has swallowed them up" (58, Oct. 1861: 388). Within the sinister terms of his vision of hell, the factory that swallows the past becomes merely one means by which the earth will devour the whole of humanity. "Oh, fair youth!" laments de Cresseron: "The parting from thee was a sadness and a violence—sadder, I think, than death itself . . . our march is towards the darkness" (60, July 1862: 49).

This general and recurring mood of darkness serves as backdrop to more mysteries than just Paul Dangerfield's awful past. Mr. Mervyn, who lives in a house once supposedly haunted, unnerves nearly everyone; the rector's daughter feels "uncertain whether he's a man or a ghost" (59, Jan. 1862: 22). Worried mostly about how to conceal his present financial crisis, the ill-fated Dr. Sturk also hides his suspicion that he once knew Dangerfield under a different name. Several other characters also feel burdened by secrets they reveal only late in the novel, and still others, like Charles Archer, are wrongly presumed dead on occasion. Such identity confusions are carried even farther in Le Fanu's next novel, *Wylder's Hand*. One major character there, whom we meet early one, soon disappears and is thought to be dead, then alive when he is apparently seen by three other characters, then once more dead when a body that resembles him is found, then alive again when the three "sightings" are announced. Finally, as even a court rules in the case, we learn that he has in fact been dead since quite early in the novel.

The House by the Church-yard appeared in the *DUM* from October 1861 to February 1863. Following the serialization of *Wylder's Hand* from June 1863 to February 1864, *Uncle Silas* began its run in July 1864, under the title "Maud Ruthyn and Uncle Silas" for two installments, and finished, from October to December 1864 as "Uncle Silas and Maud Ruthyn." This final switch, moving the emphasis increasingly from Maud to Silas, represented Le Fanu's attempt to transform his title gracefully into the one that his London publisher Richard Bentley suggested, and got, for the three-decker edition in 1864: *Uncle Silas: A Tale of Bartram-Haugh*.

Even while writing so prolifically during this period, Le Fanu still managed to sustain a high level of quality through these three novels, in part by reworking some old material. *Uncle Silas*, set in Derbyshire, had its origins in his *DUM* short story for November 1838 called "Passage in the Secret History of an Irish Countess." Elizabeth Bowen, following this bibliographic lead, has stressed the essential Irishness of the novel, *Uncle Silas* having "always struck me as being an Irish story transposed to an English setting."[4] In focusing on the Anglo-Irish nature of Le Fanu's whole career, W. J. Mc Cormack builds on Bowen's persuasive insight in his own reading of the novels, emphasizing the continuities within Le Fanu's writing during this period.[5]

---

4. Elizabeth Bowen, "Introduction," in J. S. Le Fanu, *Uncle Silas* (London: Cresset, 1947), 8.

5. W. J. Mc Cormack, *Sheridan Le Fanu and Victorian Ireland* (Oxford: Clarendon Press, 1980). Mc Cormack's excellent study is the best available on Le Fanu's life and writings.

The similarities between *The House by the Church-yard* and *Uncle Silas* prove crucial. Like the earlier work, *Uncle Silas* develops a central plot whose mysteries begin with whispered scandal and anxious premonitions and then develop to the final revelations of bigamy, murder, and suicide—all spurred on by Le Fanu's ever-present theme of financial crisis. Silas Ruthyn himself resembles Archer-Dangerfield in the ghastly whiteness of his appearance. Vampire-like, the natures and identities of both men become ambiguous "hoverings between life and death—between intellect and insanity—a dubious, marsh-fire existence, horrible to look on" (64, Oct. 1864: 426). Faced with such horrors, the characters in both novels can take nothing for granted, not even their own sanity: "Am I mad?" Maud Ruthyn asks herself. "Is this all a dream, or is it real?" (64, Dec. 1864: 672).

These questions are slippery. At one level, they reinforce Maud's credibility for us as the narrator for *Uncle Silas:* if she is able to ask such things, she cannot be mad. At another level, we feel superior to her: while she may wonder whether her terror is a dream, we know it is real, even though we have not yet learned its full nature. What we fail even to suspect is that Maud has in fact lured us inside her "real" experience with the same artifice that her creator has used throughout this whole work of fiction: with the hindsight that we lack, she narrates these events years after they have taken place, revealing this maturity only in the closing pages. In his frequent interpolations about the veracity of the "documents" he used to construct *The House by the Church-yard*, de Cresseron had done an even subtler job of obscuring the difference between fact and fantasy. Faced with these further layers of narrative deception that Maud Ruthyn or Charles de Cresseron add to their respective tales, the reader ends up more disoriented about the nature of reality than do the actual characters.

Harmony is restored by the end of both works, yet the victory seems hollow and uncertain. De Cresseron obliges with a description of a wedding party, but he also reminds his readers that the joyous, pleasant faces there "won't smile or blush any more" (61, Feb. 1863: 167). Maud's own marriage, "happy in the affection of a beloved and noble-hearted husband," has not shielded her from sorrow when her first children die in infancy (64, Dec. 1864: 679). "Maud is, by nature, a bride of Death," Elizabeth Bowen observes.[6] When she first comes to Bartram-Haugh and befriends Silas's exuberant daughter Milly, Maud feels a new and delighted sense of freedom and companionship. Yet, her experiences there ultimately leave her little of the world beyond her sense of its treachery.

As Bowen and Mc Cormack both argue, essential features from Le

---

6. Bowen, *Uncle Silas*, 9.

Fanu's whole Anglo-Irish experience work to shape the world view that dominates these two novels. With the British connection proving increasingly faithless, the Protestant Ascendancy throughout the nineteenth century saw its isolated, helpless culture crumbling away through relentless processes very like those that threaten Maud or Chapelizod.

One way to measure and explain the continuity between these two novels is to take account of Le Fanu's specifically Irish experience as related to the *Dublin University Magazine*. Although not among the original founders, he began his associations with the *DUM* early in its life, publishing his first short story in January 1838 under Isaac Butt's editorship. He had entered Trinity College in the autumn of 1832, still more concerned with personal and family difficulties than with public responses to those problems. In his father's Abington parish, however, Le Fanu's personal experiences had prepared him well for the guiding philosophy of the *DUM* and, by the end of the decade, his publishing career was well under way. His first short story in the magazine soon led to others, twelve in all, later collected as *The Purcell Papers*. Largely narrated by a rural parish priest, the stories convey Le Fanu's anxieties about the fate of the Big Houses, the lost causes and heroic defeats, the decay of the social landscape, and the inability of spiritually shaken characters to reunite the fragments of their society.

One response to this anxiety was Le Fanu's association in 1847 with Young Ireland and the *Nation*—a brief association, because he soon recoiled in horror from a political involvement he came to fear as treasonous. By early 1848, the militant rhetoric of the *Nation* threatened to develop an armed rebellion, and England responded by arresting several Young Ireland leaders. Le Fanu hailed the conviction of one of these men, John Mitchel, in a July 1848 article in the *DUM*. In July, Le Fanu warned against the seditious impulses of Irish Catholicism, "a dark and sinister theology" (32, July 1848: 118). Glancing back at this period, the *DUM* in 1862 continued to "despise the cock-a-doodle-doo of Meagher, Mitchel, and the other stage rebels" (59, Feb. 1862: 251).

Le Fanu had purchased the *DUM* in July 1861 and soon after began serializing *The House by the Church-yard*. During his editorship, until he sold the magazine in 1869, eight other novels followed: *Wylder's Hand, Uncle Silas, Guy Deverell, All in the Dark, The Tenants of Malory, Haunted Lives, Loved and Lost,* and *The Wyvern Mystery*. The sheer volume of this list is significant. As the financial demands on his journal kept dictating one novel after the next during this decade, Le Fanu's writing became progressively weaker, the plots looser, the characters thinner—and even the language finally lapsed into cliché. In the latter half of *The Wyvern Mystery*, for instance, the last of the

DUM group, the characters repeatedly fall back on one folk saying after an-other, becoming almost self-conscious parodies of human conversation.

The progression of these novels downward into careless apathy parallels the *DUM's* political commentary through the 1860s. In October 1861, the journal held a "cheery view of Ireland's prospects" (58, Oct. 1861: 512), and the tone remains optimistic through the middle of the decade. Seeking to clarify "The Irish Question in 1865," the *DUM* described the problems as gradually taking care of themselves: " . . . if existing evils are being thus naturally redressed, Ireland needs no panacea in the shape of Tenant-right, a new Education scheme, or the abolition of the Established Church. . . . What she really wants is to be let alone" (65, April 1865: 368). In December 1865, a few months after widespread arrests of most of the Fenian leaders who had renewed the threat of discontent in Ireland, the *DUM* claimed that "there is not sufficient internal discontent in Ireland to afford materials for a rebellion above the Cabbage-garden character" (66, Dec. 1865: 716), thus scornfully alluding to one of the 1848 skirmishes. And just as his political nerves had been stimulated to invective in 1848, Le Fanu again emerged from his customary silence on such matters in a series of articles which se-verely strained *DUM's* optimism.

The first of these articles, a November 1865 obituary for Lord Palm-erston, feared the political vacuum that this death might create: "An awful feeling of uncertainty for the future mingles with the national sorrow" (66, Nov. 1865: 599). In February 1866, Le Fanu warned against the extremist forces that, in his view, Palmerston has previously kept in check. By July, events seemed once more to have stabilized, and Le Fanu hoped that "the improvement of Ireland has been proceeding with the steady and cumulative action of an established law, while the disturbing influence which has thrown us back during the last ten months is simply one of those occasional checks to which all national processes are in one form or another liable" (68, July 1866: 116). The language here, however, sounds like the press release of a nervous public official, and its vague generalities and cautious qualifiers ring hollow. When Le Fanu turns, in the same article, to look more closely at that "disturbing influence," Fenianism, the tone changes markedly: "This conspiracy was as cunning and ferocious as any ever yet projected in Ireland. In the elaboration of its mystery and the energy of its internal terrorism it is unmatched" (68, July 1866: 117).

The *DUM* attributed the birth of Fenianism to the funeral for Terence Bellew MacManus in 1861, only months after Le Fanu had assumed editorial control. The huge Dublin procession in honor of the dead Young Irelander clearly showed the physical-force movement to be alive and well. By 1864,

James Stephens, as head organizer, had thousands of unarmed troops at his command in Dublin and Cork. In that same year, Archbishop Cullen tempered his opposition to Fenianism by forming a new Catholic political group, the National Association of Ireland. In announcing the association, Cullen listed the perennial Irish problems: a declining population, widespread poverty, a weak economy. Unlike the *DUM*, he sought more active redress, and one of his solutions involved disestablishing the Church of Ireland. In March 1867, the long-awaited Fenian rising finally took place, but disorganized, mismanaged, and still largely unarmed, it was easily put down. The pattern of events was clear, however, and the *DUM* was unable or unwilling to read it. In the month before the rising, the journal had suggested that the "difficulty" of administering Ireland "may, indeed, be fictitious, as created by the perverseness merely of a distracted population" (69, Feb. 1867: 231).

On the parliamentary front, Gladstone's Liberals came to power in 1868 on promises of change, and he quickly introduced a bill for disestablishment of the Church of Ireland. In 1869, when the bill passed into law, Irish nationalist forces also gained a new leader, the lawyer who had defended the accused Fenians: Isaac Butt, one of the original founders of the *DUM* and the editor who had first seen Le Fanu into print. The first Land Bill, forecasting the eventual break-up of the large landed estates in Ireland, was only a year away. But by that time the *DUM* had given up the fight. Having defended the status of the Church of Ireland ever since its inaugural issue, by October 1868 the journal was reduced to this: "No purpose sufficient to justify the effort would be served by entering, in these pages, into the rude conflict of argument going forward in every part of the country, on the question of the Irish Church" (72, Oct. 1868: 473). In its growing apathy over the course of Irish history, the *DUM* devoted less and less space to political commentary in the closing years of the decade. For 1869, the year of the long-dreaded disestablishment, only one political article can be found, titled "The Railway Problem in Ireland and Belgium" (73, Feb. 1869: 237).

In his personal response to disestablishment, Le Fanu no longer felt sufficiently involved in public events to bother with expressions of despair. Failing health had troubled him throughout the 1860s. In addition, his wife had died in 1858, and thereafter he kept largely to himself, except to see a few close relatives and friends. One such friend was the Roman Catholic book dealer Patrick Kennedy, on whom Le Fanu relied heavily for contributions. Through his interest in Celtic folklore, Kennedy sustained the *DUM*'s link to Irish issues, even after politics and religion had faded out. Once Le Fanu had stepped down as editor, the *DUM* would renew its abuse of Irish Catholicism, a "stagnant system of idolatrous worship" (75, June 1870: 638).

And for the Le Fanu of the 1840s, Catholicism and treason had similarly been synonymous terms. By 1868, however, he could privately support the selection of a "liberal Roman Catholic" as Irish Lord Chancellor under Gladstone's new administration.[7]

Paralleling his varied responses to Young Ireland in the 1840s, Le Fanu's sympathies here follow a pattern of wavering ambiguity. Not surprisingly, then, religion shares the status of every other value in his novels of the 1860s: it fails to offer his characters any kind of certainty or comfort. Attracted for a time to the religious philosophy of Emmanuel Swedenborg, Le Fanu attributed the same interest to three of *Uncle Silas*'s main characters, all of them drawn from the ranks of the ineffectual males. For Maud, Swedenborgianism makes little difference. She refers at the close of her story to a "voice from heaven" that directs her, "Write, from henceforth blessed are the dead that die in the Lord!" (64, Dec. 1864: 679). But the divine guidance, in its morbid and peculiar redundancy, fails to dispel her final mood of sorrow.

Religion thus becomes one more of many novelistic elements for Le Fanu that, in their totality, project a view that society is fundamentally, radically, and irrevocably treacherous, whether at Chapelizod or Bartram-Haugh, in Ireland or England. The continuity of that vision, as Mc Cormack argues, grows out of Le Fanu's specifically Irish experience as a member and representative of a threatened Anglo-Irish Ascendancy. Such a reading, however, minimizes the crucial changes in Le Fanu's writing following *The House by the Churchyard*. While all of his novels to appear in the *DUM* project the same vision of the world as grimly devouring, only *The House by the Church-yard*, in its choice of setting and characters, speaks directly to the Anglo-Irish Protestants that the *DUM* once claimed as its main readership. "Ireland and Irish topics have commanded the first place in our favour . . .," the journal announced in 1841; its "principal basis of support" was to be "an Irish circulation" (17, April 1841: 531 and 528). Yet sales in England and Scotland also counted heavily, especially for a novelist anxious to build up a wide and responsive public. As Le Fanu learned with *The House by the Church-yard*, such a public did not exist in Ireland. His experience with that novel quickly led him to rely much more on the sensationalist formulas that enjoyed such great success in British novels of the 1860s. To account for this sharp change of direction, we need to look beyond Ireland towards the seductive maze of the London market.

Le Fanu had arranged to publish *The House by the Church-yard* as a three-decker and at his own expense, but managed to distribute only a small

---

7. Le Fanu to Lord Dufferin, 7 Dec. 1868 (Public Records Office of Northern Ireland, Belfast: the Dufferin and Ava Papers), cited in Mc Cormack, 217.

number of copies. William Tinsley's London house then picked up the work, whereupon it came to the attention of another London publisher, Richard Bentley. In contracting for a successor from Le Fanu, Bentley specified a three-volume "story of an English subject and in modern times."[8] Le Fanu responded with *Wylder's Hand*, and events of the next two years seemed to bear out Bentley's sense of the British market. *The House by the Church-yard* having failed to gain any attention or sales, Le Fanu finally resigned himself in May 1865 to whatever price he could obtain for the remaindered sheets of his own ill-fated venture into publishing. By contrast, *Wylder's Hand* had by this time been reviewed as a significant improvement over *The House by the Church-yard*, and *Uncle Silas* as better than either of the two earlier works. While he fretted over the poor sales of *Wylder's Hand*, Le Fanu did acquire an increasingly lucrative series of contracts from his publisher to bolster his hopes that the Bentley formula would eventually lead to major success.[9]

Wylder's Hand had fulfilled Bentley's specifications while still retaining de Cresseron as narrator. In Maud Ruthyn, however, who is both main character and intended victim in *Uncle Silas*, Le Fanu found the type of narrator that Bentley's British readers were more responsive to. The shift in the sex of the narrators also signals a deeper shift in the gender alignment of the novels. Whereas *The House by the Church-yard* is dominated by male characters, *Uncle Silas*, like *Wylder's Hand* and every other Le Fanu novel of this decade, places much more emphasis on women. They have become more active participants now and, as in *Uncle Silas*, frequently control events in ways that the men cannot. Despite his formidable atmosphere of mystery and evil, Uncle Silas lacks the ongoing vitality of Archer-Dangerfield and often remains secluded off-stage, more threatening as passive and potential villainy than as an active force. His son and partner in crime, Dudley Ruthyn, is but a crude and insensitive bungler, albeit a nasty one. In the most horrifying case of mistaken identity from these novels, Dudley finally murders his own accomplice, the wicked but unsuspecting Madame de la Rougierre, as she lies sleeping in Maud's bed.

---

8. Richard Bentley to J. S. Le Fanu, 26 February 1863 (British Museum, Add. MSS. 46,642), in Walter Edens, "Joseph Sheridan Le Fanu: A Minor Victorian and His Publisher," unpublished Ph.D. thesis, University of Illinois, 1963, 164. Appendix A of Edens contains transcripts of 115 letters from the Le Fanu correspondence, most of them in the holdings of the University of Illinois library, with several others held by the British Museum.

9. Edens, 245–47, provides transcripts of British Museum copies of the Bentley contracts for *Wylder's Hand* for £200 (31 March 1863), *Uncle Silas* for £250 (7 July 1864), and *Guy Deverell* for £300 (14 Feb. 1865).

Madame herself has succeeded more consistently at intimidating Maud, largely because of her coarse sexuality. The other women, too, like Monica Knollys, Milly Ruthyn, Meg Hawkes, or Mary Quince,[10] join Maud in defining the novel's main center of energy as a female one.

Further, unlike *The House by the Church-yard*, *Uncle Silas* is much more an interior, "written" novel. De Cresseron ranges widely throughout Chapelizod and its environs and gives his story the feel of a spoken tale. He begins this way: "We are going to talk, if you please, in the ensuing chapters, of what was going on in Chapelizod about a hundred years ago" (58, Oct. 1861: 387). Maud never thinks of casually asking for the indulgence of her reader. She seeks, instead, the kind of cathartic symmetry that will allow her to make sense of her terrifying experiences, and thus brings to her tale a highly confined structure, both geographically and formally. Whereas de Cresseron, in his exterior role, eschews symmetry for seeming shapelessness, Maud holds fast to her central point within the events, places, and characters she describes, and the psychological effects of all these upon her interior consciousness give *Uncle Silas* its focus and power.

Le Fanu sought initially to place *Uncle Silas* in the *Cornhill Magazine*, whose circulation of over 80,000 readers would assure greater sales for the planned three-decker version. He mentioned these hopes to Bentley, adding: "At present the editing of the University Magazine without assistance . . . cuts up my time very much—but a success [with the *Cornhill*] would make it worthwhile to discontinue these taxes on my time."[11] When the *Cornhill* failed to oblige, *Uncle Silas* quickly began its run in the magazine that continued to tax its editor's time for the next five years. He finally sold the *DUM* in 1869 to the London printer Charles F. Adams for £1500, twice what he had paid for the magazine. But, despite this sizable return on his investment, his financial affairs during these years were constantly troubled. By 1868, debt forced him to place his Merrion Square house under heavy mortgage.

The *DUM* had failed, thus, to provide Le Fanu with the kind of medium that would establish a successful and lucrative career, something he himself had begun to recognize after only a few years as editor. And as a novelist, he saw the problem of readership further complicated by the limited Irish publishing industry itself, at mid-century largely dominated by three major figures: William Curry, James McGlashan, and James Duffy. Curry published

10. The name of Le Fanu's mother, Emma, perhaps suggested the initial letter that recurs so consistently here.

11. Le Fanu to Richard Bentley, 17 June 1864 (University of Illinois Library), in Edens, 172.

the *DUM* from 1833 to 1845, as well as Le Fanu's 1845 novel *The Cock and Anchor*. Because of increasing financial pressures that resulted in Curry's bankruptcy by early 1848, however, McGlashan became the *DUM's* publisher from 1846 to 1855, during this time issuing Le Fanu's historical novel *The Fortunes of Colonel Torlogh O'Brien*, as well as his collection *Ghost Stories and Tales of Mystery*. By 1855, though, McGlashan was showing disturbing signs of senility. James Duffy, the last of these three publishers, had weathered the financial pressures caused by the Great Famine. He did not attract Le Fanu as a publisher, however, because of the Catholic and Young Ireland material that formed the major part of his list. Moreover, by 1860 his career was largely given over to the disposal of old stock. There were, of course, other Irish houses, such as that of George Herbert. But, while Herbert sufficed to publish the *DUM* during Le Fanu's entire tenure as editor and to issue Le Fanu's anonymous political satire *The Prelude* in 1865, he lacked the stature and circulation of the others mentioned here. The alternative seemed clear; solid and respectable London houses like Tinsley or Bentley.

Bentley's influence over Le Fanu's work extended throughout much of the 1860s. Besides the 1863 letter asking for the "English subject and in modern times," Bentley had advised Le Fanu in 1867 about some changes on the manuscript for the novel *A Lost Name*. Le Fanu replied that he wished to revise and, "following your hint—to interpolate a few chapters of brighter material with some humorous & kindly characters who can be woven into the story."[12] The advice failed to render *A Lost Name* a success, however—its original edition selling fewer than 500 copies. Indeed, none of Le Fanu's work did much for the house of Bentley, or for its author. Despite a heavy advertising budget, *Uncle Silas*, Le Fanu's most successful novel, sold only 847 copies, and *Wylder's Hand* dropped to 700. Having paid Le Fanu £750 for these two works plus *Guy Deverell*, Bentley drew in a profit of but £125.[13]

One way out of this financial bog had been suggested as early as 1860, the year Wilkie Collins published *The Woman in White*, for the enormous impact of that novel helped the house of Bentley to define the formula for success. In 1863, the same year in which Richard Bentley was awaiting Le Fanu's modern English subjects, Bentley's son and co-manager George wrote in his diary: "In literature the success of . . . sensational literature as it is called is the most noticeable event. Wilkie Collins, the King of the Inventors, set the fashion of

---

12. Le Fanu to George Bentley, 20 Feb. 1867 (University of Illinois), in Edens, 225.

13. Royal A. Gettmann, *A Victorian Publisher: A Study of the Bentley Papers* (Cambridge: Cambridge University Press, 1960), 140, 123, and 83, cites ledgers from the Bentley Papers held in the British Museum.

these sensational stories. Their ingredients are bigamy & murder & sometimes theft."[14] Not everyone appreciated the fashion. The *DUM* had not liked *The Woman in White* (57, Feb. 1861: 338) and later sniffed that Collins was just a "poor imitation of Edgar Poe" (61, April 1863: 437). Le Fanu himself, in his "Postscript" to *Uncle Silas*, sought to distinguish his own work from that of the sensationalists, arguing instead for a place alongside Sir Walter Scott within "the legitimate school of tragic English romance" (64, Dec. 1864: 680).[15]

But Le Fanu had been more faithful to the Bentley formula than he could acknowledge. The "Postscript" is notable primarily for its misguided judgment of both Scott and *Uncle Silas*. Le Fanu later showed an even more faulty critical sense when he described *A Lost Name*, in an 1868 letter to Bentley, as "much the best thing I ever wrote."[16] Piling excuses upon accusations, this letter reveals Le Fanu's confusion over the nature of his own writing as but one part of a whole sense of futility and bewilderment; for the British reader, nothing that he tried seemed to work. He soon afterwards broke off dealings with Bentley, only to return a year later with an offer of "The Bird of Passage," the tale of a squire whose search for his beloved ends in bitter failure.

Le Fanu's disappointing sales and reviews fed his inherently pessimistic view of the world. In this regard, the sensationalism of his novels does separate him from Wilkie Collins, his British counterpart in the 1860s. Within the more optimistic world of *The Woman in White*, as in Collins's 1868 novel *The Moonstone*, reason, knowledge, and virtue triumph over suffering and loss. Apart from these general differences in world view, however, their work employs many of the same specific plot patterns of literary sensationalism. Winifred Hughes' 1980 study, *The Maniac in the Cellar*, isolates such recurring patterns, not only for *The Woman in White* as the "archetype of the sensation genre," but also for the work of Charles Reade and M. E. Braddon. While Le Fanu gets only brief mention for his ghost stories as "offshoots" of the sensation novelists, one of Hughes's observations on the British writers helps to account for the Bentley-inspired shift, between *The House by the Church-yard* and *Uncle Silas*, from a male- to a female-oriented work: "Whether heroine or villainess, it is always a woman who demands the spotlight in the typical sensa-

---

14. Diary entry for 31 Dec. 1863 in Vol. IV of *After Business*, an unpublished diary in 21 vols. From 1849 to 1895, cited in Edens, 98.

15. [Originally published as "A Postscript" to *Uncle Silas*, this note to the reader became "A Preliminary Word," assuming a more prominent placement at the front of the book, when the novel was published as a three-decker in 1864.—Ed.]

16. Le Fanu to George Bentley, 6 June 1868 (University of Illinois Library), in Edens, 234–35.

tion novel." Moreover, this heroine "has become enmeshed in a sordid tangle of crime, blackmail, and seduction; she has become a participant, however unwilling, as well as merely a victim."[17] The description here might well be of Maud Ruthyn, the intended victim rendered vulnerable because of her own desire to help dispel the scandalous rumors of Silas Ruthyn's past.

Hughes mentions further plot devices: bigamy, secrets, mistaken identity, forced marriages, crimes of passion, financial distress as a motive for villainy, recurring patterns to one's experience, the sheltering but unreliable mansion, like Knowl, contrasted with the sinister mansion, like Bartram-Haugh, and the return of those thought to be dead or safely removed from the scene, this last deception occasionally dependent on a staged trip to Australia. All of these, Australia included, are common features in *The House by the Church-yard, Wylder's Hand,* and *Uncle Silas.* Yet, the latter two works, written in deliberate accordance with Bentley's guidelines, carried Le Fanu far beyond his original inclinations toward sensationalism and into a full-scale treatment of the formula. *The House by the Church-yard* is an Irish novel with elements of sensationalism; *Uncle Silas* is a sensationalist novel with elements of Irishness. The overlap helps define the continuity between the two as well as their differences.

At the end of the 1860s, Le Fanu's work took another distinctive turn: towards a much greater emphasis on the short story. Having divested himself of the burdens of editing the *DUM,* he returned, with remarkable energy, to the literary form with which he had first begun his writing career over thirty years earlier. "Green Tea," appearing in 1869, charted significant new ground for the horror story. Then in 1871 Le Fanu published his best tale, "Carmilla," whose complex and alluring vampirism inspired Bram Stoker's 1897 novel *Dracula.* In their exploration of psychological horror, these later works established Le Fanu as one of the masters and originators of the modern ghost story. Clearly, then, *The House by the Church-yard* and *Uncle Silas* had not exhausted the resources of Le Fanu's genius. But, through all his subsequent writing up until his death in 1873, that genius found expression only in shorter works, and never again in his ill-fated attempts at other novels that he hoped would finally capture the British market. Had Le Fanu continued along the lines suggested by *The House by the Church-yard,* his reputation today might well place him within the first rank of modern Irish novelists.

Bentley's 1863 formula must, thus, take some of the blame for confusing the subsequent direction and purpose of Le Fanu's work during the 1860s.

---

17. Winifred Hughes, *The Maniac in the Cellar: Sensation Novels of the 1860s* (Princeton: Princeton University Press, 1980), 45, 44.

Seeking to tailor his novels to the market, Le Fanu turned to the British models that had proved so fruitful for writers like Collins. His deference to Bentley in adopting these models stands in sharp contrast to his earlier attitudes towards a readership. In its familiar references to Irish landscape, *The House by the Church-yard* had disdained compromise: "I don't apologise to my readers, English-born and bred, for assuming them to be acquainted with the chief features of the Phoenix Park . . . it is their own shame, not ours, if a nation of bold speculators and indefatigable tourists leave [Ireland] unexplored" (58, Dec. 1861: 648). Such magisterial confidence leads de Cresseron boldly through his tale, and at its end he calmly pulls on his night-cap and wishes "pleasant dreams" to his readers (61, Feb. 1863: 167). *Uncle Silas*, just two years later, has murdered sleep, and not just for the hapless Madame de la Rougierre. Even though Le Fanu's compliance with Bentley's 1863 directive had led to the symbolic power and structural control of this novel, it also contributed to the rapid decline of his subsequent fiction into aesthetic chaos and carelessness.

A further explanation for that decline lies in Le Fanu's only partial understanding of the British audience that a writer like Collins knew so much more directly and intimately. Collins would exploit that sense of rapport even further through serial publication, thus establishing a guiding sense of familiarity and community between author and reader. Even while producing his own novels in serial form, however, Le Fanu failed to realize these benefits. The *DUM*'s British readers were too distant, while its Irish readers shared with Le Fanu the uncertain identity of the Anglo-Irish culture. From neither group could he gain any sense of responsive familiarity. As editor of the *DUM*, Le Fanu felt himself in the role of spokesman for the Protestant Ascendancy. Yet, the responsibilities of that role drained off a good deal of his time and energy while failing to relieve him of the market demands that drained still more and gave little in return.

Le Fanu represented a class that found itself on the uncertain margins of Irish society. Even while the Ascendancy insisted on its Irish identity, Catholic Ireland continued to associate it with the British cause and culture, thus further diminishing any hope of unity among Ireland's literary voices, any hope of being able to create a genuinely national literature. In 1863 the narrator of *Wylder's Hand* says: "I behold in myself an abyss, I gaze down and listen, and discover neither light nor harmony, but thunderings and lightnings, and voices and laughter, and a medley that dismays me. . . . How helpless and appalled we shut our eyes over that awful chasm" (62, Oct 1863: 393). Similarly appalling to Le Fanu must have been the growing recognition that the sensationalist road to London might never provide a way back from the disappointments and uncertainties of his own personal abyss.

Sheridan Le Fanu and the Spirit of 1798

Albert Power

For many the overall impression of Joseph Sheridan Le Fanu, as a citizen of his country and of his time, is a representative of the Anglo-Irish Protestant middle class, in consequence committed to the status quo of the union between Great Britain and all Ireland. To these it will come as something of a surprise to learn that Le Fanu had a strong streak of nationalism in his blood, derived partly from heredity and partly, one must suppose, from conviction. Nowhere is this green streak more vividly displayed than in his treatment of a typical, if fictional, incident from the rebellion of 1798, concerning the exploits, trial, and ultimate escape of a caught rebel from the hangman's rope, in his verse narrative, "Shamus O'Brien."

The long, hot summer of 1798 was witness to Ireland's most brutal and intense immersal in country-wide bloodshed.

Throughout the middle months of that conflict-fraught year, bloody battle raged across several counties in Ireland. First, within the radius of a hundred miles from Dublin, in Kildare, Wicklow, Meath, Carlow and (most memorably) Wexford; then in far-off northerly Antrim and Down, and later still in Mayo in the extreme west, the banner of revolt was raised: a myriad pikes clashed with musket and cannon in an orgy of civil warfare that the emerald isle, though no stranger in recent times to conflict, has never witnessed since. In the carnage which ensued official estimates as to the death toll can be only an approximate guide. Even so, the figure accepted by many of 30,000 perishing in the embattled months between June and September gives a dim glimpse of the horror that must have prevailed during that awful time; while some scholars believe that the number of those killed, especially in the tumult of reprisal following final defeat of the rebels and prior to the granting of government amnesty, far exceeded even that frightening estimate. By contrast, the death toll in the Northern Ireland "troubles," which endured from 1969 to 1994 (with sporadic horrific later outbursts, especially the Omagh atrocity of 1998), was in the order of 3,500.

In the traditional teaching of Irish history, the events of 1798 tended to be held out as a glorious, if futile, national rebellion against the oppression of

British imperialism, which foundered on the tardiness of French help, and culminated in the tyrannical Act of Union, masterminded by the machinations of such ill-meant opponents of independence as Marquess Cornwallis, lord lieutenant of Ireland; Lord Castlereagh, chief secretary; and prime minister William Pitt. A more measured reading of the course of history demonstrates that this rush-of-blood assessment unfairly impugns the integrity of those English politicians who had sought to bring a quick end to the killing and restore lasting stability in Ireland. The fact that William Pitt was an early advocate of Catholic emancipation, his efforts thwarted by the opposition of King George III who dutifully believed that Catholic emancipation (in effect a cession of the voting franchise to all Roman Catholics and a lifting of the extant restrictions on their civil liberties), would be a violation by him of his coronation oath, is even still not widely recognized.

Nowadays, there is more general acceptance of the reality of the complex origins of the 1798 rebellion: its principal wellspring being seen as a surge of intellectual middle-class support for the sanguinary principles of the French Revolution, twinned to a contemporaneous island-wide eruption of the agrarian secret societies which had been prolific throughout Ireland at critical periods during the eighteenth century. Nowadays also, with solemn shame recognition has dawned of the sheer scale of the brutality practised as much by the United Irish rebels as by the forces of the Crown. Indeed, much in the appalling tapestry of mayhem and death woven during those dreadful summer months of 1798 would have struck a chord with the authors of the Gothic novel, at that time in its prime: the piking of the loyalists on Wexford bridge, their mangled corpses hurled dispassionately to the river below; the burning of the two hundred trapped in the barn at Scullabogue; the floggings and pitch-cappings which preceded and partly spurred the revolt; the eerie operation of spies and informers which aborted the planned uprising in Dublin; the fervor of Lord Edward Fitzgerald, scion of the noblest family in Ireland (his father was the first Duke of Leinster, whose city residence, Leinster House, is now the seat of the Irish parliament, or Oireachtas), turning his back on the privilege to which he had been born, masterminding the rebellion, then dying alone in his prison cell from pistol-shot wounds to the shoulder; the idealistic folly of Theobold Wolfe Tone, sailing with a belated French fleet into Donegal's Lough Swilly, after all the fighting was done, in the full knowledge that he would be tried and go to his death.

By 1814, when Joseph Sheridan Le Fanu was born into the family of a Church of Ireland minster in Phoenix Park, Dublin, the events of 1798 were a grim receding memory. As a member of the Anglo-Irish Protestant middle class, it would not be expected that Le Fanu would have any sentimental sympathy for the protagonists of 1798. It is therefore not surprising that his two early historical novels, *The Cock and Anchor* and *The Fortunes of Colonel Torlogh O'Brien,* are set in an epoch significantly more remote than the end of the previous century. *The Cock and Anchor* delimns the Dublin of 1709, in the turbulent aftermath of the Jacobite War of 1689–1691, during the Whig-dominated years of the vice-regency of Lord Wharton; while *Torlogh O'Brien,* shot through with many passages of melodrama and violence (not least a truly grotesque rendering of the torture of the strappado in chapter 44), depicts the Jacobite War itself. One senses that, for readers in the 1840s, when these novels were written, the immediacy of the horror of the struggle on Irish soil between James II and William III was blunted by the more recent remembrance of 1798. Prior to 1798 Ireland had enjoyed over a century of peace and moderate prosperity, despite various trade restrictions imposed by the British government and blithely acquiesced in by the underling Irish legislature. The events of 1798 shattered all that, lending to earlier times of war-spawned atrocity a welcome remoteness which enabled their worst excesses to be sampled in fiction without a shudder. To the same period, the 1840s, belong the stories that make up *The Purcell Papers*—the fictional reminiscences of Fr. Francis Purcell, regarding events mostly ghostly, which involved the old Catholic aristocracy in the years before 1690. In these stories, there is no suggestion that their author hankers for a restoration of the past times he describes or exhibits any tender regret for the fact of their passing. Rather is the time-setting itself in the nature of a *mise-en-scène* for supernatural and mysterious happenings, imparting a heightened authenticity to the narrative through the contrivance of an old document of contemporaneous recollection recently found.

Accordingly, it strikes one at first as odd to discover that, in or around 1840, Le Fanu wrote a rousing ballad about the capture, trial and daring escape from the gallows of a fictionalized doughty pikeman of '98. This is the verse narrative "Shamus O'Brien." With its racy, rambling, often awkward binary rhyming, peppered with grimace-churning colloquialism and folksy mispronunciation, this ballad is alien to anything for which Le Fanu is remembered today.

Its opening is the epitome of the almost risibly stage-Irish.

> Just after the war, in the year ninety-eight,
> As soon as the boys were all scattered and bate,
> 'Twas the custom, whenever a peasant was caught,
> To hang him by trial, barring such as was shot.

Apart from a scene of touching poignancy in which the hero's mother intercedes with the trial judge for his life, "Shamus O'Brien" is a paradigm of popular bavardage and derring-do. The extract that follows was calculated surely to bring a lump to the throat and stir the pulses in sympathy for the troubles of "old Ireland."

> Then Shamus's mother, in the crowd standing by,
> Called out to the judge with a pitiful cry:
> "Oh, judge darlin', don't!—oh, don't say the word!
> The crathur is young; have mercy, my lord!
> He was foolish, he didn't know what he was doin';
> You don't know him, my lord—oh, don't give him to ruin!
> He's the kindliest crathur, the tenderest hearted,
> Don't part us for ever, we that's so long parted!
> Judge, mavourneen, forgive him! forgive him, my lord!
> And God will forgive you. Oh, don't say the word?"
>
> That was the first minute that O'Brien was shaken,
> When he saw that he wasn't quite forgot or forsaken;
> And down his pale cheeks, at the words of his mother,
> The big tears were runnin' fast, one after th' other;
> And he tried hard to hide them or wipe them away,
> But in vain, for his hands were too fast bound that day.
> And two or three times he endeavoured to spake,
> But the strong, manly voice used to falter and break;
> Till at last, by the strength of his high-mounting pride,
> He conquered and mastered his grief's swelling tide.
> And says he, "Mother darlin', don't break your poor heart,
> For sooner or later the dearest must part.
> And God knows it's better than wandering in fear
> On the bleak, trackless mountain among the wild deer,
> To lie in the grave, where the head, hand, and breast
> From thought, labour, and sorrow for ever shall rest.
> Then, mother, my darlin', don't cry any more,
> Don't make me seem broken in this my last hour;
> For I wish, when my head is lyin' under the raven,
> No true man can say that I died like a craven!"
> Then towards the judge Shamus bowed down his head,
> And that minute the solemn death sentence was said.

In order to seek some understanding of what it was that prompted Le Fanu to compose such a work as "Shamus O'Brien," one must look to his family history and its connection with certain of the personalities in the rebellion of 1798.

The most significant link is that between Lucretia Dobbin, Joseph Sheridan Le Fanu's mother, and the capture of Lord Edward Fitzgerald on 19th May

1798. This took place only four days before the date set for the start of the rebellion, and was one of the principal causes of its disastrous collapse in Ireland's capital city. On 12th March that year most of the Leinster Directory of United Irishmen had been arrested in a government swoop, following a tip-off by an informer, at Oliver Bond's house in Bridge Street, Dublin. Lord Edward, on whom the hopes of the insurgents now largely rested, went on the run, hiding in various safe houses around the Portobello area of Dublin's Grand Canal. Now, with the rising imminent, and the government aware of its imminence but not of the date, it became ever more crucial that Lord Edward Fitzgerald, intended as commander-in-chief of the United Irish army, should keep himself free from arrest. By the same token, it was no less crucial for a quickly becoming frantic government at Dublin Castle to bring him down—and fast.

The fatal failure of security in the revolutionary movement's operations which led to the arrest of Lord Edward Fitzgerald came through Francis Magan, an impecunious barrister in the pay of the government. As is usual with such types, Magan was on friendly terms with the United Irishmen, who believed him to be cordial to their cause. A carpenter with United Irish leanings, plying his trade on the timbers of Dublin Castle overheard Under Secretary Edward Cooke unwisely announce that the Yellow Lion pub in Thomas Street was intended to be searched. The carpenter knew, though Edward Cooke did not, that this pub was the very place where Lord Edward was then in hiding. The carpenter tipped off Moore, owner of the pub. Moore besought his daughter, who had grown friendly with Lord Edward, to seek to sequester their distinguished charge elsewhere. In desperation, Moore's daughter approached a neighbour and believed supporter of the cause. This was none other than Francis Magan, the rascally cash-strapped counsel. Magan made arrangements for the alternative concealment of Lord Edward Fitzgerald, but passed on the details of his whereabouts to the government, through the medium of Under Secretary Cooke.

On the night of 18th May an armed patrol set out to ambush Lord Edward in the area near Guinness's brewery in Islandbridge; but Lord Edward, aided by his bodyguards, slipped through the net. At this point, Moore's resourceful daughter rooted out lodgings for the titled fugitive with another resident of Thomas Street, Nicholas Murphy, but, unluckily, mentioned to supposed good friend Magan where Lord Edward had moved to. Throughout most of the following day, 19th May 1798, Lord Edward hid up on the roof of Murphy's house while the yeomanry combed the neighborhood for him far below. In the afternoon, he received delivery of his revolutionary uniform: a bottle-green suit and crimson cape, topped with a florid cap of liberty. At seven o'clock, Lord Edward, having climbed down from his eyrie, was sitting on his bed reading a novel, when Murphy, the householder, came to call him for dinner. At that very moment, Major Swan, deputy mayor of Dublin, sprang into the room and declared that Lord Edward was under arrest. In a trice, Lord Edward had out his black-handled, jagged-edged stiletto and swiped at Swan, injuring him. Swan backed off and Captain Ryan, a newspaper editor doubling as yeomanry officer, rushed to the fray. The two men locked into each other, Lord Edward hacking at Captain Ryan's stomach with his knife. At last he managed to deliver a death blow. At this point, another armed officer, Major Sirr, rushed to the aid of Captain Ryan, and pistolled Lord Edward twice in the shoulder. The shot rebel was taken at once to Newgate Prison where, despite the seemingly slight character of the wound, septicemia soon set in, and Lord Edward died on 4th June 1798.

The black-handled stiletto that Lord Edward had used to defend himself was taken by Major Swan as a memento of the conflict and of his illustrious prisoner's capture. Major Swan lived in North Great George's Street, Dublin, and his wife was a relative of Lucretia Dobbin's mother. In an account written by Lucretia (then Mrs. Le Fanu), forty-nine years later, she described how she and her mother often used to visit Major Swan's house and were made to hearken to his boastful recounting of the capture of Lord Edward, with frequent reference to the dagger, "which he took pleasure in showing as a trophy."

Mrs. Le Fanu's feelings are best rendered in her own words:

> When I saw the dagger in the hands with which Lord Edward had striven in the last fatal struggle for life or death, I felt that it was not rightfully his who held it, and wished it were in other hands. Wishes soon changed into plans, and I determined, if possible, to get it. I knew the spot in the front drawing-room where it was laid, and one evening, after tea, when Major Swan and his guests were engaged in conversation in the back drawing-room, I walked into the front drawing-room, to the spot where it was. I seized it and thrust it into my bosom, inside my stays. I returned to the company, where I had to sit for an hour, and then drove home a distance of three miles. As soon as we left the house I told my sister, who was beside me, what I had done. As soon as we got home, I rushed up to the room which my sister and I occupied, and, having secured the door, I opened one of the seams in the feather bed, took out the dagger, and plunged it among the feathers. For upwards of twelve years I lay every night upon the bed which contained my treasure. When I left home I took it with me, and it has been my companion in all the vicissitudes of life. (Le Fanu, 17)

This dagger later passed into the possession of the novelist's younger brother, William Richard Le Fanu.

The association between the family of Le Fanu's redoubtable mother, Lucretia Dobbin, and the leaders of 1798 was not confined to Lord Edward

Fitzgerald, or to Lucretia. Some years earlier, in 1792, while in Paris, Lord Edward Fitzgerald met and became friendly with the barrister brothers, Henry and John Sheares. It is believed that these two most likely introduced Lord Edward to the United Irish movement. Zealots of the French Revolution, both Sheares brothers were present at the trial in Paris of King Louis XVI. John Sheares attended the guillotining of the king in the Place de la Revolution. Rumour has it that he was among the more ardent *citoyens* who rushed to soak their handkerchiefs in the dead monarch's blood once his head had been severed. Whether this is true or not, John Sheares later relished waving his red handkerchief under the nose of a youthful Daniel O'Connell (a Kerry-born Catholic barrister who was to the fore in securing Catholic emancipation in 1828 and died in 1847, his lifelong struggle for repeal of the Act of Union yet incomplete), boasting that it was "stiff with the king's life-blood."

Back in Ireland, Lord Edward Fitzgerald and the Sheares brothers rose through the ranks of the United Irishmen. Following the government pounce on Oliver Bond's house on 12th March 1798, John and Henry Sheares were among those who replaced the arrested members of the Leinster Directory. Both Sheares brothers and Lord Edward became the most vigorous proponents of an immediate on-the-ground uprising if French help, though promised and expected, did not arrive. As in the case of Lord Edward, the Sheares brothers were betrayed by one thought worthy of trust: this was Captain John Warneford Armstrong, who reported their plans to the government.

Early in May 1798, Captain Armstrong called to visit the Sheares brothers at John Sheares's house in Baggot Street and discussed with them—as *agent provocateur*—the plans for the rebellion. Next day, law enforcement swooped, and both brothers were arrested. Major Sirr, who carried out the arrests, found in Henry Sheares's writing box a proclamation in the hand of his brother, John. It began as follows: "Irishmen—your country is free. That vile Government, which has so long and so cruelly oppressed you, is no more. Some of its Most Atrocious Monsters have already paid the forfeit of their lives and the rest are in our hands."

A hurried treason trial was set in train. The proclamation written out by John Sheares, and the clear fact that both brothers had been involved in planning an uprising in Dublin, made the government confident of securing a conviction. The trial took place on 13th July 1798. It continued into the night, the courtroom lit by guttering candles and filled with angry loyalists antagonistic to the two accused. Despite a robust performance by defence counsel John Philpott Curran (whose daughter became the girlfriend of

Robert Emmet who led a doomed mini-insurrection in 1803), Captain Armstrong performed capably under cross-examination and both brothers were convicted, within seventeen minutes, by the jury.

That same night, the night before his execution, John Sheares wrote two long letters—one, in moving terms, to his sister, the other to his friend and mentor, Dr. Dobbin, Lucretia Dobbin's father. In his letter to Dr. Dobbin, John Sheares vouched that the proclamation that had been produced in court was incomplete, and that certain other parts, if tendered in evidence, would have tempered the impression created by the portion read. He also endeavored to explain that the undeniably violent language of the proclamation was intended to represent a situation in which a revolution had already taken place, not to incite the revolution itself. Taken out of context, he claimed, the proclamation conveyed a goading to violence, rather than a wish to minimize the results of revolution, as its author intended. In that part of the proclamation which either had been suppressed or lost, John Sheares had sought to make three other points.

> The three objects alluded to are these: the protection of property, preventing the indulgence of revenge, and the strict forbiddance of injuring any person for religious differences. I know it is said that I call on the people to take *vengeance* on their oppressors, and enumerate some of their oppressions; but this is the very thing that enables me to describe the difference between *private revenge* and *public vengeance*. The former has only a retrospective and malignant propensity, while the latter, though animated by a recollection of the past, has ever, and only, in view the removal of the evil and of its possibility of recurrence. Thus the assassin revenges himself, but the patriot avenges his country of its enemies by overthrowing them and depriving them of all power again to hurt it. In the struggle some of their lives may fall, but these are not the objects of his vengeance. In short, the Deity is said, in this sense, to be an *avenging* Being, but who deems him *revengeful?*

This Burkean sophistry was not designed to secure reprieve. Nor did it. The following day, 14th July 1798, John and Henry Sheares perished on the gallows, and were decapitated. They were buried in the vault of St. Michan's church (long renowned for its preservative qualities, and extolled in that connection by M. R. James in his ghost story "Lost Hearts"), where their coffins can be seen, side by side, on inspection of the crypt.

On J. S. Le Fanu's father's side, through the great dramatist Richard Brinsley Sheridan, there are also connections with 1798. It is worthy of note that, not one, but no fewer than *three* points of marital contact exist between the Le Fanus and the Sheridans. The novelist's grandfather, another Joseph, married Richard Brinsley's sister, Alicia, in 1784. (Their son Thomas was J.

S. Le Fanu's father.) Joseph's younger brother, Henry, married Betsy, another Sheridan sister. Finally, the youngest of that generation of Le Fanus,
Peter, married Frances Knowles, a cousin of Richard Brinsley Sheridan, being a daughter of Hester Sheridan who was a sister of the dramatist's father—the actor and stage manager, Thomas Sheridan.

This Thomas Sheridan had been a close friend in his time of the father
of Joseph, Henry and Peter: William Le Fanu. Early in life, Tom Sheridan
worked as manager of the Smock Alley Theatre in Dublin. However, an audience riot at the theatre, in March 1754, drove him out of business. The
impetus behind this *fracas* was a public controversy then raging, over
whether the monarch, King George II, had power to dispose of surplus reve-
nue garnered by the Irish treasury, a phenomenon in itself unique. At a performance on 2nd March 1754, the audience insisted that one of the actors,
West Digges, reprise some of his lines from a Voltaire play to which they attached a seditious implication that would embarrass the Irish government.
Thomas Sheridan forbade the actor to re-appear and repeat the lines, on the
basis that it was an affront to the dignity of theatre to engage in public pan-
dering. As soon as the audience learnt it was Sheridan who was responsible
for thwarting their desires, they went on the rampage, smashing up the pit
and setting fire to part of the backstage. After this, Tom Sheridan gave up
the Smock Alley, and made for London, leaving his Irish affairs in the hands
of his friend, William Le Fanu, the father of his two future sons-in-law and
(along with himself) great-grandfather of the novelist and ghost story writer,
Joseph Sheridan Le Fanu. William Le Fanu, who died in 1797, maintained
his role as Tom Sheridan's Irish manager until Tom's death in 1788. It is
from this connection between Thomas Sheridan and William Le Fanu that
the friendship between the two families, and the intermarriages, developed.

There was also a link of a more personal and fraught sort between Richard
Brinsley Sheridan and Lord Edward Fitzgerald. In 1791, before Lord Edward
headed off to Paris where he had his fateful encounter with the Sheares brothers, he met and fell in love with Sheridan's estranged wife, the beautiful opera
singer Elizabeth Linley. A daughter, Mary, was born of this liaison, but her
mother died of consumption only three months later. Both Sheridan and Lord
Edward were smitten with remorse at this development, and the reaction of
guilt seems to have drawn the two men together. In order to spare the child
the stigma of illegitimacy Lord Edward yielded up his daughter to Sheridan
who gladly took her into his own family. The dramatist was said to have been
broken-hearted when Mary died from a fit of convulsions in early childhood.

After Lord Edward's arrest in Dublin on 19th May 1798, his cousin,
Charles James Fox, leader of the Whig opposition in the British parliament,

together with Fox's right-hand man, Sheridan, resolved to give character evidence in his favor when Lord Edward should be brought to trial. But Lord Edward died of his wounds in prison on 4th June before ever standing trial. However, Sheridan *did* give character evidence in a court in Maidstone, Kent, on 22nd May 1798, on behalf of Arthur O'Connor, a trusted friend of Lord Edward, who had been arrested, together with a revolutionary Catholic priest, Fr. Quigley or Coigley, while on their way to France to consolidate support for the rebellion in Ireland. In due course, Fr. Coigley, on whom incriminating papers had been found, was sentenced and hanged. (King George III was insistent that a clergyman, even of the Roman cloth, should not be subjected to the additional ordeal and ignominy of drawing of the bowel and quartering of the body, then the conventional mode of execution for high treason.) At his trial on the same day as Fr. Coigley's, Arthur O'Connor was acquitted due to a lack of direct evidence. Once the verdict was pronounced an attempt was immediately made to have O'Connor re-arrested to stand trial for treason in Ireland. It appears that Sheridan had become embroiled in a plot to free O'Connor, by contriving to slip him out of the courtroom before he could be re-arrested while sentence of death was being passed upon Fr. Coigley. In the ensuing scuffle, a number of arrests were made, including of Arthur O'Connor. By dint of adroit and subtle arguing, which won him the thanks of the judge, Sheridan avoided being charged for incitement to riot. In the event, O'Connor was not returned to Ireland to stand trial for treason, and ended his days, after a long life, in easeful retirement in a *château* in Lorraine in France.

Against this background, on both parents' sides of the family, it is rather less remarkable that Joseph Sheridan Le Fanu should have flirted with the memory of 1798 in verse. When they were both young men, William Le Fanu, who enjoyed reciting his author elder brother's stories to friends, requested Le Fanu to compose a narrative poem for him. The result of this request was "Phaudrig Crohoore," likened by William to "an Irish Young Lochinvar." This features the delectable Kathleen O'Brien, who on the brink of being wed to the unloved Michael O'Hanlon, is whisked away in the nick of time by her true love, Phaudrig Crohoore. A happy conclusion is marred by the fact that, after rescuing Kathleen, Phaudrig felt the need to embark on further futile adventure. The poem ends:

> But them days are gone by, an' he is no more,
> An' the green grass is growin' o'er Phaudrig Crohoore;
> For he couldn't be aisy or quiet at all;
> As he lived a brave boy, he resolved so to fall.
> An' he took a good pike, for Phaudrig was great,
> An' he fought, an' he died in the year ninety-eight;

An' the day that Crohoore in the green field was killed,
A strong boy was stretched, an' a strong heart was stilled.

According to William Richard Le Fanu, the verse narrative "Shamus O'Brien" was written over a few days in 1840 and posted to him in instalments. However, W. J. Mc Cormack quotes a letter from Le Fanu to his mother in April 1839 in which Le Fanu states that the recital of his poem had been well received at the Historical Society in Trinity College. At the time the auditor of the Historical Society was Thomas Davis, afterwards editor of the *Nation*, the newspaper of the Young Ireland movement, whose attempted rebellion in 1848 resulted in similar failure to that of fifty years earlier, but with nothing like the same slaughter and destruction. "Shamus O'Brien" was admired by the Irish novelist Samuel Lover who recited it several times, to acclaim, in the United States. Later, Le Fanu lost the text of the poem and had to apply to his brother for a copy of it, so that it could be published in the *Dublin University Magazine*. Patrick Pearse, who led the failed but inspirational uprising in 1916, and was executed by firing squad, was known to recite "Shamus O'Brien" to his pupils at St. Enda's in Rathfarnham.

It is difficult to conjecture why Le Fanu wrote nothing like this stirring nationalist narrative poem ever again. Perhaps the disappointing outcome for the Church of Ireland of the Tithe War in the 1830s, with the statutory abolition of the ten per cent tax paid to the established church, or a recognition following the Young Ireland revolution in 1848 that there is more of grue than glamor in armed uprising, stifled that agile inspiration which had spun such popular poems as "Phaudrig Crohoore" and "Shamus O'Brien." Whatever the causes may be, mindful of all that the troubled events of 1798 yet have power to evoke, one recalls with indulgence the brief impassioned encounter through verse with Irish nationalism enjoyed in the flush of his literary youth by Ireland's unsurpassed master of the ghostly tale and the novel of macabre mystery.

Works Consulted

Browne, Nelson. *Sheridan Le Fanu*. London: Arthur Barker, 1951.

Ellis, S. M. *Wilkie Collins, Le Fanu and Others*. London: Constable, 1931.

Le Fanu, William Richard. *Seventy Years of Irish Life*. London: Edward Arnold, 1893.

Mc Cormack, W. J. *Sheridan Le Fanu and Victorian Ireland*. Oxford: Clarendon Press, 1980.

O'Toole, Fintan. *A Traitor's Kiss: The Life of Richard Brinsley Sheridan*. London: Granta Books, 1997.

Packenham, Thomas. *The Year of Liberty, The Great Irish Rebellion of 1798.* London: Weidenfeld & Nicolson, 1969; rev. 1997.

Tillyard, Stella. *Citizen Lord: Edward Fitzgerald, 1763–1798.* London: Chatto & Windus, 1997.

H. P. Lovecraft's Response to the Work of Joseph Sheridan Le Fanu

Jim Rockhill

Many have wondered why H. P. Lovecraft held such a low opinion of the work of Joseph Sheridan Le Fanu, whose work merits barely a nod in Lovecraft's seminal essay, "Supernatural Horror in Literature":

> The romantic, semi-Gothic, quasi-moral tradition here represented was carried far down the nineteenth century by such authors as Joseph Sheridan Le-Fanu [sic], Wilkie Collins, the late Sir H. Rider Haggard (whose *She* is really remarkably good), Sir A. Conan Doyle, H. G. Wells, and Robert Louis Stevenson . . .[1]

How could one of the most influential writers of weird fiction in the twentieth century fail to appreciate one of the masters of the prior century, an author whose work had been praised as exemplary by no less an authority than M. R. James, to whom Lovecraft devoted an entire chapter in the same essay?

We may ascribe part of the answer to Lovecraft's atheism, which would have taken issue with the trappings of Christianity in Le Fanu's work, though the view of Christianity displayed in Le Fanu's fiction is considerably less orthodox than one finds in either James or Machen.

An examination of Lovecraft's correspondence with Donald Wandrei, Clark Ashton Smith, and August Derleth suggests that the nature of the works to which Lovecraft had been exposed were probably equally to blame. After reading a reference to "Le Fanu's anthology 'A Stable for Nightmares'" in a letter from Donald Wandrei dated 5 January 1927,[2] Lovecraft remarked, "I wish I could get hold of Polidori's 'Vampyre' & something by Le Fanu. The latter has long been a familiar name to me, yet I have seen absolutely

---

1. First published in W. Paul Cook, ed., *The Recluse*, 1927. Revised 1933–34.

2. S. T. Joshi and David E. Schultz, ed., *Mysteries of Time and Spirit: The Letters of H. P. Lovecraft and Donald Wandrei* (San Francisco: Night Shade Books, 2002), 11.

nothing of his."[3] By 13 March 1927, Lovecraft had received Wandrei's copies of *A Stable for Nightmares* and one of Le Fanu's novels: "As soon as I have read 'All in the Dark' I'll return that and 'A Stable for Nightmares.'"[4]

These are unfortunate choices for several reasons. *A Stable for Nightmares* was a gathering of eleven anonymous and unremarkable supernatural stories published by Trusley Brothers of London for the Christmas market in 1867. Seven of those stories reappeared in an American edition in 1896, with "Le Fanu" stamped on the spine, "J. Sheridan Le Fanu . . . Sir Charles Young, Bart. and Others" on the full-title page, and no authors' names supplied for any of the stories within. One of the stories new to this edition is Le Fanu's "Dickon the Devil," the second is "What Was It?" by Fitz-James O'Brien, and the third, "A Debt of Honor," is attributed to Sir Charles Young by default. No evidence has been put forward in the past century and a half to establish that Le Fanu had anything to do with the first edition, and the author had already been dead for twenty-three years by the time the American edition appeared, not that this has prevented various anthologists and critics from assuming Le Fanu's authorship of a varying number of these stories regardless of this paucity of evidence.

Lovecraft had some suspicions concerning the authorship of these stories from the beginning: "I see that Le Fanu collection has Fitz-James O'Brien's 'What Was It?'—have you been able to identify others?"[5] Nonetheless, this first encounter with work he had first assumed to be by Le Fanu cannot have been an auspicious one.

Unfortunately, his second, more prolonged exposure was not much better. As a two-decker novel before a three-decker demanding public, *All in the Dark* (*Dublin University Magazine*, February to June 1866) did not fare well with Le Fanu's contemporaries, and in surviving notes for a lecture he delivered on Le Fanu on 16 March 1923, even the otherwise sympathetic M. R. James states, "Weakest of all the novels is *All in the Dark*—a domestic story with a sham ghost: an offence hard to forgive in any writer but much harder in Le Fanu's case, seeing that he could deal so magnificently with realness without incurring any more expense."[6]

---

3. *Mysteries of Time and Spirit*, 14.

4. *Mysteries of Time and Spirit*, 54.

5. *Mysteries of Time and Spirit*, 40.

6. M. R. James, "The Novels and Stories of J. Sheridan Le Fanu," in *A Pleasing Terror* (Ashcroft, BC Ash-Tree Press, 2001), 494. The first printing of this article in *Ghosts and Scholars* 7 omits this passage. For a more positive assessment of this novel taking into account the full context in which it was written, see Stephen Carver's "'Addicted to the

Lovecraft admitted to August Derleth that he was not impressed with the book when he first approached it on 26 March 1927—"I'll tell you about Le Fanu when I've read 'All in the Dark'—but I don't think he'll prove anything marvelous"[7]—then went on to pan the book to the same correspondent in a letter dated 26 July 1927, even though he admits that he has perhaps not read the best examples of Le Fanu's work: "What I have read of Sheridan Le Fanu was a great disappointment as compared with what I heard of him in advance—but it may be that I haven't seen his best stuff. I don't know 'Uncle Silas,' but the thing I read (I can't even recall the name) was abominably insipid and Victorian."[8]

A few years later, Lovecraft was given the opportunity to read one of Le Fanu's best novels, but again it was a work almost guaranteed to frustrate him. Although long touted as a supernatural novel based on the two early chapters devoted to "Ghost Stories of the Tiled House," Le Fanu's *The House by the Church-yard* (DUM, October 1861 to February 1863) is a sprawling portrait of life across class levels in eighteenth century Dublin bearing more of a resemblance to the darker specimens of Jacobean and Restoration comedy than it does the Gothic novel. Derleth must have belatedly realized this when he decided not to publish the edition he had announced during the early years of Arkham House.

That he was misled concerning the book's content is made clear by Lovecraft's letter to Derleth on 26 September 1929:

> Just now I am making a bold effort to keep awake over an old Victorian novel which some damn'd misguided oaf recommended to me as "weird"—J Sheridan Le Fanu's "House by the Church-yard". I had been disillusioned before by Le Fanu specimens, & this one just about clinches my opinion that poor Sherry was a false alarm as a fear monger, & I shall cut him out of any possible 2nd edition of my historical sketch [i.e., "Supernatural Horror in Literature"].[9]

Lovecraft seems to have given up attempting to read Le Fanu's novels, but continued to express a desire to read "Green Tea," "though," he confessed to August Derleth on 20 November 1931, "I can scarcely imagine a really weird tale by the author of 'The House by the Church-yard' & other Victorian

---

Supernatural': Spiritualism and Self-Satire in *All in the Dark*" included in this volume.

7. David E. Schultz and S. T. Joshi, ed., *Essential Solitude: The Letters of H. P. Lovecraft and August Derleth* (New York: Hippocampus Press, 2008), 1.75.

8. *Essential Solitude*, 1.100.

9. *Essential Solitude*, 1.216.

products which I have seen."[10] He finally received an anthology containing the story in January 1932—"Cook has just presented me with 'The Omnibus of Crime,' & I think the first thing I shall read will be the much-discussed 'Green Tea' by Le Fanu"[11]—but was initially put off by its length—"Well—I guess I'm too sleepy tonight to read 'Green Tea' after all! It's longer than I anticipated."[12]

This is the point at which we can assume that a combination of repeated disappointments, expectations too exalted to fulfill, continued difficulty in locating the author's work, impatience with Victorian manners, and distaste for Christian mysticism finally took their toll. One can also imagine Lovecraft taking exception to the sentiment characteristic of Victorian fiction; however, even though sentimental episodes appear in both of the two novels he read (and many of the anonymous stories in A Stable for Nightmares), remarkably little sentiment appears in Le Fanu's supernatural work. Even the small sample of this work we know Lovecraft to have read ("Dickon the Devil," "Ghost Stories of the Tiled House" from The House by the Church-yard, and especially "Green Tea") is remarkable for its ruthlessness, whether the victim happens to be a healthy adult, a mentally defective one, or a child.[13]

After reading sham Le Fanu in an anthology, sham supernaturalism in one of Le Fanu's own novels, and genuine supernaturalism diluted by the hundreds of pages of societal melodrama in which they appear, "Green Tea" may have seemed too little too late. To Clark Ashton Smith on 16 January 1932, Lovecraft wrote, "I at last . . . have read 'Green Tea.' It is definitely better than anything else of Le Fanu's that I have ever seen, though I'd hardly put it in the Poe-Blackwood-Machen class."[14] When August Derleth sent Lovecraft an article on Le Fanu in April 1935,[15] Lovecraft remembered

---

10. *Essential Solitude*, 1.415.

11. *Essential Solitude*, 2.435.

12. *Essential Solitude*, 2.438.

13. To cite one example of Le Fanu's restraint, few of his contemporaries would have been able to resist the temptation to draw out the scene in which Jennings is saved from suicide by the mere presence of his niece, a scene Le Fanu describes in less than 200 words. As Father Purcell states in the author's "Strange Event in the Life of Schalken the Painter," "I have no sentimental scenes to describe." The detached, clinical tone Le Fanu frequently adopts in his supernatural fiction leaves little room for digressions devoted to a pretty breast heaving in agitation, sunlit curls dancing at the stamp of a dainty foot, or bonny cheeks bedewed with tears.

14. Quoted in an annotation to *Mysteries of Time and Spirit*, 15.

15. Unfortunately, the surviving correspondence between Lovecraft and Derleth fails

not "Green Tea" but his disappointment in the novels, "Thanks abundantly for the article on Le Fanu. I have 'The House by the Churchyard'—thought it is an insufferably dull & Victorian specimen. In reading it, it was all I could do to keep awake!"[16]

If only Lovecraft had gained access to a volume of Le Fanu in full supernatural regalia his assessment may have been different, or perhaps with the aid of the critical apparatus M. R. James supplied in *Madam Crowl's Ghost and Other Tales of Mystery*—published in 1923, a mere four years prior to Lovecraft's first surviving reference of Le Fanu to Donald Wandrei—he may have seen a kindred spirit beneath those ostensibly Christian trappings. On the other hand, Heaven and Hell may have remained parochial to the cosmic materialist in Lovecraft no matter how creatively they had been couched by Le Fanu.

---

to mention the author or source for this article. Although Derleth may have had access to the issue of the *Spectator* (21 February 1931) containing E. F. Benson's "Sheridan Le Fanu," one would have expected some comment to have been made concerning Benson—whose ghost stories were known and respected by both men—had this been the article in question.

16. *Essential Solitude*, 2.693.

"A Regular Contributor": Le Fanu's Short Stories, *All The Year Round,* and the Influence of Dickens

Simon Cooke

Charles Dickens (1812–1870) was the most influential novelist of his time, and it is barely surprising to find that he had a significant impact on the fictions of Joseph Sheridan Le Fanu (1814–1873). Although Le Fanu liked to distance himself from his contemporaries,[1] Dickens's presence can be felt throughout his *oeuvre*, and, as generations of critics have observed, it is possible to detect numerous similarities between the Irish writer's techniques and those of his more famous contemporary. Several commentators have noted how Le Fanu's style displays a Dickensian tonality. "Le Fanu, like Dickens . . . is a comic writer, drawn to mixed effects: to the violent, the dreamy, the learned, and the grotesque, sometimes all at once" (*Le Fanu's Gothic* 3). These remarks by Victor Sage are suggestive, and others have made parallel observations on the treatment of character and story. Piya Pal Lapinski has argued that Le Fanu's *Carmilla* might be a re-working of Dickens's Miss Wade in *Little Dorrit,* and it is also possible to establish a connection between the two writers' treatment of plot. According to W. J. Mc Cormack, Le Fanu's convoluted *Checkmate* (1870–71) bears a relationship to the suspended uncertainties of *Edwin Drood* (226), and there are numerous occasions when Le Fanu's later novels appear to be "leaning" (226) on a Dickensian exemplar.

---

1. This is a problematic area, worthy of critical investigation in its own right. However, we can say with some certainty that Le Fanu did not encourage the idea that his work was sensational in the manner of Collins or Braddon. In the "Preliminary Word" to *Uncle Silas* he notes how the term "sensation" has been the subject of "promiscuous application" (xxvii), and goes on to comment how "romance" (implicitly *Uncle Silas*) is better read as the "legitimate" (xxvii–xxviii) continuation of the traditions of Scott.

Such criticism establishes a sense of the writers' interconnectedness although it is interesting to note that there are no far-reaching explorations of Dickens's effect on the writings of the "Invisible Prince." Such an undertaking would have to be on a colossal scale, involving a close inter-textual reading of both authors' works, embracing such vast and intricate novels as *Bleak House* and *The House by the Church-yard*, and extending over more than three decades of professional activity. No such study has yet been attempted, and it is not my intention to offer it here. However, it is possible to reconstruct *aspects* of Dickens's influence by focusing on Le Fanu's short stories for his periodical, *All the Year Round*. In the production of this material the Irish writer came under the spell of his editor: always a professional with the capacity to change and adapt his work according to its audience and context, Le Fanu responded to specific requirements, producing a series of texts which closely reflect his new employer's values and aesthetics.

The overall effect is one of complicated exchange and interchange, although it is possible to conceptualize Dickens's influence in terms of two dimensions: one was professional, involving such considerations as what could or should be published, its format, and how it would fit in the pages of the magazine; and the other was artistic, a matter of idiom and style. As with all productions for magazines both ingredients are important and worth considering in detail. What is most interesting, however, is the way in which these two elements intermingle, with practical considerations exerting a significant effect on the artistic character of Le Fanu's contributions. In the following pages I explore this situation by considering these issues and the relationship between them. Focusing on the short stories Le Fanu offered to Boz in the period 1869–70, I will attempt to reconstruct his approach to working for Dickens; how he accommodated the requirements of *All the Year Round*; and how he worked and reworked a Dickensian aesthetic in order to win himself a regular place in the periodical's columns.

Working for Dickens: The Professional Background

The working relationship between the two authors was probably initiated by the Irish writer's desire to publish in *All the Year Round*. Most of the correspondence relating to this arrangement has been lost, although surviving letters suggest that Dickens did not solicit Le Fanu's work. Rather, Le Fanu offered his submissions as just another contributor, whose writing would be judged on its merits, rather than his reputation. This new approach reflected a radical change: having acted as the proprietor and editor of the *Dublin University Magazine* and several other journals of a similar kind, Le Fanu's working for someone other than himself was in some ways a lowering of status, a shift from control to being controlled. Nevertheless, he seems to have approached this new arrangement as an important new stage in his professional life. In the absence of documentary material we have no written evidence of his thinking, but it is possible to read his desire for change as a combination of factors.

Of prime importance, perhaps, is the fact that he was "desperate for money" (Sage, "Irish Gothic" 90). In the early part of 1869 he had disposed of the *Dublin University Magazine* and had to find alternative venues from which to generate income. In the late sixties he had begun to publish in London-based periodicals such as *Temple Bar*, *Once a Week*, and *Belgravia*; but the greatest prize, in terms of its profitability, was always going to be *All the Year Round*. Launched in 1859 as the successor to *Household Words*, *All the Year Round* had a yearly circulation of a hundred thousand copies (Allingham 1), allowing the editor to pay generous fees of at least a guinea per page. Such remuneration must have been appealing to a man who is described by Sage as "canny" ("Irish Gothic" 87) and by Nelson Browne as an entrepreneurial "man of business" (27). The other London journals paid well, but *All the Year Round* was best of all, and Le Fanu may have looked to Dickens's periodical as a lucrative source of income.

His contributions to Dickens's magazine were also motivated, it can be argued, by his on-going desire to Anglicize his work. Thomas Boyle has noted how Le Fanu directed the *Dublin University Magazine* toward "the English literary mainstream" (122), and there can be no doubt that he always sought to strengthen his connection with (Protestant) England while diminishing his relationship with (Catholic) Ireland. In the early sixties he had brokered a deal with Richard Bentley which allowed his novels—notably *Uncle Silas* (1864)—to be published in England; and in working for Dickens he aligned himself with one of the pillars of the British literary establishment. Simply by shifting his work from Dublin to London he reframed his stories in the same space as that occupied by his editor, by Elizabeth Gaskell, and by Wilkie Collins. These writers exemplified the cultural tradition of "English" as opposed to "Irish" writing, and Le Fanu probably aimed to occupy the same company.

He was equally keen, in all likelihood, to establish himself as a contributor to what was widely regarded as one of the outstanding magazines of its type. Dickens's property was one of the foremost literary journals: it did not compare with the *Cornhill Magazine*, the elite periodical to which Le Fanu had offered work, probably *Uncle Silas*, and been rejected (Mc Cormack 203); but, as noted above, it did publish some of the outstanding authors of the time. Writing for *All the Year Round* had a considerable cachet, and Le

Fanu must have been aware that this journal was a step up from the more provincial pages of the *Dublin University Magazine*.

Le Fanu's determination to work for Dickens was probably motivated, then, by a combination of economic realism, professional pride and a need for some sort of cultural realignment. These factors were the pressures under which he wrote, and in quick succession he offered Dickens a novel—*The Rose and the Key*—and a series of short stories. *The Rose and the Key* was serialized after Dickens's death (*All the Year Round*, New Series, 21 January–23 September 1871), but the editor dealt directly with the short stories. These included the startling opener, "Green Tea" (October–November 1869), "The Child That Went with the Fairies" (February 1870), "The White Cat of Drumgunniol" (April 1870), "Stories of Lough Guir" (April 1870), "The Vision of Tom Chuff" (October 1870), and "Madam Crowl's Ghost" (December 1870).[2] Given a prominent position, usually at the end of the number, where they could achieve maximum effect, the stories' placement and rapid appearance strongly suggest the editor's satisfaction with the material. Known as an obsessive meddler who routinely interfered with his writers' work, Dickens's response to Le Fanu's stories is uncharacteristically accepting. He did intervene in aspects of the writing in *The Rose and the Key* (*Letters of Charles Dickens* 12.535), but surviving letters show he was willing to accept the short pieces as they stood.[3] The smoothness of this transaction gave his contributor precisely the straightforward *entrée* he sought.

However, there was nothing accidental about this situation; rather, it is probable that Le Fanu manipulated the process of submission, ensuring the best possible result. As a former "commissioning editor in his own right" (Hughes 45) whose experience exactly mirrored Dickens's own and was built on a long apprenticeship as the editor of a series of magazines, Le Fanu knew how to maximize his chances of approval, gaining a foothold in the periodi-

2. Most readers will not have access to the original issues of *All the Year Round*. All citations are therefore taken from a modern edition of *Madam Crowl's Ghost* (London: Wordsworth Classics, 1994), essentially a reprint of M. R. James's edition of 1923. All future references are cited in the text.

3. In addition to material included in Dickens's *Letters* there are two unpublished letters from Dickens to Le Fanu which deal directly with his contributions. One, dated 31 December 1869, acknowledges receipt of the "Fairy Story" ("The Child that Went with the Fairies") and advises that he is happy to retain it for publication in the journal (The National Library of Ireland, Dublin). A second letter, now in private hands, is dated 29 September 1869; it comments on Dickens's having received "Green Tea" and sent it to the printer's.

cal by giving Dickens precisely the type of material he required. He gained rapid acceptance in the pages of *All the Year Round* by responding to the editor's unwritten but implicit requirements. Dickens exerted a distinct influence on the stories, and Le Fanu *displayed* his responses—offering a series of texts which demonstrably complied with the editor's expectations.

Making the Stories Fit: The Demands of All the Year Round

One of the primary considerations was the necessity of offering stories which were in line with the magazine's format while also satisfying the taste of its audience. With no guidance from the editor, Le Fanu offered his own interpretation of the type of material he thought would gain acceptance. It is likely he was a regular reader of *All the Year Round*, and would have analyzed its range of interests as well as its formal qualities. Aimed at a middle-class audience, Dickens's periodical formed an exact parallel to the *Dublin University Magazine*, and Le Fanu would have had no difficulty at all in understanding its social and cultural orientation.

He must have been aware of the need to produce what Barbara Quinn Schmidt has described as "tight, self-contained narratives" (quoted in Wynne 26). This unspoken requirement informs the pages of *All the Year Round*, and Le Fanu's tales exactly accord with Dickens's emphasis on small-scale stories, sharp detail, concrete characters and terse narratives. Written for rapid consumption—to be scanned at home, at work, or in the daily commute on the train—his texts embody the editor's demand that his busy readers should be offered an intense reading experience. It is especially noticeable that each of the stories is underpinned by a rapidly moving narrative which takes its main characters through a series of unsettling experiences. In "Green Tea" we have the terrifying account of Jennings's encounter with the spectral monkey; in "The Child That Went with the Fairies," the tale of an abducted child and the family's grieving; and in "Tom Chuff" and "The White Cat of Drumgunniol" a series of brisk situations exploring the territories of horror and despair. The effect is generally one of condensed vividness. With the exception of "Green Tea," which extends over several numbers, the narratives are contained within an average installment of only five pages of double columns, and the overall impression is one of packaged brevity. Mindful of the limited attention span of the audience, Le Fanu conforms to the pace of *All the Year Round*'s contributions, offering work that seems breathless when compared with the more leisurely installments of monthly journals such as the *Cornhill Magazine*. Dickens needed his contributors to provide him with sharp copy, and this is precisely what Le Fanu does.

He was equally careful to present the editor with texts in close accord with the magazine's prevailing tone. Deborah Wynne has noted how Dickens developed a distinctive house-style based on a combination of informative articles, ghost stories, Gothic fantasies and thrillers, and the same sort of mixture can be observed within each of Le Fanu's contributions. His tales seem almost formulaic in their attempts to give the editor what he would hope to find, and there are numerous points of correspondence between the magazine's emphasis on realism, "melodrama," "sensationalism," "fancy," and "pathos" (Wynne 25), and Le Fanu's focus on the same qualities. Of course, Le Fanu's interest in these elements was formed long before his association with *All the Year Round,* and were an integral part of his craft. However, in his work for Dickens he foregrounds the essential ingredients, consciously shaping—or selecting—material to fit the magazine's emphasis. It could be argued, for instance, that Le Fanu's apparent factuality forms an echo with the many prosaic accounts of districts within Britain, dentists, cooking, gardening, and other miscellanea. These informative pieces create a "real" world which is re-created in the dialect narrative of "Madam Crowl's Ghost," in the geographical details of the country to the east of "the old city of Limerick" (*Madam Crowl* 50) in the opening pages of "The Child That Went with the Fairies," and in the "science" of "Green Tea." At the same time, Le Fanu unites the conventions of Sensationalism and Gothic. He re-inscribes the textures of fictions such as Collins's *The Moonstone* (*AYR*, 1868), and revisits the conventions of ghost stories by Dickens, paying special attention to "Mugby Junction: The Signalman" (*AYR*, Christmas Number 1866). By 1869 Dickens had created a dense catalogue of intricate and disturbing tales, and Le Fanu's contributions neatly conform to his employer's desire, as noted in his comments on Collins's *The Moonstone,* for stories which enact a "curious" blend of the moving and prosaic, the "wild," and the "domestic" (Lehmann 360).

These terms describe the intermingling of science and the supernatural in "Green Tea" as well as providing a clear definition of the domestic weirdness, the fusion of the familiar and the strange, that features throughout his tales. This conformity makes the tales a perfect fit within the magazine's sometimes incongruous pages, and Dickens's acceptance of Le Fanu's work is signaled, I suggest, by his positioning of the material. Deborah Wynne has explained how "Editors [of Victorian magazines] were sensitive to the possible connections which could be made between (the texts) serialized in their magazines and the various texts which made up each issue" (21). Such is also Dickens's technique, enabling him to accentuate the "rightness" of Le Fanu's tales by placing them in a series of telling juxtapositions. With its emphasis on punishment and sin the grotesque morality of "The Vision of Tom

Chuff" (AYR, 8 October 1870, 450–56) is highlighted by its relationship with the article preceding it, "A Little More Proverbial Philosophy" (446–50).[4] The "Proverbial Philosophy" advances some platitudinous aphorisms about morality and sin, and the very tameness of its conclusions helps to accentuate the wild excesses of the life and death of Tom Chuff.

The horror of the quasi-scientific "Green Tea" is similarly emphasized by the relationship of some of its installments with articles charting what appears to a parallel field. Chapters three to five (AYR, 30 October 1869, 525–28) are thrown into sharp relief by their appearance directly after "Twenty-One Months of Silence" (521–25). In this short piece the anonymous author explores "experiments of a chemical sort" (521), explaining how the "queer" condition of "mutism" is cured by the application of medical science, the very science, we might say, applied to Jennings by Hesselius. On the basis of chapters one to three it is reasonable to assume Jennings will also be cured; but when we reach the conclusion of "Green Tea" we realize that Dickens includes the other piece in order to ridicule the claims of Le Fanu's doctor. The failure of science in Le Fanu's tale is therein interrogated by its ironic positioning next to a case of medicine's success. The effects of "Green Tea" are further intensified, it can be argued, by Dickens's inclusion of "Witchcraft in the Nineteenth Century" (6 November 1869, 541–44), which is placed before chapters six to eight (548–52). With its bizarre account of an "extraordinary hallucination" in the form of a "fiery dog" (542), this account prepares the reader for the sections of "Green Tea" in which the hellishly glowing monkey progressively intensifies its presence, tormenting the unfortunate Jennings at every turn. By placing the two together an intense effect is produced, and it is possible that Dickens organized this juxtaposition in order to suggest that the unfortunate clergyman's spectral creature is in fact the product of some sort of "witchcraft."

Indeed, the framing of "Green Tea" suggests how easily Le Fanu's tale was able to intersect and interact with the existing material, producing an effect which was highly imaginative—expanding and interrogating its range of meaning—while also reinforcing the magazine's dominant characteristics. In her account of the Victorian family magazine, Wynne has noted how pe-

---

4. All the writings mentioned here were published anonymously and with the exception of Le Fanu's contributions their authorship is still unknown. The loss of most of the papers relating to All the Year Round has meant identification of the lesser writers is practically an impossible task. The only sustained detective-work is contained in Ella Ann Oppenlander's Descriptive Index and Contributor List. However she has no entries for any of the articles framing Le Fanu's tales.

riodicals were a site of "simultaneity" in which it was possible to create readings based on proximity (20); however, "Green Tea" could only function in this context because Le Fanu ensured it would make an exact fit.

Pleasing the Editor: Le Fanu and Dickensian Aesthetics

Such practical maneuverings allowed his contributions to slot into place. Dickens could find no wrong because they exactly complied with his requirements for the magazine, the tastes of the audience, and its mode of consumption. But this was only part of the equation. I further suggest that, in order to ensure his pieces were published, Le Fanu calculatedly revisited a series of Dickensian themes and ideas. Wayne Hall has noted how he gained acceptance for his early contributions to the *Dublin University Magazine* by working to "pattern his work" on the editor Isaac Butt's contributions (81), and the same can be said for aspects of his writing for Dickens. Already well-known as a practitioner of the strange and supernatural, Le Fanu set out to satisfy his editor not only by making his work publishable within the contexts of *All the Year Round* but also, more specifically, by invoking a Dickensian ambience. It is in the domain of this conscious "patterning" that we find the most tangible evidence of Dickens's "influence" on the writings of Le Fanu. Victor Sage has detected the hand of Dickens in *The Tenants of Malory* (*Le Fanu's Gothic* 154) and *Uncle Silas* (103), but Le Fanu writes most *explicitly* in a Dickensian mode in his work for *All the Year Round*. Unconscious influence is one matter, but Le Fanu's response to Dickens was entirely instrumental, creating what we would call, in the modern language of film, a "re-versioning" or "re-imagining" of his employer's writing. These manipulations are far-reaching, but are best exemplified by exploring a cross-section of texts.

In "The Child That Went with the Fairies" (*AYR*, 5 February 1870), the author plays on Dickens's interest in two key ingredients: sentimental stories of childhood which view the narrative from the child's perspective; and the conventions of the fairy-tale. In Le Fanu's text we have a child's eye view which invokes the Dickensian writing of childhood suffering. Nell is in a "trance of fear" when her siblings disappear, and her "undefined boding" (*Madam Crowl* 52) recalls the anguish and emotional discord of so many of Dickens's dysfunctional and terrorized children, from Oliver Twist (1838) and Pip (1861) to David Copperfield (1850), Tom and Louisa in *Hard Times* (1854), Little Nell in *The Old Curiosity Shop* (1841), and the figures of "Ignorance and Want" in *A Christmas Carol* (1843). Le Fanu notably re-creates a familiar Dickensian trope—the pathetic child whose inner want is signaled in the form of poverty and physical privation. Le Fanu's quoting of Dickens is apparent throughout, and it is instructive to compare two short descriptions.

The first is the Irish writer's description of the ghostly Billy, who, returning home, is as poor in death as in life: "There was light enough to see that he was barefoot and ragged, and looked pale and famished. He went straight to the fire, and cowered over the turf embers, and rubbed his hands slowly, and seemed to shiver" (*Madam Crowl* 57). And the second is Dickens's description of Ignorance and Want in *A Christmas Carol*,[5] as they appear to the horrified Scrooge: "They were a girl and boy . . . meagre, ragged [and] prostrate in their humility . . . age had pinched, and twisted them" (*Christmas Books* 108). Making a political point, Dickens's is the more powerful of the two; nevertheless, we can see how Le Fanu accentuates his child's physical oppression in an echo of what might have been his prototype. Dickens provides a vocabulary of suffering based on his imaginative representation of the Hungry Forties in Britain, and Le Fanu applies the same lexicon in his showing of the iconographies of the Irish Famine. Dickens uses a fairy tale to comment on children's sufferings, and so does his contributor.

"The Child That Went with the Fairies" might also be referenced more generally to the fairy-tale structures deployed throughout Dickens's fictions: the representation of the "beautiful" lady (*Madam Crowl* 55) and her grotesque companion are Le Fanu's own, but they form a familial similarity with characters such as Quilp, the ogre of *The Old Curiosity Shop*, Dombey—the remote and implacable "giant" of *Dombey and Son* (1848)—and numerous others. Casting his text in the form of a quasi-supernatural folk tale which is essentially another version of *The Pied Piper of Hamelin*, Le Fanu provides an apt accompaniment to Dickens's many versions of legend and fantasy. Harry Stone has explained how throughout the early part of his career Boz "was coming to regard the fairy tale and its correlates—fantasy, enchantment, legends, signs, and correspondences, indeed all the thronging manifestations of the invisible world—as potent instruments of imaginative truth" (4). That notion is as clearly exemplified in Le Fanu's text as it is in Dickens's *The Chimes* (1845) or *Hard Times*. Lacking the worst excesses of Dickensian sentimentality, Le Fanu presents his editor with a version of imaginative mediation in which the devices of the fairy-tale are directed, as they are in Dickens's own work, towards an investigation of suffering and displacement. In Le Fanu's contributions, as in his exemplar's, the surface is one of folklore and fantasy, but the subtext is always focused on the "frightful" and "miserable" (*Christmas Carol* 108).

Other stories provide the same sort of echoes, half-echoes and rewritings which are only lightly re-worked treatments of some of the editor's

---

5. The edition used here is *Christmas Books* 1.

central themes. In "The Vision of Tom Chuff" (*AYR*, 8 October 1870) Le
Fanu presents a moralizing ghost story which corresponds with Dickens's notion of spirits as some sort of moral or ethical projection, a force for retribution and reform.[6] His subject is a "surly" (*Madam Crowl* 163) drunk and thief
whose crimes, like Scrooge's, are the products of their class, although (like
Scrooge's) they "deserve" to be punished. Indeed, there are marked similarities between the nature of the retribution. Scrooge is warned by three spirits
and Tom by the spirit of his father; Scrooge reforms when he is shown his
own grave in a deserted cemetery (*Christmas Books* 124), but Tom, even
though he is taken down to Hell (*Madam Crowl* 158) is unable to make the
change. Scrooge resists damnation, but the unreformed Tom is ultimately
pushed by a malevolent spirit into the "open grave" (164). "The Vision of
Tom Chuff" is thus presented as a bold but logical reworking of its Dickensian exemplar: in *A Christmas Carol* the expectation is only that the character will reform; in Le Fanu's story, on the other hand, we have a sense of
what *would* have happened if he had not. Figured as a version of Dickens
which tests his moral certainties, Chuff's tale is written, once again, as a sort
of parallel text. It strips Scrooge's lack of awareness down to a bold simplifi-
cation by presenting a character who is simply lacking in the intelligence to
see what will happen.

At once a piece of intertextual homage and a natural extension of his
editor's moralized universe, "The Vision of Tom Chuff" is Le Fanu's gloss on
Dickens's writing, a new treatment which re-inscribes, affirms, and stretches
a Dickensian aesthetic. More oblique, though equally concerned with the
process of inter-textual re-inscription, is Le Fanu's infamous Gothic saga,
"Green Tea."

Most of Le Fanu's tales recreate aspects of Boz's writing as it appeared in
his novels, but "Green Tea" (*AYR*, 23 October–13 November 1869) can be
read as a "Dickensian ghost story," essentially a reworking of "Mugby Junction: Number One Branch Line. The Signalman" (*AYR*, Extra Christmas
Number 1866).[7] Presented as Le Fanu's first submission, "Green Tea" initi-

6. "The Vision of Tom Chuff" is a reworking of "The Drunkard's Dream" (*DUM* 12
[August 1838]: 151–57). In the original story the moral dimension of Tom's experience is more obliquely registered than it is in "Tom Chuff." The later story's treatment of the visitations also differs from the original in its greater emphasis on a
dramatic showing of the visitations. Such changes underline the idea that Le Fanu
adapted his material to fit a Dickensian exemplar.

7. The edition used here is a modern reprint edited by Deborah Thomas, *Selected
Short Fiction*.

ates his contributions to *All the Year Round* by offering the editor a text which was heavily influenced by the earlier tale and may be read, once again, as a type of homage. This claim is a bold one. Critics such as Cooke and Crawford have linked "Green Tea" to other sources, notably Samuel Warren's *Diary of a Late Physician* (1835) and de Boismont's *On Hallucinations* (1845, 1859); but its Dickensian dimension has not thus far been the subject of critical inquiry. Of course, the relationship is not necessarily an obvious one, and it could be objected that Dickens's tale is entirely dissimilar to Le Fanu's. There are, it seems, marked points of contrast. "The Signalman" concerns the anguish of a railway worker who is haunted by an unspecified "spectre" (*Fiction* 87), while "Green Tea" charts the suffering of a cleric overwhelmed by the spectral but all too physical presence of a "small black monkey" (*In a Glass Darkly* 23).[8] One focuses on a working-class man, setting its action in the "modern" industrial terrain of the railway and its associated technologies (*Fiction* 78–79); and the other on the representation of an educated bourgeois who moves in the company of aristocrats (*IGD* 110) and occupies a privileged domain in the comfort of rural Surrey (*IGD* 20) and the landscapes of an idealized, pre-industrial England. But these differences are essentially superficial, contrasting textures which conceal an underlying similarity. In "Green Tea," it can be argued, Le Fanu borrows extensively from Dickens's writing of character, situation and theme. His treatment is revealed in a close analysis of the stories' structural similarities.

These are several points of linkage between the apparently dissimilar protagonists, and Le Fanu's character can be read as a subtle reworking of Dickens's. Although distanced from the unnamed Signalman by the accident of class, the Reverend Jennings is the same type of personality, and Le Fanu models his primary characteristics, I contend, on those of the Dickensian original. Jennings clearly shares the Signalman's status as a solitary or "saturnine" (*Fiction* 80) introvert. Dickens's character is entirely self-contained, occupying a "lonesome" post (*Fiction* 78); while Jennings is mainly on his own. At the same time, neither is without friends or social graces: the Signalman treats his visitor with the utmost civility, confiding in him as if he were an intimate, and Jennings re-creates his "readiness" (*Fiction* 80) to share personal information in his conversations with Hesselius and his "good natured" (*IGD* 11) relationship with Lady Mary. Carried forward from one character to the next, these traits are used by Le Fanu to instill his creation with the psychological resonance developed in Dickens's prototype.

---

8. The edition used here is a modern reprint edited by Robert Tracy and cited in the text as *IGD*.

However, Le Fanu's more pressing concern is the question of Jennings's desire to make sense of the situation entrapping him, a situation directly borrowed from the circumstances explored in "The Signalman." Dickens formulates his tale as a drama involving his character's reading, or attempted reading, of signs, and Le Fanu writes Jennings in the same terms. Indeed, the similarities between the characters are striking: in Dickens's text the railman's task is to interpret the railway signals correctly, while in Le Fanu's Jennings's primary interest is research into the iconographies of theological (*IGD* 11) and Swedenborgian literature (15). The Signalman is obsessed with *legibility*, with reading signs which give a true representation of their messages, and Jennings is of precisely the same cast of mind. In Dickens's text the reading of the signals is entirely a matter of safety, and in Jennings's world there is a parallel demand that there should be "correspondence" between "forms" (*IGD* 15) and meanings. The problem, of course, is the incapacity of either the Signalman or Jennings to interpret what they see. Having already puzzled over the letters of Algebra (*Fiction* 80), Dickens's character is entirely unable to make sense of the "Appearance" (*Fiction* 84), and the same uncertainty, facing a more explicit and obviously troubling strangeness, afflicts the unfortunate Jennings. As the Signalman remarks, in a comment which underpins Le Fanu's story as surely as it structures Dickens's, "What does the spectre mean?" (*Fiction* 87).

Struggling to cope with this question, both characters undergo a psychological collapse, a "mental torture" (*Fiction* 87) which undermines the performance of their duties and burdens them with terrifying uncertainties. Jennings's condition is the same as the Signalman's, and Le Fanu replicates Dickens's lexical field. In "The Signalman" Dickens describes his character's anguish as a matter of nervousness or nervous breakdown, the very lineaments of cruelty, "feverish distress" (*Fiction* 87), anxiety and trouble (83, 85), and the same states of mind are represented in Jennings's unease, "irrepressible agitation" (*IGD* 26), "horror" and "despair" (29). And both are ultimately "oppressed beyond endurance" (*Fiction* 87): the Signalman takes his own life—deliberately stepping on to the track—while Jennings cuts his throat. Such is the only solution they can come up with: the Signalman is unable to rationalize or interpret the "cruel haunting" (*Fiction* 87), and Jennings is simply overwhelmed by the "dreadful" (*IGD* 29) impact of his "persecutor" (32). Unable to apply rational sense, both succumb to a belief in the unknown, finally regarding what they see as evil spirits, illegible forms whose sole function is a matter of "unfathomable malignity" (*IGD* 26).

There are nevertheless a number of possible explanations as to what the specters might mean, and as before Le Fanu bases his range of possibilities on those inscribed in the Dickensian text. The Signalman's apparition could be "supernatural" (*Fiction* 83), and Jennings is finally in no doubt of the monkey's "satanic" (*IGD* 26) purpose to make him into a "slave" of the Devil (32), and draw him ever "more interiorly into hell" (28). In "The Signalman" the Appearance seems to emanate from a quasi-medieval Hell's Mouth, a tunnel marked by a satanic "red light" (*Fiction* 79); and in Jennings's personal hell the monkey is characterized as a type of sooty incubus. Encased in a "reddish light" (*IGD* 23) with an aura of "red embers" (27), it seems to have come directly from an industrial Underworld, returning by going up the chimney (27) as surely as the Signalman's ghost returns to its tunnel.

This supernatural explanation is implied in Dickens's text, and foregrounded in Le Fanu's. Yet the characters' state of mind might equally be read as a psychological disorder. According to this line of reasoning, the two sets of apparitions are projections of some sort of inner conflict. The questions, of course, are simple ones: of what are they guilty? And what do they fear? Such speculation has particularly engaged writers on "Green Tea," there being no explicit reason as to why Jennings should have such feelings of anguish. In the words of Jack Sullivan, "he has done nothing but drink green tea" (18), and seems morally entirely innocent. However, the enigma of Jennings's "embarrassment" (*IGD* 10) can be explained by reading it as a detailed reworking of the Signalman's mental profile.

If we link these two as versions of mental illness we can see how Le Fanu follows Dickens in endowing his character with a series of difficult circumstances which might encourage psychological derangement. Buried in each text there are a series of clues suggesting the characters do have some underlying—and possibly shameful—secrets. The Signalman is described as being educated beyond his "station," having apparently cut short his studies because he had "run wild" and "misused his opportunities" (*Fiction* 81). The nature of that wildness is unspecified, but its implication is one of serious wrongdoing: he has "gone down, and never risen again . . . He had made his bed, and he lay upon it" (81). Such uncertainty might also be traced in Jennings's history, and although he is an occupant of (the apparently illegible) "Blank Street" (*IGD* 14) there is still the implication of there being something "a little ambiguous" (7) in his behavior. Hesselius further notes how his background contains issues beyond his immediate suffering which suggest a "series of transactions and alarms . . . carefully concealed" (9). But what is concealed? Dickens's use of the term "wild" would read in the context of its time as a sign of sexual impropriety, and it is possible that the apparitions witnessed by both characters are the emblems of repressed or shameful desire. This reading has often been applied to "Green Tea," notably by Glen Cavaliero (44) and Frederick Burwick (75), but its origin in the Signalman's circumstances is less obvious.

The sexual explanation is still only a possibility. The characters might equally be oppressed not by what they *have* done, but by what they *might* do. They may suppress their erotic needs but equally they try to repress their fear—or perhaps their fearful *desire*—to do something unacceptable, something, perhaps, their unconscious mind wishes they *would* do. The Signalman is afraid he will make a mistake resulting in another terrible accident (*Fiction* 87–88), and Jennings that his researches will commit some blasphemy. Viewed in these terms, the spectral beings they witness are the logical embodiment of their innermost anxieties: the Signalman's seeing of an Appearance associated with the site of an accident symbolizes the fear that *he* will cause the same thing to happen again, while the monkey, as a creature of mockery and disorder, is the emblem of Jennings's "shame" (*IGD* 7), the anxiety of somehow profaning his office. It is inevitable, then, that both apparitions try to make the characters do the very thing they least want to do: the Appearance sends misleading telegraph messages only intelligible to the Signalman (*Fiction* 84), while the monkey speaks "dreadful blasphemies" (*IGD* 31), and on at least one occasion torments the vicar when he is preaching (29).

The Signalman's ghost is thus written as an anxious product of the mind which, the more it is repressed the more it presents itself; while the monkey, as an equivalent of Dickens's original, inevitably returns to torment its "victim." Written as a classic exemplar of Freudian theory, such "cruel haunting" (*Fiction* 87) intensifies in "energy" (*IGD* 27) the more it is held in place. Indeed, Dickens provides a symbolic landscape of repression and constraint, a site of innermost containment that Le Fanu cleverly replicates in "Green Tea." The Signalman is caught in the severe and frustrating limitations of his job, while Jennings is squeezed within the narrow limits of his profession and social milieu. One is symbolically imprisoned by the narrowness of the cutting; while the other is hemmed in by the neatness of his house (*IGD* 14) and its claustrophobic screen of surrounding trees (20). Such limitations on the mind can only be unhealthy: Dickens describes the Signalman's place of work as "unnatural" (*Fiction* 84), a "dungeon" (79) imprisoning him, and the same idea of ever narrowing containment is carried forward in Le Fanu's account of Jennings's attempts to free himself merely by going away to the country (*IGD* 32).

These psychological readings provide a tangible explanation for the specters' "meaning" which stands in contrapuntal opposition to supernaturalism. A third strand is provided by the physiological interpretations favored by the original audiences of the 1860s. According to this line of reasoning, hauntings were caused not by madness or the unknown, but by illness, usually in the form of nervous disorders affecting the eye. Derived from de Boismont's *On Hallucinations* (1845, 1859) and parallel texts, this notion is modeled in "The Signalman" and developed at great length in "Green Tea." According to the narrator in Dickens's tale, the Signalman is merely suffering from "deception of his sense . . . a disease of the delicate nerves that minister to the functions of the eye" (*Fiction* 84). And the same idea is preserved by Le Fanu, framing his character's affliction as a matter of physical disorder in which the "nervous tissues" of the outer eye are inadvertently opened, allowing access to some peculiar inner vision (*IGD* 39). Dickens's narrator insists his companion can be cured of his "infection" (*Fiction* 80), noting how he will take him to "the wisest medical practitioner we could hear of in those parts . . . and take his opinion" (88); and the whole aim of "Green Tea" is to explore Jennings's predicament as if it were one of Dr Hesselius's case-studies.

We can see, in short, how "Green Tea" provides a pendant for "The Signalman," recreating its underlying ideas and implications, and offering the editor an elaborate new treatment of his bleak and troubling tale. As noted earlier, such patterning was likely a calculated strategy: "Green Tea" may have been sent to the offices of *All the Year Round* as a sales pitch and was certainly the piece that won him favour. On the basis of this work it was clear Le Fanu could write in an appropriate idiom and supply more of the same. The serial concluded on 13 November 1869, and on 24 November, in reply to the author's request for further opportunities, Dickens wrote to "assure" him that he would "be truly glad to count upon [him] as a regular contributor" (*Letters* 12.442). The editor was faithful to his word, and the arrangement survived his death in 1870. *The Rose and the Key* appeared in 1871, and Le Fanu followed it up with stories such as "Sir Dominick's Bargain" (1872).

Taken as a whole, his contributions allowed him to develop his association with *All the Year Round*, creating a niche which placed him in the mainstream of mid-Victorian fiction and gave him access to a wide audience. Such was undoubtedly his intention, and reading his stories as contributions to a journal allows us to refigure his status and recharacterize his achievement. Traditional criticism of Le Fanu has stressed his distinctiveness, but he can also be viewed, as the previous pages have shown, as a highly professional writer who knew how to shape his material to fit a particular context. Such an approach stresses the notion of Le Fanu the craftsman, who could give a potential employer what he was looking for. He does this with Bentley, and he takes the process much further in his homage to Dickens.

Much has been written of the concept of haunting in Le Fanu's work. His work, as critics have observed, is overshadowed by the ghosts of a crumbling Protestant culture, by the specters of religious doubt and the shades of personal fearfulness. But his contributions to *All the Year Round* can be read, finally, as haunted readings of another writer's work, sharply-crafted pieces which, although they are unmistakeably the work of Le Fanu, are visited, with uncanny persistence, by the ghost of Dickens.

Works Cited

Manuscripts

Unpublished letters: The National Library of Ireland, Dublin; and from a private collection.

Printed works

All the Year Round (New Series), Conducted by Charles Dickens. London: Chapman and Hall, 1868–70.

Allingham, Philip. "All the Year Round." *The Victorian Web.* victorianweb.org/periodicals/ayr.html. Accessed 7 June 2010.

Boyle, Thomas F. "The *Dublin University Magazine*." *British Literary Magazines: The Romantic Age, 1789–1836.* Ed. Alvin Sullivan. Westport, CT: Greenwood Press, 1983. 119–23.

Browne, Nelson. *Sheridan Le Fanu.* London: Barker, 1951.

Burwick, Frederick. "Romantic Supernaturalism: The Case Study as Gothic Tale." *The Wordsworth Circle* 34:2 (Spring 2003): 73–80.

Cavaliero, Glen. *The Supernatural in English Fiction.* Oxford: Oxford University Press, 1995.

Cooke, Simon. "'Metaphysical Medicine': de Boismont's Possible Influence on 'Green Tea.'" *Le Fanu Studies* 6:1 (May 2011): www.lefanustudies.com.

Crawford, Gary William. "Le Fanu's *In a Glass Darkly* and Samuel Warren's *Diary of a Late Physician*." *Le Fanu Studies* 1:1 (May 2006) www.lefanustudies.com.

Dickens, Charles. *The Christmas Books.* Vol. 1. Ed. Michael Slater. Harmondsworth, UK: Penguin, 1982.

———. *Selected Short Fiction.* Ed. Deborah A. Thomas. Harmondsworth, UK: Penguin, 1976.

———. *The Letters of Charles Dickens.* Vol. 12. Ed. Graham Storey. Oxford: Clarendon Press, 2002.

Hall, Wayne E. *Dialogues in the Margin: A Study of the* Dublin University Magazine. Washington DC: Catholic University of America Press, 1999.

Hughes, William. "The Origin and Implications of J. S. Le Fanu's 'Green Tea.'" *Irish Studies* 13:1 (February 2005): 45–54.

Lapinski, Piya Pal. "Dickens's Miss Wade and Le Fanu's Carmilla: The Female Vampire in *Little Dorrit.*" *Dickens Quarterly* 11:2 (August 1994): 81–87.

Le Fanu, J. S. *In a Glass Darkly.* Ed. Robert Tracy. Oxford: Oxford University Press, 1999.

———. *Madam Crowl's Ghost.* Ed. M. R. James. 1923. Rpt. Ware, UK: Wordsworth, 1994.

———. *Uncle Silas.* Introduction by W. J. Mc Cormack. Oxford: Oxford University Press, 1988.

Lehmann, R. C., ed. *Charles Dickens as Editor.* London: Smith, Elder, 1912.

Mc Cormack, W. J. *Sheridan Le Fanu.* 3rd ed. Stroud, UK: Sutton, 1997.

Oppenlander, Ella Ann. *Dickens' "All the Year Round": Descriptive Index and Contributor List.* Troy, NY: Whitston, 1984.

Sage, Victor. "Irish Gothic: C. P. Maturin and J. S. Le Fanu." In *A Companion to Gothic,* ed. David Punter. London: Blackwood, 2001.

———. *Le Fanu's Gothic: The Rhetoric of Darkness.* Basingstoke, UK: Palgrave Macmillan, 2004.

Stone, Harry. *Dickens and the Invisible World: Fairy Tales, Fantasy and Novel-Making.* London: Macmillan, 1979.

Sullivan, Jack. *Elegant Nightmares: The English Ghost Story from Le Fanu to Blackwood.* Athens: Ohio University Press, 1978.

Wynne, Deborah. *The Sensation Novel and the Victorian Family Magazine.* New York: Palgrave, 2001.

A Shared Vision: Le Fanu's *In A Glass Darkly* and Carl Theodor Dreyer's *Vampyr*

Gary William Crawford

Much of the criticism of Carl Theodor Dreyer's film *Vampyr* (1932) remarks how different the film is from Le Fanu's *In a Glass Darkly* (1872) on which it is based. Carlos Clarens's view is representative: "Dreyer and his screenwriter, Christen Jul, jettisoned most of the original plot, retaining only the basic theme, that of the vampire who continues to live after death, feeding on the blood of the young" (105–6). The best study of Le Fanu and Dreyer is in S. S. Prawer's *Caligari's Children: The Film as Tale of Terror*. He begins his chapter thus: "It needs no *politique des auteurs* to persuade us that Carl Dreyer's films convey a vision of the world which is predominately that of their director" (138). This essay, in regard to Le Fanu and Dreyer, counters that view. I contend that Dreyer, in making his film, shared Le Fanu's vision, even though he did not merely copy it.

I utilize David Bordwell's chapter on *Vampyr* in his book *The Films of Carl Theodor Dreyer*, Mark Nash's essay, Ebbe Neergaard's book, David Rudkin's monograph *Vampyr,* and recent studies of *In a Glass Darkly* to show how Dreyer visually reinterpreted Le Fanu's narrative structure through a series of comparable cinematic techniques.

Turning first to David Bordwell on *Vampyr*, I see that he regards point of view and juxtaposition of cinematic images as crucial to a sense of mystery that is the central point of the film, and as I will show, central to the Le Fanu original. Bordwell says that structurally the cinematic narrative of *Vampyr* is based on "absent cause," "contradictory spaces," and "narrative recoil."

The idea of absent cause comes early in the film when Allan Grey,[1] who like Le Fanu's Dr. Hesselius, is a student of the occult, takes a room at the

---

1. Note that three different versions of the film exist in German, French and English. In the English version, the name of the central character was David Gray, hence the different names given to the character by some critics.

small hotel of the village of Courtempierre. When he is visited by the vampire's victim's father, and receives from him a package that is "to be opened upon my death," the cause of the visitation is absent.

The following sequence shows Grey led by shadows that have no sources to the lair of the doctor. Here the logical cause and effect pattern is not present. Likewise the cinematic shots are built on "contradictory spaces." This is to say that what is seen within the frame is contradicted by what is outside the frame. This technique occurs through much of the film and suggests even further the mystification of the Le Fanu.

I quote Bordwell on his commentary on the opening sequence of *Vampyr*. He notices a dismantling of time and space:

> Such dismantling is most apparent from the way *Vampyr*'s editing flagrantly disrupts the spatio-temporal continuum. Like *Jeanne d'Arc*, *Vampyr* depends on a cross-cutting which perpetually fragments narrative continuity. The crosscutting frees up the spatio-temporal relations, making the film more perceptually opaque. From the very start, it juxtaposes spaces whose precise relationship has not been defined: David Gray's arrival at the inn is interrupted by cutaways to the old man with the scythe, while his wanderings are juxtaposed with repeated shots of the crooked angel that surmounts the inn. (98)

What provides sense to the film is "narrative recoil" where some of the questions are answered, but not all. These cinematic techniques are like, as I will show, Le Fanu's narrative strategy. As Bordwell concludes, "A dense, shadowy work, the film insistently challenges our perception, forcing us to struggle to grasp its spaces, its time, its logic. The complexity of this spectatorial activity makes *Vampyr*, in all its snares and bafflements, the fascinating film that it is" (116). Mark Nash studies *Vampyr* in relation to Tzvetan Todorov's *The Fantastic: A Structural Approach to a Literary Genre* and argues that Dreyer's film is based on the tension between the natural and the supernatural; and point of view in the film conveys this. Most of the film is seen from the point of view of Allan Grey, and he is described in the opening title of the film as a dreamer, for whom the line between the supernatural and the natural is blurred. Cause and effect are broken down the deeper he gets into the vampirism in the village of Courtempierre, and this is conveyed in cinematic terms, such as cross-cutting of shots.

In utilizing his cinematic techniques, Dreyer relies on the viewer's response to the mysteries in the film. Ebbe Neergaard quotes Dreyer in this connection:

> Imagine that we are sitting in an ordinary room. Suddenly we are told that there is a corpse behind the door. In an instant the room we are sitting in is completely altered; everything in it has taken on another look; the light,

the atmosphere have changed, though they are physically the same. This is because we have changed, and the objects are as we conceive them. That is the effect I want to get in my film. (27)

Dreyer utilized a specific technique to convey this feeling: he discovered that if he placed a piece of gauze over the lens of the camera and shined a light into it, it gave an overall misty, white quality to the film. So the film is really photographed, in a sense, "through a glass, darkly."

David Rudkin provides a shot by shot analysis which argues basically the same thing as Bordwell. His techniques present the same problems of "absent cause," which are not fulfilled logically until the conclusion of the film. Rudkin writes of the ending, the

> supreme irony of *Vampyr*, and the richest clue to its poetic intention: what Grey sees from within his coffin is a living world that he inhabits no more, yet is bound to him in a continuous syntax of integrated and coherent space. Such a coherence we have craved since the film began, and we have been denied. Now at last, we are vouchsafed it, a secure and rational geometry, at one and the same time binding, and severing, the living and the dead (75).

The opening scenes at the inn and at the evil doctor's lair create a sense of mystification. We cannot make sense of the images we see. At the inn where Grey takes a room, there are several shots that convey death. Outside the inn by the river, Grey tries to enter but the door is locked. There are several cuts to the figure of an angel above the hotel sign, and there are also shots of an old man with a scythe ringing a bell to call the ferry. The music is ominous and one can sense that Dreyer is trying to present an image of the Grim Reaper, Death.

In Grey's room at the inn, he looks at a painting on the wall of a mourning scene in which a priest, mourners, and a skeleton that is Death foreshadows the death scenes at the chateau with the vampire's victim. Dreyer cuts to a shot of the man with the scythe as Grey looks out of the window. The music during these shots is very ominous. What creates a sense of mystery and terror is the cross-cutting of images inside the inn and outside the inn. We hear the tolling of the bell calling the ferry in this sequence, and there are several cuts to a shot of the angel above the hotel sign.

While Grey sleeps, the door of his room opens, and a light from the floor fades up, suggesting the supernatural. The locked door magically opens and an old man enters. He opens the window shade in the room and then looks up, exclaiming "Quiet!" He then turns to Grey, who has been awakened by this visitation, and looks into the camera as if to look at Grey and says, "She must not die! Do you hear?" He leaves a small package on the bedside table, and he writes on it, "To be opened upon my death." Then he crosses to the door and bows slightly as he opens the door and leaves; and then the light from the floor fades out, and the light in the room returns to its original state.

There is no explanation for any of this material, which provides yet another instance of the absent cause. A title says that Grey sensed that a soul was in dire need, and that he must heed that call. He follows shadows that have no sources to a strange building that looks like a factory, and there is cross cutting to the shadow of a man who is digging a grave in reverse. At the doctor's lair the shadow of a man with a peg leg seems to have no source until it sits down properly with its owner. There follows a shot of an old woman with a cane as the music becomes more foreboding. There are shadows of men and women dancing to a polka played by the shadows of musicians that are stopped by the old woman calling "Quiet!"

Nothing is explained during this entire sequence, and the shots are deliberately illogical.

The appearance of the doctor is marked by confusing shots of corridors and rooms. The old woman, we later learn, is the vampire and is in collusion with the doctor and the peg-legged man to kill whom we later discover is the vampire's victim. The old woman who is the vampire hands the doctor a bottle of poison. One clearly sees that even though nothing is explained, the idea of Death is repeatedly conveyed, and clearly we see that the film is about life and death.

Influencing Vampyr, Le Fanu's In a Glass Darkly appropriately also focuses on life-and-death issues. The opening sequence of "Carmilla," in which Carmilla's mother exclaims, after a carriage accident, that she is on a journey of "life and death" (253) presents the central theme of Le Fanu and the Dreyer film. Similarly, in Vampyr's screenplay, Dreyer and Christen Jul wrote that the river at Courtempierre was the dividing line between life and death (7).

In dealing with these ideas, Le Fanu's work is, as Jack Sullivan has noted, very modern (12); and Dreyer actually determined to make a film in the style of the "isms" of the time, such as German expressionism and French surrealism; and both of these movements are historically related to the Gothic. In their biography of Dreyer, Dale D. Drum and Jean Drum point this out; the film is a break from the realism of his previous films (156). It is a critical commonplace that the Gothic novel presaged modernism, and Le Fanu's In a Glass Darkly is a key transitional development in the history of the movement.

In the terms of the narrative in the Le Fanu and the Dreyer film, life and death concerns are presented from the outset. In the film, as Tom Milne writes of the opening scenes, "the whole sequence, with its dissolving surfaces as though people were literally being seen through a glass darkly, and its profound silences broken only by the unearthly tolling of the bell and the remote echo of a human voice, is like a mysterious ceremonial of death" (108). It is as if both the author and the filmmaker pose the question, what can man really know of his precarious position in the face of death? From the beginning of *In a Glass Darkly*, death makes its presence. We learn, through Dr. Hesselius's medical secretary, that Hesselius has died. Posthumously he edits Hesselius's papers, the first case history being the story of the Rev. Mr. Jennings, who is haunted by a spirit demon in the form of a monkey until he commits suicide. The multiple, contradictory, and unreliable narratives of "Carmilla" reveal that Laura, the narrator, receives news that her friend Bertha, who was to pay Laura a visit, has died.

In the terms of narrative in Le Fanu, the idea of mystery in the face of death appears. Victor Sage has noted, in his discussion of frames in Le Fanu, that they "create a peephole into a forbidden, or a forgotten world, created dialectically out of its very canceling rhetoric" (23). *In a Glass Darkly* is a tangled skein of narratives, and Le Fanu's point is that all of the narrators are unreliable. They contradict each other in subtle ways, creating a pervasive sense that all is mystery. In Dreyer's film, the juxtaposition of apparently unconnected images creates a prevailing sense of mystery in the viewer. By turning away from the orderly Hollywood film narrative, in which all is logical, Dreyer creates a film that is true to Le Fanu's original. It is as if in both the author and the filmmaker, a question is posed, "What can we know in the face of death?"

We see Dreyer's characters, the vampire's victim who cries out for death, and her sister who faces the murder of her father, come to grips with the reality of death. Dreyer uses close-ups of faces to convey their anguish. The camera angles and the cross-cutting convey a pervasive sense of mystery. The multiple and contradictory and unreliable narratives of Le Fanu convey this in a parallel way.

Some critics have noted the fact that rather than using the King James translation of St. Paul, "through a glass, darkly," Le Fanu writes *In a Glass Darkly*, suggesting a mirror which underscores the isolation and self-haunting of the protagonists of the tales. All the characters in Dreyer and Le Fanu are alone. We only have their isolated narratives and their isolated viewpoints.

It is astonishing how many narrators there are in *In a Glass Darkly*. There are four narrators in "Green Tea," two in "The Familiar," five in "Mr. Justice Harbottle," two in "The Room in the Dragon Volant," and three in "Carmilla." The multiple narratives serve as a discourse on the reality of the supernatural. The conflicting and contradictory viewpoints are like a set of Chinese boxes. One narrative is enclosed within the other, and the entire book is unified in that it is a collection of linked short stories.

There is one unifying figure in the stories and the film: the character of Dr. Martin Hesselius in the fiction and the character of Allan Grey in the film. Since the five tales of *In a Glass Darkly* are from the files of Hesselius, and Allan Grey is the central character of *Vampyr*, the reader and the viewer are given the point of view of these students of the supernatural. Dr. Hesselius takes part in the action of the tale "Green Tea," but he is shown to be a fraud. He does not help the Rev. Mr. Jennings; in fact, he is responsible for opening the way for him to commit suicide. Allan Grey is not a fraud, but, like a somnambulist, he goes through the entire film with a blank, slightly surprised expression on his face. (Julian West, the screen name of the actor and financier of the film, Baron Nicolas de Gunzburg, is not a trained actor, but Dreyer utilizes him well.) Most of the actors in the film are amateurs whom Dreyer chose for what he called their "mental resemblance" to the characters.

These characters are faced with the supernatural and with death. The vampire's victim in *Vampyr*, Léone, and the Rev. Mr. Jennings, the victim of "Green Tea" cry out in despair. Léone cries out "I'm lost!" and the Rev. Mr. Jennings says to Hesselius "while I talk to you, and implore relief, I feel that my prayer is for the impossible, and my pleading with the inexorable" (31).

I will turn now to a discussion of the narrative of *In a Glass Darkly* and along the way, show how it is echoed in *Vampyr*. In the first story, "Green Tea," for instance, the Rev. Mr. Jennings is haunted to his death by what appears to be a spirit-demon in the form of a monkey. But Le Fanu implies that the monkey has no objective reality by offering several other possibilities for the supernatural phenomena: the appearance of the monkey may be merely a hallucination resulting from the mentally stimulating effects of green tea; it may be, in the scientific-metaphysical jargon of Dr. Hesselius, an opening of "the interior sense"; it may be one of the demons that Mr. Jennings reads about in the writings of Emanuel Swedenborg; and, in psychological terms, it may be the symbolic representation of the Rev. Mr. Jennings's religious doubts. The point of all these conflicting explanations is that no one explanation is satisfactory. Similarly, in *Vampyr* there is no reason that the innocent Léone is being victimized by an old woman who lives after death as a vampire.

Furthermore, in "Green Tea," as in each story in *In a Glass Darkly*, Le Fanu places each of these contradictory explanations for the supernatural phenomena within the narrative viewpoints of several characters. By offering several different spectral and psychological explanations, each of these narrators and their informants contradicts the other and is thereby rendered unreliable. There are questions about narrative reliability in the face of death. Can the reader know the real truth amid the many versions of the "truth" the narrators provide? In the dark vision of the world that *In a Glass Darkly* and *Vampyr* present, nothing, or everything, is real.

As Jack Sullivan writes of "Green Tea,"

> Le Fanu's world view is not based on a coherent or knowable determinism—there is neither the benign workings of Providence nor the naturalism of Zola or Dreiser. The sense of doom in these stories emanates from a uniquely hostile cosmos vaguely suggestive of the purblind doomsters which later pursue Thomas Hardy's characters. But Le Fanu is not interested in programmatic philosophical consistency. In trying to get at the source of the horror, various characters suggest various possibilities—all of them bleak—yet final solutions elude them, as they elude the reader. One event leads inexorably to another once the pursuit begins, but the reason behind it is known only to the otherworldly invaders. (19)

The cause is absent to the innocent victim, just as there is absent cause, as David Bordwell noted earlier in this essay, in *Vampyr*. What, may we ask, is happening in *Vampyr*? These questions can be very disconcerting to viewers, and this sense of confusion was felt by the spectators at the premiere of *Vampyr* in Berlin in 1932: they hissed and booed during the showing and there was a minor riot at the box office when the film was shown in Vienna with patrons demanding their money back. Dreyer's experiment with the film medium was misunderstood.

Le Fanu's book was also misunderstood by critics when it appeared in 1872. The anonymous contemporary reviewer of the book in the *Saturday Review* expressed an impatient puzzlement: "Mr. Le Fanu, having written four or five foolish and vulgar ghost stories, presents them to the world as belonging to 'metaphysical speculation,' or 'religious metaphysics,' or 'metaphysical medicine' " (222). And the Swedenborgianism of "Green Tea" appears to be just one more inadequate solution to the problematic cause of Jennings's haunting.

Similarly, in "The Familiar," we cannot know what precisely haunts Captain Barton to his death; and as in "Green Tea" the narrators are unreliable and contradictory. Here Le Fanu raises the question of the reliability of his main narrator by having him admit that much of what he reports is based on mere conjecture; and in some instances, Le Fanu leads the reader to believe that his narrator's reports are not only conjectural, but sheer fabrications. We can never know the force that drives Captain James Barton to his death.

The supernatural entity that appears to drive Captain Barton cannot be known either—it may be the ghost of a man or a spirit in the shape of an owl. Barton's entire story is clouded under what the Rev. Herbert admits is an "impenetrable mystery" (82). At the outset of the tale, Barton disbelieves in supernatural agencies, including God; but after he is haunted by the ghost of a sailor he murdered, Barton is subsequently terrified into believing in the spectral. What finally kills Barton is unknown; it may be his fiancée's pet owl, which terrifies him, and it may be the ghost of the man. Barton's servant only hears confusing sounds and voices and sees the owl crash through the skylight in his room. His master is found dead with a look of absolute horror on his face. Here the face of Barton is like the agonized face of the vampire's victim in *Vampyr*. The close ups of the actress Sybille Schmitz, who plays Léone, in which she alternately becomes a victim and a victimizer, are some of the most significant images of the film.

In "Mr. Justice Harbottle," Le Fanu utilizes five narrators and five separate supernatural manifestations witnessed by five different characters. The central spectral court that tries Justice Harbottle for his crimes on the bench appears in a dream sequence. But the most significant borrowing from Le Fanu in the film is the live burial of young Richard Beckett in "The Room in the Dragon Volant," which parallels Allan's splitting into two selves and experiencing his own burial.

As in Le Fanu, Grey can see the vampire and the doctor's cohorts through his coffin's transom as he is carried to a graveyard. The sequence is a dream, which may be regarded as the death of consciousness.

Finally, in "Carmilla," we have the vampire theme. Like the lesbian implications in Le Fanu, Dreyer's vampire is an old woman who was evil and unrepentant during life and is a vampire in death. In Dreyer vampirism represents a sickness of the soul.

The primary narrator of Le Fanu's novella is certainly unreliable. Written as a letter to "a town lady," Laura admits confusion and misunderstanding about her experiences. Similarly, the victim Léone's confusion and sense of loss is similar. There is the famous sequence in the film of Léone's feeling agony about her plight, and then suddenly lusting after her own sister with a hard, cruel smile showing her teeth. The excerpts from the book that Léone's father leaves to Allan Grey, *Der Vampyre* by Paul Bonnat, relate to the viewer the characteristics of the vampire and parallel the events of the film.

As David Bordwell has pointed out, *Vampyr* is a pale, bloodless film in which the sets are white and seen through a pale white mist, through a glass darkly, as it were. The final death of the doctor, who is locked as if by magic in a cage in a flour mill where white flour smothers him, is another example of this spectral whiteness. This sequence cross-cuts to the escape of Allan Grey and Léone's younger sister Gisèle in a boat on the white fog-shrouded river. Allan and Gisèle cross the river of life and death, and shots of the machinery of the mill coming to a stop at the end illustrate the shutting down of the machinery of the vampire story and serve as Dreyer's ending.

As I contend here, Dreyer was not making a film that was solely his own. He saw things in Le Fanu that he interpreted in cinematic terms. The camera work and editing are like the contradictory and unreliable narratives in the fiction. Dreyer transformed Le Fanu's strikingly modern original into a modern expressionist film that is today regarded as a film masterpiece in general and a horror film classic in particular.

Works Cited

Bordwell, David. *The Films of Carl-Theodor Dreyer.* Berkeley: University of California Press, 1981.

Clarens, Carlos. *An Illustrated History of the Horror Film.* New York: Capricorn Books, 1968.

Crawford, Gary William. "Sheridan Le Fanu's *In a Glass Darkly:* Ironic Distance and the Supernatural." M.A. thesis: Mississippi State University, 1977.

Drum, Jean, and Dale D. Drum. *My Only Great Passion: The Life and Films of Carl Th. Dreyer.* Lanham, MD: Scarecrow Press, 2000.

Dreyer, Carl Theodor, and Christen Jul. *Vampyr: The Screenplay.* The Criterion Collection, 2008.

Le Fanu, J. Sheridan. *In a Glass Darkly.* Oxford: Oxford University Press, 1993.

Milne, Tom. *The Cinema of Carl Dreyer.* New York: A. S. Barnes, 1971.

Nash, Mark. "Vampyr and the Fantastic." *Screen* 17:3 (1976): 29–67.

Neergaard, Ebbe. *Carl Dreyer: A Film Director's Work.* Trans. Marianne Helweg. London: British Film Institute, 1950.

Prawer, S. S. *Caligari's Children: The Film as Tale of Terror.* Oxford: Oxford University Press, 1981.

Rudkin, David. *Vampyr.* London: British Film Institute, 2005.

Sage, Victor. *Le Fanu's Gothic: The Rhetoric of Darkness.* Basingstoke, UK: Palgrave Macmillan, 2004.

Sullivan, Jack. *Elegant Nightmares: The English Ghost Story from Le Fanu to Blackwood.* Athens: Ohio University Press, 1978.

[Unsigned.] Review of *In a Glass Darkly. Saturday Review* (17 August 1872): 222–23.

Dreyer, *Vampyr,* and Sheridan Le Fanu

Mark Le Fanu

A glance at the classic Danish film *Vampyr* (1932) should begin with a glance at its begetter, Carl Th. Dreyer (1889–1968), whose relatively restricted output (especially in the later part of his career, only five features completed in over thirty years) has not prevented him from being spoken about as one of the greatest film directors of all time. The accolade rests not so much on some surmised technical prowess as on the recognition of a very special spiritual integrity: everything he touched—and he touched many different genres in the course of his lifetime—he made inimitably his own. Proud, shy and reticent in his personal life, he gave everything he had to the burgeoning craft of cinema. Somehow or other, the profundity and heroism of that sacrifice are communicated as a felt value in his movies. Each of them has a beautiful seriousness.

The bulk of Dreyer's filmography—nine films out of a total of fourteen, stretching from his debut in 1919 to *La Passion de Jeanne d'Arc* in 1928—belongs to the silent epoch. The vagaries of Danish film production (the industry, which subsequently collapsed, had enjoyed a brief golden age just prior to the first world war) meant that no sooner had he established himself at home than he had to seek his fortune abroad, wherever he could find backers: in practice this meant Germany and France. *La Passion de Jeanne d'Arc*, his last effort in the twenties is one of the finest of all silent films—an epitome of the art-form as it had developed up to that point—but it was not a success with the public. Notoriously, *Vampyr*, too, was to fail to find an audience, even more disastrously than *Jeanne d'Arc* did, so it is worth emphasizing that this strange, hermetic and experimental film was originally conceived of, if not exactly as a "potboiler" (the concept is impossible in Dreyer's case), then at least as something possessing—he hoped—healthy money-making possibilities. After the great Expressionist outburst at the beginning of the decade that had issued in masterpieces like *The Cabinet of Dr Caligari* (Robert Wiene, 1919) and *Nosferatu* (F. W. Murnau, 1922), vampires, horror and darkness were back in vogue again toward the end of the twenties—both in Europe and the USA. In films such as *The Lodger* (Alfred

232

Hitchcock, 1926) and *The Cat and the Canary* (Paul Leni, 1927) Dreyer discerned, or thought he could discern, instances of a genre where broad popular appeal was allowed to exist within the framework of artistic integrity.

The material Dreyer and his co-scenarist Christen Jul chose to base their screenplay on (the director always worked from literary sources) was a collection of tales entitled *In a Glass Darkly* by the nineteenth-century Irish Huguenot writer Joseph Sheridan Le Fanu—one tale in particular standing out from the collection, "Carmilla," a strikingly modern vampire story with a scarcely concealed lesbian subtext. The writer of these lines professes kinship with Le Fanu, so perhaps it will be understandable that I have always secretly harbored the hope that Dreyer possessed a special fondness for this author. Alas, scholarship is unable to confirm the surmise one way or the other. Casper Tybjerg, Dreyer's current biographer, has found no irrefutable evidence on the matter, and indeed other, more prosaic, considerations may have been to the fore. Following on from the legal trouble Murnau had had with the Bram Stoker estate on the release of *Nosferatu* back in 1922, one thing that *had* to be got right by Dreyer and his backers was that the material should be out of copyright. And here as luck would have it (Le Fanu died in 1873), Dreyer found himself on safe ground.

At all events, it is a somewhat contentious question how much *Vampyr* really is based on "Carmilla." The French film historian Maurice Drouzy who has written extensively on the director and knew many of his collaborators at first hand is only one of a number of authorities who believe that the debt is quite marginal. "While certain directors don't hesitate to pillage literature without naming their sources" [I quote from Drouzy's book on the director written in the early 1980s] "Dreyer, here, was engaged in an exactly opposite manouevre, that of attaching his own ideas to an innocent third party. Why didn't he, I wonder, own up to the fact that he invented the whole thing?" Drouzy's answer—that Dreyer needed the literary camouflage to protect the deepest personal meaning of the film from the public's and critics' gaze—is suggestive, and we will come back to it. Still, it is fair to add that Drouzy's take on the adaptation, or as he would say, the pseudo-adaptation, is not necessarily the last word. Other writers—notably S. S. Prawer in *Caligari's Children: The Film as Tale of Terror* (1980) and David Rudkin in his excellent monograph on the film recently contributed to the British Film Institute Classics series—have been more patient with the mysterious ways by which literary sources "infiltrate" a scenario, not always head-on, yet in the end decisively, through their accumulation of often-surprising detail. A crucial linkage here is that the vampire, in both book and film, should be female. In "Carmilla" she is young and beautiful, whereas in *Vampyr* of course—it is one of the most striking things everyone remembers from the film—she is a stout, aged witch with a walking stick. As Prawer points out, the cue for this change may have been provided by the original, in the figure of Carmilla's terrifying mother, briefly introduced early in Le Fanu's tale before just as suddenly vanishing. Nor, despite many alterations of tone and emphasis, is the intimate, adolescent and sexual subtext of the tale entirely absent from the movie—mediated, here, by the bifurcation of Le Fanu's ripe, innocent heroine Laura into a pair of languid sisters, Léone and Gisèle, one of whom, in becoming a vampire herself, takes over the central figure of Carmilla, whom Dreyer and Jul chose to dispense with.

In the end, the issue is probably not whether or not the film is one hundred per cent faithful to the original (plainly it is not), but what *Vampyr* signifies in its own terms, as an autonomous aesthetic object. Its elliptical dreamlike logic seems to demand, more than many films do, some definitive shot at interpretation. What is it exactly that we have watched here? Can we piece together what the film means? A critic who failed to ask these kinds of questions would be failing in his duty I think, and indeed it is one of the attractive aspects of Maurice Drouzy's approach to Dreyer that he doesn't hesitate to give us a reading. We may or may not agree with him in the event; we may feel, as with many interpretations, that there is something reductive and simplistic in its conclusions. But at least it is there and examinable. The essence of Drouzy's case, as I have already said, is that the film is profoundly autobiographical. He claims that it plays out as a fantastical psychodrama the ambivalence and pain Dreyer felt all his adult life about his fate as an abandoned, and subsequently adopted, child. In the film, the vampire Marguerite is Dreyer's hated Danish foster mother (Marie Dreyer in real life), while Léone is his beloved birth mother whom the hero of the film fails to rescue from suicide; yet who nonetheless survives, re-born, in the figure of her twin sister Gisèle—whom (just to round off the Oedipal circle) our hero in due course falls in love with.

In forwarding his thesis, Drouzy makes much play with proper names. Marguerite elides into Marie Dreyer (perhaps not so close a match after all?); Gisèle and Léone are pressed together to become—at a pinch—Joséphine, the first half of the name of Dreyer's birth mother. Her complete name, Joséphine-Bernhardine, is supplied, conveniently, by the names of the castle-owner's servant, Joseph, an important secondary figure in the film; and the castle owner himself, named Bernard. The reader may harbor legitimate doubts about the usefulness of this kind of Freudian detective work, while at the same time recognizing that names *are* an interesting aspect of the film. The fact that the vampire is given a surname is quite striking in the first place: her complete name, Marguerite Chopin, certainly has a ring to it. Then there are the different names that the hero is known by: in real life the actor Baron Nicolas de Gunzburg (who incidentally was the film's independent financial backer), in the movie he is—depending on which print one sees—"Julian West," or else "Allan Grey," or, finally, "David Gray" (it is interesting that the surname of these last two should be spelled slightly differently). The explanation for all this may well be straightforward—attributable to nothing more odd than the different linguistic versions of the film, French, German and English, that Dreyer was preparing for the international market. Yet, on the other hand, if we think about it, this pluralism really does seem to symbolize something important about the film, and that is the way that the characters dissolve into each other, taking on separate personas, imitating in so doing the logic of dreams, in which identity is always fluid, and you—the dreaming subject, the inventor of these phantasms—can never be quite sure whom you're dealing with.

So a fascinating aspect of the film is the way that the hero himself, and not just the Gisèle/Léone pair, is also "bifurcated," not only, though most obviously, in the scene in which, after he has tripped up and fallen in the meadow, we see his soul in double exposure leaving his body; but also in some other, earlier scenes where a kind of "relay effect" is introduced by allowing the servant Joseph to take over from Gray the reading of the vampire manuscript—in effect usurping Gray's function as authorial presence and chief guide to events (a substitution reinforced toward the film's ending, where intriguingly it is Joseph, not Gray, who digs up the coffin and drives the fatal stake through Marguerite Chopin's heart).

The tendency toward multiple narratorship glimpsed here takes us back, if we so wish, to Le Fanu's original manuscript. The five separate tales that make up the 1872 collection *In a Glass Darkly*—"Green Tea," "The Familiar," "Mr. Justice Harbottle," "The Room in the Dragon Volant," and finally "Carmilla"—are presented as coming from the working papers of a certain Dr. Hesselius, a "metaphysical physician" or, as perhaps we should say, a psychiatrist (at least some early form of this profession)—papers which in turn are being edited and prepared for publication by the said doctor's literary amanuensis, during the early part of the nineteenth century. The fictive scholarly apparatus with which Le Fanu goes on to surround each of the stories complicates them in a remarkably modern way—which Dreyer and his scenarist may well have picked up on. So, for example, to take one of these tales at random, in "Mr. Justice Harbottle," we have the following narrative relay: (1) the original case study is said to have been communicated by Dr. Hesselius to his medical colleague Van Loo of Leyden in the form of a letter;

(2) the letter informed his friend that two versions of this story of a haunting were current; only one of these versions is extant—and this version actually is the less interesting one! (3) It is this lesser version, then, communicated to Hesselius by a certain Mr. Harman, that is now being edited for publication by the amanuensis. But before readers have proceeded into the story very far they discover that the author of the "less interesting" version had in turn received it from an "elderly witness" of his acquaintance, so that it is the words of *this* (unnamed) man finally (4) that we are reading on the page.

This may then be the place to remind ourselves of the significance of the fact that, as hinted before, not one but two tales from In a Glass Darkly are strongly represented in the film, with all the opportunities this gives for further narrative dispersement. The other great source besides "Carmilla" for *Vampyr* is the long post-Napoleonic adventure story "The Room in the Dragon Volant," a rambling Balzacian chronicle of crime and sexual intrigue set in the milieu of French high society. It's from this text that Dreyer borrowed the location of the film—an ancient inn near a mysterious chateau in the neighborhood of Paris—along with a number of suggestive details, the most telling of which involves the cameo near the climax of the tale, in which the dashing English hero is screwed down into a coffin while still alive, paralyzed (because of his drugged state) and unable to communicate with possible helpers. Such mute and hypnagogic trances evidently interested Dreyer highly—and not always in the context of terror. The question of immortality (and what one might call its opposite, pseudo-immortality) fascinated Dreyer throughout his life, both within and without the traditional Christian framework. The meditation it encompasses is the central idea explored in what is probably his greatest movie, *Ordet/The Word* (1955), from Kai Munk's play, which ends, stupendously, with the resurrection from her coffin of the young heroine Inger after she has supposedly died in childbirth. Impossible, blasphemous and yet—in the context the film provides for it—true, just and compelling. *Ordet* partakes of none of the malignity and madness that we find in *Vampyr*. A different kind of poetic sublime is being explored in this film. But with vampires, too, it is the pathos of immortality that moves us most when we admit to being moved—the restlessness of their undead souls, the sadness of their longing to be done with it all, even as they feed on the blood of live mortals.

The vampire genre gave Dreyer the chance to explore, too, less grandly metaphysical aspects of immortality, specifically the idea of *out-of-body experiences*—the notion (terrifying or exalting depending on circumstances) that the soul may survive, even for a short period, the physical death of the subject, rising out of the body to look down upon it from "above," as happens in *Vampyr* in the extraordinary sequence (borrowed as we have said from "The Room in the Dragon Volant") in which David Gray, nailed into a casket, seems to observe his own progress to doom as the coffin is wheeled through the streets of Courtempierre towards the cemetery. (Bergman in his turn may have been thinking of this *doppelgänger* episode when he came to stage the wonderful dream early on in *Smultronstället/Wild Strawberries* [Ingmar Bergman, 1957] in which old professor Isak Borg, played by Viktor Sjöström, confronts his ghostly double in the coffin that slides out of the broken carriage.) It is a fair guess, anyway, that at one time or another many of us have dreamed of such ghostly encounters with ourselves; just as we regularly dream, too, of the beloved dead—friends and relatives departed from us, yet who for the duration of the dream are back and "alive" in our company, doing their best to prove that they are immortal.

On waking, alas, it is different. Then we see that death really is irrevocable. Under cover of the film's discreet symbolism, the two sides of the equation are both present: the dreamlike hope for continuance coupled to the knowledge of irremediable loss. Dreyer's birth mother, a servant seduced by her Swedish master, killed herself in a particularly horrible way when Dreyer was two years old, by eating a box of phosphorous matches. We have glanced at the question earlier on in this essay whether Drouzy's autobiographical reading of the film is or is not to be judged "far-fetched." Yet if proof for Drouzy's contention is needed, it is perhaps provided by the extraordinary moment (one of a number of such moments accruing round this strikingly-conceived character) when we come across the vampire sister, Léone, staring at the poison bottle by her bedside with a mixture of longing and horror. Drouzy doesn't say it explicitly so we may be allowed to say it for him, that it is difficult if not impossible to avoid here a fleeting reminiscence of Dreyer's birth mother Joséphine-Bernhardine's last moments on earth. It is the *intensity* of the shot that permits this intimation: the idea that we are in the presence, if only momentarily, of something personal, secret and momentous. (No one involved was to know when the film was being shot that the actress who takes the part, Sybille Schmitz—one of the few professionals in the cast—was herself to end her life tragically by suicide.)

Vampyr was Dreyer's first sound film, made at a time when the technology of sound was still at a quite early stage of its development, and the aesthetics of the movie still belong in obvious and important ways to the silent epoch. There is very little spoken dialogue. No harm in that: by the end of the twenties, the visual vocabulary of silent film had reached, internationally, an extraordinary level of refinement and sophistication. Indeed it could be argued that a significant percentage of the most beautiful films of all time belong to the period in question. Yet I am thinking not only of the prodigies of lighting here (Dreyer himself was a great private connoisseur of the Danish and Dutch masters of *chiaroscuro*) but also of the film's suppleness of camera movement which, following the innovations of F. W. Murnau in the middle of the 1920s, took off in a major way during the rest of the decade. *Vampyr* is full of terrifically *soigné* traveling shots that explore space and locale with freedom and daring. At the same time, the compositions are daringly de-centered: a head may appear in the bottom left-hand corner of the picture, for example, cut off from the body attached to it, forcing the viewer to construct in his mind's eye the missing elements of the body as if in a jigsaw puzzle. As in other instances of the avant-garde art of the period, there is a deliberate effort of estrangement; the question "what exactly are we watching here?" becomes (if you go along with it) one of the film's primary aesthetic pleasures.

To return to the soundtrack for a moment, *Vampyr*'s opacity—one might almost say crudity—of dialogue is arguably in itself an "aesthetic value," contributing importantly to the film's uncanny dreamlike atmosphere. (We do talk in dreams, of course, but somehow speech is not dream's primary element.) In later vampire movies—for example, the famous Hammer cycle of the sixties and seventies—talk is naturalized into the dramatic fabric of the scenario, at the expense, however, of atmosphere and mystery, introducing indeed, at times, an unwanted comic element: such movies slide easily into camp. It would be wrong to imagine that Dreyer was uninterested in speech. On the contrary, later films of his show, among other things, a complete mastery of the medium of sound. But in *Vampyr* Dreyer intuited, correctly I believe, that, concerning atmosphere, the crucial contribution would continue to be made (where it had always been made in the days of so-called silent film), through the medium of music. And in fact, Wolfgang Zeller's delicately eerie score is one of the film's quiet triumphs.

And yet the words *are* important—maybe just because there are so few of them! Taken together, they represent in this film a kind of collective cry from the abyss: against a background of generalized evil, somebody, somewhere, is dying, and that person needs to be saved. The central figure around whom such a "pathos of salvation" accrues is Léone, of course, but throughout the film further hints and possibilities are continually dangled before the viewer. When Gray first arrives at the inn, for example, he hears the sound of weeping emanating from a nearby room. A man's voice is trying to console a woman who cries out in her grief: "Oh my little boy, why did I have to lose him . . . why, why?," an episode followed immediately afterwards by another incident in which a nervous stranger (he later turns out to be Léone's father

Bernard) appears in Gray's room and stammers out this mysterious message: "She mustn't die, do you hear? . . . She's dying, dying"—all this long before we *meet* any of the characters in the film, male or female, about whom such appeals might be referable (indeed as far as the dead child is concerned, there is no further mention to his fate). The inherent drama of such petitions coupled to their vagueness of object, seem to me to belong profoundly to the logic of dreaming. An immense underground feeling of pity suffuses the film. Here, finally, is the *psychological coherence* that lies at the heart of *Vampyr*, however contrived are its narrative byways.

The movie premiered in Berlin in the summer of 1932 but as stated above it was not a public success: on its opening night it was barracked by a section of the audience, anticipating thereby the notorious reception at Cannes, some thirty years later, of Dreyer's last sublime masterpiece *Gertrud* (1964). Nor did the film's lukewarm welcome at Copenhagen nearly a year later help to restore the director's equilibrium. The independence he enjoyed as a producer, while providing him with vital aesthetic freedom, had worn him down physically and mentally. As Drouzy records, the shooting of *Vampyr* was a draining and indeed fearful experience for all involved, taking its toll on Dreyer's personal life. In the wake of its commercial failure there were inevitable money problems. His marriage came under threat and for a time he entered a psychiatric clinic (by strange coincidence, the name of this establishment, at Saint-Mandé near Paris, turned out to be the Institut Jeanne d'Arc). At the same time, contacts re-established with his old production company, Société Général de Films, issued only in abortive projects—a doomed Italian co-production in Somalia—before being ruptured altogether. We are entering what Drouzy calls *les années noires de Dreyer*, the bulk of the 1930s, when rather little is known about his movements. He rested, and read, and wrote articles. Ten years were to pass before a new man emerged at the far side of his crisis—re-moralized, re-invigorated, and ready to enter the fight again.

Bibliographical Note

"Dreyer, *Vampyr* and Sheridan Le Fanu" is a revised version of an essay written to accompany the DVD release of *Vampyr* for The Criterion Collection in 2008. The DVD disc, besides possessing an excellent visual quality (from a restoration made in 1998) contains a number of extras that may be of interest to readers of the above essay, including a visual commentary on the film composed by Professor Casper Tybjerg, a vintage (1966) documentary on Dreyer's career, and an audio voice-over. Tybjerg's biography of Dreyer, long awaited, is due to be published in 2012. The old biography by Maurice Drouzy mentioned in Mark Le Fanu's essay was published in France in 1982 (Editions du Cerf). Two other studies mentioned in the current essay are *Caligari's Children: The Film as Tale of Terror* by S. S. Prawer (Oxford University Press, 1980) and *Vampyr* by David Rudkin (British Film Institute, 2005), both excellent. Finally, the Oxford World's Classics edition of Sheridan Le Fanu's 1872 collection of tales *In a Glass Darkly* (1993, revised 2008), the text on which *Vampyr* was based, contains a scholarly introduction by Professor Robert Tracy, along with extensive and helpful textual apparatus.

IV. Contemporary Reviews

Contemporary Reviews

Compiled by the Editors

The Cock and Anchor (1845)

————*Dublin University Magazine* 26 (November 1845): 607–25.
It has that sterling merit which needs no flattery, and which can bear the censure of bold and free criticism, without detracting from its praise. [. . .] It is impossible to peruse even a chapter of it, without having the mind stamped with the conviction that the writer is a man of genius, and this is impressed even upon its faults. [. . .]

We take our leave of *The Cock and Anchor* rejoiced that to the literature of Ireland there has been made an addition, in every way calculated to do it honor.

The Fortunes of Colonel Torlogh O'Brien (1847)

————*Dublin University Magazine* 30 (September 1847): 276–78.
But why should we go on prophesying about the future, when even at this moment Ireland has writers of whom she may be justly proud—some of the power and ability sufficient at all events, to make her name respected; and, amongst the many proofs which we can bring forward of the truth of what we

---

[The following excerpts from contemporary reviews of Le Fanu's works have been chosen based on several criteria. Herein the reader will find expressed opinions that vary from perceptive to myopic, sympathetic to hostile, conscious of the author's attempts to push beyond the apparent genres in which his work has been marketed and impatient with the liberties he has taken with his audience's expectations. Several of the reviews, including some of the unflattering ones, have conscientiously considered the work under review on its own terms before attempting to place it within a broader moral, social, or literary context. Others have attacked the work assigned to them with a fervor born of hidebound preconceptions that communicate more about the reviewer's prejudices than they do about the book. The latter phenomenon, applied to famous works as well as those still struggling to emerge from shadow, will doubtless continue as long as people continue to produce artefacts for public consumption.–Ed.]

assert, is the book called *The Fortunes of Colonel Torlogh O'Brien.* It is utterly impossible for us to discuss at length, or to enter into any lengthened examination of the incidents of this story [. . .] Scattered through its pages, there are passages of wonderful power, one glance at which is enough to show us that the writer is no ordinary man. There are also some exquisitely drawn portraits, pictures of indeed rare beauty [. . .] That it is very exquisitely drawn there can be no manner of doubt, immeasurably superior, in our opinion, to the little Nells and Kates, or the Lady Floras and Miss Lucindas of the fashionable fictions. But the author of *Torlogh O'Brien* has a pencil of power, to delineate the fearful events of war, as well as the softer lineaments of beauty. [. . .] We could go on for ever culling extracts as beautiful, or more beautiful, than those we have just given from this extraordinary book; but space forbids. We cannot avoid noticing, in this author also, a similar fault to that which pervades his work which we had reviewed before it. There is an evident clumsiness or carelessness, as the case may be, in the management of the incidents of his narrative; passages of wonderful power, descriptive scenes of rare beauty, are huddled one upon another with a lavish extravagance, which, while it attests the power of the author, speaks but little for his skilfulness in arranging his materials. Before a man sits down to write a novel, in our humble judgement, he ought to have some definite idea of a plan or plot to which he should adhere, instead of leaving such matters wholly to chance, or the impulse of the moment. *Torlogh O'Brien* must be the production of a man who knows how to wield his pen, and in a workmanlike manner too. There is genius of no common order flung forth carelessly upon its pages; but, notwithstanding all this, there is a want about it which a little consideration and forethought would easily have supplied. A novel ought to be something more than a rapidly-shifting succession of scenes, however powerful and beautiful. There ought to be something in the progress of the story and in the devolution of its incidents to excite our interest. With these few observations, we must take our leave of *Torlogh O'Brien.* There is nothing whatever to prevent the author from producing a novel equal, if not far superior, to any by the first men of the day, if he will only attend to a few suggestions which, with every desire for his future success, and in all spirit of kindliness, we have presumed to offer.

Ghost Stories and Tales of Mystery (1851)

————*Warder* 30 (25 January 1851): 5.

[T]here is force, and wild romance, and deep knowledge of the human heart in these stories. We take "The Watcher" as the direst and most unexplained mystery of the four. Even here there is a gleam of psychological light [. . .]

The second story belongs to the annals of the Irish peerage. It is entitled "The Murdered Cousin," and is related by the Countess D——, cousin of the victim. Of this, and the third of the series, "Schalken the Painter," our space forbids us to say a word. What remains at our disposal shall be devoted to the longest and most remarkable of the tales, "The Evil Guest" [. . .] The merit we pointed out in the commencement of our observations, is here conspicuously apparent. Not a specter—not the tip of a goblin's tail, justifies the admission of the story into a volume entitled as this; yet, in the literal violation of the rule, such is the author's management of his materials, such his power over the subtle element of the imagination, anybody must admit that its spirit is observed, and that without the supernatural presence, there is a flit of ghostly wings delightfully audible through the gloomy halls of Gray Forest.

[. . .] It will be seen that the somber coloring suitable to the season, prefaces these tales. Dashes of a lighter tint here and there, however, relieve the landscape; and passages of genuine tenderness and picturesque beauty pass like alleys through the green masses of foliage, letting in sunshine and the air of heaven upon its gloom. We regret being unable to extract any of these; but refer the reader to the volume itself, for this purpose, as well as to enable him to gain that peculiar appreciation of the author's style, which a continuous perusal of his own creation can so satisfactorily impart, and which no description, no panegyric, no isolated specimen can fully convey.

The House by the Church-yard (1863)

———*Warder* 41 (1 March 1862): 5.

The author of this Chapelizod romance seems to have no rival among living English writers in his perception of what may be looked for on the other side of that screen which separates the material from the immaterial portion of creation. He describes what he finds or fancies he finds there with a certain awe, as one looking into an apartment filled with fearful shapes, and giving an impression of what he sees to those beside him, not like the showman of Mdme. Tussaud's chamber of horrors, glibly and unfeelingly descanting on a subject, awful to his audience but not to him. The tales of "Ultor de Lacy" and "Borrhomeo the Astrologer" are among the happiest specimens of supernatural fictions; from their style and spirit we are induced to believe that they may claim brotherhood with the story under notice. In giving the foremost place in this department of literature to the author of those and the Ghost Stories (?) of the old days of the magazine, we are not insensible to the wonderful weird power that made itself felt in one or two passages of *Zanoni*.[1]

---

1. [A long, popular novel (1842) mixing romantic, occult, philosophical, and historical

————*Athenaeum* (14 February 1863): 225–26.

By way of complicating the interest, a digression is made into the fortunes of many individuals; a *soupçon* of bigamy is raised, which is perfectly unnecessary, and excites neither interest nor sympathy: indeed, most of the characters, both male and female, are mere marionettes, stiff and stupid. A great deal of irrelevant comic business is also introduced, which is forced and wearisome, and in extremely bad taste. There are, however, one or two well-drawn scenes, which show that Mr. Le Fanu has power to write simply and forcibly, and to do something very much better than *The House by the Church-yard*. The sketch of Dillon, the profligate surgeon of genius, is extremely clever, and worth the whole batch of the *dramatis personae*. [Geraldine Jewsbury]

Wylder's Hand (1864)

————*Athenaeum* (12 March 1864): 371–72.

Wylder's Hand, by the author of *The House by the Church-yard*, is a great improvement on that novel. It fulfils the promise which it gave, and avoids most of the faults. *Wylder's Hand* is a clever story: the reader will be carried on by too strong an interest to have time to pause for criticism. When the book is closed, and he has time to consider, he may perhaps object to some of the details, but the fact will remain that the novel is one of sterling interest. It is well put together, and the mystery is very cleverly kept up. The reader is just sufficiently taken into the confidence of the author to be able to feel a strong sympathy with the personages concerned, whilst at the same time there is sufficient concealment to stimulate curiosity; and, on the whole, the *dénouement* is adequate to the preparation [. . .] There are some touches of imagination, which though they have nothing absolutely to do with the story, heighten the interest and are extremely effective. Tamar, the old nurse, and the spectral figure of Uncle Lorne are powerful sketches; the descriptions of places, too, are so well managed that rocks, trees, pathways, and even the very furniture of certain rooms, add to the weird, ghostly awe inspired by the dark, nameless crime that haunts the story, gradually gathering distinctness and becoming palpable, until in the end it stands revealed and confessed.

---

elements. Its author, the prolific Victorian writer and politician Sir Edward Bulwer-Lytton (1803–1873), is perhaps best known today for the supernatural story "The Haunted and the Haunters; or, The House and the Brain" (1859) and the opening of his novel *Paul Clifford* (1830), which provided inspiration for the San Jose State University's annual Bulwer-Lytton Fiction Contest: "It was a dark and stormy night [etc.]."–Ed.]

Uncle Silas (1864)

————*Athenaeum* (7 January 1865): 16–17.

The story of *Uncle Silas* is one of great imaginative power, and is superior to either of the former works by the same author (*The House by the Church-yard* and *Wylder's Hand*). Indeed, it fulfils—more than fulfils—the promise of excellence that lay in those stories. The shadow on the first page of the story creeps slowly on, becoming darker as it advances, until the terrible reality comes into sight, which has been preparing from the beginning, like some old Greek tragedy of domestic crime and wrong, tracking the steps of a guiltless victim. Mr. Le Fanu has the gift of working up the imagination of his readers, until every description of still life—a room, a picture, a piece of furniture, the entire house—becomes instinct with significance. The incidents in *Uncle Silas* are strong and strange; but the imaginative element so interpenetrates the whole, that the terror of the story is softened, and never becomes crude and horrible. The shadowy dread with which the reader is inspired will, however, do more to make him feel *eerie* than if he were set to "sup full with horrors" on fifty mortal murders. [. . .] The author's artistic imagination touches every object, however small or apparently insignificant, giving them a meaning like a song without words. One thing we *can* guarantee—the reader will be frightened at his own shadow when he goes to bed after finishing the book; and we certainly commend our readers to this remarkable and powerful novel. [Geraline Jewsbury]

————*Saturday Review* 19 (4 February 1865): 145–46.

Mr. Le Fanu interposes none of those quiet gray and green tints which Sir Walter Scott employs as a background or foil to his more striking situations. He would probably consider a chapter devoted to rural manners or antiquarian lore a mere waste of power. He is feverishly intent on producing a series of Rembrandt effects. He is always darkening the stage, and turning on the lime light. Seen through this ghostly medium, all the characters, from the principals to the merest supernumerary, appear more or less weird or unearthly. Mr. Le Fanu depicts a state of society utterly at variance with the prosaic experience of every-day life. The English country-house becomes a veritable Castle of Otranto. The British squire has a soul above Southdowns and a quarter sessions, and is either a dreamy mystic or a polished fiend. The peasantry are in league with the powers of darkness. There is a twist of mystery about the most ordinary personages and transactions. Men of business glide about in glossy black cloth, with vulpine features and hands as brown as a mummy. There are demoniac millers, haggish housekeepers, and tremulous butlers. Mr. Le Fanu possesses an apparently limitless fund of epithets warranted to make the flesh of the most impassive reader creep. He splashes them about wholesale; but perhaps the choicest assortment is reserved for the portrait of a French governess, who is the prime agent of evil in the story, and whose malpractices exceed all that has been ascribed to her class in the wildest hallucinations of the *Morning Advertiser*. [. . .] In one respect it may be admitted that this work differs essentially from those of what is loosely called the sensation school of novelists. It has none of the ingenious dovetailing and neat workmanship with which those writers have made us familiar. Mr. Le Fanu is too assiduously bent on operating on his reader's nerves, and sending a shiver through his frame, to take much trouble in elaborating details or securing for his narrative strict logical sequence. He is satisfied with dashing in broad picturesque effects, and leaving his reader to supply any link that may be wanting in his chain of incident.

————*Times* (London) (14 April 1865): 4–5. Rpt. *Warder* 43 (15 April 1865): 4.

We have called Mr. Le Fanu's novel of *Uncle Silas* a strange tale, but it so far fulfils all conditions of the best class of sensational stories that nothing is related which might not have happened, and the most absolute consistency is maintained in the different characters described. There is scarcely any creation in modern novel-writing more striking or more wonderfully sustained than the character of Uncle Silas himself. Anchorite, hypocrite, sybarite, with his gentle, luxurious, valetudinarian habits and real hardness; his hollow phrases of religion, dove-tailed with scraps of sentimental French philosophy and poetry; and the subtle cunning and avarice underlying all this which gleams forth faintly from time to time to puzzle the unsuspicious, and to keep the reader in a state of perpetual distrust, in spite of that outward justification which half satisfies the other personages of the novel. [. . .] Shakespeare's famous line, "Macbeth hath murdered sleep," might be altered for the occasion; for certainly *Uncle Silas* has "murdered sleep" in many a past night, and is likely to murder it in many a night to come, by that strange mixture of phantasies like truth and truths like phantasy which make us feel as we rise from the perusal as if we had been under a wizard's spell. [Caroline Norton][2]

2. [Noted feminist and author Caroline Elizabeth Sarah Norton (1808–1877) was Le Fanu's second cousin. He had earlier dedicated *Wylder's Hand* (1864) to her: "To Hon. Mrs. Norton, whose kindness will overlook its many faults, this Tale is inscribed by the Author."—Ed.]

Guy Deverell (1865)

————*Athenaeum* (21 October 1865): 536–37.

Guy Deverell is a tale which is well told and light in hand; it is easy to read, and will draw the reader on to the end. It is not a sensation novel, and those who have read *Uncle Silas* will be surprised, and perhaps a trifle disappointed, to find the broad natural daylight in which the whole story stands revealed. There is certainly a "green chamber" which plays an important part in the catastrophe; but it is not a haunted room, and the book may be read in the loneliest nook, at any house of the night, without shock to the nerves of a timid reader. There are two highly-wrought and very powerful scenes in *Guy Deverell* which prove that Mr. Le Fanu can do something better than evoke eerie terrors [. . .] [Geraline Jewsbury]

All in the Dark (1866)

————*Athenaeum* (30 June 1866): 860.

If readers take up Mr. Le Fanu's new novel with the idea of finding any weird or ghostly interest, they will not meet with it. Mr. Le Fanu seems to repudiate all that is sensational, and not only to repudiate, but to "make a mock of it," as nurses say to naughty children. [. . .] The story, of course, ends cheerfully; it is too slight to have borne anything heavier or graver than the perplexities and cross-purposes of a farce. In his next story we would entreat Mr. Le Fanu to be more sparing in his use of slang and of the conventional dialect familiarly known as "humming and hawing," which is more annoying in print than even in speech. [Geraldine Jewsbury]

————*Saturday Review* 22 (14 July 1866): 59.

To the harassed reader vainly casting about for pleasant food of the three-volume order, but forced to feed mainly on dry husks and dreary chaff, the advent of a book bright, natural, and cheery is a real boon; and the opening chapters bring him into a state of mind highly conducive to a general flow of Christian philanthropy, and eminently favorable to the author. Even supposing that, as he advances, the promise of the beginning is not fulfilled, and that the interest gradually dies away until nothing is left but flowerless sticks and fleshless bones, still, even then, the first gradual falling-off is accepted with wonderful charity and with a yet more wonderful belief in better things to come. A running commentary of imaginary supplements and lively interpretations fills up the vacuum and maintains the credit of the author, and, if things are going rather ill, it is cheerfully believed that they will soon go very well, and that bad times will mend. First impressions are strong, and a story powerfully begun and tamely ended does to some readers convey the notion of force throughout, the vigor of the commencement spreading itself over the weakness of the finale, and making the whole seem vigorous alike. Happily, however, for the best interests of art, these accommodating readers, willing to do half of the author's work unrewarded, are rare. The more exacting and less imaginative public for the most part demands that a good beginning shall have a corresponding ending, and that the tone of a work of art shall be, at the least, harmonious and uniform; fustian and velvet being a bad mixture of material, and the *coda* of a rondo turning off into the *motif* of a jig being questionable harmony. [. . .]

It is grievous to see good material thus wasted, for the want, not so much of power to make the best use of it, as of diligence to work out its capabilities. If the author of *All in the Dark* would give himself more time, we can hardly doubt that he would do really well, for he does not want for ability; but even a heaven-born genius cannot produce anything worth having in the haste and carelessness in which this book has evidently been written. That this is a general fault with modern authors pleads in no wise for the pardon of Mr. Le Fanu. [. . .] [O]ur fast young authors and authoresses, in deadly terror lest they should be forgotten or distanced, turn out their three volumes with a jaunty celerity positively appalling to those of the older school whose period of incubation was spread over a year's length at least, and who thought they had done wonders when they left to posterity a dozen works written, corrected, revised, and retrimmed in twice a dozen years. [. . .] The backbone of *All in the Dark* is a very slender one, and the collateral growths are neither many nor intricate. [. . .] It is a pity that Mr. Le Fanu has adopted this worse than unsatisfactory manner of work. He might do good things if he would; but neither he nor any one else can afford to reap unripe harvests; and if people will build their temples of unbaked clay they cannot expect them to stand for longer than a very briefest summer.

The Tenants of Malory (1867)

————*Athenaeum* (28 September 1867): 397.

The book is thoroughly amusing, from the skill with which the drama is opened at an admirably-described Welsh watering-place, the singular complications of the narrative, and the extreme comicality of the chief actor and incidents of the third volume. Something more than ordinary commendation is due to a novel that pleases at the outset, interests deeply in its progress, and occasions an abundance of laughter towards the conclusion. And to the praise which these merits will command must be added grateful acknowledgement of the originality of Mr. Le Fanu's villainous attorney, Jos.

Larkin, and of his vagabond, Dingwell, *alias* the Honorable Arthur Verney.
[John Cordy Jeaffreson]

A Lost Name (1868)

————*Athenaeum* (9 May 1868): 657.
Even wilder and more powerful than the first strange story by which Mr. Le
Fanu made for himself an honorable place amongst writers of prose fiction, *A
Lost Name*, through lack of artistic construction, fails to hold the reader's fancy
in the first volume; but the later parts of the tale atone for the defect of its
opening chapters, and the book upon the whole is so notable a work, that we
are constrained to speak of it with more than ordinary commendation,
although its interest depends upon one of those mysterious murders which
have drawn from us more than one strong declaration of critical disapproval. [.
. .] The author of *Uncle Silas* might do so much to raise the taste of novel-
readers that we feel no less regret than surprise in seeing him pander to that
morbid appetite for the horrible which would die out if writers of his calibre
and influence would only refrain from giving it new stimulants. But *A Lost
Name* has qualities that command recognition, even when they are employed
for a bad end. [. . .] [N]o reader who has been drawn into the fascinating
perplexities and doubts of the puzzle is likely to lay side the book, which is
most absorbing where its actors and incidents are most repulsive. And in
saying this for the tale, we bear witness that its main purpose is completely
accomplished. But a novelist of Mr. Le Fanu's ability should write for higher
ends than those of sensational art. [John Cordy Jeaffreson]

————*Times* (London) (21 September 1868): 4.
"True to nature," whether nature simple, or nature complex, or nature
mysterious; true to nature even while seeming to exaggerate or caricature
nature—there is the real secret of the power of the novelist; and where the
consistency of nature is lost sight of the dullest reader feels instinctively a
certain deficiency which makes the novel more vapid to him than any
poverty of plot of sameness of story could otherwise make it.

From such defect, perhaps, no writer of the present day is so free as Mr.
Le Fanu. His characters stand out distinct and definite, with a breadth of
coloring and mastery of outline such as prove him a skilled anatomist of the
human heart. Its inmost variations are known to him, whether in the depth
of malicious perversity or the high religious soaring that brings us into
neighborhood with angels. His *Uncle Silas* may rank with the most masterly
creations in the long generations of novels, and there is scarcely a character
in any of the numerous volumes he has given to the public that is not in-

stinct with the same creative skill. With respect to the novel by this prolific and popular writer now under notice we may safely affirm that it is the greatest success he has yet achieved. *A Lost Name* is equal from the first page to the last. The interest never swerves one tittle from the expectation formed of them in the opening sketches which introduce them to the reader. [. . .] [T]hese things do not amuse us as a romance, but affect us as a reality. They pain and gladden us; they alarm and make us anxious; they thrill us with an intensity that makes us absolutely forget we have only to lay the book down and say to them, "Come like shadows, so depart."

When we say that the plot, the style, and the scattered passages of feeling and thought are alike worthy of the warmest commendation we have said enough, and leave the mass of readers in this holy-day season to ascertain for themselves why *A Lost Name* should help to make the name of the author famous. [Caroline Norton]

Haunted Lives (1868)

————*Athenaeum* (7 November 1868): 598–99.

Bearing a strong family resemblance to the author's previous novels, *Haunted Lives* is, in some respects, very different from them; and so far as the points of difference are concerned, the present story must be commended for decided superiority to its precursors. Acting apparently on a critical suggestion made in our review of *A Lost Name*, Mr. Le Fanu has demonstrated his ability to tell a story that hardly in any degree derives its interest from sensational incident or repulsive crime; and throughout the intricacies of its very ingenious and extremely complicated plot he exhibits a nicety and exactness of workmanship of which the most elaborate and finely wrought of his earlier tales contain only occasional indications. The "story" is altogether out of the regions of the commonplace; but though wildly improbable, it is so cunningly manipulated and fully charged with realistic force that the reader accepts its improbabilities without a protest, as maters no less worthy of credence than surprise.

In giving this summary of the plot we are doing Mr. Le Fanu a service; for readers enlightened beforehand as to the scheme and ending of the tale, will derive much more pleasure from its pages than readers who fall without preparation into the hands of the novelist, who is far too good a hand at keeping his own counsel. The style of the story is admirable, but its method is most injudicious. [. . .] Novelists should be chary of mystifying their readers; for in proportion as they are flattered and delighted by the author who admits them into his confidence, readers are prone to resent the action of the story-teller who is continually throwing them on false scents, and is bent chiefly on enjoying himself at their expense, when he ought rather to be bent on amusing them at the expense of some of his characters. Mystification, obstinately maintained throughout the greater part of three volumes, invariably causes some amount of irritation and weariness, and is apt to convert what might have been an exhilarating entertainment into a humiliating practical joke. [John Cordy Jeaffreson]

————*Spectator* (7 November 1868): 1314–15.

Mr. Sheridan Le Fanu deteriorates more rapidly than any novelist of our acquaintance. In his first or second novel, *The House by the Church-yard,* he showed power of a very original and sustained kind, power which in a slightly modified form was not wanting to *Uncle Silas.* The plot of that book was, perhaps, sensational, but it was neither improbable nor impossible, and no one who read it will ever forget that figure of the strange old man, with his pallid face and Talleyrand[3] manner, who could feel remorse yet commit deliberate crime mainly to gratify a love of fastidious luxury. One might imagine a Duc de Praslin[4] of that type, and Uncle Silas even without that help was so well explained as to be conceivable. The work in *Wylder's Hand* was feebler or more careless, but still the characters were strongly marked, and the plot had something of the interest of a combat between gladiators; but since that story Mr. Le Fanu has produced nothing worth reading, and in *Haunted Lives* he has descended almost to the level of the *London Journal.* There is not a character in the book bearing the faintest resemblance to a human being, the dialogue resembles nothing so much as the shaking of the iron plate which makes thunder in theatres, and the plot would be hissed by an audience accustomed to melodrama. So wretchedly poor is the performance, indeed, that had it been the work of a young author we should have passed it without notice, as we do scores of such novels in a year; but Mr. Le Fanu cannot have suddenly

---

3. [Charles Maurice de Talleyrand-Périgord (1754–1738) was a French diplomat of swaying loyalties, as famous for his hedonistic, expensive lifestyle as for his controversial politics.—Ed.]

4. [Charles Laure Hugues Théobald, duc de Choiseul-Praslin (1804–1847) was a French nobleman and politician, infamous for the brutal murder of his wife, being sentenced first to house-arrest despite the weight of evidence against him, then, once imprisoned, managing to secure a large enough dose of laudanum to commit suicide while awaiting trial. Scandal surrounding the duke's affairs, the brutality of the murder, and perceived preferential legal treatment for the nobility epitomized for some the rampant inequalities in French society leading to the 1848 Revolution in France a few months later.—Ed.]

254 REFLECTIONS IN A GLASS DARKLY

lost a capacity so marked as his, and an honest expression of annoyance may shame him into once more putting it forth. It is carelessness, not want of power, which has allowed him to descend from Uncle Silas to De Beaumirail, from sculpture to hasty modeling in mud. [. . .]

The Wyvern Mystery (1869)

————Saturday Review (2 October 1869): 457–58.
The name of Mr. Le Fanu is a guarantee for a ghastly kind of sensationalism, vigorous if one will, though unwholesome and bad of style; but though his former works were coarse as well as horrid, they were not so coarse, not so intolerably vulgar, as this *Wyvern Mystery*, into which he has infused some of the most objectionable qualities of his peculiar school. The story is insincere as well as ugly, the leading crime in it being more of the will than of the deed; Mr. Le Fanu sheltering himself behind the stale defense of appearances only, and so shirking the fulfillment of his own odious program. [. . .] The book is too undeserving of anything like a careful analysis to make it worth while to point out the many instances of bad workmanship, slovenliness, and incongruous statements made through haste or a change of plan midway, with which the story abounds; neither do we care to copy into our own columns the hideous vulgarities with which the speeches of the two "squires" bristle. To those who are fond of garbage we can recommend this *Wyvern Mystery*; while we warn against it all who care for purity, refinement, scholarly workmanship, or artistic beauty.

————Spectator (2 October 1869): 1157–58.
Mr. Le Fanu has written nothing nearly so clever as this since he wrote *Uncle Silas*. Indeed, this book has more of literary power, though less of melodramatic effect than that, and might, we think, rank in some respects next to, though much beneath, his first and best book, *The House by the Church-yard*. In this story the chief defects of plot, which, while promising a good deal in parts, and keeping the reader's interest on the stretch for a good portion of the story, subsides before the end in a way to make him feel that he has been rather unfairly dealt with. [. . .]

But why does not Mr. Le Fanu read over his MS., at least once before publishing, even if he cannot correct his own proofs? Nothing can be more slovenly than the English sometimes is, and the minute inconsistencies in the plot also. [. . .] Yet the story is powerful enough to deserve finish. Mr. Le Fanu has evidently taken more pains with the principal figures than he has done in any of his stories since the first. The glitter and shimmer of the ghastly moral effects in which he most delights, are not so prominent, and do not so completely kill by their predominance the better literary power in him, as they have too often done in his recent novels. [John Cordy Jeaffreson]

Checkmate (1871)

————*Athenaeum* (18 February 1871): 206–7.
The lovers of sensation will find a rich banquet in Mr. Le Fanu's volumes; but we cannot recommend the perusal of them to any that do not wish to be haunted afterwards by a very nightmare of fantastic crime. [. . .] Whether his conscience and his self-respect will enable him to look back with complacency on the highly-seasoned garbage he has submitted to an omnivorous public, is perhaps another question. [Robert Collyer]

————*Spectator* (25 February 1871): 224–25.
We confess to a literary weakness for Mr. Le Fanu. In the first place, he has a flavor of genius which never entirely leaves him, though he does draw upon it recklessly and in a manner a very much greater genius could not bear, by writing one "lurid" novel after another in rapid succession. The *House by the Church-yard* is a book full of humor and buoyancy, as well as of great talent for the ghastly, and through none of his long subsequent series of sensation stories have come near to that in power, you seldom miss the trace of a certain amount of skill and ability; though you may be ashamed of yourself for being amused and fascinated by his ghastly ingenuities, yet you are amused and fascinated, whether ashamed or not. [. . .] The last novel of Mr. Le Fanu's we reviewed in these columns was very like the last expiring effort of a man of talent, so utterly trashy was the sensation element of the tale, and so little relieved by any indication of larger power. [. . .] But *Checkmate* shows, we are happy to say, a relapse into talent,—not talent of a high kind, for there are but two or three pages showing anything of Mr. Le Fanu's old humor in the book, amongst which the sketch of Sir Reginald Arden's recovery from his fit and that of Lady May Penrose's disappointment must hold the principal places, and most of the characters are faintly and carelessly drawn, but still talent,—a certain amount of real ingenuity in inventing lurid mysteries, and a certain amount of dash in the delineation. If you want a good trashy novel,—not trashy enough to inspire a vexed contempt,—not good enough to challenge criticism or any attempt to compare it with real life, but just trashy enough to make you feel you are only amusing yourself and need not even think of such a thing as passing a serious judgment on the book, and just good enough to oblige you to be extremely entertained with the resource and ingenuity shown by the author

in giving so marvelously lurid a glare to the life of our own day,—*Checkmate* is the very book for your purpose. In fact, *Checkmate* is the very model of a story to waste time over without weariness, if that process ever be allowable, and forget without a pang of compunction as soon as you have finished it. [. . .] There is more real power of invention in Mr. Le Fanu, and there is a certain case of manner and polish of style about his villains which greatly adds to their value as villains. And the vivacity of the book is throughout considerable. [. . .] But the strong point of *Checkmate* is undoubtedly the almost inexpressible grandeur of the evil genius of the book. Mr. Le Fanu has always been great in these sinister beings, who in his tales usually appear for the first time in a middle life of great ability and incisiveness,—which sinister rumors begin more and more to connect with a youth of crime. But he has hardly yet done anything quite so complete as the Mr. Longcluse of *Checkmate*, of whom we may fairly say that "take him for all, we shall not look upon his like again." [. . .] Here is, indeed, a gloomy grandeur of soul to set off this great being's versatility in crime with a gleam of lurid light!

————*Saturday Review* (18 March 1871): 351–52.
[. . .] At the same time we warn them that we are criticizing an author who has contrived to write three full volumes without writing a single line that can either instruct or (we should think) amuse any human being. It is indeed a marvel that he should not accidentally have stumbled into something good. It has been said that the dullest talker, if he will only persevere in his strivings after wit, must, without intending it, say a good thing now or then. Chance, however, is as little indulgent towards Mr. Le Fanu as nature. He has written some twenty-five thousand lines, and yet he has not, we believe, turned out a single one worth reading and remembering. We should be curious to learn whether he has always been able to write such dreary novels as the one before us, or whether his skill has been acquired solely by laborious practice. [. . .] It is, we fear, to little purpose that we protest against such odious writing as this, for in novel-writing, as well as in wax-work shows, a Chamber of Horrors is found to pay only too well. Madame Tussaud[5] has at all events the decency to keep her horrors in a chamber to

---

5. [Marie Tussaud, *née* Anna Maria Grosholtz (1761–1850) was a French-born crafter of wax mannequins who learned her trade while serving as housekeeper to a physician skilled in creating wax anatomical models. She turned these skills to the recreation of French celebrities, then the death masks of those executed during the French Revolution before leading a long, tour of Europe. Settling in London, she increased the scope of her exhibits between 1831 and 1835, thus establishing the first of her famous waxworks museums.—Ed.]

themselves. It would be something if Mr. Le Fanu would gather his repulsive descriptions into a chapter, or rather a volume, to themselves, and not scatter them up and down his book.

Chronicles of Golden Friars (1871)

————*Athenaeum* (15 July 1871): 79–80.

If we except some unusual traces of haste, which has betrayed Mr. Le Fanu into certain faults of diction and slips of chronology, from which he is generally free, we may say that he is quite himself in the group of novelettes before us. These tales possess at least two distinct merits: in the first place they set a good example of concentration within a manageable length; and secondly, the locality is so wisely chosen, in the heart of the romantic, but fresh and healthy north-country, that we may defy even the grisly imagination of Mr. Le Fanu to produce upon us any morbid effect. [. . .] "The Haunted Baronet," we suspect, is intended to be the center of attraction: the tale certainly reads like a bad dream, and is so far a triumph in its peculiar line; the directions for finding the supernatural being who plays Mephistopheles to Sir Bale Mardyke's Faust; the swelling of the dark spot in the stone, the springing of strange flowers by the way, the half-human parroquets and jays, all contribute to the nightmare effect of this charismatic story. At the same time, we confess to an impression that the less ghostly portions of the book have a greater merit, and, for ourselves, we prefer the last tale ["The Bird of Passage"] to the other two. We have said that marks of haste are too visible in all of them. [. . .] But in spite of these demerits, we are inclined to think there are many worse books than *Chronicles of Golden Friars*. [Dr. John Doran].

————*Saturday Review* (12 August 1871): 223.

Mr. Le Fanu, and we speak after a certain acquaintance with his writings, has at any rate one merit. He had fewer lines to a page than most other novelists. He raises in the mind of his critic that feeling of gratitude which comes over a man who some Sunday, instead of having his usual commonplace sermon of half-an-hour, is let off with a very foolish sermon of fifteen minutes. We gladly acknowledge, therefore, that Mr. Le Fanu has the merit of brevity. His pages are small, his type is large, his lines are not too close together, his *Chronicles* are divided into three stories and eighty-three chapters, and the beginning and ending of each story and of each chapter are honored with an ample allowance of blank space. Everything, in fact, has been done to promote the convenience of the reader, and to procure his speedy release. When we have said this, we have said all that we can say for

Mr. Le Fanu and his *Chronicles of Golden Friars,* unless indeed it be any satisfaction to the public to know that they are inscribed to a lady of title. Brief though the three volumes are, we must confess through disgust and weariness that we left the third volume unopened. We felt that we were getting so hopelessly confused between the glass-eyed villain and the ghosts of the first story and the haunted baronet and the ghosts of the second story, that our brain could not stand any further mixture.

The Rose and the Key (1871)

————*Athenaeum* (28 October 1871): 558–59.

Mr. Le Fanu is, on the present occasion, less grisly and not quite so effective as usual. [. . .] We could have spared, for the sake of those steps in the narrative, over which he would have guided us so well, some of the space allotted to the inner life of Garewoods, a place the character of which we understand almost before we reach it. But no doubt it would have cost our author no slight pang to have omitted any of the circumstances which gradually reveal to the poor victim the nature of her imprisonment. [. . .] Altogether, the story is an exemplification of the vivid detail so characteristic of our author, but in other respects is not one of his most successful efforts. [John Collyer]

In a Glass Darkly (1872)

————*Saturday Review* (17 August 1872): 222–23.

Mr. Le Fanu, having written some four or five foolish and vulgar ghost stories, presents them to the world as belonging to "metaphysical speculation," or "religious metaphysics," or "metaphysical medicine." He informs us that he has the stories from "the immense collection of papers" left by Dr. Martin Hesselius, a man whose "knowledge was immense, his grasp of a case was an intuition." Happily for the non-scientific world, the Doctor "writes in two distinct characters." [. . .]

As for "the analysis, diagnosis, and illustration," and "the force and originality of genius," with which they are made, we must take Mr. Le Fanu's word; of course we have no opportunity given us of judging. But when he asks us to believe, after we have read through the stories, that the learned Doctor "describes what he saw and heard as an intelligent layman might," here at least we are able to exercise our own judgment. If Mr. Le Fanu can find readers so silly as to delight in all the horror, as senseless as they are coarse, which he here serves up to them, he is welcome. But at all events let him not, while pretending to praise an imaginary author, have the assurance to claim for himself that he "describes as an intelligent layman might." It may be, however, that

Mr. Le Fanu's readers look upon everyone as intelligent who uses words beyond their comprehension. A man must needs be intelligent, for instance, who writes of "the lumen of the eyes," or of the "odylic and magnetic influence of the moon," who is quite familiar with "the primary distinction between the subjective and the objective," and speaks not of Brussels, but of "Bruxelles lace." Nevertheless, Mr. Le Fanu would have shown a little more modesty, and quite as much intelligence, if he had allowed his readers to find out his great powers for themselves, and had not added to his work a preface which is in fact a puff of himself. It is idle, we fear, to expect that Mr. Le Fanu will give up his ghosts and goblins, his gallows and coffins, his murderers and vampires, and his spectral forms, whether they come in the shape of a "small monkey, perfectly black, with a character of malignity—unfathomable malignity," or whether they come in the shape of "a sooty-black animal that resembled a monstrous cat, and that continued toing and froing with the lithe, sinister restlessness of a beast in a cage." There are some writers, indeed, who, ever dealing in horrors, yet are excused for their bad taste on account of the morbidness of their imagination. Before we can allow, however, Mr. Le Fanu to plead that his imagination is morbid, we shall require him to prove that he has, properly speaking, any imagination at all. In the most ignorant and debased of savage tribes there could scarcely be found an old woman who could not tell stories as full of childish horrors as Mr. Le Fanu's, and tell them in a language that was at all events intelligible. Some of the mountain tribes in India believe in ghosts who reside in trees, and who are only to be propitiated by a dance being executed round the tree in which they reside. "Among the more superstitious tribes," we read in the Annals of Rural Bengal, "it is customary for each family to dance round every single tree, in order that they may not by any chance omit the one in which their god may be residing." Now, if any one man first struck out the thought that a ghost resided in a tree and required to be propitiated by a round dance, he indeed might justly lay claim to some amount of imagination. But when generation after generation had thus propitiated these ghosts, we should just as soon think of attributing imagination to a savage whom we found dancing round his hundredth tree as to Mr. Le Fanu, who, following in the track probably of his old nurse or of Mrs. Radcliffe, is bringing in his hundredth specter. Any one, if he were put to it, could find enough imagination to make up a story with the churchyard materials which Mr. Le Fanu delights to use, though it is not every one who, having performed this easy feat, would proceed to write a preface in praise of his own intelligence.

Mr. Le Fanu evidently thinks that in such imaginative works as his claim to be, the best way to win his reader's belief is to follow De Foe in his circumstantiality. Unfortunately, however, though he shows no imagination in his fiction, he shows a good deal of imagination in his facts, and while pretending to deal minutely with bygone days, proves at once that his ignorance of them is complete. His study of literature began, we should imagine, with the first novel that he wrote. The pelican, we are told, feeds her young on food which she plucks from her own breast. Mr. Le Fanu, on the contrary, would seem to feed the later offspring of his brain on sustenance solely derived from his first-born. We ought not, however, to fail to do him the justice of admitting that he now and then introduces a Latin word which suggests a certain acquaintance with the Latin Grammar, and a fine-sounding phrase which suggests a certain acquaintance with the *Daily Telegraph*. Like the editor of that paper, moreover, he has a great command over the moon, and in one of his stories passes with extraordinary rapidity from a night that is bright with moonlight to the next that is as dark as pitch. The scene of one of his stories is laid in the year 1794. It is certainly somewhat strange to find that in that year, of all years, a gentleman who was suffering from "depression, misery, and excitement" was advised "to try a short tour of the Continent," and went by way of Dover to Calais. It was not exactly the year in which a cure for excitement was to be looked for in France, or in which "a crowd of idlers stood upon the jetty at Calais to receive the packet." We are willing to forgive Mr. Le Fanu for the improbability of the ghost who was among the idlers, and who, Englishman, or rather English ghost, that he was, yet talked in "a broad provincial *patois*." We should be curious to learn, by the way, what *patois* is not provincial. Mr. Le Fanu may bring in his ghosts where he pleases, and when he pleases, and may make them talk even in the peculiar language which he writes, but he must not be allowed without rebuke to show an ignorance of modern history of which a writer of school histories might well be ashamed. In one of the stories, along with the specter of the black monkey with the "unfathomable malignity," we have cabs and omnibuses. Now, though we think that the old women from whom alone, till we came across Mr. Le Fanu's writings, we had heard of such specters, had sense enough to place them in far earlier times, yet we shall let him, if he pleases, take his money specter into what he calls a 'bus. Nevertheless, if his story requires that 'busses and cabs and monkey specters shall come together, we have a right to insist that he shall not pretend that his story was written quite so far back as "about sixty-four years ago." Even Dr. Hesselius, though "his knowledge was immense, and his grasp of a case was an intuition," can scarcely be allowed in the year 1808 to have known of a 'bus. Perhaps, however, the prophetic knowledge or intuition which he showed in this matter may have been a part of the "metaphysical speculation," or "religious metaphysics," for which he was so famous.

As for the five stories contained in these three volumes, there is not one of them which is not hopelessly absurd. The hero of the first tale, a country vicar haunted by the black monkey, cuts his throat with a razor. The hero of the second, haunted by the ghost who at one time spoke "the provincial *patois*," and at another time apparently took the shape of an owl, was killed in his bed by this most intrusive apparition. In the third story an old judge of the last century, after hanging the husband of his mistress, gets tried in a ghostly court, and is at last found hanged himself. Ever since, "this direful old man," the judge, has haunted a house in Westminster carrying "in his ringed and ruffled hand a coil of rope." These three stories fill up the first volume, with the help of such extracts from "metaphysical medicine" as the following:—

> So soon as the spirit-action has established itself in the case of one patient, its developed energy begins to radiate, more or less effectually, upon others.

The fourth story, which is the longest, contains some horrors in Mr. Le Fanu's best style. The hero is made, without knowing it, to order his own grave and his own coffin. He is thrown into a kind of trance, in which, though he cannot move, he yet knows all that is going on. He is laid in the coffin, and hears very distinctly "the working of a turnscrew, and the crunching home of screws in succession. Than these vulgar sounds," he remarks in Mr. Le Fanu's best style, "no doom spoken in thunder could have been more tremendous." Happily, before the noble murderers could make off with the £30,000 which the hero, after the fashion of young Englishmen, had taken with him on his first visit to Paris, they were surprised. The hero is let out of the coffin, becomes "a sadder if not a wiser man," and has "deep reason to be thankful to the all-merciful Ruler of events for an early and terrible lesson in the ways of sin."

Our readers will have had enough by this time of Mr. Le Fanu's stories, and may be thankful to be spared an account of the most foolish and the most offensive of all his tales—that, namely, of the Vampire. When an author has the grave opened of a person who had been buried one hundred and fifty years, and describes how "the leaden coffin floated with blood, in which, to a depth of seven inches, the body lay immersed," we are, we think, more than justified in declining to analyze his silly and miserable story. We should hope that this time he will find that he has miscalculated the taste of the subscribers to the seaside lending libraries, for whom he probably writes. They will no doubt stand a good deal, but possibly Dr. Martin Hesselius and his raw-head and bloody-bones horrors will prove too much even for their powers of endurance.

Willing to Die (1873)

———*Athenæum* (24 May 1873): 659.

The late Mr. Le Fanu's most recent book is, in some respects, a contrast to many which have preceded it. There is less of that ghostly atmosphere in which the author used to revel, and more carefulness, perhaps, in the delineation of character. The autobiographical form in which it is cast presents, of course, greater facilities for such minuter study as far as the leading figure is concerned. [. . .] So expert a story-teller as Mr. Le Fanu of course maintains the interest of his incidents to the end, and does not forfeit any claim he has gained to our attention by prematurely revealing the key to their complications.

The Purcell Papers (1880)

———*Athenaeum* (15 May 1880): 630–31.

A critic is naturally inclined to handle gently the posthumous work of one who has in life often given his readers hours of entertainment, but the collection of short stories by the late Sheridan Le Fanu stands in need of no such allowances. The turn he always showed for the marvellous and the horrible is abundantly exhibited in the present volumes, which contain some stories, such as "Drunkard's Dream," "Passages in the Secret History of an Irish Countess," and "A Chapter in the History of a Tyrone Family," which exceed in mystery and realism any of his longer tales, and read like nothing so much as the ghastly stories of real Irish life which occur in the pages of Froude,[6] plus a supernatural element in which history is lacking. As a set off to these horrors there are some humorous tales redolent of national fun. "The Quare Gandher" [sic], "Jim Soolivan's Adventures" [sic], Billy Malowney's Taste of Love and Glory" will unbind the severest critic.

———*Saturday Review* (19 June 1880): 802–3.

The literary ambition of the Fat Boy in *Pickwick* was to make the old lady's blood run cold. The genius of the late Mr. Sheridan Le Fanu (the author of *Uncle Silas, Wylder's Hand, In a Glass Darkly*, and other romances) was also of a chill and curdling nature. No author more frequently caused a reader to look over his shoulder in the dead hour of the night. None made a nervous visitor

---

6. Editors' Note: J(ames) A(nthony) Froude (1818–1894) was a historian who produced one notorious novel, *The Nemesis of Faith* (1849), early in his career. He was particularly noted for his scholarship on Tudor history and *The English in Ireland in the Eighteenth Century* (1872), a book highly critical of what he perceived as the chaotic society built by the Anglo-Irish Ascendancy.

feel more uncomfortable in the big, bleak bedrooms of old Highland houses. Mr. Le Fanu did not deal with actual ghosts. His apparitions were much more fearful wild-fowl. "What a sell it would be for a ghost," said a clever but slangy little boy, "if he appeared to a lunatic!" The behavior of the lunatic, so unlike that of a sane person in the presence of the supernatural, would indeed be likely to vex and discomfit a specter accustomed to rational society. Mr. Le Fanu's ghosts, on the other hand, had a way of turning out to be the family idiot, the monstrous birth, or other horror of the flesh and blood which fine old families are supposed to keep in a secluded corner of fine old castles. These substantial apparitions were more horrible in Mr. Le Fanu's books than the airy banshees or immaterial bogey of civilization. You had first the horror caused in well-regulated minds by the supernatural—which is an evanescent feeling, for familiarity with the bodiless breeds indifference, if not contempt. Next you had the revulsion of feeling caused by the discovery that the supposed ghost was something human and yet not human, something wild and semi-bestial, like the "Alastor" or avenging fiend that haunted the House of Atreus. Indeed, if Mr. Le Fanu had dealt in classical and mythological horrors, he would doubtless have hinted that the hateful and hungry spirit whom Cassandra beheld in vision was only old Thyestes in his dotage, moping and prowling in the scenes of murder and worse than murder.[7]

To these amiable and attractive qualities of fancy Mr. Le Fanu added considerable power of dealing with the real old-fashioned supernatural. [. . .] *Carmilla* is a tale that every parent should make haste not to place in the hands of the young. Neither Poe nor Richepin[8] ever invented anything more horrible than the dusky, undulating nocturnal shape of her who was a fair woman by daylight and an insatiate fiend at night. Mr. Le Fanu's skill in the weaving of plots was greater, we think, than that of Mr. Wilkie Collins, as his humor was more spontaneous and less mechanical. *Wylder's Hand* is a very well managed story. *Guy Deverell* might, we venture to think, have been improved by a very simple device. The wicket baronet should have died (of

---

7. Editors' Note: The reviewer refers in these two sentences to the avenging spirit hovering over the House of Atreus following generations of treachery and murder, leading into the Trojan War, and culminating in the events described in Aeschylus's *Oresteia*.

8. [Jean Richepin (1849-1926) was a French writer whose work is frequently marked by frank expression, violence, and the grotesque. His collection of macabre stories *Les Morts bizarres* appeared in 1876, though only one of its stories is currently available in translation: "Constant Guinard" in *The Dedalus Book of French Horror: The 19th Century*, edited by Terry Hale (Sawtry, UK: Dedalus, 1998).–Ed.]

apoplexy) in the secret chamber of his vicious pleasure, whereby we should have gained a mystery, and been spared a murder. [. . .]

The Purcell Papers are a collection of Mr. Le Fanu's early stories and sketches. They vary much in power, though a certain simpleness and sobriety of style is common to all of them. Nothing spoils a ghost story more than a florid, or pretentious, or too ingenious style. The narrator ought to seem absorbed in his topic: his tale should be plain and unvarnished. Mr. Le Fanu's manner in the more serious, not to say sepulchral, of the Purcell stories is just what it ought to be. [. . .] Mr. Le Fanu appears to have studied the horrors of visions in which "we dream of the devil and wake in a fright";[9] or lie benumbed with dread while some fancied horror approaches us. "The Fortunes of Sir Robert Ardagh" are "all about the devil," as the small boy said, when asked to give some account of the tract presented to him by a pious relative. The same ghostly foe is very nicely managed in "The Drunkard's Dream," where "the bad place" is treated with much delicacy of touch and originality of design. This is a story which to quote De Quincy's amateur, "one can recommend to a friend." [. . .]

A judicious reader of The Purcell Papers may enjoy many moments of what are called "creepy" sensations. The book is ill-timed for summer, and London; it should be read in winter, when the nights are long, and in some country house where banshees are still strictly preserved, and brownies are as common as ground-game.

—————Spectator (31 July 1880): 978–80.

[. . .] Mr. Le Fanu's humor was rich and spontaneous, but it did not prove so durable a quality of his literary work as his genius for the weird, to which it presented so vivid a contrast. We know nothing better of its kind in our literature than the broad effects of this contrast in The House by the Churchyard; but it is evident that while his power in delineating weird effects was at the root of his genius, his humorous productiveness was more transient, and hardly maintained itself to the end. It was in the region of the weird that he gave both his first and his last sign of true genius.

---

9. [Allusion to a line from the poem "The Jackdaw of Rheims," in The Ingoldsby Legends (First Series, 1840) by "Thomas Ingoldsby," pseudonym of the English clergyman Richard Harris Barham (1788–1845).—Ed.]

The Watcher and Other Weird Stories (1895)

————*Athenaeum* (16 February 1895): 214.

[. . .] The late Mr. Le Fanu had always a special gift for the weird and the terrible. Since the days of "Monk" Lewis there has not been a writer who was fonder of blue lights and "eerie" sensations. He was *sui generis* in his time, and like Bartoline Saddletree,[10] "we ken what that amounts to." In other ages, if he had not been burnt for a wizard, he would at least have been accredited with the loss of his shadow. In the present tasty volume, beneath the sign of the owl, we are presented with half a dozen sufficiently grim stories of Irish life. [. . .]

A Chronicle of Golden Friars and Other Stories (1896)

————*Academy* (London) 50 (7 November 1896): 346–47.

Sheridan Le Fanu does not invite modern criticism. His books live, and that is the best proof of their worth. Only great critics, or impertinent ink slingers, would attempt to appraise their value. One lesson, at any rate, they teach: that the best novelist is he who has a story to tell, and is not ashamed to tell it simply. [. . .] Percy Addleshaw.

---

10. [A character in Sir Walter Scott's (1771–1832) seventh Waverley novel, *The Heart of Midlothian* (1818).–Ed.]

V. Studies of Individual Works

"Green Tea": The Archetypal Ghost Story

Jack Sullivan

In 1839, a new kind of ghost appeared in English fiction. The appearance, in Joseph Sheridan Le Fanu's "Strange Event in the Life of Schalken the Painter," went unnoticed, for Le Fanu was an unknown, and his tales were published anonymously. By a strange coincidence, "The Fall of the House of Usher" came out the same year, but Poe's more celebrated tale is a landmark of a different order, an exercise in cosmic paranoia rather than a tale of the supernatural. Le Fanu's creations were real ghosts who stubbornly refused to confine themselves to the shabby psyches of aristocratic neurotics, yet somehow managed to emerge from within as well as invade from without; who (unlike Mrs. Radcliffe's ghosts) could not be explained away, yet who would have nothing to do with what Oliver Onions once called "the groans and clankings of the grosser spook."[1] "Schalken the Painter" was as revolutionary in execution as in the peculiar nature of its two ghosts. The story tells of the abduction, rape, and final seduction of a young woman by a living corpse, all from the point of view of the girl's befuddled uncle and horrified fiancée. Le Fanu handled both the necrophilia and the supernaturalism in the tale with a new anti-Gothic restraint. As if reluctant to reveal its sordid and marvelous secrets, the plot develops itself entirely through suggestion and indirection, building toward an extraordinary dream sequence involving the transformation of a coffin into a Victorian four-poster bed. It is a chilling performance.

Yet "Schalken the Painter" is not the most refined or the most representative of Le Fanu's tales. It is rather the promising start of a long, influential career in ghostly fiction. The culmination of that career is "Green Tea," the story of a man who literally has a monkey on his back, can serve as an ideal introduction not only to Le Fanu's other tales, but to the entire ghostly school that he spawned. It is a thoroughly modern tale, and its modernity, so

---

1. Oliver Onions, "Credo," *The Collected Ghost Stories of Oliver Onions* (New York, 1971), x.

unexpectedly daring, is the key to understanding the contradictions between plot and theme in more ambivalent tales such as "The Mysterious Lodger" and "The Familiar."

Le Fanu first published "Green Tea" in Dickens's magazine *All the Year Round* (1869) and later reprinted it in *In a Glass Darkly* (1872), a remarkable collection of his late tales which includes "Mr. Justice Harbottle," "The Familiar," "Carmilla," and (somewhat inappropriately since there is no supernatural episode) "The Room in the Dragon Volant." With the possible exception of "Carmilla," no other Le Fanu tale has been so widely discussed. Its visibility, so unusual for Le Fanu, can probably be accounted for by its novel concept. V. S. Pritchett, Edna Kenton, William Buckler, Nelson Browne, and E. F. Benson have all sung the praises of Le Fanu's demonic monkey.[2] Speaking for all of them, Buckler states that "Green Tea" "is generally given first place in the canon of his work," while Pritchett extends the generalization by calling it one of "the best half-dozen ghost stories in the English language."

The structure of "Green Tea" is a perfect illustration of M. R. James's model for the modern ghost story:

> Let us, then, be introduced to the actors in a placid way; let us see them going about their ordinary business, undisturbed by forebodings, pleased with their surroundings; and into this calm environment let the ominous thing put out its head, unobtrusively at first, and then more insistently, until it holds the stage.[3]

Le Fanu was the first to use this strategy, and he applies it with particular deftness here. The victim in "Green Tea," the Reverend Mr. Jennings, is introduced to the reader by the central narrator, Dr. Martin Hesselius, who in the course of the tale becomes Jennings's therapist. We first see Jennings at a congenial, tedious dinner party, conversing with Hesselius. They are discussing a German first edition of Hesselius's "Essays on Metaphysical Medicine." The conversation is learned but also abstracted and rather silly. Only one sentence appears to have any relevance to a possible ghostly experience: it is a hint involving the motivations for Jennings's odd curiosity concerning Hessellius' exotic research: "I suppose [says Hesselius] you have

2. V. S. Pritchett, *The Living Novel and Later Appreciations* (New York, 1947), 121-28; Edna Kenton, "A Forgotten Creator of Ghosts," *Bookman* (New York, 1929): 528-35; *Minor Classics of Nineteenth Century Fiction*, Vol. II, ed. William E. Buckler (Boston, 1967), 27-28; Nelson Browne, *Sheridan Le Fanu* (New York, 1951), 78-80; E. F. Benson, "Sheridan Le Fanu," *Spectator* (21 Feb. 1931): 263-64.

3. M. R. James, "Introduction," *Ghosts and Marvels* (London, 1927), vi.

been turning the subject over again in your mind, or something has happened lately to revive your interest in it."[4]

The conversation, with its pedantry and innuendo, is a prefiguration of M. R. James's dialogue, as are the clues which reinforce its implications. Something indeed "has happened." Although Jennings is a reserved, "perfectly gentleman like man," he has a few revealing quirks. For one thing, he has a peculiar tendency to flee from the pulpit during his own sermons: "After proceeding a certain way in the service, he has on a sudden stopped short, and after a silence, apparently quite unable to resume, he has fallen into solitary, inaudible prayer, his hands and eyes uplifted and then pale as death, and in the agitation of a strange shame and horror, descended trembling, and got into the vestry-room, leaving his congregation, without explanation, to themselves" (180). The situation becomes so critical that Jennings resorts to having an alternate clergyman waiting in the wings "should he become thus incapacitated." Hesselius also notices a "certain oddity" in Jennings's dinner conversation: "Mr. Jennings has a way of looking sideways upon the carpet, as if his eye followed the movements of something there" (180). The final oddity is revealed by the hostess, Lady Mary Heyduke, when she remarks that she used to quarrel with Jennings over his addiction to green tea. Hesselius agrees that Jennings was once "extravagantly" addicted to the stuff, but insists that "he has quite given that up" (183).

Le Fanu, a careful artist, was undoubtedly aware of the ludicrousness of all this. The notion that humor is anathema to horror is one of the persistent clichés of anthology introductions. It is also one of the most erroneous, as anyone who has read Bierce or Hartley can attest. Humor, particularly when ironic or absurd, is inextricably fused with supernatural horror in fiction. I have found the linkage to be consistent throughout the field: the reader automatically integrates the two elements as he reads. In "Green Tea," the first apparition scene skirts the same arbitrary borderline between the laughable and the horrible as the clues which anticipate it. The absurdity of the premise—the lethal apparition is, after all, a monkey—weakens the impact not at all; indeed the strange power of the tale lies in the irony that something intrinsically ridiculous can drive a man to destroy himself.

Jennings, of course, is not amused by this creature. His account of the first apparition is peculiarly unnerving and deserves to be quoted at length as a paradigm of Le Fanu's apparition scenes:

---

4. *Best Ghost Stories of J. S. Le Fanu*, ed. E. F. Bleiler (New York, 1964), 182. Unless otherwise noted, further quotations from Le Fanu's tales will be documented by citing page numbers from the Bleiler edition.

"The interior of the omnibus was nearly dark. I had observed in the corner opposite to me at the other side, and at the end next the horses, two small circular reflections, as it seemed to me of a reddish light. They were about two inches apart, and about the size of those small brass buttons that yachting men used to put upon their jackets. I began to speculate, as listless men will, upon this trifle, as it seemed. From what centre did that faint but deep red light come, and from what—glass beads, buttons, toy decorations—was it reflected? We were lumbering along gently, having nearly a mile still to go. I had not solved the puzzle, and it became in another minute more odd, for these two luminous points, with a sudden jerk, descended nearer and nearer the floor, keeping still their relative distance and horizontal position, and then, as suddenly, they rose to the level of the seat on which I was sitting and I saw them no more.

"My curiosity was now really excited and before I had time to think, I saw again these two dull lamps, again together near the floor; again they disappeared, and again in their old corner I saw them.

"So, keeping my eyes upon them, I edged quietly up my own side, towards the end at which I still saw these tiny discs of red.

"There was very little light in the 'bus. It was nearly dark. I leaned forward to aid my endeavour to discover what these little circles really were. They shifted position a little as I did so. I began now to perceive an outline of something black, and I soon saw, with tolerable distinctness, the outline of a small black monkey, pushing its face forward in mimicry to meet mine; those were its eyes, and I now dimly saw its teeth grinning at me.

"I drew back not knowing whether it might not meditate a spring. I fancied that one of the passengers had forgot this ugly pet, and wishing to ascertain something of its temper, though not caring to trust my fingers to it, I poked my umbrella softly towards it. It remained immovable—up to it— *through* it. For through it, and back and forward it passed, without the slightest resistance.

"I can't in the least, convey to you the kind of horror that I felt." (193–94)

Throughout this passage, the emphasis is on the way Jennings perceives the apparition rather than on the apparition itself. Jennings's reaction is the important thing, as is the reader's: we are forced to see this strange abomination exactly as Jennings sees it. It scarcely matters whether the thing is "real" or hallucinated; in a good horror tale this distinction is effaced. Supernatural horror in fiction has little to do with the materiality of spooks. What counts is the authenticity of the experience. The scene works because of the intricate perspectival character of the writing, a technique which anticipates Henry James's *The Turn of the Screw* and "Sir Edmund Orme." The most remarkable aspect of Le Fanu's perspectivism is his use of synecdoche, a poetic mechanism which allows him to straddle the boundary between the explicit and indirect. His use of the device is more radical in other tales, notably "The Haunting of the Tiled House" in which the unearthly force is represented solely by a disembodied hand. Here we visualize the creature in terms of its eyes, although "these two full lamps" dimly illuminate the rest of the shape.

Jennings stumbles from the omnibus "in a panic," discovering to his "indescribable relief" that the thing is gone. Like all of Le Fanu's victims, he convinces himself that it was all a fleeting "illusion." But on the way home he looks up "with loathing and horror" to see it creeping along beside him on a brick wall. From this point on, the creature persecutes Jennings with incredible tenacity. As in the first apparition scene, the sufferer's emotions are communicated consistently through his reaction to the demon's eyes. During the initial phase of the persecution, the eyes are "dazed and languid," "jaded and sulky," "sullen and sick." Yet they have "unfathomable malignity" and above all, "intense vigilance." "In all situations, at all hours," says the unfortunate Jennings, "it is awake and looking at me; that never changes" (196).

Thus begins this extraordinary obsession, chronicled in graded steps: thee "stages" in a hellish "journey." In the "Second Stage," the demon mysteriously disappears for a month, during which time Jennings again experiences an illusory respite. But then it returns with "new energy," "brooding over some atrocious plan." This phase of the persecution is characterized by many such disappearances: "it has sometimes been away so long as nearly two months, once for three," Jennings tells his therapist. "Its absence always exceeds a fortnight, although it may be but by a single day. Fifteen days having past since I saw it last, it may return now at any moment" (197). At once arbitrary and mysteriously calculated, this time span induces the maximum amount of anxiety, causing the patient to look progressively "like death." It is a typically cruel touch, which Le Fanu is fond of using in situations of otherworldly harassment (cf. "The Familiar"). Another painful characteristic of the second phase is Jennings's new inability to attain relief by simply shutting his eyes: "I know it is not to be accounted for physically, but I do actually see it though my eyes are closed" (199). As part of its new militancy, the creature will "squat" in Jennings's prayer book during holy services, obscuring any passage he attempts to read his congregation. It is presumably during these occasions that Jennings flees from the pulpit.

In the third and final stage, the demon "speaks" to Jennings. Unlike Gothic writers, with their fatal predilection for chatty specters, Le Fanu shrewdly avoids any attempt to reproduce its actual words.[5] Instead, he al-

---

5. On rare occasions when Le Fanu directly quotes a demon's speech, he is careful to

lows Jennings to suggest the sound metaphorically, through a kind of ghostly music: "It is not by my ears it reaches me—it comes like a singing through my head" (200). Although Jennings never quotes the lyrics of this "song," he lets us know that they are thoroughly unpleasant, particularly during his abortive attempts at prayer: "'The faculty, the power of speaking to me, will be my undoing. It won't let me pray, it interrupts me with dreadful blasphemies. I dare not go on. I could not. Oh! Doctor, can the skill and thought, and prayers of man avail me nothing!'" (200). They indeed avail him nothing. In these tales, prayer is utterly ineffectual—as are faith and good works. Like most Le Fanu, "Green Tea" does not end happily. In the final phase, the demon tries to persuade his victim to commit suicide. Jennings, who after three years of demonic persecution does not need much persuading, ends his "journey" by cutting his throat. Suicide is the only way out for him, and he is unique among Le Fanu's victims in perceiving this. As in Greek tragedy, the final horror is not rendered directly but is reported by a messenger, in this case Jennings's servant. As always, Le Fanu avoids being too direct: he leaves the awful details to the reader's imagination, yet still gets in a good bloody scene by having Hesselius clinically inspect the "immense pool of blood on the floor" of Jennings's "sombre and now terrible room" (204).

"Green Tea" is every bit as twisted, disturbing and unresolvable as it seems. Nevertheless, by imposing orthodox explanations and theoretical systems on the story, critics have done what they could to dissipate its mystery and menace. The orthodoxies divide into two camps, the Freudian and the Christian, each of which has a predictable explanation for Jennings's persecution. To Peter Penzoldt, Jennings's monkey is simply "the product of schizoid neurosis"; to V. S. Pritchett, it is "dark and hairy with original sin," and its persecutions symbolize "justified" retribution for specific sins; to Michael Begnal, the monkey is sent to punish a clergyman who has "lost his faith" and whose "intellectual pride" has "cut him off from God."[6]

The problem with such theories is that they convert possibilities into solutions. M. R. James, who modeled his stories after Le Fanu's, once stated, "It is not amiss sometimes to leave a loophole for a natural explanation, but I would say, let the loophole be so narrow as not to be quite practicable." This teasing, enigmatic quality, so obvious to any writer in the genre, is missed by theory-obsessed critics. In "Green Tea," the Freudian "loophole" is narrow

---

include diabolical transformation a key element in the story. Thus Carmilla speaks, but only in her non-vampiric phases.

6. Penzoldt, 77; Pritchett, 122–23; Michael H. Begnal, *Joseph Sheridan Le Fanu* (Lewisburg, PA, 1971), 40; James, vi.

indeed. We are not given enough information about the near-anonymous Jennings to conclude that he is "schizoid" or "sexually repressed." We are told only that he is shy and unassuming.

The Christian interpretation is even flimsier. There is no doubt that Jennings's obsession is somehow connected with an intense, unspeakable feeling of guilt. The text contains many references to this feeling: he collapses from the altar "in the agitation of a strange shame and horror" (180); he looks at Hesselius "guilty" during their conversation (182); he even cries "God forgive me!" during a later conversation (192). What the text does not tell us is what Jennings needs to be forgiven for, what crime he has committed to merit such a hideous, ultimately lethal punishment. As we shall see, the only character who could conceivably be accused of "intellectual pride" is Dr. Hesselius. Indeed, if we assume with Begnal that Jennings committed a mortal sin by researching the non-Christian religious beliefs of the ancients, we must ask why Hesselius is not also pursued to the grave by the avenging monkey, for he is guilty of the same heterodox research. Nor is there any evidence that Jennings has lost his faith; on the contrary, he is a pious, devout Christian who ceases to pray only when the monkey literally prevents him from doing so by shrieking blasphemies in his ear.

The truth is that Jennings has done nothing but drink green tea. The very title of the tale registers the fundamental irony: the awful disjuncture between cause and effect, crime and punishment. What emerges is an irrational, almost Kafka-esque feeling of guilt and persecution. Like Joseph K., Jennings is ceaselessly pursued and tormented for no discernible reason. A persistent experience in modern fiction is a situation in which the main character wakes up one morning on a tightrope and does not know how he got there. This is precisely the predicament Jennings finds himself in. Although S. M. Ellis calls Le Fanu a "tragic" writer,[7] "Green Tea" is closer to modern tragic-comedy. Jennings never experiences even a flash of tragic recognition; on the contrary, he never knows why this horrible thing is happening. There is no insight, no justice and therefore no tragedy. There is only absurd cruelty, a grim world view which endures in the reader's mind long after the hairs have settled on the back of the neck.

Though ultimately deterministic, this world view is not based on a coherent or knowable determinism—there is neither the benign workings of Providence nor the naturalism of Zola or Dreiser. The sense of doom in

---

7. S. M. Ellis, *Wilkie Collins, Le Fanu and Others* (London, 1931), 165. "Tragic" is more applicable to the novels than to the tales. (Ellis finds "a sort of stately inevitableness" in *The House by the Church-yard*.)

these stories emanates from a uniquely hostile cosmos vaguely suggestive of the purblind doomsters which later pursue Thomas Hardy's characters. But Le Fanu is not interested in programmatic philosophical consistency. In trying to get at the source of the horror, various characters suggest various possibilities—all of them bleak—yet final solutions elude them, as they elude the reader. One event leads inexorably to another once the pursuit begins, but the reason behind it is known only to the otherworldly invaders. Causality is present, but Le Fanu's victims experience only Crass Causality, blind and mechanical, yet efficiently murderous once the cosmos gives someone a bad throw of the dice. Jennings dimly perceives the magnitude of the forces massed against him in one of his final, most pathetic speeches:

> But as food is taken in softly at the lips, and then brought under the teeth, as the tip of the little finger caught in a mill crank will draw in the hand, and the arm, and the whole body, so the miserable mortal who has been once caught firmly by the end of the finest fibre of his nerve, is drawn in and in, by the enormous machinery of hell, until he is as I am. Yes, Doctor, as I am, for a while I talk to you, and implore relief, I feel that my prayer is for the impossible, and my pleading with the inexorable. (200)

Jennings is horribly right in his perception that the workings of the grisly machinery are "inexorable" and that his "prayer is for the impossible."

Despite the resemblance of all this to Hap in its most perverse manipulations, there is an ominous point at which the analogy breaks down. Once Le Fanu's hellish machine begins grinding, it does so with Hardyesque remorselessness, but also with a strange awareness of purpose which goes beyond the half-consciousness of the Immanent Will. If Hardy's cosmos is struggling to attain consciousness, Le Fanu's has already attained it, or is at least well along the way. If there is no benevolent or rational purpose behind things, there does seem to be a sinister purpose. James Barton, another Le Fanu victim, speaks of this conspiracy in Manichaean terms in "The Familiar." Jennings, lacking even tentative answers, is obsessed with "machinery" and process, with the "stages" of his torment:

> "In the dark, as you shall presently hear, there are peculiarities. It is a small monkey, perfectly black. It had only one peculiarity—a character of malignity—unfathomable malignity. During the first year it looked sullen and sick. But this character of intense malice and vigilance was always underlying that surly languor. During all that time it acted as if on a plan of giving me as little trouble as was consistent with watching me. Its eyes were never off me. I have never lost sight of it, except in my sleep, light or dark, day or night, since it came here excepting when it withdraws for some weeks at a time, unaccountably.

"In total dark it is visible as in daylight. I do not mean its eyes. It is *all* visible distinctly in a halo that resembles a glow of red embers and which accompanies it in all its movements.

"When it leaves me for a time, it is always at night, in the dark, and in the same way. It grows at first uneasy, and then furious, and then advances towards me, grinning and shaking, its paws clenched, and, at the same time, there comes the appearance of fire in the grate. I never have any fire. I can't sleep in the room where there is any, and it draws nearer and nearer to the chimney, quivering, it seems, with rage, and when its fury rises to the highest pitch, it springs into the grate, and up the chimney, and I see it no more.

"When first this happened, I thought I was released. I was now a new man. A day passed—a night—and no return, and a blessed week—a week—another week. I was always on my knees, Dr. Hesselius, always thanking God and praying. A whole month passed of liberty, but on a sudden, it was with me again . . .

"It was with me, and the malice which before was torpid under a sullen exterior, was now active. It was perfectly unchanged in every other respect. This new energy was apparent in its activity and its looks, and soon in other ways.

"For a time, you will understand, the change was shown only in an increased vivacity, and an air of menace, as if it were always brooding over some atrocious plan. Its eyes, as before, were never off me. (196–97)

The victim of "an atrocious plan," intricately conceived and faultlessly executed, Jennings is denied even an inkling of the ultimate purpose behind that plan.

In this sense, Jennings is in a bleaker predicament than Poe's Roderick Usher, who is powerless largely because he thinks he is. Usher's main problem seems to be a kind of self-inflicted catatonia: since the horrors in Poe's tale are completely localized in a single house, they would presumably lessen if Usher would take the narrator's advice and go somewhere else; but the famous twist is that the house cannot be separated from Usher's mind, as Usher himself reveals to us in his allegorical poem and in his abstract paintings of subterranean tunnels.[8] More than anything else, Usher needs a therapist. But Jennings, who has a therapist, is entirely helpless, for the horror which pursues him is more than a psychological phenomenon. Therapy does him no good; he is victimized by something finally independent of his psyche. In the passage describing the monkey's leap up the chimney, Le Fanu is careful to depict a fiend who is extraordinarily alive, the active incarnation of some unrelenting principle of hatred. The symbiotic connection

8. The most extreme psychoanalytical view of the tale is John S. Hill, "The Dual Hallucination in 'The Fall of the House of Usher,'" *Southwestern Review* 48 (1963): 396–402.

between setting and psyche, so important in "The Fall of the House of Usher" and "M. S. Found In a Bottle," does not apply here. Le Fanu's settings are often evocative in themselves (see "Sir Dominick's Bargain"), but they are irrelevant to the main action: his doomed heroes are pursued wherever they go, are tormented in the most unlikely places; their ghostly tormentors see no need to confine themselves in depressing Gothic houses and are likely to appear anywhere, often in broad daylight. (In "The Familiar," James Barton is chased by the Watcher, a specter who is fond of appearing not only in daylight, but in crowds; nor does he mind traveling long distances when Barton tries to skip the country.)

This is not to say that Le Fanu is unconcerned with psychology. On the contrary, his tales deal repeatedly with dark states of consciousness. The difference between "Green Tea" and Edmund Wilson's version of *The Turn of the Screw* is that this inner darkness is a sinisterly accurate measure of the outer world rather than a neurotic projection. Like the madness of Lear, the derangement of Jennings's mind is a mirror image of a derangement in the cosmos, although Jennings has neither the insight nor the catharsis of Lear. That the infernal region in Jennings's psyche reflects not only reality, but the fundamental reality, is hinted at in a passage in Swedenborg's *Arcana Caelestia*, which Hesselius translated from the Latin:

> "When man's interior sight is opened, which is that of his spirit, then there appear the things of another life, which cannot possibly be made visible to the bodily sight. . . .
>
> "By the internal sight it has been granted me to see the things that are in the other life, more clearly than I see those that are in the world. From these considerations, it is evident that external vision exists from interior vision, and this from a vision still more interior, and so on. . . .
>
> "If evil spirits could perceive that they were associated with man, and yet that they were spirits separate from him, and if they could flow in into the things of his body, they would attempt by a thousand means to destroy him; for they hate man with a deadly hatred." (186)

Placing the passage in context with Jennings's experience, it becomes apparent that the doors of perception open straight into hell; they are kept mercifully shut for the most part, but can be flung open by the most absurdly inadvertent act, in this case by the drinking of green tea.

It is just as well that little has been made of Le Fanu's connection with Swedenborg,[9] for Le Fanu's version represents a distortion, or at least a darkening of the original. The passage which Hesselius translates goes on to say

---

9. Neither Ellis nor Browne does any more than mention the connection.

that the "wicked genii" do not attack those who are "in the good of faith." The Christian is "continually protected by the lord." But this protection does not work for Jennings (who writes *"Deus misereatur mei"* in the margin of the Swedenborg text). Without the saving light of a benevolent deity, Le Fanu's mystical psychology is far more malevolent than Swedenborg's: what we have in this psychological landscape are increasingly deeper layers of consciousness, each one increasingly diabolical—an infinite darkness.

The darkness in Le Fanu is quite different from the "blackness of darkness"[10] in Poe or the "great power of blackness"[11] Melville found in Hawthorne. In Poe, darkness is a thick, palpable texture, opaque and impenetrable, which permeates mind and matter like an endless sewage. In Hawthorne, darkness is a moral quality deriving from the traditional symbolic equation of darkness with evil. Both writers paint with a wide brush, darkening their prose immediately with adjectives like "gloomy" and "inscrutable." Though brilliantly evoked, theirs is often a melodramatic world where colors have allegorical rigidity. In Le Fanu, where the fiend is as likely to appear in the full light of the Sunday church service as in the gloom of a moldering house, where he is comfortable squatting in a prayerbook rather than seething in the sinner's bosom, colors are used sparingly, sometimes monochromatically. Much of the traditional color symbolism remains: the blacks and reds often suggest as much evil and violence as they do in *Macbeth*; the lurid halo emanating from the monkey like "a glow of red embers" gives off the same satatic light as Ethan Brand's lime kiln.

For the most part, however, Le Fanu's colors elude allegorical equations. Unfettered by an orderly moral universe, they have a half-tinted quality which is somehow more unsettling than the extravagant darkness and storminess of the Gothic writers:

> The sun had already set, and the red reflected light of the western sky illuminated the scene with the peculiar effect with which we are all familiar. The hall seemed very dark, but, getting to the back drawingroom, whose windows command the west, I was again in the same dusky light.
>
> I sat down, looking out upon the richly-wooded landscape that flowed in the grand and melancholy light which was every moment fading. The corners of the room were already dark; all was growing dim, and the gloom was

---

10. Edgar Allan Poe, "The Pit and the Pendulum," *The Complete Tales and Poems of Edgar Allan Poe* (New York, 1938), 246.

11. Herman Melville, "Hawthorne and His Mosses," reprinted in "Reviews and Letters by Herman Melville," *Moby Dick*, ed. Harrison Hayford and Hershel Parker (New York, 1967), 540.

insensibly toning my mind, already prepared for what was sinister. I was waiting alone for his arrival, which soon took place. The door communicating
with the front room opened, and the tall figure of Mr. Jennings, faintly seen
in the ruddy twilight, came, with quiet stealthy steps, into the room.

We shook hands, and taking a chair to the window, where there was still
light enough to enable us to see each other's faces, he sat down beside me,
and, placing his hand upon my arm, with scarcely a word of preface began his
narrative . . . .

The faint glow of the west, the pomp of the then lonely woods of Richmond, were before us, behind and about us the darkening room, and on the
stony face of the sufferer—for the character of his face, though still gentle
and sweet, was changed—rested that dim, odd flow which seems to descend
and produce, where it touches, lights, sudden though faint, which are lost
almost without gradation, in darkness. The silence, too, was utter: not a distant wheel, or bark, or whistle from without; and within the depressing still-
ness of an invalid bachelor's house. (191)

What do we make of this strange twilight, dim, and translucent one minute,
"grand and melancholy" the next; "every moment fading," yet reappearing
suddenly, only to be "lost, almost without gradation, in darkness"? The
passage seems naturalistic enough, at least up to a point (The sunset has
"the peculiar effect with which we are all familiar.") Yet the lights and
shadows become so blurred and undefined as to become almost
interchangeable. Faint points of light seem to go on and off like stars
suddenly going out and reappearing in a cloudy sky. In the next to last
sentence, with its twisted, almost Jamesian syntax, this "odd glow" is
associated with Jennings's face. The "almost" here suggests a subtle
gradation, a hierarchy of twilight worlds, each of which gives off its own
unearthly lights, swallowing them up again almost instantly.

Jennings has accidentally summoned a creature from one of these
worlds, and his face shows the price he has paid: it has assumed the same
deathlike appearance as Jennings's new companion; it even emits the same
strange lights. Le Fanu's imagery suggests the shifting, dissolving colors of a
nightmare. Ambiguous and undefined, his colors are like those in our
dreams, much harder to recall than the Technicolor images of Poe or
"Monk" Lewis.

The reader can experience the relief of waking, simply by closing the
book and turning on every light in the house. The doomed protagonists are
not so fortunate. In Jennings's case, his demise seems to be hastened by the
incompetence of his therapist. Hesselius deserves close examination, for he
appears to be the first psychiatrist in English literature. Since he is pre-
Freudian by at least thirty years, he has a hard time defining just what he is,

calling himself at various times a medical philosopher, a philosophical physician and even a doctor of Metaphysical Medicine. He is distinctly a therapist, however, claiming to have diagnosed "two hundred and thirty cases more or less nearly akin to that I have entitled 'Green Tea'" (208). This is a staggering thought, suggesting that Hesselius has dealt with a large number of what are surely the most bizarre patients in the annals of psychiatry. If the prefaces to *In a Glass Darkly* are to be taken seriously, he has had to confront such things as living corpses, demonic monkeys, and lesbian vampires.[12]

All this has been hard on him, as his ineptness in treating Jennings all too clearly reveals. After Jennings unfolds his tale, Hesselius is at an obvious loss as to what to do. At one particularly strained point, immediately following the oration on "the enormous machinery of hell," Hesselius can only say: "I endeavoured to calm his visibly increasing agitation and told him that he must not despair" (200). This is fatuous advice: there is every reason to despair, especially in the absence of any concrete suggestions. Following Jennings's depressing account of a near-suicide attempt, Hesselius's advice is even worse:

> "Yes, yes; it is always urging me to crimes, to injure others, or myself. You see, Doctor, the situation is urgent, it is indeed. When I was in Shropshire, a few weeks, ago" (Mr. Jennings was speaking rapidly and trembling now, holding my arm with one hand, and looking in my face), "I went out one day with a party of friends for a walk: my persecutor, I tell you, was with me at the time. I lagged behind the rest: the country near the Dee, you know, is beautiful. Our path happened to lie near a coal mine, and at the verge of the wood is a perpendicular shaft, they say, a hundred and fifty feet deep. My niece had remained behind with me—she knows, of course, nothing of the nature of my sufferings. She knew, however, that I had been ill, and was low, and she remained to prevent my being quite alone. As we loitered slowly on together, the brute that accompanied me was urging me to throw myself down the shaft. I tell you now—oh, sir, think of it!—the one consideration that saved me from that hideous death was the fear lest the shock of witnessing the occurrence should be too much for the poor girl. I asked her to go on and walk with her friends, saying that I could go no further. She made excuses, and the more I urged her the firmer she became. She looked doubtful and frightened. I suppose there was something in my looks or manner that alarmed

---

12. With the exception of "Green Tea," none of these confrontations are ever dramatized. Though frequently mentioned in prologues, Hesselius never appears as a character in any of the other tales. Even in "Green Tea," the therapy is interrupted by the patient's suicide before we are able to assess its effectiveness. Unlike Machen's Dr. Raymond, Blackwood's John Silence or Hodgson's Carnacki (all of whom he anticipates), Hesselius is a background rather than a luminary figure.

her; but she would not go, and that literally saved me. You had no idea, sir, that a living man could be made so abject a slave of Satan," he said with a ghastly groan and a shudder.

There was a pause here, and I said, "You *were* preserved nevertheless. It was the act of God. You are in his hands, and in the power of no other being: be confident therefore for the future." (201)

Jennings's concern for the little girl's reaction, even at the climax of his own suicidal despair, strengthens our feeling that he is a scrupulously sensitive, compassionate man, undeserving of this torment. But the passage is more revealing of Hesselius.

"You see, doctor, the situation is urgent, it is indeed" is a chilling under-statement, yet all the philosophic physician can do is offer platitudes—the solace of a deity who is either indifferent or as impotent as Hesselius himself. The advice is more than merely unctuous and ineffectual: the claim that Jennings is "in the power of no other being" is demonstrably false.

Nor does his epilogue, "A Word for Those Who Suffer," do anything to enhance his professional credibility. This final chapter is in the form of a let-ter of Professor Van Loo of Leyden, a chemist who has suffered from Jennings's malady and whom Hesselius claims to have cured. It is a suspi-ciously self-serving document:

Who, under God, cured you? Your humble servant, Martin Hesselius. Let me rather adopt the more emphasised piety of a certain good old French surgeon of three hundred years ago: "I treated, and God cured you." . . .

There is no one affliction of mortality more easily and certainly reducible, with a little patience, and a rational confidence in the physician. With these simple conditions, I look upon the cure as absolutely certain.

You are to remember that I had not even commenced to treat Mr. Jennings' case. I have not any doubt that I should have cured him perfectly in eighteen months, or possibly it might have extended to two years. . . .

You know my tract on "The Cardinal Functions of the Brain." I there, by the evidence of innumerable facts, prove, as I think, the high probability of a circulation arterial and venous in its mechanism, through the nerves. Of this system, thus considered, the brain is the heart. The fluid, which is propa-gated hence through one class of nerves, returns in an altered stage through another, and the nature of that fluid is spiritual, though not immaterial, any more than, as I before remarked, light or electricity are so.

By various abuses, among which the habitual use of such agents as green tea is one, this fluid may be affected as to its quality, but it is more frequently disturbed as to equilibrium. This fluid being that which we have in common with spirits, a congestion found upon the masses of brain or nerve, connected with the interior sense, forms a surface unduly exposed, on which disembod-

ied spirits may operate: communication is thus more or less effectually established. Between this brain circulation and the heart circulation there is an
intimate sympathy. The seat, or rather the instrument of exterior vision, is
the eye. The seat of interior vision is the nervous tissue and brain, immediately about and above the eyebrow. You remember how effectually I dissi-
pated your pictures by the simple application of iced eau-de-cologne. Few
cases, however, can be treated exactly alike with anything like rapid success.
Cold acts powerfully as a repellent of the nervous fluid. Long enough continued it will even produce that permanent insensibility which we call numb-
ness, and a little longer muscular as well as sensational paralysis.

I have not, I repeat, the slightest doubt that I should have first dimmed
and ultimately sealed that inner eye which Mr. Jennings had inadvertently
opened. . . . It is by acting steadily upon the body, by a simple process, that
this result is produced—and inevitably produced—I have never yet failed.

Poor Mr. Jennings made away with himself. But that catastrophe was the
result of a totally different malady, which, as it were, projected itself upon
the disease which was established. His case was in the distinctive manner a
complication, and the complaint under which he really succumbed, was hereditary suicidal mania. Poor Mr. Jennings I cannot call a patient of mine, for
I had not even begun to treat his case, and he had not yet given me, I am
convinced, his full and unreserved confidence. If the patient do not array
himself on the side of the disease, his cure is certain. (206–7)

The immediate point of interest here is the earnest but tortured attempt to
reconcile medical science with mystical experience, a commonplace exercise
in nineteenth- and early twentieth-century weird fiction.[13] In relation to the
story, however, the epilogue is not so earnest. It raises a variety of questions.
Why did Hesselius not share any of these insights with his patient, a man on
the verge of self-destruction? Why did he not tell him that his cure would be a
"simple process"? Why did he not describe this process and thereby relieve
Jennings's paranoia? Leaving aside the believability of this "absolutely certain"
cure why did he not produce the magical "iced eau-de-cologne" and douse the
wretched man with it? The final dismissal of Jennings's case as "hereditary
suicidal mania," without any evidence, is an ugly rationalization. The wonder
is that Jennings, unremittingly persecuted for three years, did not kill himself

---

13. Of all the writers who attempted this fusion—Stevenson, Bulwer-Lytton, Machen,
Blackwood, Hodgson, and Wells (among others)—only Wells seems to have recognized that the polarities must be reconciled with the aesthetic demands of the story as
well as with each other. Compare Wells's "The Plattner Story" with Bulwer-Lytton's
"The House and the Brain": one is an integrated work of fiction, the other a story
interrupted (and subverted) by an essay.

sooner; if anything, the evidence indicates an unusually strong psyche.

But the oddest thing about this addendum is its failure to explain its author's behavior in the period between Jennings's narration and his suicide. After giving his account, Jennings understandably breaks down weeping (despite Hesselius's disingenuous "He seemed comforted"). Hesselius does have one concrete bit of comfort to offer: "One promise I exacted, which was that should the monkey return, I should be sent for immediately" (202). Taking his doctor at his word, Jennings tries to contact Hesselius "immediately" after the monkey's next appearance, which is predictably soon:

> Dear Dr. Hesselius—It is here. You had not been an hour gone when it returned. It is speaking. It knows all that has happened. It knows everything— it knows you, and is frantic and atrocious. It reviles. I send you this. It knows every word I have written—I write, but I fear very confused, very incoherently, I am so interrupted, disturbed. (203)

Hesselius, however, is not to be found. Intentionally making his whereabouts unknown, he has fled when he is most needed to an unknown address where he intends to dabble with his metaphysical medicines "without the possibility of intrusion or distraction" (202). He seems to need therapy himself, so shut off is he from the consequences of his actions. The immediate consequence is that Jennings, feeling totally alone, cuts his throat.

Hesselius is only marginally concerned with the well-being of his patient. His chief motivation—which reaches a state of frenzied anticipation—is his determination to validate his theories. As the epilogue implies, he is less saddened than annoyed by his patient's death; by that act, Jennings has robbed him of his big chance.

We can reasonably conclude that Le Fanu did not mean us to take this epilogue on the same level of seriousness as Hesselius assumes we do. His claims, accusations, and actions are dubious enough in themselves; set against the powerful authenticity of Jennings's narrative, they make sense only as dramatic irony. Unless seen as ironic, the "Word for Those Who Suffer" becomes an aesthetic blunder. There is nothing organic about this final chapter; it seems distinctly tacked on, a needless diatribe which ruins the tale if taken at face value. But seen as ironic, it underscores the hopelessness of Jennings's predicament.

As the less than reliable narrator of a horror tale, Hesselius is part of a tradition which begins with Poe's narrator in "The Tell-Tale Heart" and culminates in the governess's account in *The Turn of the Screw*. This is not to say that Hesselius is a Gothic villain—a frothing madman or an ostentatious evil doctor. Like everything else in the story, he is difficult to pin down: earnest and well-meaning in the opening pages, he seems progressively more ineffectual, even senile, at worst evincing a precarious ego which distorts his judgment. In other respects as well, the narrative problems are more complex than those in Poe. Hesselius is not the only narrator of "Green Tea." The tale has a prologue as well as a conclusion; as William Buckler has shown, the prologue is also problematic:

The story is filtered to the reader through three "carefully educated" men of science: the supposed editor, or "medical secretary"; Dr. Hesselius, the narrator; and Professor Van Loo, chemist and student of history, metaphysics, and medicine, to whom a correspondent would presumably write with conscientiousness. And yet each is a fallible authority: the editor is a confessed "enthusiast" who has taken Dr. Hesselius as his "master"; Dr. Hesselius, besides suffering from an acutely sensitive ego, obviously has no authority within the medical fraternity, is theoretical and categorical, and seems unduly intent upon rationalizing the perfect record of his "cures," and Dr. Van Loo, according to the narrator, has suffered from a similar "affection," while, according to the editor, he is an "unlearned reader."[14]

Though accurate and concise as a summary, Buckler's introduction does not attempt to resolve the obvious question it raises: why does Le Fanu bother with this narrative filtering device at all? This is a difficult question to answer, for "Green Tea" is unlike other tales which saddle us with unreliable or multiple narrators: we get little sense of the moral complexity found in Stevenson, the pathological involutions found in Poe, or the fanatically refined sensibility found in Henry James.

As an intentionally fuzzy narrative, "Green Tea" is similar to several tales in Ambrose Bierce's *In the Midst of Life* and *Can Such Things Be?* Like Bierce's "The Moonlit Road" and "The Suitable Surroundings," "Green Tea" seems arbitrarily burdened with narrators and editors.[15] Yet the seeming arbitrariness of the narrative scheme imparts a unique atmosphere to these tales. Le Fanu anticipates Bierce in his evocation of a world where things refuse to fit together, where terrible things happen to the wrong people for the wrong reasons, where horrors leap out of the most trivial or ridiculous contexts. The disjointedness of the narrative pattern reinforces our sense of a nightmare world where everything is out of joint. Why should we expect aesthetic

---

14. Buckler, 27.

15. Although brief, "The Moonlit Road" achieves an almost mind-numbing complexity by emerging from three fragmented points of view, including that of the murder victim as communicated through a medium. "The Suitable Surroundings" juxtapose time sequences as well as narrators, in each case creating a maximum of confusion which gives the tale a peculiarly delayed impact.

order when monkeys can chase people into their graves, green tea can cause damnation, and therapists can suddenly drop out of sight when patients are on the precipice of suicide? Besides instilling a sense of underlying chaos, the filtering device also gives the impression of narrative distance, a useful effect in any kind of ironic fiction, but particularly necessary in the ghost story, where too much narrative directness can instantly blunt the desired impact. Jennings must seem like a thoroughly helpless creature, dwarfed by diabolical forces beyond his comprehension (let alone control) and gradually receding from our vision into hell. What could serve this purpose better than to have his narrative manipulated by three verbose doctors who are more concerned with selling their theories than with protecting his sanity?

Le Fanu's complicated narrative skein also helps create the "loophole" of ambiguity mentioned by M. R. James. It is at least *possible* that Hesselius's claims are justified, that his unorthodox medications would have banished Jennings's monkey, and that his infallibly is "absolutely certain." (Although this certainty would not efface the supernatural elements in the story, it would have the disappointing effect of a natural explanation: demonic forces might still exist in some sense, but would be so easily subdued by infallible German doctors as to be in effect naturalized.) For the many reasons mentioned, however, we doubt Hesselius's word: the easy way out is a remote possibility but "not quite practicable." Even if Hesselius were believable as the medical equivalent of a Dickensian benefactor (dispensing cures instead of money at the end), we would still be left with the terrible irony of Jennings destroying himself just as he is about to be delivered.

Either way, "Green Tea" is a horror tale. It is Le Fanu's most extreme, yet most controlled performance. Although the "well managed crescendo" admired by M. R. James occurs in most of his tales, nowhere is it more attenuated and cumulative than in "Green Tea." In "Schalken the Painter," "Justice Harbottle," and others, the initial apparition comes fairly quickly; here the "journey" is more leisurely and spread out; the distance traveled is greater. By taking his time, Le Fanu makes Jennings's "doors of perception" experience all the more painful and catastrophic. Similarly, the heavy use of ambiguity and dramatic irony suggests a dislocated, strangely modern world where reality is grim enough to outpace our most exaggerated fantasies. Though written in the late nineteenth century, "Green Tea," as E. F. Benson has happily put it, is "instinct with an awfulness which custom cannot stale."[16] Those who find ghost stories to be boring or silly will probably interpret "awfulness" in a different way than Benson intended. But the rest of us know exactly what he means.

---

16. Benson, 263–64.

Introduction to *The House by the Church-Yard*

Elizabeth Bowen

The House by the Church-yard was first published in 1863,[1] one year before Joseph Sheridan Le Fanu's other great novel, *Uncle Silas*. Of the two, *Uncle Silas*, with its small cast and highly-concentrated psychological interest, may accommodate itself better to readers today: it being just over a century since both books were written, *Uncle Silas* may seem the more "modern." Those whose addiction to Le Fanu derived from the fascinations of *Uncle Silas* may (I do not say must) experience a set-back when first they embark on *The House by the Church-yard*—less taut, less apparently sure in "tone," disconcerting in its oscillations between sinister grimness and full-blooded jocosity and, here and there, threatened by diffuseness. Such, frankly, was, at the outset, the reaction of the writer of this introduction. It took some time for the excellences, chief among which are the almost uncanny force and total originality of *The House by the Church-yard*, to seep through. That having happened, the novel obtained a grip nothing can dislodge.

Le Fanu, one may take it to be known, was an Irishman. When I had the privilege of writing an introduction to *Uncle Silas*, I spoke of its being an essentially Irish novel in an English setting. Something profoundly, temperamentally, differentiates it from the English-Victorian novel of mystery and suspense—such as Wilkie Collins' *The Woman in White*. The oblique and more than semi-mistrustful view of character (or characters), the unopposed great part played by obsession, the acceptance of more or less permanent insecurity as the basis for life, all belong to, all emanate from, the further side of the Irish sea. Le Fanu's Irishness, it could be argued, stood out the more strongly when, for the purposes of a story, he set himself to treating with English characters in England. *The House by the Church-yard*, I have now to admit, contradicts that. That the *mise-en-scène* is, and the entire cast, with

---

1. [*The House by the Church-yard* first appeared as a three-decker novel in 1863 (London: Tinsley Brothers); it was originally serialized in the *Dublin University Magazine* from October 1861 to February 1863.—Ed.]

one exception, are Irish doubles the author's own native characteristics. Le Fanu, here, is steeping his story in what was to him a pre-natal atmosphere, an atmosphere so normal, so natural to him that we can—one might feel— for at any rate the duration of the story, conceive of no other as being possible. The point of view, the evaluations, the mood, the dilemmas are all Hibernian—what one does wonder is, how far they were comprehensible to his English readers? For Le Fanu's Ireland is far from being "stage-Ireland," it is Ireland as he knew her to be, for better or worse.

The happenings in the action of *The House by the Church-yard* pre-date by just less than a hundred years the time of the telling of the tale: 1767 is the date specified. The narrator is an anonymous old man,[2] whose curiosity as to a by-gone drama was, he explains to us, originally stirred, during his boyhood, by the coming to light in a village church-yard of a skull with two deep clefts, plus a round hole in the back of it. This old man (or rather, the Le Fanu behind him) cheats liberally—albeit with an effectiveness by which the cheating is twenty times justified—in the matter of what goes into his narrative: no matter of burning into the letters and diaries to which he purports to have had access could account for the authenticity, the sometimes fearful vividness, down to the last detail, he gives to what took place before he was born—or indeed, thought of—or for his omniscience as to not only the doings but feelings and thoughts of people on whom he had not, and never could have, set eyes. Not one scene in the book seems at-one-remove; on the contrary, the action of *The House by the Church-yard* unfolds itself directly, immediately, close-up to you and me. The good old man, with his singsong expressions of nostalgia for an epoch he fancies—perhaps rightly?— to have been more *simpatico*, more agreeable, than his own, early on is faded out of *The House by the Church-yard*. This I feel entitled to promise you—lest he put you off. (Why, incidentally *did* Victorian writers burden themselves and their novels with "intermediaries?" Why does Emily Brontë use them in *Wuthering Heights*?)

The House by the Church-yard is set in what since has come to be known to James Joyce devotees as the *Anna Livia* country: Chapelizod, in the Liffey valley. Few making a Joyce tour, as now organized, will omit Chapelizod from their itinerary. Its name is now the poor place's remaining glory; apart from that it has come to be little more than a lusterless over-run from Dublin. Even by the 1860s it had, according to our narrator, lapsed, being dominated if not by satanic mills by frowsty, smoke-engendering factories. Bearable in his

---

2. [The novel was originally presented as written by Charles de Cresseron, a name adapted from the de Cresserons of Le Fanu's French ancestry.—Ed.]

boyhood, it had been at its heyday in the 1760s: that is, when the events related in *The House by the Church-yard* were taking place. "In those days, Chapelizod was about the gayest and prettiest of the outpost villages in which old Dublin took a complacent pride. The poplars which stood in military rows, here and there, just showed a glimpse of formality among the orchards and old timber that lined the banks of the river and the valley with a lively sort of richness. The broad old streets looked hospitable and merry, with steep roofs and many coloured hall-doors . . . Then there was the village church, with its tower dark and rustling, from base to summit, with thick piled, bowering ivy." Equivalents of the vanished prettiness and propriety of Chapelizod still are to be found—long may this be so!—in up-river Lucan and, still more, in the more-intact, further up-river Leixlip (Co. Kildare).

Poplars were not the only military feature: the Chapelizod of the time of *The House by the Church-yard* had the prestige and enjoyed the panache of being the headquarters of the Royal Irish Artillery, or R. I. A.—not pray, to be confused by English readers with the I. R. A.! The barracks, the parade ground with its great gate, were along the riverside. The officers lodged on the drawing-room floors of sedate little houses on the aforesaid streets. The commander, "fat, short, radiant General Chattesworth," abode, with his lively spinster sister and pretty young daughter, in a nearby mansion, Belmont, overlooking the river from the heights—many such are, I am glad to say, still to be found in this neighborhood. General Chattesworth is, we find, overshadowed socially only by the local peer, Lord Castlemallard, a dreamy bore.

The cast of *The House by the Church-yard,* in the main male, is largely though not wholly military. Civilians are represented by Dr. Walsingham, the Protestant rector, his genial Catholic opposite number Father Roach, the physician Toole (whose relations with Sturk, the army surgeon attached to the R. I. A. are not so ideal as they should be), Irons, the lantern-jawed parish clerk, and, not by an means least, the dark-avised Nutter, miller, whose chief income is derived from his agency of the surrounding Castlemallard properties. To these are added two men of mystery: haunted young Mr. Mervyn, who arrives with a coffin and stays on, in a perpetual brooding frenzy which leads ladies to think he may be an *âme damnée*, and suave, sophisticated, middle-aged Mr. Dangerfield, Englishman, who moves in for no declared purpose, renting a riverside villa delightfully known as The Brass Castle. Dangerfield is Lord Castlemallard's agent in England, where—Irish peers enjoyed the best of both worlds!—properties are more extensive and valuable. A second putative *âme damnée* is handsome Captain Devereaux, of the R. I. A. The R. I. A. contribute to our story also, most notably, corsetted, on-the-make Captain Cluffe, Lieutenant Fireworker O'Flaherty (one of the

"ferocious O'Flaherty's" from Galway) and dear, ingenuous, generous, fat little First Lieutenant Puddock . . . In spite of this bevy of males, if one may so
call it, *The House by the Church-yard* could have been sub-titled "a novel
without a hero."[3] There is, actually, no one central character of either sex.
As "heroines," Lilias Walsingham and Gertrude Chattesworth amicably divide the honors; yet, neither girl plays a major part in the plot—one of them
is to be made momentous, and deeply moving, by her illness and death.
Gertrude's Aunt Rebecca is more in the forefront—handsome, something of
a volcano. Miss Magnolia Macnamara and her mother are comics (something in the splenetic Thackeray manner). It is two at the first glance incon-
spicuous matrons, Mrs. Nutter and Mrs. Sturk, who are to become most
drastically involved, in whirlpools of menace, terror, piteous anxiety, darkling mystery. And there is an evil-precipitating adventuress out from Dublin, Mary Matchwell.

With near-genius, with which goes a friendly equalitarianism in regard to
them, Le Fanu keeps this host of characters in play. Never for long does any
one of them leave the story. His hero-less plot is kept spinning by a diversity
of criss-crossing passions. He *does*, one has to admit, introduce a villain,
though so subtly, and with so many light and deluding touches, that this creature's enormities hardly are to be suspected until the end. Rivalries and an-
tagonism are at work, pressures exerted. A criminal drama, set in another
land, proves unfinished; it continues to operate in and round Chapelizod . . .
All this sounds like, and indeed is, the stock material of one kind of fiction.
What, then, causes *The House by the Church-yard* to soar above endless other
novels of what might otherwise be its kind? I would suggest, Le Fanu's curious, near-visionary manner of seeing and way of writing, his what one might
call depth-charge perceptions into feeling and motive, his sympathy with the
off-beat, with deviation, his nonetheless uncompromising sense of what *is*
ethical, and, most of all, the acute, sometimes almost unbearable emotion,
always too astringent to be emotionality or sentiment, with which he suffuses
his key scenes. He is aware of the monstrous, and makes a not wholly ironical
bow to it: his Black Dillon, that perverse young surgeon of genius cynically
weltering in the stews of Dublin, plays but a brief part but is unforgettable.

This novel has rare, few, lovely and on the whole heartbreaking lyrical
episodes. It is also roared through by an intense sociability. Bravura rates
high, and "gaieties"—in the full and enthusiastic connotation those have in

---

3. [An allusion to William Makepeace Thackeray's satirical *Vanity Fair: A Novel without a Hero*, issued in twenty illustrated monthly parts between January 1847 and July
1848 before publication in the standard hardcover format of the time.—Ed.]

Ireland—are dear to his pen. We have the shooting match, with its merry onlooking troops of ladies, the fair at Palmerstown, the military ball, the *al fresco* entertainment given by the R. I. A. to the neighborhood, fifes, bugles, and other supporting instruments joyously loudening the air of the lady-adorned, tree-shaded riverside. The dinner party at Belmont, at which interesting Mr. Dangerfield first appears, is rendered with every shade of social precision.

Note three particularly Irish attributes of Le Fanu's, all of them to the fore in this novel. (1) His feeling for, acceptance of, and matter-of-fact though nonetheless terrifying treatment of the supernatural, as exemplified by the hauntings of The Tiled House, young Mr. Mervyn's dwelling. (2) His depiction of servants, together with more irregular hirelings who surround households, such as "the Widow Macann . . . who carried ten pailfuls of water up from the river to fill the butt in the backyard every Tuesday and Friday for a shilling a week and 'a cup o' tay with the girls in the kitchen'." The intimacy, the complicity, the often-shared desperations of the employer-employed relationship, as it is in Ireland, can seldom have been, and may never be, better drawn. (3) His sense of the illimitable majesty of death, and its train of incurable desolations. We see a young student, agonized by sympathy, trying to tender comfort to an old clergyman bereft of his dear daughter:—

> "Oh, Dan—Dan—she's gone—little Lily."
> "You'll see her again, sir—oh, you'll see her again."
> "Oh, Dan! Dan! Till the heavens be no more they shall not awake, nor be raised out of their sleep. Oh, Dan, a day's so long—how am I to get over the time?"

In *The House by the Church-yard,* some enchanting lyrics, such as the one beginning:—

> The river ran between them,
>   And she looked upon the stream,
> And the soldier looked upon her,
>   As a dreamer on a dream.

are sung or recalled. And a long moralistic ballad is intoned in a pub, taking off thus:—

> There was a man near Ballymooney,
>   Was guilty of a deed o' blood,
> For thravellin' alongside wiv ould Tim Rooney,
>   He kilt him in a lonesome wood.

Where did Le Fanu get these from, I wonder—did he write them? They stand, in their ways, for what might be called the opposite poles of the book—whose first event is a torchlit midnight burial, surrounded by secrecy, odor of disgrace and unspoken horror, and whose last is a sunlit, splendid young-aristocratic wedding. A damaged skull, we recall, set the story going. By the end, we have learned whose the skull was—yes, we *have* learned, but without greatly caring. That this should be so is, I feel, a tribute to and not a reflection upon *The House by the Church-yard*. So much has been stirred up, such an orchestrated variety of sensations has been lived through, so much that was unexpected has teased our nerves and so much that is tender and beautiful touched our senses and delighted our spirits, since the story began, that the original mystery has been swept away—on the much water that has, but now, flowed under the bridges.

Three Ghost Stories: "The Judge's House," "An Account of Some Strange Disturbances in an Old House in Aungier Street," and "Mr. Justice Harbottle"

Carol A. Senf

As someone who has spent years studying Bram Stoker, I was familiar with his frequently anthologized short story "The Judge's House." Consequently, when I read "An Account of Some Strange Disturbances in an Old House in Aungier Street" and "Mr. Justice Harbottle" by Joseph Sheridan Le Fanu, I immediately detected some similarities. All three stories are classic ghost stories that feature the character of a corrupt judge who returns to haunt people residing in his house. Indeed, because of these similarities, many scholars of the Gothic are inclined to comment on Le Fanu's influence on Stoker and to emphasize the similarities in the two. Even though they are members of different generations (Le Fanu was born in 1814 and died in 1873 while Stoker was born in 1847 and died in 1912), the two were Dublin residents, graduates of Trinity College, members of the Anglo-Irish Ascendancy, lawyers who never practiced law, friends of the William Wilde family, and creators of ghost stories. Stoker's posthumously published short story "Dracula's Guest" (1914) has several similarities to Le Fanu's "Carmilla" (including the location in Styria and the presence of a beautiful woman vampire) and may have been excised from *Dracula* for this very reason. While scholars continue to note Le Fanu's influence on Stoker, it's difficult to pinpoint the nature and extent of that influence.

Because of these connections, the standard critical response is that Le Fanu influenced Stoker. In *Vampires, Mummies, and Liberals: Bram Stoker and the Politics of Popular Fiction*, David Glover comments on that influence, noting that Le Fanu's "vampire story 'Carmilla' (1872) was an important precursor of *Dracula*" and goes on to comment specifically on Le Fanu's influence on other Stoker works: "In fact, traces of Le Fanu's distinctive Anglo-Irish Gothic mode are evident throughout Stoker's writing, especially in some of his shorter fiction such as the 1891 tale 'The Judge's House,' which comes close to pastiche" (29).

Albert Power and Peter Denman also notice a strong similarity in the stories with Power commenting on "a very strong similarity" between "Aungier Street"(1853) and "The Judge's House" (1891):

> Both stories concern the supernatural prowlings of a wicked "hanging judge;" in each case the house possesses a lurid portrait of the judge which exerts a disturbing influence on the house's occupants; and in each case also the judge becomes embodied in the form of a grotesque and menacing rat. (Power 17)

Stoker biographer Paul Murray also comments on the "obvious influence of Sheridan Le Fanu, especially his 'Mr. Justice Harbottle' and 'Aungier Street' on 'The Judge's House'" (152), while Walter Kendrick goes so far as to accuse Stoker of plagiarism:

> But only amnesia or plagiarism can account for the resemblance of Bram Stoker's "The Judge's House" (1914) to Joseph Sheridan Le Fanu's "An Account of Some Disturbances in Aungier Street." Le Fanu's story first came out in the *Dublin University Magazine* in 1853; *In a Glass Darkly* republished it in 1872. Stoker must have read it somewhere; two stories that center on a hanging judge reincarnated as a giant rat in a spooky old house can hardly have arisen from separate bursts of genius. (193)

Even though Leslie Shepard explores Stoker's library and observes that a printed catalogue of the books that Florence Stoker sold after her husband's death refers to a "volume of stories by J. Sheridan Le Fanu" (412), it's difficult to determine exactly which Le Fanu works Stoker read. Shepard doesn't mention which book of short stories was in Stoker's library though Murray notes that *The Watcher and Other Weird Stories* (1894) was in Stoker's library (61). This volume of stories was posthumously published in 1894, but Stoker could have read Le Fanu's work in earlier publications.

Despite the strong tendency to lump the two writers together and to explore Le Fanu's influence on Stoker, this essay is more interested in examining the three stories as separate and individual works and in examining what each has to say about ghost stories. Because this volume focuses on Le Fanu, the essay will begin with "The Judge's House" even though "Aungier Street" and "Mr. Justice Harbottle" were published first.

"The Judge's House"

"The Judge's House," originally appeared in the *Illustrated Sporting and Dramatic News* (5 December 1891) and was republished in *Dracula's Guest and Other Stories* (1914). More spare than either of the Le Fanu stories, it focuses on Malcolm Malcolmson, a student of mathematics who rents a house where he can study for exams, and a small supporting cast: the local lawyer and agent, who tells Malcolmson that the house "has been so long empty that some kind of absurd prejudice has grown up about it" (30); the superstitious innkeeper, Mrs. Witham, who tells him about the man whose house it had been; the charlady, Mrs. Dempster, a rationalist and skeptic who observes that she isn't "afraid of all the bogies in the kingdom" (31); a physician Dr. Thornhill; and the ghostly judge. Moreover, while all three stories ask readers to consider whether the ghost is real or a manifestation of psychological trauma, Le Fanu's first-person narrators may be unreliable. Stoker, on the other hand, chooses a rather spare third-person limited point of view, exploring only Malcolmson's perspective. He also chooses a straightforward chronological telling of Malcolmson's life from the time he rents the old house in Benchurch until his death a matter of days later.

Stoker presents Malcolmson as a rational man who rents a house in a small town where he doesn't know anyone so "there would be nothing to distract him" (29). Warned by the agent that the house has a bad reputation and told by Mrs. Witham that "there was a general feeling that there was *something*" (30) about it, Malcolmson responds that he doesn't have time to worry about such things:

> A man who is reading for the Mathematical Tripos has too much to think of to be disturbed by any of these mysterious "somethings," and his work is of too exact and prosaic a kind to allow of his having any corner in his mind for mysteries of any kind. Harmonical Progression, Permutations and Combinations, and Elliptic Functions have sufficient mysteries for me! (31)

Upon hearing the sounds of rats, Malcolmson explores his living quarters, at which point he notices "some old pictures on the walls." He is also intrigued by the "rope of the great alarm bell on the roof, which hung down in a corner of the room on the right-hand side of the fireplace" (31), a rope that also appears in the portrait. Perhaps most disconcerting is the fact that, while most of the rats scamper away when they see him coming, one huge rat isn't the least bit frightened. Lining up his books to throw at the giant rat, Malcolmson discovers that only one book frightens it away, the "Bible my mother gave me!" (37).

Observing that the large rat escapes behind one of the portraits on the wall, Malcolmson has the portrait cleaned and discovers that it depicts "a judge dressed in his robes of scarlet and ermine" (41). He also learns from Dr. Thornhill that the alarm rope is "the very rope which the hangman used for all the victims of the Judge's judicial rancour!" (39). Neither he nor Malcolmson seems particularly worried that the judge will have any power over the young student, and readers are still free to consider whether anything supernatural is occurring or whether Malcolmson is simply overwrought. Only in the final pages does Stoker tip the scales to focus on the existence of supernatural evil when he shows the painting come to life. Looking at the portrait, Malcolm sees the judge "seated in a great high-backed carved oak chair," and a rope hanging "down from the ceiling, its end lying coiled on the floor. With a feeling of something like horror, Malcolmson recognized the scene of the room as it stood" (41).

While the portrait is disconcerting, readers might conclude that it is merely a representation of a powerful evil that had existed in the past. However, Stoker reinforces the existence of a supernatural force when the portrait becomes alive: "In the centre of the picture was a great irregular patch of brown canvas. . . . The background was as before, with chair and chimney-corner and rope, but the figure of the Judge had disappeared" (42). Of course, what frequently distinguishes ghost stories from psychological exploration is that the ghost eventually manifests itself in the present, and Stoker paces himself carefully to enable the reader to participate in the final terrifying moments of Malcolmson's life when he and the reader realize that the portrait has come to life: "Slowly and deliberately the Judge rose from his chair and picked up the piece of the rope of the alarm bell which lay on the floor, drew it through his hands as if he enjoyed its touch, and then deliberately began to knot one end of it, fashioning it into a noose" (43). Malcolmson, who had not previously believed in ghosts, finds himself in the presence of a force far more powerful than he, a force against which his skepticism offers no protection:

> He felt the Judge's icy fingers touch his throat as he adjusted the rope. The noose tightened—tightened. Then the Judge, taking the rigid form of the student in his arms, carried him over and placed him standing in the oak chair, and stepping up beside him, put his hand up and caught the end of the swaying rope of the alarm bell. As he raised his hand the rats fled squeaking, and disappeared through the hole in the ceiling. Taking the end of the noose which was round Malcolmson's neck he tied it to the hanging-bell rope, and then descending pulled away the chair. (44)

What remains at the conclusion is the body of the dead student and the portrait, on whose face is "a malignant smile" (45).

What conclusions can readers draw from this rather spare story? The most obvious is that supernatural forces exist and can impose their will on ordinary human beings. Things that cannot be explained rationally are therefore not figments of a diseased imagination or manifestations of a guilty conscience. The second is that these supernatural forces are not agents of cosmic justice but of a human evil so persistent that it refuses to die. During his life the judge had dispensed random cruelty rather than justice and was "held in great terror on account of his harsh sentences and his hostility to prisoners at Assizes" (30). Malcolmson thus becomes one more victim of his cruelty, for Stoker suggests that, like many of the prisoners that the judge had sentenced, he is an innocent victim who had done nothing to deserve his punishment.

Two other points are worth noting. The first is that the judge, like most ghosts, is apparently an incarnation of the past. Thus it's possible that Stoker was thinking of a particular period in the past. At least the house that he describes evokes a particular period:

> It was an old rambling, heavy-built house of the *Jacobean* style, with heavy gables and windows, unusually small, and set higher than was customary in such houses, and was surrounded with a high brick wall massively built. Indeed, on examination, it looked more like a *fortified house* than an ordinary dwelling. (29; emphasis added)

The use of the word Jacobean and the reference to a fortified house might evoke the period in Ireland's history when Catholics and Protestants battled for both religious and political power. Or Stoker might have used these words to express the age of the judge's house. In addition, Stoker suggests that only one thing seems to have any power over the judge, the bible Malcolmson's mother had given him. One wonders whether Stoker intended readers to draw a conclusion about the power of religion (*Dracula*, for example, is full of references to the power of religion) or the power of human relationships. If so, the story is really too spare to draw much of a conclusion, and Malcolmson appears to lack faith in both God and his family.

"An Account of Some Strange Disturbances in an Old House in Aungier Street"

The two Le Fanu stories are more complex and more subtle. Moreover, despite the fact that many critics call "Mr. Justice Harbottle" a revised version of "An Account of Some Strange Disturbances in an Old House in Aungier Street," they are sufficiently different to warrant discussing them separately.

"Aungier Street" first appeared in the *Dublin University Magazine* in December 1853. Gary William Crawford, who writes frequently on Le Fanu, describes it in *J. Sheridan Le Fanu: A Bio-Bibliography* as far superior to "Mr. Justice Harbottle" and as one of "Le Fanu's best spectral tales":

The theme of the story is one that Le Fanu would develop further later in his career: the subjective and objective, or supernatural and rational, view of human perception. The subtle ambiguities of a tale in which two students rent an old haunted house is explored as they try to rationalize what appears to be supernatural: the appearance of the ghost of a judge who committed suicide years earlier. (20)

Peter Denman and Edward Wagenknecht also explore the similarities in the tales. Wagenknecht refers to "Mr. Justice Harbottle" as a "much more elaborate and more psychological treatment of the same subject," but adds that it is "not therefore necessarily more effective" because of its greater complexity. (14)

Since almost all ghost stories confront residents of the present with representatives of the past, Wagenknecht's suggestion that Le Fanu had a particular historical figure in mind when he created his "hanging judge" is especially worth considering:

> This is the same "hanging judge," probably suggested by Judge Jeffreys and here called Judge Horrocks, whom Le Fanu treated later in "Mr. Justice Harbottle." A thoroughly corrupt man as well as a cruel one, he had specialized in hanging others and finished by hanging himself . . . A particularly horrifying and effective touch is supplied by his having used the skipping-rope owned by his housekeeper's little daughter, who was probably his also, to do away with himself, "and the child never throve after, and used to be starting up out of her sleep and screeching in the night time." (13–14)

Wagenknecht asserts that George Jeffreys (1648–1689), described as follows in *Who's Who in British History*, was a possible model for Judge Horrocks:

> [H]e was actively involved in the prosecutions following the Popish Plot scare (1678–9). . . . He became Chief Justice of the King's Bench in 1683. . . . His ruthlessness when trying those who had participated in Monmouth's . . . rebellion earned the session the name of the "Bloody Assizes": more than 300 were executed, and several hundred others were transported to the West Indies. (458)

The narrator learns that the previous owner, known as Judge Horrocks, "resided there, entertaining good company, with fine venison and rare old port," earned "the reputation of a particularly 'hanging judge'," and "ended by hanging himself, as the coroner's jury found, under an impulse of 'temporary insanity,' with a child's skipping-rope" (70). If Wagenknecht is correct in his historical allusion, it is reinforced primarily by the references to the judge's cruelty and by the fact that Le Fanu's narrator mentions the date

1702 though he undermines the historical allusion by indicating that the house was old even then.

While "Aungier Street"[1] describes an encounter with the ghost of a hanging judge, it is far less grim than Stoker's story primarily because the two students are not physically harmed. Nonetheless the first-person account asks readers to consider whether ghosts are real or manifestations of psychological trauma and also whether they are capable of impacting the present.

The first-person narrator downplays the seriousness of the story:

> It is not worth telling, this story of mine—at least, not worth writing. Told, indeed, as I have sometimes been called upon to tell it, to a circle of intelligent and eager faces, lighted up by a good after-dinner fire on a winter's evening, with a cold wind rising and wailing outside, and all snug and cosy within it has gone off . . . indifferent well. (69)

Indeed, the reader might conclude that Le Fanu's narrator is simply interested in describing what makes a good ghost story. He mentions almost as an aside, however, that his cousin Tom Ludlow was changed by the experience, and that brief mention suggests a greater power than the narrator wants to admit. Though both young men are studying medicine when they encounter the ghostly visitor, Tom "preferred the Church . . . and died early, a sacrifice to contagion, contracted in the noble discharge of his duties" (69). The reader must wonder what makes the cheerful and unexcitable Tom change from pursuing a rational profession to choosing a spiritual one. In fact, this subtle strategy is similar to what Le Fanu uses in "Carmilla" when, after the exorcism, he has Laura, his first-person narrator admit that she remains haunted by Carmilla:

> To this hour the image of Carmilla returns to memory with ambiguous alternations—sometimes the playful, languid, beautiful girl; sometimes the writhing fiend I saw in the ruined church; and often from a reverie I have started, fancying I heard the light step of Carmilla at the drawing-room door. (*In a Glass Darkly* 319)

Thus both stories suggest that the past is more powerful than people in the present choose to admit.

---

1. Note that the story has been published by several slightly different titles. [The story's most common title, beginning with M. R. James's inclusion of it in *Madam Crowl's Ghost and Other Stories*, has been, "An Account of Some Strange Disturbances in Aungier Street"; however, the title as it appears on the first page of the story in the December 1852 issue of the Dublin University Magazine reads "An Account of Some Strange Disturbances in an Old House in Aungier-street."–Ed.]

As he does in "Carmilla," Le Fanu employs a first-person narrator in "Aungier Street." The story begins when the two young medical students are living rent-free in a house owned by Tom's father. Although the house itself is large, the young men decide to live in only three rooms: "The front drawing-room was our sitting room. I had the bedroom over it, and Tom the back bedroom on the same floor, which nothing could have induced me to occupy" (69–70). Here the narrator contrasts himself with his more rational cousin and admits to feeling some apprehension about the bedroom that had belonged to the judge. Confessing that Tom "ridiculed my tremors" he adds that the "sceptic was, however, . . . destined to receive a lesson" (71).

The narrator soon begins to experience nightmares in which a picture appears "mysteriously glued to the window-panes." The portrait is of "an old man, in a crimson flowered silk dressing-gown . . . with a countenance embodying a strange mixture of intellect, sensuality, and power, but withal sinister and full of malignant omen" (71–72). The cousins then discuss what caused the bad dreams: "Was this singular apparition—as full of character as of terror—therefore the creature of my fancy, or the invention of my poor stomach? Was it, in short, subjective (to borrow the technical slang of the day) and not the palpable aggression and intrusion of an external agent?" (72). Their conversation raises the issue of whether the apparition is real or whether it is produced by physical ailments, and Le Fanu continues to toy with these ambiguities until Tom returns and confesses that he had seen the apparition three times. At this point the young men decide to leave the apparently haunted house, and the housekeeper observes that sleeping in the judge's bedroom brings people bad luck. These details undermine the assertion that the eyes the narrator sees at night were "nothing but a pair of inverted teacups" (76). Rational scientific explanations don't really explain what takes place here.

Le Fanu also enables the reader to share the narrator's experience of hearing something on the stairs:

> There was a slow, heavy tread, characterised by the emphasis and deliberation of age, descending by the narrow staircase . . . and, what made the sound more singular, it was plain that the feet which produced it were perfectly bare, measuring the descent with something between a pound and a flop, very ugly to hear. (74)

Horror grows the following evening, when the narrator hears the same sound and, opening his door, sees "a black monster, whether in the shape of a man or a bear . . . facing me, with a pair of great greenish eyes shining dimly out" (75). Eventually the apparition becomes "the most monstrous grey rat I ever beheld or imagined" (77) with "a perfectly human expression of malice"

(77). What is more horrifying, however, is that the rat resembles the portrait of the evil judge: "I felt it then, and know it now, the infernal gaze and the accursed countenance of my old friend in the portrait, transfused into the visage of the bloated vermin before me" (77).

"An Account of Some Strange Disturbances in an Old House in Aungier Street" is an elegant tale that asks readers to contemplate what constitutes an effective ghost story as well as what happens to these young men. By having the more rational of the two young men come to believe in the marvelous and change his vocation, he also reinforces the existence of a world beyond the material. Finally, like Stoker, he suggests that human evil from the past continues to haunt the present.

"Mr. Justice Harbottle"

Described by James Walton as "a case history, a primitive apparition-narrative or 'true relation,' a moral fable, a modern ghost story" (125), "Mr. Justice Harbottle" is the most complex of the three stories. According to Robert Tracy's note in the Oxford World's Classics edition of *In a Glass Darkly*, it "appeared as 'The Haunted House in Westminster,' without chapter divisions, in *Belgravia* (January 1872)" (326). A much more complicated tale, it is one of a number of cases collected by the German physician Martin Hesselius and published in the collection, *In a Glass Darkly*. A forerunner of the modern psychiatrist, Hesselius is himself framed by an editor who provides his own commentary on the cases and notes frequently that the record is fragmented. The editor introduces himself as a scientist in the "Prologue" to "Green Tea," the first story of *In a Glass Darkly*:

> Though carefully educated in medicine and surgery, I have never practiced either. . . . Neither idleness nor caprice caused my secession from the honourable calling which I had just entered. The cause was a very trifling scratch inflicted by a dissecting knife. This trifle cost me the loss of my two fingers . . . and the more painful loss of my health. I have never been quite well since, and have seldom been twelve months together in the same place.
>
> In my wanderings I became acquainted with Dr. Martin Hesselius, a wanderer like myself, like me a physician, and like me an enthusiast in his profession. (*In a Glass Darkly* 5)

The reader might therefore expect both Hesselius and his editor to be skeptical by training and to look for either psychological or physical causes of traumatic events.

Furthermore, although "Mr. Justice Harbottle" also features a hanging judge who returns to haunt the people who reside in his home, it is a much more complex story because it includes more characters, multiple plots, and a more complex narrative structure. Unlike the straightforward Stoker story and the slightly more complex "Aungier Street," it can be divided into two distinctly separate sections, the first dealing with people who have seen the judge's ghost, the second with the judge himself.

The editor opens the "Preface" by noting "two accounts of the remarkable case of the Honourable Mr. Justice Harbottle, one furnished to me by Mrs. Trimmer of Tunbridge Wells (June, 1805); the other at a much later date, by Anthony Harman, Esq." (83). The editor explains that he prefers "the former . . . because it is minute and detailed, and written . . . with more caution and knowledge" and "because the letters from Doctor Hedstone, which are embodied in it, furnish matter of the highest value to a right apprehension of the nature of the case" (83). The editor explains that Mrs. Trimmer's record, "which Doctor Hesselius thought the better of the two" (84), has disappeared. Thus readers can contemplate whether the original version by Mrs. Trimmer provides a more rational explanation or a more supernatural one.

The story proper begins with Mr. Harmon's description of what had happened to a friend "thirty years ago" (84) and notes his friend's appropriateness as a witness: "He was a dry, sad, quiet man, who had known better days, and had always maintained an unexceptionable character. No better authority could be imagined for a ghost story" (84). Harmon's reference to his friend's unemotional character, the editor's mention of Dr. Hedstone, and a brief mention of a "sceptical kitchen-wench" who sees "a monstrous figure, over a furnace, beating with a mighty hammer the rings and rivets of a chain" (116) all suggest that the information is accurate, not a figment of anyone's diseased imagination.

Harmon begins by explaining that his friend "had taken lodgings in this house, on account of their extraordinary cheapness . . . and was the only tenant" (85). Despite the reasonable rent, the man decides, after seeing two ghostly visitors, one of them carrying a coil of rope, to change his lodgings. He describes his visitors as "a slight dark man, particularly sinister, and somewhere about fifty, dressed in . . . a very antique fashion, such a suit as we see in Hogarth" (85). The second visitor is an older man who "wore a flowered-silk dressing-gown and ruffles . . . and on his head a cap of velvet, such as, in the days of perukes, gentlemen wore in undress" (85). The reference to William Hogarth, a satirical English artist who lived from 1697 to 1764, and to the days when men wore powdered wigs suggests that these visitors are from the past.

The friend isn't harmed by his ghostly visitors but decides that he cannot stay in the house. At this point Harmon provides additional information about the original inhabitant of the house, which he had seen when he was a boy:

> When I saw it, it had long been untenanted, and had the gloomy reputation beside of a haunted house. Cobwebs floated from the ceilings or spanned the corners of the cornices, and dust lay thick over everything. The windows were stained with the dust and rain of fifty years, and darkness had thus grown darker.
>
> When I made it my first visit, it was in company with my father . . . in the year 1808. I was about twelve years old, and my imagination impressible, as it always is at that age. (87)

By emphasizing gloom, cobwebs, and abandonment, Harmon establishes the house in question as a typical haunted house.

Harmon's reference to 1808 is interesting here, but Le Fanu is careful to make the judge a member of an even earlier generation:

> My father was an old bachelor of nearly sixty when he married. He had, when a child, seen Judge Harbottle on the bench . . . a dozen times at least before his death, which took place in 1748, and his appearance made a powerful and unpleasant impression, not only on his imagination, but on his nerves. (88)

Both Wagenknecht and Tracy suggest that Le Fanu may have been thinking of George Jeffreys. However, the reference to 1748 makes Jeffreys, who died in 1689, an unlikely candidate. Tracy's footnote mentions one other possibility, the "central figure in Hogarth's 'The Bench' (1758) portraying the then Chief Justice Sir John Willes" (326). An additional footnote provides Tracy's explanation why Le Fanu might have mentioned the session of 1746:

> The date partly explains Harbottle's alertness to a possible political conspiracy. In July 1745, Bonnie Prince Charlie landed in Scotland, rallied many of the clans and their chieftains to his side, captured Edinburgh, and invaded England, intending to gain the throne for his father, 'James III,' the Stuart claimant, by driving out the Protestant George II. . . . The Prince reached Derby before opposing forces had gathered to attack him; he retreated, and was finally defeated at Culloden (16 April 1746). (328, note 88)

While these are interesting arguments, they are in my opinion red herrings, the result of literary critics reading *into* the text rather than reading the text itself. Le Fanu's threatening judge is not the Chief Justice or Lord Chancellor but "one of the judges of the Court of Common Pleas" (86). Thus he would seem to represent the law in general rather than a particular judge.

Moreover, Harmon's narrative presents Judge Horrocks as cruel and unscrupulous but not especially motivated by politics.

> This old gentleman had the reputation of being about the wickedest man in England. Even on the bench he now and then showed his scorn of opinion.

He had carried cases his own way, it was said, in spite of counsel, authorities, and even of juries, by a sort of cajolery, violence, and bamboozling, that somehow confused and overpowered resistance. . . . He had the character of being . . . a dangerous and unscrupulous judge; but his character did not trouble him. The associates he chose for his hours of relaxation cared as little as he did about it. (88)

Indeed, Harmon also suggests the judge's sensuality. His description of one of the judge's soirees, "his dubious jollifications, such as might well make the hair of godly men's heads stand upright, for that night" (90), confirms that licentiousness, and it appears that he sends Lewis Pyneweck to the gallows because he has taken Pyneweck's wife as his mistress, not from political ideology.

The remainder of the story explores the judge's life after he sends the innocent Pyneweck to the gallows. Not only does he imagine that he sees Pyneweck wherever he goes, but he also imagines that he is tried "for the murder of one Lewis Pyneweck of Shrewsbury, citizen, wrongfully executed for the forgery of a bill of exchange . . . by reason of the willful perversion of the evidence" (102). The judge in his case, "Chief-Justice Twofold . . . a dilated effigy of himself" (108), informs Harbottle that he will be executed on March 10, and the judge commits suicide on that date, hanging himself with the jump rope belonging to the daughter of Pyneweck's wife. Mother and child are the first to see a ghost in the house. The little girl sees a man in the Judge's sedan-chair, and her mother sees a stranger in the house holding "a coil of rope, one end of which escaped from under his elbow and hung over the rail" (115).

While the ghostly figures in Judge Harbottle's house frighten those who see them, they are less malicious than the ghost in Stoker's "The Judge's House." The living Justice Harbottle had been indifferent to the issue of justice and interested only in himself, but his ghost is unwilling or unable to harm the living. Indeed, if either violence or justice is dispensed in this story, it is dispensed against Judge Harbottle himself. As Harmon notes, the judge apparently tells several others of being tried for his crimes, and the editor mentions that Harbottle had written to people about what happened to him. There is, however, no written record: "What of the paper I have cited? No one saw it during his life; no one, after his death. He spoke of it to Dr. Hedstone; and what purported to be 'a copy,' in the old Judge's handwriting, was found. The original was nowhere. Was it a copy of an illusion, incident to brain disease? Such is my belief" (104). Thus, the version of the story in the collection In a Glass Darkly is extremely open ended about whether the judge was insane or driven by external forces to commit suicide. Tracy's footnote observes that the previous paragraph, which mentions the judge's insanity, "does not appear in *Belgravia*" (330, note 104), an indication that Le Fanu was uncertain about whether he wanted to emphasize the super-natural aspects of his story or the psychological.

The conclusion is definitely open-ended, with four people seeing ghostly figures in the house, but with the editor attempting to provide a more scientific conclusion:

> There was medical evidence to show that, in his atrabilious state, it was quite on the cards that he might have made away with himself. The jury found accordingly that it was a case of suicide. But to those who were acquainted with the strange story which Judge Harbottle had related to at least two persons, the fact that the catastrophe occurred on the morning of the 10th March seemed a startling coincidence. (117–18)

This logical conclusion may explain why the judge committed suicide (and ironically this jury may be as prejudiced as the juries that the judge had "stacked" against certain prisoners), but it doesn't address the fact that, after his death, other people see someone resembling the judge in his former home. Thus, despite the presence of rational explanations in the story, Le Fanu suggests there are "more things in heaven and earth than are dreamt of in modern philosophy."

What conclusions can readers draw from reading "Mr. Justice Harbot-tle"? Its multiple plots and complex narrative structure reinforce the difficulty of discovering the truth even though all the versions suggest that something supernatural occurs in Justice Harbottle's home. Though some witnesses see one individual and others two, and some witnesses identify their visitors as representing an earlier historical period, even the scientists and skeptics agree that something does happen. Perhaps it is only logical that individuals who know the judge's history tend to associate the ghostly figure with him.

Conclusions

Despite the strong tendency to explore Le Fanu's influence on Stoker, the three short stories are sufficiently different to warrant being examined as separate and individual works. Comparing them should convince readers that, while sharing certain plot elements and characters, the three stories do not demonstrate plagiarism or even a lack of creativity on either writer's part.[2] Like most writers, Le Fanu tends to wrestle with the same problems

---

2. Citing Julia Briggs, *Night Visitors: The Rise and Fall of the English Ghost Story* (London: Faber & Faber, 1977), 51, Barbara T. Gates observes, "Critics of Le Fanu have

and issues, though neither he nor Stoker can be accused of writing the same book over and over. Indeed both writers experimented with the popular genres available to them. Though remembered today primarily as writers of a peculiarly Irish Gothic, both wrote romances and historical fiction as well as Gothic literature, and Stoker experimented with utopian fiction, science fiction, and travel literature as well. There is little ambiguity about the presence of the supernatural in any of the three stories this essay has explored, however. While Stoker's judge is the most obviously malicious of the three, both Stoker and Le Fanu use visitors from the past to demonstrate that inhabitants of the modern world are still impacted by what took place in the past. A recent essay by Sally C. Harris explores that impact, and her assessment of Le Fanu applies to Stoker as well:

> Le Fanu was well aware of this inevitable intrusion of the history of a nation on its present inhabitants; nineteenth-century Ireland was suffering from the political events of the seventeenth century and, it can be argued, suffering for events as far back as the twelfth. By ignoring history, people are unlikely to recognize the threat it poses to their present stability. In Victorian Ireland, the Anglo-Irish were in danger of losing not only their position in society, but also their land if the Irish uprisings were successful. The aristocracy needed to understand the past injustices in order to recognize the present threat. Another danger in ignoring a nation's past is that the crimes it has already committed may be repeated only to affect future generations. (Harris, unpaged article)

Although Harris grounds her assessment in terms of Le Fanu's Irishness, readers should not forget that Gothic literature is characterized by its writers' awareness that they cannot escape from the past.

Alison Milbank provides a slightly different interpretation of Le Fanu's treatment of the past:

> The narratives, too, have cloudy or untraceable origins, involving complex chains of transmission. The text-within-text motif is taken to extremes in "Mr. Justice Harbottle," which purports to be a record of a case collected by . . . Doctor Hesselius, checked by the editor of his work for the present publication with Hesselius's own sources in a (lost) account by a Mrs. Trimmer, which itself referred to a letter to a Mr. Heyne, and with an alternative account by a Mr. Harmon, who himself got the story from one of his pensioners. This Chinese-box arrangement of texts shows a failure to penetrate and deal with the

---

contended that he revamped these stories because plotting came hard for him." This observation appears in Gates's "Blue Devils and Green Tea: Le Fanu's Haunted Suicides," *Studies in Short Fiction* 24:1 (1987): 15–23.

origin of the evil let loose in the stories. Further, it bastardises the text by denying it an ultimate paternity, and questions along with it the basis of patriarchal authority whether in society or religion. (107)

Even though Milbank's observation here cannot be applied to Stoker's more straightforward treatment of the relationship between past and present, she addresses the significance of the Gothic interest in the past. While ghosts may be used simply to terrify readers, ghost stories often explore the negative impact that the past has on the present even when the ghosts don't physically harm the people with whom they come in contact.

Exploring the three stories, readers should consider that the ghosts in all three stories are judges who had, while living, been associated with cruel and arbitrary treatment of the people under their control. Even though several critics argue that Le Fanu was thinking of a specific historical figure or at least of a particular historical period—generally the eighteenth century—the stories are effective even for people who are unaware of the historical connection. Readers can identify with the innocent victims in these stories (specifically children and students), a connection that reinforces the extent to which powerful and unscrupulous people can manipulate the law to their own advantage. That "The Judge's House" is often included in popular anthologies also reinforces that people today remain concerned that individuals associated with the law are not necessarily interested in dispensing justice. Of course, readers may also respond to the fact that the ghostly figures in the stories are associated with rats. To paraphrase Freud, sometimes a rat is only a rat. The popular interpretation of the Occam's razor principle—that the theory with the fewest new assumptions—is the correct one may be applicable to these three stories as well. Readers continue to respond to these stories because we fear the arbitrary application of power, the possibility that powerful supernatural forces do exist, the likelihood that forces beyond our control can lead to mental illness, and the suspicion that we have no more control over the forces of nature than we have over history.

Works Cited

Crawford, Gary William. *J. Sheridan Le Fanu: A Bio-Bibliography*. Westport, CT: Greenwood Press, 1995.

Denman, Peter. "Le Fanu and Stoker: A Probable Connection." *Éire-Ireland* 9 (Autumn 1974): 152–58.

Gates, Barbara T. "Blue Devils and Green Tea: Le Fanu's Haunted Suicides." *Studies in Short Fiction* 24:1 (1987): 15–23.

Glover, David. *Vampires, Mummies, and Liberals: Bram Stoker and the Politics of Popular Fiction*. Durham, NC: Duke University Press, 1996.

Harris, Sally Harris. "The Haunting Past in J. S. Le Fanu's Short Stories." *Le Fanu Studies* 1 (November 2006).

Kendrick, Walter. *The Thrill of Fear: 250 Years of Scary Entertainment*. New York: Grove Weidenfeld, 1991.

Le Fanu, Joseph Sheridan. "An Account of Some Strange Disturbances in Aungier Street." In *Madam Crowl's Ghost and Other Stories*. Ed. M. R. James. London: Wordsworth, 1994. 69–86.

———. "Mr. Justice Harbottle." In *In a Glass Darkly*. Oxford: Oxford University Press/World's Classics, 1993. 83–118.

Milbank, Alison. "Doubting Castle: The Gothic Mode of Questioning." In David Jasper and T. R. Wright, ed. *The Critical Spirit and the Will to Believe: Essays in Nineteenth-Century Literature and Religion*. New York: St. Martin's Press, 1989. 104–19.

Murray, Paul. *From the Shadow of Dracula: A Life of Bram Stoker*. London: Jonathan Cape, 2004.

Power, Albert. "Bram Stoker and the Tradition of Irish Supernatural Literature." *Bram Stoker Society Journal* 3 (1991): 3–27.

Shepard, Leslie. "The Library of Bram Stoker." In *Bram Stoker's Dracula: Sucking through the Century, 1897–1997*, ed. Carol Margaret Davison. Toronto: Dundurn Press, 1997. 411–14.

Stoker, Bram. "The Judge's House." In *Dracula's Guest and Other Stories*. London: Wordsworth, 2006. 29–46.

Wagenknecht, Edward. *Seven Masters of Supernatural Fiction*. Westport, CT: Greenwood Press, 1991.

Walton, James. *Vision and Vacancy: The Fictions of J. S. Le Fanu*. Dublin: University College Dublin Press, 2007.

Who's Who in British History. Ed. Juliet Gardiner. London: Collins & Brown, 2000.

Introduction to *Uncle Silas*

M. R. James

This masterpiece of its kind first appeared in its present form in the *Dublin University Magazine* in 1864 under the title of *Uncle Silas and Maud Ruthyn*. This serial publication was followed by a three-volume edition by Bentley, and one-volume issues since then have been frequent.

But there had been two previous publications of a short story which embodied the main lines of the plot. The first was "An Episode in the History of an Irish Countess" in the *Dublin University Magazine* of 1838, the fifth of a series called the Purcell Papers. It was reissued—I think without any change except in the title—in *Ghost Stories and Tales of Mystery with illustrations by* "Phiz" (Dublin, James McGlashan, 1851), where it appears as "The Murdered Cousin." Both these were anonymous, but it will be seen that Le Fanu in his Preface to *Uncle Silas* acknowledges or claims them as his own. *The Purcell Papers* were republished as a collection in 1880 in three volumes (Bentley), with a Prefatory Memoir of Le Fanu by A. P. Graves.

It is not uninteresting to glance at "The Murdered Cousin" and compare it roughly with *Uncle Silas*. It occupies forty-six not very full pages in the 1851 volume. The narrator is "the late Countess D—" otherwise "Lady Margaret," and the scene is laid in Ireland; apparently we are in the eighteenth century or the very early years of the nineteenth. Sir Arthur Tyrell is the wicked uncle. The victim of the murder of which he had been accused is one Hugh Tisdall. One of the features which is elaborated in the story and not in the book is the appearance, some months after the murder, of a letter from Tisdall written on the day of his death to a friend, and describing an attempt of Sir Arthur's to drug or poison him. This letter is given in full. In the account of Tisdall's murder there is one of Le Fanu's odd careless mistakes; for the cause of death is represented as being wounds in the head, while a little later we hear of the throat being cut with a razor.

On her father's death Lady Margaret is duly committed to the care of Sir Arthur and moves to his house of Carrickleigh, in Galway, where she is welcomed by her cousin Emily, who is by no means of the hoyden type, but cultivated and charming. She is of course the equivalent of Milly in our book, and her brother Edward corresponds to Dudley. There is the proposal and refusal, the pretended departure of Edward, the discovery that he has not really left the house; the introduction of a "tall, raw-boned, ill-looking eld-erly Frenchwoman" (who remains nameless) as Lady Margaret's attendant. The letter which Lady Margaret writes in despair to an old friend, begging to be rescued, is interpreted by Sir Arthur, who confronts her with it. "The sus-picions expressed in this letter are the hallucinations and alarms of a moping lunatic. I have defeated your first attempt, madam; and by the holy God, if you ever make another, chains, darkness, and the keeper's whip shall be your portion." That is his peroration—no feeble one—and after it events move swiftly. The final scene is almost as effective as in the longer novel. It is Emily who, sharing Lady Margaret's room and sleeping—drugged, it seems—in her bed, is killed. Sir Arthur and his son escape; the Frenchwoman is exe-cuted as an accessory. There is a vague reference to "the terrible, the tre-mendous retribution which, after long delays of many years, finally overtook and crushed Sir Arthur and Edward;" a tantalizing remark of the sort that Le Fanu is apt to throw out, as in "The Evil Guest," where we read that "a retri-bution so frightful and extraordinary overtook" the lady villain "that we may hereafter venture to make it the subject of a separate narrative."

Such was the first draft of Uncle Silas. There is little in it, with the ex-ception of the murder scene, which is comparable in merit with the novel. Yet taken by itself it is a sufficiently absorbing story.

When he wrote Uncle Silas Le Fanu had already produced four long sto-ries. Two of these, The Cock and Anchor and Torlogh O'Brien, were early works, separated by an interval of fourteen or fifteen years from the long series which he began in 1861. In that year he brought out The House by the Church-yard, and in 1863 Wylder's Hand. I have always thought that in some ways The House by the Church-yard is the best of all his books: but it cannot be denied that Uncle Silas is the better known and has enlisted more suffrages. It is in-deed more compact and clearer in plot: its population is more easily grasped: there is not the multiplicity of threads which make the earlier book—some would say confusing, I say, rich and attractive. And it does possess very great excellences. Let me reckon up some of the features which I remember to have caught my fancy when I first read the book, some time in the early eighties, I suppose. There was Maud Ruthyn herself. Surely that character is well kept up throughout? Of course there is always the improbability of the recollection of long dialogues spoken many years before they were written down, but that is a convention in which one can very easily acquiesce. What matters is that the girl should write as a sensible pleasant woman would write in later years, when she was able to detach herself enough from her girlish self to be amused at it and critical of it. That I think Le Fanu has made her do, and he has made her sensible and pleasant. It was a role, by the way, which he rather liked; in his last novel *Willing to Die* the pen is held by a lady very like Maud Ruthyn, and so it is in the admirable story of "Carmilla."

Monica Knollys: I do not know if the wise sharp-tongued humorous lady of mature age has often been better drawn. What good language she uses! How well she tells the story of Charke's murder! For Dr. Bryerly too I have a particular respect. His talk to the housekeeper when he comes at dead of night to watch by Austin Ruthyn's body is one of those outbursts in which I think Le Fanu reaches a great height of eloquence, and shows the poet that was in him.

But naturally, among the characters, my chief admiration was centered on Uncle Silas himself and yet more on Madame de la Rougierre. The horrid veneer of French culture combined with pietism that appears in Silas's talk and letters is inimitable: "Chaulieu and the evangelists" as Lady Knollys puts it. It is she too who drops a hint about Silas which I think was, in the back of Le Fanu's mind, the key to the situation, though, true to his artistic instinct, he does not dwell on it. "Perhaps," she says, "other souls than human are sometimes born into the world and clothed in flesh." "Venerable, bloodless, fiery-eyed," Uncle Silas is a figure who stamps himself on the memory.

"On a sudden, on the grass before me, stood an odd figure—a very tall woman in gray draperies, nearly white under the moon, courtseying extraordinarily low, and rather fantastically." That is the way in which Madame de la Rougierre is introduced, and from that moment whenever she is on the scene she rivets the attention. It is a most careful study; the language she speaks is but one of many successes in the portrait. What a hideous atmosphere she carries with her! The hints of a dreadful past, the growing certainty that she is an accomplice in an obscure plot, the relief when she vanishes from Knowl, the ghastly shock when she is discovered in the attic at Bartram-Haugh—to me all these episodes seem to be really masterly in the working out. Among smaller details I have vainly tried to find the source—if any—of the Breton ballad of the lady with the pig's head which is introduced with such sinister effect in Chapter VII. Some reader will, I hope, be able to throw light on it.[1]

Throughout the story many little scenes are managed which serve to put

---

1. [Women with the face or head of a pig have not been uncommon in popular literature since at least the sixteenth century, and Le Fanu would probably have been familiar with the various rumors, stories, and illustrations devoted to the Pig-Faced Lady of Manchester Square—so memorably depicted by the English caricaturist and illustrator George Cruikshank (1792-1878)—who supposedly lived in seclusion in early nineteenth century London. The "Breton ballad" praised by James has not, thus far, been traced to an earlier source, and was probably composed by Le Fanu.—Ed.]

us into the right frame of mind, expectant of tragedy. There is the talk of the Swedenborgian in the third chapter, there is the account of the family ghosts of Knowl, the fortune-telling gipsy, the mysterious "Fly the fangs of Belisarius;" but of course it is the march of the main story with its short glimpses of light followed by increasing darkness, the gradual withdrawal of friends and closing up of avenues of escape, that ought to enlist and does enlist our terrified interest. The climax, I have always thought, is in every way worthy of what has gone before, and the swift ending of the book is artistically right, I am sure. Vulgar Victorian curiosity, I confess, always makes me wish to know exactly what Uncle Silas and Dudley said to each other when they discovered their mistake: but this is more than we could reasonably expect to be told, even if Dickon Hawkes heard it and repeated it, years after, Lady Ilbury might well have hesitated to write it down.

Two curious literary phenomena in connection with *Uncle Silas* are worth recording, I think. It is difficult not to feel when one reads Sir Arthur Conan Doyle's early novel *The Firm of Girdlestone* that we have there an adaptation conscious or unconscious of Le Fanu's plot. All the main elements are present: the young heiress entrusted by the dying father to his old friend—an austere sectarian; the attempt to marry her to the guardian's repulsive son; her seclusion, when that fails, in a desolate house; the murder carried out on the wrong victim. More than the framework, however, no one could claim for Le Fanu: the setting and the under-plots make a completely new story of it, and a very readable one.

Not long ago a London firm issued a cheap edition of *Uncle Silas* which I bought. It was a thinner volume than I was accustomed to, and it was not long before I found that at least one-third of the text had been tacitly omitted. I thought and think that this was unfair to the public, and I wrote to the firm in question, suggesting that at least they ought to have called their issue an abridged edition; but no reply was vouchsafed, and I do not think the hint has been taken.

I count it a very happy idea to include *Uncle Silas* among the World's Classics. There are not many stories which succeed in creating and in sustaining with the right intensity the atmosphere of mystery and the crescendo of impending doom, and whose *dramatis personae* are at the same time so unremote and so easily realized. I wish the book many readers, and I wish that all of them may find in it the same delight that it has often brought me.

M. R. JAMES.
ETON, *April*, 1926.

Conversations in a Shadowed Room:
The Blank Spaces in "Green Tea"

John Langan

Given the extent to which J. Sheridan Le Fanu's posthumous reputation rests on his achievements as a writer of ghost stories, an investigation of his approach to the ghost story is worth undertaking. While much good work has and continues to be done on Le Fanu's fiction, a substantial amount of it treats his use of the ghost story as a coded way for him to engage a variety of topics. As William Hughes has pointed out, recent readings of Le Fanu's supernatural fiction have tended to relate it to his identity as a Protestant Irish writer, as a manifestation of this in-between state (45). To be sure, such study offers important insights, but it does not do much to help us understand Le Fanu's ghost stories as ghost stories, which is to say, as specific manifestations of a recognizable narrative kind. W. J. Mc Cormack, Le Fanu's biographer, has noted that the writer's "best fiction . . . is amenable to formal and stylistic criticism to a degree surprising in sensationalism," calling attention to its "recurrent imagery" and "symmetrical patterns" (144). While I hesitate to raise the flag of a new formalism, a more formally-attentive approach offers a fresh appreciation of the ghost story *qua* ghost story, and therefore of what it means for Le Fanu to employ it.[1] Rather than severing his work from the context of its

---

1. Despite my hesitancy, the formal analysis in which this paper engages would appear to place it, broadly speaking, under the heading of the "New Formalism" explored by Marjorie Levinson in her 2007 *PMLA* article, "What Is New Formalism?" While I applaud Levinson's effort to map the contours of this emerging (or re-emerging) critical continent, I find her survey riven by what seem to me its competing drives to categorize and contend with its territory. Although I am not prepared to pledge my allegiance to any of the states she names, Jonathan Loesberg's "Cultural Studies, Victorian Studies, and Formalism" (1999) offers much to consider. Levinson's summary of Heather Dubrow's New Formalism "at its best" as displaying "Enlightenment's demand for scrupulous attention to the formal means that establish the

314 REFLECTIONS IN A GLASS DARKLY

composition,[2] such an analysis yields a clearer view of the ways in which narrative details are linked to the fiction's time and place.

While several of Le Fanu's stories would serve for such study, "Green Tea" (1869) is a particularly rich text. One of Le Fanu's best-known works, praised by writers ranging from M. R. James to Elizabeth Bowen to V. S. Pritchett,[3] this story of a doomed clergyman employs the type of ghost story I would call the haunted individual, in which a supernatural entity pursues a woman or man, frequently in the interest of revenge or retribution. It is a variety of the larger category that is built around a trio of revelations: that the character is haunted; why the individual is haunted; what the individual's fate is to be. "Green Tea" follows this general construction, but the specifics of its architecture distinguish it. This is a story whose central components echo each other to the point that they collapse into one another. Bracketed by a pair of commentaries which focus on the unintended consequences of seemingly innocuous acts, the story moves through a quartet of spaces whose cluster of shared details reveals them as iterations of the same fundamental place. Within that space, the narrative brings Swedenborgian ideas together with Rosicrucianism and mixes in Victorian Britain's ever-expanding geopolitical hegemony. Jack Sullivan has argued that the story's particulars are so random as to fail to cohere around any thematic center, but this is not the case (29–31). "Green Tea" draws on the broad range of Victorian efforts to bring more and more things under the sway of official, institutional knowledge, from the geographical to the historical to the metaphysical. The story's arrangement layers those attempts one over the other, and in so doing associates them with one another, and with the narrative's supernatural elements. In so doing, the story lays bare a deep anxiety about the results of such exploration and categorization, namely, that it might reveal not plenitude, but the void, and that this void might have a correspondence within

---

conditions of possibility for experience—textual, aesthetic, and every other kind" is certainly congruent with my own interests here (Levinson 562).

2. Which appears to be the principle anxiety underlying Levinson's criticism of a more formal approach.

3. For James, see "Some Remarks on Ghost Stories" (1929) and "Ghosts—Treat Them Gently!" (1931), both of which have been reprinted as appendices in the recent Penguin edition, *The Haunted Doll's House and Other Ghost Stories* (2006); for Bowen, see her "Introduction" to the 1947 edition of Le Fanu's novel, *Uncle Silas: A Tale of Batram-Haugh*, reprinted in 2006 by the Nonsuch Press; for Pritchett, see his "Introduction" to the 1947 edition of Le Fanu's *In a Glass Darkly*, published by John Lehmann.

us. Le Fanu's "Green Tea" emerges as a meditation on and mediation of absence, especially of firm epistemological ground on which to stand.

Hughes has discussed the story's debt to medical narratives of the day
(especially Samuel Warren's *Passages from the Diary of a Late Physician*
[1854]), and much of the introductory material in "Green Tea" positions it
as a medical narrative (Hughes 46). The story is introduced by an unnamed
narrator who describes himself as "carefully educated in medicine and sur-
gery," neither of which he has practiced (Le Fanu 178). The reason for this
is not "idleness nor caprice," but a "very trifling scratch inflicted by a dissecting knife," which resulted in "the loss of two fingers, amputated promptly,
and the more painful loss of my health" (178). This chronic illness led to the
narrator's having "seldom been twelve months together in the same place"
(178). This man already has lived his own medical narrative, one that has
ended unhappily. Significantly for the story that follows, he has suffered consequences whose severity seems disproportionate to their cause.

During his "wanderings," the narrator became acquainted with a German physician, Martin Hesselius, also a wanderer, although Hesselius's travels are due to a combination of curiosity and, if not wealth, then "easy
circumstances" (178). So taken was the narrator with Hesselius that he became his secretary, remaining with him for two decades. During this time,
the narrator was impressed by Hesselius's case histories, which he wrote "in
two distinct characters" (178). In the first, the doctor "describes what he saw
and heard as an intelligent layman might;" this is succeeded by a discussion
of the case "in the terms of his art and with all the force and originality of
genius" (178–79). Not only is Hesselius a brilliant doctor, he is a gifted
writer. Of these documents, a few have struck the narrator "as of a kind to
amuse or horrify a lay reader with an interest quite different from the peculiar one which it may possess for an expert" (179). The lay reader's interest
does not preclude the expert's, but the narrator's account of his motives
shifts the emphasis on what we are about to read from the clinical to the
emotional, even prurient. For this reason, he is offering us the story we are
about to read, which he has excerpted from Hesselius's notes of "a tour of
England about sixty-four years ago"[4] (179). The story was spread over several
letters to one of Hesselius's friends, a chemist, "Professor Van Loo of Leyden," which were written "some in English, some in French, but the greater
part in German" (179). Therefore, the narrator has acted as translator and
editor, "omit[ting] some passages, and shorten[ing] others, and disguis[ing]
names"; although, he makes it clear, he has "interpolated nothing" (179).

---

4. Given the story's publication date of 1869, this would place the action of Hesselius's narrative sometime within the first decade of the nineteenth century.

With this reassurance, the story proper begins. Of course, the framed narrative we are presented with is also typical of the ghost story, and of Gothic-inflected literature in general (cf. Kilgour 18–19). Hesselius's ability to write in two distinct "characters" calls to mind the Gothic's concern with doubles and doubling, a concern manifest in the tale that follows in still more dramatic fashion (cf. Kilgour 31–43). Thus, at the outset, the medical narrative, in which the emphasis is on the physician's ability to solve challenging cases, and the ghost story, whose emphasis is on the confrontation with the mysterious and unknown, converge. The result is a kind of cross-pollination in which the supernatural apparition may be figured as a disease, while medical investigation takes on something of the character of mystical exploration.

Hesselius's story opens with a description of an Anglican clergyman, the Reverend Mr. Jennings, whom he met at a small party thrown by a mutual friend. Jennings is High Church, a bachelor, well-off financially, and subject to a strange, ongoing health problem. While officiating at Sunday services in his parish, he has

> stopped short, and after a silence, apparently quite unable to resume, he has fallen into solitary, inaudible prayer, his hands and eyes uplifted, and then pale as death, and in the agitation of a strange shame and horror, descended trembling, and got into the vestry-room, leaving his congregation, without explanation, to themselves. (180)

After one of these incidents, Jennings returns to his "narrow" house in London, where his friends observe that he seems to be fine (180). Hesselius, however, notes that the clergyman gives "an impression a little ambiguous," which owes itself in part to his "way of looking sidelong at the carpet, as if his eye followed the movements of something there" (180). Jennings observes the doctor observing him, and soon the two are in conversation. Hearing Hesselius's name, Jennings identifies him as the author of "Essays on Metaphysical Medicine," which, Hesselius tells us, "suggest more than they actually say" (182). Flattered to be recognized, Hesselius offers to send Jennings a copy; the clergyman accepts, gratefully. Shortly thereafter, he departs for home.

So the physician, who addresses the life of the body, meets the clergyman, who addresses the life of the soul. The division between the two professions is less pronounced than might first appear. Hesselius already has described himself as a "medical philosopher," who seeks out cases upon which he lavishes as much time and attention as they require; in this regard, he distinguishes himself from ordinary physicians (180). Nor is that all that separates him: Hesselius explains that when he refers to "medical science," he does so "in a much more comprehensive sense than its generally material treatment would warrant" (181). For Hesselius, "the entire natural world is but the ultimate expression of that spiritual world from which, and in which alone, it has its life" (181). His view has "practical bearing upon medical science;" although exactly what that bearing is is not immediately clear (181). Certainly, his declaration of the deep connection between matter and spirit is a dramatic instance of the convergence of medical and ghostly narratives.

Hesselius's philosophy may be what allows him to "penetrate [Jennings's] thoughts without his being aware of it," and thus to arrive at a series of intuitions about the clergyman which he tests on their hostess after Jennings's departure (182). Hesselius declares that Jennings is a bachelor—not so surprising—that he was working on a book he has abandoned; that he formerly drank a good deal of green tea; and that one of his parents saw a ghost (183–84). He is correct on every count. It is a performance worthy of Sherlock Holmes, albeit without the explanation with which Holmes accompanies his insights. With the exception of Hesselius's mentioning them together, none of these facts appears related to any other. Part of the action of the story to come will consist in establishing their relations.

Following their initial encounter, Hesselius furthers his acquaintance with the Reverend by sending him his book on metaphysical medicine. Jennings responds with an invitation to the doctor to visit him at home. The relationship between the two, inaugurated by discussion of the doctor's writing, is advanced by its exchange. Hesselius accepts the offer and calls on Jennings's house on "Blank Street" (185). The name of the street might be taken as narrative convention, a way of mimicking the appearance of medical propriety. In fact, the address is the first of several blank spots in the narrative, gaps literal and figural.

Hesselius waits for Jennings in the back study. Unlike the location of their first encounter, Hesselius describes this space at length. The room is thickly carpeted, the top carpet a "Turkey," and it has "two tall slender windows, and rich dark curtains," not to mention extensive bookcases, which, "standing out, placed the windows, particularly narrow ones, in deep recesses" (185). With the exception of the windows and "two narrow looking glasses . . . set in the wall," the bookcases fill the walls; as Hesselius remarks, the room is "almost a library" (185). James Walton has argued that the room's mirrors must be facing one another, to create a *trompe l'oeil* effect he finds throughout Le Fanu's work (Walton 363). The evidence from the story is uncertain, though it seems more likely that the mirrors are opposite the windows, to heighten the room's lighting. Given its narrow, recessed windows, even with such an arrangement, the room is likely dimly-lighted. In discussing Le Fanu's "Schalken the Painter" (1839; revised 1851), Walton has described Le Fanu's "using Dutch portraiture as a projection of his own uncanny realism," especially as regards his use of shadow (353). Something similar is happening here. We are in the first of a quartet of crepuscular spaces, all of which will be associated with writing.

Nor is this all there is to the library. It is the place where knowledge is catalogued and categorized, no doubt a fitting place for a physician and a clergyman to meet. Yet the mention of the "Turkey" carpet brings into the scene associations of the structures that support such libraries, both the economics of trade and colonialism that drive Victorian Britain's economy, and the intellectual endeavors that add new volumes to the collection.

His attention drawn by a series of books placed face-down at the foot of one of the bookcases, Hesselius discovers "a complete set of Swedenborg's 'Arcana Caelestia,' in the original Latin" (185). Hughes has pointed out the importance of Swedenborg (1688–1772) to a reading of this story, although he has done so in rather general terms (48). In fact, Swedenborg's ideas have considerable bearing on "Green Tea." As Eric Sutton has written, Swedenborg's

> aim was to discover the seat and nature of the soul. To this end, he entered upon an examination of the human body wherein the soul reigned as in its own kingdom. As he advanced from an enquiry into the form and function of bodily organs to a very full study of the brain and central nervous system, it became clear to him that the microscope and scalpel could disclose only the ultimate materials of which the organism is composed. (Sutton 8–9)

In his quest for a physiological basis for the spiritual, Swedenborg resembles Hesselius the "medical philosopher." Both men embody the effort to bring the metaphysical under the sway of scientific investigation so much a part of later Victorian culture (most dramatically exemplified by the Spiritualist enterprise).[5] Swedenborg's *Arcana Caelestia* was written after an intense religious crisis that led to a vision of Christ and an ongoing series of revelations about the nature of the spiritual world. Published in London in eight volumes from 1749 to 1756, the *Arcana* was not initially credited to Swedenborg; it would be 1768 before he was disclosed as its author (Joksvig 230). The result of Swedenborg's conversations with various disembodied entities about the immaterial world, the *Arcana* is a kind of encyclopedia-cum-travel guide-cum-theological tract; as such, it has remained one of Swedenborg's most popular works. It is not difficult to imagine its appeal to a writer of supernatural fiction such as Le Fanu; here is material for dozens of stories. For an Anglican

---

5. For more on Spiritualism, see Janet Oppenheim's *The Other World: Spiritualism and Psychical Research in England 1850–1914* (1985) and Alex Owen's *The Darkened Room: Women, Power, and Spiritualism in Late Victorian England* (1990).

clergyman to have these volumes in his library, though, is of more ambiguous significance. While some of the theology his works contained was heretical, Swedenborg did not claim to be a reformer; rather, he continued to describe himself as a scientist. Broadly speaking, his emphasis on Divine Love is consonant with fundamental orthodox Christian teaching.

Upon examining Jennings's copy of the *Arcana*, Hesselius sees that the clergyman has bookmarked several passages. Of the nine quotations that follow, the first two deal with the opening of "man's interior sight," which permits the viewing of "the things of another life;" while the remaining seven treat the nature and behavior of evil spirits, whose "delight" is "to do evil to man, and to hasten his eternal ruin" (186). Upon the bottom of the last page he reads, Hesselius notices penciled words. Assuming them to be Jennings's commentary on Swedenborg, Hesselius begins to read, only to stop when he recognizes its *"Deus misereatur mei"* ("May God have pity on me") as the start of a prayer (187).[6]

Moving on to other pages in the *Arcana* that discuss how "evil spirits, when seen by other eyes than those of their infernal associates, present themselves, by 'correspondence,' in the shape of the beast (*fera*) which represents their particular lust and life, in aspect direful and atrocious," Hesselius notices Jennings reading over his shoulder via one of the narrow mirrors (187). The doctor is surprised to see the Reverend's "face so dark and wild that I should hardly have known him" (187). This is the first of a trio of reflections in the narrative. In a reversal of its intended function, the mirror returns an image of the inner man, of the turmoil afflicting the clergyman. Hesselius turns to address Jennings, who attempts to laugh off his spying and states that Hesselius is undoubtedly acquainted with Swedenborg's work. The doctor agrees, admitting its influence on his book on metaphysical medicine. The clergyman claims to have read "very little" of the *Arcana* (which seems obviously untrue), though he declares the volumes "rather likely to make a solitary man nervous" (188). Why, he does not specify, but given what we have read, we might hazard a guess.

Following this meeting, almost two months will pass before Hesselius learns the secret of the Reverend Mr. Jennings's complaint. In the meantime, he will have had word of the clergyman's unsuccessful attempt to return to his parish in a note from him that promises further contact. When that contact comes, it does so in the form of another missive inviting Hesselius to visit Jennings's country home in Richmond as soon as possible. To this end,

---

6. Most likely, a variation on Psalm 43 or Psalm 46, either of which might be included as part of the clergyman's Lauds.

Jennings has instructed the servant at his house on Blank Street to have a carriage ready at the doctor's convenience. Hesselius decides to make the trip then and there, and before long is in sight of the Reverend's country home.

It is "a very old-fashioned brick house, darkened by the foliage of [the] trees, which overtopped and nearly surrounded it. It was a perverse choice, for nothing could be imagined more triste and silent" (191). In the figure of the ominous house, of course, we have one of the hallmarks of ghost and indeed Gothic narratives[7] (cf. Bayer-Berenbaum 23–27). Hesselius has arrived just after sunset, "and the red reflected light of the western sky illuminated the scene with the peculiar effect with which we are all familiar" (191). The red light of the gloaming is the second of the story's three reflections, and with the sinister house, it sets the mood for the scene. Nor is that all: originating from a point out of view, its source literally occult, the light is an analogue for the story's supernatural elements. That it is the light of the sun that has gone down in the west associates it with the coming of night and, by extension, with death. As on his previous visit to the clergyman, Hesselius is led to the back room, "whose windows commanded the west" and keep the doctor "in the same dusky light" (191). "The corners of the room were already dark," Hesselius says, "all was growing dim" (191).

This space recalls the other back room in Jennings's urban dwelling. Like that room, this one is shadowy. Shortly, it, too, will be linked to the act of writing. At the very least, the room seems the double of its urban counterpart, but in its accumulation of similarities, it is as much repetition, as if these two spaces overlap, are in some sense the same space. When Jennings enters the room, he is "faintly seen in the ruddy twilight" (191). Walton has argued that "figures of Death-in-Life, set off against the darkness, can be said to constitute the nuclear image in Le Fanu's fiction" (361). Whether they are at the absolute center of his work, we have one such image here. The evocation of the Reverend emerging from the darkness, limned in red light, recalls Walton's observation about the importance of Dutch portraiture to Le Fanu; specifically, the scene calls to mind Rembrandt, the abundant darkness and lurid lighting serving as indexes of the clergyman's spiritual/psychological state. While as yet we still have no clear idea of the exact nature of the Reverend's ailment, what we already have observed concerning the red light's significance offers clues. For one thing, the source of his affliction is in some sense removed, hidden. For another, it is connected to death.

---

7. McCormack has written about the significance of houses to Le Fanu's work (and life) in his biography; important to his overall work as they may be, this house seems to serve little purpose beyond establishing the atmosphere for the scene to come.

In this shadowy setting, Hesselius finally learns the story and secret of the Reverend Mr. Jennings's ailment. That narrative has its roots in a book on which the clergyman was working. Once again, in perhaps the most dramatic way, the story's plot turns on writing. The Reverend was studying "the religious metaphysics of the ancients" (192). Hesselius describes the field as "wide and very interesting," but Jennings declares it "not good for the mind—the Christian mind, I mean" (192). What Jennings calls "paganism" "is all bound together in essential unity, and, with evil sympathy, their religion involves their art, and both their manners, and the subject is a degrading fascination and the Nemesis sure" (192). Jennings fails to specify which branch of paganism he was investigating; although his reference to "the Nemesis," the Greek goddess of retribution, steers us in the direction of ancient Greece.

The Reverend's book project aligns him with the resurgence of interest in classical Greece whose most profound manifestation was the German poets and writers of the eighteenth and nineteenth centuries, such as Winckelmann, Goethe, Schiller, Hölderlin, and Nietzsche, and in which such English figures as Keats, Arnold, and Eliot participated, as well. This engagement with the ancient world is paralleled by the developments in German Biblical hermeneutics and theology that led to Strauss's *Leben Jesu* (*Life of Jesus*) (1846). In each case, the sacred is subject to history, circumscribed by an attempt to bring it under the sway of a different kind of understanding. Both branches of research feed the developing discipline of anthropology, which had seen notable volumes added to its growing body of literature during the 1860s, among them Jacob Burckhardt's *Die Kultur der Renaissance in Italien* (*The Civilization of the Renaissance in Italy*) (1860) and Edward Burnett Tylor's *Researches into the Early History of Mankind and the Development of Civilization* (1865).

It is difficult not to see these approaches to sacred material as representing the other half of the impulse behind Swedenborg's *Arcana*, to say nothing of Spiritualism. In both instances, religious matter is submitted to a categorization that promises new insights into it. Different as their aims might be, these impulses are a manifestation of the broader urge to catalogue that is so fundamental to and ubiquitous within Victorian culture.

However, in Jennings's description of his scholarship as "not good for the mind," and specifically "the Christian mind," because of paganism's "essential unity" and "evil sympathy," the story sounds a cautionary note. The Christian mind, presumably, depends on the recognition that the world is not essentially unified, that evil is in discord, not sympathy, with it. It appears the price of the kind of intensive research in which the clergyman is involved is an increasing identification with its subject, to the jeopardy of one's dearest beliefs. The result of that degrading fascination is a fear of retribution that is figured in pagan terms, as if the contamination of the pagan is inescapable.

So the first of Hesselius's mysterious deductions about the Reverend, that he was at work on a book, is confirmed. The next part of Jenning's account will bear out Hesselius's claims about his choice of beverages. While writing his study, Jennings says, he consumed "a good deal" of tea, first "the ordinary black tea," in ever-stronger doses, and then "a little green tea" (192). The "effect" of green tea Jennings found "pleasanter, it cleared and intensified the power of thought so," and so he drank it "frequently" (192). Given that it is from this drink that the story takes its title, and given the apparent significance the doctor assigns it, its history is pertinent. Ultimately Chinese in origin, green tea's associations are Far-Eastern, and thus freighted with rumors and legends concerning the mysterious Orient.[8] The British began purchasing the tea directly from China in 1651; by 1720, Britain had exclusive right to import Chinese tea. British desire for tea would contribute to a trade deficit with China that would lead to the first Opium Wars (1839–42), when the British sought to force the Chinese to accept opium to pay for their debt (the Chinese, understandably, preferred silver) (Evans 93–120). The spread of tea culture and tea cultivation is a direct consequence of the development and growth of the British Imperium. Jennings's narrative makes explicit the immediate connection between writing a book and drinking green tea. The latter facilitates the former. Their connections extend beyond the practical to the thematic. Both the anthropological study the Reverend undertakes and the tea he consumes during it are the result of exploration broadly conceived, of the cultural past and the geographical present.

During his own explorations, Jennings "met with a man who had some odd old books, German editions in Medieval Latin, and I was only too happy to be permitted access to them" (193). What those books are is anyone's guess; that Jennings does not name them to Hesselius may be significant. Their titles are another blank spot in the text, a gap in the narration that might be irrelevant, might offer more explanation for its incidents were it available. After visiting the man in "a very out-of-the-way part" of London, and staying later than he had intended, the Reverend took an omnibus home to Richmond (193). The time was "twilight;" the "interior of the omnibus was nearly dark" (193). Across and at the other end of the 'bus from him, Jennings could make out a pair of "small circular reflections, as it seemed to me of a reddish light" (193). Jennings moved to the opposite end of the 'bus and discovered the lights to be the eyes of "a small black monkey,

---

8. In this regard, the green tea is in keeping with what Bayer-Berenbaum has identified as a larger tradition of Orientalism within the Gothic (44–45).

pushing its face forward in mimicry to meet mine" (194). The monkey was "grinning" at the clergyman (194).

For a third time, we are in a shadowy space. Where there were a pair of mirrors in the Reverend's house on Blank Street, reflected light inside his country house, here there are a pair of "small circular reflections." Certainly, the omnibus is as narrow as any room in any narrow house. And while there are no books on the 'bus, Jennings's need to take it arises from his having consulted those "odd old books, German editions in Medieval Latin." Jennings sits in a shadowy place narrating the story of another shadowy space that evokes a third shadowy place. If there is a nuclear image in "Green Tea," this narrow, crepuscular space is it. It underwrites the trio of shadowed rooms the story has presented so far, as well as the fourth and final space waiting ahead.

As for what occurs in its latest instance: perhaps the most surprising thing about Jennings's encounter with the monkey—at least, initially—is how nonplussed he is by it. He assumes it to be an abandoned pet. In fact, monkeys had been kept as pets in Britain starting from the Middle Ages, when they were largely the province of the nobility. By the seventeenth century, they had made inroads with the general populace, which led to their becoming popular pets during that century and the next (Thomas 123). In his use of the monkey, Le Fanu may have in mind the 1675 portrait of John Wilmot, Earl of Rochester, and his pet monkey. In the picture, the Earl proffers the monkey a laurel crown while the monkey offers him a page ripped from a book.[9] (In the same year the portrait had been painted, Wilmot had written *A Satyr against Mankind*, an excoriation of human folly and praise of animal virtue.)

Of course, encountering a primate in a story written in the later nineteenth century, it is impossible not to think of Darwin. Hughes has argued against this, insisting that "the grinning ape in 'Green Tea' is a reflection not of the Darwinian debates . . . but of the Swedenborgian studies which had preoccupied the nominally Anglican author following the death of his wife, Susanna, in 1858" (Hughes 51). Swedenborg is significant to the story, but this does not preclude the monkey having other associations. Indeed, given the widespread debates that saturated British culture during the 1860s, the decade in which "Green Tea" was composed, it would be strange if the story were not aware of Darwin.

The monkey is associated with exploration (and commerce) literal and

---

9. The portrait may be seen at the National Portrait Gallery in London, which added it in 1888. As of this writing, I have not been able to trace the portrait's history before then; since 1888 dates well after Le Fanu's death; however, it makes my speculation concerning Le Fanu's possible reference to it all the more speculative.

figural, geographic and scientific—the geographical facilitating the scientific. As the 1860s had witnessed, the results of such investigation could be profoundly unsettling and upsetting. Wilmot could denigrate human behavior in comparison to the animal, safe in the gap that stretched between the two and gave his satire its bite. Close that gap, though, and the contrast becomes muddled.

Attempting to gauge the monkey's temper, Jennings prodded it with his umbrella, only to have the umbrella pass through the monkey "without the slightest resistance" (194). Horrified, he fled the 'bus, to discover that the monkey had accompanied him. It has been with him ever since, for over three years during which its behavior has grown steadily more hostile. Initially, the monkey "had but one peculiarity—a character of malignity— unfathomable malignity" (196). It appeared "sullen and sick," and did nothing more—or less—than watch Jennings ceaselessly (196). Always visible, the monkey was surrounded at night by "a halo that resembles a glow of red embers" (196). That crimson glow picks up the red of the gloaming and its freight of associations, and adds to them a more infernal aspect. Occasionally, the monkey has left Jennings, usually for slightly longer than two weeks, although it has been away for up to three months. When it is about to leave, it grows agitated and a fire appears in the chimney. The monkey leaps into the fire, up the chimney, and is gone.

The first time this happened, Jennings says, he thought he was "released" (197). Within a month, however, the monkey had returned, its appearance marked by a change in its demeanor. Where previously it had been sluggish, "torpid," now the monkey was active, energetic (197). "Its power of action . . . had increased," and was manifest when Jennings, having resolved "some questions that were pending between me and the bishop," assumed the duties of his parish (198). The monkey accompanied him into the church, "in the reading desk—in the pulpit—within the communion rails;" soon, "it reached this extremity, that while I was reading to the congregation, it would spring upon the book and squat there, so that I was unable to see the page" (198). Here is another book, in this case, the Lectionary. Yet where the story's other texts have served to encourage communication among its characters, the Lectionary appears only to be obscured, to sever the clergyman from his congregation. The monkey's act is the literalization of what we saw taking place in Jennings's speech, in his use of the classical figure of the Nemesis to describe the pernicious effects of his classical scholarship. As the Nemesis reference takes the place of a Christian one, so does the monkey, whose appearance is linked to the Reverend's classical studies, physically take the place of the written Christian text.

Unable to perform his duties, Jennings absented himself from his position to seek medical attention. For the three months of his treatment for what he still considered a variety of hallucination, Jennings did not see the monkey. Believing himself cured, he returned to his church, only to find the monkey returned, as well. Once more, its reappearance brought with it a heightening in its malevolent activity. Now, the monkey would "spring on a table, on the back of a chair, on the chimney-piece, and slowly . . . swing itself from side to side, looking at me all the time" (199). This movement had within itself "an indefinable power to dissipate thoughts, and to contract one's attention to that monotony, till the ideas shrank, as it were, to a point, and at last to nothing;" so pernicious is this effect that "unless I had started up, and shook off the catalepsy I have felt as if my mind were on the point of losing itself" (199). Nor could Jennings escape the monkey by closing his eyes; it was visible to him whether his eyes were open or shut. Needless to say, the monkey is hypnotizing him.

To make matters worse, for the last year, Jennings tells Hesselius, the monkey has been speaking to him, "in words and consecutive sentences, with perfect coherence and articulation" (200). He has not heard the monkey's speech via his ears; rather, "it comes like a singing through my head" (200). It is this development the clergyman fears the most. The monkey "won't let me pray, it interrupts me with dreadful blasphemies;" it "is always urging me to crimes, to injure others, or myself" (200–201).

The Reverend concludes his narration with an account of a recent excursion taken in the company of his niece and some friends. In the course of their outing, the group came across the entrance to a coal mine, "a perpendicular shaft, they say, a hundred and fifty feet deep"[10] (201). It is the story's latest blank, one the ever-present monkey "was urging me to throw myself down," and had his niece not remained with him there, despite his protestations that she continue with the rest of the company, Jennings would have obeyed it (201). The monkey, Jennings has said, "is prevailing little by little, and drawing me more interiorly into hell"[11] (198). He does not hold out much, if any, hope for himself.

---

10. In the figure of the mineshaft, Le Fanu may have in mind Swedenborg's declaration that the "hells are everywhere, both under the mountains, hills, and roads, and under plains and valleys. The aperture or gates to the hells . . . appear to the sight as holes and clefts of rocks; some stretching wide and large, some straight and narrow, some rugged. They all when looked into appear dark and gloomy, but the infernal spirits that are within them are in a light of similar quality to that from a fire of coals" (Warren 699).

11. We might recall Milton's Satan's "Myself am hell" (*Paradise Lost* 4.75).

By the end of the Reverend's narrative, the story's freight of details has expanded to take in monkeys and hypnotism. The monkey's associations are numerous and complex, spanning the shores of science and religion. As we have mentioned, the monkey cannot avoid Darwinian echoes; as such, it is representative of a fundamental assault on the priority of human beings in the natural schema. Nor are its metaphysical associations any more reassuring. In Swedenborg, the ape is associated with mimicry, with the uncomprehending replication of human action.[12] Whether we view the monkey as Darwinian allusion, Swedenborgian figure, or both, its reflective eyes foreground its relationship to the Reverend Mr. Jennings. To say the least, it is a relationship that calls the integrity of his character into question.

As does the hypnotism the monkey practices on him. As a term, hypnotism was still relatively new at the time "Green Tea" was composed, having been coined in 1843 by James Braid in his *Neurypnology* (Tinterow 269). Mesmerism, however, many of whose operative principles Braid's work debunked, had been in vogue since English anti-French sentiment faded in the wake of Napoleon's final defeat. In the same year of 1843, John Elliotson founded the *Zoist* magazine to bring together work on "cerebral physiology and mesmerism" (193). Whatever name it operated under, the placing of one human will under the control of another raised numerous anxieties about the stability (or lack thereof) of the psyche, which were summarized by the question, Could a hypnotist compel a subject to perform an action s/he would not otherwise? For the monkey to be hypnotizing Jennings is for it to be threatening him in a particularly intimate, interior way.

In terms of the story's construction, the monkey and hypnosis join Swedenborg's *Arcana*, anthropological research, and green tea in being grouped together within the narrow, shadowy space that is the story's core location. All are further joined by their association with the act of writing. The details are layered one over the other, until it is as if each is a metonym for the same fundamental urge, the urge to know, whose essential trope is that of letters on the page.

Though Jennings has accepted the monkey's reality, Hesselius remains cautious. Indeed, in contrast to the Reverend's despair, Hesselius is reassuring to the point of being blasé. "Even if the thing that infests you be," he tells

---

12. See Swedenborg's *True Christian Religion*, which in passage 568 contains a reference to people who "are like cunning apes which perform actions like those of men, but the human heart is wholly lacking," and which in passage 574 asks, "How many are there of the human race who are not born satyrs and priapi or four-footed lizards; and who among these, if not regenerated, does not become an ape?"

Jennings, "you seem to suppose a reality with an actual independent life and will, yet it can have no power to hurt you, unless it be given from above," i.e. God (200). The monkey's "access to your senses depends mainly upon your physical condition," Hesselius goes on, "it is only that in your case, the '*pa-ries,*' the veil of the flesh, the screen is a little out of repair, and sights and sounds are transmitted" (200–201). He reminds the Reverend that he is in God's hands "and in the power of no other being: be therefore confident for the future" (201). Hesselius then leaves the clergyman for the night, pledging to spend it in "careful consideration of the whole case" (201). He will return the next day with the results of his deliberations. In the meantime, he extracts a promise from Jennings, that "should the monkey at any time return, I should be sent for immediately" (202). Jennings having agreed to his request, Hesselius departs. On his way out, he warns Jennings's servant "that his master was far from well, and that he should make a point of frequently looking into his room" (202).

In order to be "quite secure from interruption," Hesselius returns to his lodgings long enough to pick up "a traveling desk and carpet bag," then heads for an inn called "The Horns," within whose "good thick walls" he plans to consider the Reverend Mr. Jennings's case (202). This he does, not returning to his rooms until one o'clock the following afternoon. When he walks in the door, Hesselius finds "a letter in Mr. Jennings's hand upon my table" (202). The letter had arrived at eleven the night before. Opening it, Hesselius reads a desperate message. The monkey, Jennings writes, has returned, and "knows all that has happened. It knows everything—it knows you, and is frantic and atrocious. It reviles" (203). "I am so interrupted, disturbed," the clergyman writes, recalling the doctor's wish to be *unin*terrupted, which in turn calls to mind the clergyman's description of the monkey interrupting his prayers with its blasphemies (203). Hesselius hurries out to see him.

He arrives too late, greeted first by "a tall woman in black silk," who "looked ill, and as if she had been crying," then by a pair of men, both of whose hands are "covered with blood" (203). The worst has come to pass. The clergyman has "made away with himself," opening "his throat with his razor" (204). There is an "immense pool of blood on the floor" of Jennings's bedroom, while "one of the great elms that darkened the house was slowly moving the shadow of one of its great bows upon this dreadful floor" (204). We have reached the last of the quartet of dark spaces. Its red pool of blood corresponds to the light of sunset, the reflection of the monkey's eyes. All of them are symbolic of death, more, of doom. By the same process of layering that associated the other details encountered in this place, those details are brought into conjunction with the pool of blood, with the clergyman's suicide. Through the associative principle that allowed us to see Swedenborg's metaphysical catalogue and green tea as deriving from that root drive to know, that drive in turn is linked to self-destruction. Such pessimism about the benefits of knowledge is typical of the ghost story, and of the larger category of the Gothic, but in this instance, it has a more specific target, namely, the constellation of cultural activities that constitute Victorian culture.

The Reverend's story, though, is not over. His servant relates the story of Jennings's final night, which the clergyman spent "talking a great deal to himself" (204). The servant checked on him regularly until six the following morning, when the servant assumed Jennings was finally asleep. By eleven, however, the servant grew suspicious, forced the door, and found Jennings dead. "Dejected and agitated," Hesselius leaves the house, offering us a diagnosis as he goes: "It is the story of the process of a poison, a poison which excites the reciprocal action of spirit and nerve, and paralyses the tissue that separates those cognate functions of the sense, the external and the interior" (205).

With Jennings's suicide and its aftermath, the ghostly portion of the narrative ostensibly has come to a close. What follows is the medical portion of it. While the ghost story may be content to end in mystery, the medical narrative requires an explanation. Indeed, a practitioner of metaphysical medicine such as Hesselius would appear to be well-suited to account for the clergyman's story. The medical strand is deployed to contain the ghostly, to render it more intelligible.

Thus, "Green Tea" concludes with Hesselius's expansion and clarification of this diagnosis. His explanation rests on the hypothesis that the brain is the center of a parallel circulatory system that flows through the nervous system. The fluid transmitted along this route is "spiritual, though not immaterial;" by "various abuses," one of which is "the habitual use of such agents as green tea," it is possible to disturb the "equilibrium" of this fluid, causing it to congest on the brain and thus "unduly" expose a section of the brain to the influence of "disembodied spirits"[13] (206–7). The "seat of interior vision is the nervous tissue and brain, immediately about and above the eyebrow;" once that "inner eye" is opened, it requires specialized treatment to close, namely, the application of cold, which "acts powerfully as a repellant of the nervous fluid" (207). "By acting steadily upon the body" over a course of "a year and a

---

13. Le Fanu's description of this fluid is sufficiently similar to Mesmer's ideas about a mesmeric fluid which is responsible for mesmerism to make it a likely source for Le Fanu (cf. Kaplan 17).

half to two years," Hesselius is certain he could have cured Jennings (206). He has, he boasts, cured "fifty-seven such cases," never failing (206). In case Hesselius's correspondent might consider the narrative he has been relating a conspicuous exception to that record, Hesselius is sure to remind him that "I had not even commenced to treat Mr. Jennings' case" (206).

Nor is that all. The opening of the clergyman's inner eye was not, Hesselius states, his true problem; rather, "the complaint under which he really succumbed, was hereditary suicidal mania," which projected itself upon the disease which was established" (207). Hesselius brings his story to a close by repeating that Jennings was not his patient, because "he had not yet given me, I am convinced, his full and unreserved confidence" (207). "If the patient do not array himself on the side of the disease," Hesselius concludes, "his cure is certain" (207).

The reference to the inner eye returns us to Swedenborg and his remarks concerning interior vision. Given Hesselius's location of the eye "immediately about and above the eyebrow," it is difficult not to think of Hinduism's third eye, which likewise allows discernment of the spiritual world. In addition, Le Fanu may have been aware of the writings of Robert Fludd, an early seventeenth-century "Paracelsist physician practicing in London" whose "philosophy was in line of descent from Renaissance Magia and Cabala, with the addition of Paracelsist alchemy and strong influences of John Dee" (Yates 73). From 1617 to 1619, Fludd published his *History of the Macrocosm and Microcosm*[14] (78–80). Among the illustrations Fludd included with the book is one of the inner eye, which he locates in the same area as Hesselius. Like Swedenborg (and Hesselius) after him, Fludd represents the attempt to chart the points of contact between the material and immaterial worlds. Of course, given what we have seen of Hesselius's failure of vision, his dilation upon the third eye is especially ironic.

In his characterization of the clergyman's story as that of a "poison," we are brought back to the very beginning of "Green Tea," to our nameless editor's infection and loss of his physical health. With the Reverend Mr. Jennings, the teacup has replaced the dissecting knife. The horrific symmetry of such a diagnosis is tempered by the doctor's assertion that what ultimately did in Jennings was not the opening of his inner eye, but the displacement

---

14. Interestingly, the work was published in Latin through the German university at Oppenheim; its foreign publication would result in Fludd having to defend himself from charges the book contained passages of black magic that made it unsuitable for British publication (Yates 9, 77). While the *History* is not medieval, it may lie behind those unnamed volumes Jennings consults.

upon that condition of his true problem, "hereditary suicidal mania." Hesselius's reasoning is circular: since Jennings cut his throat, he must have been predisposed to do so, or else he would not have. Granted, Jennings's narration of the monkey's insistence that he throw himself down the mineshaft, taken together with his declaration that the monkey is always urging him to injure himself, might be taken to indicate a tendency towards suicide. Yet these must be considered alongside the other acts the monkey spurs him towards, generic "crimes" and injury to others.

More, this explanation has most force if the monkey is a hallucination, symptom of a purely material complaint. Yet Hesselius's entire practice of medicine rests on the premise that the material is only part of existence, that it is the "ultimate expression of that spiritual world from which, and in which alone, it has its life." This would appear to validate the monkey's existence independent of the Reverend Mr. Jennings and to allow for the possibility of its agency, a possibility the Swedenborg quotations endorse. Indeed, those quotations underscore the malevolence of such spirits as the clergyman sees, and their desire to bring human beings to ruin. Despite his confession of Swedenborg's influence on his work, Hesselius either has come up short in his understanding of the man's writings, or has chosen to disregard those portions of them that have most bearing on the case at hand. Even if we give Hesselius the benefit of the doubt, assume that the other cases to which he refers have shown him how much of Swedenborg is accurate and applicable, his decision to leave a man as desperate as Jennings on his own is ill-advised at best. Nor does his departing the lodging at which he told the Reverend to contact him in favor of one of which Jennings is ignorant do much to bolster our estimation of his judgment, while his insistence that the clergyman was not actually his patient is obviously defensive.

Far from fulfilling its narrative obligation, Hesselius's conclusion leaves the reader confused, thinking that the doctor has not understood the story of which he has been part. He has failed the Reverend Mr. Jennings, a fact of which he appears to be aware, and which his explanation intends to disguise. Of course, the disguise is so clumsy that it calls more attention to what it attempts to conceal than would a simple admission of culpability. Instead of explaining and containing the ghostly portion of the narrative, the medical framework has been contaminated by it, whatever certainties it might have hoped to offer undermined. The notion of the infection has coursed throughout the story, from the framing narrator's loss, to the clergyman's inability to escape a pagan perspective, to Hesselius's diagnosis; it is one of the tropes tying the story's various elements together. In this way, the story demonstrates Linda Bayer-Berenbaum's assertion that "Gothic terror is dependent upon a merger of the natural and supernatural that undermines a sound, predictable reality" (35).

"Green Tea," then, relates a pair of failures. On the one hand, there is the clergyman, whose inability to fend off the advances of an evil spirit leads to an act of self-destruction and -damnation. His faith has not stood him in good stead, either as a means of ridding himself of the demonic monkey, or as a source of comfort that might allow him to continue to bear its depredations. On the other hand, there is the physician, whose inability to appreciate the case that has presented itself to him has made him complicit in another man's ruin. However splendid his theories on paper, they have not helped in the world of flesh and blood. There is no use in taking physic, nor does prayer appear terribly efficacious.

Sullivan has suggested that the true horror of "Green Tea" is its vision of an incomprehensible world, and there is some truth to such a reading (Sullivan 50). Sullivan contends that such an attitude is quintessentially modern, and while this assertion has merit, "Green Tea" also articulates profound contemporary fears about the advances in all fields of knowledge that were both the engine driving Victorian culture forward and the symbol of that process (48–51). At the heart of such fears, the story locates a deep nervousness about the self, both in terms of its ability to fulfill its duties to God and self, and in terms of its ability to fulfill its duties to others. What if, the story asks, all the actions we undertake to better our understanding of ourselves and our world should have the opposite effect? What if the self that undertakes these challenges is at root insufficient, unable for the tasks of the day?

In that relentless interrogation, the story has its power. Rather than the reassuringly rote deployment of formulaic plot, the ghost story in Le Fanu's hands is a lever that unsettles the firmest foundations of society and self. Absence is its subject, and if this makes a story such as "Green Tea" especially relevant to the context of its composition, it also helps to account for the story's continuing appeal. This reading of "Green Tea" opens intriguing avenues for exploration of Le Fanu's other stories, particularly "Mr. Justice Harbottle" (1872) and "Carmilla" (1872). It also suggests new approaches to the ghost stories of writers including Dickens, Collins, and Stevenson.

The monkey looks at us; we look back, and see that its eyes are mirrors.

For Fiona

Works Cited

Bayer-Berenbaum, Linda. *The Gothic Imagination: Expansion in Gothic Literature and Art.* Rutherford, NJ: Fairleigh Dickinson University Press, 1982.

Evans, John C. *Tea in China: The History of China's National Drink.* Westport, CT: Greenwood Press, 1992.

Hughes, William. "The Origins and Implications of J. S. Le Fanu's 'Green Tea.'" *Irish Studies Review* 13:1 (February 2005): 45–54.

Jonsson, Inge. *Emmanuel Swedenborg.* Trans. Catherine Djurklou. New York: Twayne, 1969.

Kaplan, Fred. *Dickens and Mesmerism: The Hidden Springs of Fiction.* Princeton: Princeton University Press, 1975.

Kilgour, Maggie. *The Rise of the Gothic Novel.* London: Routledge, 1995.

Le Fanu, J. Sheridan. "Green Tea." In *Best Ghost Stories of J. S. Le Fanu.* Ed. E. F. Bleiler. New York: Dover, 1964. 178–207.

Levinson, Marjorie. "What Is New Formalism?" *PMLA* 122 (March 2007): 558–69.

Mc Cormack, W. J. *Sheridan Le Fanu and Victorian Ireland.* Oxford: Clarendon Press, 1980.

Sullivan, Jack. *Elegant Nightmares: The English Ghost Story from Le Fanu to Blackwood.* Athens: Ohio University Press, 1978.

Sutton, Eric A., ed.. *The Living Thoughts of Swedenborg.* London: Cassell, 1944.

Thomas, Keith. *Man and the Natural World: Changing Attitudes in England 1500–1800.* Harmondsworth, UK: Penguin, 1984.

Tinterow, Maurice M. *Foundations of Hypnosis: From Mesmer to Freud.* Springfield, IL: Charles Thomas, 1970.

Walton, James. "Vision and Vacancy: 'Schalken the Painter' and Le Fanu's Art of Darkness." *Papers on Language and Literature* 40 (Fall 2004): 353–83.

Warren, Samuel, ed. *A Compendium of the Theological Writings of Emanuel Swedenborg.* New York: Swedenborg Foundation, 1974.

Yates, Frances A. *The Rosicrucian Enlightenment.* London: Routledge & Kegan Paul, 1972.

Introduction to *Uncle Silas*

Elizabeth Bowen

I.

*U*ncle Silas is a romance of terror. Joseph Sheridan Le Fanu lets us know that he expanded it from a short story (length, about fifteen pages) which he wrote earlier in his literary life and published, anonymously, in a magazine—under the title of "A Passage in the Secret History of an Irish Countess." As he does not give the name of the magazine, I have not, so far, been able to trace the story.[1] I should make further efforts to do so could I feel that its interest was very great: its initial interest, that is to say, *qua* story. It holds, it is true, the germ of the later novel—or, at least, of its plot. But about that plot itself there is little new. The exterior plot of *Uncle Silas* is traditional, well worn by the time Le Fanu took up his pen. What have we? The Wicked Uncle and the Endangered Heir. I need not point out the precedents even in English history. Also, this is the Babes in the Wood theme—but in *Uncle Silas* we have only one babe—feminine, in her late adolescence, and, therefore, the no less perpetual Beauty in Distress. Maud Ruthyn has her heroine-prototype in a large body of fiction which ran to excess in the gothic romances but is not finished yet—the distraught young lady clasping her hands and casting her eyes skyward to Heaven: she has no other friends. . . . No, it is hard to see that simply uncle and niece, her sufferings, his designs, compressed, as they were at first, into a number of pages so small as to limit "treatment" (Le Fanu's *forté*) could have made up into anything much more than the conventional magazine story of the day.

What *is* interesting is that Le Fanu, having written the story, should have been unable, still, to discharge its theme from his mind. He must have continued, throughout the years, to be obsessed, if subconsciously, by the niece and uncle. More, these two and their relationship to each other became magnetic

---

1. ["Passage in the Secret History of an Irish Countess" first appeared in the November 1838 issue of the *Dublin University Magazine*.—Ed.]

to everything strangest and most powerful in his imagination and temperament. The resultant novel, our *Uncle Silas*, owes the pressure, volume and spiritual urgency which make it comparable to *Wuthering Heights* to just this phenomenon of accretion. Accretion is a major factor in art. Le Fanu could not be rid of the niece and uncle till he had built them a comprehensive book.

Something else draws my interest to the original story: its heroine, by the showing of the title, was Irish, by marriage if not birth. Joseph Sheridan Le Fanu (1814–1873, grand-nephew of Sheridan the dramatist) was Irish; or rather Anglo-Irish. And *Uncle Silas* has always struck me as being an Irish story transposed to an English setting. The hermetic solitude and the autocracy of the great country house, the demonic power of the family myth, fatalism, feudalism and the "ascendancy" outlook are accepted facts of life for the race of hybrids from which Le Fanu sprang. For the psychological background of *Uncle Silas* it was necessary for him to *invent* nothing. Rather, he was at once exploiting in art and exploring for its more terrible implications what would have been the norm of his own heredity. Having, for reasons which are inscrutable, pitched on England as the setting for *Uncle Silas*, he wisely chose the North, the wildness of Derbyshire. Up there, in the vast estates of the landed old stock, there appeared, in the years when Le Fanu wrote (and still more in the years *of* which he wrote: the early 1840s) a time lag—just such a time lag as, in a more marked form, separates Ireland from England more effectually than any sea.

Le Fanu was not, in his generation, alone in seeing the possibilities of the country house from the point of view of drama, tension and mystery. We may comment on "atmosphere": almost all the Victorians who were novelists used it without fuss. Wilkie Collins, for instance, wrings the last drop of effect from the woodgirt Hampshire mansion in *The Woman in White*, with its muffling, oppressive silence and eerie lake. The castles, granges and lonely halls back through romantic fiction are innumerable. One might, even, say that Le Fanu showed himself as traditional, or unoriginal, in his choice of setting as in his choice of plot. Only, while his contemporaries, the by then urbanized Victorian English, viewed the ancestral scene from the outside, the Irishman wrote out of what was in his bones.

Uncle Silas is, as a novel, Irish in two other ways: it is sexless, and it shows a sublimated infantilism. It may, for all I know, bristle with symbolism; but I speak of the *story*, not of its implications—in the story, no force from any one of the main characters runs into the channel of sexual feeling. The reactions of Maud, the narrator-heroine, throughout are those of a highly intelligent, still more highly sensitive, child of twelve. This may, to a degree, be accounted for by seclusion and a repressive father—but not, I think, entirely: I should doubt whether Le Fanu himself realized Maud's abnormality as a heroine. She is an uncertain keyboard, on which some notes sound clearly, deeply and truly, others not at all. There is no question, here, of Victorian censorship, with its suggestive gaps: Maud, on the subject of anything she *does* feel, is uninhibited, sometimes disconcerting. And equally, in the feeling of people round her we are to take it that, child-like, she misses nothing. The distribution of power throughout the writing is equal, even: the briefest scene is accorded brimming sensuous content. We must in fact note how Maud's sensuousness (which is un-English) disperses, expends itself through the story in so much small change. She shows, at every turn, the carelessness, or acquiescence, of the predestined person: Maud is, by nature, a bride of Death. She delays, she equivocates, she looks wildly sideways; she delights in fire and candlelight, bedroom tea-drinking, cozy feminine company, but her bias is marked. The wind blowing her way from the family mausoleum troubles our heroine like a mating cry. Her survival after those frightful hours in the locked bedroom at Bartram-Haugh is, one can but feel, somewhat ghostly: she has cheated her Bridegroom only for the time being. Her human lover is colorless; her marriage—unexceptionable as to level and felicity—is little more than the shell of a happy ending. From the parenthesis in her "Conclusion" (Maud writes down her story after some years of marriage) we learn that the first of her children die.

Is, then, *Uncle Silas* "morbid"? I cannot say so. For one thing morbidity seems to me little else than sentimentality of a peculiar tint, and nothing of that survives in the drastic air of the book. For another, Maud is counterpoised by two other characters, her unalike cousins Monica Knollys and Milly Ruthyn, who not only desire life but are its apostles. And, life itself is painted in brilliant colors—colors sometimes tantalizing, as though life were an alternative out of grasp; sometimes insidious, disturbing, as though life were a temptation. I know, as a matter of fact, of few Victorian novels in which coziness, gaiety and the delights of friendship are so sweetly rendered or played such a telling part. Le Fanu's style, translucent, at once simple and subtle, is ideal for such transitions. He has a genius for the unexpected—in mood as well as event. One example—a knowing twist of his art—is that Maud, whose arrival at Bartram-Haugh has been fraught with sinister apprehension, should, for the first few months, delight in her uncle's house. After Knowl—overcast, repressive, stiff with proprieties—Bartram-Haugh seems to be Liberty Hall. She runs wild in the woods with her cousin Milly; for the first time, she has company of her own age. Really, it is the drama of Maud's feelings, rather than the melodrama of her approaching fate, which ties one to *Uncle Silas*, page after page, breathless, unwilling to miss a word.

336 REFLECTIONS IN A GLASS DARKLY

II.

Le Fanu either felt or claimed to feel uneasy as to the reception of *Uncle Silas*. He mentions the genesis of the novel, not for its interest as a creative fact, but in order to clear himself, in advance, of the charge of plagiarism: his long-ago short story having been anonymous. And, in the same "Preliminary Word" he enters a plea that the novel be not dismissed as "sensation" fiction. *Uncle Silas* was published in 1864: the plea would not be necessary to-day. Sensationalism, for its own sake, does, it is true, remain in poor repute; but sensation (of the kind which packs *Uncle Silas*) is not only not disdained, it is placed in art. The most irreproachable pens, the most poetic imaginations pursue and refine it. The status of the psychological thriller is, to-day, high. *Uncle Silas* was in advance of, not behind, its time: it is not the last belated Gothic romance but the first (or among the first) of the psychological thrillers. And it has, as terror-writing, a voluptuousness not approached since. (It was of the voluptuousness in his own writing that Le Fanu may, really, have been afraid.) The novel, like others of its now honored type, relies upon suspense and mystification: I should be doing wrong to it and the reader were I to outline the story or more than hint at its end. To say that a rich, lonely girl is placed, by her father's will, in charge of an uncle who, already suspected of one murder, would be the first to profit by her death is, I think, at once sufficient and fair. But, the real suspense of the story emanates from the characters; it is they who keep the tale charged with mystery. The people in *Uncle Silas* show an extraordinary power of doubling upon or of covering their tracks. Maud seldom knows where she stands with any of them; neither do we. They are all at one remove from us, seen through the eyes of Maud. The gain to a story of this nature of being told in the first person is obvious (but for the fact that the teller, for all her dangers, must, we take it, survive, in order to tell the tale). All the same, it is not to this device that Le Fanu owes the main part of his effects—you and I, as readers, constantly intercept glances or changes in tones of voice that Maud just notes but does not interpret aright. No, Maud has little advantage over you or me. Temperamentally, and because of her upbringing, she is someone who moves about in a world of strangers. She is alternately blind and unnecessarily suspicious. Her attitude towards every newcomer is one of fatalistic mistrust; and this attitude almost, but not quite (which is subtle) communicates itself to the reader. We do not, for instance, know, for an unreasonably but enjoyably long time, whether Milly, for all her rustic frankness, may not at heart be a Little Robber Girl, or Lady Knollys a schemer under her good nature.

You perceive [says Maud] that I had more spirit than courage. I think I had the mental attributes of courage; but then I was but an hysterical girl, and in so far neither more nor less than a coward.

No wonder I distrusted myself; no wonder my will stood out against my timidity. It was a struggle, then; a proud, wild struggle against constitutional cowardice.

Those who have ever had cast upon them more than their strength seems framed to bear—the weak, the aspiring, the adventurous in will, and the faltering in nerve—will understand the kind of agony which I sometimes endured.

And later, on receiving comforting news:

You will say then that my spirits and my serenity were quite restored. Not quite. How marvellously lie our anxieties, in filmy layers, one over the other! Take away that which has lain on the upper surface for so long—the care of cares—the only one, as it seemed to you, between your soul and the radiance of Heaven—and straight you find a new stratum there. As physical science tells us no fluid is without its skin, so does it seem with this fine medium of the soul, and those successive films of care that form upon its surface on mere contact with the upper air and light.

Who are the characters whom, in *Uncle Silas*, this at once nervous and spiritual girl confronts? There is her father, Austin Ruthyn of Knowl, scion and reigning head of an ancient family, wealthy, recluse, widower, given up to Swedenborgian religion. There is Mr. Ruthyn's spiritual director Dr. Bryerly—"bilious, bewigged, black-eyed"—whose nocturnal comings and goings seem to bode no good. There is Mr. Ruthyn's first cousin Lady Knollys, woman of the world, who comes to stay at Knowl and interests herself in Maud. There is Maud's French governess Madame de La Rougierre, who, arriving early on in the story, gibbers in moonlight outside the drawing-room window.

Half-way through, story and heroine cross sixty miles of country. Austin Ruthyn is dead: his place in Maud's life is taken by his younger brother Silas, of Bartram-Haugh—reformed rake, widower and, again, religious recluse. Silas's marriage to a barmaid had dealt the first, though not yet the worst, blow to Ruthyn family pride. Children of the marriage are Milly ("a very rustic Miranda," her father says) and Dudley, a sinister Tony Lumpkin. In the Bartram-Haugh woods dwell an ill-spoken miller and his passionate daughter. . . . In both great houses there is the usual cast of servants—at Knowl, correct, many and reassuring; at Bartram-Haugh few and queer. On from this point, characterization, in any full sense, stops: we are left with "types," existing, solely and flatly, for the requirements of the plot. A fortune-hunting officer, three clergymen, two lawyers and a thoughtful peer, Maud's future husband, come under this heading.

That last group, uninspired and barely tinted in, represents Le Fanu's one economy. In the main, it could be a charge against him that too many of the characters in *Uncle Silas* are overcharged, and that they break their bounds. There is abnormal pressure, from every side; the psychic air is often overheated. And all the time, we must remember, this is a story intended to be dominated by the figure of *one* man: Uncle Silas. All through, Uncle Silas meets competition. He is, I think, most nearly played off the stage by Madame de la Rougierre. Apart from that he is (as central character) at a disadvantage: *is* he, constantly, big enough for his own build-up? Is there or is there not, in scenes in which he actually appears, a just perceptible drop into anti-climax? Le Fanu, in dealing with Uncle Silas, was up against a difficulty inherent in his kind of oblique, suggestive art. He has overdrawn on his Silas in advance. In the flesh, Uncle Silas enters the story late: by this time, his build-up has reached towering heights. It is true that most of the time at Bartram-Haugh he remains off stage, and that those intervals allow of batteries being recharged. At Knowl, still only a name, he was ever-present—in the tormented silences of his brother, the hinting uneasy chatter of Lady Knollys, and Maud's dreams.

> I don't [Lady Knollys admits, to Maud] understand metaphysics, my dear, nor witchcraft. I sometimes believe in the supernatural, and sometimes I don't. Silas Ruthyn is himself alone, and I can't define him because I don't understand him. Perhaps other souls than human are sometimes born into the world, and clothed in flesh. It is not only about that dreadful occurrence, but nearly always throughout his life; early and late he has puzzled me . . . . At one time of his life I am sure he was awfully wicked—eccentric indeed in his wickedness—gay, frivolous, secret and dangerous. At one time I think he could have made poor Austin do almost anything; but his influence vanished with his marriage, never to return again. No; I don't understand him. He has always bewildered me, like a shifting face, something smiling, but always sinister, in an unpleasant dream.

Here is Maud, on arrival at Bartram-Haugh, fresh from her first meeting with her uncle:

> When I lay down in my bed and reviewed the day, it seemed like a month of wonders. Uncle Silas was always before me; the voice so silvery for an old man—preternaturally soft; the manners so sweet, so gentle; the aspect, smiling, suffering, spectral. It was no longer a shadow; I had now seen him in the flesh. But, after all, was he more than a shadow to me? When I closed my eyes I saw him before me still, in necromantic black, ashy with a pallor on

which I looked with fear and pain, a face so dazzlingly pale, and those hollow, fiery, awful eyes! It sometimes seemed as though the curtain opened, and I had seen a ghost.

"What a sweet, gentle, insufferable voice he has!" exclaims, later, Lady Knollys, who, for Maud's sake, has tried to reopen relations with Bartram-Haugh. And, towards the end, we hear the beleaguered Maud: "There were the sensualities of the gourmet for his body, and there ended his human nature, as it seemed to me. Through that semi-transparent structure I thought I could now and then discern the light or glare of his inner life . . . . Was, then, all his kindness but a phosphoric radiance covering something colder and more awful than the grave?"

Of the French governess, what is one to say? She is Uncle Silas's rival or counterpart. She is physical as opposed to metaphysical evil. No question of "semi-transparent structure" here—the Frenchwoman is of the rankest bodily coarseness: one can smell her breath, as it were, at every turn. In the *Uncle Silas* atmosphere, bleached of sex, she is no more woman than he is man; yet, somehow, her marelike coquetry—that prinking with finery and those tales of lovers—is the final, grotesque element of offence. As a woman, she can intrude on the girl at all points. She is obscene; and not least so in the alternate pinchings and pawings to which she subjects Maud. While the uncle gains in monstrousness by distance, the governess gains in monstrous by closeness.

Madame de la Rougierre is unhandicapped by a preliminary build-up: she enters the story without warning and makes growth, page by page, as she goes along. Le Fanu, through the mouths of his characters, is a crack marksman in the matter of epithets: nothing said of the governess goes wide. He had, it is true, with this Frenchwoman a great vein to work on: with Wilkie Collins and Dickens he could exploit the British concept of the foreigner as sinister. Her broken English (with its peculiar rhythm, like no other known broken English, specially coined for her) further twists, in speech, the thoughts of her hideous mind. Like Uncle Silas, Madame de la Roguierre is, morally, of an unrelieved black: considering how much we are in her company it is wonderful that she does not become monotonous—the variations Le Fanu *has* contrived to give her are to be admired. "When things went well," we are told, "her soul lighted up into sulphureous good-honour." The stress is most often upon this woman's mouth—a "large-featured, smirking phantom" is Maud's first view of her, through the drawing-room window. We have her "wide, wet grin." She would "smile with her great carious teeth."

This creature's background is never fully given. Indeed, her engagement, as his daughter's companion, by Mr. Ruthyn of Knowl, is, with his obstinate tolerance of her presence, one of the first anomalies of the plot.

III.

Uncle Silas, as a novel, derives its power from an inner momentum. In the exterior plot there are certain weaknesses—inconsistencies and loose ends. In this regard, the book has about it a sort of brilliant—nay, even inspired—amateurishness; a sort of negligent virtuosity in which Le Fanu shows his race. This may be the reason why *Uncle Silas* has never yet quite made the popular grade. It has not *so far*, that is to say, moved forward from being a favorite book of individual people into the rank of accepted Victorian classics.

It cannot, I think, be said that most Victorian novels are guiltless of loose ends. But, in their elaborate plots with their substructures, crowds of characters and varied, shifting scenes, there is usually more to distract the eye: reader as well as author may well overlook something. *Uncle Silas* is, in this matter, defenseless in its simplicity: it has no sub-plots and contains comparatively few people. The writing is no less simple: this, its beauty apart, is its great virtue. The effect of the simplicity is, that every sentence of Le Fanu's—or, at least, its content—incises itself deeply upon one's memory: one can forget not the slightest hint or statement or question. And, the excitingness of the story keeps one on the stretch, at once watchful and challenging, like a child listener. Like the child, one finds oneself breaking in, from time to time, with: "But—? . . . But, I thought you *said*—?"

The omissions or inconsistencies of the plot are not psychological; they are practical or mechanical. They do not, to my mind, detract from or injure the real story, because they are not on its realest plane. However, there they are. I do not feel it to be the function of this Introduction to point them out to the reader in advance—I intend, therefore, only to mention one, which could hardly escape the most careless eye. *Who* was the concealed witness who relayed to Maud the conversation between Madame de la Rougierre and Dudley Ruthyn at Church Scarsdale? A witness who must, by the way, have been no less observant and subtle than Maud herself, for no inflection, gesture or glance is lost. We are never told who it is. The most likely bid is Tom Brice, the girl Beauty's lover and, at one time, Dudley's hanger-on. Tom might have told Beauty, who might have told Maud. But the account does not sound as though it had come through the mouths of two peasants. . . . . Elsewhere, the fact that the degree and origin of the Frenchwoman's relationship with the Bartram-Haugh Ruthyns is never stated may worry some readers. We are left to infer that she *was*, already, their agent from before the time she arrived at Knowl.

The plot is obfuscated (sometimes, one may say, helpfully) by an extraordinary vagueness about time. This is a book in which it is impossible to keep a check on the passage of weeks, months, years. The novel is dominated by one single season in whose mood it is pitched: autumn. Practically no other season is implied or named. (Yes, we have a Christmas visit to Elvaston, and a mention, elsewhere, of January rain. And after Madame de la Rougierre's departure from Knowl Maud, in the joy of her release, is conscious of singing birds and blue skies—but those could be in September.) The whole orchestral range of the novel's weather is autumnal—tranced, dripping melancholy, crystal morning zest, the radiance of the magnified harvest moon, or the howl of the straining of gales through not yet quite leafless woods. The daylight part of Maud's drive to her uncle house is through an amber landscape. The opening words of the novel are, it is true, "It was winter . . ." But our heroine, contradictory with her first breath, then adds: "the second week in November." By this reckoning Maud, in telling Lady Knollys that Madame de la Rougierre had arrived at Knowl "in February" is incorrect. The Frenchwoman, we had been clearly told, arrived "about a fortnight" after the opening scene. . . . No, there is nothing for it: one must submit oneself to Le Fanu's hypnotizing, perpetual autumn. One autumn merges into another: hopeless to ask how much has happened between! Yet always, against this nebulous flow of time stand out the moments—each unique, comprehensive, crystal, painfully sharp.

The inner, non-practical, psychological plot of *Uncle Silas* is, I suggest, faultless: it has no inconsistencies. The story springs from and is rooted in an obsession, and the obsession never looses its hold. Austin Ruthyn of Knowl, by an inexorable posthumous act, engages his daughter's safety in order to rescue his brother's honour. Or rather, less Silas's honour than the family name's. Silas Ruthyn is a man under a cloud: he has never yet been cleared of a charge against him. Austin's having committed Maud to his brother's keeping is to demonstrate, to the eyes of a hostile world, his absolute faith in his brother's innocence. By surviving years under his lonely roof, Maud, whose next heir he is, is to vindicate Silas. Maud has, during her father's lifetime, agreed in principle to the trust. (She has still, be it said, to hear the terms of the will, and to learn the full story of Silas from Lady Knollys.)

> I think [Austin says to his daughter] little Maud would like to contribute to the restitution of her family name. . . . The character and influence of an ancient family is a peculiar heritage—sacred but destructible; and woe to him who either destroys or suffers it to perish.

Call this *folie de grandeur*, or a fascination of the Almanach de Gotha. It is the extreme of a point of view less foreign to Le Fanu than to his readers. It was a point of view that they, creatures of an industrialized English nineteenth century, were bound to challenge, and could deride. It could only hope to be made acceptable, as mainspring and premise of his story, by being challenged, criticized—even, by implication, derided—in advance, and on behalf of the reader, by a person located somewhere *inside* the story. The necessary mouthpiece is Dr. Bryerly. Dr. Bryerly's little speech to Maud is a piece of, as it were, insurance, on Le Fanu's part. "There are people," remarks Dr. Bryerly, "who think themselves just as great as the Ruthyns, or greater; and your poor father's idea of carrying it by a demonstration was simply the dream of a man who had forgotten the world, and learned to exaggerate himself by his long seclusion." True—and how effective. The reader's misgivings, his fear of being implicated in something insanely disproportionate, have been set at rest. He is now prepared to lean back and accept, as Le Fanu wished, the idea on one—but that a great—merit purely: its validity for the purposes of the tale.

One more comment, before we leave the plot. In the disposition of characters (including what I have called functional types) about the field of the story, Le Fanu shows himself, as a novelist, admirably professional, in a sense that few of his contemporaries were. Not a single, even the slightest, character is superfluous; not a one fails to play his or her part in the plot, or detains us for a second after that part is played. One or two (such as the house party guests at Elvaston) are merely called in to act on Maud's state of mind. But Maud's mind, we must remember, reflects, and colors according to its states, the action of the interior plot. No person is in the story simply to fill up space, to give the Victorian reader his money's worth, or to revive flagging interest—Le Fanu, rightly, did not expect interest to flag.

IV.

The background, or atmosphere, needs little discussion: in the first few pages one recognizes the master-touch. The story of *Uncle Silas* is, as I have indicated, as to scene divided between two houses: Knowl and Bartram-Haugh. The contrast between the two houses contributes drama. Knowl, black and white, timbered, set in well-tended gardens, is a rich man's home. It is comfortable; fires roar in the grates; pictures and paneling gleam; the servants do all they should. As against this, Knowl is overcast, rigid, haunted: Mr. Ruthyn is closeted with dark mysteries; there are two ghosts, and, nearby, the family mausoleum, in which Maud's young mother lies and to which her father is to be carried under the most charnel circumstances of death.

Maud, sitting with Lady Knollys after Austin's death, hears the wind come roaring her way through the woods from the mausoleum. The wind, Lady Knollys can but point out, comes, too, from the more really threatening direction of Bartram-Haugh. Uncle Silas's house, already the scene of one violent death, is, beforehand, invested with every terror. Bartram-Haugh, as first seen, demands a John Piper drawing:

> I was almost breathless as I approached. The bright moon shining fully on the white front of the old house revealed not only its highly decorated style, its fluted pillars and doorway, rich and florid carving and balustraded summit, but also its stained and mossgrown front. Two giant trees, overthrown at last by the recent storm, lay with their upturned roots, and their yellow foliage still flickering on the sprays that were to bloom no more, where they had fallen, at the right side of the courtyard, which, like the avenue, was tufted with weeds and grass.

"The mind is," as Maud elsewhere remarks, "a different organ by night and by day." Next morning's awakening is reassuring—a wakening of bright morning through bare windows, a cheerful breakfast, superb if neglected stretches of parkland, a blackberrying walk. Exploration, with Milly, of whole closed derelict floors and internal galleries brings only a fleeting memory of the ill-fated Charke. The psychological weather of those first Bartram-Haugh chapters is like the out-of-doors weather: gay and tingling. Till Milly is sent away, nothing goes wholly wrong.

From *that* point, the closing is continuous. The ruined rooms, the discovery of the ogress-governess in hiding, introduce the beginning of the end. . . . All through Le Fanu's writing, there is an ecstatic sensitivity to light, and an abnormal recoil from its inverse, darkness. *Uncle Silas* is full of outdoor weather—we enjoy the rides and glades, cross the brooks and stiles, meet the cottagers and feel the enclosing walls of two kingdom-like great estates. Though static in ever-autumn, those scenes change: there is more than the rolling across them of clouds or sunshine. Indeed we are looking at their reflection in the lightening or darkening mirror of Maud's mind.

V.

Uncle Silas is a romance of terror, written more than eighty years ago. Between then and now, human susceptibilities have altered—some may have atrophied, others developed further. The terror-formula of yesterday might not work-to-day. Will Uncle *Silas* act on the modern reader?

I think so, and for several reasons. Le Fanu's strength, here, is not so much in his story as in the mode of its telling. *Uncle Silas*, as it is written, plays on one constant factor—our childish fears. These leave their work at the base of our natures, and are never to be rationalized away. Two things are terrible in childhood: helplessness (being in other people's power) and apprehension—the apprehension that something is being concealed from us because it is too bad to be told. Maud Ruthyn, vehicle of the story, *is* helpless apprehension itself, in person: this is what gets under our skin. Maud, simplified (in the chemical sense, reduced) for her creator's purpose, is, we may tell ourselves, an extreme case. She has a predisposition towards fear: we are to watch her—and *be* her—along her way towards the consummation of perfect terror—just as, were this a love story, we should be sharing her journey towards a consummation of a different kind. Proust has pointed out that the predisposition to love creates its own objects: is this not true of fear? At the start, Maud, in her unconscious search, experiments with Dr. Bryerly: she fears him. He acts as the forecast shadow of Uncle Silas—and, that he may play this role for the first act, he is given all the necessary trappings. Then, the Doctor discloses a character in point-blank reverse: he is levelheaded, a man of daylight, unfailing good counselor, champion, friend. But by that time, what the Doctor is does not matter: using the love-fear analogy, he is an off-cast love. He has been superseded by Uncle Silas, past whom Maud has no further to look.

Maud has suspected in Dr. Bryerly a supernatural element of evil: his influence on her father appeared malign. This brings us to another terror-ingredient: moral dread. Should one call this timeless, or is it modern? Let us say, it is timeless, but that its refinement in literature has been modern. (By modern I mean, modern at the best.) Henry James inspired, and remains at the head of, a whole school of moral horror stories—I need not point out that it is the stench of evil, not the mere fact of the supernatural, which is the genuine horror of *The Turn of the Screw*. Our ancestors may have had an agreeable-dreadful reflex from the idea of the Devil, or a skull-headed revenant popping in and out through a closed door: we need, to make us shiver, the effluence from a damned soul. In *Uncle Silas*, there is no supernatural element in the ordinary sense—the Knowl ghosts exist merely to key Maud up. The genuine horror is the non-natural. Lady Knollys, in her chatter, suggests that Silas may be a non-human soul clothed in a human body.

What Maud dreads, face to face with Silas, is not her own death.

Physically, Maud's nerve is extremely good. She stands up to Madame de la Rougierre, to whom her reactions are those of intense dislike, repugnance and disdain. She is frightened only of what she cannot measure, and she has got the governess taped. With the same blend of disdain and clear-sightedness, she stands up to Dudley. She shows, I think, remarkable non-chalance in re-exploring the top rooms alone, in the late dusk, after Milly's departure. As the plot thickens round her and door after door clangs to, she shows herself fanatically disposed, up to the very last minute, to give her uncle the benefit of the doubt. Were she, in fact, a goose or a weakling, the story would lack the essential tension: *Uncle Silas* would fail. As it is, we have the impact of a crescendo of hints and happenings on taut, hyper-controlled and thus very modern nerves. *Is there to be a breaking-point? If so, why, how, when?* That, not the question of Maud's bodily fate, sets up the real excitement of *Uncle Silas*.

The let-up, the pause for recuperation, even the apparent solicitude: these are among the sciences of the torture chamber. The victim must regain his power to suffer fully. The let-ups in *Uncle Silas*—the fine days, the walks, the returned illusions of safety—are, for Maud and the reader, artfully timed. Nothing goes on for long enough either to dull you or to exhaust itself. And the light, the open air, the outdoor perspective enhance, by contrast, the last of the horror-constants—claustrophobia. On the keyboards of any normal reader, *Uncle Silas* will not, I think, fail to strike one or another note: upon the claustrophobic it plays a fugue. The sense of the tightening circle, the shrinking and darkening room . . . .

Just as the outer plot of *Uncle Silas* is traditional, or unoriginal, Le Fanu does draw also, for fear or horror, out of the traditional bag of tricks—the lonely ruinous house, the closed room, the burning eyes, the midnight voices, the hired assassins, and so on. Maud herself, exploring Bartram-Haugh in the dusk, has in mind the romances of Mrs. Radcliffe. The induction of misery and despair preparatory to slaughter is Elizabethan. . . . In so far as *Uncle Silas* uses physical horror, the use is extremely sophisticated: Maud's quick and almost voluptuous reactions to sound, sight, touch and smell make her the perfect re-agent. The actual *sound* of a murder, a messy butchery, has probably never, in any gangster story, been registered as it is here.

* * *

The function of an Introduction is, I think, to indicate the nature of a book and to suggest some angles for judgment. That judgment the reader himself must form. *Uncle Silas* will, in this new edition, reach, among others, a generation of readers who have grown up since the novel was last in print. They may read into it more than I have found. That it will have meaning for them I do not doubt.

"Addicted to the Supernatural": Spiritualism and Self-Satire in Le Fanu's *All in the Dark*

Stephen Carver

In the spring of 1848, the Fox family of Hydesville, a desolate New York hamlet, was nightly plagued by disembodied knocking. Events escalated on the evening of March 31, when John and Margaret Fox heard loud noises emanating from the room above in which their children, Katherine and Margaretta, were sleeping. This time the mysterious sounds appeared to indicate intelligence, apparently interacting with Katherine. When the child snapped her fingers or clapped her hands the entity, which she called "Mr. Splitfoot," would rap back in reply. Mrs. Fox bravely attempted to make contact, while her husband went for help. That night, a group of frightened neighbors watched Mrs. Fox communicate with the "spirit" in the upstairs room, which knocked with such violence that one eyewitness, William Duesler, recorded that he "felt the bedstead jar when the sound was produced" (Capron and Barron 15). As the presence could only affirm, deny and enumerate, Mrs. Fox asked a series of speculative questions to determine its identity and intent. This séance revealed that the ghost was benign, and that of a murdered peddler.[1]

In the heavily evangelized "burned-over district" of Upstate New York, news travelled fast. Older brother David Fox soon devised a laborious alphabetical method of communicating with spirits (the forerunner of Elijah Bond's "Ouija Board"), while older sister Mrs. Leah Fish began to market the family's clairvoyance. This notoriety was greatly enhanced by the recent publication of Andrew Jackson Davis's *The Principles of Nature, Her Divine Revelations, and A Voice to Mankind*, in which the "Poughkeepsie Seer" prophesized that "the truth that spirits commune . . . will ere long present

---

1. The Rev. Simeon Stefanidakis of the First Spiritual Temple cites a signed affidavit written by Mrs. Fox on April 4, 1848, in "The Hydesville Events, March 31, 1848." This may originate from interviews conducted by a Mr. E. Lewis of New York, who published a pamphlet on the phenomenon within days of its occurrence.

itself in the form of a living demonstration" (Davis 1.675–76). The Fox sisters demonstrated and, initially supported by radical New York Quakers, their "Spiritualism" quickly became a national sensation. Frank Podmore, of the Society for Psychical Research, estimated that there were over a hundred practicing mediums in New York alone by 1850 (Podmore 1.183), while Augustus de Morgan likened the spread of mediums to smallpox (Brandon 43).

Like many British intellectuals, de Morgan was converted by the Boston medium Mrs. Maria B. Hayden, who performed séances in London in 1853 at a guinea-a-head. Mrs. Hayden brought the new and widely reported "faith" to the United Kingdom, and she was soon followed by even more flamboyant mediums, most notably Daniel Dunglas Home. Despite skeptical voices, including Dickens (who denounced Hayden in *Household Words*), the fundamentally optimistic, pseudo-religious theatricality of Spiritualism found easy purchase in the Victorian psyche. But as tables tapped and tilted across fashionable Europe, one particular expert in the supernatural had had quite enough.

In the words of M. R. James, the Victorian Gothic writer Joseph Sheridan Le Fanu "stands absolutely in the first rank as a writer of ghost stories" (James vii). Dickens was an avid reader, and he also sought the Irish author's advice on "spectral illusions" (Gates 109). The symbolic and allegorical application of Swedenborgianism in much of Le Fanu's writing indicated a sophisticated approach to the concept of life after death in reality and literature that Dickens respected. Le Fanu's supernaturalism was complex, a combination and deconstruction of the discourses of his core Huguenot values, radical Romantic philosophy, Enlightenment science, and the literary Gothic tradition. It is therefore hardly surprising that the master of the supernatural should find the contemporary craze for Spiritualism trivial, if not downright annoying. Following Browning's lead in "Mr. Sludge, 'The Medium' " (1864), Le Fanu set out to address the effects of "that foolish spiritrapping" in his 1866 serial *All in the Dark* (Le Fanu 18).[2]

All in the Dark was serialized in the *Dublin University Magazine* from February to June 1866, sitting between *Guy Deverell* (1865) and *The Tenants of Malory* (1867). It was published by Bentley in two volumes—rather than the more usual "three-decker" format—and was not a commercial success, leading the author to confess to George Bentley that "I am half sorry I wrote 'All in the Dark' with my own name to it" (Mc Cormack 233). In an apparent stylistic digression, *All in the Dark* is an easy going Victorian romance. There

---

2. *All in the Dark* is not an easy novel to locate, so I am working from the single volume Downey & Co edition of 1898.

is no intrigue, no torture, no suicides, libertines, mad governesses, mysterious rooms, and definitely no foul play. Instead, a young bourgeois Everyman must conquer financial insecurity and the English class system to win the hand of a lady.

There are, however, ghosts.

Le Fanu critics generally disregard *All in the Dark*. Nelson Browne dismisses it as "the history of a village wooing," adding that it "provides little to attract the general reader" (56–57). W. J. Mc Cormack similarly describes it as "a colourless tale of village wooings," and finds it "universally disappointing" (232), while Norman Donaldson takes a hacking swing, asserting that "The consensus declares it to be the poorest of Le Fanu's novels" (x).

This common, indifferent critique could, however, indicate a contextual misinterpretation. If anything, *All in the Dark* initially suffered from a branding problem, representing, as it did, a radical change of style on the part of the author of *Uncle Silas*, and one with which his public were not in tune. "I am now quite convinced it is a great disadvantage to give the public something quite different from what your antecedents had led them to expect from you," Le Fanu told Bentley, adding "although it may be better" (Mc Cormack 233). The popular historical novelist William Harrison Ainsworth had similarly suffered at the hands of his own author function a few years previously with his semi-autobiographical serial *The Life and Adventures of Mervyn Clitheroe* (1852). A contemporary setting combined with a satiric deconstruction of his more familiar Gothic style found no favor with his fans, and Ainsworth was forced to abandon his new style in favor of the formulaic romances that fed his family (Carver 346–47). Only Nicholas Rance seems to get the point regarding *All in the Dark*, placing the quirky novel within a "contemporary extra-literary debate" concerning ghosts and the latest religious import from America. *All in the Dark*, argues Rance, is a "squib on spiritualism" (60–61).

All in the Dark is no mere squib however. It is much more complex than the critical heritage allows. It is, indeed, a satire, and it enables Le Fanu to express his opinions on a credulous bourgeoisie "addicted to the supernatural" (37). In addition, the text also, rather more slyly, interrogates its author's own work and the genre which it defines. *All in the Dark* is a *Northanger Abbey* for the Victorian Gothic, but it is a parody that did not, apparently, suit the times, when ghost stories were voraciously consumed, and hauntings were reported in the press like any other news story. On closer reading, however, *All in the Dark* is at once both a Gothic comedy and a serious cultural critique.

All in the Dark is abstractly narrated in the first person by an unidentified cousin of the protagonist, the orphan William Maubray. Maubray is at Cambridge, and is supported by his aunt, Miss Dinah Perfect of Gilroyd Hall, Saxton. Saxton is a real village in North Yorkshire, although the affected naming of the "Hall," in fact "an old red-brick house of moderate dimensions" (1), suggests either a Victorian bourgeois modernization of the more traditional Gothic space, or a downright pastiche. The Perfects are a once great but now waning bloodline, usurped by the Trevors of Revington who are, in turn, not as landed as they once were either. In a motif common to Le Fanu, both families can be read as symbols of the dying caste of the Protestant Anglo-Irish, while the setting resembles Southern Ireland over Northern England.

Maubray is in love with the rather frosty Violet Darkwell, Dinah's other ward, but as a penniless student he cannot propose marriage. Violet, meanwhile, has attracted the attention of the wealthy Vane Trevor, and Dinah is hopeful of a union. The novel's principle proairetics therefore concern Maubray's attempts to undermine Trevor, gain an independent income, and win Violet. This is the "village wooing," and is a pretty standard "rags to riches" romance. Maubray eventually gets the girl, inherits Gilroyd, and gains a title. But the text is doubled. There is a parallel narrative inverting and subverting the realist.

Setting the scene for a contemporary Gothic burlesque, the narrator describes the story as a "romance of the shrubbery" in gentle suburban mockery of Radcliffe (44). He also cites Lewis, comically comparing the cadaverous Dinah to the "apparition of the Bleeding Nun" (27). In an Austenesque move, intertext combines with subtext in the relationship between Maubray and his aunt and her relationship with "those wonderful queer books from America" (37):

> It was about this period, as we all remember, that hats began to turn and heads with them, and tables approved themselves the most intelligent of quadrupeds; chests of drawers and other grave pieces of furniture babbled of family secrets, and houses resounded with those creaks and cracks with which Bacon, Shakespeare, and Lord Byron communicated their several inspirations in detestable grammar, to all who pleased to consult them.
>
> Aunt Dinah was charmed. Her rapid genius loved a short-cut, and here was, by something better than a post office, a direct gossiping intimacy opened between her and the people on t'other side of the Styx. She ran into this as into her other whimsies might and main, with all her heart and soul. She spent money very wildly, for her, upon the gospels of the new religion, with which the transatlantic press was teeming. (5–6)

Aunt Dinah has become a Spiritualist, and while Maubray privately considers this to be "All bosh and nonsense" (19) he is, however, a consumer of Gothic narrative (no doubt including the work of Le Fanu):

The student, as I have said, had a sort of liking for the supernatural, and although now and then he had experienced a qualm in his solitary college chamber at dead of night, when, as he read a well-authenticated horror, the old press creaked suddenly, or the door of the inner-room swung slowly open of itself, it yet was "a pleasing terror" that thrilled him.[3] (40)

This sensibility drives the ambivalently supernatural dimension of the plot, while also foregrounding the narratological receptivity of Victorian culture for the occult through their familiarity with the discourse of the literary Gothic.

Dinah's head, we are told, is "full of the fancies and terrors of a certain American tome," that is identified as the eight-volume *Revelations of Elihu Bung, the Pennsylvanian Prophet* (5). This would appear to be a lampoon of Andrew Jackson Davis, while also an amalgam of American Spiritualist literature in general. If Le Fanu had a particular target in mind for "Elihu Bung" it was probably Daniel Dunglas Home (1833–1886). Home was a Scottish *émigré* settled in Connecticut who went on to become, in the words of historian Ruth Brandon, "probably the most famous name in Spiritualism" (Brandon 52). Home had followed Maria Hayden to England in 1855, and conducted hundreds of séances, attracting the endorsement of some very public figures, including Robert Owen, Sir Edward Bulwer-Lytton, Thomas Adolphus Trollope, James John Garth Wilkinson (who edited Swedenborg), and Elizabeth Barrett Browning. Home was a natural showman, and was reported to levitate as well as communicate with spirits. He never charged his clients a fee—instead he accepted their "hospitality." Robert Browning detested Home, and based "Mr. Sludge" upon him, while Sir Arthur Conan Doyle described him as "a very great man" (Stashower 92).

Unlike Browning, Le Fanu is not so much interested in mediums as their influence on amateurs and dedicated followers of fashion. Dinah is doing it herself, in common with many Victorians who were following the advice of publications like the weekly magazine the *Spiritualist*, which suggested that

Inquirers into Spiritualism should begin by forming spirit circles in their own homes, with no Spiritualist or professional medium present. Should no results be obtained on the first occasion, try again with other sitters. One or

---

3. "A pleasing terror" is a phrase nowadays attributed to M. R. James, and is the title of the Ash-Tree Press edition of his complete supernatural writings. It is quoted from James's article "Some Remarks on Ghost Stories," published in the *Bookman* (London) in December 1929. Le Fanu is paraphrasing Byron: "thy breakers—they to me / Were a delight; and if the freshening sea / Made them a terror—'twas a pleasing fear" ("The Dark Blue Sea," *Childe Harold's Pilgrimage*).

more persons possessing medial powers without knowing it are to be found in nearly every household. (Brandon 43)

In an insightful critique of the "effects theory" of popular culture, Dinah's irritating but essentially harmless beliefs become destructive when she believes her spirit guide, "Henbane," to have prognosticated her doom.

In popular history and, indeed, contemporary Spiritualism, "spirit guides" are often associated with Blavatsky and Olcott's Theosophical Society, founded in New York in 1875, but they have in fact been around much longer. "Henbane"—literally a ruinous and/or poisonous chicken—indicates Le Fanu's awareness that mediums claimed to pierce the veil via an intermediary, a "control" or "spirit" guide, a benevolent and sociable spirit who would facilitate introductions, locate, and steer dead relatives to séances. The fashion was for Native American guides, and this probably originated from the Shaker sects, many of whom believed that "Indian" spirits visited them. The Shakers eagerly embraced Spiritualism while, ironically, their established belief in clairvoyance may well have influenced the Fox family. It could also be conjectured that James Fenimore Cooper may well have had some influence, *The Last of the Mohicans* (1826) being one of the most widely read American novels of the nineteenth century.[4]

Dinah's absolute certainty that "By half-past twelve o'clock to-morrow night I shall be dead!" leads her friend and physician Dr. Drake to diagnose "hysteria" (14, 24). While the narrator equally treats Dinah as basically delusional, he does note the psychology of fear and its very real effects on behavior. "There seemed something real and grisly in Aunt Dinah's terror," which "a little infected" everyone at Gilroyd (24). This is a serious point, although handled with humor, while still teasing the reader with supernatural semiotics. Gothic becomes slapstick when Dinah and Drake blunder into each other in the darkened drawing room, each taking the other to be the spirit guide: "Tall and thin, and quite unrecognisable by him, was the white figure at the door, with a taper elevated above its head, and which whispered with a horrid distinctness the word 'Henbane!'" (29).

This scene is a subversion of Le Fanu's familiar Gothic application of *chiaroscuro* (a Renaissance term for light modeling in painting), as a textual metaphor and narratological device that, as Victor Sage describes, "dominates the twilight world in which his characters live" (118). The effect is multi-layered. There is suspense, and the familiar competing frames of explanation that characterize a Gothic narrative. In Sage's terms, this is also a

---

4. James Fenimore Cooper regularly attended Leah Fox's New York séances, as did Washington Irving and Henry Longfellow.

"transgressive" moment, an "epiphany of darkness" when "an older universe of 'superstition' and barbarity rushes momentarily into the vacuum left by civilized, 'modern,' reasonable doubt" (4). Le Fanu's Gothic is replete with such moments, only here it is *mise-en-scènically* closer to Laurel and Hardy's *Habeas Corpus* (1928) than the "Strange Event in the Life of Schalken the Painter" (1839).

We are constantly wrong-footed by Le Fanu. The arrival of Dr. Drake and his weird sister immediately suggests a creepy charlatan and his accomplice—in the manner of "Mr. Sludge"—or, at the very least, fellow readers of the *Spiritualist*. Le Fanu toys with us until the first séance, where Dr. Drake appears to be working the room in a form familiar to Victorian skeptics, as well as viewers of *Most Haunted:*

> All being prepared, fingers extended, company intent, Aunt Dinah propounded the first question—
> "Is there any spirit present?"
> There was a long wait and no rejoinder.
> "Didn't you hear something?" inquired the doctor. William shook his head.
> "I thought I *felt* it," persisted the doctor. "What do *you* say, Ma'am?" addressing himself to Winnie, who looked, after her wont, towards her mistress for help.
> "Did you feel anything?" demanded Miss Perfect, sharply.
> "Nothing but a little wind like on the back of my head, as I think," replied Winnie, driven to the wall.
> "Wind on her head! That's odd," said Miss Perfect . . . "*very* odd!"[5] (31)

The question is put again, and answered by an upward heave of the table. "Tilt, Ma'am," triumphantly exclaims Winnie (the maid), while Drake gives Maubray's foot a conspiratorial squeeze (32).

Maubray doesn't quite get it yet, and throughout the séance he performs a textual function not unlike Alcibiades' sneezing fit in Plato's *Symposium*. At the beginning of the candle-lit proceedings—as prescribed by Elihu Bung and which Dinah is taking terribly seriously—Maubray "exploded into something so like a laugh, though he tried to pass it off for a cough" (30). Maubray's inability to disguise his giggles by noisily clearing his throat, constantly undermine the solemnity of the occasion to the point of farce. Drake is playing a more sophisticated game, which Maubray fails to understand, and the farce is increased by his attempts to subvert Drake's subversion by refuting

---

5. The *Spiritualist* also advised that a cool breeze was often the first sign of a presence at a séance.

every supernatural communication the doctor fakes in order to cure Dinah's death wish (another Le Fanu leitmotif). Dinah, meanwhile, tries to keep up. The scene is a masterpiece of comic timing, worthy of the author's great uncle, Richard Brinsley Sheridan:

> "Doctor Drake was changing his position just at the moment, and I perceived no other motion in the table—nothing but the little push he gave it," answered William.
>
> "Oh, pooh! yes, of course, there was that," said the doctor a little crossly; "but I meant a sort of a start—a crack like, in the leaf of the table."
>
> "I felt nothing of the kind," said William Maubray.
>
> The doctor looked disgusted, and leaning back took a large pinch of snuff. There was a silence. Aunt Dinah's lips were closed with a thoughtful frown as she looked down upon the top of the table. (32)

Drake finally manages to "excommunicate" Maubray by recalling that he might have read somewhere that the spirits avoid unbelievers. With Maubray banished, the increasingly exasperated Drake asks Henbane, "Is her [Dinah's] death to take place at the time then appointed?" He manufactures a response to his own question with such enthusiasm that he fires the table across the room, along with his slipper. Dinah lets this go, but then disallows the goal on a technicality:

> "That's a tilt," said the doctor, "that means *no*—a very *emphatic* tilt."
>
> "I think it was a *jump*," said my aunt, sadly.
>
> "No, Ma'am, no—a tilt, a tilt, I'll take my oath. Besides a *jump* has no meaning," urged he with energy.
>
> "Pardon me: when a question is received with marked impatience a jump is no unfrequent consequence."
>
> "Oh, ho!" groaned the doctor reflectively. "Then it counts for nothing."
>
> "Nothing," said Miss Perfect in a low tone. "Winnie, get the table up again." (35)

Drake then proposes lexicographical communication, and manages to spell out "A-D-J-O-U-R-N-E-D," gilding the lily by adding "S-I-N-E D-I-E" and almost spoiling everything:

> "It ends with *die*?" said my poor aunt, faintly.
>
> "*Sine die*, Ma'am. It means indefinitely, Ma'am; your death is postponed without a day named—for ever, Ma'am! It's all over; and I'm very happy it has ended so. What a marvellous thing, Ma'am—give her some more water, please—those manifestations are. I hope, Ma'am, your mind is quite relieved perfectly, Ma'am."

> Miss Dinah Perfect was taken with a violent shivering, in which her very teeth chattered. Then she cried, and then she laughed; and finally Doctor Drake administered some of his ammonia and valerian, and she became, at last, composed (36).

The doctor's relief is palpable—it is almost as if he looks furtively out of the text, catches the reader's eye and delivers a pantomime wink.

Dinah, meanwhile, who 'notwithstanding her necromancy, was a well-intending, pious Churchwoman,' opens the Book of Kings and leads the group in prayer (36). Throughout the novel, Dinah swayeth and wavereth between the Bible and Elihu Bung, the discourses of Christianity and Spiritualism wrestling for supremacy rather than synergy. In the second act crisis, when she disinherits Maubray, Dinah significantly reads from both texts for guidance, but places Elihu Bung on top of the pile.

Drake does wink, in fact, at Maubray, but the young man is beginning to take Spiritualism quite seriously because of its shared codes with the literary Gothic: "'And you are convinced it's true?' urged William, who, like other young men who sit up late, and read wild books, and drink strong coffee, was, under the rose, addicted to the supernatural" (37). Maubray wants to believe. He also, we are later told, "drew altogether upon the circulating library for his wisdom" (53). Drake's response is, however, noncommittal, diplomatic and pragmatic: "Why, you see, as Shakespeare says, there are more bubbles between heaven and earth than are dreamt of by the philosophers . . . I wish to live at peace with my neighbours; and I'd advise you to think over this subject, old fellow, and not to tease the old lady up stairs about it" (38). Drake's doctrine of tolerance could be the moral of the story, were Le Fanu not teasing so mercilessly.

Drake's reverse psychology ultimately backfires however, as Dinah feels her beliefs to be vindicated and continues to consult Henbane on all matters. This leads to a rift with Maubray, when he refuses to follow Henbane's pronouncement that he must enter the Church in order to satisfy a clause in an obscure family will that would grant him an income of fifteen hundred a year (Le Fanu's standard way of evaluating social rank). It is difficult not to read Maubray's horror as an indictment of all who use religion for profit, such as, for example, fake mediums: "to go into the Church without any kind of suitability, is a tremendous thing, for mere gain, a dreadful kind of sin" (104). This conflict pushes Maubray away from Gilroyd and into a Sheridanesque comic "double" plot in which he works as a private tutor under an assumed name, and is mistakenly taken to be an aristocrat *incognito* by his employers, who try to marry off their daughter.

Regarding the supernatural, however, the impressionable Maubray continues to swing between incredulity and credulity in much the same way that his aunt oscillates between religions. This is a subtle and textured textual dialectic that encompasses Enlightenment Reason versus Romantic superstition, Anglo-Irish Protestantism against both Catholicism and nouveau-American Evangelism, novel and anti-novel (Realist versus Gothic), and the contemporary scientific debate on the nature of apparitions.

Moving from the comedy of the séance, Le Fanu puts Maubray through three major supernatural experiences at Gilroyd. Unlike the séance, these scenes are Gothic and narratologically unstable, the style returning to that of *The Purcell Papers*—"I am now going to relate a very extraordinary incident," the narrator explains, "but upon my honour the narrative is true":

> He thought that he heard a heavy tread traverse the room over his head; he heard the same slow and ponderous step descend the narrow back stair, that was separated from him only by the wall at the back of his bed. He knew intuitively that the person thus approaching came in quest of him, and he lay expecting, in a state of unaccountable terror. The handle of his door turned . . . then the door swung slowly open, and in the deep shadow, a figure of gigantic stature entered, paused beside his bed, and seized his wrist with a tremendous gripe. (41)

This episode is left tantalizingly unresolved while Maubray falls in love with Violet, tangles with Vane Trevor, and falls out with his aunt. The apparition returns towards the end of the story, after Dinah and Maubray are reconciled. The frame is the same as the first "vision," the narrator prefacing with "again he had a dream so strange that I must relate it." This time the apparition is Dinah's "double," balefully moaning "Oh, my God! William, I'm dead—don't let me go!" (272). As before, Maubray "distinctly felt the grasp of a cold hand upon his wrist" which "vanished as he recovered the full possession of his waking faculties, leaving, however, its impression there" (275). The style of the classic Le Fanu ghost story is unmistakable— narrative frames of explanation compete while *mise-en-scène* is eerie and unsettling. There is no apparent trace of humor.

To contemporary Victorian readers, however, this scene would be familiar to the point of cliché. As Srdjan Smajić notes: "By the 1860s the strategy of providing suggestive evidence in support of the ghost-seer's vision, yet leaving the question of the ghost's existence undecided, was familiar and predictable—and open to parody" (53). This can be seen, for example, in the article "The Latest Thing in Ghosts," which appeared in Once a Week in 1862. (*Once a Week* was published by Bradbury & Evans, who also owned *Punch*.) Taking his lead from Poe's "How to Write a Blackwood Article"

(1840), the anonymous author[6] offers a creative writing master class on the genre, positing the following scenario as a springboard:

> The ghost of a relative appears before you one night . . . The exact time of the visitation is 12.45 a.m. . . . When you can articulate, you gasp out, "Why, George! What is the meaning of this? How did you get here?" The spirit shakes its head solemnly . . . rises from the sofa, gazing at you fixedly all the time, and disappears. Now, if you understand ghosts—as everyone ought to by this time—you grieve for your friend at once, and prepare your mourning. (102)

Poor old George, of course, dies on the stroke of 12:45 A.M. In this context, the supernatural components of *All in the Dark* are intentionally contrived to surreal and ridiculous proportions—the haunting is, in fact, hyper-real.

Following the rules, Dinah dies (natural causes) shortly after the manifestation of her double. With a gallows humor that characterizes the narrative, Winnie is moved to comment that her mistress makes "a very pretty corpse" (297). The narrator then reveals himself again, in a *Purcell*-esque prelude to the final act, adopting a legalistic, evidentiary perspective in the manner of the *ipsissima verba* that frame many of the Purcell and *Hesselius* stories:

> I come now to some incidents, the relation of which partakes, I can't deny, of the marvellous. I can, however, vouch for the literal truth of the narrative; so can William Maubray; so can my excellent friend Doctor Wagget; so also can my friend Doctor Drake, a shrewd and sceptical physician, all thoroughly cognizant of the facts. If, therefore, anything related in the course of the next two or three chapters should appear to you wholly incredible, I beg that you will not ascribe the prodigious character of the narrative to any moral laxities on the part of the writer.[7] (319)

Maubray is, again, haunted, although in an epistemological lampoon of Gothic ambivalence that anticipates "Green Tea" (1869), he wonders if "all the strong tea he had drunk with old Winnie that night helped to make him nervous" (325). Most notably, this episode plays with Poe, following, and sometimes paraphrasing, "The Raven" (1845) as the increasingly nervous Maubray attempts to rationalize the phenomena that torment him. There is also a dash of Lewis Carroll:

> "Oh! I see; nothing but the shadow, as I move the candle. Yes, only that and nothing more . . . The fire's gone out; the room is cooling, and the wood of

---

6. Possibly "Charles Felix," recently identified as Charles Warren Adams.

7. See Sage (2004), Chapter 1, for a detailed analysis of Father Purcell's rhetorical strategies.

that ridiculous cabinet is contracting. What can it do but crack? I think I'm growing as mad as—" he was on the point of saying "as poor Aunt Dinah," but something restrained him, and he respectfully substituted "as a March hare." (325–26)

In a room locked from the inside, Maubray awakes to find a boot he left outside the previous night placed upon his aunt's final letter like an ominous paperweight. He reads the sign in the context of the Gothic/Spiritualist *zeitgeist*: "Here was a symbol such as he could not fail to interpret. The heel of his boot on the warnings and entreaties of his poor dead aunt! Could anything be more expressive?" (330). In the 1866 Christmas edition of *All the Year Round*, Dickens will make a similar semiotic move in "The Signalman."

As Gilroyd is "a haunted house, and he the sport of a spirit," Maubray turns to the Church for answers, seeking the advice of the Anglican rector, Dr. Wagget (335).[8] Wagget's opinion of "that spiritualism" alchemically blends Enlightenment moral rationalism with a tacit admission that the Reformed Church relies as much on the supernatural as any other religion. On one hand he rejects the occult as dangerous, if not downright Satanic, while on t'other he keeps his metaphysical options open:

> "I don't say there's *nothing* in it . . . there *may* be a great deal—in fact, a great deal too much—but take it what way we may, to my mind, it is too like what Scripture deals with as witchcraft to be tampered with. If there be no familiar spirit, it's *nothing*, and if there be *what* is it? . . . nothing would induce *me* to sit at a *séance*. I should as soon think of praying to the devil . . . The spirit world is veiled from us . . . and we have no right to lift that veil; few do with impunity." (299–300)

What is it indeed? Here, Dr. Wagget apparently serves a similar textual function to Le Fanu's Father Purcell. As Sage has convincingly argued, the motives of the framing narrative of *The Purcell Papers*, in particular the priest's commitment to accuracy, "are evidently not just scientific or a form of disinterested post-Enlightenment anthropology: they are magical and sublime and they involve evidences of the resurrection from the dead" (13). Having delivered his warning to the curious, Wagget's enthusiasm for ghost stories therefore gets the better of him: "'Ha! It *is* the very *best* case I ever

---

8. In the majority of supernatural narratives, haunted protagonists invariably turn to *priests* rather than Anglican ministers like Dr. Wagget. This is a deeply embedded cultural code signifying Catholicism and, therefore, superstition. See, for example, William Peter Blatty, *The Exorcist* (1971), and Jay Anson, *The Amityville Horror* (1977).

heard of or read. Everyone knows, in fact, there *have* been such things. *I* believe in apparitions. I don't put them in my sermons, though, because so many people *don't*, and it weakens one's influence to run unnecessarily into disputed subjects'" (332). He finally compromises both belief-systems by concluding that: "If these things *be*, they form part of the great scheme of nature, and any evil that may befall you in consequence is as much a subject for legitimate prayer as sickness or any other affliction" (332). As it was in nineteenth century culture as a whole, the subject of apparitions remains, thus, unresolved, the position of the Church ambivalent.

By 1866, this was hardly a new debate. As Smajić has argued, an essentially Positivist discourse that "ghost sightings can effectively be explained in physiological terms, namely as optical illusions" runs through Victorian culture, its origins in literature and science. Smajić traces this back to George Berkeley's *An Essay Towards a New Theory of Vision* (1709), and cites Scott's *Letters on Demonology and Witchcraft* (1830), and physicist Sir David Brewster's *Letters on Natural Magic* (1832) as influential "ghost-debunking works" (Smajić 4).[9] When the narrator of Dickens's "The Signalman" shows the haunted railwayman that "this figure must be a deception of his sense of sight . . . originating in disease of the delicate nerves that minister to the functions of the eye" he is indicating an awareness of the on-going scientific debate (23).

The influence of Scott's theory of the supernatural cannot be overstated, and was certainly still common cultural currency in the mid-nineteenth century. Charles Mackay, for example, still cites Scott's *Letters on Demonology* at length when providing examples of spurious "haunted houses" in *Extraordinary Popular Delusions and The Madness of Crowds* (1852)—ghosts being, of course, very popular delusions just then. Scott was concerned with the emotional effects of apparently (though ultimately explicable) "preternatural" experiences on character. As he wrote in his *Remarks on Frankenstein*:

> The author's principal object . . . is less to produce an effect by means of the marvels of the narrations, than to open new trains and channels of thought, by placing men in supposed situations of an extraordinary and preternatural character, and then describing the mode of feeling and conduct which they are most likely to adopt. (613)

The reference to "supposed situations" signals the final removal of the fantastic from the Gothic discourse as far as Scott is concerned, and informs much of his admiration for Radcliffe rather than Walpole or Lewis: "A principal characteristic of Mrs. Radcliffe's romances," he later wrote, "is the rule which the author imposed upon herself, that all the circumstances of

---

9. Brewster attended one of D. D. Home's London séances, and was not impressed.

her narrative, however mysterious, and apparently superhuman, were to be accounted for on natural principles, at the winding up of the story" (Scott xxiv). Scott then applied this rationalization of the supernatural to supposedly "real" hauntings and apparitions in his *Letters on Demonology.* "Even Sir Walter Scott is turned renegade," James Hogg complained in "The Mysterious Bride," as "a great number of people now-a-days are beginning broadly to insinuate that there are no such things as ghosts" (943).

Le Fanu resolves Maubray's haunting by calling the Ghostbusters. Drake and Wagget keep watch while Maubray retires. They polish off a bottle of Old Tom (lightly sweetened gin)—offering another layer of possible explanation for what follows—and Drake nods off, while Wagget significantly expounds on "the precise point on which two early heresies differed" (340). As fire, candles and Wagget dim, a sudden noise is heard, and: "On turning in the direction of the noise, the clergyman saw a gaunt figure in white gliding from the room" (341). The rector is "awfully frightened" and subsequently refrains from visiting Gilroyd after nightfall (348). The doctor is, however, made of sterner stuff and once more stands vigil. When the ghost once more appears, he gives chase.

George Henry Lewes went beyond Victorian optics and Scott's epistemology, and took a semiotic approach to apparitions. "When a man avers that he has 'seen a ghost'," he argued, "he is passing far beyond the limits of visible facts, into that of inference. He saw *something* which he *supposed* to be a ghost" (383). Structurally speaking, the ghost, like the sign, is arbitrary, its meaning established through collective cultural connections. The revenant is an ancient cross-cultural myth and a Gothic archetype. As noted recently in Tod Williams's movie *Paranormal Activity 2* (2010), for example, when people encounter the unexplained they frequently "go straight to ghosts." The chain of inference, in fact, would seem to have no end. The "Hammersmith Ghost" of 1803, for example, turned out to be a cobbler with a grudge dressed in a sheet. Thomas Milward, a local bricklayer, was mistaken for the apparition by an amateur ghost breaker and shot. Milward's corpse was taken to the Black Lion Pub, which is widely reported to be haunted by *him* to this day (Anon, "The Strange Case of the Hammersmith Ghost," par. 4–6).

D. D. Home was never exposed, and the debate regarding the veracity of his powers remains ongoing, although the published diaries of Viscount Adare, *Experiences in Spiritualism with Mr. D. D. Home* (1869), unintentionally reveal him to be dominating and manipulative, while his converts appear complete fantasists. Forty years after the Hydesville events, Maggie Fox confessed that she and Katie had contrived the mysterious noises using their feet and apples on strings. This statement was quoted at length by R. B.

Davenport in *The Death-Blow to Spiritualism* (1888). By then it was too late. Boston millionaire Marcellus Seth Ayer had founded The Working Union of Progressive Spiritualists in 1883, and the alcoholic Maggie was quickly discredited by the new church. Jack the Ripper was getting all the press anyway.

The Gilroyd apparition was, in fact, William Maubray, somnambulist, clad in bed sheets and nightshirt, the hand that gripped him his own. Dr. Drake had solved the mystery, testing his hypothesis and facilitating a cure through shock treatment: he woke up the "ghost." Maubray also finds a final written statement from his aunt, in which she renounces Spiritualism and resolves to "make for future the Bible my only guide" (353). The Reverend Dr. Wagget provides the moral to the story: "If apparitions be permitted, they are no more supernatural than water-spouts and other phenomena of rare occurrence, but, *ipso facto, natural*" (355). The family is no longer "in the dark."

Le Fanu died fifteen years before Maggie Fox recanted, which is a pity, as he would no doubt have found her confession hilarious. *All in the Dark* takes ghosts out of the Gothic and into the real world of charlatan celebrities and their credulous converts. At a deeper level, Le Fanu also explores the narrative form itself, his own work in relation to it, and the borderlands between faith, fact, and fiction. Autobiographically speaking, Maubray's financial insecurity mirrors Le Fanu's own, and before the *deus ex machina* of the inherited title, he considers writing with an insight that suggests the voice of the author over his character: "Literary work, the ambition of so many, not a wise one perhaps for those who have any other path before them, but to which men will devote themselves, as to a perverse marriage, contrary to other men's warnings, and even to their own legible experiences of life in a dream" (244). There is also an echo of the mature author in Dr. Wagget, a complex man who loves to hear and tell ghost stories.[10] James Joyce similarly dramatized—and satirized—himself in youth (Stephen Dedalus) and middle age (Bloom) in *Ulysses* (1922).[11] Narratologically, Le Fanu is also following the inward turn of the nineteenth century Gothic, in which, as Jackson demonstrates, "there is a gradual transition from the marvelous to the uncanny" (24). The Gothic fictions of De Quincey, Poe, and Le Fanu all progressively make the psychological move, in a transitioning cultural paradigm where the supernatural is giving way to the natural but is not yet fully displaced.

Mc Cormack reads *All in the Dark* as a failed attempt at "bourgeois real-

---

10. Mc Cormack also makes some biographical connections worth pursuing, but not the ones I identify (232–33).

11. The "dirty deed" in "Phornix" and "Fiendish" (Phoenix) Park that underpins *Finnegans Wake* is also intertextually related to *The House by the Church-yard*.

ism," arguing that the author was "ill-suited" to adopt the "new style" to which this novel allegedly aspires (232). Yet this would be a paradigm shifting without a clutch. Le Fanu knows exactly what he is doing. He is satirizing the supernatural, and using the narrative codes against themselves, just as the discourses of science, religion, fantasy and realism are colliding in the public arena. *All in the Dark* catches the epistemological crisis of mid-Victorian culture perfectly, and is as much a part of Le Fanu's elegant Gothic project as *The Purcell Papers* and *In a Glass Darkly*.

For Gracie

Works Cited

Adare, Viscount (Windham Thomas Wyndham-Quin). *Experiences in Spiritualism with Mr. D. D. Home*. London: Thomas Scott, 1869.

Anon. "The Latest Thing in Ghosts." *Once a Week* 6 (June 1862): 99–103.

Anon. "The Strange Case of the Hammersmith Ghost." *Real British Ghosts*. Available from: http://www.real-british-ghosts.com/hammersmith-ghost.html (Accessed 14 January 2011).

Brandon, Ruth. *The Spiritualists*. London: Weidenfeld & Nicolson, 1983.

Browne, Nelson. *Sheridan Le Fanu*. London: Arthur Barker, 1951.

Browning, Robert. "Mr. Sludge, 'The Medium.'" In *Dramatis Personae*. London: Chapman & Hall, 1864.

Capron, E. W., and Barron, H. D. *Explanation of the Mysterious Communion with Spirits*. New York: Auburn, 1850.

Carver, Stephen. *The Life and Works of the Lancashire Novelist: William Harrison Ainsworth, 1805–1882*. New York: Edwin Mellen Press, 2003.

Davenport, Rueben Briggs. *The Death-Blow to Spiritualism*. New York: C. W. Dillingham Co., 1888.

Davis, Andrew Jackson. *The Principles of Nature, Her Divine Revelations, and a Voice to Mankind*. Boston: Colby & Rich, 1847. 3 vols.

Dickens, Charles. *Mugby Junction: The Extra Christmas Number of All the Year Round*. London: Chapman & Hall, 1866.

Donaldson, Norman. "Introduction to the Dover Edition." In J. Sheridan Le Fanu, *The Rose and The Key*. New York: Dover, 1982.

Gates, Barbara T. *Victorian Suicide: Mad Crimes and Sad Histories*. Princeton: University Press, 1988.

Hogg, James. "The Mysterious Bride." *Blackwood's Edinburgh Magazine* 28 (174) (December 1830): 943–50.

Jackson, Rosemary. *Fantasy: The Literature of Subversion*. London: Routledge, 1981.

James, M. R. "Prologue." In J. Sheridan Le Fanu, *Madam Crowl's Ghost and Other Tales of Mystery*. London: G. Bell, 1923.

Le Fanu, J. S. *All in the Dark*. London: Downey & Co, 1898.

Lewes, George Henry. "Seeing is Believing." *Blackwood's Edinburgh Magazine* 88 (540) (July 1860): 381–95.

Mackay, Charles. *Extraordinary Popular Delusions and The Madness of Crowds*. 2nd. ed. London: National Illustrated Library, 1852.

Mc Cormack, W. J. *Sheridan Le Fanu and Victorian Ireland*. Oxford: Clarendon Press, 1980.

Paranormal Activity 2. Dir. Tod Williams. Paramount Pictures, 2010.

Podmore, Frank. *Modern Spiritualism*. London: Methuen, 1902. 2 vols.

Rance, Nicholas. *Wilkie Collins and Other Sensation Novelists*. London: Macmillan, 1991.

Sage, Victor. *Le Fanu's Gothic: The Rhetoric of Darkness*. London: Palgrave Macmillan, 2004.

Scott, Walter. "Remarks on *Frankenstein; or the Modern Prometheus*, 1818." *Blackwood's Edinburgh Magazine* 1 (2) (March 1818): 613–20.

Scott, Walter. "Prefatory Memoir of the Life of the Author." In *The Novels of Mrs. Anne Radcliffe*. London: Hurst, Robinson & Co, 1824. i–xxxix.

Scott, Walter. *Letters on Demonology and Witchcraft*. London: Routledge, 1884.

Smajić, Srdjan. *Ghost-Seers, Detectives, and Spiritualists*. Cambridge: Cambridge University Press, 2010.

Stashower, Daniel. *Teller of Tales: The Life of Arthur Conan Doyle*. London: Penguin, 1999.

Stefanidakis, Rev. Simeon. "The Hydesville Events, March 31, 1848." Available from: First Spiritual Temple http://www.fst.org/spirit4.htm (Accessed 5 January 2011).

In the Name of the Mother: Perverse Maternity in "Carmilla"

Jarlath Killeen

Where is mamma?" (255).[1] These are the first words spoken by Carmilla in Joseph Sheridan Le Fanu's 1871 story, but they could have been uttered by two of the other female characters, Laura, the protagonist, and Bertha Rheinfeldt, the ward-niece-daughter of General Spielsdorf, the stake-wielding, vampire-hating zealot. This is a story with a number of absent mothers, and the main events of the plot are set in train by the "disappearance" of Carmilla's mother on a mysterious "life and death" journey, "forcing" her to leave her daughter in the care of Laura's father (253), thus precipitating disaster for the nearby villagers and near-death for Laura herself. Moreover, while Laura clearly regrets the absence of a mother in her life, and twice informs the reader that her mother died "in my infancy" (245), Carmilla also feels in need of some mothering, possibly because her own mother treats her like a piece of property and seems to abandon her everywhere they go. That Carmilla believes herself mother-deprived is evident from her reactions to being deserted. Even if we grant that there is some premeditation involved in depositing Carmilla at the homes of both Laura and the General, she still genuinely appears dismayed by being so discarded: "learning that her mamma had left her here, till her return in about three months, she wept" (255). Again, this may be a charade put on in order to gain Laura's affection, but it is interesting that when she is unceremoniously abandoned with the General she places special emphasis on her desire to see her mother: "In the next room," said Millarca, "there is a window that looks upon the hall door. I should like to see the last of mamma, and kiss my hand to her" (302). Unfortunately, her mother does

---

1. Quotations will be taken from Sheridan Le Fanu, "Carmilla," *In a Glass Darkly*, ed. Robert Tracy (Oxford: Oxford University Press/World's Classics, 1993), 243–319, and placed in parentheses in the main text.

not seem at all anxious to get a last glimpse of her daughter. " 'She is gone,' said Millarca, with a sigh. . . . 'She did not look up' " (302).

Carmilla seems sincerely to regret that her mother did not provide her with a parting glance before moving on. This sense of some tension between mother and daughter is an echo of something Laura notices, spying Carmilla's mother throwing "on her daughter a glance which I fancied was not quite so affectionate as one might have anticipated" (254). Bertha Rheinfeldt is another motherless orphan, although the General's rhetorically inflated way of talking about her puts himself in the place of her parents. She is his more-than-niece, his "darling daughter" (249).[2] We are never told what happened to put Bertha in the General's care, so her missing mother's absence, like that of Carmilla's mother, remains mysterious and unexplained.

Three daughters, three missing mothers. Of course, the dearth of mothers in a Gothic story is not all that surprising because the Gothic is a genre that appears particularly obsessed with absenting them. As Ruth Bienstock Anolik points out in her article "The Missing Mother," "the mothers of most Gothic heroines are dead long before the readers meet the daughters,"[3] and this is certainly true for the mothers of Isabella in *The Castle of Otranto* (1764), Emily in *The Mysteries of Udolpho* (1794), Jane Eyre (1847), Lucy Snowe in *Villette* (1853), Laura Fairlie in *The Woman in White* (1859), Mina Murray in *Dracula* (1897), and, of course, Maud Ruthyn in Le Fanu's *Uncle Silas* (1864). These motherless girls are forced to seek for mother-substitutes where they can find them, often with disastrous results. The absence of the mother in Gothic narratives is compounded by the fetishization of the mother in much Victorian fiction where the figure of the mother is generally transformed into the now notorious angel of the house apostrophized in John Ruskin's "Of Queen's Gardens" (1864), where she is idealized as "enduringly, incorruptibly good."[4] The missing mother becomes an ideal lost and in need of being re-found. Carolyn Dever points out that the number of absent or dead mothers in Victorian fiction is startling, even given the threat to women posed by childbirth, and far exceeds the numbers dying in reality. Dever believes that the absence of the mother causes particular problems for fictional daughters, that it "creates a

---

2. Le Fanu may be echoing the very strange relations between Elizabeth and the family of Victor Frankenstein in Mary Shelley's novel, who is pointedly described as Victor's "more than sister."

3. Ruth Bienstock Anolik, "The Missing Mother: The Meanings of Maternal Absence in the Gothic Mode," *Modern Language Studies* 33:1–2 (Spring–Autumn 2003): 25.

4. John Ruskin, "Of Queen's Gardens," in *Sesame and Lilies* (New York: Charles F. Merrill, 1891), 138.

mystery for her child to solve, motivating time and again the redefinition . . . of female decorum, gender roles, and sexuality" and that "maternal loss prompts anxieties that undermine a protagonist's efforts to construct an identity."[5] The missing mothers of Laura and Carmilla may propel them into ever-closer union as a means to solve the mystery of self-identity.

If mothers are mostly missing, they are certainly also missed. William Veeder recognizes what he calls an "unconscious yearning for a mother" in Laura,[6] and when Carmilla and Laura meet they immediately fall into a familial closeness, so much so that at times Carmilla behaves as if she is actually Laura's dead mother come back to this isolated *schloss* to claim her daughter. On the face of it, the notion that Carmilla's interest in Laura is as much maternal as sexual seems rather outrageous. However, it is important to bear in mind that "Carmilla" is a very slippery text, a close reading of which generates far more questions than answers, and one which tends to cause confusion and querulousness in its readers. Not the least cause of this confusion is the strange relationship between Carmilla and Laura, a relationship that leaves the story's protagonist as puzzled at the end as it does at the start. Put simply, Laura can't make out why Carmilla is so interested in her, and why she treats her as if she is a lover as well as a friend, and also cannot understand the meaning of the enigmatic statements Carmilla is prone to making, her strange (indeed, bizarre—even for a vampire!) way of talking. At one point, covering her "friend" in kisses, Carmilla whispers, "You are mine, you shall be mine, you and I are one for ever" (264). This is the kind of thing that might be expected from the lips of the love-crazed teenagers Edward Cullen and Bella Swan in Stephenie Meyer's *Twilight* (2005),[7] where it would be rather less puzzling (though still rather silly), or from Catherine or Heathcliff in *Wuthering Heights* (1847) where the characters would find nothing odd about such possessiveness or unwarranted intensity. But unlike these characters, Laura cannot understand what Carmilla means, or why she is saying such things to her. When Carmilla tells her that, "in the rapture of my enormous humiliation I live in your warm life, and you shall die—die,

5. Carolyn Dever, *Death and the Mother from Dickens to Freud* (Cambridge: Cambridge University Press, 1998), xi, xii.

6. William Veeder, "'Carmilla': The Arts of Repression," in *Gothic: Critical Concepts in Literary and Cultural Studies*, ed. Fred Botting and Dale Townshend (London: Routledge, 2004), 3.125.

7. Of course, Edward, like Carmilla, is not really a teenager and both have been alive for more than a century. However, they are both imaged as adolescent and it makes most sense to think of them as perpetual teens.

sweetly die—into mine" (263), Laura tries to puzzle these phrases out but finds that these "agitations and her language were unintelligible" (264). The only explanation Laura can think of is that she and Carmilla are blood relations, and she asks Carmilla directly: "Are we related . . .?" (264).

It is not really clear why a blood relationship would permit or explain Carmilla's over-familiarity with the body (and mind) of her hostess, or why Laura thinks that it would help explain it—though it is obvious that she is desperate to decipher the meaning of both her guest's character and her words—but a couple of pages later we find that, indeed, they *are* related, by blood, through the Karnstein family. When her mother's portrait of Mircalla Karnstein (dated 1698) is returned from the cleaners, Laura is shocked to find that it is the spitting image of her guest: "[the portrait] was quite beautiful; it was startling; it seemed to live. It was the effigy of Carmilla!" (272). Laura "is descended from the Karnsteins; that is, mamma was" (273), and Carmilla confesses that she too is a Karnstein by blood, "a very long descent, very ancient" (273). This means that Laura and Carmilla, maternally (as well as eternally), belong to one another. This maternal blood connection is dangerous for a number of reasons, not least that General Spielsdorf informs both Laura and her father (rather insensitively, I would have thought), that the Karnsteins were "a bad family" with "blood-stained annals" (305), this bad blood now flowing in the bodies of both girls. To Carmilla's apparently innocent question, "Are there any Karnsteins living now," Laura replies "None who bear the name" (273), which conveniently passes over the fact that she is herself a living and breathing Karnstein (especially since we never actually discover what her patronymic is). These details confirm a maternal blood connection between Laura and Carmilla (and Laura's father tells us that his "dear wife was maternally descended from the Karnsteins" [294]), so that the biological chain connecting Mircalla/Millarca/Carmilla, Laura, Laura's mother, and the Karnstein clan, is maternal all the way down.

The maternal blood link between Laura and Carmilla is a significant one, partly because it goes some way to explain the intensity of the relationship between them. Although there is obviously a strong homoerotic element to this relationship, that they are related through maternal blood is, perhaps, even more significant than the probability that they desire each other sexually. Although sometimes disgusted by Carmilla's overt homoerotic caresses,[8] Laura admits that, "I felt rather unaccountably towards the beautiful stranger. I did

---

8. On the homoerotic in the story see Richard Dyer, "Children of the Night: Vampirism as Homosexuality, Homosexuality as Vampirism," *Sweet Dreams: Sexuality, Gender and Popular Fiction*, ed. Susannah Radstone (London: Lawrence & Wishart, 1988), 47–73.

feel, as she said, 'drawn towards her'" (260), a reaction that may be due not only to a (repressed) sexual desire for her guest (though also that),[9] but to their familial connection. Victorian doctors were particularly interested in what daughters inherited from their mothers, and most seem to have believed that a mother's hereditary disorders were likely to be passed on to their daughters and on down the female line. For this reason, many warned mothers with a background of family illness (whether physical or mental) to refrain from reproduction if at all possible as the threat of "infection" was particularly high. Insanity was a condition believed to be passed from mother to daughter with terrifying ease, since, as the Victorian physician Henry Maudsley insisted: "insanity descends more often from the mother than the father, and from the mother to the daughters more often than to the sons."[10] Famously, in *Jane Eyre* this assumption forms the basis of Mr. Rochester's conviction that Bertha Mason is mad and needs to be locked up. He finds out that, "Her mother, the Creole, was both a madwoman and a drunkard! . . . Bertha, like a dutiful child, copied her parent in both points."[11] As Elaine Showalter argues, "Brontë's account echoes the beliefs of Victorian psychiatry about the transmission of madness: since the reproductive system was the source of mental illness in women, women were the prime carriers of madness."[12] Given that Laura and Carmilla are also maternally connected via the "bad blood" of the corrupt Karnsteins, the likelihood of their being infected by family malignancy is, therefore, quite high.[13] They are indeed "related," a relation in which Laura's mother's always already corrupted womb forms the nexus, a womb perhaps imaged in the blood-filled Karnstein coffin in which Carmilla floats fetus-like towards the end of the narrative: "the leaden coffin floated with blood, in which to a depth of seven inches, the body lay immersed" (315).

So, they are definitely maternally related, but Carmilla also behaves as if she wants to be considered *in loco matris* quite a number of times in the story. As well as caressing Laura lovingly during her stay in the *schloss*, Carmilla re-

---

9. On Laura as a "repressed" lesbian, see Veeder 120.

10. Henry Maudsley, *The Physiology and Pathology of the Mind* (London: Macmillan, 1867), 216.

11. Charlotte Brontë, *Jane Eyre*, ed. Michael Mason (London: Penguin, 2003), 326.

12. Elaine Showalter, *The Female Malady: Women, Madness and English Culture, 1830–1980* (London: Virago, 1987), 67.

13. On insanity and "Carmilla," see Helen Stoddart, "'The Precautions of Nervous People Are Infectious': Sheridan Le Fanu's Symptomatic Gothic," in *Gothic: Critical Concepts in Literary and Cultural Studies*, ed. Fred Botting and Dale Townshend (London: Routledge, 2004), 106–14.

sorts to "murmured words" which "sounded like a lullaby" to Laura, "soothed" her "resistance into a trance" (264). This maternal behavior is merely a repetition of the actions of eight years previous. During Laura's first nightmare when she was six, Carmilla appeared to her at the side of the bed, "with her hands under the coverlet" (the sexual link emerges immediately). Laura is "whimpering" at the time, and preparing for "a hearty bout of roaring" (that is, behaving like an anxious baby rather than someone aged six), when this mother-substitute begins to soothe her: "she caressed me with her hands, and lay down beside me on the bed, and drew me towards her, smiling; I felt immediately delightfully soothed, and fell asleep again" (246). Victorian parenting manuals all make it clear that Carmilla is behaving precisely as a bad mother would in such circumstances. The main advice given concerning children who woke in the night and wailed for their mother emphasized the necessity of allowing children to "cry it out" rather than soothe and comfort. Samuel Smiles warned that crying was beneficial to children and that infants "cry in default of exercise, or rather, for exercise."[14] Mrs. Beeton's Book of Household Management (1859–61) was particularly scathing of any mother (or nurse) who made the mistake of actually getting into bed with a crying baby:

> We must strenuously warn all mothers on no account to allow the nurse to sleep with the baby, never to lay down with it by her side for a night's rest, never to let it sleep in the parents' bed, and on no account keep it, longer than is necessary, confined in an atmosphere loaded with the breath of many adults.[15]

Of course, Laura is six years old at this time and not a baby, but, deprived of her mother's care in her early days and years, she has clearly not grown out of her infantile desires and needs.

Given that Carmilla has broken the maternal rules, what happens next is not as much a surprise as might be imagined. Laura records that she "was wakened by a sensation as if two needles ran into my breast very deep at the same moment" (246). This is unexpected, not, though, because a breast is being bitten, but because, initially at least, it appears to be the wrong breast. Given that Carmilla has taken on the mothering role, then it should be her breast that is gnawed (as a prelude to suckling), rather than her daughter's. At this moment, a horrific transformation takes place and when the maternal Carmilla bites into

---

14. Samuel Smiles, Physical Education; or, The Nurture and Management of Children (Edinburgh: Oliver & Boyd, 1838), 95.

15. Mrs. Beeton's Book of Management, abridged edition, ed. Nicola Humble (Oxford: Oxford University Press/World's Classics, 2000), 488.

the breast of her child she becomes a hybrid of mother and baby. Veeder points out that, "As a vampire [Carmilla] is infantile as well as maternal. She is a demonic shadow mother to motherless girls; but these girls function as Carmilla's 'mother' when her vampiric, sexual needs drive her to suck from their breasts."[16] Le Fanu lived through a period of major change in breastfeeding practices in Britain. Whereas in the eighteenth century wet nursing was all the rage, by the turn of the nineteenth century women were increasingly being told to suckle themselves (*except* when they came from a family of bad blood), and by the mid-nineteenth century the majority of children were being breast fed by their own mothers. Valerie Fildes, probably the foremost expert on breastfeeding history, maintains that, "the incidence of private wet nursing steadily decreased as the [nineteenth] century progressed."[17] In this story we have a woman who certainly behaves like a (bad) mother, who soothes her child's crying, sings a lullaby to her to put her back to sleep, rocks her in her arms, but, instead of then making her breast available for suckling, perversely attacks the breast of her needy offspring. Carmilla would seem to be not so much the murdering mother *á la* Lady Macbeth, who would, "even as the baby was smiling up at me . . . have plucked my nipple out of its mouth and smashed its brains out against a wall," but the devouring mother who turns on her children in order to consume them for her own nourishment.[18] This is a reversal she continues thirteen years later when she turns up again in Laura's house and begins to suckle on her loving "daughter" nightly.

Carmilla is certainly gaining sustenance by feeding on her daughter-turned-mother Laura. She also appears in serious need of some kind of nourishment. Carmilla is the kind of Victorian mother who would never have been encouraged to breastfeed her children anyway. As well as inheriting bad blood from the Karnsteins, she displays a number of the symptoms of biological pollution. Sally Shuttleworth has demonstrated that quite a number of women were advised not to breastfeed by the medical establishment, including those who manifested signs of physical weakness (evident in pallor, insipidity, languidness), as they would be sure to pass on this weakness to their children through blood and milk. Shuttleworth quotes Sarah Ellis's *The Women of England, their Social Duties and Domestic Habits* (1838) which lamented that, "By far the greater portion of the young ladies . . . of the present day, are distin-

---

16. Veeder 213.

17. Valerie A. Fildes, *Wet Nursing: A History from Antiquity to the Present* (Oxford: Blackwell, 1988), 204.

18. For an interesting examination of the "archaic mother," see Barbara Creed, *The Monstrous-Feminine: Film, Feminism, Psychoanalysis* (London: Routledge, 1993), 16–29.

guished by a morbid listlessness of mind and body, except when under the influence of stimulus, a constant pining for excitement."[19] Carmilla displays
many signs that she is a woman whose "uterine economy"[20] is seriously awry.
The perpetual tiredness she complains of, the "listless" look she manifests
(271), her "languid—very languid" movements (263), the "bodily languor"
(265) evident in her actions are all indications of a serious biological disorder.
Indeed, the need to feed, both on Laura's blood and on that of the local village
girls, suggests a cannibalistic longing on Carmilla's part that can also be found
haunting the Victorian literature on maternity. One case, which repeatedly
crops up in this literature, is that of a mother who was driven by an ovarian
ailment to kill, consume and then pickle her poor husband.[21] Certainly, Carmilla displays many of the symptoms of a woman whose menstrual cycle is
causing her to act in bizarre ways. The vision of Carmilla standing at the end
of Laura's bed covered with blood evokes the image of the menstruating
woman, and unruly menstruation was blamed for many "problems" experienced by Victorian women.[22] In her doctoral thesis on the "menstruous-
monstrous," the tendency for the menstruating woman to be considered freak-
ish in Western culture, Maria Parsons directs particular attention to the theories of Dr. Edward Tilt, whose *The Change of Life in Health and Disease: A
Practical Treatise on the Nervous and Other Afflictions Incidental to Women at the
Decline of Life* (1857) diagnosed what he called "pseudo-narcotism" in some
menstrual patients, a condition that would cause listlessness, weakness,
drowsiness, a delicate and limpid complexion, and sleep walking—each of
which symptoms are displayed by Carmilla.[23] When she has somehow managed to escape from a locked room without opening the door, it is put down to
the fact that she is somnambulant, and she certainly confesses that she walked
in her sleep when she was young (286). This sense that Carmilla's weirdness is
connected to her menstrual cycle is reinforced by repeated references to the
moon, whose association with and partial control over menstruation was

---

19. Sally Shuttleworth, "Demonic Mothers: Ideologies of Bourgeois Motherhood in
the Mid-Victorian Era," in *Rewriting the Victorians: Theory, History, and the Politics of
Gender*, ed. Linda M. Shires (London: Routledge, 1992), 34–35.

20. Ibid. 32.

21. Ibid. 33.

22. Marie Mulvey-Roberts, "Menstrual Misogyny and Taboo: The Medusa, Vampire,
and the Female Stigmatic," in *Menstruation: A Cultural History*, ed. Andrew Shail and
Gillian Howie (London: Palgrave, 2005), 159.

23. Maria Parsons, "'The Menstruous-Monstrous': Female Blood in Horror" (Ph.D.
diss.: Trinity College Dublin, 2009), 110ff.

widely believed. Carmilla appears on a night when Mademoiselle De Lafontaine declares that the moon shines "with a light so intense . . . that it indicated a special spiritual activity," a night when it is "full of odylic and magnetic influence" (251). Such associations between menstruation and vampirism have implications for the version of woman being imaged by Carmilla, as they essentially make the menstruating woman a figure of monstrosity, danger and horror. There is a long history of associating the menstruating woman with supernatural and monstrous power, configuring her as polluted and abjected, and this is particularly the case when the woman is in her adolescent years. As Shelley Stamp Lindsey emphasizes, "Poised between natural and supernatural realms . . . the menstruating adolescent girl occupies a liminal state, an object of both aversion and desire,"[24] and this is precisely the reaction Laura experiences when close to Carmilla. Although she is fearful and rather disgusted by Carmilla's physical and mental closeness, she confesses, "I did feel, as she said, 'drawn towards her,' but there was also something of repulsion" (260).

Given all these monstrous, horrific associations connecting Carmilla, menstruation, vampirism, insanity, uterine irrationality and biological corruption, her perverse maternal/infantile relationship with Laura would seem to be a version of the corrupted image of the mother and child that "experts" on child rearing and maternity cautioned against again and again throughout the nineteenth century. Carmilla is the monstrous mother who feeds on her own children; she is also an evil baby who drains the energy from the mother who gives her suck. That she feeds on Laura's breast only when Laura is asleep recalls a striking passage from *Mrs. Beeton's Book of Household Management*. This domestic manual for women contained a long and involved chapter, written not by Mrs. Beeton herself, but by a surgeon friend, on "the Rearing, Management, and Diseases of Infancy and Childhood." Perhaps the most memorable piece of advice dished out by this surgeon was the warning against allowing an infant to continue to breast feed after the mother had gone to sleep:

> The evil we now allude to is that most injurious practice of letting the child *suck* after the mother has *fallen asleep*, a custom . . . which, as we have already said, is injurious to both mother and child. It is injurious to the infant by allowing it, without control, to imbibe to distension a fluid sluggishly secreted and deficient in those vital principles which the want of mental energy, and of the sympathetic appeals of the child on the mother, so powerfully produce on the secreted nutriment, while the mother wakes in a

24. Shelley Stamp Lindsey, "Horror, Femininity, and Carrie's Monstrous Puberty," in *The Dread of Difference: Gender and the Horror Film*, ed. Barry Keith Grant (Austin: University of Texas Press, 1996), 284.

state of clammy exhaustion, with giddiness, dimness of sight, nausea, loss of appetite, and a dull aching pain through the back and between the shoulders. In fact, she wakes languid and unrefreshed from her sleep, with febrile symptoms and hectic flushes, caused by her baby vampire, who, while dragging from her, her health and strength, has excited in itself a set of symptoms directly opposite, but fraught with the same injurious consequences—"functional derangement."[25]

It is highly likely that this memorable image influenced Le Fanu in writing the scene where a sleeping Laura is bitten on the breast by her baby vampire Carmilla. As a menstruating, adolescent, quasi-mother, suckling child, and vampire, Carmilla is a very complicated figure.

One image of Carmilla sucking from Laura's breast is echoed just over twenty-five years later by that of the vampiric Lucy Westenra and the children she kidnaps in Bram Stoker's *Dracula* (1897), a novel very much influenced by Le Fanu's story. In this scene, the Crew of Light are waiting in the cemetery for the vampire Lucy to return. In the darkness they see her carrying a child, but are unsure what she is doing to it because at first it appears as if the child is nursing on Lucy's breast. However, on closer inspection in the moonlight—an indication that there is something of the menstruous-monstrous about Lucy's vampirism as well—they discover that she is in fact sucking on the child, like Carmilla on Laura, in a reversal of the "natural" relations between mother and child:

There was a long spell of silence, big, aching, void, and then from the Professor a keen "S-s-s-s!" He pointed, and far down the avenue of yews we saw a white figure advance, a dim white figure, which held something dark at its breast. The figure stopped, and at the moment a ray of moonlight fell upon the masses of driving clouds, and showed in startling prominence a dark-haired woman, dressed in the cerements of the grave. We could not see the face, for it was bent down over what we saw to be a fair-haired child. There was a pause and a sharp little cry, such as a child gives in sleep, or a dog as it lies before the fire and dreams . . . With a careless motion, she flung to the ground, callous as a devil, the child that up to now she had clutched strenuously to her breast, growling over it as a dog growls over a bone. The child gave a sharp cry, and lay there moaning.[26]

Lucy is certainly a horrifying creature here as far as the novel is concerned, and there is no real indication that there is any alternative to Van Helsing's

25. *Mrs. Beeton's Book of Management* 489.

26. Bram Stoker, *Dracula*, ed. Maurice Hindle (London: Penguin, 2003), 225-26.

insistence that they stake her, cut off her head, and stuff her mouth full of garlic. It may seem logical, then, to read the scene between Carmilla and Laura as indicative of the monstrously unsympathetic nature of the female vampire, and to conclude that her perverted motherhood warrants destruction as Lucy's does. The men in the story certainly come to this conclusion, and General Spielsdorf speaks of Carmilla's "accursed passion" (249) and calls her a "fiend" (295), a "monster" (306).

To come to the same conclusion as the General, however, would be to ignore the fact that Le Fanu consistently treats Carmilla far more sympathetically than Stoker does his female vampires.[27] Interestingly, a similar scene is found in *Breaking Dawn* (2008), the fourth book in the *Twilight* series, after Bella has given birth to her own vampire baby and takes it into her arms. The baby immediately bites her breast:

> By the time I looked, it was too late. Edward had snatched the warm, bloody thing out of her limp arms. My eyes flickered across her skin. It was red with blood—the blood that had flowed from [the baby's] mouth, the blood smeared all over the creature, and fresh blood welling out of a tiny double-crescent bite mark just over her left breast.[28]

Although this is certainly a horrific scene, the baby is not configured as evil because of its actions. It simply needs nurturing, and Bella does not reject it.[29] Similarly, although Laura feels pained and frightened by the nightly visits of Carmilla and the bites on her breast, even after she discovers that Carmilla is a vampire she does not disown her or ever mention approving of the actions taken by her father and the General in wiping her out. Indeed, even after hearing the story of how Millarca caused the death of Bertha, and witnessing Carmilla's transformation in the graveyard after being attacked by the General, she is more disturbed by Carmilla's disappearance than apparently capable of joining the dots together and working out that her guest is the source of the plague they have all been suffering from: "I was glad, being unspeakably fatigued when we reached home. But my satisfaction was changed to dismay, on discovering that there were no tidings of Carmilla" (314).

Although the nightly attacks on her cause a certain amount of pain, the

27. See Nina Auerbach, *Our Vampires, Our Selves* (Chicago: University of Chicago Press, 1995), 38–53.

28. Stephenie Meyer, *Breaking Dawn* (London: Atom, 2008), 324. My thanks to Meghanne Flynn for this reference.

29. Indeed, it goes on to become the unfortunately named Renesmee, and a major and much-loved character in the rest of the novel.

result of them is the same as breastfeeding itself: they draw "mother and daughter" closer together in an unbreakable bond (because by sharing milk the infant and mother share blood—the Karnstein blood they are connected through anyway). As Carmilla emphasizes to her "mother-daughter" Laura, "I live in you; and you would die for me, I love you so" (274). Moreover, blood-letting was considered by some experts in child care as beneficial rather than dangerous, and the application of leeches was encouraged by many doctors as a means of effecting cures for almost every childhood ailment.[30] The Karnstein blood is passed from breast to mouth between Laura and Carmilla in a sensual and loving manner, drawing mother and child ever closer in a perpetual union. By consuming Laura's blood "milk," Carmilla is in effect taking Laura's identity into her own body and they are to all intents and purposes "one flesh" after the feeding takes place. Hence Carmilla's claim that "I have been in love with no one, and never shall . . . unless it should be with you" (273). In the mingling of blood they both become brides as well as lovers and parents as well as children. This mingling of the identities of the two girls is especially important here because both parties are adolescents and not infants, so their return to the state of maternal feeding effectively instigates a rejection of the integrity of the adult self that is achieved in the maturing process.[31] They are essentially "going back" to a state of oneness at the maternal breast thus rejecting the abjection of the mother—and the mother's fluids—that Julia Kristeva has argued is central to the process of human subjectivity.[32] That they are both adolescents is significant to this act of "regression" since Kristeva theorizes this phase as an "open psychic structure" in which the abject and the repressed can return.[33]

Laura and Carmilla are engaged in a profoundly counter cultural act of "regression," not to the womb, but to the maternal breast. In "Mourning and Melancholia" (1917), Sigmund Freud argues that although the loss of the mother is

30. See Christina Hardyment, *Dream Babies: Child Care from Locke to Spock* (London: Jonathan Cape, 1983), 68–69.

31. Of course, while Laura is nineteen, Carmilla is not "literally" a teenage girl anymore given that she has been alive for two centuries. However, as pointed out earlier in note 7, she certainly appears to be adolescent.

32. Julia Kristeva, *Powers of Horror: An Essay in Abjection* (New York: Columbia University Press, 1982), 90–112.

33. Julia Kristeva, "The Adolescent Novel," in *Abjection, Melancholia and Love*, ed. John Fletcher and Andrew Benjamin (London: Routledge, 1990), 8. See also Karen Coates, *Looking Glasses and Neverlands: Lacan, Desire, and Subjectivity in Children's Literature* (Iowa City: University of Iowa Press, 2004), 142.

necessary to subjectivity, it is also profoundly traumatic, and that in order to overcome this trauma, the child symbolically "eats" the mother so as to take her into the self and make her part of the self: "the ego wants to incorporate the object into itself, and, in accordance with the oral or cannibalistic phase of libidinal development in which it is, it wants to do so by devouring it."[34] Freud's point is that in order for the child to become an individual s/he *must* symbolically "kill" the mother by devouring her. Here, Carmilla as mother does the *opposite*, so that by "devouring" her adolescent "daughter," she prevents the process of subjectivity and maturation from coming to a conclusion just at the moment when nineteen year old Laura is about to cross the threshold into adulthood. Laura is prevented from entering fully into adult life and being molded into the kind of individual that her father wants her to be—Laura is devoured back into the pre-Oedipal matrix, but perhaps for very good reasons.

In this context we should also note that the figure of the mother prepared to kill her own children had very complex connotations in the mid-Victorian period. Of course, the infanticidal mother was most often construed as monstrous within the culture, however, she could also be configured as heroic, a defender of her children against the monstrous designs of male culture. Josephine MacDonagh notes a division between, "on the one hand, those who saw child murder as a crime committed by sexually deviant, unmarried women, and, on the other hand, those who held it to be a crime provoked by archaic or corrupt institutions, which themselves required reform."[35] Against a corrupt and corrupting society, and especially against the miseries going to be inflicted on daughters by fathers and future husbands, the "eating of your own child may be a means of keeping them alive in a hostile environment."[36] Mothers who kill are therefore not always the threats to the safety of their children: sometimes they are their children's saviors.

The division between the monstrous and the saving mother may help to explain one of the most puzzling incidents in the narrative, the strange event of Laura's second waking nightmare:

> One night, instead of the voice I was accustomed to hear in the dark, I heard one, sweet and tender, and at the same time terrible, which said, "Your mother warns you to beware of the assassin." At the same time a light unexpectedly

---

34. Sigmund Freud, "Mourning and Melancholia," in *The Standard Edition of the Complete Psychological Works of Sigmund Freud*, trans. and ed. James Strachey (London: Hogarth Press/Institute of Psycho-Analysis, 1986), 14.249-50.

35. Josephine McDonagh, *Child Murder and British Culture, 1720-1900* (Cambridge: Cambridge University Press, 2003). 4-5.

36. Ibid. 23.

sprang up, and I saw Carmilla, standing, near the foot of the bed, in her white nightdress, bathed, from her chin to her feet, in one great stain of blood. (283)

Laura's absent-present mother here decisively re-enters the story, to warn about an attempt on someone's life. But who is in danger? "I wakened with a shriek, possessed with the one idea that Carmilla was being murdered" (283). Laura interprets the dream as a warning about an impending danger to Carmilla rather than to herself. Subsequent criticism has tended to assume that Laura is simply mistaken, that Carmilla is the assassin being warned against, and that Laura is the intended victim. However, it is not clear on what basis such an interpretation is warranted. It is, after all, Carmilla who *is* "assassinated" at the end of the story by a gaggle of male authorities. Moreover, the word "assassin" has a resonance with an earlier statement by Carmilla when describing the moment when her life changed forever: "I was all but assassinated in my bed, wounded here" she touched her breast, "and never was the same again" (276). In this comment, Carmilla is the assassinated, not the assassin. Moreover, the vision of Carmilla in her white nightdress stained red with blood images menstruation, sexual consummation, and childbirth, and therefore carries a symbolic power linking the vampiric and blood-drinking Carmilla to maternity, and therefore to Laura's mother, placing them on the same side, *both* warning Laura about impending danger. If this is (at least potentially) the case, the question arises of who is being warned against.

Perhaps the threat of the story is not by Carmilla towards Laura, but towards Laura *and* Carmilla, who, in their sharing of maternal blood and in their languid and limpid femininity appear to have returned to the undifferentiated state of pre-Oedipal oneness. Their embrace and acceptance (a partial acceptance in Laura's case) of what Margrit Shildrick calls the "leaky body" of the woman makes both female characters monstrous and dangerous to a culture whose central, idealized figure is the whole, clean, differentiated body of the man.[37] While the men in the story see the vampire Carmilla as disgusting and threatening, Laura hesitates between repulsion and attraction, between the whole body and the leaky body, between father and mother. Carmilla's continued existence—and her mission to bring other (adolescent) women (who have just begun to leak menstruously) into her body through consumption—means she constitutes a serious threat to masculine authority over these women. As is emphasised by Amy D'Antonio in her study of breast feeding in Victorian culture:

---

37. Margrit Shildrick, *Leaky Bodies and Boundaries: Feminism, Postmodernism and (Bio)Ethics* (London: Routledge, 1997). I owe this reference to Maria Parsons.

The nursing dyad, in which mother and child are physically and psychologically unified, stands as perhaps our most powerful image of the pre-symbolic state of boundlessness. And . . . the unbounded nursing dyad appears in Victorian popular fiction as an object of both longing and loathing, of sacralization and vilification. The nursing mother whose dyadic position precludes identifying her as an individual represents the possibility of return to an infantile state of boundlessness in her union with her child. The nursing child, infecting its mother with its own disregard for the symbolic norms and boundaries of self that order civilized society, acquires the same contagious monstrosity accorded to . . . border-transgressing vampires who make new monsters of boundlessness by sucking on their victims.[38]

This nursing dyad also threatens the distinctions between nature and culture so central to our civilization, since it appears as both liminal and "amphibious" (317)—like a vampire—and therefore cannot even safely be dismissed to a realm outside of cultural divisions. The nursing mother and her child cross boundaries and refuse to stay still. They are leaky rather than solid, bodies in process and flux rather than stable and classifiable. As Carmilla points out to Laura, as adolescent girls they are in the course of bodily change and are comparable to "caterpillars." While they will (eventually) become butterflies "when the summer comes . . . in the meantime there are grubs and larvae," in the process of transformation (270). Carmilla's intervention will ensure that neither Laura nor Bertha grow up, never come out of the transition phase, and always remain in flux, in-between, liminal.

This is a powerful reason for the men in the story to need to dispatch the vampire. As she absorbs adolescent girls into her own leaky body, they lose masculine power over them. It is important in this light, that far from showing any attraction to the male, adult world, Laura consistently depicts her father as a far more distant and forbidding (and perhaps even ridiculous) figure than Carmilla. In fact, all the men in the story seem particularly insufferable to Laura and are often depicted in her narrative as threats to her independence. Veeder traces the ways in which the narrative constantly diminishes men in favor of women, by using a fairly small range of adjectives to describe them, particularly the term "old," which functions to distinguish between Laura, Carmilla and the men who constantly intervene in their lives. The physician is "pallid and elderly" (247), the priest who exorcises her room is an "old man" with a "quavering voice" (247–48), "old General

---

38. Amy D'Antonio, "Devouring Anxiety: Victorian Breastfeeding and the Modern Individual" (Ph.D. diss.: Arizona State University, 2009), 4–5.

Spielsdorf" (244) is a "hardy old fellow," Laura's father is the "kindest man on earth, but growing old" (245).[39]

Laura's father is a particularly problematic figure in the story behaving in what can only be described as a bizarre manner throughout the narrative. For example, given that Laura finds the resemblance between the portrait of Mircalla Karnstein and Carmilla to be so striking and proclaims it an "absolute miracle" (a strong expression), the reaction of Laura's father of this revelation is downright outlandish (272). This "beautiful" guest (he refers to her beauty on a number of occasions) turns out to look exactly like one of his dead wife's female ancestors, yet he seems hardly fazed by the fact: "My father laughed, and said "Certainly it is a wonderful likeness," but he looked away, and to my surprise seemed but little struck by it, and went on talking to the picture cleaner . . . while I was more and more lost in wonder the more I looked at the picture" (272). This is only one instance where Laura's father behaves with what seems like sheer stupidity. Faced with the fact that his guest has apparently walked through a locked door twice, he puts it all down to somnambulism as if this could possibly provide an explanation. In fact, he seems intent on elaborating an excuse in order to draw any possibility of suspicion away from Carmilla herself. He declares that he wishes "all mysteries were as easily and innocently [a strange word in the context of sleep-walking!] explained as yours, Carmilla . . . And so we may congratulate ourselves on the certainty that the most natural occurrence is the one that involves no drugging, no tampering with locks, no burglars, no poisoners, or witches—nothing that need alarm Carmilla, or any one else, for our safety" (287). This, after his daughter has complained about nightly attacks, half the village is dropping dead claiming mysterious appearances by a pale woman in the night, and a strange, pallid and beautiful girl who looks exactly like a dead ancestor of his wife has just apparently performed a magician's trick.

This incident helps to highlight other moments when he behaves in an odd manner. When the story opens, he and his daughter have been waiting for a visit from General Speilsdorf and his ward/niece Bertha Rheinfeldt for some weeks, but when he receives a letter informing him that they won't be coming and that Bertha has died, he "quite forgets" to tell his lonely child what has happened, and then abruptly blurts out "the poor young lady is dead" (249). His behavior later in the story is even stranger, however. When he hears the good General is finally on his way to see him—his best friend, a man he has not seen for at least six months, and whose ward has tragically expired since their last meeting—Laura's father is not delighted but "on the

---

39. Veeder 122-23.

contrary, he looked as if he wished him at the bottom of the Red Sea" (291), and decides that instead of waiting for the General to arrive, he will head out with his very sick daughter on an excursion to Karnstein, the now-deserted village where his wife's ancestors once lived, and have a picnic in the graveyard where their crypt is rumored to be. On Laura's perfectly reasonable questions concerning his behavior and her own physical state, he responds in a very mysterious manner: "You shall know all about it in a day or two; that is, all that *I* know," a response that Laura rightly feels is weird: "He turned and left the room, but came back before I had done wondering and puzzling over the oddity of all this" (291). We then find out that he has instructed that Carmilla, the suspicious new arrival, should follow them soon after, and intends that they will all meet in Karnstein later on. Why he should feel a sudden desire to travel to the deserted village of his wife's ancestors just when his daughter is on the verge of death is never made clear, though he indicates he has "business" with the priest there. Is this business the destruction of Carmilla? Is it instead a marriage with her?

The opposition between the "leaky" Carmilla, the maternal dyad of vampire and victim, and the solid rationalist men, including Laura's father, the General, Baron Vordenburg, and the various doctors and priests we are briefly introduced to, help to explain why it is *now* that Carmilla enters the lives of both Bertha and Laura, because the narrative strongly hints that they are both about to be married off. That Laura's father intends to marry her to the General is indicated a number of times in the story, particularly in the scene where he attempts to prevent the General from meeting with Laura while she is so ill. He is particularly anxious that the General does not see Laura in her present state—"I wish that you had been perfectly well to receive him" (291)—which, together with his later comment that he hoped that the General was going to "claim the title and estates" of the Karnsteins, suggests he wants to unburden himself of his daughter on an "old" and rather frightening man (294).[40] Moreover, given that the General was previously meant to visit with his ward (who is about the same age as Laura), some kind of reciprocal sexual/marriage exchange may have been on the cards. It is only Carmilla's "killing" of Bertha that prevents her from being brought to Laura's home for this exchange, and then, just before Laura is about to be severed from the mother forever and forced into adulthood through marriage and therefore penetration by a male and breaking of the hymen by the General (who appears to like decapitating women), Carmilla reappears and also prevents this marriage from taking place.

---

40. This possibility is also noticed by Elizabeth Signorotti, "Repossessing the Body: Transgressive Desire in 'Carmilla' and *Dracula*," *Criticism* 58 (1996): 617.

Of course, the slippery and ambiguous language of the story means that these impending marriages are only hinted at rather than described openly, but this is a tale that returns time and again to the need for readers to pay close attention and interpret carefully. As Veeder has pointed out, "techniques to make us active readers occur throughout 'Carmilla' . . . exegetical situations proliferate."[41] The active reader can surely read the male manipulation going on behind Laura's rather naïve and ignorant eyes.[42]

Certainly, fathers and father figures are generally very threatening and/or stupid in the story. The inanities or suspicious behavior of Laura's father have already been outlined, but there are a host of incompetent male figures populating this narrative, often with suitably comic names. Moreover, even in the narrative frame, male incompetence and/or malevolence are evident. The story was originally published as a two-part serial in the short-lived periodical, the *Dark Blue*, without a narrative frame, but when Le Fanu came to add it to *In a Glass Darkly* (1872), he appears to have forgotten that in a number of places in her narrative, Laura assumes she is writing to a woman: "a town lady like you" (265). "Carmilla," as it appears in the collection, is supposed to be complied from a series of letters sent by Laura to Doctor Martin Hesselius, the metaphysical doctor, and extracted from his "case notes"—indeed, the Editor tells us that the doctor has written a medical paper to explain the story, but which he declines from providing to the present reader as it would have no interest for the "laity" (243). Because of this new placing, the story which still contains indications of being written by one woman to another, now appears to have somehow been placed with Hesselius, who effectively usurps the position of the original female addressee. Of course, this is more or less simply an editorial slip-up on Le Fanu's part, but interpretively it carries symbolic weight in a story where men are generally seen to be threatening towards women and wanting them out of the way. Moreover, while the male Editor tells us that although he thinks Laura a competent and "intelligent" narrator, he also bizarrely insists that, "she, probably, could have added little to the Narrative which she communicates

---

41. Veeder 119.

42. One understandable response to this argument might be that an over-active reader might indeed see all kinds of nefarious motivations behind the actions of Laura's father, but that this would be projection rather than interpretation. See Richard Haslam, "Irish Gothic: A Rhetorical Hermeneutics Approach," *Irish Journal of Gothic and Horror Studies* 2 (2007). http://irishgothichorrorjournal.homestead.com/index.html. Obviously, I think that the story itself constantly draws attention to cognitive gaps and invites such interpretive speculation.

in the following pages," another act of male containment of female authority and power (243).[43]

That Laura's father is prepared to "sacrifice" her to the General—for some vague, probably sexual and financial reasons of his own—places him as one of a long line of men in Irish Protestant fiction who are willing to dispatch their children for the sake of the tribe. According to Margot Gayle Backus, fiction by Irish Protestants frequently returns to the trope of child sacrifice, where parents are ready to symbolically sacrifice their own children in order to perpetuate the colonial order. The dedication of Laura's father to the maintenance of his English identity, and his class and religious superiority over the Catholic peasants of the nearby village, requires that Laura be married off to the right kind of man. Such parents privilege the heterosexual nuclear "capitalist family cell" terrified by religious, ideological and gender threats to this order.[44] However, I think it unfair to align "Carmilla" with highly conservative, status quo preserving narratives as it presents its male figures in a very unsympathetic light. "Carmilla" is a story that seems genuinely suspicious about the kind of child sacrifice necessary to maintain privilege and well-disposed to challenges to that order.[45] The emphasis in the story on the mother and child dyad, as an alternative to the singular project of adulthood, provides a cogent reason for the ultimately positive version of the vampire given by Le Fanu. 1861 was not only the year when *Mrs. Beeton*'s image of the vampire baby sucking on her maternal victim's breast first impinged on the public. It was also the year when Johann Jakob Bachofen produced his great study of *Das Mutterecht* which insisted that the earliest societies were matriarchal, and that modernity was in great need of a return to a system of social organization centered around the mother in order to recover from the kind of

---

43. A number of critics have pointed to this authorial slip-up, including W. J. Mc Cormack, *Dissolute Characters: Irish Literary History through Balzac, Sheridan Le Fanu, Yeats and Bowen* (Manchester: Manchester University Press, 1993), 146; Veeder 217; Richard Haslam, "Joseph Sheridan Le Fanu and the Fantastic Semantics of Ghost-Colonial Ireland," in *That Other World: The Supernatural and the Fantastic in Irish Literature and Its Contexts*, ed. Bruce Stewart (Gerrards Cross, UK: Colin Smythe, 1998); Signorotti 619.

44. Margot Gayle Backus, *The Gothic Family Romance: Heterosexuality, Child Sacrifice, and the Anglo-Irish Colonial Order* (Durham, NC: Duke University Press, 1999), 127-34.

45. Jim Rockhill has pointed out to me that "Carmilla" is not the only Le Fanu story concerned with such acts of "child-sacrifice," and that two other stories deal with the question more explicitly, and also feature motherless young women: "Strange Event in the Life of Schalken the Painter" (1839) and "Ultor de Lacy" (1861).

general existential anxiety Max Weber has called "disenchantment."[46] Many historians have argued that there was a general feeling throughout Europe in the second half of the nineteenth century that a return to the mother was necessary, a desire evident not only in academic and anthropological studies of motherhood, but in the increase in apparitions of the Virgin Mary. Throughout the century, reports of Marian apparitions came in from all around Europe, including from La Salette (1846), Lourdes (1858), Pontmain (1871), and Knock (1879). As Joseph Cleary has pointed out in relation to these apparitions, while "the meaning and function of the Great Mother patently varies from one to the other . . . what they all appear to share in common is a certain dissatisfaction with some or other element of the project of modernity."[47] The absent mother, the apparitional mother, operates as a grand critique of the alienating forces of modernity—especially as they instantiate in the blundering male fools that populate this story, from Laura's patently idiotic father, to the sexually lecherous General Spielsdorf, to the incompetent doctors, to the vampire-obsessed Baron Vordenburg.

For Le Fanu personally, the preternatural woman may act as a version of his dead wife Susanna, but scholars have noted that he was haunted by a sense of what James Walton calls "the void," and what Victor Sage terms a "rhetoric of darkness" throughout his writing.[48] According to Walton, Le Fanu's interest in the more occult versions of Western knowledge (Swedenborgism, spiritualism, Boehmism), and his specialism in supernatural narratives like "Carmilla," were both propelled by an epistemological and theological "vacancy" negating Anglican orthodoxy and forcing him to take up different avenues to find existential peace again. In "Carmilla" the means of obviating the emptiness of the adult self is by return to the plenitude of the mother-child dyad, and an "amphibious" existence in process and flux rather than one dedicated to rationality and certitude. Certainly, Laura is critically divided: between her present father and her absent mother, between England (her father's homeland) and Styria/Hungary (home of her

---

46. Max Weber, "Science as Vocation," in From Max Weber: Essays in Sociology, trans. and ed. H. H. Gerth and C. Wright Mills (New York: Oxford University Press, 1946), 155.

47. Joseph Cleary, "Into Which West? Modernity, Moving Images and the Maternal Supernatural," Outrageous Fortune: Capital and Culture in Modern Ireland (Dublin: Field Day Publications, 2007), 183.

48. James Walton, Vision and Vacancy: The Fictions of J. S. Le Fanu (University College Dublin Press, 2007); Victor Sage, Le Fanu's Gothic: The Rhetoric of Darkness (London: Palgrave Macmillan, 2004).

mother), between modernity and superstition, the present and the past, the rational and the irrational, this world and the next. Carmilla represents—as a Karnstein, like Laura's mother—precisely what is missing within her home; she resides "in the west" (263), a mythical Irish zone often identified with the feminine and the maternal, what Cleary calls "that much mythicized landscape that has dominated literary representations of the Celtic regions in Europe since at least the nineteenth century . . . the magical 'Celtic West' made famous by Sydney Owenson's national tales, by Arnold and Renan, by Synge and Yeats; it is a version of the West as the place of the romantic sublime stretching with remarkable consistency from the Celtic exoticism of Ossian and Scott to the Irish Literary Revival."[49]

The supernatural vampire-mother Carmilla is a kind of over-determined, overloaded, mythically overflowing version of the oceanic mother into whose blood-relationship the adolescent longs to return. She is a representation of all that is considered "superstitious" and "archaic" by modernity, "the appalling superstition that prevails in Upper and Lower Styria, in Moravia, Silesia, in Turkish Servia, in Poland, even in Russia; the superstition, so we must call it, of the Vampire" (315). In her relations with Carmilla, Laura experiences what Rita Felski has called a "mythic plenitude" as opposed to the life of isolation and loss to which her life with her father had condemned her.[50] Although Laura appears to choose her father against Carmilla, the glimpse Le Fanu provides of her future suggests that this decision is not an easy one. That Laura is forever haunted by Carmilla, continues to hear her step outside the drawing room door, and is actually dead by the time the narrative reaches the Editor is highly suggestive of the possibility that she has ultimately revoked that choice of the father (who is never even given a name) and returned to her mother/Carmilla/feminine plenitude.

With the destruction of Carmilla, the male forces of bureaucratic modernity, the "Imperial Commission" with its "official papers" (316), might seem to have won against the leaky, adolescent vampire. However, the story ends on a profoundly ambivalent note. After all, we are plainly told that those who are bitten by the vampire will themselves become vampires and therefore there is no reason to suppose that Laura and Bertha are not now vampires as well—indeed, Laura's final line indicates that "often from a reverie I have started, fancying I heard the light step of Carmilla at the drawing-room door" (319), and she is herself dead by the time the story is being published. This line might even indicate that far from being finally vanquished, Carmilla is still lurking somewhere. Moreover, even granting the destruction

---

49. Cleary 189.

50. Quoted by Cleary 197.

of Carmilla, where is Carmilla's mother, the black woman in the coach and the man in black at the General's party? If they have not been defeated, has the threat of vampirism (the maternal past) really been suppressed?

That the existence of such a thing as a vampire has been verified by a number of highly important members of the modern establishment is problematic enough. Although, it is true, these men have acted in order to banish the vampire and its superstition forever, if it is a mere fragment of folklore what is it doing existing in the first place? Reasonable men do not believe in vampires, as is demonstrated by Laura's father throughout the story. If the vampire really exists, is modernity safe from revenants? The story echoes the events which first started the craze for vampire narratives in the mid-eighteenth century—and its setting in Styria, which is quite near Hungary, suggests that Le Fanu may have been aware of this celebrated case. In 1732 the London Journal published a report about "blood suckers" in a Hungarian village where the dead had apparently been rising from the grave to feed on the blood of the living. Upon investigation by a venerable team of Hungarian authorities, including doctors, army captains and lieutenants, and legal experts, this claim was apparently authenticated and the authorities dispatched the vampires in the usual manner (stake through the heart, burning). The report on the matter was signed by the authorities involved, and sent to the "Imperial Council of War."[51] When these happenings were reported in the London newspapers they caused a flurry of commentary on the relations between superstition and rationality, the past and the present, the atavistic and the future-oriented, with most insisting that those involved simply had to be mistaken as such things as vampires did not and could not exist. The 1730s "vampire controversy" provided a paradigm for later discussion and narrative depiction of vampires, ranging believers against skeptics, and depicting a band of good and true rational male authorities against the irrational folkloric survival. Laura's father acts as the voice of the skeptics in "Carmilla," dismissing folkloric beliefs as a peasant "infection" (269). It is hardly a coincidence that the exhumation and "execution" of Carmilla is carried out in a similar manner to that of its eighteenth-century Hungarian precursor, and is witnessed by a multitude of "official" men who could verify the truth of what they were saying: "My father has a copy of the report of the Imperial Commission, with the signatures of all who were present at these proceedings, attached in verification of the statement" (316). Superstition, like the maternal body of Carmilla herself, has infiltrated the official records: banishing the vampiric maternal dyad has not really worked.

---

51. A very interesting examination of this event, its reporting in England, and its impact on the understanding of the vampire, is found in Markman Ellis, *The History of Gothic Fiction* (Edinburgh: Edinburgh University Press, 2000), 162–65.

Crossing Boundaries, Mixing Genres in *The Wyvern Mystery*

Sally C. Harris

In an 1870 letter to Joseph Sheridan Le Fanu, Charles Dickens wrote, "I quite agree with you that no story should be planned out too elaborately in detail beforehand, or the characters become mere puppets and will not act for themselves when the occasion arises" (257). As Bert G. Hornback notes in his comment on his reproduction of the letter (259), this letter seems to refer to *The Rose and the Key* (1871). In *Willing to Die* (1872), his last novel, Le Fanu also points toward this approach. In the first section, "To the Reader," the narrator, Ethel Ware, opens with these lines:

> First, I must tell you how I intend to relate my story. Having never before-hand undertaken to write a long narrative, I have considered and laid down a few rules which I shall observe. . . . I adopt them, because they will enable me to tell my story better than, with my imperfect experience, better rules possibly would. In the first place, I shall represent the people with whom I had to deal quite fairly. . . .
>
> My narrative shall be arranged in the order of events; I shall not recapitulate or anticipate. (1)

She hopes to "be clear and true" so that the reader will forgive her "clumsiness" in writing (2). To the narrator, faithfulness to the story and to the characters is more important than adhering to rules of narrative or genre. Here again, the importance of representing characters honestly is stressed, albeit by a character herself. Written just a few years before these two novels, *The Wyvern Mystery* (1869) provides a good example of characters breaking novelistic conventions to "act for themselves." They are characters represented "quite fairly," one may say. Because characters act of their own accord, they can break free from the traditional conventions of specific genres, leading to multiple genres within one work. In *The Wyvern Mystery*, Le Fanu shows us, as he does with boundaries in so many other areas of life, that boundaries in fiction are permeable.

In *Le Fanu's Gothic: The Rhetoric of Darkness*, Victor Sage claims that Le Fanu uses "textual hybridity," reviving Gothic rhetoric and "the discourse of the old Gothic romance, mediated through German folktale, to defamiliarize the contemporary Victorian plot of romantic love, studying erotic passion as a morbid and perverse condition which leads to death" (5, 6). In Le Fanu's works, it seems nothing can stay in its place but must always be breaking boundaries to defamiliarize Victorian as well as twenty-first century readers. *The Wyvern Mystery* is no different. In this study, I explore the ways characters break into or escape from walled in and confined houses. When characters breach these boundaries, the traditional expectations for a genre are undermined and there is a shift in genre, emphasizing that genres, like the characters, cannot be confined to or kept from a specific house or wing of fiction. They break though the defining walls and hedges to challenge the prevailing norm. Throughout *The Wyvern Mystery*, historical, Gothic, realistic, and fairy-tale elements emerge, battling for primacy in the house of fiction.

Le Fanu himself did try to explain the genre of his works. In the often-quoted passage from the preface to *Uncle Silas* (1864), Le Fanu writes that he would rather have his novels associated with "the legitimate school of tragic English romance, which has been ennobled, and in great measure founded, by the genius of Sir Walter Scott" (xxviii). His earlier novel *The Fortunes of Colonel Torlogh O'Brien* (1847) is more similar to Scott's historical romances than Le Fanu's later novels set in England. However, earlier in his preface to *Uncle Silas*, Le Fanu refers to the "death, crime, and, in some form, mystery" that are in the "unapproachable 'Waverly Novels.'" He explains, though, that "no one, it is assumed, would describe Sir Walter Scott's romances as 'sensation novels'" (xxvii). Even here Le Fanu recognizes the difficulty of defining a novel as a specific genre because elements from other genres creep in. Thus, it seems that rather than try to limit the boundaries of a genre, Le Fanu is calling for them to be opened. Only a month before the first installment of *The Wyvern Mystery* (*Dublin University Magazine*, February to November 1869), the author of an unattributed review of Charles Lever's *The Bramleighs of Bishop's Folly* in the *Dublin University Magazine* indicates that Lever's novel "is not what is denominated, in the critical parlance of the day, a sensational tale. It has no terrible crime and no frightful mystery. It has no fiend in human shape. But Mr. Trollope, as well as Mr. Lever himself in former works, has shown that these are not necessary to a bustling story full of interest" (105). If not the author of the review,[1] Le Fanu, as editor, would certainly have been aware of these attempts to differ-

---

1. The *Wellesley Index* has not attributed this review.

entiate sensational novels from realistic ones. Despite his attempts at shunning labels, Le Fanu was considered a sensational writer by most critics. Indeed, *Uncle Silas* seems to have more in common with Gothic novels and sensation than historical romance: an orphan, an evil uncle, decaying mansions, a devious marriage plot, and a murder plot. *The Rose and the Key* has some of these elements, too, with the added sensational elements of an asylum and an illegitimate son. *Wylder's Hand* (1864) includes family houses, inheritances, the threat of marriage for money, and murder. *The Wyvern Mystery* adds fairytale elements as well as realism to some of these Gothic and sensational qualities, intertwining multiple genres within the work.

Based on Le Fanu's earlier story "A Chapter in the History of a Tyrone Family" (1839), *The Wyvern Mystery* moves the events from Ireland to England and delves deeper into the effects of bigamy, or at least divided loyalties of the heart. "Tyrone Family" recounts the tale of a young Fanny Richardson "*ipsissima verba*" (29). Although the fictional collector of stories, Father Purcell, has changed her name when copying her papers, he claims that the teller is "far too deeply and sadly impressed with religious principle to misrepresent or fabricate what she repeated as fact" (30). At the end of Fanny's tale, Father Purcell even mentions that "many will recognise" the tale although it "refers to a somewhat distant date," and that he has not taken "any liberties with the facts" but "adhered to the truth" (135). This story, then, is purported to be historical. Relating her true history, Fanny Richardson recounts her marriage to Lord Glenfallen who then takes her to his ancient estate. In an episode that seems to have informed Charlotte Brontë's Bertha and bigamy plot in *Jane Eyre*,[2] Fanny is attacked in the middle of the night by a blind Dutch woman claiming to be Lord Glenfallen's wife. Lord Glenfallen denies this accusation, and the blind woman is imprisoned and executed. However, Lord Glenfallen is tormented by some inner battle, and he slashes his throat.

There are a few elements of this story that are interesting to note in relation to *The Wyvern Mystery*. First, Lord Glenfallen raises the connection between himself and Bluebeard from Charles Perrault's 1729 collection of fairytales; Lord Glenfallen claims, "I shall be your *Bluebeard*" (75). Additionally, upon their first arriving at the house, he calls it "the enchanted castle" (62). These references signal a combining of the historical and fairytale, one that ends up destroying Bluebeard rather than his wife. Two other episodes incorporate another genre and place "Tyrone Family" in the realm of supernatural legend. The first occurs when Fanny and her family are expecting her older sister home for the first time since her marriage. She has been ill

---

2. For example, see Sage, Beaty, and Kenton.

and is visiting home to improve her health. When the family hears wheels on the drive and clatter at the gates, they believe she has arrived. Even the dogs bark to announce the arrival. The doors are opened in greeting, but no one is there, and Fanny learns that her sister died less than an hour before the noise at the gates. The second event is less fantastic, but still has preternatural qualities. Fanny, when she is being conducted around Lord Glenfallen's house for the first time, is momentarily frightened by a black drape falling across the opening of a room which she is about to enter. Trying to make light of her jumpiness, Fanny apologizes to the servant for being startled. Martha, however, has not seen the drape, and when Fanny turns back, it is no longer there. Supernatural legends and fairytales emerge within Fanny's historical account. Even within the early short story on which *The Wyvern Mystery* is based, genres—albeit story-telling rather than novelistic genres—are intertwined. Of these three episodes, only the last makes it into *The Wyvern Mystery* intact. The visiting wraith is omitted completely, and the Bluebeard references are less overt. The transformation from short story that combines history, fairytale, and fantastic to a novel indicates another interweaving of genres. Even as it transitioned from short story to novel, *The Wyvern Mystery* showed signs of crossing boundaries among genres.

In *The Wyvern Mystery*, it is the setting and characters themselves who seem to impose boundaries for a specific genre. Other characters who "act for themselves" rather than within the limits of what others have prescribe breach those boundaries, mixing the genres. By using isolated houses as the main locations for different parts of the plot as well as the characters' fear of or potential for escape and break-in, Le Fanu shows that limiting a novel and its characters to one genre is impossible if the characters are to be represented truly, acting for themselves. Of the four main locations in *The Wyvern Mystery*, only one seems readily accessible, and that is Wyvern itself. The one description of approaching Wyvern is given early in the novel. As Alice returns from a visit to her aunt, her carriage turns down "the short, broad avenue that leads through two files of noble old trees to the grey front of the many-chimneyed Wyvern" (10). The openness of Wyvern contrasts with the inaccessibility of Carwell Grange. On her first visit there, Alice's carriage drives for two miles under a spreading forest. Then, it enters a "ruder track, with a rather steep ascent" (8), and the driver must dismount to walk the horses to the house. Once there, Alice sees the "piers of stone" marking the entrance to the house under "leafy darkness," and she must peek through a gate with a missing wicket (8). Later, as Alice and Charles arrive at Carwell Grange together, the road and the structures get steeper and narrower as well as more overgrown:

Winding always upward, and steeper and steeper, was the narrow road. The wood gathered closer about them. The trees were loftier and more solemn, and cast sharp shadows of foliage and branches on the white roadway. . . . At last through the receding trees that crowned the platform of the rising grounds they had been ascending, gables, chimneys, and glimmering windows showed themselves in the broken moonlight; and now rose before them, under a great ash tree, a gatehouse that resembled a small square tower of stone, with a steep roof, and partly clothed in ivy. No light gleamed from the windows. (41–42)

Throughout the novel, the journey and entrance to Carwell Grange are described similarly, emphasizing the isolation and dilapidation of the house, distinguishing it from the old but well kept and accessible Wyvern.

The two other primary spaces of action, Marjory Trevellian's cottage and Noulton Farm, are not quite as isolated as Carwell Grange, but they are hedged in by borders. Marjory's cottage is "in the sequestered country, about twelve miles south of Twyford, in a pretty nook formed by a wooded hollow close by the old by-road to Warhampton" (238). Although closer to the road than Carwell Grange, Marjory's house is still isolated since it is only an "old by-road" and is at least two miles from the nearest village. Marjory's old cottage is "shrunk and warped by time" with an "ivy-bound porch" (239). It is this antiquity that leads the narrator to claim, "one might fancy it the very farmhouse in which Anne Hathaway passed her girlhood" (239). Marjory's house is isolated by its location and bordered by time, as if to get there one must travel back centuries. Noulton Farm also has boundaries but of a different nature from Marjory's cottage: "Noulton Farm is a melancholy but not an ugly place. There are many trees about it. They stand too near the windows. The house is small and old, and there is a small garden with a thick high hedge round it" (259). Although the house is closer to a town—Willie and Sergeant-Major Archdale complete their journey there on the autobus— it is surrounded by trees and hedges, an attempt to keep out others or perhaps keep in the inmates. These changes in location indicate a change in genre, and the movement from one location to another is instigated by one character acting in a way that disregards the boundaries another has established.

In *Victorian Renovations of the Novel*, Suzanne Keen argues that many Victorian authors shifted genres within a work in order to create what she calls a "narrative annex" so that the characters may develop or experience more than they would be able to if confined to one specific genre (1–3). This seems as if it might help to explain the shifting locations and, thus, genres in *The Wyvern Mystery*. It does shed some light on Le Fanu's shifting genres. However, the events at Wyvern, Carwell Grange, and Marjory's house cannot be considered annexes because the narratives in those locations are too

long and they comprise the main action of the plot rather than a place outside of the main action for the character to grow. Even with these differences, there is a similarity between Keen's annexes and the settings in *The
Wyvern Mystery*: they show crossovers of genre. Just as Keen's geographical
annexes are different genres allowing a character to break free from the primary genre of the novel, the geographical locations in *The Wyvern Mystery*
represent different genres, changing for each new location as the characters,
by their own actions, cross boundaries.

The novel opens with Alice leaving Oulton to return to Wyvern. Oulton, Lady Wyndale's home, is never clearly described, and other than the
leave-taking in chapter one, no other scene occurs there so it does not become a marker for a genre. Alice's journey from there to Wyvern, including
her side trip, is the main introduction to the multi-genred novel. When Alice asks her driver to turn off the main road to Wyvern, the reader gets a
sense of the danger—Alice leaves the straight and narrow path. Even Dulcibella "dimly apprehended that they were about to deviate from the straight
way home" (5). Although it may be more fear of the squire than fear of what
lies down the new path that unnerves Dulcibella, the danger is still recognized. Here is the possibility of the Gothic: a young woman with only her
servant on a strange road as night falls. The Gothic obliges, and Alice's way
is blocked by another vehicle with a mysterious woman. Allowed to pass, Alice makes it to Carwell Grange, the dilapidated old manor that seems to rise
out of the forest. Here is the Gothic danger for Alice, yet she is turned away
on her first visit because the "master" is not at home. This enables Alice to
retrace her way out of the Gothic setting and return on her "direct journey
to Wyvern" (10). Already, the reader begins to see signs of the multiple genres. In *Misreading Jane Eyre*, Jerome Beaty argues that *Jane Eyre* "redefines the
novel" by "inbreeding and crossbreeding conventions and varieties of the
Gothic and governess novels with an admixture of still others" (72). Similarly,
there is "crossbreeding" of the Gothic with other conventions in *The Wyvern
Mystery*, and Alice's journey to Wyvern with her side trip to Carwell Grange
introduces the reader to this crossing of genres at the beginning of the novel.

In the third chapter, the reader, now aware of the possibility of the
Gothic, arrives with Alice at a setting with a different atmosphere from Carwell Grange. The more accessible Wyvern estate seems to be most closely
associated with historical novels, which, as his preface to *Uncle Silas* indicates, was a genre Le Fanu admired. As noted above, the description of the
entrance to Wyvern is broad; it does not isolate the house like the entrances
to the other houses in the novel. The estate is large, and there are many who
must pay rent to the squire. It is a vestige of the old, English aristocracy:

Wyvern is a very pretty old house. It is built of a light grey stone, in the later Tudor style. A portion of it is overgrown with thick ivy. It stands not far away from the high road, among grand old trees, and is one of the most interesting features in a richly wooded landscape . . . [and is] one of the prettiest countries to be found in England. (11)

Unlike the Gothic castles nestled in the forests, Wyvern is by the "high road," and visitors can approach it quite easily. Inside Wyvern, there are old portraits on the walls, and the three Fairfields left are single men over forty. It is in relation to Wyvern that the narrator conveys most of the history about the characters. We learn that Squire Fairfield was widowed thirty years ago, Charles and Henry fear their father, and that fear arises from their childhood days. We also learn that Charles had been "wild and wasteful" but has now "sobered" (11). Later, the narrator describes the estate as belonging "time out of mind, to the Fairfield family" (30) and explains that "the character of the Fairfields has the vices, and some of the better traits of feudalism" (31), also connecting the estate with the historical genre. The history of the young heroine and her lowly family is told also. Owing partly to the cruelty of the old Squire Fairfield's exacting demand for rents from the vicarage, Alice is orphaned, yet he has compassion enough to take her in. Here, it seems, is the making of a novel about an old family in England and the potential salvation of its estate because of the transforming quality the orphan has on the hardened family. The Fairfield line will continue as a mixture of English aristocratic heritage and English clerical heritage. These narrative divergences from the plot in order to relate the history of the characters emphasize Wyvern's association with English history: it is a "good old English house [with] none o' your thin brick walls and Greek pillars, and scrape o' rotten plaster" (18). As master of the estate, Squire Fairfield perceives his story as one of retaining the old English values in the face of modern corruption and the "courtiers' ways" (18). Despite Squire Fairfield's attempts to keep his "good old English house" in the ways of old days when "a gentleman that kept a house and hounds here was more, by a long score, than half a dozen Lunnon lords" (18)—to keep the house in the realm of the historical—he doesn't succeed.

Upon Alice's arrival after her side trip to the decaying Carwell Grange, the Gothic creeps across the boundaries of historical Wyvern. When the old squire decides to propose to Alice, the Gothic threat begins. The squire sees his proposal as a way to take care of Alice and give meaning to his life. It also means holding on to the traditional values: Alice is "better . . . than the best o' them painted, fine ladies that's too nice to eat beef or mutton, and can't call a cabbage a cabbage, . . . and would turn up their eyes, like a duck in thunder, if a body told 'em to put on their patterns, and walk out . . . to look over the poultry" (18–19). Although the squire sees his offer of marriage as honorable, it appears grotesque and threatening to Alice. Drunk, the squire has Alice play vulgar tunes and stands over her. She fears he has gone insane, and he approaches her like a "phantom" (21). The narrator even exclaims that the "squire boisterously 'bussed' the young lady, as he had threatened" (22); although he merely kisses her, it is a threat to Alice. She acts as if she's in the role of threatened Gothic heroine. Emphasizing Alice's role as Gothic heroine, the squire locks Alice in her wing as he has done since before she could remember. However, Alice's hero comes to rescue her. Her "darling Ry" (28) signals to her, and she opens the ground floor window to let him into her locked wing. Charles does not take Alice with him, though. Like Adeline, the Gothic heroine in Radcliffe's *The Romance of the Forest*, Alice must take flight alone, crossing the commons (instead of the forest) in a carriage with only her servant and the driver. Despite Squire Fairfield's attempts to keep his historic lineage and maintain feudal power by locking out what he sees as romances or "Romeo and Juliet tragedies" (23) and locking in the woman who can help continue the Fairfield history, the Gothic does break in. Although Alice may see the Gothic threat from the squire, he actually does not conform completely to the Gothic villain. There is no threat of incest[3] or of destroying Alice's virtue. He wants to marry Alice legally. From Alice's perspective, though, he is a threat. She does not conform to the squire's perception and acts of her own will rather than according to the confines of the historical genre that Squire Fairfield imposes on Wyvern. He cannot keep the Gothic from crossing the boundaries. They are breached; the genres cannot be kept isolated.

From Wyvern, Alice flees what she sees as a threat only to enter what readers might perceive as the real Gothic based on the above description of Carwell Grange. It is here, though, that genres cross boundaries most easily, enabling all of the genres in the novel to meet. Gothic, realism, supernatural, and fairytale battle for primacy. The man who was once considered the hero is hiding a dark secret and, in fact, hiding Alice. He has had an earlier attachment, and although he claims he never married Bertha Velderkaust, she claims he did. Thus, Alice's virtue and honor are threatened. If Bertha is correct, then Alice's virtue has already been destroyed and she is a fallen

---

3. One could argue that because the squire took in Alice and raised her at Wyvern, there is a type of incest implied. However, there is no biological connection, and Alice does not see his proposal as an incestuous threat. If she did, there would be references to her marriage to Charles as incestuous.

woman—the fulfilled Gothic tragedy. The reader is never told the truth from any reliable character, though, and, at least while she's at Carwell Grange, Alice's role is ambiguous. Charles's role is uncertain, too. Jerome Beaty argues that "first-time readers of *Jane Eyre* . . . may not be sure whether Rochester is Gothic villain or Byronic hero" (75). Similarly, readers of *The Wyvern Mystery* may not be certain whether Charles has rescued Alice or has trapped her.[4] What makes the intermingling of genres at Carwell Grange even more interesting is that Charles himself cannot determine to which genre he belongs. Although he acts like a loving husband who would defend and rescue Alice from the clutches of a man who threatens her virtue, namely his father at Wyvern, he recognizes his threat to her. Conflating himself with Charles, the narrator says, "How easy it would have been comparatively to disclose all to Alice before leading her into such a position! He did not believe that there was actual danger in this claim. He could swear that he meant no villainy" (95). The confusion Charles feels is evident in these sentences; "such a position" indicates danger, and "meant no villainy" indicates that Charles has done something wrong. It seems, though, that he is trying to persuade himself there is no danger. However, he must believe there is some danger since he does attempt to protect Alice from his secret past by keeping her well hidden and, in a Bluebeard-like fashion, making her promise not to go into public or tell anyone where they are. Because Charles acts like Bluebeard by extracting the promise from Alice, he is now associated with the Gothic villain instead of the hero he earlier seemed to be. Charles's conscience gets to him, and he screws up his courage to tell Alice about Bertha, only to fail. Seeming to be both villain and hero, he can fill neither role fully. When Bertha attacks Alice, Charles does hit Bertha to defend his beloved, yet his reaction is mixed:

> And—did he *strike* her? Good God!—had he struck her? How did she lie there bleeding? For a moment a dreadful remorse was bursting at his heart—he would have kneeled—he could have killed himself. Oh, manhood! Gratitude! Charity! Could he, even in a moment of frenzy, have struck down any creature so—that had stood to him in the relation of that love? What a rush of remembrances and hell of compunction was there!—and for a rival! She the reckless, forlorn, guilty, old love cast off, blasted with deformity and privation, and now this last fell atrocity! Alice was clinging to him the words

---

4. This similarity between *Jane Eyre* and *The Wyvern Mystery* is just one of the many. In fact, it seems that Le Fanu consciously and overtly connects his novel to Brontë's by retaining the first name Bertha for the hidden woman who threatens the heroine. He does change the last name to return her to her Dutch origins as in "Tyrone Family."

"Darling, darling, my Ry, my saviour, my Ry," were in his ears, and he felt as if he hated Alice—hated her worse even than himself. (156)

Charles's mixed reactions reflect his mixed state of romantic hero and Gothic villain. Later, again through the narrator's words, it is clear that Charles recognizes the stalemate caused by his confused roles: "Why was he not a little more or a little less wicked? If the latter, he might never have been in his present fix. If the other, he might find a way out of the thicket—'hew his way out with a bloody axe'—and none but those whose secrecy he might rely on be the wiser!" (166). Charles's actions are his own, and they do not conform to the expected role of either Gothic hero or Gothic villain. He, too, feels this conflict.

Although Charles's role does not conform clearly, the setting does reflect the Gothic genre. In addition to the Gothic exterior, the interior of Carwell Grange is like the sprawling houses in Gothic novels. As Ellen Moers says in *Literary Women*, "indoors, in the long, dark, twisting, haunted passageways of the Gothic castle, there is travel with danger, travel with exertion—a challenge to the heroine's enterprise, resolution, ingenuity, and physical strength" (129). Alice discovers these winding passageways and ancient rooms on her first exploration of the house with Charles: "they walked through the hall, and by a staircase, and through a second smaller hall, with a back stair off of it" (43). Later, she is taken to her room by Mildred, and "there was that about [the house] which, if Alice had been in less cheerful and happy spirits, would have quelled and awed her. Thick walls, windows deep sunk, double doors now and then, wainscoting, and oak floors warped with age" (43–44). When Alice arrives at her room, the preternatural episode from "Tyrone Family" emerges. As she is about to enter her bedroom, she sees a black curtain fall across the doorway. In this case, it seems, the supernatural establishes a boundary, creating its own space within the house— Alice's room. In fact, the witch-like Bertha, blind but agile, walks through a wall into Alice's room as if she were an apparition. Even Mildred Tarnely associates Bertha with the devil: "Satan's her name. Lord help us" (113). Bertha simply knows the secret passages and can cut through the wallpaper covering the door, but the eerie atmosphere adds something of the supernatural Gothic, reminiscent of *The Monk*.

Despite the Gothic threat at Carwell Grange, Alice does not conform to the expected role of the Gothic heroine, and her own perceptions and actions bring in an element of realism. Unlike many Gothic heroines, Alice is oblivious to the threat Charles and his previous mistress pose to her virtue and her life, thinking that her only concern is Charles's creditors and his health. Concerns about money, debts, and illness address topics usually found in realistic novels. Once she has left what she perceives as the threat at Wyvern, Alice actually approaches her life as if she were in a realist novel: she grows their vegetables, uses the utmost economy, and worries for Charles's health. These are the incidents of "ordinary occurrence" used by writers of the "Real School" (150) that David Masson writes about in his 1859 essay "British Novelists since Scott." At Carwell Grange, though, it also seems as if there is "a world of semi-fantastic conditions," like those used by writers in the "Ideal School" (Masson 150): a supernatural drape falls across an entry way, a blind woman agilely finds her way through a blocked passage, a wife is hidden from public view, and the husband must secretly stay away for weeks. However, the ordinary does creep in as Alice must make do with broken dishes to avoid incurring more debt, plan to provide food for the household, and nurse the ailing Charles. Alice's realistic perceptions of her new, married, and debt-ridden life enable realism to cross the boundary established by the Gothic setting as well as the Gothic threat from Charles and Bertha. In *The Wyvern Mystery*, Le Fanu shows that the "Real School" can intertwine with the "Ideal School," merging the ordinary and the extraordinary within one location.

Although there are some realistic aspects of fiction, Charles and Alice attempt to make something of the fairytale out of Carwell Grange, once again intertwining genres. Before they even arrive at Carwell Grange, Charles claims: "we'll live like the old baron and his daughters in the fairy tale" (39). While showing Alice the garden, he again connects their lives to a fairytale: "This is the garden—I tell you lest you should mistake it for the forest where the enchanted princess slept, surrounded by great trees and thickets" (48). This time, though, it seems as if he's trying to avoid connection with "Sleeping Beauty," which is collected in Perrault's tales with "Bluebeard." He shifts and wants Alice to recognize the reality so she does not imagine she's in the enchanted garden. Confusingly, he then compares Alice to a fairy, but indicates that not even a fairy could make flowers grow in the shadowed garden. Once again, he uses reality to undermine the fairytale. Although Carwell Grange is Gothic and Charles implies that he and Alice have escaped to their own kingdom as in a fairytale, realism keeps crossing the boundaries, entering the story in the midst of the reader's Gothic expectations and Charles's fairytale hopes.

The next geographic location in the novel focuses on new characters. At a narrative level, this new section appears unrelated to the rest of the Wyvern and Carwell Grange plot although readers might expect a foundling narrative. What readers find, though, is the fairytale genre. Of course, many Victorian novels include references to fairytales. Dickens's "Frauds on the Fairies" emphasizes the importance he placed on fairytales, and *Hard Times* critiques a world in which fairytales are prohibited. However, Le Fanu does more than just reference the fairytales; he creates a bounded space that seems to keep Willie in a fairytale. Marjory Trevellian's cottage is the location for the fairytale genre. Even the description of the cottage has a fairytale quality to it. As noted above, the location is isolated and the cottage itself "antique." It is also in a "wooded hollow" (238). This seclusion connects it to cottages in fairytales such as "Little Red Riding Hood," also from Perrault's tales. Emphasizing the transition to the fairytale genre, Marjory calls Willie "her Fairy, and her Prince" (239) and has a wealth of fairytales she can tell him. There is even the fairytale injunction: Willie is never to speak to or play with any boys or he will be taken away from Marjory. Willie calls Marjory "Granny," connecting her with Gammer Grethel who tells the fairytales in Edgar Taylor's translations of the Grimm Brothers' tales.[5] Another character who seems to be drawn from fairytales is Tom Orange. Like the magical character who brings gifts to the protagonist of the fairytale in Ruskin's "The King of the Golden River" or the fairy godmother in "Cinderella," another story from Perrault's tales, he enters the scene to perform magic for Willie and tells tales of wondrous places. Yet, there are hints of realism even here. Tom Orange always makes sure he gets his "shilling 'tip' " from Marjory Trevellian, and his clothes are poor. Willie, of course, doesn't notice these aspects, but when Tom Orange crosses into the space on which Willie and Marjory have imposed their fairytale perception of life, he brings these realistic elements with him. Tom Orange, although fanciful, is a true representation of a character, and because of this, he does not conform completely to the expectations of the fairytale genre.

The main breach into Marjory and Willie's fairy world, though, is by Sergeant-Major Archdale. This no-nonsense, realistic character drags Willie out of his fairy world and into the world of realism. When Archdale arrives at Marjory's cottage, Marjory and Willie try to keep the fairy world safe. Willie hides himself in a press, and Marjory locks it, putting the key in her pocket. Archdale, who speaks in a "military fashion" with a "chill, stern voice" (254), reads the reality of the clues—the warm teapot, the table setting for two, and the packed carpet bag—to infer logically that the boy he is to take into his charge is there. Despite both Willie's and Marjory's attempts to keep Archdale's realism out of their lives, Archdale has breached the lines and is able to get Marjory to hand over the key to the press so that he may intrude into Willie's little world. Again, a character's ability to act of his own

5. Taylor's first translation of the Grimms' collection was published in 1823, and he published more translations of the Grimms' stories before 1839, which were reprinted multiple times throughout the century.

will and breach the boundaries others have established enables the genres themselves to break into the defining limits of other genres. Realism seems to win here, and ignoring Willie's cries, Archdale drags him from fairy land.

The ensuing events at Noulton Farm are most closely connected with the realism represented by Archdale. The family at Noulton Farm is small, just Mary and her father: "Miss Mary Archdale was ill. . . . [and] was the only child of the ex-sergeant, who was a widower" (259). The state of the family indicates a realistic setting, addressing the difficult situations of some lower-middle-class fictional families such as might be found in one of Elizabeth Gaskell's novels such as *North and South*. Life at Noulton Farm has nothing of the old English grandeur of Wyvern and, thus, is not fitting subject matter for a traditional historical romance in the tradition of Scott. Rather, the middle-class organ maker who is willing to turn a blind eye to Henry's illicit behavior and his sick daughter define the boundaries of this part of the story. After Willie crosses into this realistic genre, he and Archdale enter "a small parlour," and Archdale "[hangs] his hat on a peg in the hall, and [places] his cane along the chimney-piece" (259). The two then sit down to tea at the kitchen table, and Archdale puts on his glasses and reads the paper, actions reminiscent of every-day, middle-class life. When she has finished "a-spitting blood," Mary joins them at the tea table. Although one would expect a father to be more sympathetic toward his daughter's ailment, in a very Gradgrindian way, Archdale coldly discusses her illness:

> "Not well just now?"
> "No, sir."
> "You take the bottle regularly?"
> "Yes, sir."
> "You'll be better in the morning belike."
> "I'm sure I shall, sir." (259)

This is a household based on realism, nothing sensational such as parental confessions of love or sorrow and nothing fairy-like such as giant mushrooms or magical performances. Neither is there anything as Gothic as giant fireplaces with vaulted ceilings and a threatened maiden. This is, to return to Masson's words, an "ordinary occurrence." In addition to the father and daughter, only two other servants live at Noulton: the woman who works in the kitchen and Tony, a young boy from the workhouse who performs menial and general jobs. The introduction, as brief as it is, of a character from the workhouse also connects this space with realism.

Even into this well-barricaded house of realism, though, fairytales can enter. By bringing little Willie to Noulton, Archdale seems to have weakened his fortress. One evening while in the garden, little Willie sees Tom

Orange and rushes to the boundary hedges to speak with him. Although threatened with sixty lashes if he talks to Tom Orange, little Willie does, and Tom Orange manages to bring the fairytale genre into the boundaries of Archdale's realism. Like the magical character in fairytales, Tom Orange presents little Willie with a challenge. He must escape the house and meet him where the "two osiers grow" (263), and they will take a long journey. In *The European Folktale: Form and Nature*, Max Lüthi explains that in fairytales, "otherworld beings appear at the moment they are needed" (18), just as Tom Orange appears over the hedge at exactly the right moment: Willie is to join him on the very night that Mary, his only companion at Noulton, dies. As in other fairytales where the otherworld characters "come to meet" the hero (Lüthi 8), Tom Orange finds Willie. Willie, like the fairytale hero who "calmly accepts their advice, [and] receives their help" (Lüthi 8), does what Tom Orange asks without questioning him. In this tale, though, the hero is not promised marriage to the fairest princess but promised that he will "see mammy again, and come to a nice place where he should always be happy as the day is long, and mammy live with him always, and Tom look in as often as his own more important business would permit" (Le Fanu, *Wyvern* 263).[6] Willie breaks through the hedges of realism and begins his journey, meeting the hero's challenges head on. He and Tom act according to their nature, not according to Archdale's limiting rules. Characters acting of their own will, moving from one space to another, once again, make it impossible for a novel to remain within the boundaries of one limited genre.

As Thomas Pavel notes in *Fictional Worlds*, "The mobility and poor determinacy of fictional frontiers is often part of a larger pattern of interaction between the domain of fiction and the actual world" (84). He explains this further: "Fictional domains can acquire a certain independence, subsist outside the limits of actuality, and sometimes strongly influence us, not unlike a colony established overseas that develops its own unusual constitution and later comes to affect in various ways the life of the metropolis" (84). Although this statement refers to fiction crossing the boundary into reality, the same happens within the multi-genred fictional world of *The Wyvern Mystery*. In fact, the end of the novel returns to Wyvern and restores an heir to the Fairfield country seat. When one genre crosses the boundary of another, it precipitates a journey. When the Gothic enters the historical Wyvern, Alice and Charles leave. When the ordinary events of realism enter the Gothic Carwell Grange, Alice and her son leave. When the unfanciful realism enters

---

6. For further reading on the ways in which *The Wyvern Mystery* incorporates fairytales, see Harris's "*The Wyvern Mystery*: A Realistic Fairy Tale."

Marjory's fairy realm, Willie must travel to Noulton. And when the fairy realm enters Noulton, Willie journeys home to his "Granny." Carwell Grange, Marjory's cottage, and Noulton Farm are like the "colon[ies] established overseas" which will affect the homeland of Wyvern. The final journey to Wyvern comes immediately on the heels of Willie's return to his fairy home. He is able to return to the historical home of the Fairfields,[7] and his mother, Alice, returns with him. The multiple elements of the different genres, Pavel's "unusual constitution," have returned to Wyvern, Pavel's "metropolis."

It seems, though, that each genre is not quite complete. Although Alice has returned to Wyvern, it is without her hero. Thus, the Gothic plot with the restitution of the heroine to her rightful position and married to her hero is only partially fulfilled. That Charles and Lady Wyndale are dead emphasizes the realism of the plot, which is only partially realized at the end because of the seemingly fantastic way in which Wyvern is restored to Willie and Alice. Even Tom Orange, the fantastic character who ushers in fairytale elements incorporates the realism of emigrating to Australia, probably to avoid previous charges of poaching. The last sentence of the novel points to the partial fulfillment of each: "Marjory Trevellian lives with the family at Wyvern, and I think if kind old Lady Wyndale were still living the consolations of Alice would be nearly full" (272). The genres are "nearly" complete, but not fully. Elements of fairytale, Gothic, and realistic genres rather than their complete conventional traditions combine to keep the Fairfield line at Wyvern, restoring order to the estate—and possibly to the historical romance that Le Fanu so admired.

---

7. It is never completely clear that legally the estate should be passed to Willie. That would be based on the assumption that Charles is right about never being married to Bertha. Although there is "ample proof to support his [Willie's] claim" to Wyvern (271), that support is probably based on Alice and Charles's marriage without searching for proof that Charles and Bertha had been married. Bertha is dead and cannot contest the claim. The fact that at times Charles seems to waver in his conviction that he and Bertha never married implies there might still be some doubt. Even Harry's confession to Bertha that she never married Charles is suspect because Harry is determined to inherit the estate, and on his death bed, Harry maintains "that his brother was really married to Bertha Velderkaust" (271). This statement, of course, could be his justification for having hidden Willie to take control of the estate, and there might not be truth in it. There is no doubt, though, that Willie is Charles's son, and, even if illegitimate, another Fairfield is master of Wyvern.

Works Cited

Beaty, Jerome. *Misreading* Jane Eyre: *A Postformalist Paradigm*. Columbus: Ohio State University Press, 1996.

"Charles Lever's Last Novel." *Dublin University Magazine* 73 (January 1869): 105–6.

Dickens, Charles. "Frauds on the Fairies." *Household Words* No. 184 (1 October 1853): 97–101.

———. *Hard Times*. Ed. Kate Flint. New York: Penguin, 2003.

———. Letter to J. S. Le Fanu (26 May, 1870). In "Five New Dickens Letters." Ed. Bert G. Hornback. *Michigan Quarterly Review* 10 (1976): 255–60.

Gaskell, Elizabeth. *North and South*. Ed. Angus Easson. London: Oxford University Press, 1973.

Harris, Sally C. "A Realistic Fairy Tale: *The Wyvern Mystery*." *Le Fanu Studies* 3:1 (2008). [online]

Keen, Suzanne. *Victorian Renovations of the Novel: Narrative Annexes and the Boundaries of Representation*. Cambridge: Cambridge University Press, 1998.

Kenton, Enda. "A Forgotten Creator of Ghosts: Joseph Sheridan Le Fanu, Possible Inspirer of the Brontës." *Bookman* (New York) 69 (1929): 528–34.

Le Fanu, Joseph Sheridan. "A Chapter in the History of a Tyrone Family." In *The Purcell Papers*. Vol. 3. 1880. New York: Garland, 1979.

———. *The Fortunes of Colonel Torlogh O'Brien: A Tale of the Wars of King James*. 2nd ed. London: Routledge, 1851.

———. *The Rose and the Key*. Ed. Frances A. Chiu. Kansas City, MO: Valancourt, 2007.

———. *Uncle Silas*. New York: Oxford University Press, 1981.

———. *Willing to Die*. London: Chapman & Hall, 1876.

———. *Wylder's Hand*. New York: Dover, 1978.

———. *The Wyvern Mystery*. Stroud, UK: Sutton, 2001.

Lewis, Matthew Gregory. *The Monk*. Mineola, NY: Dover Thrift, 2003.

Lüthi, Max. *The European Folktale: Form and Nature*. Trans. John D. Niles. Philadelphia: Institute for the Study of Human Issues, 1982.

Masson, David. "From 'British Novelists Since Scott': Lecture IV of *British Novelists and Their Styles*, 1859." In *Victorian Criticism of the Novel*, ed. Edwin M. Eigner and George J. Worth. Cambridge: Cambridge University Press, 1985. 148–58.

Moers, Ellen. *Literary Women*. Garden City, NY: Doubleday, 1976.

Pavel, Thomas G. *Fictional Worlds*. Cambridge, MA: Harvard University Press, 1986.

Perrault, Charles. *Histories, or Tales of Past Times. Translated into English*. 1729. Facsimile in Jaques Barchilon and Henry Pettit. *The Authentic Mother Goose Fairy Tales and Nursery Rhymes*. Denver: Swallow Press, 1970.

Radcliffe, Ann. *The Romance of the Forest*. Ed. Chloe Chard. London: Oxford University Press, 1999.

Ruskin, John. *The King of the Golden River*. Chicago: Henneberry, 1895.

Sage, Victor. *Le Fanu's Gothic: The Rhetoric of Darkness*. Basingstoke, UK: Palgrave Macmillan, 2004.

Taylor, Edgar, trans. *German Popular Stories and Fairy Tales, as Told by Gammer Grethel*. From the Collection of M.M. Grimm. London: Bell & Daldy, 1872.

"I Resolved To Play the Part of a Good Samaritan": Metafiction in "The Room in the Dragon Volant"

William Hughes

In the Introduction to *Le Fanu's Gothic: The Rhetoric of Darkness* (2004), Victor Sage rightly concludes that "some of [Le Fanu's] most powerful work is in the two collections he produced at the end of his life, *In a Glass Darkly* (1871) and *Chronicles of Golden Friars* [1871]" (2). *In a Glass Darkly*—unlike *Chronicles of Golden Friars*—has, however, achieved an unquestionably canonical status in the academic teaching of Gothic. Its place there is both validated and maintained not merely through scholarly editions, such as that originally produced for Oxford University Press in 1993 by Robert Tracy, but also by way of critical analyzes of the individual tales within the volume by scholars as diverse as W. J. Mc Cormack, Richard Davenport-Hines, and Diane Mason. This analysis, though, is somewhat unbalanced. Of the five narratives which make up *In a Glass Darkly*, "Carmilla"—"The most famous and influential lesbian vampire story" (9), according to the anthologist Pam Keesey—has received by far the majority of critical attention. A modicum of critical consideration has, admittedly, been paid to "Green Tea" by critics such as Richard Haslam and Jack Sullivan, the latter proclaiming it "the archetypal ghost story." "Mr. Justice Harbottle" has been analyzed, albeit obliquely, by Peter Denman as a possible source for Bram Stoker's 1891 short story "The Judge's House." The remaining stories, "The Familiar" and "The Room in the Dragon Volant" have received little more than passing attention in surveys of the breadth of Le Fanu's fiction such as Audrey Peterson's 1984 study, *Victorian Masters of Mystery* (125, 154). Peterson is spectacularly inaccurate in her account of the latter narrative, both misnaming and misspelling the narrative's hero and rescheduling a soldier as a member of the French police (154).

The longstanding critical neglect of "The Room in the Dragon Volant"— a story that has been addressed at length in only a single article by Ken Scott, published as early as 1968—is curious to say the least. "The Room in the Dragon Volant" is arguably the most complex of Le Fanu's short stories. The penultimate tale of *In a Glass Darkly*, it differs from its four compatriots not merely through its eschewing of any supernatural content but also on account of the intense self-reflection that characterizes its retrospective, first-person narrative. In this substantial short story there is no pagan temptation, such as that which afflicts the Reverend Mr. Jennings in "Green Tea." Nor, indeed, is there any vengeful ghost or predatory vampire to parallel those found in "The Familiar," "Mr. Justice Harbottle" or "Carmilla." The strange and almost fatal catalepsy that afflicts Richard Beckett, who as an elderly man narrates this singularly unpleasant episode from his youth, is explained unequivocally at the conclusion of "The Room in the Dragon Volant" as being the consequence of human greed, bold opportunism and the naïve vanity that blinds the hapless protagonist to the all too worldly motivations of his associates. Beckett is poisoned, not haunted. His attackers, likewise, are subjected to the regular processes of secular law rather than to a supernatural retribution meted out by the dead they once wronged.

Yet this is no simple tale of crime and retribution. Rather, it is a crafted and deliberate work that explores the machinations of fiction as much as it does those of crime, a rudimentary metafiction that anticipates the self-consciousness of postmodern writing by way of a fictional narrator whose reminiscence demonstrably functions in the manner of a fictional narrative; which in turn depicts a younger man who views his world by way of the clichés of contemporary fictional discourse, and perceives himself in the person of a fictional character. There is more to contemplate in "The Room in the Dragon Volant" than the mere "pleasant dramatic irony" (154) with which the dismissive Audrey Peterson characterizes the tale: Ken Scott's identification of the hero's adoption of "a romantic posture in his attack on life" (25) is a far fairer assessment of the narrative's at times pointed focus. Yet Scott's argument may be taken further, and his article's deflection of attention away from Beckett's knowingness and towards the text's reconciliation of "apparent antitheses" (26) may also be corrected somewhat by a reconsideration of how Le Fanu's narrator is, in his own mind, as much a "skilfully wrought entity" (26) as the story he advances for the reader's consideration.

Metafiction (1984), Patricia Waugh's still-pertinent study of a recurrent device characteristic in particular of postmodern fiction, provides a telling definition of crafted self-conscious writing which might profitably be applied to Le Fanu's nineteenth-century short story. Waugh states that "Metafiction is a term given to fictional writing which self-consciously and systematically draws attention to its status as an artefact in order to pose questions about the relationship between fiction and reality" (2). In "The Room in the Dragon Volant," Waugh's concepts of "fiction" and "reality" may be considered to elide readily into the narrator's variously historical and contemporary perceptions of both the self and its actions. As Beckett narrates his adventure his retrospection, and the sporadic commentary upon his former self which he interpolates into his reminiscence, accentuate repeatedly how artificial his perception of events has actually been—and how evident this artifice may be to an older and wiser self whose implicit counterpart is the contemporary reader, one who appreciates that elaborate fictional situations cannot, by definition, be truly "real." There is more at stake here, though, than a world-wise, older Beckett recalling and narrating his youthful naïveté with a mixture of evident embarrassment and indulgent incredulity. "The Room in the Dragon Volant" engenders also the problematic situations that may arise when actions or motivations are perceived (or, perhaps, "read") simultaneously—and, at times, cynically—from multiple perspectives within the curtilage of the fiction. Beckett's contemporaries—not merely the villainous St. Alyres, but also implicitly the other fellow travelers of his youth—readily perceive not merely the actuality of the world he portrays, but also the somewhat imaginative interpretation that the idealistic, adventurous and impetuous ingénue is inclined to veneer it with. As the imbrication of the older and younger versions of Beckett in the narrative would suggest, the retrospective Beckett is himself similarly aware, making him in essence a fictional character self-consciously narrating the fiction of the character in which he once perceived himself and his motivations.

In a very postmodern way, Beckett depicts himself as being in retreat from the integrated and discreet identity that one might associate with the term "self," and progressively envisions his youthful existence through the generic concept of the performative "role" (Waugh 3). The narrative of "The Room in the Dragon Volant," despite its superficial unity as a memoir narrated by a single participant, is subtly faulted. The retrospective tone emphasizes, for the most part, a narrated voice which demands to be associated with the younger Beckett. The younger Beckett, of course, *cannot* in reality be the narrator, the younger man's time having passed, the events he describes having become the history, the reminiscence, of what Beckett himself terms "a sadder if not a wiser man" (241). That elder figure, though at times humorous, is still able to pointedly place the actions of his former self within the contexts of consequences and knowledge unavailable to that self. If the temporal implications of retrospective narration are perhaps too subdued an index of the narrative's crafted metafictional nature, then the sporadic interjection of a form of ironic commentary by the elder Beckett further enforces the tension between past and present, between he who experiences and he who narrates, be they both the same person. The spontaneity of youth, the high adventure of romance, the very matter of the perception voiced by the ostensibly younger Beckett is a mere façade: "The Room in the Dragon Volant" toys consistently with the problem of false and mistaken perception, with the implication that many things that appear as realities are merely distorted reflections which conceal actualities of a more sinister outline.

As a self-conscious narrative with Gothic inflections, "The Room in the Dragon Volant" bears obvious comparison to Jane Austen's *Northanger Abbey* (1818). Both works are fictions which reveal their generic coordinates through the eyes of a deluded central figure as the plot advances. Just as Austen's Catherine Morland perceives Radcliffean dangers in Bath and the English West Country, so Richard Beckett implicates himself into an extravagant, and indeed troubadourean, *affair d'amour* in early nineteenth century France. En route to Paris, he hastily deduces the misery of a broken marriage from a few harsh words overheard by chance, and configures himself as the romantic hero fated to save the beautiful Countess de St. Alyre from a supposedly loveless bondage to an older man. Catherine Morland's suspicions regarding the likely fate of the unfortunate Mrs. Tilney are equally without foundation, deductions made from too incautious an involvement with ambiguous information that yields too readily to a mind inflamed by Gothic fiction. Both *Northanger Abbey* and "The Room in the Dragon Volant" demonstrate, further, how other characters might "read" the imaginative or generic script which motivates and makes predictable the actions of those who recklessly exchange mundane worldly reality for the excitement of literary fantasy. The knowing—if not actually provocative—behavior of Henry Tilney in verbally anticipating (124–126) the discovery of the supposedly concealed manuscript in Catherine Morland's bedroom (133–136) in the somewhat un-Gothic edifice of the novel's title has its parallels in how the St. Alyres draw upon, and indeed stimulate, Beckett's own desire for romantic intrigue in "The Room in the Dragon Volant." If not as overtly or consistently comedic as *Northanger Abbey*, "The Room in the Dragon Volant" ought to be regarded as a crafted piece of writerly introspection whose implications project, perhaps, a little further beyond the merely satirical.

Beckett is, explicitly, an incautious consumer of fiction, and this—with his undoubted vanity—lies at the root of his utter predictability within the narrative. Rather than simply live his life, the youthful hero is engaged in a consistent role playing, a constant viewing of the self from outside, as if it were a character in a novel or an actor upon the public stage (cf. Scott 25). This process is pursued as much during moments of private delectation as it

406 REFLECTIONS IN A GLASS DARKLY

is performed upon the public stage of social intercourse. Only just engaged on his romantic enterprise, Beckett recalls:

> I took a turn or two up and down my room, and sighed, looking at myself in the glass, adjusted my great white "choker," folded and tied after Brummel, the immortal "Beau," put on a buff waistcoat and my blue swallow-tailed coat with gilt buttons; I deluged my pocket handkerchief with Eau-de-Cologne (we had not then the variety of bouquets with which the genius of perfumery has since blessed us); I arranged my hair, on which I piqued myself, and which I loved to groom in those days. That dark-brown *chevelure*, with a natural curl, is now represented by a few dozen perfectly white hairs, and its place—a smooth, bald, pink head—knows it no more. I was making a very careful toilet. I took my unexceptionable hat from its case, and placed it lightly upon my wise head, as nearly as memory and practice enabled me to do so, at that very slight inclination which the immortal person I have mentioned was wont to give his. A pair of light French gloves and a rather club-like knotted walking stick, such as just then came into vogue, for a year or two again in England, in the phraseology of Sir Walter Scott's romances, "completed my equipment." (128; italics in original)

The closing reference to Scott makes perfect sense in context. Edward Waverley, the titular hero of Scott's 1814 historical novel, enters the ruthless political strife of the 1745 Jacobite rebellion as if it were a chivalric crusade and he a romantic and invulnerable hero. The eighteenth-century Waverley is just such a man as Le Fanu's nineteenth-century Beckett, and is similarly inconvenienced and dispossessed as a consequence of his naïveté and inability to distinguish between fiction and harsh reality. Even if it might be contended that the Beckett, who travels in 1815, may not have actually read *Waverley*, published just a year before, it is clear that the interjecting, elder Beckett—who specifically draws the reader's attention to his somewhat unromantic decrepitude—is indeed capable of drawing a parallel between Scott's hero and his own younger self. Beckett is explicitly a reader of romances, and admits that he "had two or three idle books, it is true, as travelling companions" (128). The prefix "idle" is apt to suggest content which is entertaining rather than didactic or morally uplifting, and that epithet might justifiably be applied also to the young man himself. Traveling listlessly in France in the turbulent aftermath of Napoleon's defeat in 1815, he is one of many "English excursionists anxious, let us say, to improve their minds by foreign travel" (120). The narrator's interjection here draws attention to the euphemism: Beckett is a bored wealthy dilettante, "having just succeeded to a very large sum in consols" (119). He is in search of adventure, intrigue and possibly romance in a country whose political instability and strangeness of customs easily aligns it to the imaginative Europe of Gothic fiction, or the turbulent Scotland of *Waverley*. It is all too tempting. Beckett, both incautious reader and vain performer, is seemingly destined by his own enthusiasm to reschedule everything he sees in post-Napoleonic France in terms of an adventure in which he must participate.

Arguably, however, every other character in "The Room in the Dragon Volant" sees the world differently to Beckett, though some of them are represented as being insightful enough to perceive his own imaginative relationship both with the contemporary environment and with the people that surround him. In the perception of these others—to whom we may also append the (historically later) reader of Le Fanu's novella—the heroic and amorous Beckett is simultaneously "novel-reader," "figure of fun," "dupe" (238) and (but for the timely intervention of another character less-inclined to romantic dreaming) "victim" and ultimately "corpse." For all Beckett's occasional indulgent interjections, there is—as this last role indicates—precious little humor in this unpleasant narrative of vanity and opportunism.

The events that lead Beckett deeper and deeper into his personal fantasy do indeed resemble those of a popular novel. The spectacular carriage accident which first brings the English traveler into contact with the St. Alyres, notably, has its parallel in "Carmilla," where it is utilized to bring the vampire—another predatory traveling impostor—into the unwary circle of Laura's family (252–53). It is not the accident so much as Beckett's own self-conscious perception of his supposedly spontaneous reaction to its stimulus that brings the matter into perspective, however. After calmly noting the discomfiture of the horses and the deployment of the servants, Beckett recalls with somewhat more interest how:

> A pretty little bonnet and head were popped out of the window of the carriage in distress. Its *tournure*, and that of the shoulders that also appeared for a moment, was captivating: I resolved to play the part of a good Samaritan; stopped my chaise, jumped out, and with my servant lent a very willing hand in the emergency. Alas! the lady with the pretty bonnet wore a very thick, black veil. I could see nothing but the pattern of the Bruxelles lace, as she drew back. (120)

As Beckett's rhetoric suggests, there is a degree of performance here: the pointed use of "very" is a wonderful touch. The reader is prompted to wonder whether this alleged good Samaritan's actions might have been so impetuous had the lady's *tournure* or silhouette been somewhat less "captivating": even with these, a delay between observation and action is discernible. The lack of detail in the perception and recollection of the suddenly revealed heroine, the suggestion rather than revelation of her beauty, is a specific tool in the protracting of Beckett's aroused interest. First "the demure, pretty little bonnet" (121), and then the frustratingly opaque "black veil that baulked my romantic curiosity" (121), become a substitute for the as yet unseen face of a character whom Beckett is already clearly accelerating into the role of a potential heroine for his own personal romance. This is a face seen only in its absence, as in a glass darkly. Fittingly, when he does finally perceive the credible beauty concealed by "the envious veil" (122) it is through the reflective medium of a clear rather than dark mirror, albeit one ominously contained within "a tarnished frame" (122). Even in this final actualization, the heroine appears to Beckett framed somewhat in the manner of "a half-length portrait" (122), again an idealization, an abstraction, a fiction presented to his eager, consuming gaze.

The lady, of course, is—in keeping with her visibly genteel station in life, for he understands her to be the Countess de St. Alyre—traveling with a male escort, "a lean old gentleman," even "an invalid" (120), whom Beckett immediately and explicitly assumes to be her husband (121) rather than her father or guardian. An interview with the family's temporarily engaged coachman, whose favor is momentarily bought with Beckett's gold, fails to confirm this. As the coachman informs Beckett, "They are the Count, and the young lady we call the Countess—but I know not, she may be his daughter" (126): Beckett, notably, underplays somewhat this unwelcome distraction from his developing romantic fantasy.

Beckett's impetuous assumption regarding the relationship that pertains between the Count and Countess is expanded upon greatly as he progressively fabricates his mental romance. For the moment, though, he contents himself with merely adding further significance not merely to the mysterious lady's unexceptionable expression of gratitude for his practical assistance with the horses—indulgently described by him as a "little speech in such pretty broken English" (120)—but also attributing to her an interest in his own attentions and attractions of which he surely could not be aware, given the opacity of her veil. Beckett, simultaneously the besotted young man and his older, more sober counterpart, recalls:

> I was conscious of being good-looking. I really believe I was; and there could be no mistake about my being nearly six feet high. Why need this lady have thanked me? Had not her husband, for such I assumed him to be, thanked me quite enough, and for both? I was instinctively aware that the lady was looking on me with no unwilling eyes; and, through her veil, I felt the power of her gaze. (121)

The final sentence is, of course, as logically ridiculous as it is romantically conventional. The youthful narrator's apparent bondage to naïve credulity is only saved from utter bathos by the judicious interposition of some quiet irony on the part of the elder Beckett, who concludes that, as the lady's carriage draws away, "a wise young gentleman followed her with ardent eyes, and sighed profoundly as the distance increased" (122).

Love at first sight is a very dangerous emotion. It evades the wiser judgments customarily associated with empiricism and experience. Beckett's subsequent pursuit of his mysterious female love-interest might well be described as "stalking" in modern terminology: it is, certainly, not the behavior one would associate with a gentleman. Having instructed his coachmen to discreetly shadow the emblazoned carriage of the St. Alyres to its destination, Beckett is ultimately placed in such a position as to be able to indulge in a highly sexualized moment of voyeurism, an intimate encounter between himself and the focus of his interest. Passing the lady's private drawing room, he unexpectedly perceives "the very bonnet with which I had fallen in love" (122) and then, as its owner moves into the light, the visage its veil has hitherto occluded, reflected in a mirror. He recalls:

> The face was oval, melancholy, sweet. It had in it, nevertheless, a faint and undefinably sensual quality also. Nothing could exceed the delicacy of its features, or the brilliancy of its tints. The eyes, indeed, were lowered, so that I could not see their colour; nothing but their long lashes and delicate eyebrows. (122)

Beckett's protracted gaze problematizes both the woman he consumes and his own status as a potential or aspiring lover. The opening sentence englobes her with all the condescending ownership of the male gaze, and reduces her to a tabulation of romantic and erotic signifiers. His attention, indeed, approaches the fetishistic: he admits, "I saw even the blue veins that traced their wanderings on the whiteness of her full throat" (123). To linger for so long, and in such intimate detail, upon one apparently unaware of his presence places Beckett beyond the chivalric deference to women no doubt exemplified by the heroes of the fiction he customarily reads. The object of his attention, though, is equally problematized. The lady's downcast eyes ought, conventionally, to indicate her modesty, yet the earlier suggestion of her underlying sensual nature undermines this: clearly, she is no passive, innocent heroine. The younger Beckett, though, sees none of this, being lost already in his reverie. He concludes, simply, that "The face was, indeed, one to fall in love with at first sight. Those sentiments that take such sudden possession of young men were now dominating my curiosity" (123). The elder Beckett, no longer numbered among the ranks of "young men" has, once again, dryly commented upon the excesses of his naïve counterpart.

Like Austen's Catherine Morland, Beckett is reading the mundane and

410   REFLECTIONS IN A GLASS DARKLY

accidental incidents he encounters during his everyday life as if they were the intense, meaningful and progressive scenarios that prototypically accumulate in the pursuit of a fictional *dénouement*. In this artificially episodic perception, each scenario ought rightly to proceed by the predictable logic of fiction, generating its successor and implicating its central protagonist yet further into an inevitable conclusion, a coming together of the separated. Anything dissonant to that perspective, or not conducive to the fantasy Beckett has so happily involved himself in, he is inclined if not to dismiss then simply to ignore. He is the passive—albeit hopeful—recipient of all that romantic fate throws in his path.

In this respect, Beckett's fictional co-ordinate in the romances of his youth ought rightly to be not the hero but the heroine. Beckett is, admittedly, directly and knowingly manipulated by the St. Alyres, but he positions himself also in sympathetic and receptive positions which may be associated as much with desirable and vulnerable heroines as they are with their besotted though ultimately heroic swains. Having pursued the St. Alyres to a rural *auberge*, the Belle Etoile, Beckett positions himself at a suitably picturesque window: "As I completed my preparations the light failed me; the last level streak of sunlight disappeared, and a fading twilight only remained, I sighed in unison with the pensive hour, and threw open the window, intending to look out for a moment before going downstairs" (128–29). It is in this rather elaborately posed position that he chances to overhear first the raised voices of the two St. Alyres, who are in the room beneath, and then latterly a song from the Countess's own lips, the words of which—according to the tradition of Ann Radcliffe—he must conventionally assume are meant for his ears alone. The colloquy is marked by its mode of delivery rather than its actual content, however; for, as Beckett admits, to the latter he is not privy. The narrative continues:

> I perceived instantly that the window underneath mine was also open, for I heard two voices in conversation, although I could not distinguish what they were saying.
>
> The male voice was peculiar; it was, as I told you, reedy and nasal. I knew it, of course, instantly. The answering voice spoke in those sweet tones which I recognized only too easily. The dialogue was only for a minute; the repulsive male voice laughed, I fancied, with a kind of devilish satire, and retired from the window, so that I almost ceased to hear it. (129)

As the elder Beckett confesses, this is hardly an exceptional incident, for all the evocative polarity vested in his choice of words: "It was not an altercation; there was evidently nothing the least exciting in the colloquy" (129). But it *is* the foundation upon which an imaginative distress might be erected, a cause that might justify the chivalric Englishman's interest or intervention. He continues: "What would I not have given that it had been a quarrel—a violent one—and I the redresser of wrongs, and the defender of insulted beauty! Alas! so far as I could pronounce upon the character of the tones I heard, they might be as tranquil a pair as any in existence" (129). Whilst the final sentence might be an ironic commentary upon the convention of marital harmony, it functions more obviously as yet another reminder that Beckett, once intrigued, is quite prepared to ignore any detail inconvenient to his fantasy.

The song which Beckett subsequently overhears, and which is tellingly entitled "Death and Love, together mated" (129), has an evident symbolic value for the lovesick swain, given the comparative ages of the couple beneath. Yet again, though, he ignores the implicit warning contained in his own depiction of the singer's voice as being "a little mocking in its tones" (129). The implication that it might be *he* that is being mocked, rather than the elderly count, does not cross Beckett's mind. Nor, indeed, does he hear with any concern the proleptic opening lines of the ballad, these being:

> Death and Love, together mated,
> Watch and wait in ambuscade; (129)

The elderly man and the young woman do, indeed, "wait in ambuscade" upon the hapless Beckett and his love will bring his death should the plot function at all like a novel. Beckett, living his plot is not aware that his fellow characters are engaged in writing it, and reading his likely reactions to their behavior. The whole drawing down of the window "with a rattle that might easily have broken the glass" (130) terminates his access to the colloquy and thus piques his interest yet more. He has now constructed for her a whole fictional character, utterly attuned to his romantic nature and adventurous leanings. Without as much as a protracted conversation with the Countess, he empowers himself sufficiently to determine both her enduring nature and her current fate:

> That beautiful Countess, with the patience of an angel and the beauty of a Venus and the accomplishments of all the Muses, a slave! She knows perfectly who occupies the apartments over hers; she heard me raise my window. One may conjecture pretty well for whom that music was intended—ay, old gentleman, and for whom you suspected it to be intended. (130)

Of course, Beckett is correct in all but the detail of the Countess's slavery. It is he that is now enslaved, bound by the expectations of his own reading, and the excitement of the *chase d'amour*. When the elder Beckett dryly comments that his younger self "moralised, wisely" (130), the pause occasioned by his comma enforces quite the opposite interpretation—the bitter and ironic reflex, as it were, of hindsight.

From this point, the narrative proceeds more or less directly towards its inevitable conclusion—the coming together of Beckett and the supposed Countess. If the original accident was exactly that—an accident—the events at the Belle Etoile signal the point at which the conspirators begin to arrange, for their own ultimate benefit, the very dramatic events which Beckett wishes to immerse himself in. For Beckett, of course, the whole thing is seemingly spontaneous, a dream coming true, a romantic pursuit with him as the hero, the Count as the villain, and the Countess as the wronged heroine. Again, he pauses to muse under the sympathetic light of the evening sky:

> It was now night, and a pleasant moonlight over everything. I had entered more into my romance since my arrival, and the poetic light heightened the sentiment. What a drama, if she turned out to be the Count's daughter, and in love with me! What a delightful—*tragedy*, if she turned out to be the Count's wife! (131; italics in original)

At this point, the arrival of a further impostor—the Marquis d'Harmonville, *alias* Monsieur Droqville, *alias* Planard—adds further evidence to the accreted case that Beckett has constructed for himself. An accomplice of the St. Alyres, it is he who confirms the very information which Beckett wishes to hear, and has not yet been able to obtain from the servants and ostlers of the hotel, namely that the Count

> " . . . is the very soul of honour, and the most sensible man in the world, except in one particular."
> "And that particular?" I hesitated, I was now deeply interested.
> "Is that he has married a charming creature, at least five-and-forty years younger than himself, and is, of course, horribly jealous."
> "And the lady?"
> "The Countess is, I believe, in every way worthy of so good a man," he answered, a little drily. (138)

Beckett's hesitation indicates on one level his evident romantic interest, and on another draws attention to his prescient knowledge that this must, indeed, be the case, lest his fantasy not work out in the true style of love abused, thwarted and finally won. The closing remark by d'Harmonville, indeed, hints that the Countess may herself be less of a fool than her purported husband, a woman who may potentially not be so "worthy" as her jealous husband in the eyes of strict sexual morality. The stage is now set, and by his question Beckett has furnished the plotters with the confirmation which they need to draw him into an assignation with the Countess, and a fatal appointment with a grave in the Parisian cemetery of Père La Chaise.

A second encounter with d'Harmonville, this time in Paris, is distinguished not by a dry deflection but rather by a more inviting reminder of the uneasy relationship between the jealous Count and the "Too handsome" (158) woman to whom he is married. Beckett recalls the exchange:

"I should wish so much to be presented to the Count; you tell me he's so—"
"So agreeably married. . . ." (159)

And if this teasing were not evident enough, d'Harmonville takes pains to depict the elderly gentleman as being "'the very man for a philosopher, like you! And he falls asleep after dinner, and his wife don't. But, seriously, he has retired from the gay and the great world, and has grown apathetic; and so has his wife; and nothing seems to interest her now, not even—her husband!'" (159). Later, in a manner somewhat reminiscent of a scene in *Jane Eyre*, Beckett is told his fortune, and given further evidence of the apparently parlous state of the St. Alyre marriage (173) by the mysterious occupant of an oracular palanquin. This, though he does not perceive it, is nothing more than the repetition of stock phrases from his romantic pursuit of the Countess, including her last frenetic words to him on departing, "*I may never see you more, and, oh! that I could forget you. Go—farewell—for God's sake, go!*" (176; italics in original). It is the Countess herself, indeed, and she in disguise, who repeats those words to him as the oracle's interpreter. A deliberate ploy on the part of the plotters—which Beckett later understands was "intended to re-animate my interest . . . in the beautiful Countess" (241)—it is enough to spur him on to a fatal meeting with the disguised Countess (178–84), and a subsequent tryst with her (195), without his recognizing that d'Harmonville himself had systematically placed him next to the masked intriguer in the first of these fatal encounters. Even the episode of the oracular palanquin has a literary context: Beckett recalls that a similar occasion, enacted a century earlier, is recorded "among my books of French anecdote and memoirs . . . marked, by my own hand" (201).

Little more needs to be said regarding Beckett's progress: he is a willing victim, and anticipates the twists and turns of the plot without realizing that he is from this juncture a character as well as narrator, and that the St. Alyres are the master novelists whose work is so ably described by the retrospective pen of the elder Beckett. His only assertive action, enacted spontaneously, is ironically to physically defend the St. Alyres from the angry attention of the brother of one of their victims (146), this gaining him a love token from the Countess and the melodramatic outburst whispered to him as a touchstone at the palanquin (147, 176). Of course, he does—he *must*—

pursue her to Paris, and it is from the environs of that chaotic yet romantic city that he is led literally to the final plot, a grave as well as an intrigue, in which he is almost buried alive, a cataleptic victim of his own vanity. There is a momentary flicker of clear-sightedness on his part, as he waits at the scene of the final elopement. Having heard of a number of robberies and disappearances associated with the Dragon Volant, the hotel in which he is staying (202), he muses:

> . . . there came upon me an odd thought, which you will think might well have struck me long before. It seemed on a sudden, as it came, that the darkness deepened, and a chill stole into the air around me.
>
> Suppose I were to disappear finally, like those other men whose stories I had listened to! Had I not been at all the pains that mortal could, to obliterate every trace of my real proceedings, and to mislead everyone to whom I spoke as to the direction in which I had gone? (219)

This, of course, he dismisses and, indeed, he overlooks moreover the implications of his own subsequent assessment of the Countess as "an ally so clever and courageous" (219). The truth is that Beckett is literally following in the footsteps of those men, and utilizing—he believes for his own purposes—the secret passageways by which those past disappearances were so successfully effected.

The corpse that Beckett almost becomes is, in many respects, the supreme fiction envisaged within the narrative. He literally *is* to be written into the role of another character, a falsified and "purely fictitious" (239) name to be inscribed upon the coffin he occupies, this final scripting being calculated to erase once and for all his two previous roles on the French social stage, as English ingénue and dedicated lover. His retrospective testimony, it might be added, fixes him permanently as Beckett, correcting finally this intriguing fiction of false identity even where it shames the naïveté that almost condemned him to eternity under the name of Pierre de la Roche St. Armand (222).

Others, though, perceive Beckett with less sinister motives than those held by the St. Alyres. The Englishman's own manservant, St. Clair, is induced to solicit information from the servants at the inn, and, naturally, believes to the letter his master's statement that "It is, of course, the venerable peer, and not the young lady who accompanies him, that interests me" (127). Yet, as Beckett admits, even this is a literary rather than professional relationship. On sending the servant out in pursuit of this information, Beckett comments:

> It was a commission that admirably suited the tastes and spirits of my worthy St. Clair, to whom, you will have observed, I had accustomed myself to talk

with the peculiar familiarity which the old French comedy establishes between master and valet.

I am sure he laughed at me in secret; but nothing could be more polite
and deferential. (127)

The contrast between St. Clair and the laconic coachman to the St. Alyres
could not be more pointedly accentuated. The obviously significant, utterly
complicit, series of "wise looks, nods and shrugs" (127) which St. Clair
returns to his master's request are, indeed, a world away from the "slightly
sarcastic" (125) disdain of the Count's retinue.

Likewise, the warlike Colonel Gaillarde, a truculent *ancien militaire*
whose investigations have connected the St. Alyres with the disappearance
of his own brother, is indulgent to Beckett even though it is the Englishman
who permits the escape of the St. Alyres to Paris. Gaillarde, as it were, is a
man grotesque enough to have come from the melodramatic stage: on con-
templating the St. Alyres his behavior is exaggerated to say the least

> You can't conceive a more diabolical effigy of hate and fury than the Colo-
> nel; the knotted veins stood out on his forehead, his eyes were leaping from
> their sockets, he was grinding his teeth, and froth was on his lips. His sword
> was drawn, in his hand, he accompanied his yelling denunciations with
> stamps upon the floor and flourishes of his weapon in the air. (145)

On this occasion the Count and Countess are both "in travelling costume"
(145), the latter's garment, of course, featuring the veil that is both an
invitation to intrigue and a disguise for treachery. Later, when actually
attending a costume ball, Gaillarde is so remarkable as to demand comment.
Beckett recalls:

> . . . I saw a gaunt figure stalking towards us. It was not a masque. The face
> was broad, scarred and white. In a word it was the ugly face of Colonel Gail-
> larde . . . There were strips of very real sticking-plaster across his eyebrow
> and temple, where my stick had left its mark, to score, hereafter, among the
> more honourable scars of war. (173)

Gaillarde is, however, the most genuine of the French citizens encountered
by Beckett en route to, and within, Paris. Despite Beckett's attempts to
configure the Frenchman through the façade of the "effigy" and the
"masque," Gaillarde's anger is unfeigned, his passion ultimately true. It is
Gaillarde, moreover, who correctly "reads" the armorial bearings that adorn
the St. Alyre coach. These include the figure of a stork which "was standing
upon one leg, and in the other claw held a stone" (121). Beckett, despite
being a character in his own fantasy, fails to comprehend the symbolism of
the armorial shield as being anything more than "a pretty device" that "no

doubt indicates a distinguished family" (125). In a novel, symbolically, such a thing *ought* rightly to act as a warning, a significant device to inform the reader even if the character is too purblind to appreciate its prescience. Where Beckett reads the figure simply as "the emblem of vigilance" (121), Gaillarde is more perceptive: "A red stork—good! The stork is a bird of prey; it is vigilant, greedy, and catches gudgeons. Red, too!—blood red! Ha! ha! The symbol is appropriate" (134). The stone may crush or bury Beckett, just as easily as the family it emblematizes may greedily devour him as it has so many other impressionable young men. The arms, it must be added, are themselves a masque, a façade of respectability through which the unwary gallant might be entranced. The Countess, whose spectacular diamonds are revealed to be counterfeit, "had figured some years before as one of the cleverest actresses on the minor stage of Paris, where she had been picked up by the Count and used as his principal accomplice" (241).

Despite the sympathy of his close associates, after Beckett is released from catalepsy, and testifies at the trial of the St. Alyres he becomes a quite different type of literary figure—a comic buffoon rather than an elegant hero:

> Having had an escape, as my friend Whistlewick said, "with a squeak" for my life, I innocently fancied that I should have been an object of considerable interest to Parisian society; but, a good deal to my mortification, I discovered that I was the object of a good-natured but contemptuous merriment. I was a *balourd*, a *benêt*, *un âne*, and figured even in caricatures. I became a sort of public character, a dignity "Unto which I was not born," and from which I fled as soon as I conveniently could . . . (240)[1]

Clearly, this is not the sort of fiction with which Beckett wishes to be implicated. His reaction, notably, is to escape from role play and to give thanks for his deliverance into a more real world (242).

"The Room in the Dragon Volant," then, is discernibly a different work to the more conventional ghost stories embodied in *In a Glass Darkly*. Its referents in Le Fanu's *oeuvre* are less the Gothic short stories of that volume and more the protracted locked-room and country house mysteries that the author produced in three-volume format for his English publishers. Simultaneously, though, "The Room in the Dragon Volant" has its counterpart in late-eighteenth century narratives of romance, adventure and intrigue both within and beyond the Gothic. It is, curiously, a historical novel as well, and yet it equally concerns those who resist the contemporary and retreat to the imaginative history of popular fiction. "The Room in the Dragon Volant" is,

---

1. French: "a numbskull, a booby, a jackass" (Le Fanu 344).

to recall the title of its containing volume, a reflection of the customarily transparent processes of perception and recollection, now revealed as seen, in a glass, darkly.[2]

Works Cited

Austen, Jane. *Northanger Abbey*. Bound with *Lady Susan, The Watsons*, and *Sanditon*. Ed. John Davie. Oxford: Oxford University Press, 1998. 1–205.

Davenport-Hines, Richard. *Gothic: Four Hundred Years of Excess, Horror, Evil and Ruin*. London: Fourth Estate, 1998.

Denman, Peter. "Le Fanu and Stoker: A Probable Connection." *Éire-Ireland* 9 (1974): 152–58.

Haslam, Richard. "Joseph Sheridan Le Fanu and the Fantastic Semantics of Ghost-Colonial Ireland." In *That Other World: The Supernatural and the Fantastic in Irish Literature and Its Contexts*, ed. Bruce Stewart. Gerrards Cross, UK: Colin Smythe, 1988. 1.267–86.

Keesey, Pam. "Introduction." In *Daughters of Darkness: Lesbian Vampire Stories*, ed. Pam Keesey. Pittsburgh: Cleis Press, 1993. 7–17.

Le Fanu, J. S. "Carmilla." In *In a Glass Darkly*. Ed. Robert Tracy. Oxford: Oxford University Press, 1993. 241–319.

Le Fanu, J. S. "The Room in the Dragon Volant." In *In a Glass Darkly*. Ed. Robert Tracy. Oxford: Oxford University Press, 1993. 119–242.

Mason, Diane. *The Secret Vice: Masturbation in Victorian Fiction and Medical Culture*. Manchester: Manchester University Press, 2008.

Mc Cormack, W. J. *Sheridan Le Fanu*. 3rd ed. Stroud: Sutton, 1997.

Peterson, Audrey. *Victorian Masters of Mystery: From Wilkie Collins to Conan Doyle*. New York: Frederick Ungar, 1984.

Sage, Victor. *Le Fanu's Gothic: The Rhetoric of Darkness*. Basingstoke, UK: Palgrave, 2004.

Scott, Ken. "Le Fanu's 'The Room in the Dragon Volant.'" *Lock Haven Review* 10 (1968): 25–32.

Sullivan, Jack. "'Green Tea': The Archetypal Ghost Story." In *Literature of the Occult*, ed. Peter B. Messent. Englewood Cliffs, NJ: Prentice-Hall, 1981. 117–38.

Waugh Patricia. *Metafiction: The Theory and Practice of Self-Conscious Fiction*. London: Methuen, 1984.

---

2. The allusion within the volume's title, of course, is to 1 Corinthians 13: 12, "a glass" in this context implying a mirror rather than a window.

"The Child That Went with the Fairies": The Folk Tale and the Ghost Story

Peter Bell

J. Sheridan Le Fanu's weird tale "The Child That Went with the Fairies," one of the last he wrote, first appeared in February 1870 in the weekly *All the Year Round*, then still edited by Charles Dickens. It was anonymously published, its author not being identified until M. R. James published the fruits of his investigations into Le Fanu's unattributed stories in *Madam Crowl's Ghost* in 1923. The tale remained relatively obscure until Richard Dalby included it in his 1971 anthology *The Sorceress in Stained Glass and Other Ghost Stories*, followed in 1975 by E. F. Bleiler in *Ghost Stories and Mysteries*, the second volume of Le Fanu's stories published by Dover, eleven years after the companion volume *Best Ghost Stories* containing the author's more famous tales. It concerns that topic of perennial fascination to the Victorian and Edwardian imagination: the fairy folk, good folk or little people—far removed from the sentimental nursery stereotype, and handed down in sinister legends common to Irish, Welsh, Scottish, and Northumbrian culture.

It is one of only two stories on the theme written by Le Fanu; the other, "Laura Silver Bell," appeared in *Belgravia Annual* two years later in 1872. While the latter is set amidst the Northumberland hills, an area he used in several other tales, "The Child That Went with the Fairies" is set to potent effect at the very heart of the region where the young Le Fanu first imbibed an awe of Irish folklore from a noted raconteur, Miss Ann Bailey, of Lough Guir in Limerick. Such lore also frequently infused his ghost stories, including his earliest, "The Ghost and the Bone-Setter." It is interesting that toward the end of his life he returned to the myths that had been so formative an influence. "The Child that Went with the Fairies" is especially notable for its blending of the folk tale and the ghost story.

Limerick's legends featured, in the same year, in two further copies of *All the Year Round*, both in April, likewise printed anonymously. "Stories of Lough Guir" comprises five linked tales; although they do not concern the fairy myth, the preamble, citing Ann Bailey's yarns, describes the area as "a kind of centre

418

of the operations of the Munster fairies." When a child is stolen by the "good people," it is "conjectured to be the place of its unearthly transmutation from the human to the fairy state." A compelling image of the strange Ann Bailey emerges: "plain, but refined and ladylike, with that kindly mystery in her sidelong glance and uplifted finger, which indicated the approaching climax of a tale of wonder." Jim Rockhill, in his perceptive introduction to the Ash-Tree Press edition of Le Fanu's complete works, has drawn attention to a passage in *Seventy Years of Irish Life*, the memoir of Le Fanu's brother, William, which recounts an incident from their childhood testifying to actual local belief in superstitions about fairy abduction (xviii–xix). "The White Cat of Drumgunniol" is an eerie ghost story about a family curse, with a terrifying Poe-like cat, a motif present also in "Laura Silver Bell." E. F. Bleiler has rightly emphasized Le Fanu's skill "as a reworker of the folklore of his native land." M. R. James, introducing the stories in *Madame Crowl's Ghost*, explained that he had "placed the most striking and sensational of them at the beginning." Significantly, out of twelve selected "The Child That Went with the Fairies" has the honour of fourth place, after "Madam Crowl's Ghost," "Squire Toby's Will," and "Dickon the Devil," and ahead of "The White Cat of Drumgunniol" and the impressive ghost story "An Account of Some Strange Disturbances in an Old House in Aungier Street."

There is an interesting temporal coincidence between Le Fanu's reawakened interest in the superstitions of his youth and the publication of that classic literary and artistic tribute to faerie: Richard Doyle's *In Fairyland: A Series of Pictures from the Elf World*. With a publication date of 1870, Longman in fact issued the book at the end of 1869, in time for the Christmas market; post-dating being not unusual in the era 1860–1900. Given that Le Fanu's story appeared very soon after, in February 1870, it is tempting to speculate that it may have been influenced by Doyle's book; this, however, is improbable, for it would leave insufficient time for editorial process. It is conceivable, though, that within aesthetic circles news of the latest work by the greatly respected Doyle, with its keynote poem, William Allingham's "The Fairies," had already circulated. More likely, the theme's topicality among writers and artists underlined its timely relevance; conceivably Le Fanu submitted it, or Dickens solicited it, with that in mind. The Irish aesthetic fascination with the theme was highlighted in an exhibition at the National Gallery of Ireland in 2007: "The Fantastic in Irish Art." This remarkable display of literature and art, with many illustrated books, covered a variety of macabre and fantastic cultural themes, in which the fairies held prominent place: it included Richard Doyle, as well as his uncle, Charles Doyle, father of Sherlock Holmes's creator and one time believer in fairies himself, Arthur Conan Doyle. Likewise, the subject was popular in London at this time as well as Dublin, exemplified by the great acclaim accorded to *In Fairyland*, rendering the subject eminently suitable for *All the Year Round*.

Richard Doyle's representation of the little people had a long pedigree, going back a quarter of a century to an illustrated new edition of the Brothers Grimm, *The Fairy Ring* of 1846, and numerous similar publications up to his 1870 masterpiece, product of a lifelong passion for fairy tales. The Dublin Exhibition brochure emphasized the sanitized nature of Doyle's portrayal of such macabre myths: "an escape from the real concerns of modern life," his fairies "were presented as rather benevolent, occasionally cruel, but never a threat to human beings"—mischievous elves and gnomes furnished any violent element in his view of fairyland. William Makepeace Thackeray, whose books Doyle illustrated, praised the way his fairies exuded a "burlesque which never loses sight of beauty." This may sound a far cry from the chillingly macabre tone of Le Fanu's tale, but the comments understate the capriciously grotesque element in Doyle's imagery—the juxtaposition of the burlesque and the grotesque. There is no beauty, as Edgar Allan Poe mused, "without some *strangeness* in the proportion." It is this aspect which Le Fanu—whose vision echoed in so many ways that of his American contemporary—deftly captures. Allingham's poem, interestingly, conveys more of the sinister and tragic than Doyle's illustrations, closer to Le Fanu. Commencing on an ominous note—"Up the airy mountain, Down the rushy glen, We daren't go a-hunting, For fear of little men"—its longest verse expresses the horror and tragedy underlying the legend:

> They stole little Bridget
> For seven years long;
> When she came down again
> Her friends were all gone.
> They took her lightly back,
> Between the night and morrow,
> They thought that she was fast asleep,
> But she was dead with sorrow.
> They have kept her ever since
> Deep within the lake,
> On a bed of flag-leaves
> Watching till she wake.

"The Child That Went with the Fairies" skillfully embellishes the popular myth: a child abducted from a rural community, deemed to have "gone to the fairies." A simple plot, maybe, but such is Le Fanu's art that the hackneyed yarn is imbued with a lasting sense of the strange and terrible;

leaving the reader with a feel of the genuine horror primitive communities cherished. He imparts to the familiar legend the Gothic ambience that underpins so effectively his ghost stories and mysteries. Fundamental is the setting, eerily established in the opening paragraph: "Eastward of the old city of Limerick, about ten Irish miles under the range of mountains known as the Slieveelim hills . . . there runs a very old narrow road." Running beside "bog and pasture, hill and hollow, straw-thatched village, and roofless castle," it is "singularly lonely." It traverses "a deserted country," sketched in bleak terms:

> A wide, black bog, level as a lake, skirted with copse, spreads to the left, as you journey northward, and the long and irregular line of mountains rises at the right, clothed in heath, broken with lines of grey rock that resemble the bold and irregular outlines of fortifications, and riven with many a gully, expanding here and there into rocky and wooded glens, which open as they approach the road. (*Ghost Stories and Mysteries* 136)

Le Fanu thus invests the scene with the kind of sinister ambience that Arthur Machen would later paint in his eerie descriptions of the Welsh mountains, where he set his own grim fables of the little people.

In this uninviting land is the abode of the widow Mary Ryan and her four children, a mean cabin bedecked with the amulets one finds warding off the Devil in a Gothic fantasy: it is circled by a ring of mountain ashes; horseshoes are nailed above the door; over lintel and thatch "grew, luxuriant, patches of that ancient cure for many maladies, and prophylactic against the machinations of the evil one, the house-leek;" and "in the *chiaroscuro* of the interior, when your eye grew sufficiently accustomed to that dim light, you might discover, hanging at the head of the widow's wooden-roofed bed, her beads and a phial of holy water." Here were the "defences and bulwarks against the intrusion of that unearthly and evil power, of whose vicinity this solitary family were constantly reminded by the outline of Lisnavoura, that lonely hill-haunt of the 'Good People.'" Its "strangely dome-like summit rose not half a mile away, looking like an outwork of the long line of mountain that sweeps by it." Here Le Fanu introduces the motif of dreaded Lisnavoura, which is dramatically repeated, again and again, as the tale gathers force.

Mary Ryan, returning from her chores, discovers that her three younger children, two sons and a daughter, have disappeared, unnoticed by her elder daughter, Nell, who has been keeping house. Dispatched to find them, at first Nell is angry, but as the scene's brooding vacancy besieges her, "now a different feeling overcame her, and she grew pale." With "an undefined boding" she looks to Lisnavoura, "now darkening to the deepest purple against the flaming sky of sunset." In these brief, subtle lines Le Fanu captures many things: fear of the wild, a dread of twilight when the fairies are abroad, and above all Nell's terror that the old tales might be true: "How many stories had she listened to by the winter hearth, of children stolen by the fairies, at nightfall, in lonely places! With this fear she knew her mother was haunted." Le Fanu adds a nice Gothic touch, the classic superstitious response: as Nell looks to Lisnavoura "in a trance of fear," she "crossed herself again and again, and whispered prayer after prayer."

Especially effective is the way Le Fanu paints the terrifying vacancy by focusing on the contrast between sound and silence. We are introduced to the children as birds are singing among the branches "in the thinning leaves of the melancholy ash-trees," their playful voices mingling with the evening chorus. This establishes a link between innocence and the perilous beauty of the wild. Searching for her siblings, Nell anxiously calls "but no answer came from the little haggard, fenced with straggling bushes." Though she listens in increasing dread "the sound of their voices was missing." Beyond the house all is "silent and deserted." She listens "with a sinking heart," hearing "nothing but the farewell twitter and whistle of the birds in the bushes around." It is at this point that the awful recognition that the children had gone with the fairies dawns on her.

Expert in suspense, sudden shifts in narrative expectation, Le Fanu offers a moment's hope, yet tinged with doom: the children are espied approaching, but it is "from the westward, and from the direction of the dreaded hill of Lisnavoura," on the road "which some little way off made a slight dip, which had concealed them." Then comes the real shock: there are only two "and one of them, the little girl, was crying." The youngest, the little boy Billy, is missing. His brother and sister have a fearful tale to relate. It is rendered the more horrifying for being mediated through a prism of naivety, their struggle to convey a shocking experience they can scarcely comprehend; the terror is thus reinforced by reliance on a not quite coherent second-hand account:

> "Where is Billy—where is he?" cried the mother, nearly breathless as soon as she was within hearing.
>
> "He's gone—they took him away; but they said he'll come back again," answered little Con, with the dark brown hair.
>
> "He's gone away with the grand ladies," blubbered the little girl.
>
> "What ladies—where? Oh, Leum [aka Billy], asthora! My darlin', are you gone away at last? Where is he? What took him? What ladies are you talkin' about? What way did he go?" she cried in distraction.
>
> "I couldn't see where he went, mother; 'twas like as if he was going to Lisnavoura." (139)

Having established authentic ambience with local dialect and the terrified children's stumbling words, Le Fanu resumes the narrative voice: "the two children, sometimes speaking together, often interrupting one another, often interrupted by their mother, managed to tell this strange story, which I had better relate connectedly and in my own language." He highlights the eerie scene, the fading autumn evening, contrasting the gloom again with the children's gay voices: "Under the great old ash-trees, whose last leaves were falling at their feet, in the light of an October sunset, they were playing with the hilarity and eagerness of rustic children, clamouring together, and their faces were turned toward the west and storied hill of Lisnavoura." Childhood innocence is thus overshadowed by the sinister domain of the fairies. The tranquility is rudely shattered by "a startling voice with a screech" behind them, and they behold "a sight, such as they never beheld before." This is the cue for the story's critical phase, the appearance of the fairies and their abduction of the youngest child, golden-haired Billy. Except for Machen's dimly glimpsed horrors, no picture of the little people has been so menacingly drawn as in this masterly sequence by Le Fanu, in which he brings to the fore his genius as a purveyor of horror.

Le Fanu achieves his impact, again, through contrast: the fairies look both fair and foul, their glamour tinged with ugliness, their pleasing allure disguising dreadfulness. Le Fanu alternates skillfully between these poles, building the suspense: the reader already senses more amiss than the naïve children, entranced by the magnificence of the horse-drawn carriage—a common image in faerie art. It is "old-fashioned and gorgeous," of an "antique splendour," "a spectacle perfectly dazzling," its trappings "scarlet, blazing with gold." The horses are surreal, awe-inspiring: "huge, and snow-white, with great manes, that as they tossed and shook them in the air, seemed to stream and float, sometimes longer and sometimes shorter, like so much smoke." But the coach, "glowing with colours, gilded and emblazoned," has lackeys fearful to behold. Le Fanu here switches from the fabulous to the grotesque: they are "ludicrously out of proportion with the enormous horses." They display "sharp, sallow features, and small, restless fiery eyes, and faces of cunning and malice that chilled the children," and the driver "was scowling and showing his white fangs underneath his cocked hat, and his little blazing beads of eyes were quivering with fury in their sockets as he whirled his whip round and round again over their heads, till the lash of it looked like a streak of fire in the evening sun, and sounded like the cry of a legion of 'fillapoueeks' in the air."

Worse is to come. When the coach stops the children become "so frightened that they could only gape and turn white in their panic." Then it seems their fears are premature: for "a very sweet voice from the open window of the carriage reassured them, and arrested the attack of the lackeys." A "very grand-looking" and beautiful lady smiles on them, such that they "all felt pleased in the strange light of that smile." Ominously, she declares, bending her "large and wonderfully clear eyes" on Billy: "The boy with the golden hair, I think." This is the cue for the supreme horror, a masterly touch by Le Fanu, for the children glimpse through the carriage's glass window, "another woman inside, whom they did not like so well." Here, Le Fanu excels as a master of the macabre:

> This was a black woman, with a wonderfully long neck, hung round with many strings of large variously-coloured beads, and on her head was a sort of turban of silk striped with all the colours of the rainbow, and fixed in it was a golden star.
>
> This black woman had a face as thin almost as a death's head, with high cheekbones, and great goggle eyes, the whites of which, as well as her wide range of teeth, showed in brilliant contrast with her skin, as she looked over the beautiful lady's shoulder, and whispered something in her ear. (141)

Having sketched this horror, the tale reverts to the fair-faced woman and her appeal to the gullible children. Dramatic irony is skillfully deployed: the reader knows what horror lurks behind the fair façade, but the children despite their qualms remain charmed. The lady's voice is "as sweet as a silver bell," her smile as beguiling as "the light of an enchanted lamp." She casts a look of "ineffable fondness" over Billy and lifts him to her lap—he seeming to "ascend in her small fingers as lightly as a feather"—and lavishes kisses on him, such that his siblings "would have been only too happy to change places with their favoured little brother." But there "was only one thing that was unpleasant, and a little frightened them, and that was the black woman, who stood and stretched forward, in the carriage as before." The culmination of this scene, must surely be one of the finest cameos of the macabre in supernatural literature:

> She gathered a rich silk and gold handkerchief that was in her fingers up to her lips, and seemed to thrust ever so much of it, fold after fold into her capacious mouth, as they thought to smother her laughter, with which she seemed convulsed, for she was shaking and quivering, as it seemed, with suppressed merriment; but her eyes, which remained uncovered, looked angrier than they had ever seen eyes look before. (141)

It is easy to see why M. R. James was impressed and recognized within the anonymous draft the hallmark of Dublin's dark prince. Indeed, the scene anticipates James's own style, derived so much from Le Fanu, in the way it so subtly conjures the hideous. The contrast between finery and grotesquerie, the fair and the morbid, the alluring and repulsive, and the grotesqueness of the central horror—so briefly yet, for that reason, so appallingly glimpsed— all this demonstrates the powerful Gothic intelligence apparent in Le Fanu's better-known classics.

The culminating abduction is chillingly finessed, having the air of a strange visionary dream. From the departing carriage, with the captive Billy on her knee, the fair woman casts to his still enthralled siblings one "large russet apple" after another, each vanishing as they run to retrieve it, until they reach the "old crossroad":

> It seemed that there the horses' hoofs and carriage wheels rolled up a won-derful dust, which being caught in one of those eddies that whirl the dust up into a column, on the calmest day, enveloped the children for a moment, and passed whirling on towards Lisnavoura, the carriage, as they fancied, driving in the centre of it; but suddenly, it subsided, the straws and leaves floated to the ground, the dust dissipated itself, but the white horses and the lackeys, the gilded carriage, the lady and their little golden-haired brother were gone. (141–42)

Notable is the image of Lisnavoura, which throughout the tale is a motif repeated like a mantra—ten times in all. The children contemplate the sudden emptiness as "the upper rim of the clear setting sun disappeared behind the hill of Knockdoula, and it was twilight." They feel "the transition like a shock," and "the sight of the rounded summit of Lisnavoura, now closely overhanging them, struck them with a new fear." Lisnavoura, domain of the fairies and ominous against the sunset, constantly repeated, lends the prose a compelling poetic timbre, rather in the mode of Poe, with whom Le Fanu shared in so many ways a vision of the grotesque.

If Le Fanu's story had ended here it would still have been a masterly piece, a clever adaptation of a traditional folk tale; but there is an impressive coda, to which he brings all his dexterity as a master of the ghost story. Con-ventionally, the fairy myths end with the child returned to human society, albeit subtly changed, or else confined permanently to fairyland; but this story's resolution is more complex, and it is, as Bleiler has observed, "to Le Fanu's credit that he left it a mystery." Mary Ryan "never more saw her dar-ling," but the children do see "something of the lost little boy." Sometimes they glimpse "the pretty face of little Billy peeping in archly at the door, and smiling silently at them," yet as "with cries of delight" they run to embrace him, he "drew back, still smiling archly, and when they got out into the open day, he was gone, and they could see no trace of him anywhere." Or he would "peep for a longer time, sometimes for a shorter time, sometimes his little hand would come in, and, with bended finger, beckon them to follow," but always "smiling with the same arch look and wary silence—and always he was gone when they reached the door." Gradually, his visitations "grew less and less frequent, and in about eight months, they ceased altogether, and little Billy, irretrievably lost, took rank in their memories with the dead." Just as we anticipate that here the story must end, Le Fanu provides one final, harrowing glimpse: in the gray wintry dawn, some year and a half later, his sister wakes to the sound of the latch softly lifting, revealing her lost brother softly closing the door behind him. She cries to her sister that he has come back, but the vision is pathetic, frightening: barefoot and ragged, pale and famished, he makes for the fire and cowers over the embers, slowly rubbing his hands, shivering. He turns toward them but "it seemed to her, in fear," and in "the glare of the embers reflected on his thin cheek," he seems to regard her—but nothing more; for then he "rose and went on tiptoe, quickly to the door, in silence, and let himself out as softly as he had come in." "After that," the single-sentence paragraph bleakly states, "the little boy was never seen any more by any one of his kindred." Despite efforts by "fairy doctors" and holy ritual to find his body so that it could rest beneath a headstone where "the survivor might kneel and say a kind prayer for the peace of the departed soul," in the end "no grave received him." The story ends starkly on the haunting motif of Lisnavoura:

> But there was no landmark to show where little Billy was hidden from their loving eyes, unless it was in the old hill of Lisnavoura, that cast its long shadow at sunset before the cabin-door; or that, white and filmy in the moonlight, in later years, would occupy his brother's gaze as he returned from fair or market, and draw from him a sigh and a prayer for the little brother he had lost so long ago, and was never to see again. (143)

Le Fanu ends his tale on a note that is simultaneously disquieting and tragic. In a few spare paragraphs he transcends the folk convention, converting the fable into a moving reflection on grief: the hope, infused with the sad conviction it cannot be so, that a loved one will somehow return. Grief was an emotion that consumed the writer after the death of his beloved wife, and found its way into much of his writing, suggesting that his stories in the genre offered lifelong catharsis. What lends the ending heightened poignancy is that the beloved lost boy evidently rests not in peace: his family are impotent before a fate they cannot comprehend, terrifying, pathetic, tragic. It is, as Rockhill has shrewdly observed, "a sadly beautiful tale," with the victim "neither fully in this world or the one into which it was abducted, peeping and creeping into our own until fading into oblivion."

"The Child That Went with the Fairies" is something of an undervalued gem. Although it may be a lesser tale, overshadowed by better known masterpieces, it contains in its concise four thousand words many of the elements that define Le Fanu's genius. It establishes an eerie setting; it expertly builds suspense; it is macabre and frightening; it convincingly and subtly portrays the supernatural; it is replete with grief and tragedy; and to the very end it conveys a sense of numinous mystery. The story is interesting and unusual in several ways. Although it is excellent simply as an authentic relay of the old folk-tale, it transcends the legend. It works into it powerful elements of the ghost story, seamlessly and naturally; and stands as a fine example of the ghost story as metaphor for existential crisis: the pathos of bereavement and grief, and a sense of mankind's apprehension before the inexplicable. Le Fanu's other foray into fairy lore "Laura Silver Bell" is a fine horror tale, which, as Rockhill has noted, "blurs the line between the natural and the supernatural . . . to work marvels," but remains little more than a macabre realization of the convention, recounting an unbaptized girl's bewitchment by a fairy lord who appears glamorous to her, but to other observers grotesque. "The Child That Went with the Fairies" on the other hand, has greater depth, conveying a far more harrowing sense of tragedy.

That Le Fanu, toward the end of his life, should have returned to the folk tales of his youth is notable. This might be attributable merely to age, but it could also betoken awareness of the theme's topical interest; and it should not be forgotten that folklore infused many of his other stories. The tale is one of the earliest, and most effective, fictionalizations of the fairy myth—twenty years before John Buchan and Arthur Machen, who shared a similar awe of landscape and its interplay with ancient traditions of the little people. Only Machen, perhaps, has imbued the myth with greater terror, but Le Fanu's tale, for all its brevity, has comparable mastery of the grotesque. Whilst there may be sufficient in Welsh tradition to have inspired Machen, it is possible he was influenced also by this tale, even though it was not identified as Le Fanu's until 1923 by M. R. James. It is also interesting that Sarban's magnificent fairy lore fantasia "Ringstones" (1951) gains much of its power from its location in the Northumberland hills, where "Laura Silver Bell" also was set. Rockhill has remarked, concerning Le Fanu's late ventures into Limerick folklore, that it is "a pity he did not live long enough to redevelop these along more elaborate lines as he had his earlier works," praising his command of "the curious intermixture of natural and supernatural phenomena, fairy tale and ghost story." These are certainly conclusions supported by his most fully elaborated example: "The Child that Went with the Fairies."

Works Cited

Bell, Peter. "Of Sacred Groves and Ancient Mysteries: Parallel Themes in the Writings of Arthur Machen and John Buchan." *Faunus: The Journal of the Friends of Arthur Machen* 21 (Spring 2010): 26–45.

Dalby, Richard. *The Golden Age of Children's Book Illustration.* London: Michael O'Mara, 1991.

Doyle, Richard. *In Fairyland.* London: Longman, 1870.

Le Fanu, J. S. *Ghost Stories and Mysteries.* Ed. E. F. Bleiler. New York: Dover, 1975.

———. *Madam Crowl's Ghost and Other Stories.* E. M. R. James. Ware, UK: Wordsworth, 1994.

Rockhill, Jim. "A Dream of the Shadow of Smoke: The Final Years and Supernatural Fiction of Joseph Sheridan Le Fanu 1870–1873." In *Mr. Justice Harbottle and Others* by J. S. Le Fanu. Ashcroft, BC: Ash-Tree Press, 2005.

Wilson, Neil. *Shadows in the Attic: A Guide to British Supernatural Fiction, 1820–1950.* Boston Spa: The British Library, 2000.

[Unsigned.] "The Fantastic in Irish Art." Exhibition Catalogue. Dublin: National of Ireland Gallery of Ireland, 2007.

The "Smashed Looking-Glass": Fragmentation and Narrative Perversity in *Willing to Die*

Victor Sage

The hybrid Gothic rhetoric of Le Fanu's *Willing to Die* is either an epistemological puzzle created in the service of an intriguing narrative perversity, or, as some have argued, a piece of rank clumsiness we have to forgive an author at the end of his life. I confess I prefer the first hypothesis; the evidence (which includes my own readerly pleasure) favors it, I believe, and I want to demonstrate the point in this discussion and consider some of its implications.[1]

---

1. See, for example, W. J. Mc Cormack's standard critical biography, *Sheridan Le Fanu and Victorian Ireland* 227, in which he describes Ethel Ware as "a vacillating, passive female voice, almost drained of personality." The strong suggestion here is that this voice is the voice of an author, who, towards the end of his life, cannot make up his mind about Catholicism, and who has patched together this novel in haste. There are thirty-five references to *WTD* in the index to Mc Cormack's work, which shows that the novel is a continual point of reference, and even fascination; yet, perhaps paradoxically, several of them hint in passing at the feebleness of this novel. Perhaps the most important of these is the interesting discussion on 247–49, which quotes the view of Wolff, that a certain number of late Victorians resorted to "'the fantasy of a bisexual God' whose feminine characteristics often overwhelm the traditional masculine ones of God the father," a notion, which, Mc Cormack comments, might provide the unifying principle in the imagination of the later Le Fanu, which "otherwise might appear to be a ragbag filled with random and unrelated obsessions." Le Fanu is probably a latent homosexual, he suggests, and this gives to the writer's work a "consistency and unity of feeling achieved through literary forms of little or no complexity and buoyancy." This last remark hints at the formal weakness of these books. They are romances, it is implied, not novels. The implication is that the aesthetic price the author has paid for his choice of form is high: these long, "homogeneous," "hermetically-sealed," late narratives, the writer suggests, lack the dynamism of a concrete, historical, social world, which is revealed by realism. Their characters are the victims of abstract emotions. There is a strong whiff of nostalgia here for the masculine virtues

The problem arises at the very outset in the way the first-person narrator, Ethel Ware—who is also, as we would say, a beginning writer—sets out the rules of her own narrative. She will write in two modes:

> My narrative shall be arranged in the order of events; I shall not recapitulate or anticipate.
>
> What I have learned from others, and did not witness, that which I narrate, in part, from the limits of living witnesses, and, in part, conjecturally, I shall record in the historic third person; and I shall write it down with as much confidence and particularity as if I had actually seen it; in that respect imitating, I believe, all the great historians, modern and ancient. But the scenes in which I have been an actor, that which mine eyes have seen, and my ears heard, I will relate accordingly. If I can be clean and true, my clumsiness and irregularity, I hope, will be forgiven me. (WTD 1.2)

Ethel sets herself a stern task here as the writer of her text, making a clear distinction throughout between the first-hand witness and the historian who "compiles" his or her narrative, from other, second-hand, witness-statements. Ethel calls this her "conjectural" mode. The redundancy of this rhetorical procedure is justified by a simple, elementary proposition, which seems to represent a naïve historical ideal: to follow the order of events without recapitulation or anticipation. As anyone who has tried to write either history or fiction knows, such a rigorously "historical" self-prescription, even for a historian, would be so hard to follow, that it is likely to be violated at the first opportunity, or perhaps even abandoned before it

---

of classic European mimesis: "In this pattern there is no sense of a Hegelian dialectic in which reality perpetuates itself through contradiction and destruction; rather, it is the *praecox* phenomenon of schizophrenia which offers a comparison to Le Fanu's logic. There is little evidence in the fiction or elsewhere that he was conscious of these features of his imagination" (247). This rather reductive version of an unselfconscious retreat from the representation of "history" into the occult psychology of the author, perhaps serves a biographical aim better than a critical one. For the evaluative significance of the idea of "retreat," its implications for genre, and its co-appearance with the aesthetics of realism in the critical commentary on Le Fanu's later work, see my *Le Fanu's Gothic: The Rhetoric of Darkness*, Introduction, 1–8. For another, different set of arguments about the place of this theme of female renunciation in Le Fanu's fiction, see Gaid Girard, *Joseph Sheridan Le Fanu: Une écriture fantastique*, an account which also relates this theme to the phenomenon of split female narrators in Le Fanu, esp. 392–410; see also my detailed review of this book, 281–86, especially 285–86.

has properly begun. But for Ethel honesty is a sacred trust, and she is wedded to the re-creation of first-hand witnessing.[2]

Ethel is the author of her narrative, but she isn't the author of her text. This rule of reading is a familiar convention in the management of first person-narratives. But in this case the implied author, to whom these rules of redundancy do not apply, has vanished into the disarming crispness of her *ingénue* rhetoric, and we have been seduced at a stroke, as soon as we accept her rules. The game with the reader is actually quite a different one. Yet it is as if the author, in effacing himself at the level of writing, has perversely contracted himself at least to pay lip-service to Ethel's eccentric and self-willed narrative methods, obeying at least the form, if not the matter, of her rigorous epistemological distinction, and thus endorsing the naïvety of her composition, and the apparent weakness of its switches into remote witnessing mode.

But every restriction which Ethel imposes forms a rhetorical opportunity at the other, "conjectural" level of the text, and, on the face of it oddly, some of the most powerful scenes in the novel fall into this category of (epistemologically weak), reconstructed third-person narration. For, indeed, Ethel's obsession with order (and the value of order) leads paradoxically to a recreation of doubt and mystery; as if events and people, particularly those witnessed by the direct method of the senses, despite the sharpness of their images, retain a film of inexplicability and a shading of horror which is a part of them or their after-image, and cannot be struck from the record, or altered in any way. In Volume 1, Chapter 3 of the novel, for example, called, "The Thief in the Night," and which features the death of her beloved sister Helen, Ethel, despite or perhaps because of, her rage for narrative order, finds herself at a loss to narrate and resorts to analogy:

> Of what happened next I have a strangely imperfect recollection. I cannot tell you the intervals, or even the order, in which some of the events occurred. It is not that the mist of time obscures it; what I do recollect is dreadfully vivid; but there are spaces in the picture gone. I see faces of angels, and faces that make my heart sink; fragments of scenes. It is like something reflected in the pieces of a smashed looking-glass. (WTD 1.44)

---

2. In reality, we are not reading History, but Fiction. But History anyway cannot really be reduced to testimony. To put Ethel's insistence on testimony as the *prima materia* of her "history," in context, here is the opposite argument. "But to know an event historically, Arthur Danto has reminded us, is precisely to know it in a way that a witness cannot. It is to assume an enabling continuity—a different language, another knowledge" quoted in Ina Ferris, *The Achievement of Literary Authority* 194. This book also has implications for the dichotomy between Gothic Romance and History.

The point here is that Le Fanu, the author, who is an admirer of Scott, knows perfectly well that this trope of the looking glass is an ancient metaphor for mimetic representation: to see it smashed, as Ethel does, in order to describe faithfully the difficulty of her narrative at this point, is to hint at another form of representation beyond, or beneath, realism and realism's demand for whole forms.[3] Le Fanu's interest in fragmentation is well-attested, and by the time he wrote this, his last novel, he had been experimenting in narrative fragmentation in a variety of modes, short and long, for forty years or so. He is particularly attracted, from his early stories, to the twice-told tale; to the presentation of the same events from different points of view and different registers. Thus, Ethel Ware, his *ingénue* writer and eye-witness, is allowed to stumble here into the fictional aesthetic of the novel through her own innocent confession of narrative ineptitude, her own sense of falling short of the high standards of "true" (i.e. "historical" or sequential) representation, which she herself has apparently set.

Ethel is thus composing a spiritual portrait of herself as a pilgrim, piecing the fragments of the mirror-image together from the broken fragments of perceived events. Thus the primary order is the one in which she herself is present. But there is more to her sense of the rigid order of things than at first appears. The smashed looking-glass is an entry into a series of images, suspended in a quite different medium from that of Enlightenment causality ("plot") or the powerful analogy between fiction and (the narrative of) "history" as linear forms, which might be familiar to the Victorian reader through a reading of Scott. One of Le Fanu's favorite analogies, on the other hand, repeated by the narrators of previous novels, is between the action of memory and the resurrection of the dead; and Ethel has already strikingly drawn on the transgressive and occult aspects of this figure: "In the volume of memory, every page of which, like "Cornelius Agrippa's bloody book" has power to evoke a spectre, would you yet erase a line? We can willingly part with nothing that ever was part of mind, or memory, or self. The lamentable past is our own for ever" (*WTD* 1.8). These are the terms of a haunted ontology, or in the awkward post-Derridean play, "hauntology." The fragmented space of narrated memory preserves and acts out the bond between

---

3. The classic discussion is M. H. Abrams, *The Mirror and the Lamp*. For an early use by Le Fanu of the mirror as a fantasmagorical way of representing History, see Sage 40ff. For further discussions in the context of Irish Gothic, see the section "Representation and History" in *Melmoth the Wanderer*, ed. Victor Sage (Harmonsworth, UK: Penguin, 2000), xix–xxiii; and my account of Maturin's "broken or distorting mirror" in *A Companion to the Gothic*, ed. David Punter, 85. On Le Fanu's narratives as "two-way mirrors," see Girard 373; 387 et al.

the witness and the revenant. The status of Ethel's writing is a complex traf-
ficking between her self-imposed silence, which results in a private form of
speech, forbidden but just at the point of acknowledgement, and the composition of a public record. Here is how she writes of the far-off memories
which her narrative stimulates, and their revenant specter, her dead sister
Helen, awakened by her grief and intense longing:

> A sense of profanation shuts the door, and we "wake" our dead alone. I
> could not have told you what I am going to write. I did not intend inscribing
> here more than the short, bleak result. But I write it as if to myself, and I will
> get through it.
>
> To you it may seem that I make too much of this, which is, as Hamlet
> says, "common." But you have not known what it is to be for all your earthly
> life shut out from all but one beloved companion, and never after to have
> found another. (*WTD* 1.44–45)

Who is shut out from whom here? The reader ("you") is addressed like a very
close confidante; and this intimacy of an unspoken conversation between two
aspects of the remembering speaker, silent thought and self-expression, known
imperfectly to herself, echoes both Maud in *Uncle Silas* and Laura in
"Carmilla." But here the insistence on the courage needed at the moment of
composition of a long narrative, not just a brief witness statement, gives it an
extra layer: (1) it interrupts the process of memory and re-dramatizes it, as she
appeals to a silent someone, present like a confessor, witnessing her conversion
of her inability, or unwillingness, to speak, into silent writing; and (2) the
accompaniment to that composition, a kind of musing commentary on what
she writes, forms a commentary which is included in it.

Writing as portrayed in several of Le Fanu's earlier novels, is already a
kind of fantasmagoria, a magic lantern show, in front of which the readers
sit, as one of his favorite phrases goes, "all in the dark"—i.e. unable to know
what is coming next: the relation between the reader and the text is figured
as a darkness like that of primitive superstition or belief, in which the images
which rise to the memory are like those bright pictures of the original fantasmagoria of the 1790s, conjured from the abyss by Robertson, after the
nuns had been evicted in 1790, in the old Capuchine Convent at Paris.[4] The
difference here is Ethel's extreme insistence on the strict, indeed the ines-

---

4. See M. Milner, *La Fantasmagorie* 18–20. For the connection between the fantasmagoria and the Gothic romance, see Terry Castle; see also Castle for the more detailed
The Female Thermometer 140–67. See my detailed analysis of the mirror motif as a
form of fantasmagoria in the frame of *The Fortunes of Colonel Torlogh O'Brien* in *Le
Fanu's Gothic* 40–46.

capable, order of things, as *the order in which they happened to her*. That order is necessarily a fragment. Robertson's magic lantern show was free and random, a set of images, surrounded by darkness, without a plot, except the "plot" of revenancy; Ethel's memories, comparably, are a set of autobiographical conjurings which send us on a journey down into the underworld—her *facilis descensus* (2.215; "easy descent") as she calls it, after Virgil—towards Avernus, the underworld of ruin and death, from which she cannot deviate, or turn aside. And from it, like the Sybil of Cumae, she is allowed a hard climb back up.

She apparently sacrifices everything to the sequential order of this journey, in order to preserve her own initial ignorance, keeping the reader also (at all costs) in the dark; and thus, increasingly in the second and final volumes, according to her rules, the reader becomes aware that she has to interpolate "conjectural" explanations of what has gone on, which we have been rigorously denied during the novitiate of its first volume and a half. In this way, the novel preserves the primary reactions—particularly the trust, fear and horror—of the child, and later, the adolescent subject, to the images of people she encounters in her rustic solitude.

There is a debt here to Ann Radcliffe's trademark pursuit of uncertainty, in *The Mysteries of Udolpho*, in which "explanation" is separated from "epiphany": we are given the image first, encountered by both reader and character under maximum conditions of uncertainty and curiosity, and hundreds of pages later, the explanation, which is natural, rather than supernatural. Radcliffe will go to any lengths to keep these two writerly modes apart, tormenting the reader's sense of plausibility. The principle of this preservation of the first impressions of the ignorant she also refers to, later, as a Latin formula for a naïve form of the Sublime: *Omne ignotum pro magnifico*—"The unknown is taken for the sublime" (*WTD* 2.140).

Let me just briefly illustrate some of these points from the opening sequences of the narrative. In fact, we actually do meet most of the characters and the intrigue in the novel's first volume through the medium of Ethel's incomprehension. After a few pages, the reader meets Laura Grey, the just-appointed governess of the two little girls, Helen and Ethel, at the same time as they do; and Ethel declares that "we were in high good humour with our young lady-superioress, and she seemed to like us" (I, 1, 26). The narrative is doubled here: the term "lady-superioress" (or abbess), slipped in by the older Ethel, enforces the thematic idea that Malory is an anchoritic solitude. Laura, however, culled by Ethel's careless mother from an advert in *The Times* is the center of some kind of intrigue, which she consistently refuses to share with the persistently curious Ethel, even though, after Helen's death, they become close friends. Much later, she presses Laura for "her story;" Laura produces a fake idea of the "average history" and installs herself neatly behind it:

> "My story! What does it signify? I suppose it is about an average story. Some people are educated to be governesses; and some of us take to it later, or only by accident; and we are amateurs, and do our best. The Jewish custom was wise; everyone should learn a mechanic's business. Saint Paul was a tent-maker. If fortune upsets the boat, it is well to have anything to lay hold of— anything rather than drowning; an hospital matron, a companion, a govern-ess, there are not many chances, when things go wrong, between a poor woman and the workhouse."
> "All this means, you will tell me nothing," I said. (*WTD* 1.69)

The sleight of hand evidently doesn't work on Ethel, and only sharpens her sense of the mystery. But Laura's words, despite herself, do contain something: a prophetic metaphor of a shipwreck. That is exactly what will happen right on their doorstep in the estuary at Malory to both Laura and to Ethel, when the *Conway Castle* is literally wrecked in front of their eyes and goes down with all hands but one. In fact, Ethel (alongside the reader) learns much later, Laura is a ruined aristocrat, the fiancée of the son of Lord Rillingdon, Mr. Jennings, who loves her, but whose father will never now marry him to her, since the crash of her family fortunes. She has been forced to work as a governess, but even so, even in this retirement from the world, Rillingdon *père* is afraid she will disrupt his new plans to marry off his son elsewhere. One day he appears on the road to Malory, and Ethel christens him, the "man in the chocolate-coloured overcoat." He tries to warn Laura off his son, threatening her, while Ethel, told to walk on a little, tries to read their lips and body-language at a distance. Laura seems to reject and resist the old man, but absolutely refuses to tell Ethel (or the reader) anything.

There are other mysterious "figures" which appear in this remote land-scape. Soon after Laura's appointment, Ethel's careless and neglectful Fa-ther, nagged by her totteringly high-church, more than half-Catholic Mother, takes on a Mr. Carmel, who appears at the house. Here is how Ethel first sees him against the darkness of the garden at Malory: "The figure stood out against this background like a pale old portrait, his black dress almost blended with the background; but, indistinct as it was, it was easy to see that the dress he wore was of some ecclesiastical fashion not in use among Church of England men" (*WTD* 1.29). The image of Dutch painting is un-canny here: Ethel may figure herself as an anchorite, but she is a Protestant, brought up by old Rebecca Torkill, and can spot the old enemy when he ap-pears. The separate mysteries of Laura Grey and Edwyn Carmel twine together for Ethel in chiaroscuro: " . . . the delicate features of the pale ecclesiastic, and Miss Grey's pretty and anxious face, were lighted, like a fine portrait of Schalken's, by candle only" (*WTD* 1.48). It seems Laura is very afraid and distrustful of Mr. Carmel:

> "I like that unconscious air of command, but I don't perceive those signs of cunning and reserve. He seemed to grow more communicative the longer he stayed," I answered.
>
> "The darker it grew," she replied. "He is one of those persons who become more confident the more effectually their countenances are concealed. There ceases to be any danger of a conflict between looks and language—a danger that embarrasses some people."
>
> "You are suspicious this evening," I said. "I don't think you like him."
>
> "I don't know him, but I fancy that, talk as he may to us, neither you nor I have for one moment a peep into his real mind. His world may be perfectly celestial or serene, or it may be an ambitious, dark, and bad one; but it is an invisible world for us." (*WTD* 1.84–85)

Laura acts out a traditional distrust of the Jesuits here. Edwyn Carmel is the stereotype of the pale, feminine Oxford Puseyite from *Punch*, a generation on, who has "gone over" to Rome and become a Catholic priest. Carmel, who is charged with teaching the teenage Ethel Italian, gives her a little book of saints' lives. Is he trying to convert her? Laura thinks so; but Ethel is more sympathetic to what she sees as his ascetic discipline. Carmel is clearly not a man of action, but his mind belongs to the Church, and therefore he is another totally opaque figure for Ethel and the reader to deal with. He is, however, associated with the sinister Jesuit, Monsieur Droqville, who has targeted Ethel's family. One day, Droqville appears for the first time with Carmel on the road from Cardyllion to Malory, and, as this stranger suddenly turns and addresses Ethel, who is watching him, the reader suddenly anticipates the abandoned child's horror of the bogey man in a fairy tale:

> "Suppose your father and mother have placed you in my sole charge, with a direction to remove you from Malory, and take you under my immediate care and supervision, today; you will hold yourself in readiness to depart immediately, attended by a lady appointed to look after you, with the approbation of your parents,—eh?" (*WTD* 1.94)

That "Suppose" turns instantly into an order. Ethel, however, for all her dreaminess to us readers, instantly reacts to repel and threaten Droqville with the local policeman. They run home, she and Laura, and lock themselves in. But it's only a test, a "mystification," as he explains to Carmel afterwards, in a conversation at which Ethel couldn't have been present, to search out any weakness in her. She has, unfortunately for his plans, passed the test. This is a good example of how the method works: the image is allowed all its impact, and then what is going on is "explained" sometime later (*WTD* 1.95).

And later, Carmel, in what is a major crux of the novel, seems, to Ethel at least, to be involved in Droqville's Jesuit plot to get part of the estate of Ethel's grandmother, Lady Lorrimer, a plot whose success ruins Ethel's father, and results in his suicide. We learn the true hideousness of this plot via a blatantly conjectural scene, in which, having been at Lady Mardyke's ball at Carsbrook, Ethel the narrator, not the protagonist, leaves like a malign eavesdropper, taking the reader with her, in the carriage of Droqville, and penetrates the mysterious house in which her dying grandmother is being held, and the scene unfolds from the point of view of an unseen witness. This is offered as evidence of the vile nature of what Droqville is up to, but we are not given its source. As Ethel comments elsewhere, in a remark which applies to the narrative technique of the novel: "Under excitement so tremendous as mine, people, I think, are more than half spiritualized. We seem to find ourselves translated from place to place by thought rather than effort" (*WTD* 2.209). But the novel turns the stereotype of Catholic skull-duggery on its head: Carmel is a failed Jesuit, really, as his mentor, Droqville, makes clear when he declares to his face (in another scene Ethel couldn't have been at) that he is unable to give him a reference to the Order; and he is eventually shipped off to a missionary post in South America, where he (willingly) dies in the service of his church. Ethel cruelly rejects his friendship on suspicion of his involvement with this sordid plot, which for the reader is never quite cleared up, but we have to assume that his failure absolves him from inner involvement on a "need to know" basis, though, from the eye-witness evidence Ethel does give us, he must have known in a general way what was going on and could have spilt the beans. But despite these doubts, which are allowed to belong permanently to the reader, Carmel turns out to be that thing of pure gold, a friend; subsequently trying to warn her on a number of occasions about the danger she is in from his "alter ego," Richard Marston's attentions, and helping to rescue her in her hour of need, by throwing into the river the dagger with which (using her writing hand) she stabs Droqville. Ethel ends by regarding Carmel as a friend, even a soul mate, forgiving him in her own mind, but too late to be able to confess this to his face. The novel's title alludes to the "feminine," pale, consumptive Carmel, bound for an early death, who has dedicated himself to his Church.

There are some thematic aspects of this special intimacy between speaker and reader, which are important to this novel, a work which acts as

a summation of Le Fanu's studies of women. The isolation of women is en-
forced from childhood, through the lack of knowledge offered them by their
parents about what is going on in the world, and with which they sometimes
perversely collude as a form of resistance. Women become aware of their
value, but also their confinement, as objects of exchange.[5] That confinement
is sometimes embraced, and its solitude gives to women's friendships a peculiar intensity. We see this precisely in Maud Ruthyn in *Uncle Silas*, who is
brought up without a mother by pious but superstitious servants, and sent to
live with her uncle, to redeem the family honor under the terms of her father, Austin's will; and "Carmilla's" Laura, lonely in her remote Styrian
schloss, again without a mother, brought up by servants and governesses, who
longs for a friend and who is never told anything by her impercipient father.

The plot of Romance becomes an anchoritic theme in some of the novels that follow *The House by the Church-yard*. Consider, for example, the
summary fate of Margaret Fanshawe in *The Tenants of Malory*, who is represented figuratively as a nun, kept in isolation by the shame of her father's
debts, up to the brief moment when she is spied, courted and ruined by, the
"vindictive adoration" of Cleve Verney, who impregnates her and keeps her
in secret as his mistress until she wastes away and dies. Or Rachel in *Wylder's
Hand* who retires as an "anchorite" to Redman's Farm, only to become the
principal witness of her brother's murderous plot. The connection between
perversity, renunciation, and morbid psychology is never far away. This begins often as an innocent "perversity," as in the case of spirited young Maud
Vernon in *The Rose and the Key*, who finds her preferred happiness, away
from the marriage market, on a sketching tour of North Wales with a female
companion; but is "recognized" and pursued by a suitor, and ends up in a
private lunatic asylum, committed there by her monster of a mother, Barbara, entirely for her own reasons. There is, as the narrator of *Tenants of
Malory* puts it, "something recluse in the human soul," evidenced in the sol-
ipsistic disavowal of Le Fanu's males, and the always-ready capacity of his
women to withdraw from life and "die" to it, like nuns who take vows of silence and become the brides of Christ. Women so easily, it seems, become
those who "stand and wait": "In the passion avowed, so often something of
simulation; in the feeling disowned, so often the true and beautiful life"
(*Tenants of Malory* 196).[6]

---

5. See Girard's complex analysis of the representation of this in "Strange Event in the
Life of Schalken the Painter," 405–10.

6. For the full context of the "perversity" of this sentiment, see Sage, Chapter 6, 131–
56. But for other relevant works and materials in Le Fanu, see also Girard 392ff.

The second aspect of this novel that needs to be put in context at this point is its setting, and its use of the codes of the picturesque, which overlap with the names and sometimes indicate the natures of its characters in the earlier symbolic schemes of Le Fanu. It is worth remembering briefly here that, after the relative commercial failure of *The House by the Church-yard*, Le Fanu accepted as a gentlemen's agreement the stipulation of his publisher, Richard Bentley, that his novels from then on, though publishable first in the *DUM*, should be "The Story of an English subject in modern times"; and this restriction is built explicitly into the 1863 contract for *Wylder's Hand*. Le Fanu then shaped his fiction faithfully according to this demand, developing different sites as codes for the "Cyclopean" history of *The House by the Church-yard* and the haunted, in his novels, without violating the terms of the agreement with Bentley.[7] One of these haunted sites, which Bentley didn't seem to notice, or positively approved of because Wales was thought of as "England," is the countryside around Beaumaris ("Cardyllion" in the novel), and in particular "Malory" (probably named after Sir Thomas Malory the late-medieval writer of romances), which is Cor Penmon in the south-eastern corner of Angelsey, on the Northern coast of the Menai Straits opposite Conway, which is called "Ware" in this environmental code. Thus Ethel Ware, the heiress, takes her name from the town of Conway, and she clearly "belongs" in this landscape, in more than a merely subjective, emotional sense: this is a tantalizing reference to a lost landowning heritage. This allusion combines with another, more "Gothic" layer of signification: the ancient Druid heritage of Anglesey, or Mona, where the last battle of the Druids against the Romans, recorded by Tacitus, took place across the tidal channel of the straits. Near Cor Penmon, there is a sixth-century Augustinian priory ("Penruthyn" in the code). The sublime site of the house and grounds at Penmon, set down almost on the waters of the sound, opposite the Cambrian Mountains on the other side of the water, the graveyard round the back of the house on the landward side, the very distinctive, tiny, "Steward's House" in the corner of the garden, in which Mr. Carmel is allowed by Ethel's father to stay and from which he is ousted by the injured Richard Marston, are all transcribed, with slight foreshortening and alteration here and there, from the actual landscape.

The disaster of the *Conway Castle* in the novel, from which emerges Richard Marston, its demonic hero and Ethel's future lover, is also portrayed as a local event involving Conway, connected with Ethel through its code-

---

7. For a more detailed account of the effects of this arrangement, see my "Censorship and the Codes of the Picturesque" 74–82.

name (i.e. "Ware"). ("Marston," on the contrary, is a literary code probably named after the rough English sixteenth-century satirist and playwright, the initiator of revenge tragedy). His alter ego, the pale, "dying Catholic priest, Mr. Carmel," with whom Ethel feels such tantalizing affinities, is named after a headland in the northwest of Anglesey, itself, "Englished" (and Christianized) recalling a biblical site in the Middle East. The local landowners are called, fictionally, the Verney family, who have their own pew in the church at Cardyllion.

Le Fanu knew this area well from his own boyhood, when he and his brother were sent across for their summer holidays to get them away from the troubles of the Tithe War.[8] Later, after the death of his wife, he and his daughters used to go to Beaumaris for their summer holidays, staying at No. 10, Victoria Terrace, a house facing the Sound and the Cambrians, with a little green in front of it, the one in the novel, on to which in this novel Marston and Laura Grey's secret lover, Jennings, sidle to arrange their duel.

The other setting of the novel is "Golden Friars," in the Lake District, in present-day Cumbria, perhaps Keswick, at the head of Derwentwater, another haunted landscape common to the stories in *Chronicles of Golden Friars* (1871). In the past, Ethel's mother suddenly, on a "violent whim" refused Sir Harry Rokestone, and married Ethel's father, Francis Ware instead, a lightweight adventurer who fails in everything he seeks to achieve, and ruins them systematically until he commits suicide through debt and failure. Sir Harry has a house in an isolated valley just off the head of Derwentwater called Dorracleugh. After Mabel Lorrimer's sudden change of heart, the old man retires from life. There is a vague plan to appeal to him for help. Ethel is in a boat on the lake with her mother and grandmother, and they pass the entrance to this valley, catching a glimpse of someone:

> Never did I see a spot with so awful a character of solitude and melancholy.
>
> In the gloom we could see a man standing alone on the extremity of the stone pier, looking over the lake. The figure was the only living thing we could discover there.
>
> "Well, dear, now you see it. That's Dorracleugh—that's Harry Rokestone's place," said Lady Lorrimer. "What a spot! Fit only for a bear or an anchorite!" (*WTD* 2.108)

This remark connects the landscape and settings together with the plot, via the theme of perverse renunciation. It is to this place, after the deaths of Lady Lorrimer and the suicide of Francis Ware, that the action of the novel shifts, as Ethel, orphaned by the deaths of both her parents and her

---

8. See Enid Madoc-Jones.

grandmother, is rescued from ruin in London (and from a working career as a teacher or governess) by the figure on the end of the pier, the faithful recluse, Sir Harry, standing and waiting.

The title of this novel under discussion, *Willing to Die*, is thus full of these resonances, as well as the more familiar masculine and heroic sense of its title-phrase. That heroic sense, of course, is present in Richard Marston, the novel's demonic man of action, who cannot wait for anything; a discredited, unscrupulous scion of the aristocracy, who seeks to get back his fortune by any means available to him, including that of lying to Ethel Ware, Marston is always willing to die. He is the only passenger to emerge from the wreck of the *Conway Castle* in the Sound at Malory, and thus, in a sense, suffers death by water right in front of Ethel, entering her anchoritic life at Malory by pure and violent chance. But even there she has noticed the strange expression on the face of this revenant:

> But I lay long awake in the dark, haunted by the ceaseless rocking of that dreadful sea, and the apparition of that one pale, bleeding messenger from the ship of death. How unlike my idea of the rapture of a mortal just rescued from shipwreck! His face was that of one to whom an atrocious secret has been revealed, who was full of resentment and horror; whose lips were sealed. (*WTD* 1.150–51)

Marston is a challenge to the notion of Providence, the very scheme of the nineteenth century romance plot. It seems he has been reserved for Ethel, emerging from the underworld as her own special demon lover:

> I sometimes think that we women are perverse creatures. For us there is an occult interest about the guilty and audacious, if it be elevated by masculine courage and beauty, and surrounded by ever so little of mystery and romance. Shall I confess it? The image of that wicked Mr. Marston, notwithstanding all Laura's hard epithets, and the startling situation in which I had seen him last, haunted me often, and with something more of fascination than I liked to confess. Let there be energy, cleverness, beauty, and I believe a reckless sort of wickedness will not stand the least in the way of a foolish romance. I think I had energy; I know I was impetuous. Insipid or timid virtue would have no chance with me. (*WTD* 1.277)

Marston literally replaces Carmel as the force in Ethel's young life, even uncannily occupying the same bench and talking in the same intimate way as the old tutor through the window to Ethel and Laura, like a revenant, as Ethel points out. But all events, like people in this book, have "another side" to them. Ethel has no idea, at the time that she is a witness to this scene, that he has been stalking Laura, threatening her secret liaison with Jennings by picking a duel with him, because he seeks to take her over, seeing in her a landed connection. Ethel in teenage fashion entirely misreads the situation and thinks that Laura is jealous of the attention he is giving to her, Ethel, but in reality, Marston (like a demonic Swedenborgian "spirit") has "recognised" her, seeing his true prey at last, and is simply switching his allegiance. This scene is narrated to us by Ethel the witness in its order of occurrence, its misunderstanding perfectly intact, and perfectly opaque to the reader. Or should we say, relatively opaque, because by this time we are used to the fact that when Ethel the witness tells us things, they are often temptingly incomplete, and subject to a "correction" by a "conjectural" scene, whose "eavesdropping" is informed by knowledge revealed later to Ethel the writer.

It takes Ethel the conjectural eavesdropper to reveal to us the nature of the occult relationship between Carmel and Marston: at one point Marston pursues him to some lodgings he has borrowed from a friend in The Temple and the two engage in a dialogue reported by Ethel the narrator which Ethel the witness wasn't at, but, we assume, has heard from either or both, afterwards. Marston wants him to help him seduce Ethel. Carmel asks him to put out the light: "'Why, what are you afraid of?' said Marston. 'You haven't, I hope, got a little French milliner behind your screen, like Joseph Surface, who, I think, would have made a very pretty Jesuit. Why should you object to light?'" (WTD 2.212). Darkness is the medium of both these characters. The coded references which Ethel makes here are to Le Fanu's great uncle, Sheridan's play *School for Scandal*, and the lot of the two brothers, Charles and Joseph Surface. Charles is an open, innocent debtor who can't keep his money or anyone else's, but who is benign. Joseph, the good one, is a pure fraud, all Puritan front, who turns out, in the climactic stage revelation referred to here, to have been concealing a mistress.[9] So Marston, acknowledging the close relation between them, here casts himself as Charles, and Carmel as Joseph. But in fact, it is Carmel in this novel who is in the end, although presented as the Gothic stereotype of hypocrisy, the good one; and Marston who is his Gothic double, possessed like Joseph of a hypocrisy so deep, that he is, that impossible thing, an unconscious hypocrite, as Ethel goes on to demonstrate to us, in the motif of his "suspended smile." This is a specially horrible smile that reveals all, but Ethel is not allowed to see, until long after she has committed herself to him. Marston has two sides to his being (like Joseph Surface) and they do not touch each other at all. He is convincingly handsome and convincingly schizophrenic. With an asset stripper's

---

9. See Sage 6, 119, 127–29, 151–52, and 168 for the early nineteenth century "Gothicizing" of the part of Joseph Surface.

forethought, he reappears, woos and wins Ethel, after her ruin, who has been rescued by Harry Rokestone who takes her to another anchoritic solitude at Dorracleugh. It turns out that Marston is Sir Harry's nephew, already disgraced in his uncle's eyes and disinherited by the commission of a crime for which he is never apprehended, having been saved by Sir Harry and his faithful steward, Blount.[10] This was the point he was at, it seems, when the shipwreck happened, which offers us a mundane explanation of his facial expression when Ethel first sees him. We have to wait until Vol. 3, Chapter 65 before she finally encounters, full-on, the serpent's smile.[11]

In the meantime, however, we learn (conjecturally), that, knowing or thinking he knows, that Sir Harry has never executed his will, Marston has stolen it from the safe, and, after rapidly making sure that his uncle is dead, carries it off to a rural hotel, where no one can witness him, and destroys it. But he reckons without our conjectural eavesdropper, who, hovering invisibly at his elbow, takes us through every move he makes, as he makes sure that there are no remains decipherable by anyone coming after him, penetrating even the unconscious level of his hypocrisy:

> Richard Marston was a man of redundant courage, and no scruple. But have all men some central fibre of fear that can be reached, and does the ghost of the conscience they have killed within them sometimes rise and overshadow them with horror? Richard Marston, with his feet on the fender and the tongs in his hands, pressed down the coals upon the ashes of the will, and felt faint and dizzy, as he had done the night of the shipwreck, when, with bleeding forehead, he had sat down for the first time in the steward's house at Malory. (*WTD* 3.210)

Ethel the writer takes over from Ethel the witness here, to render, in her epistemologically impossible, conjectural eavesdropper's mode, the return of the repressed. Le Fanu uses the Gothic language of haunting to describe the "central fibre of fear."

---

10. Blount is another reversal of stereotype from Le Fanu's earlier romances: the "Methodist hypocrite," Joseph Larkin, who is part of a "firm" of blackmailers and extortionists. For analysis of this earlier type, see my book, 174–77, which also involves Le Fanu's anti-Semitism. This is exactly how Marston sees Blount in this novel; but despite his introduction as an "ill-dressed clown," in this fictional reincarnation, he proves a faithful retainer and a friend to Ethel in her adversity. In the end, it is he who defeats Marston by producing a signed, executed copy of an earlier version of Sir Harry Rokestone's will.

11. See, for example, the motif of the evil smile and its association with the snake in "The Evil Guest," in Le Fanu's *Ghost Stories and Tales of Mystery*.

This passage helps us interpret the novel's final paragraphs, the acme of perversity: "Over an image partly dreamed and partly real, shivered utterly, but still in memory visible, I pour out the vainest of all sorrows" (*WTD* 3.279). For Ethel, using the language of the looking-glass, Marston's image is irrevocably "shivered." She can only conjecturally piece together the splinters, though she can call him up to haunt her, like a phantom, by the action of memory. Marston's plans to become Baron Rokestone are foiled by the existence of another will, signed by Sir Harry, which reduces to a pittance the reasonable generous inheritance which Marston would have had, had he not stolen the will and destroyed it. Having given himself, as Ethel puts it, "with a vindictive elation" (3.253), the airs and graces of the heir-apparent, and pretended to be concerned about his uncle and the correct management of his estates; and, having ingratiated himself with everyone concerned, Marston is obliged to stay on in a hell of his own making, while Ethel immediately flees, and therefore he cannot pursue her, otherwise, she conjectures, he would have found her and brought her back; but he must take charge as the front man for the local populace at his uncle's funeral, gaining all of the responsibility and none of the profit, under the thumb of the old Methodist, Lemuel Blount, whom he secretly despises as a hypocritical self-interested hanger-on, but who has kept a sharp eye on him for his uncle, all along. An elegant punishment.

Marston has betrayed Ethel comprehensively, having told her he was already married, and he has caused her to flee him immediately without divulging her whereabouts to London, where, having determined to make her own way as a governess, she has taken up again by the chance of a confidential advert in *The Times* with her old governess Laura Grey, who has eventually married her "Mr. Jennings" (actually a Viscount) and is now Lady Rillingdon. They all go abroad together to India for a couple of years. Ethel has inherited all the estate, which Blount and Tarlcot look after for her, but she comes home to Malory, the scene of her conventual childhood, with her sister Helen's grave and her own grave-plot ready, next to her, behind the house. Having initially offered Marston an annual income from her own, she received a letter from him, rejecting it and asking for her forgiveness. Crazily, she is still in love with him. She has heard of Marston's death from fever at Marseilles when the novel comes to rest where it began. Here are her final reflections on her own perverse obsession with putting together the shivered fragments of herself and her dead "hero of romance":

> In the wonderful working that subdues all things to itself—in all the changes of spirit, or the spaces of eternity, is there, shall there never be, from the first failure, evolved the nobler thing that might have been? I care for no other. I can love no other; and were I to live and keep my youth, through eternity, I

think I never could be interested or won again. Solitude has become dear to me, because he is in it. Am I giving this infinite true love in vain? I comfort myself with one vague hope. I cannot think that nature is so cynical. Does the loved phantom represent nothing? And is the fidelity that nature claims, but an infatuation and a waste? (WTD 3.280–81)

The empirical course of history has no meaning for Ethel, and her story cannot follow it. She can of course use the shadow play of memory to resurrect his phantom; but only to see those features of the one side of his schizophrenia, (i.e. "the nobler thing that might have been") which she has pieced together through love, willing them to survive the shattering of the representational looking-glass. But as she explains, no such mixed characteristics will survive the last day. She is the bride of Christ, but in that empirical glass of history her Christ is the Serpent, hanging over her: "a cunning, selfish face gloating down on me, with a gross, confident, wicked simper" (3.216). The ambiguity of her rhetorical questions about infatuation, and waste, and whether the "loved phantom" represents nothing or not—do they expect the answer yes or no?—is finally divided between her reader and herself.

Works Cited

Abrams, M. H. *The Mirror and the Lamp: Theory and the Critical Tradition.* London: Oxford University Press, 1971.

Castle, Terry. "The Spectralisation of the Other in *The Mysteries of Udolpho.*" In *The New Eighteenth Century,* ed. Felicity Nussbaum and Laura Brown. London: Methuen, 1987.

Castle, Terry. *The Female Thermometer.* London: Oxford University Press, 1995.

Ferris, Iva. *The Achievement of Literary Authority.* Ithaca, NY: Cornell University Press, 1991.

Girard, Gaid. *Joseph Sheridan Le Fanu: Une écriture fantastique.* Paris: Champion, 2005.

Le Fanu, J. Sheridan. *Ghost Stories and Tales of Mystery.* Dublin: James McGlashan, 1851.

———. *Willing to Die.* London: Hurst & Blackett, 1873. 3 vols.

Madoc-Jones, Enid. "Sheridan Le Fanu and North Wales." *Anglo-Welsh Review* 17 (1969): 167–73.

Mc Cormack, W. J. *Sheridan Le Fanu and Victorian Ireland.* 2nd ed. Dublin: Lilliput Press, 1991.

Milner, M. *La Fantasmagorie: Essai sur l'optique de fantastique*. Paris: Presses Universitaires Françaises, 1982.

Sage, Victor. "Introduction." In *Uncle Silas* by J. S. Le Fanu. Harmonsworth, UK: Penguin, 2000.

———. "Irish Gothic: C. R. Maturin and J. S. Le Fanu." In *A Companion to the Gothic*, ed. David Punter. Oxford: Blackwell, 2000. 81–93.

———. "Censorship and the Codes of the Picturesque: The Druidic, the Cyclopean, and the Cultural Other in Le Fanu's Later Fiction." In *Fictions of Unease: The Gothic from Otranto to the X-Files*, ed. Andrew Smith, Diane Mason, and William Hughes. Bath, UK: Sulis Press, 2002.

———. *Le Fanu's Gothic: The Rhetoric of Darkness*. Basingstoke, UK: Palgrave Macmillan, 2004.

———. Review of Gaid Girard's *Joseph Sheridan Le Fanu*. *Irish University Review* 37:1 (22 March 2007): 281–86.

Bibliography

A. Primary Bibliography

1. Shorter Prose Fiction

[in order of first publication, revisions as noted]

"The Ghost and the Bone-Setter." *Dublin University Magazine* (January 1838).

"The Fortunes of Sir Robert Ardagh." *Dublin University Magazine* (March 1838).

"The Last Heir of Castle Connor." *Dublin University Magazine* (June 1838).

"The Drunkard's Dream." *Dublin University Magazine* (August 1838).

"Passage in the Secret History of an Irish Countess." *Dublin University Magazine* (November 1838). A revised version of the story appeared as "The Murdered Cousin" in *Ghost Stories and Tales of Mystery*. Dublin: James McGlashan, 1851.

"The Bridal of Carrigvarah." *Dublin University Magazine* (April 1839).

"Strange Event in the Life of Schalken the Painter." *Dublin University Magazine* (May 1839). A revised version of the story appeared as "Schalken the Painter" in *Ghost Stories and Tales of Mystery*. Dublin: James McGlashan, 1851.

"Jim Sulivan's Adventures in the Great Snow." *Dublin University Magazine* (July 1839).

"A Chapter in the History of a Tyrone Family." *Dublin University Magazine* (October 1839).

"An Adventure of Hardress Fitzgerald, a Royalist Captain." *Dublin University Magazine* (February 1840).

"The Quare Gander." *Dublin University Magazine* (October 1840).

"Spalatro." *Dublin University Magazine* (March–April 1843).

"The Watcher." *Dublin University Magazine* (November 1847). A revised version of the story appeared as "The Familiar" in *In a Glass Darkly*. London: Richard Bentley, 1872.

"The Fatal Bride." *The Dublin University Magazine* (January 1848).

"Some Account of the Latter Days of Richard Marston, of Dunoran." *Dublin University Magazine* (April–June 1848). The story reappeared as "The Evil Guest" in *Ghost Stories and Tales of Mystery*. Dublin: James McGlashan, 1851.

"The Mysterious Lodger." *Dublin University Magazine* (January–February 1850).

"Billy Malowney's Taste of Love and Glory." *Dublin University Magazine* (June 1850).

"Ghost Stories of Chapelizod." *Dublin University Magazine* (January 1851).

"Some Gossip about Chapelizod." *Dublin University Magazine* (April 1851).

"An Account of Some Strange Disturbances in an Old House in Aungier-street." *Dublin University Magazine* (December 1853).

"Ultor de Lacy." *Dublin University Magazine* (December 1861).

"Borrhomeo the Astrologer." *Dublin University Magazine* (January 1862).

"An Authentic Narrative of a Haunted House." *Dublin University Magazine* (October 1862).

"My Aunt Margaret's Adventure." *Dublin University Magazine* (March 1864).

"Wicked Captain Walshawe, of Wauling." *Dublin University Magazine* (April 1864).

"Squire Toby's Will." *Temple Bar* (January 1868).

"Green Tea." *All the Year Round,* New Series (23 October–13 November 1869).

"A Strange Adventure in the Life of Miss Laura Mildmay." *Cassell's Magazine* (Weekly Edition) 1869. The novella reappeared with the interpolated story "Madam Crowl's Ghost" in *Chronicles of Golden Friars.* London: Richard Bentley, 1871.

"The Child That Went With the Fairies." *All the Year Round,* New Series (5 February 1870).

"The White Cat of Drumgunniol." *All the Year Round,* New Series (2 April 1870).

"Stories of Lough Guir." *All the Year Round,* New Series (23 April 1870).

"The Bird of Passage." *Temple Bar* (April–June 1870).

"The Haunted Baronet." *Belgravia* (July–November 1870).

"The Vision of Tom Chuff." *All the Year Round,* New Series (8 October 1870).

"Madam Crowl's Ghost." *All the Year Round,* New Series (31 December 1870). The story reappeared as an episode in "A Strange Adventure in the Life of Miss Laura Mildmay" when that short novel was reprinted in *Chronicles of Golden Friars*. London: Richard Bentley, 1871.

"The Dead Sexton." *Across the Bridge: The Christmas Number of Once a Week* (31 December 1871).

"Carmilla." *Dark Blue* (December 1871–March 1872). A revised version of the story was reprinted with the addition of a series introduction in *In a Glass Darkly*. London: Richard Bentley, 1872.

"The Haunted House in Westminster." *Belgravia* (January 1872). A revised version of the story appeared as "Mr. Justice Harbottle" in *In a Glass Darkly*. London: Richard Bentley, 1872.

"The Room in the Dragon Volant." *London Society* 21 (February–June 1872).

"Sir Dominick's Bargain." *All the Year Round* (6 July 1872).

"Dickon the Devil." *London Society* 22 (Christmas 1872).

"Laura Silver Bell." *Belgravia Annual* (December 1872).

"Hyacinth O'Toole." *Temple Bar* (August 1884).

2. Verse

"Scraps of Hibernian Ballads" *Dublin University Magazine* (June 1839). An essay incorporating "Phaudhrig Crohoore."

"Shamus O'Brien." *Dublin University Magazine* (July 1850).

"Duan na Claev." *Dublin University Magazine* (February 1863).

"Abhain au Bhuideil." *Dublin University Magazine* (March 1863).

"A Doggrel in a Dormant Window." *Dublin University Magazine* (December 1864).

"Beatrice." *Dublin University Magazine* (November 1865–January 1866).

3. Novels and Collections

[serialization and first book publication]

The Cock and Anchor. Dublin: William Curry; London: Longmans; and Edinburgh: Fraser, 1845.

The Fortunes of Colonel Torlogh O'Brien. Serialized in eleven monthly parts by James McGlashan between April 1846 January 1847. Dublin: James McGlashan, 1847.

Ghost Stories and Tales of Mystery. Dublin: James McGlashan, 1851.

The House by the Church-yard. Serialized in *Dublin University Magazine* (October 1861–February 1863). London: Tinsley Brothers, 1863.

Wylder's Hand. Serialized in *Dublin University Magazine* (June 1863–February 1864). London: Richard Bentley, 1864.

Uncle Silas. Serialized in *Dublin University Magazine* (July–November 1864). London: Richard Bentley, 1864.

The Prelude. Dublin: G. Herbert, 1865.

Guy Deverell. Serialized in *Dublin University Magazine* (January–July 1865). London: Richard Bentley, 1865.

All in the Dark. Serialized in *Dublin University Magazine* (February–June 1866). London: Richard Bentley, 1866.

The Tenants of Malory. Serialized in *Dublin University Magazine* (February–October 1867). London: Tinsley Brothers, 1867.

Haunted Lives. Serialized in *Dublin University Magazine* (May–December 1868). London: Tinsley Brothers, 1868.

Loved and Lost. Serialized in *Dublin University Magazine* (September 1868–May 1869).

A Lost Name. Serialized in *Temple Bar* (May 1867–May 1868). London: Richard Bentley, 1868.

The Wyvern Mystery. Serialized in *Dublin University Magazine* (February–November 1869). London: Tinsley Brothers, 1869.

Checkmate. Serialized *Cassell's Magazine* (6 August 1870–25 February 1871). London: Hurst and Blackett, 1871.

Chronicles of Golden Friars. London: Richard Bentley, 1871.

The Rose and the Key. Serialized in *All the Year Round* (21 January–23 September 1871). London: Chapman & Hall, 1871.

In a Glass Darkly. London: Richard Bentley, 1872.

Willing to Die. Serialized in *All the Year Round* (21 September 1872–26 April 1873). London: Hurst & Blackett, 1873.

The Purcell Papers. Ed. Alfred Perceval Graves. London: Richard Bentley, 1880.

The Poems of Joseph Sheridan Le Fanu. Ed. Alfred Perceval Graves. London: Downey, 1896.

Madam Crowl's Ghost and Other Tales of Mystery. Ed. M. R. James. London: G. Bell, 1923.

Spalatro: Two Italian Tales. Mountain Ash, Wales: Sarob Press, 2001.

B. Secondary Bibliography

Allen, Nicholas. "Sheridan Le Fanu and the Spectral Empire." In *The Ghost Story from the Middle Ages to the Twentieth Century*, eds. Helen Conrad O'Briain and Julie Anne Stevens. Dublin: Four Courts Press, 2010.

Ashman, Anne. "A Psychobiographical Study of Death, Mourning, and the Swedenborgian After-Life in the Later Works of Joseph Sheridan Le Fanu." Ph.D. diss.: University of Aberdeen, 2005.

Begnal, Michael H. *Joseph Sheridan Le Fanu*. Lewisburg, PA: Bucknell University Press, 1971.

———. "A Source for 'Distant Music.'" *James Joyce Quarterly* 17 (1980): 303.

Briggs, Julia. *Night Visitors: The Rise and Fall of the English Ghost Story*. London: Faber & Faber, 1977.

Bleiler, E. F. "Introduction." In *Best Ghost Stories of J. S. Le Fanu*. New York: Dover, 1964.

———. "Introduction." In *Ghost Stories and Mysteries* by J. S. Le Fanu. New York: Dover, 1975.

Browne, Nelson. *Sheridan Le Fanu*. London: Arthur Barker, 1952.

Cavaliero, Glen. *The Supernatural in English Fiction*. Oxford: Oxford University Press, 1995.

Cox, Michael. "Introduction." In *The Illustrated J. S. Le Fanu*. Wellingborough, UK: Equation, 1988.

Crawford, Gary William. *J. Sheridan Le Fanu: A Bio-Bibliography*. Westport, CT: Greenwood Press, 1995.

Crawford, Gary William, and Brian J. Showers. *Joseph Sheridan Le Fanu: A Concise Bibliography*. Dublin: Swan River Press, 2011.

Davenport-Hines, Richard. *Gothic: Four Hundred Years of Excess, Horror, Evil and Ruin*. London: Fourth Estate, 1998.

Denman, Peter, "Le Fanu and Stoker: A Probable Connection." *Éire-Ireland* 9 (1974): 152–58.

Edens, Walter Eugene. "Joseph Sheridan Le Fanu: A Minor Victorian Novelist and His Publisher." Ph.D. diss.: University of Illinois, 1963.

Gates, Barbara. T. "Blue Devils and Green Tea: Le Fanu's Haunted Suicides." *Studies in Short Fiction* 24:1 (1987): 15–23.

Girard, Gaïd. *Joseph Sheridan Le Fanu: Une écriture fantastique*. Paris: Champion, 2005.

Hall, Wayne E. *Dialogues in the Margin: A Study of the* Dublin University Magazine. Washington, D.C.: Catholic University of America Press, 1999.

Harrington, John P. "Swift through Le Fanu and Joyce." *Mosaic* 12:3 (1979): 49–58.

Haslam, Richard. "Joseph Sheridan Le Fanu and the Fantastic Semantics of Ghost-Colonial Ireland." In *That Other World: The Supernatural and the Fantastic in Irish Literature and Its Contexts*, ed. Bruce Stewart. Gerrards Cross, UK: Colin Smythe, 1988. 1.267–86.

Hughes, William. "The Origin and Implications of J. S. Le Fanu's 'Green Tea.'" *Irish Studies* 13:1 (February 2005): 45–54.

James, M. R. "Some Remarks on Ghost Stories." *Bookman* (London) (December 1929): 169–72. Rpt. in M. R. James. *A Pleasing Terror.* Ashcroft, BC: Ash-Tree Press, 2001. 475–80.

———. "Ghosts—Treat Them Gently!" *Evening News* (17 April 1931). Rpt. in M. R. James. *A Pleasing Terror.* Ashcroft, BC: Ash-Tree Press, 2001. 481–83.

Jedrzejewski, Jan. "Introduction." In *The Cock and Anchor* by Joseph Sheridan Le Fanu. Gerrards Cross, UK: Colin Smythe, 2000.

Kilroy, Thomas. "Introduction." In *The House by the Churchyard* by J. S. Le Fanu. Belfast: Appletree Press, 1992.

Lapinski, Piya Pal. "Dickens's Miss Wade and Le Fanu's Carmilla: The Female Vampire in *Little Dorrit.*" *Dickens Quarterly* 11:2 (August 1994): 81–87.

Le Fanu, T. P. *Memoir of the Le Fanu Family.* Privately printed, 1924.

Madoc-Jones, Enid. "Sheridan Le Fanu and North Wales." *Anglo-Welsh Review* 17 (1969): 167–73.

Mc Cormack, W. J. *Dissolute Characters: Irish Literary History through Balzac, Sheridan Le Fanu, Yeats and Bowen.* Manchester: Manchester University Press, 1993.

———. *Sheridan Le Fanu and Victorian Ireland.* Oxford: Clarendon Press, 1980. The second, enlarged edition (Dublin: Lilliput, 1991) offers the text of the first edition virtually unchanged, with the unfortunate omission of the photographs originally placed near the end of the book; nonetheless, in addition to a brief new preface, this edition contains an indispensable third appendix, "A notebook of 1858: transcript and commentary," exploring Le Fanu's recorded thoughts following the death of his wife. The third edition (Phoenix Mill, UK: Sutton, 1997) contains the full, expanded text and reinstates the photographs.

————. "Sheridan Le Fanu and Greater Chapelizod." In *The Shadow of James Joyce: Chapelizod & Environs*, ed. Motoko Fujita. Dublin: Lilliput Press, 2011. 77–82.

Power, Albert. "Le Fanu's *The House by the Churchyard* and the Influence of Richard Brinsley Sheridan." *Wormwood* 9 (16 November, 2007): 32–43

Punter, David. *The Literature of Terror: A History of Gothic Fictions from 1765 to the Present Day*. London: Longman, 1980. Rev. ed. 1996 (2 vols.).

Ridenhour, Jamieson. "Introduction." In *Carmilla* by J. S. Le Fanu. Kansas City, MO: Valancourt, 2009.

Rockhill, Jim. "As on a Darkling Plain: The Life and Supernatural Fiction of Joseph Sheridan Le Fanu from 1814–1861." In *Schalken the Painter and Other Ghost Stories 1838–1861* by J. S. Le Fanu. Ashcroft, BC: Ash-Tree Press, 2002.

————. "A Mind Turned In upon Itself: The Life and Supernatural Fiction of Joseph Sheridan Le Fanu from 1861–1870." In *The Haunted Baronet and Others—Ghost Stories 1861–1870* by J. S. Le Fanu. Ashcroft, BC: Ash-Tree Press, 2003.

————. "A Dream of the Shadow of Smoke: The Final Years and Supernatural Fiction of Joseph Sheridan Le Fanu, 1870–1873." In *Mr. Justice Harbottle and Others—Ghost Stories 1870–1873* by J. S. Le Fanu. Ashcroft, BC: Ash-Tree Press, 2005.

Sage, Victor. "Censorship and the Codes of the Picturesque: The Druidic, the Cyclopean, and the Cultural Other in Le Fanu's Later Fiction." In *Fictions of Unease: The Gothic from Otranto to the X-Files*, ed. Andrew Smith, Diane Mason, and William Hughes. Bath, UK: Sulis Press, 2002.

————. Horror Fiction in the Protestant Tradition. New York: St. Martin's Press, 1988.

————. "Introduction." In *Uncle Silas* by J. S. Le Fanu. Harmonsworth, UK: Penguin, 2000.

————. "Irish Gothic: C. P. Maturin and J. S. Le Fanu." In *A Companion to Gothic*, ed. David Punter. London: Blackwell, 2001.

————. *Le Fanu's Gothic: The Rhetoric of Darkness*. Basingstoke, UK: Palgrave Macmillan, 2004.

Scott, Ken. "Le Fanu's 'The Room in the Dragon Volant.'" *Lock Haven Review* 10 (1968): 25–32.

Selerie, Gavin. *Le Fanu's Ghost*. Hereford, UK: Five Seasons Press, 2006.

Signorotti, Elizabeth, "Repossessing the Body: Transgressive Desire in 'Carmilla' and *Dracula*." *Criticism* 58 (1996): 607–32.

Simmons, William P. "Through a Mind Darkly: Some Thoughts on J. S. Le Fanu and the Psychology of the Ghost Story." *Wormwood* 6 (8 May 2006): 24–32.

Smith, Andrew. "Colonial Ghosts: Mimicry, History, and Laughter." In *The Ghost Story 1840–1920: A Cultural History*. Manchester: Manchester University Press, 2010.

Stoddart, Helen. "'The Precautions of Nervous People Are Infectious': Sheridan Le Fanu's Symptomatic Gothic." In *Gothic: Critical Concepts in Literary and Cultural Studies*, ed. Fred Botting and Dale Townshend. London: Routledge, 2004. 106–14.

Stribling, Miles. "Introduction." In *Spalatro: Two Italian Tales* by J. S. Le Fanu. Mountain Ash, Wales: Sarob Press, 2001.

Sullivan, Jack. "Beginnings: Sheridan Le Fanu." In *Elegant Nightmares: The English Ghost Story from Le Fanu to Blackwood*. Athens: Ohio University Press, 1978. 32–68.

Sullivan, Kevin. "The House by the Churchyard: James Joyce and Sheridan Le Fanu." In *Modern Irish Literature: Essays in Honour of William York Tindall*, ed. R. J. Porter and J. D. Brophy. New York: Iona College Press/Twayne, 1972. 315–34.

———. "Sheridan Le Fanu: The Purcell Papers 1838–1840." *Irish University Review* 2:1 (Spring 1972): 5–19.

Tracy, Robert. Introduction and Annotations. In *In a Glass Darkly* by J. S. Le Fanu. Oxford: Oxford University Press/World's Classics, 1993.

Veeder, William. "'Carmilla': The Arts of Repression." In *Gothic: Critical Concepts in Literary and Cultural Studies*, ed. Fred Botting and Dale Townshend. London: Routledge, 2004. 3.117–41.

Wagenknecht, Edward. *Seven Masters of Supernatural Fiction*. Westport, CT: Greenwood Press, 1991.

Walton, James. *Vision and Vacancy: The Fictions of J. S. Le Fanu*. Dublin: University College Dublin Press, 2007.

Wurtz, James F. "Introduction." In *The Cock and Anchor* by J. S. Le Fanu. Kansas City, MO: Valancourt, 2010.

Zeender, Marie-Noelle. "Joseph Sheridan Le Fanu and Swedenborg: An Inquiry into the Origin of 'The Mysterious Lodger.'" *Études Irlandaises* 5 (1980): 75–89.

C. Internet Resources

In addition to these articles and those reprinted in this volume, the following websites have also published fine studies devoted to Le Fanu:

The Irish Journal of Gothic and Horror Studies—irishgothichorrorjournal. homestead.com

Le Fanu Studies—www.lefanustudies.com

Wormwoodiana—wormwoodiana.blogspot.com

Sources

The editors and publisher are grateful to the following parties for permission to reprint the essays reprinted in this volume (those articles for which permission is not indicated are believed to be in the public domain):

Alfred Perceval Graves, "A Memoir of Joseph Sheridan Le Fanu," *The Purcell Papers* (Richard Bentley & Son, 1880), v–xxxi. The editors have made slight abridgements to this article, marked [. . .], where the author's brother, William Richard Le Fanu, offered a fuller and more accurate version of the same anecdote (see "Anecdotes from *Seventy Years of Irish Life*" in this volume).

W. R. Le Fanu, *Seventy Years of Irish Life* (London: Edward Arnold, 1893). Page numbers cited in the text.

S. M. Ellis, *Wilkie Collins, Le Fanu and Others* (London: Constable, 1931); rpt. Freeport, NY: Books for Libraries Press, 1968. Page numbers cited in the text.

Brian J. Showers, "A Void Which Cannot Be Filled Up: The Obituaries of Mr. J. S. Le Fanu, Esq.," *Le Fanu Studies* 2:1 (May 2007). Revised for this appearance. Reprinted by permission of the author.

M. R. James, "M. R. James on Le Fanu," printed in *Ghosts & Scholars* 7 (1985): 24–27; corrected and reprinted in *The Fenstanton Witch and Others* (The Haunted Library, 1999), 35–39. Adapted from manuscript notes for a lecture given at The Royal Institution of Great Britain on 16 March 1923. Reprinted by permission of N. J. R. James; and courtesy of Rosemary Pardoe. © 1985, 1999 N. J. R. James.

Edna Kenton, "A Forgotten Creator of Ghosts—Joseph Sheridan Le Fanu, Possible Inspirer of the Brontës," *Bookman* (New York) (July 1929): 528–35.

E. F. Benson, "Sheridan Le Fanu," *Spectator* 126 (21 February 1931): 263–64.

Peter Penzoldt, extract from "Chapter 1: Joseph Sheridan Le Fanu (1814–1873): The transition from the Gothic Novel to the Short story of the supernatural—Sir Walter Scott—Bulwer-Lytton—Captain Frederick Marryat," *The Supernatural in Fiction* (New York: Humanities Press, 1965): 67–91. First published London: Peter Nevill 1952. All attempts have been made to contact the copyright holder of this material. The copyright holder is invited to contact the publisher.

V. S. Pritchett, "An Irish Ghost," *The Living Novel and Other Appreciations* (Random House, 1964), 121–27. © V. S. Pritchett, 1964. Reprinted by permission of PFD (www.pfd.co.uk) on behalf of the estate of V. S. Pritchett.

M. R. James, "Prologue" and "Epilogue," *Madam Crowl's Ghost and Other Tales of Mystery* (London: G. Bell & Sons, 1923). The editors have made slight abridgements to this article.

Patricia Coughlan, "Doubles, Shadows, Sedan-Chairs, and the Past: The 'Ghost Stories' of J. S. Le Fanu," *Critical Approaches to Anglo-Literature*, ed. Michael Allen and Angela Wilcox (Gerrards Cross, UK: Colin Smythe, 1988), 17–39. Revised for this appearance. Reprinted by permission of the author.

Kel Roop, "Making Light in the Shadow Box: The Artistry of Le Fanu," *Papers on Language and Literature* 21 (Fall 1985): 359–69. All attempts have been made to contact the copyright holder of this material. The copyright holder is invited to contact the publisher. Reprinted by permission of the original publisher.

Wayne Hall, "Le Fanu's House by the Marketplace," *Éire-Ireland* (Spring 1986): 55–72. Reprinted by permission of the author.

Albert Power, "Sheridan Le Fanu and the Spirit of 1798," originally published in the *Bram Stoker Society Journal* No. 11 (1999): 3–12. Revised for this appearance. Reprinted by permission of the author.

Jim Rockhill, "H. P. Lovecraft's Response to the Work of Joseph Sheridan Le Fanu," originally published as "Lovecraft on Le Fanu" on *Wormwoodiana*, wormwoodiana.blogspot.com (30 October 2010). Revised for this appearance. Reprinted by permission of the author.

Simon Cooke, "'A Regular Contributor': Le Fanu's Short Stories, *All the Year Round*, and the Influence of Dickens." Original to this volume. Printed by permission of the author. The author is indebted to Professor Philip Allingham, Faculty of Education, Lakehead University, Ontario, Canada, for advice on research sources relating to *All the Year Round*.

William Hughes, "'I Resolved to Play the Part of a Good Samaritan': Metafiction in 'The Room in the Dragon Volant.'" Original to this volume. Printed by permission of the author.

Peter Bell, "'The Child That Went with the Faeries': The Folk Tale and the Ghost Story." Original to this volume. Printed by permission of the author. Especial thanks to Richard Dalby for advice in researching this essay.

Victor Sage, "The 'Smashed Looking-Glass': Fragmentation and Narrative Perversity in *Willing to Die*." Original to this volume. Printed by permission of the author.

Biographical Notes

Editors

Gary William Crawford is a scholar, poet, and short story writer. He is the author of scholarly books, such as *Ramsey Campbell* and *Robert Aickman: An Introduction*. He is the founder of Gothic Press, which has published such books as *Akin to Poetry: Observations on Some Strange Tales of Robert Aickman*, in addition to the print journal *Gothic* and the free online journal *Le Fanu Studies*. He also maintains free online secondary databases of Le Fanu, Robert Aickman, Ramsey Campbell, Fritz Leiber, and Walter de la Mare. His Stoker nominated poetry collections are *The Shadow City* and *The Phantom World*. His short story collections are *Gothic Fevers* and *Mysteries of Von Domarus and Other Stories*. He lives in Baton Rouge, Louisiana.

Jim Rockhill has edited the complete supernatural fiction of Joseph Sheridan Le Fanu for Ash-Tree Press (2002, 2003, 2004) and Bob Leman for Midnight House (2002), served as coeditor to Jane Rice's collected weird tales for Midnight House (2003), and assisted with many other volumes, including *Battered Silicon Dispatch Box's compilation of the complete adventures of* Seabury Quinn's occult detective *Jules de Grandin (2001)*. His reviews and articles appear in *The Freedom of Fantastic Things*, *Warnings to the Curious*, *Supernatural Literature of the World*, *Encyclopedia of the Vampire*, the journals *All Hallows*, *Dead Reckonings*, *Le Fanu Studies*, *Lost Worlds*, and various websites.

Brian J. Showers is originally from Madison, Wisconsin. He runs the Swan River Press and has written short stories, articles, and reviews for magazines such as *Rue Morgue*, *Ghosts & Scholars*, *Le Fanu Studies*, and *Supernatural Tales*. His short story collection, *The Bleeding Horse* (Mercier Press), won the Children of the Night Award in 2008. He is also the author of *Literary Walking Tours of Gothic Dublin* (Nonsuch, 2006) and *Old Albert—An Epilogue* (Ex Occidente, 2011); with Gary W. Crawford he coauthored *Joseph Sheridan Le Fanu: A Concise Bibliography* (Swan River Press, 2011); and is the editor of *Haunted Histories and Peculiar Places* (forthcoming). He lives in Dublin.

Contributors

Douglas A. Anderson's first book was *The Annotated Hobbit* (1988; revised and enlarged 2002), and he is a founding coeditor of *Tolkien Studies: An Annual Scholarly Review*, of which eight volumes have appeared. His anthologies include *Tales Before Tolkien* (2003), *H. P. Lovecraft's Favorite Weird Tales* (2005), and *Tales Before Narnia* (2008). He writes regular columns on older fantasy and supernatural literature in the journals *Wormwood* and *Fastitocalon* and contributes to the blog *Wormwoodiana*.

Peter Bell is a historian living in York, England. As well as academic works on the international history of the 1930s, he has written for the *Ghosts & Scholars M. R. James Newsletter*, *Faunus* (the Journal of the Friends of Arthur Machen), *Wormwood*, and *All Hallows*, and his work has been published by Ash-Tree Press, the Swan River Press, Side Real Press, and Ex Occidente Press.

E[dward] F[rederic] Benson (1867–1940) was the son of Edward White Benson, Archbishop of Canterbury. He attended King's College, Cambridge, and was a member of the Chitchat Society when M. R. James debuted his first ghost story, "Canon Alberic's Scrap-book," in 1893. While Benson is perhaps most popular for his humorous "Mapp & Lucia" novels, readers of the present volume might know him best as the author of numerous memorable "spook" stories collected in such classic volumes as *The Room in the Tower* (1912), *Spook Stories* (1928), and *More Spook Stories* (1934).

Elizabeth Bowen (1899–1973) was born at 15 Herbert Place in Dublin. As coincidence would have it, Le Fanu himself lived just a few doors away, albeit half a century before Bowen's birth. Like Le Fanu, at an early age Bowen moved to the rural southwest of Ireland. In 1930 she inherited the family estate in County Cork, Bowen Court, where she entertained such writers as Virginia Woolf, Eudora Welty, and Seán Ó Faoláin. Her novels, short stories, and nonfiction—notably *The Cat Jumps and Other Stories* (1934), *The Death of the Heart* (1938), *The Demon Lover and Other Stories* (1945), *The Heat of the Day* (1949), *Collected Impressions* (1950), and the posthumous collections *The Collected Stories of Elizabeth Bowen* (1980) and *The Mulberry Tree: Writings of Elizabeth Bowen*, edited by Hermione Lee (1999)—continue to be read and appreciated to the present day. Her ghostly fiction, which made regular appearances in the anthologies of Cynthia Asquith, is akin to that of Henry James in its psychological probity, but briefer, wittier, and more ironic, with a streak of feline cruelty.

Stephen Carver is a freelance writer and editor. He also teaches literature and creative writing at the Centre for Continuing Education, University of East Anglia. He was formally Associate Professor of English Literature at the University of Fukui, Japan (2002–05) and Lecturer in Critical Theory and Creative Writing at the Norwich School of Art and Design (2005–10). He is the biographer of the Victorian writer William Harrison Ainsworth and is presently working on his first novel, as well as an essay on Tim Burton and Postmodern Gothic and a book about lesser-known nineteenth-century authors. Carver's late mother and wife are both Spiritualists.

Simon Cooke, Ph.D, has spent most of his working life as a teacher and writer. From 1986 to 2000 he was a tutor in English and the History of Art in the School of Continuing Studies, University of Birmingham, where he also held a senior position as the Director of the Certificate in Modern Art. He has also worked as lecturer and researcher for Coventry University and the University of Exeter, and is currently employed as a teacher and adviser working for a college in Coventry. A recipient of several scholarships and academic awards, Cooke has published numerous articles and papers in the related fields of Victorian fiction, art, and illustration. His book, *Illustrated Periodicals of the 1860s*, was published in 2010, and his essays have appeared in journals such as the *Dickens Studies Annual*, *Victorian Periodicals Review*, *VIJ*, *Le Fanu Studies*, the *Thomas Hardy Journal*, and the *Dickens Quarterly*.

Patricia Coughlan, a professor of English at University College, Cork, has published widely on Irish writing, including several essays on early modern colonial discourse, Irish Gothic, and twentieth-century work (Beckett, Bowen, Kate O'Brien). Edited or coedited collections include *Spenser and Ireland* (1990), *Modernism and Ireland: The Poetry of the 1930s* (1995), and *Irish Literature: Feminist Perspectives* (2008). Recent work on contemporary literature includes articles on Banville, Peig Sayers and life-writing, Edna O'Brien, Ní Chuilleanáin, Ronan Bennett, and others. In 2002–03 she held a Government of Ireland Senior Research Fellowship. During the 2000s she led a state-funded research project on women in Irish society. She is currently completing a study of subjectivity, gender and social change in contemporary Irish literature.

S[tewart] M[arsh] Ellis (1878–1933) was a critic and biographer whose many books and articles include the first bibliography of Le Fanu's work (*Irish Booklover* 8, 1916) and studies examining the darker branches of fiction during the Romantic and Victorian period, such as *William Harrison Ainsworth and Friends* (1911), *Mainly Victorian* (1925), and *Wilkie Collins, Le*

Fanu and Others (1931). The latter focuses not only on Collins and Le Fanu but also on Charles Allston Collins, Mortimer Collins, R. D. Blackmore, and Mrs. J. H. Riddell.

Alfred Perceval Graves (1846–1931) is remembered today mainly for his poetry. His early works were published in the *Spectator*, the *Athenaeum*, and the *Dublin University Magazine*; it was through his work for the latter journal that he made the acquaintance of Le Fanu. After Le Fanu's death in 1873, he edited two volumes of the author's work: *The Purcell Papers* (1880) and *The Poems of Joseph Sheridan Le Fanu* (1896). Graves's son, Robert, was also a poet of note whose most celebrated work is *The White Goddess* (1948).

Wayne Hall serves as Vice Provost for Faculty Development at the University of Cincinnati, where he also holds the position of professor in the Department of English and Comparative Literature. His early research on modern Irish literature led to the publication of two books: *Shadowy Heroes: Irish Literature of the 1890s* (Syracuse University Press, 1980) and *Dialogues in the Margin: A Study of the Dublin University Magazine* (Catholic University of America Press, 1999). Over the past ten years, and following the path created by his administrative work, his research has focused on scholarly teaching and the scholarship of teaching and learning, with particular focus on instructional technology, e-portfolios, and teaching strategies for large-enrollment classes.

Sally C. Harris is a lecturer of English literature and writing at the University of Tennessee, Knoxville. She has published a number of essays on Le Fanu and continues to study his use of the supernatural as well as his narrative techniques. In addition to her work on Le Fanu and Victorian fiction, she is interested in the development of detective fiction.

William Hughes is Professor of Gothic Studies at Bath Spa University, Bath, UK. A specialist in the writings of Bram Stoker, he is the author of *Beyond Dracula: Bram Stoker's Fiction and Its Cultural Context* (2000) and two critical guides to *Dracula* published by Palgrave (2009) and Continuum (2009). He has also edited critical editions of Stoker's *The Lady of the Shroud* (2001) and *Dracula* (with Diane Mason, 2007). With Andrew Smith he has coedited a number of scholarly collections relevant to the Gothic, most notably *Bram Stoker: History, Psychoanalysis and the Gothic* (1998), *Fictions of Unease: The Gothic from Otranto to The X-Files* (with Andrew Smith and Diane Mason, 2002), *Empire and the Gothic: The Politics of Genre* (2003), *Queering the Gothic* (2009), and the forthcoming *EcoGothic*. He is the editor of *Gothic*

Studies, the refereed journal of the International Gothic Association, and is writing a monograph on Victorian hypnotism.

M[ontague] R[hodes] James (1862–1936) was Provost of King's College, Cambridge, and later of Eton College. In addition to being a noted medieval scholar and expert in biblical apocrypha, he is the author of four collections of highly influential ghost stories: *Ghost-Stories of an Antiquary* (1904), *More Ghost Stories of an Antiquary* (1911), *A Thin Ghost and Others* (1919), and *A Warning to the Curious* (1925). He is known as an admirer of Le Fanu's work and cites him as an influence in his own. In 1923 he edited *Madam Crowl's Ghost and Other Tales of Mystery*, a volume of Le Fanu's uncollected stories, which helped pave the way for a revival of the author's work.

Edna Kenton (1876–1954) was an American critic, novelist, and feminist associated with the Chicago and New York literary scenes, best known today for her essays on Henry James and her account of her association with *The Provincetown Players and the Playwrights' Theatre, 1915–1922*, ed. Travis Bogard and Jackson R. Bryer. (Jefferson, NC: McFarland, 2004), the amateur theater group that launched the career of Eugene O'Neill. Her essay "Henry James to the Ruminant Reader: *The Turn of the Screw*," *Arts* 6 (November 1924) was one of the key texts in focusing critical attention toward the clever manipulations and psychological dimensions in that work.

Jarlath Killeen is a lecturer in Victorian Literature at Trinity College, Dublin. He is the author of *The Faiths of Oscar Wilde* (Palgrave, 2005), *Gothic Ireland* (Four Courts, 2005), *The Fairy Tales of Oscar Wilde* (Ashgate, 2007), and *Gothic Literature, 1825–1914* (University of Wales Press, 2009), and editor of *Oscar Wilde* (Irish Academic Press, 2010).

John Langan's essays have appeared in the *Lovecraft Annual, Studies in the Fantastic, Fantasy Commentator*, and *Lovecraft Studies*. He is the author of a novel, *House of Windows* (Night Shade, 2009), and a collection of stories, *Mr. Gaunt and Other Uneasy Encounters* (Prime, 2008). He lives in upstate New York with his wife and son.

Mark Le Fanu is a London-based film scholar who has written extensively on international cinema, including critically acclaimed books on Tarkovsky and Mizoguchi. He contributes to the journals *Sight & Sound* (London) and *Positif* (Paris).

W[illiam] R[ichard] Le Fanu (1816–1894) was born at the Royal Hibernian Military School, Phoenix Park, Chapelizod. As a railroad engineer he assisted with the construction of Ireland's Great Southern and Western railway system, earning promotion as Deputy Commissioner of Public Works in 1863. Although a prolific diarist, William only has one publication to his name: *Seventy Years of Irish Life: Being Anecdotes and Reminiscences* (1893). In addition to containing a wealth of information about his better-known older brother, it remains a readable and charming portrait of nineteenth-century Irish life.

W. J. [Bill] Mc Cormack recently retired as Keeper of the Edward Worth Library (1733), Dublin; before that he was Professor of Literary History at the University of London (Goldsmiths College). Among his publications are *Sheridan Le Fanu and Victorian Ireland* (Clarendon Press, 1980), *Dissolute Characters: Irish Literary History through Balzac, Sheridan Le Fanu, Yeats and Bowen* (Manchester University Press, 1993), *From Burke to Beckett: Ascendancy, Tradition and Betrayal in Literary History* (Cork University Press, 1994), *Fool of the Family: A Life of J. M. Synge* (Weidenfeld & Nicolson, 2000), *Roger Casement in Death: or Haunting the Free State* (University College of Dublin Press, 2002), *The Silence of Barbara Synge* (Manchester University Press, 2003), and *Blood Kindred: W. B. Yeats, the Life, the Death, the Politics* (Pimlico, 2005). He is finishing a biography of the Ulster poet John Hewitt (1907–1987).

Peter Penzoldt (1925–1969) was born in Munich, Germany. His seminal work *The Supernatural in Fiction* was originally written as a doctoral thesis at the University of Geneva in Switzerland and was expanded for publication three years later at the prompting of Penzoldt's friend Algernon Blackwood. Penzoldt moved to the United States in 1950, teaching modern languages first in San Francisco, then at Sweet Briar College, Virginia, where he remained for the remainder of his life. *The Supernatural in Fiction* was his only major publication. See Douglas A. Anderson's biographical sketch of the author published in *All Hallows* No. 43 (Summer 2007): 72–73.

Albert Power is a Gothic scholar and writer. For several years he was editor of the *Journal of the Bram Stoker Society*. He has written for Tartarus Press's *Wormwood*, and his novella, *Mad Matinée in Baku*, was published in 2010 by Ex Occidente Press.

Sir V[ictor] S[awdon] Pritchett (1900–1997) was an English man of letters famed equally for his essays, short stories, novels, biographies, autobiography, and the books he edited. Random House published his *Complete Short Stories* and *Complete Collected Essays* in 1991 to wide acclaim. His output of weird fiction is small but choice, with his "A Story of Don Juan" reprinted frequently since its first appearance in Cynthia Asquith's *The Second Ghost Book* (London: J. Barrie, 1952).

Victor Sage is Emeritus Professor of English Literature at the University of East Anglia, Norwich. A novelist and short story writer, he has also written on Protestantism and the horror tradition, Dickens, Beckett, and other nineteenth- and twentieth-century Irish writers. He has edited Maturin's *Melmoth the Wanderer* and Le Fanu's *Uncle Silas* for Penguin Classics. His latest book was *Le Fanu's Gothic: The Rhetoric of Darkness* (2004). He is working on *A Cultural History of European Gothic* for Polity Press.

Carol A. Senf is a professor at the Georgia Institute of Technology, where she is also Associate Chair of the School of Literature, Communication, and Culture. She has written one article on Le Fanu ("Women and Power in *Carmilla*," *Gothic*, 1987) and frequently on Bram Stoker and his work: *The Critical Response to Bram Stoker* (Greenwood Press, 1993), *Dracula: Between Tradition and Modernism* (Twayne, 1998), *Science and Social Science in Bram Stoker's Fiction* (Greenwood Press, 2002), and *Bram Stoker* (University of Wales Press, 2010) as well as a number of shorter works.

Jack Sullivan, Professor of English and Director of American Studies at Rider University, is the author of *Hitchcock's Music* (Yale University Press), winner of the 2007 ASCAP Deems Taylor Award. He is also the author of *New World Symphonies* (Yale University Press) and editor of *Words on Music* (Ohio University Press) and the *Penguin Encyclopedia of Horror and the Supernatural*. He has written for the *New York Times*, the *Wall Street Journal*, the *Washington Post*, *Opera*, the *American Record Guide*, the *Hitchcock Annual*, the *Chronicle of Higher Education*, and others.

Index